WHY GORBACHEV HAPPENED

ROBERT G. KAISER

A TOUCHSTONE BOOK
Published by Simon & Schuster
New York   London   Toronto   Sydney   Tokyo   Singapore

TOUCHSTONE
Simon & Schuster Building
Rockefeller Center
1230 Avenue of the Americas
New York, New York 10020

First Touchstone Edition 1992
TOUCHSTONE and colophon are registered trademarks
of Simon & Schuster Inc.
Designed by Levavi & Levavi
Manufactured in the United States of America

1   3   5   7   9   10   8   6   4   2

Library of Congress Cataloging-in-Publication Data
Kaiser, Robert G.
Why Gorbachev Happened: His Triumphs and His Failure/
Robert G. Kaiser.
p.   cm.
Includes bibliographical references and index.
1. Gorbachev, Mikhail Sergeyevich, 1931–   . 2. Soviet
Union—politics and government—1985–   . 3. Heads of
State—Soviet Union—biography.   I. Title.
DK290.3.G67K35   1991
947.085′4′092—dc20   91-6986
CIP
ISBN: 0-671-73692-2
ISBN: 0-671-77878-1 (pbk)

THIS BOOK IS FOR

THOMAS POWERS

A friend may well be reckoned the masterpiece of Nature.

RALPH WALDO EMERSON

SOVIET UNION

MILES
0   500   1000   1500

LITHUANIA   LATVIA   ESTONIA
●Tallinn
Vilnius ●Riga
Leningrad
◉Minsk
BELORUSSIA
MOLDAVIA
Kishinev ◉Kiev   ★ Moscow
UKRAINE
Volga River
RUSSIA
●Novocherkassk
●Privolnoye
●Stavropol
Kuban R.
GEORGIA
◉Tbilisi
Yerevan ◉
ARMENIA
AZERBAIJAN   ●Baku
Aral Sea   KAZAKHSTAN
Lake Balkhash
TURKMENISTAN   UZBEKISTAN
◉Ashkhabad
Tashkent ●   ●Frunze   ●Alma Ata
Dushanbe ●   KIRGHIZIA
TADZHIKISTAN

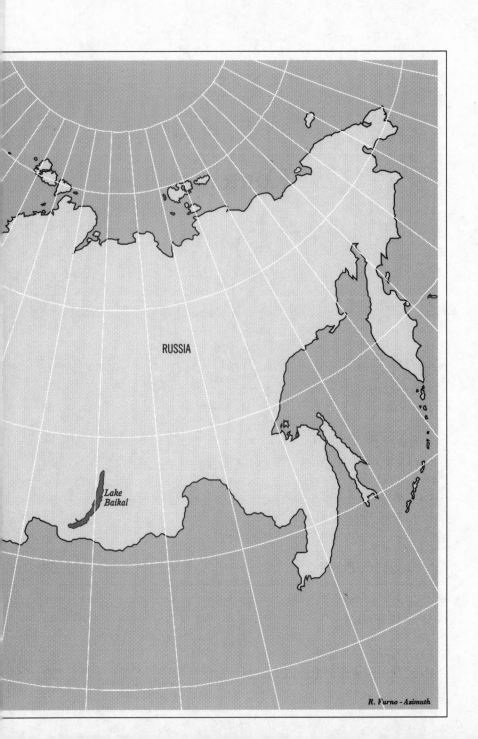

RUSSIA

Lake
Baikal

R. Furno - Azimuth

Contents

There is nothing more difficult to take in hand, more perilous to conduct, or more uncertain in its success, than to take the lead in the introduction of a new order of things.

NICCOLO MACHIAVELLI,
The Prince

Revolution

In just less than seven years, Mikhail Gorbachev transformed the world. He turned his own country upside down. He woke a sleeping giant, the peoples of the Soviet Union, and gave them freedoms they had never dreamed of. He also gave them back their own horrific history, which his predecessors had hidden and distorted for sixty years. He tossed away the Soviet empire in Eastern Europe with no more than a fare-thee-well. He ended the cold war that had dominated world politics and consumed the wealth of nations for nearly half a century. Finally, he disbanded the Soviet Communist Party, the vast institution that had made his political career possible, then watched helplessly as the collection of peoples and cultures which he considered one country fell into pieces. The revolution he had started had flown out of his control, and he was compelled to step aside, leaving to others the job of building something new on the wreckage of the Soviet Union. These are the most astounding historical developments any of us is likely to experience. Why did they happen?

This book is an attempt to answer that question—to explain why Gorbachev came to power, why he was the kind of man who could do what he did, why his comrades in the Soviet Union's Communist Party let him do it, why the Soviet empire at home and abroad crumbled as quickly as it did, and why he lost control of his revolution and was forced from office at the end of 1991. This is unabashedly a book about the accomplishments of a great man, a giant in modern history. But a large part of the story concerns that man's shortcomings and failures.

I've written the book with an imaginary reader in mind, a curious, intelligent person with no particular expertise in Soviet affairs or Russian history with whom I have struck a deal: Give me a weekend, or a few evenings by the fire, and I will try to give you a graspable explanation of these most amazing historical events—a combination of biography, history, sociology, and theory that allows it all to add up, to make sense.

This is a personal book, written by a lucky reporter who has been given the chance to study the Soviet Union at close range for twenty years. I've lived in Russia, written books about Russia, met and helped to interview Mikhail Gorbachev, all thanks to *The Washington Post,* where I've worked since I was a college student. In the amazing years of Gorbachev, friends and colleagues who know of my interest in Russian affairs have turned to me for explanations of successive astounding developments; to try to respond, I started formulating the ideas that fill these pages.

There were many moments when I could not easily explain the latest amazement. This was the case each time Gorbachev defied the most basic laws of Sovietology—the bedrock presumptions on which we in the West built our explanations of the Soviet system. He shattered them, one at a time.

For example, we knew that in the Soviet Union individuals were inevitably subjugated to the state and the Communist Party. We knew the authorities would inevitably use their power to stamp out dissident behavior and censor nonconformist ideas. They had to preserve the myths that propped up their system—myths about a "workers' state" where the Communist Party played a "leading role" and preserved the "dictatorship of the proletariat." Without the myths the autocrats who ran the country could not justify their power, so the myths would be preserved at all costs. The country's leaders would respect the rites and taboos that had symbolized their power from the time of Stalin onward—ceremony would submerge substance, and ritualized praise for the system and its triumphs would drown out realistic criticism.

We knew that some features of the system were immutable—the centrally planned economy, for example, or the tightly controlled

multinational empire, in which ethnic Russians would always dominate Latvians, Armenians, Uzbeks, and the rest. We knew that the
Soviet state would risk a great deal to maintain discipline in its East
European empire—this was proven in 1968, when Czechoslovakia was
invaded, and in 1981, when martial law was imposed to crush the
Solidarity trade union in Poland. We knew all these truths to be self-
evident.

After living in the Soviet Union for three years in the 1970s, I had
convinced myself that the inertia governing the society was so powerful that there was little hope of ever really changing it. The system
was cruel, stupid, and inefficient, but it met the basic needs of the
country, and it suited a nation of sheeplike followers (the metaphor
was Pushkin's) whose fears of anarchy and disorder far outweighed
their interest in democracy or freedom. Russians loved their suffering,
I decided (many of them said so), and would persevere.

I didn't pay enough attention to the epigram I chose to begin my
first book on Russia. It was a quotation from Peter the Great, one of
the reformer czars to whom Gorbachev will be compared in the history
texts of the twenty-first century and beyond. "Russia," said Peter, is
"a country in which things that just don't happen happen." When I
first heard that line from Lev Kopelev, a giant among Russia's postwar
intellectuals, I thought it captured the bigger-than-life aspects of Russia, the exaggerations that typify so much of the national life and
culture, from the multiple endings of Tchaikovsky symphonies to the
size of Siberia. The Gorbachev experience puts Peter's remark in a
more serious context, where it belongs. Peter's own contribution—
creating a beautiful new capital on a swamp at the edge of the Gulf of
Finland,* yanking Russia into Europe by the scruff of the neck—was
unimaginable before it happened, like Gorbachev's reforms. The
events of recent years suggest that Russia really does have possibilities
not offered to other peoples, nor predictable by conventional modes
of analysis.

The most obvious "thing that just doesn't happen" in the Gorbachev
revolution was Gorbachev himself. Where did such a remarkable Soviet Communist come from? When I lived in Moscow in the early
1970s and began to realize what dolts Leonid Brezhnev and his colleagues were, I used to daydream about how a really interesting and
radical Soviet leader might emerge (though I never really expected

---

* St. Petersburg originally, Leningrad in the Soviet period, then (after 1991) St. Petersburg again.

that one would). Nikita Khrushchev offered a model of sorts—a loyal henchman of Stalin's, he had shown unexpected creativity and courage once he became leader himself. Could that pattern be repeated? The Soviet system reminded me of the United States Army—a bureaucracy in which those who get ahead are those who know best how to please and flatter their superiors without threatening them. A man's true personality would only emerge when he reached the very top, where he had no more superiors to flatter. If the comparison was apt, a radical Soviet leader would have to emerge from a conventional earlier career.

Gorbachev validated that theory in spades. By outward appearances he was an unexceptional Party man; his face and manner were a little handsomer and more vigorous than many comrades', but he fit a familiar mold. He had put in the necessary long years in the provinces, enduring periods of stupefying boredom to reach the senior leadership in Moscow. He had shown signs of a real political personality, earning a reputation as a Party leader who could mingle effectively with ordinary people, and obviously impressing his comrades with his intelligence. But he was never threatening. As we will see, his advancement up the ladder of power depended at every stage on the patronage of powerful elders.

We now know that Gorbachev was exceptionally intelligent and creative. No one who meets him forgets the intense eyes that are a harbinger of that intelligence. His ability to improvise, to outthink his rivals and then outmaneuver them, was a hallmark of his years in power. Unusually bright people were rare among senior Communists since Stalin wiped out the intellectuals who were Lenin's first comrades; intelligence couldn't coexist easily with loyalty to a Party dominated by ritual and myth. Gorbachev obviously harbored a great ambition for power from an early age—we will see signs of it from adolescence onward. The Party offered this son of peasants extraordinary opportunities to improve himself. Ambition may have enabled him to endure the petty humiliations and the lies of Party life that a less driven man would have found intolerable. His great self-assurance, also a rare quality among Soviet politicians, must have helped him believe that a careful, patient ascent could take him all the way to the top.

Another surprising trait is Gorbachev's courage. Only great courage allowed him to try to turn his country in a new direction, to challenge and eventually destroy the ideological orthodoxy that he inherited, and to separate the Communist Party from state power, ending the Party's "leading role" and finally ending the Party itself.

He had the courage to accept the implications of his own observations. From an early age, Gorbachev had unusual opportunities to see for himself the wide gulf that often separated Party propaganda from reality. He lived through the brutal collectivization of agriculture and appreciated its cruelty; at Moscow State University he had the chance to read foreign political philosophy and constitutional law; he had unusual chances to travel to Western Europe and sample "imperialism" at firsthand. Experiences like these enabled him to separate his own ideas from official ones, and to see the inadequacies of the official ones.

The most important use a politician can make of courage is to lead —to actually strike out in a new direction, shouting "Follow me!" over his shoulder. We see that so rarely that it is a compelling spectacle every time it appears. Gorbachev's ability to lead assures his place in history. And yet, when the revolution he initiated spun out of his own control in 1991, his courage failed him. Or perhaps he had reached its limits.

Gorbachev's brand of reformism caught much of the Western world by surprise, but he was actually part of a reform tradition inside the Communist Party almost as old as the Party itself. Nikolai Bukharin, one of Lenin's closest comrades, was a godfather to this group; in 1938 Stalin arrested Bukharin, and in 1988 Gorbachev rehabilitated him. Countless members of Gorbachev's generation absorbed the reformist spirit of Khrushchev's famous "secret speech" at the 20th Communist Party Congress in 1956, when he denounced Stalin's crimes and implied that the Party had to find a new path. That speech initiated "The Thaw," a period of relaxed censorship and control that produced a flowering of poetry and literature, and shaped a generation— Gorbachev's generation, the "children of the 20th Party Congress."

These were people born in the 1920s and 1930s who grew up believing in communism and in Stalin. But as they came of age in the late forties and fifties, they shared yearnings for change—for modernization and liberalization. Their elders saw the Great Patriotic War— the Soviet name for World War II—as a great event in the history of the country that solidified the Bolshevik revolution and established the Soviet Union as a great world power. But the children of the 20th Congress seemed more conscious of the devastation that the war caused, and less interested in the superpower status it conferred.

Khrushchev's Thaw gave them hope that change was coming, and encouraged them to dream that the country might begin to confront its own problems, beginning with poverty, isolation, and Stalinist paranoia. Then, before they knew what had happened, the Thaw was gone, replaced by the long freeze of Leonid Brezhnev's eighteen years in power. Members of this generation saw Gorbachev as their own redeemer—"our last chance," as many of them described him. They meant the last chance to expiate their guilt for allowing the optimism of the late 1950s to disappear before it had brought meaningful change. Numerous children of the 20th Congress will play important roles in this story.

One interesting member of the group is Alexander Bovin, a famous commentator on *Izvestia,* the government newspaper, who worked in the Party *apparat* for Khrushchev and Yuri Andropov, probably Gorbachev's most important patron. In 1990 I told Bovin I was trying to figure out how to understand Gorbachev. "Understanding Gorbachev," Bovin said without a moment's hesitation, "means understanding the Soviet Union."

Many in the West never grasped the uncertain nature of Soviet history. We tended to see a monolithic, totalitarian power hellbent on world domination; for many years we also saw a Soviet Union that seemed to be advancing that goal relentlessly. Those were flawed images. One of the most important reasons why Gorbachev was possible was that the Soviet system never worked as well as advertised. By the time he was a candidate for national leadership, it was stumbling badly. His prescriptions for radical change were acceptable to many of his countrymen because they understood that their country had fallen into a disastrous state.

The collapse of communism in what we used to call the Soviet bloc was more the result of exhaustion and decay than of Gorbachev's innovations. Sometime in the 1970s the Stalinist model, on which the Soviet Union and all its satellites were operating, ran out of steam. The combination of directives from "the center," exhortation, and discipline that had produced a steady expansion of the economies of those countries since the end of World War II just stopped working. The system could not survive the modern age; it failed to respond to modern technology and could not counter the cynicism and worldly wisdom that grew with the breakdown of Stalinist isolation from the outside world.

In 1987 I saw Milovan Djilas, the brilliant Yugoslav who first exposed Stalinism from an insider's perspective in his book *The New Class,* and asked him if the trend toward liberalization in Eastern Europe, then just beginning, would continue. Yes, he said firmly, "the crisis will continue." Not the crisis, I said, but liberalization—would it continue? "Liberalization, crisis, it's the same thing," Djilas replied. It was one of those metaphysical remarks that make East European intellectuals so appealing. After thinking about it for a long time, I decided that Djilas was absolutely right. The crisis in the Soviet bloc was largely a crisis brought on by alienation. The leadership in each of those countries stuck by the familiar words and rituals, but the people no longer put any stock in them. Liberalization was a response to alienation—an attempt by ruling élites to win back popular support, even enthusiasm, from cynical publics. The élites were willing to try this approach because all else had failed—their societies were on the verge of collapse.

Gorbachev's most fundamental new idea was his oft-stated belief that the Soviet Union could only solve its many problems if the people of the country felt a stake in the way it was run. I suspect it came to him even before he was appointed a Central Committee secretary in 1978—the beginning of his Moscow political career. The people were alienated, he said again and again; they had to be given a new reason to work and to care about their country. In a revealing comment to newspaper editors in July 1987, for example, Gorbachev spoke of "our fulcrum":

"This fulcrum is really to rouse people and to make use of the rich political, cultural, and scientific potential that has accumulated in our society in the years of Soviet power." Speaking to a similar meeting a year later, he was more explicit: "In all spheres of life, including the spiritual sphere, we will have to overcome a very basic factor —alienation, which, unfortunately, occurs under socialism when it is deformed by authoritarian-bureaucratic distortions. Alienation . . . can be overcome only [with] democratization and openness (*glasnost*) . . ." Or, as he said on another occasion, "A house can be put in order only by a person who feels that he owns the house."

Gorbachev first began talking publicly about the need to democratize society to give Soviet citizens a sense of being in control of their country and their destiny and to assure "the accountability of all executive organs" in December 1984, three months before he was chosen general secretary of the Soviet Communist Party.

If Gorbachev was an old believer in increased popular participation, did he realize from the beginning where the democratization of Soviet society might lead? Probably not. I am convinced—and will try to show why—that for more than two years after coming to power he thought he could remain a loyal Party man and persuade the Party to follow a more democratic line without entirely relinquishing the Communist Party's "leading role," even if it would inevitably be diluted. What is remarkable is that when he realized this would not be possible —when he came to understand that democracy was going to undermine Party control, not bolster it—he did not change course. He must have understood that there was no way to proceed with the modernization of Soviet society and preserve the position of the Party. By then he was more committed to trying to save his country than to saving the political organization in which he had grown up. But when democratization threatened to tear apart the Soviet Union, and perhaps to undermine his own power, Gorbachev briefly turned away from it. Then, in 1991, he lost his way.

Gorbachev's relationship with the Communist Party isn't easy for a Westerner to understand. I'm not certain I understand it. There is no question about the Party's influence on the man: A thirty-year career in Party work gave him a vocabulary and a political style that were instantly recognizable to any Soviet citizen as the mark of a Party man. He was never able to stop giving overlong speeches, for example; nor could he get far beyond the stale formulations of the Party phrasebook, the vocabulary of *Pravda* and of Central Committee directives. On some subjects—relations among the Soviet Union's many nationalities may be the best example—Gorbachev was permanently hobbled by his faith in the Party propaganda he had absorbed. There were moments when Gorbachev the great reformer reverted to Gorbachev the *apparatchik* and put on appalling performances. One ugly example was when he led a chorus of brutal denunciations of Boris Yeltsin at a Party meeting in November 1987 that could have been presided over by Stalin himself. By 1990, when public opinion was turning against him, these traits had become a serious liability for Gorbachev, but he couldn't suppress them entirely. Then, in 1991, a newly fearful Gorbachev sent murderous troops into the Baltic states in a crude show of force that made him look like a typical *apparatchik* from the worst old days. After bitter denunciation of those harsh actions at home and abroad, Gorbachev again turned back toward reform. But by the time he made that last course correction in mid-1991, events had raced ahead of him.

Many Russians spoke of "two Gorbachevs," the *apparatchik* and the reformer, who often struggled with one another. This is a useful way of thinking about him. Gorbachev led a revolution, but for a long time he also tried to preserve the prerevolutionary political arrangement—a Party-run state—that the revolution would ultimately destroy. This was a form of political schizophrenia. "He wanted . . . to marry a hedgehog and a grass snake," as Yeltsin put it years later. Curiously, the Russians who were Gorbachev's strongest initial supporters were intellectuals who had no real sympathy for the Party; they were easily put off when he reminded them of his own Party personality. But the *apparatchik* in whose interest, at least initially, he was trying to preserve the Party's role never liked him—perhaps because they understood the contradiction in Gorbachev's approach better than he did.

Gorbachev will have the historical status of a transitional leader—one who bridged two eras by keeping a foot in both. Gorbachev's ability to be both Party man and revolutionary was what enabled him to shatter the Stalinist system. If there hadn't been two Gorbachevs, there would have been no Gorbachev of the kind we will now remember. At the same time, Gorbachev's inability to renounce his roots in the Party limited his freedom of action, and eventually limited his capacity to manage the forces that his revolution unleashed. His upbringing in the Party may also have given him a desire for personal power that ultimately undermined his attempt to transform his country. Because he was a Party man he succeeded; because he was a Party man he failed—that is the ultimate paradox of Gorbachev.

The pattern of events during the Gorbachev era could be described as the work of two (or more) Gorbachevs. As I will try to show in telling the story, it falls naturally into phases—periods of calm followed by intense, almost manic activity, then calm again. Gorbachev's perceptions evolved through every phase; you could see his mind change, his sense of the possible grow—and sometimes shrink.

My method will be to concentrate on key moments, turning points. I will try to give you a sense of each of them. I will do this, whenever possible, by using the words of participants, particularly of Gorbachev himself, who had a habit from the outset of saying what he thought—not always, and not always completely candidly, but remarkably often. I hope I can show you how Soviet politics in the age of Gorbachev really worked—Kremlinology for everyman.

Most Kremlinology is written like medical literature, in a jargon accessible only to the initiated. That isn't necessary, and I intend to avoid it. Kremlinology is just a fancy word for political analysis, and political analysis is just an attempt to understand human behavior. In this book I want to explain some dramatic human behavior.

This is not a full-blown history of the Gorbachev revolution. The hardback edition of this book was published eight months before Gorbachev left office, so it could not cover the dramatic final acts of his reign. This paperback edition covers the entire story (its introduction and conclusion have also been modified slightly to keep up with events), but it touches only lightly on many of the subjects that will preoccupy future historians, from foreign policy to the intricacies of economic reforms.

My goal is to explain how a lifelong Communist and successful Party official could change in less than six years from a modest reformer to the revolutionary leader who ended seventy-three years of Communist Party rule in Russia, and then lose his way as conflicting nationalisms pulled his country apart. I hope I can also explain how Gorbachev nudged the Soviet Union into increasingly dramatic change, then lost control and watched helplessly as the Soviet Union disintegrated. Finally, I want to demonstrate why, despite his great intelligence, courage, and ingenuity, Mikhail Gorbachev could not transform the Soviet Union into a prosperous modern nation—or preserve it as one nation.

Gorbachev succeeded brilliantly in maneuvering his country out of the Stalinist straitjacket that had made it such a miserable and unsuccessful society. But the Soviet Union needed more than an escape route. It also required a new destination, and means to reach it. Once freed from the Stalinist past, the society discovered just how damaged and just how divided it was. Gorbachev discovered the limits of his own imagination. He found that he could not appease the new forces of freedom that he had unleashed. Ultimately, a romantic adventure story that once seemed to promise a happy ending instead turned into another Russian melodrama. In a startling twist in the plot, the conservative counterreaction that Gorbachev had long feared finally materialized in the coup of August 1991—and was crushed three days later. The coup ultimately crushed Gorbachev as well, giving the melodrama an ending but leaving fifteen new nations in Europe and Asia to start a fresh adventure in uncharted territory.

—WASHINGTON, D.C.
January 1992

AN INDEPENDENT MAN

Mikhail Sergeyevich Gorbachev had an oddly charmed early life—not because he was pampered or prosperous, but because he stumbled into a series of opportunities that shaped the person who would change the world. Those opportunities easily might not have arisen; just as easily, he could have missed them. There was nothing foreordained about the course his life followed. But from the beginning Gorbachev was resourceful and ambitious. He took advantage of the opportunities that came his way to invent himself.

Gorbachev is the first Soviet leader whose life story is not shrouded in myth and mystery. A good deal is known about his early years, thanks to the anecdotes he himself has recounted and to the memories of others who knew him as a child, in school, and at Moscow State University. The story includes numerous clues as to why Gorbachev turned out to be such an unusual Soviet Communist.

He was born in the Kuban, part of the Cossack lands of southeast Russia—perhaps the first lucky coincidence of his life. The Kuban is a special place, seven hundred miles from Moscow. The farmers in most of Russia are the descendants of serfs—slaves—who worked the land for centuries until Alexander II, the great reformer czar, abolished serfdom in 1861. But the peasants of the Kuban were Cossacks who had never been serfs. The region was famous for the independent and sometimes rebellious spirit of its people. The two most renowned leaders of peasant revolts in seventeenth- and eighteenth-century Russia, Stepan Razin and Yemelyan Pugachev, were Cossacks. After the Bolshevik Revolution in 1917, many Cossacks refused to accept the new regime, and fought against the Reds in the ensuing civil war. Thousands were killed when the Bolsheviks prevailed. For centuries, Western travelers and many Russians have noted the striking difference between the self-confident Cossacks and the more docile peasants who had known serfdom.

The circumstances into which Mikhail Sergeyevich was born on March 2, 1931, are not easy for a Westerner to imagine. His native village, Privolnoye, was crude and poor, a cluster of huts and outbuildings on the vast, open plain of the North Caucasus. Its people lived a hard life, with no amenities. Even today the backwardness of the Russian countryside startles foreign visitors; in 1931 conditions were grim. There were no paved roads, no electricity, and precious few motor vehicles. At the time of Gorbachev's birth the North Caucasus *krai,* or region, was enduring horrific suffering. In the first months of 1931 Stalin's frenzied drive to reorganize the countryside into giant collective farms was coming to its successful if bloody conclusion. Thousands of wealthier peasants, derisively called *kulaks,* had been driven from the land or killed to remove the rural bourgeoisie and make way for this new form of socialized agriculture. In Privolnoye— which means "free," as in "free and easy"—the collective farm was organized within days or weeks of Gorbachev's birth. Its first chairman, named that spring, was Gorbachev's maternal grandfather, Pantelei Gopkolo, an active supporter of collectivization.

A surviving photograph taken when Gorbachev was four shows a serious boy with precisely the same penetrating stare that strikes anyone who meets him today. He could have seen a great deal with those eyes. The first years of his life were a time of murderous famine around Privolnoye; thousands died, a disproportionate number of them young children. Gorbachev was six in 1937, the worst year of Stalin's Great Terror, so he was old enough to absorb the traumas that struck his own family during those terrifying times.

For many years Gorbachev did not reveal the skeletons in his family closet. He finally did so in November, 1990, in a speech to cultural and intellectual personalities in the Kremlin. He disclosed that in

1933, his paternal grandfather was arrested for failing to "fulfill the plan for sowing [grain]," and was "sent off to Irkutsk [in Siberia] to cut timber," leaving behind a "tormented family" that soon became destitute: "Half the family died of starvation." Then Grandfather Gopkolo, the first chairman of the collective farm and later "an authorized representative of the Ministry of Procurements, someone of standing for this time" was imprisoned and "interrogated for fourteen months, and he confessed to things that he had not done, and so on. Thank God, he survived."

When Grandfather Gopkolo returned to Privolnoye his home had become "a plague house," Gorbachev continued, "the house of 'an enemy of the people,' where even relatives and close friends could not visit him for fear of following in his footsteps"—presumably into the hands of the political police who had arrested him.

This was a chilling memory, one Gorbachev carried inside himself for more than fifty years before discussing it in public. Apart from the personal pain, a grandfather who was an "enemy of the people" was a liability to the young man—a stigma that could have frustrated his own ambitions.

In 1941, when Gorbachev was ten, his father, Sergei—a Communist Party member—and all the other able-bodied men in the village were drafted into the army to fight the Germans. Sergei Gorbachev did not return home for five years. (Gorbachev's little-mentioned younger brother, Alexander, was born several years after Sergei's return from the front, when Gorbachev was already seventeen.) In August 1942, when Gorbachev was eleven, the Nazis occupied the area around Stavropol, the nearest large town to Privolnoye. Gorbachev's own village escaped the fighting, but the Germans visited regularly to forcibly confiscate food. One villager told Hedrick Smith that two or three local Jewish families were taken away and shot during the occupation, which must have traumatized the Stavropol region. It lasted for five months.

By this time Gorbachev was certainly an alert young man, avidly taking in the world around him. The war interrupted his education and forced him to go to work. During and after the war, youngsters of twelve were required to work as much as fifty days a year—long, hard days—and school did not begin each fall until the harvest was complete. Gorbachev worked in the fields with his mother, Maria Panteleyevna, and other women and children of Privolnoye. Maria Panteleyevna still lives in the village, in a white brick house with electricity and a television set, watched over by the local KGB. She is still remembered as an outspoken person who aggressively stated her opinions at meetings of the collective farm and local Party organization. Villagers who knew her as a younger woman ascribe Gorbachev's outspoken, confident manner to his forceful mother.

In his adolescent years when Gorbachev was becoming a man, his father was away at the front. He apparently lived with his mother and her parents. His grandmother was a religious woman, who had young Mikhail baptized as a child. His grandparents kept religious icons, hiding them behind more acceptable political portraits on the wall of their cottage. Grandfather Gopkolo is described by villagers as a great inspiration to Gorbachev, and introduced the boy to the Russian classics with volumes borrowed from the collective farm's library.

The earliest recorded event hinting at young Mikhail's ambition to better himself was his decision to go on from Privolnoye's village school to the secondary school in Krasnogvardeiskoye (literally, Red Guard town, one of many in the region renamed after the civil war) ten miles from home. To pursue his education he had to walk those ten miles every Monday morning; he spent all week in town, sleeping in a bed he rented from an elderly couple, then walked home every Friday evening and spent the weekend working in the fields.

David Remnick of *The Washington Post* visited the area in 1989 and wrote an extraordinary account of Gorbachev's high school years based on conversations with people who remembered him. Remnick found Yulia Karagodina, Gorbachev's high school sweetheart, who recalled: "He was fearless for someone that age. I remember him correcting teachers in history class, and once he was so angry at one teacher he said, 'Do you want to keep your teaching certificate?' He was the sort who felt he was right and could prove it to anyone, be it in the principal's office or at a Komsomol meeting."

The current principal of the high school showed Remnick Gorbachev's grades, preserved in an ancient ledger book—all 5's (the Russian A) except for one 4 in German. Others recalled that he was a natural leader and serious student.

One of Gorbachev's favorite teachers was Yulia Sumtsova, who pressed her charges to read the Russian classics and to act in school plays. Gorbachev decided to try the student theatricals, and liked them. Student theater became a preoccupation, and the handsome young man with thick, dark hair was soon a leading man. He played the Grand Prince Zvezdich in Mikhail Lermontov's *Masquerade,* and the lovelorn Mezgir in Alexander Ostrovsky's fairy tale *The Snow*

Girl, among others. By Yulia Karagodina's account, it was on the stage that she and Gorbachev found "young love." He also found something he was good at and enjoyed—enjoyed so much that he toyed with the idea of acting as a career. "There was a time," Karagodina told Remnick, "when he even talked with me . . . about trying for a theatrical institute," the obvious way to begin a career in the theater.

While still a student in secondary school Gorbachev discovered that he could use his theatrical skills off the stage, too. The political actor who came to dominate global politics in the late 1980s was evident to Yulia Karagodina forty years earlier:

"He could be so cool and businesslike sometimes. Once at a Komsomol meeting [Gorbachev became the leader of the school's Young Communist League], in front of everyone at the local movie house, he was angry with me for not finishing on time a little newspaper that we put out. And despite our friendship, he reprimanded me in front of everyone, saying that I'd failed, that I was late. He was shouting a bit, disciplining me. Then afterward it was as if nothing had happened. He said, 'Let's go to the movies.' I was at a loss. I couldn't understand why he did what he did, and I said so. He said, 'My dear, one thing has nothing to do with another.' "

Still a teenager, he could already play the part of the *apparatchik.* This is a side of Gorbachev that we will meet again often.

In his last years of school Gorbachev was working for the local machine-tractor station, whose tractors and combines were assigned to the kolkhozes in the area. He was an assistant combine operator— dirty, difficult work requiring long days in the sun. The collective in Privolnoye had an unusually good harvest in 1949, and Gorbachev, together with his comrades at the machine-tractor station, was honored for his contribution with the Order of the Red Banner of Labor, a significant state honor. The next year the young man who presided so efficiently over the Komsomol organization in school applied to become a "candidate member" of the Communist Party. And he applied for a place at Moscow State University.

It would be difficult to exaggerate the length of the leap the eighteen-year-old Gorbachev proposed to make from Privolnoye to the capital and to the country's leading university. This was a common ambition for rural young people at the time, but very few were able to fulfill it. Gorbachev's background as a peasant, a Komsomol activist, and a winner of the Red Banner of Labor no doubt helped him win a place at Moscow State.

His trip to Moscow showed Gorbachev how the war had ravaged his country. The view from the train left a strong impression, which he recalled years later. "I traveled through Stalingrad [now Volgograd], which had been destroyed; through Voronezh, which had been destroyed; and Rostov was destroyed. Nothing but ruins everywhere. I traveled as a student and saw it all. The whole country was in ruins."

At Moscow State University, Gorbachev told an Italian interviewer in 1987, "I entered the law faculty, but at the outset I wanted to enter the physics faculty," adding that he was also interested in mathematics, history, and literature. His country school may not have prepared him well for entrance exams in Moscow, or perhaps he was simply assigned to the law faculty. It would have been an odd choice for an ambitious young man. Lawyers had (and have) low status in Soviet society, and during the Stalinist dictatorship the legal system was a malleable appendage to the Party.

Yulia Karagodina recalled that Gorbachev the law student "wrote letters to me telling me how much he liked Moscow and the abundance of things and the fascinating people. There was never a sense in his letters that he felt any lack of confidence because he was a village boy." Alas, those letters were lost to posterity when the man Karogodina later married burned them in a fit of jealousy. Others who studied with Gorbachev recall his seriousness and determination to catch up with better-prepared graduates of urban high schools. He often returned at one or two in the morning to the room he shared with six or seven other boys in an ancient and dilapidated dormitory complex, where he and ten thousand other students lived.

"Gorbachev the student was not only quite intelligent and gifted, he was also a straightforward man, whose intelligence never led him to arrogance. He was able and eager to listen to the person with whom he was conversing. Loyal and personally honest, he gained an authority that was informal, spontaneous. Not that he wasn't sure of himself. He had the self-awareness of a man who knows that everything that he possesses is due to his own efforts, his own talent, his own diligence, and that he has obtained nothing through the protection of others or from social origin."

These are the impressions of Zdenek Mlynar, a Czech who was a fellow student and roommate of the combine operator from Privolnoye. "We lived in the same student quarters for five years, and were in the same field of study. We prepared for exams together, and both of us finally obtained a degree with honors. We were more than schoolmates. We were known to all as a couple of good friends."

Mlynar became an active reformist Communist in the Czech regime of Alexander Dubcek that was crushed by Soviet invasion in 1968; he later emigrated to Vienna. He has been repeatedly interviewed since disclosing his friendship with Gorbachev in 1985, but his most interesting memories are those he disclosed first, in an article for the Italian Communist Party newspaper *L'Unità* published in April 1985, just a few weeks after Gorbachev became Soviet leader.

Mlynar portrays a young man eager to learn and to study, who did his own thinking and was prepared to share thoughts with his foreign friend. "From the Marxist philosophy lessons Gorbachev picked as his favorite maxim Hegel's assertion that 'truth is always concrete,' " Mlynar wrote. "He always liked to repeat that when a teacher or student muttered general principles, totally ignorant of how little they matched reality."

Reality interested Gorbachev; Mlynar recounts that his friend told him the truth about the suffering of ordinary people during the war —as opposed to "the wartime romanticism of the soldiers" who were their classmates. And Gorbachev explained the difference between the collective farm laws they studied in class and real life in the countryside, where the law had "a minor role" and a larger part was played by "ordinary violence in 'assuring labor discipline' on the collective farms."

Mlynar suggests that Gorbachev was an independent thinker even in 1952, when Stalinist paranoia was intense. He recounts their studies of Party history, in which they were taught that "every idea that diverges from the line prescribed from above had to be viewed as an 'anti-Party deviation,' whose supporters were liquidated, executed, and canceled from history. It was precisely at that time that Gorbachev told me: 'But Lenin did not arrest Martov; he let him emigrate from the country'."

The reference was to Julius Martov, an early comrade of Lenin's who broke away to become a leader of the Menshevik faction after the 1917 revolution. Lenin turned against the Mensheviks, banning and crushing them in 1922, but in 1920 he allowed Martov and other Mensheviks to leave Russia unharmed. Mlynar, a Communist himself, rightly seizes on the significance of Gorbachev's small but telling heresy. Gorbachev's reference to Martov suggested that Lenin was more humane than Stalin, whose unforgiving line they were taught at the university. As Mlynar put it, "These words meant that the student Gorbachev doubted that men could be divided into supporters of a given line, or criminals"—though that was precisely Stalin's position at the time.

Perhaps more remarkable than the fact Gorbachev held such an opinion was his willingness to share it spontaneously "with a school companion, let alone a foreigner," as Mlynar notes. Had Mlynar mentioned Gorbachev's remark to a police informant in those mad times, it could have ended the young Russian's political career.

Gorbachev's outspokenness led to another incident remembered somewhat differently by various contemporaries. In the version of Rudolf Koltchanov, now a newspaper editor in Moscow and then a Gorbachev roommate, they were in a course on "Marxism and Issues of Language." The professor habitually read from the works of Stalin. Koltchanov recalls that Gorbachev once stood up and said, "Respected professor, we can read for ourselves. What is your interpretation of the reading, and why don't we discuss it?" Gorbachev was summoned to the dean's office but not punished.

Vladimir Lieberman, a war veteran eight years older than Gorbachev, who was also his classmate, has provided a somewhat different account. Lieberman recalls that he and Gorbachev jointly sent an anonymous note up to the professor complaining about his reading. The professor angrily denounced the author of the note as anti-socialist. Gorbachev then rose calmly to acknowledge authorship of the offending document, noting that he was a strong Communist and Komsomol activist. By either account, Gorbachev behaved with startling courage for a Soviet student of that time.

Mlynar was the first foreigner that Gorbachev ever got to know. In his 1986 biography of Gorbachev, Zhores Medvedev, a Soviet emigré, notes that rooming arrangements for foreign students in Moscow—in the early fifties, and for many years afterward—were not left to chance. "Only 'trustworthy' Soviet students are distributed amongst the better rooms allocated to foreigners," Medvedev wrote, adding that it was "not unlikely that Gorbachev would have been asked to give periodic reports on his roommate" to the secret police.

It is difficult for Western readers to appreciate how exotic it was for a young farm boy from the North Caucasus to be rooming with a relatively sophisticated Czech. Mlynar recounts a telling anecdote. In the summer of 1951, when Gorbachev was home—as he was each summer to work again on the combine—Mlynar sent him a postcard from Czechoslovakia. In Privolnoye, "the police commander had gone to find him personally in the fields to deliver that suspicious item—a picture postcard from abroad." Such was its rarity and significance!

There must have been more to his relationship with Mlynar than postcards. The opportunity to spend five years with someone raised in old Europe, someone much more sophisticated and worldly than himself, gave Gorbachev an experience that separated him from all but a handful of his contemporaries.

The course of study on the law faculty also gave Gorbachev unusual exposure to foreign influences. Most of the curriculum was conventional and tedious, involving study of the totally corrupted Soviet legal system. Gorbachev learned, for example, that the famous show trials of the late 1930s, at which Stalin's henchmen convicted Nikolai Bukharin and other leading Bolsheviks of mythical crimes of treason and betrayal, were a sterling example of socialist legality. But he also read the American constitution, the history of Roman law, Rousseau, Hobbes, Thomas Aquinas, and Machiavelli. He took a famous two-year course on political ideas taught by Professor Stepan Kechekyan, a distinguished intellectual who had been educated before the revolution. Mlynar remembers that "Gorbachev was impressed by those other ideas" he was exposed to in Kechekyan's lectures.

Law offered another academic opportunity to Gorbachev that has proved useful to him in later life—a chance to study oratory. Almost uniquely among the academic disciplines in the Soviet Union, law schools teach students how to give speeches, conduct interrogations, think on their feet. The former schoolboy actor must have enjoyed this training, which—judging by his performances at home and abroad years later—helped him considerably.

For all his curiosity and self-confidence as a student, the young Gorbachev was a conventional and ambitious Communist. "Gorbachev took Marxism very seriously," Mlynar recalled. "We were convinced that Marxism was the final answer that would change the world." That conviction "was a rare thing among Soviet students," Mlynar said. In a later interview with *Time* magazine, Mlynar added that Gorbachev "like everyone else at the time was a Stalinist. In order to be a true reforming communist, you have to have been a true Stalinist."

Fridrikh Neznansky, who worked in the Komsomol with Gorbachev during their university years and who emigrated to the West in 1978, has recounted how Gorbachev got his first job as a Komsomol organizer (*komsorg* in Party argot) in the university. By his unflattering account, Gorbachev picked the eve of a Komsomol meeting to go out on the town with the young man who had the job of *komsorg* and get him drunk. At the meeting next day, Gorbachev denounced the other fellow for drinking to excess in a manner not befitting a Communist. Gorbachev was then chosen to replace the drinker—according to Neznansky. If true, this story suggests that Gorbachev learned the basic *apparatchik*'s lesson—that the right end justifies most means—at an early age.

In 1952 Gorbachev became a full member of the Communist Party. He remained active in Komsomol affairs. Neznansky has said he often heard "the steely voice of the Komsomol secretary of the law faculty, Gorbachev, demanding expulsion from the Komsomol [of some member] for the slightest offense, from inappropriately telling political anecdotes to shirking being sent to a collective farm." Lev Yudovich, another classmate who now lives in the West, has a similar memory of a young Gorbachev in charge of ideology and propaganda for the law-faculty Komsomol who often took a hard line.

There are no recorded recollections of Gorbachev's participation in the darkest moments of Stalin's last mad months, when he mobilized the party and the Komsomol to join in the campaign against the "Doctors' Plot," the imaginary conspiracy of Jewish physicians against Stalin and other Kremlin leaders. In the last months of his life in late 1952 and early 1953, Stalin was apparently preparing to deport the entire Jewish population of the European parts of the Soviet Union to the remote Far East; the frenzied propaganda campaign to prepare for that giant pogrom involved the entire party apparatus.

On one occasion Gorbachev stood up for a Jewish classmate who was under attack. Vladimir Lieberman has recounted to Hedrick Smith his memory of a Party meeting at the university where another student "suddenly jumped on my neck, mentioning that in spite of my good marks I had lots of foibles, and in particular, I was talking too much." Gorbachev cut off the attacker and chastised him for being "a spineless animal" and an opportunist. Gorbachev's rebuke deterred others from joining in criticizing the Jewish student.

Asked by an interviewer for *Time* if Gorbachev had ever taken part in the anti-Semitic campaign, Mlynar did not deny that he had, but said his old friend had done nothing to make any individual suffer. "I know that Gorbachev was not involved in any affair that had tragic consequences," as he put it.

Just as Gorbachev's high school girlfriend was amazed by his ability to shift from *apparatchik* to friend, so Mlynar remembers a liberal-minded and independent Gorbachev while other classmates draw a harsher portrait of a tough Party man. It is as if two strains in his character have been in conflict since he was a teenager; by all indications, the conflict has never been resolved.

In his third or fourth year at the university, Gorbachev got to know a handsome young woman who was a year behind him. Raisa Maximovna Titorenko was a philosophy student, which in those days meant she studied primarily Marx, Lenin, and the other "philosophers" of socialism, but also read the classics. They met at a ballroom-dancing class; Gorbachev and his friend Koltchanov had dropped by to make fun of several of their friends who were in the class. "We were ready to say, 'You call yourselves real men and look at all this,' " Koltchanov has recalled. "But then one of our friends in the class, Volodya Kuzmin, introduced Mikhail Sergeyevich to his dance partner. It was Raisa Maximovna. I think for Gorbachev it was love at first sight. Just like in the movies. She was just so striking. And, as I think he discovered later on, she was extremely smart."

She was bright and cultivated—she knew music and painting as well as literature—and according to accounts of their contemporaries was much sought-after by other young men. Mlynar, who married a Czech girl who was Raisa Maximovna's roommate, said the red-haired Raisa was won over in part by Gorbachev's "lack of vulgarity." This sounds like a polite, Czechoslovak way of suggesting that unlike many Russian men who treated women boorishly, Gorbachev showed Raisa genuine respect. His regard for her is obvious today whenever they appear in public together.

They married in 1954. Accounts of their friends suggest that they were able to spend a wedding night alone together, but then both returned to their crowded dormitory rooms in the same complex. For Gorbachev's last year at the university, they apparently got a room together in a new dormitory for married students. Friends remarked that the polished Raisa would refine the country boy from Privolnoye, as indeed she did. The two have been inseparable for more than thirty-five years.

•   •   •

Joseph Stalin died on March 5, 1953, toward the end of Gorbachev's third year at the university. His demise was a cataclysmic event in the life of the Soviet Union. The Great Teacher, the Great Shepherd, the Father of the Peoples, the Shining Sun of Humanity, the Friend and Teacher of All Toilers—the man who literally invented the society they lived in was suddenly gone. The night Stalin died, Gorbachev and a number of his classmates joined the teeming mobs in the streets of Moscow. "Most of us were out all night in the freezing cold, trying to see the body at the House of Columns" in the center of the city, Rudolf Koltchanov, a Moscow newspaper editor who lived with Gorbachev in the old dormitory, told Remnick of the *Post*. "When we all got back to the room, in the early hours of the morning, we were sitting on our beds. We tried to talk, but mostly we were just silent, thinking. Some were crying, though I remember that I wasn't, and neither was Mikhail Sergeyevich. We were so accustomed to life under Stalin. We might find it strange and terrible now, but that was how it was. And then someone spoke with the question that everyone had on their minds: 'What are we going to do now?' he said."

One answer to that question was that they were going to begin to think more freely—not overnight, of course, but surprisingly soon. Stalin's death lifted an oppressive intellectual cloud, releasing long-suppressed critical energies. Gorbachev's generation of university students—freshly grown up, still at the age of discovery—was best positioned to take advantage of the new atmosphere.

During that first summer after Stalin's death, when Gorbachev was presumably back in Privolnoye, working on the combine, Lavrenti Beria was arrested in Moscow. Beria had been Stalin's terrorist henchman in Moscow since 1938 as commissar for internal affairs, sharing responsibility for the deaths of millions; his removal from power symbolized the new leadership's decision to move away from terror. By the time Gorbachev returned to Moscow in September to begin his fourth year (of five) at the university, the period known as "The Thaw" (named for an Ilya Ehrenburg novel of that name) was beginning.

"In the first three years after Stalin died," recalled Fyodor Burlatsky, a contemporary of Gorbachev's and now a prominent Moscow editor, "a whole new spirit developed—it infected student life, the intelligentsia, and Gorbachev too." It was a spirit of skepticism infected with hope—hope that Stalin's heavy-handed dictatorship, which had lasted a quarter century, could be followed by a more open society. Beria's demise, the diminution of the role of the secret police, and the new government's public disavowal of Stalin's last mad acts, including the "Doctors' Plot," signaled a relaxation of controls that many intellectuals quickly sought to exploit. Professors at Moscow State University were among those who eagerly opened a new period of debate about the first principles of Soviet society. It was a time of possibilities and—to borrow a Gorbachev phrase from thirty-five years later—of new thinking.

It is impossible to say precisely how this new atmosphere changed young Gorbachev's outlook, but the influence had to be enormous. As his old roommate Koltchanov put it, what they learned in class was only a fraction of their education. "The dorm room may have been the greatest classroom for all of us. We talked about everything from girls to more serious things: the latest exhibition or the latest artistic awards or historical event."

But none of Gorbachev's university friends has recalled him talking about the arrests of both his grandfathers—his own direct exposure to the cruelties of Stalinism. If Stalin's death gave him any personal satisfaction, Gorbachev kept it well hidden.

When the talk was over, and the last examinations were behind him, Gorbachev and his bride left Moscow for Stavropol, the principal city of his native North Caucasus. He was twenty-four when he left, fully a man, shaped by powerful forces and events, including collectivization, Stalin's great terror, war, and Stalin's death. Five years at Moscow State University had polished the country boy. He has never lost the soft "g" of his Privolnoye origins, but it became less noticeable in Moscow. He read great books—and a great deal of Stalinist tripe. He learned about Europe from Zdenek Mlynar, and about free thinking from many of his contemporaries in that time of ferment. He learned from his legal studies that there was a rich history of political ideas not related to Stalinism; he learned the concept of the rule of law. And he experienced the reality of arbitrary dictatorship, notably during Stalin's last crusade against "cosmopolitans," when Jewish professors disappeared from the faculty of Moscow State and the Komsomol organization joined in the national witch hunt for "followers" of the members of the "Doctors' Plot." He found that his ambitions could be rewarded—with political office in the Komsomol, with the hand of the smart and attractive woman he fell in love with. In about ten years he had remade himself from village lad to educated lawyer, from farmer to a man with serious prospects. To repeat from Mlynar's description: "He gained an authority [at university] that was informal, spontaneous. . . . He had the self-awareness of a man who knows that everything he possesses is due to his own efforts, his own talent."

•   •   •

Like his decision to study law, Gorbachev's choice of a first job has never been fully explained. He might have preferred to stay in Moscow for graduate study or political work—country boys who have discovered the capital are rarely eager to return home. But the rules then in effect gave Gorbachev little freedom of choice; he had to be chosen for graduate study, and apparently he wasn't. So he had to accept the work assignment given to him, which called for his return to Stavropol in the North Caucasus.

If he was as clever as he was ambitious, Gorbachev may have realized that Stavropol was actually the right place to begin a serious political career. *Apparatchiks* can spend their entire working lives as bureaucrats or experts in Moscow, but political leaders usually made names for themselves in the provinces before coming to "the center," as Moscow is called on the periphery. Gorbachev may also have known from the time he first left home for the university that the Stavropol Komsomol—which apparently helped him get into Moscow State—expected him to return when he finished his degree. In any event, that is what happened.

"I was assigned to go and work for the procuracy [the state prosecutor] of Stavropol *krai*," Gorbachev told an audience in 1990. "I took up the job and began work. But that very same month I was transferred to Komsomol work . . . so I missed out on a lawyer's career." It was the beginning of a twenty-three-year career as a provincial Party official.

Gorbachev was assigned to head a department in the Komsomol committee in Stavropol, then a city of about 120,000 inhabitants. It wasn't much of a job for a new graduate of the Moscow State University law faculty. The Komsomol is one of the dreariest of Soviet institutions. It is a kind of junior Communist Party for fourteen- to twenty-seven-year-olds; all young people who want to join the Party must pass first through the Komsomol. The Komsomol's huge bureaucracy has few specific functions beyond exhorting the membership to work harder and more responsibly. It is part of the great apparatus that for decades socialized Soviet citizens into the political culture of their country. As a department head, Gorbachev was probably responsible for keeping tabs on the Komsomol organizations in a number of local institutions, and for helping out with the organizing and propagandizing. Inevitably, he had to perform boring tasks surrounded by dull people.

During Gorbachev's first year in that job Nikita Khrushchev shattered the family china in Soviet communism's closet. At the 20th Party Congress in February 1956—apparently without warning his colleagues in the leadership—Khrushchev denounced Stalin's crimes in his famous secret speech, so called because it wasn't published in the Soviet press. But it was quickly conveyed to party and Komsomol activists, first in closed meetings where the speech was read, soon afterward in specially printed editions. There is no record of Gorbachev's reaction to the speech, but his contemporaries who shared that experience are confident of its importance in his life, as in theirs.

The secret speech accelerated the processes of change initiated by Stalin's death. It opened the way to fundamental reconsideration of Communist doctrine, but its most important consequences were more practical. It ended the period of intense paranoia and fear that lasted from the mid-1930s until Stalin died, interrupted only by the exhilarating but devastating war years. The Party was transformed from a monolith living in constant fear of the leader to a new kind of debating society. At the same time the thaw of the mid-fifties allowed for Russia's reentry—however tentatively—into the outside world. If Khrushchev could denounce Stalin, and the Soviet Union could be opened to foreign tourists (tens of thousands came for the World Youth Festival in Moscow in 1957, a turning point for the sensibilities of many young Soviets at the time), if new art and poetry could reawaken the famous Russian soul, then it was not fruitless to dream of real change and progress.

The secret revelations of the 20th Party Congress became public five years later at the 22nd, and on that occasion Mikhail Gorbachev was a delegate in the hall. His career had progressed with remarkable speed in the intervening five years under the sponsorship of the man who gave him his first Komsomol position, Vsevolod Murakhovsky. After just a year in the Komsomol, Gorbachev was named first secretary of the city organization. Two years later he moved up again, becoming head of the department of propaganda and second secretary of the Komsomol for the entire Stavropol region, or *krai*. After another two years he was named first secretary, a post that gave him membership on the Communist Party bureau, the local equivalent of the national Politburo. Each of these promotions appears to have been made or recommended by Murakhovsky.* Gorbachev was then the leading Komsomol official and sixth-ranking Communist in an important agricultural region of the country, and he was just twenty-nine.

---

* Gorbachev's relationship with Murakhovsky has continued ever since. In October 1985, seven months after Gorbachev was named Party leader, Murakhovsky came from Stavropol to Moscow to become deputy prime minister.

As a delegate to the 22nd Party Congress Gorbachev took part in one of the great Soviet political dramas of the modern era. Numerous senior Party officials went to the podium in the huge new Palace of Congresses—an architectural monstrosity that Khrushchev had built inside the Kremlin's walls—to denounce Stalin and provide detailed recitations of his crimes. Many of the denouncers had held high office when the crimes were committed. The Congress created a sensation. As Khrushchev later recorded in the memoirs he dictated into a tape recorder, he and his colleagues were quite terrified at the possible consequences of the decision to speak openly about the past, fearing the reactions of the public. "We were scared—really scared. We were afraid the thaw might unleash a flood, which we wouldn't be able to control and which could drown us." Nevertheless, in 1961 they made a decisive break with their own history. Stalin's body was removed from the mausoleum in Red Square; Stalingrad became Volgograd, and hundreds of other places and institutions named for Stalin were re-named; thousands of monuments to the Father of the Peoples came down all over the Soviet Union.

After the Congress Gorbachev went back to Stavropol to lead a series of meetings to explain the Party's decisions to Komsomol activists. It must have been an interesting experience for this young man to tell even younger comrades that Stalin should now be seen as a criminal, not a savior. His audiences in Stavropol undoubtedly included the sons and daughters of many families that had suffered directly from Stalin's crimes, but that fact would not have prepared them for this dramatic public turn in the Party line.

Several months later, Gorbachev left the Komsomol to begin working directly for the Party. His new job appeared to be a demotion. He may have wanted to get out of the Komsomol, an organization that never really *did* anything, to get his hands on real problems. Or his patrons in Stavropol may have made it clear that this was the moment for him to move into the main political channel that led to higher office, the Party itself. Whatever the reason, Gorbachev became Party organizer of a newly formed agricultural production unit in the Stavropol region—a bureaucratic creation born of Khrushchev's latest attempt to find an efficient way to manage the country's chaotic agriculture.

Gorbachev's job was to coordinate the agricultural production of perhaps two dozen collective farms, a considerable portion of the Stavropol region. The job was made more difficult by the fact that other officials shared the same responsibility; the latest reorganization had not created clear lines of authority. Gorbachev appears to have realized quickly that he was poorly prepared for serious responsibilities in agriculture; he registered as an "external" or correspondence student at the Stavropol Agricultural Institute in September 1962, for a five-year course that would give him an advanced degree as an agronomist-economist.

Gorbachev was promoted so quickly from this new job that there are grounds to wonder if he took it on the understanding that he would soon have bigger responsibilities. He got them in December 1962, less than a year after he had left the Komsomol, when he was named a department head of the Stavropol region Party organization in charge of Party "cadres," or personnel.

There was great drama in the North Caucasus in 1962 that deserves mention here, though it is unknown how it may have affected Gorbachev. In the town of Novocherkassk, about 180 miles from Stavropol, workers in a factory that made electric locomotives led a popular revolt, set off by simultaneous announcements that the prices of butter and meat were going up, and their wages were being reduced. The uprising that June 2 was unique in the postwar era: a leaderless group of ordinary people spontaneously protested the conditions of their lives, ripped up the rails of the main line that passed through town, massed in the town square, raided Party headquarters, and chanted hostile slogans: "Down with Khrushchev!" and "Use Khrushchev for sausage meat!" Troops opened fire on the crowd, killing men, women, and children—seventy or eighty killed in all, according to the vivid account of the uprising assembled after the fact by Alexander Solzhenitsyn, and published in the third volume of *The Gulag Archipelago*.

Senior Party leaders from Moscow including Anastas Mikoyan and Khrushchev's number-two man, Frol Kozlov, flew to the scene and supervised the official response. Afterward all trace of the event was wiped away: The wounded were exiled to Siberia, according to Solzhenitsyn. So were the families of the dead and of the wounded. So was every identifiable participant in the protest—except for nine men who were shot after a trial, and two women sentenced to fifteen years in prison camps. People in the town were told that the deaths were caused not by soldiers but by armed "saboteurs" of unknown origin.

A mob in the streets—nothing frightened the Soviet leaders more. Citizens were supposed to put up with the privations of the Stalinist system, to accept sloganeering in place of sausage. Any sign of rebellion had to be snuffed out, then obliterated. The events in Novocherkassk were never mentioned in the press, nor even discovered by foreign scholars for years. But word of what happened must have traveled the 180 miles to Stavropol that June. We can only wonder what the young Gorbachev, fresh from explaining to Komsomol activists why Stalin had been denounced at the 22nd Party Congress, might have made of this grisly tale from Novocherkassk.

The job as head of the department of cadres was a sensitive one for a thirty-one-year-old; the fact that Gorbachev got it was a sign that he had won the patronage—and the confidence—of the new Party boss in Stavropol, Fyodor Kulakov.

Murakhovsky had been an invaluable patron in the first stages of his career; Kulakov now became Gorbachev's mentor for a much longer period. Over the next sixteen years, Gorbachev moved up the ladder from Stavropol to Staraya Ploshchad (Old Square) in Moscow —home of the Central Committee of the Communist Party—under Kulakov's wing, though also with the help of others.

Kulakov had arrived in Stavropol as the new first secretary of the *krai*'s Communist Party just before Gorbachev was named first secretary of the Komsomol there. The appointment was a demotion for Kulakov, who had previously served in Moscow as minister of grain products for the Russian Federation, the largest of the Soviet Union's fifteen republics. Kulakov, with other senior officials responsible for agriculture in the capital, had fallen into Khrushchev's disfavor and been sent to the countryside. But he was an ambitious man determined to restore his standing by succeeding in Stavropol.

Gorbachev worked on cadre—personnel—matters for the next four years. Zhores Medvedev—whose account of Gorbachev's years in Stavropol I have drawn on heavily here—suggests that the job was unusually important because so many of the Soviet Union's most popular resorts were located within the borders of Stavropol *krai*. Numerous members of the senior leadership spent vacations in Mineralnye Vody (Mineral Waters), Kislovodsk, and other towns in the mountains southeast of Stavropol, so Party authorities in Moscow would have been especially sensitive to the selection of local officials in the area. Medvedev writes that Gorbachev probably made useful contacts in Moscow during consultations with representatives of the senior leadership. During those four years Gorbachev continued his correspondence studies in agriculture. Raisa Maximovna also studied for an advanced degree by correspondence from the Moscow State Pedagogical Institute. (She spent much of her time in the early sixties on a research project on the sociology of the local peasantry, which became her doctoral dissertation.)

While Gorbachev was working on personnel matters in Stavropol, the Party's senior leadership was making a critical personnel change in Moscow, and the young official in Stavropol may have known something about it. After months of plotting, senior comrades removed Khrushchev from office in October 1964. Kulakov, Gorbachev's patron, may have been involved in the conspiracy. By some accounts, key conspirators, led by the party's chief ideologist, Mikhail Suslov, discussed their plans during a fishing and hunting holiday in the Stavropol region, where all were guests of the local first secretary, Kulakov.

Whether he knew in advance or not, Gorbachev apparently approved of Khrushchev's removal. According to his old Czech friend Mlynar, Gorbachev in 1967 openly expressed disdain for Khrushchev's erratic and "entirely subjective" behavior. He told Mlynar that Khrushchev was not a true reformer, because he insisted on maintaining total control from the center, and allowed for no genuine devolution of powers to local officials.

Khrushchev's political demise in 1964 brought Kulakov's ascent; he returned to Moscow to become head of the agricultural department of the Party's Central Committee. Another member of the Khrushchev leadership, Leonid Efremov, was now exiled to Stavropol, where he replaced Kulakov as first secretary. Both moves appeared to serve Gorbachev's interests. His chief patron was now a formidable power in Moscow; his new boss in Stavropol was a cultivated, liberal man, an intellectual by Party standards, who also took a shine to the second secretary for cadres.

Gorbachev's independent-mindedness must have been strengthened by two remarkable trips that he—apparently accompanied by Raisa—made to France and Italy during those Stavropol years. In both cases, they had a chance to see and touch and smell for themselves something that most Soviet citizens at the time considered the ultimate exotica —life "in the West." They visited France in 1966 as members of a small group of Party functionaries invited by Jean-Baptiste Doumeng, a French businessman known for his leftist politics. By Gorbachev's own account, he was able to spend several weeks driving more than three thousand miles around France in a Renault. Later the Gorbachevs traveled to Italy as guests of the Communist Party there, making a thorough tour of Sicily, then visiting a series of cities including

Turin and Florence, and many smaller towns. "I remember best the meetings in small towns and workers' settlements with Italian workers," Gorbachev said years later.

That a young Party official like Gorbachev would have two such opportunities to absorb Western realities in the mid-1960s was extraordinary. The Soviet leaders of those years were generally uneducated and unsophisticated, and knew little if anything about actual living conditions in the capitalist world. Svetlana Alliluyeva, Stalin's daughter, has recorded the revealing remark that Suslov made to her in 1966 when she was seeking permission to travel abroad, and Suslov was trying to dissuade her: "Take my family and my children—they never go abroad, don't even want to. Not interested!" Suslov embodied the narrow-minded Party puritanism of the time, which was typical—nearly universal—among senior officials.

So Gorbachev's unusual opportunities to see for himself what went on in the West set him apart from most of his colleagues. More important, a chance to get a close look at life in the "imperialist camp" inevitably undermined the distorted view of the outside world drawn in Soviet propaganda. For a young man who had adopted Hegel's maxim that "truth is always concrete," the concrete reality of France and Italy had to make a profound impression. The essential civility of daily life in those countries, the efficiency of basic services, the abundance of food and clothing, housing, automobiles, and other modern conveniences all made for a stunning contrast with the life the Gorbachevs knew in Stavropol. Westerners who haven't seen a provincial Soviet city cannot easily imagine the poverty, the scruffiness, and the deprivation that are endemic.

The Gorbachevs also could have noticed a startling difference between the manner and bearing of ordinary Frenchmen and Italians and comparable Russians on the streets of Stavropol or Moscow. The French and Italians display the sense of personal sovereignty, the individualism and confidence that are typical of their cultures, whereas Russians seen on the street tend to be bundled up, figuratively and literally, as they scuffle through their tedious daily rounds. Yes, these sound like large generalizations, but they are accurate. Indeed, their accuracy was demonstrated by the radically changed flavor of Moscow crowds in the late 1980s, when—after several years of *glasnost* and *perestroika*—a visitor could see a new energy level and self-confidence on the sidewalks of the capital. I was taken aback by the change.

Back in Stavropol, Gorbachev's brisk ascent continued. In 1966 he became first secretary of the Party organization for the city of Stavropol; in 1967 he received his degree in agronomy and economics; in 1968 he was named second secretary of the Party organization for the entire region, a big promotion that left him in charge of agriculture for all of Stavropol *krai*. After just one full harvest cycle—and very poor results, thanks to terrible weather—he was promoted again. When Efremov went back to Moscow in 1970, Gorbachev, still not forty, was named first secretary of the Stavropol *krai* Party Committee.

This appointment transformed Gorbachev's status. He joined an élite group of several hundred men (and a handful of women) at the pinnacle of Soviet society. He was now in line, as Party boss of an important region, to be elected a full member of the Central Committee, as he was in 1971. Suddenly Gorbachev would enjoy an elaborate array of privileges, from access to special foodstuffs and tailors to trips abroad in official delegations. He would be able, if he chose, to live far outside normal Soviet society; he could build a handsome dacha somewhere in the *krai,* let servants look after his homes, live like the potentate he had now become.

For the 2.3 million residents of Stavropol *krai,* his word would have the force of law. In the Brezhnev era, a Party first secretary was a prince in his own domain. When Gorbachev became national leader and encouraged such revelations, the Soviet press described astounding corruption involving numerous first secretaries around the country who took full advantage of the opportunities the system offered. There were few if any effective controls.

But by all indications the corrupt, fat life held no appeal for Mikhail Gorbachev. His performance as first secretary over the subsequent eight years established him as a *rara avis* among Soviet leaders of the Brezhnev era: an honest and unpretentious man seemingly determined to do a good job. A version of the Gorbachev that the world came to know in the eighties was first encountered by the residents of Stavropol in the early seventies—an energetic, involved, relatively informal leader willing to get his hands dirty, talk out problems with ordinary people, and encourage others to take responsibility.

Gorbachev, with Raisa and their daughter Irina, born in 1959, lived modestly in a one-story house of brick and stucco on Dzerzhinsky Street in Stavropol. According to *Time* magazine's biography, citizens soon learned that they could avoid the traditional bureaucratic impediments and deal directly with the first secretary by accosting him on his daily walk to work at Party headquarters on Lenin Square. He regularly gave residents of more remote areas access to the boss during visits he made to towns and villages in the region. The Gorbachevs were regulars at the local theater, and he often attended soccer games at the town stadium.

Gorbachev experimented with something akin to *glasnost* in Stavropol. He published the documents from Party meetings, and arranged regular briefings for the local press. Alexander Mayatsky, a former editor of *Stavropolskaya Pravda,* the local Party organ, told *Time* that Gorbachev discouraged the local editors from checking everything they wanted to write with the Party leadership, encouraging them to make their own decisions. Mayatsky said Gorbachev occasionally approached him on the street to suggest he pursue some topic Gorbachev considered important. "If Gorbachev found something interesting, you had the impression that it would occupy him day and night, waking and sleeping."

One of the duties he found interesting, or at least important, was the cultivation of the Politburo members who regularly came to Stavropol *krai* on holiday. The three he probably saw most often were Yuri Andropov, who served as head of the Committee on State Security, the KGB, during the years Gorbachev was Stavropol's first secretary; Alexei Kosygin, the premier in those years; and Suslov, who had been first secretary in Stavropol during World War II and was the last of Stalin's active comrades in the leadership. In the Brezhnev years Suslov was the protector of traditional orthodoxy in the Party.

All three suffered from diabetes and kidney ailments that brought them regularly to Kislovodsk to take advantage of the baths and mineral waters at the special sanitoria for senior officials maintained there by the Party, government, and KGB. These three senior leaders shared another attribute; all were relatively austere men who did not succumb to the temptations of the sweet life that Brezhnev and his more intimate cronies so enjoyed.

Party protocol would have required Gorbachev to meet each of them when he arrived in Stavropol *krai,* to escort each to his sanitorium, and then to return later during the visit to make sure all was well. It seems a fair assumption that all of them would have appreciated Gorbachev's confident, intelligent manner, and the obvious fact that he shared their distaste for ostentatious displays of status and power.

The relative importance of these new relationships and Kulakov's continued patronage of Gorbachev's career is not clear. Several senior officials, all formerly associated with Andropov, have assured me that Andropov soon became Gorbachev's most important patron. But others, also well connected, insist Kulakov remained more important. In 1970, when Gorbachev was elevated to the post of first secretary, Kulakov was a candidate (nonvoting) member of the Politburo—a strong position from which to support the ascent of his protégé in Stavropol. In 1971 Kulakov became the youngest full member of the Politburo, and in the subsequent five years, he rose steadily in the hierarchy. By 1976 and 1977 he was widely considered a potential successor to Brezhnev. (Andropov became a full member of the Politburo in 1973.)

It was in those years that Kulakov did Gorbachev perhaps the largest and most significant favor of Gorbachev's career. Achieving the rank of *krai* first secretary at the age of thirty-nine was a considerable accomplishment, but to rise further in the hierarchy Gorbachev would have to make a name for himself beyond the borders of Stavropol and beyond the walls of its sanitoria for high officials. He needed some kind of grand accomplishment that could attract national attention. Kulakov created one for him.

Kulakov's own ticket to the pinnacle of power was to be his success as manager of the country's agricultural output. An unusually good harvest in 1976 gave him a boost, and in that same year he organized an important new experiment to demonstrate improved harvesting methodology. Soviet agriculture has traditionally been plagued by horrendous losses; 20 to 30 percent of every year's crop can be lost because of sloppy harvesting, poor transportation of harvested grain, inadequate storage facilities and the like. Kulakov's experiment, designed at an agricultural institute in Rostov, was designed to speed the harvesting of ripe grain so that more would be captured precisely when it was ready for harvest, thus reducing unnecessary losses.

At the time, Kulakov—like all senior leaders of the Communist Party—was also a member of the Supreme Soviet, the ritualistic national legislature whose members invariably gave unanimous approval to all Politburo policies. He represented part of Stavropol *krai*, and he decided to conduct the harvesting experiment in his own constituency, one of the country's richest farming areas. Of course it was also Gorbachev's territory.

Kulakov picked the Ipatovsky district, where winter wheat was grown on a flat plain. Success of the experiment would depend largely on the enthusiasm and organization of those who had to conduct it. Kulakov counted on his own supporters in the area, and especially on Gorbachev, to provide them.

And they did. The experiment was conducted by an unusually large brigade of men and machines—at least fifteen combines, fifteen trucks to collect and carry the grain from the fields, mobile living facilities to allow work to continue night and day, and a large body of workers divided into groups specializing in each aspect of the harvesting. Numerous Party workers, including professional agitators and organizers, were assigned to provide moral support. After elaborate preparations in the winter and spring, work began at the beginning of July—the earliest moment when winter wheat was ripe.

Traditionally, the harvest in Ipatovsky had taken several weeks. In 1977 it took nine days. The plan for the region called for Ipatovsky to deliver 120,000 tons of wheat to the state; the effectiveness of the new harvesting methods allowed the district to deliver 200,000 tons instead. The entire undertaking was a complete success.

For the first time in his life, Gorbachev was featured in *Pravda,* the Party newspaper, in a major interview on the front page. The Central Committee hurriedly published a congratulatory resolution, urging other regions to copy Ipatovsky's success. This follow-on campaign came so quickly that it must have been carefully orchestrated in advance, as if the propaganda surrounding the harvest—and implicitly boosting Kulakov—was more important than the harvest itself.

The Ipatovsky experiment put feathers in the caps of both Kulakov and Gorbachev. The Politburo greeted Kulakov's sixtieth birthday the next February by awarding him the title Hero of Socialist Labor, reserved for those held in the highest regard. Gorbachev was awarded the Order of the October Revolution—a less grand but still respectable honor. It was also given to the entire Stravropol *krai.*

In 1978 Ipatovsky did even better, completing its harvest in seven days and delivering 240,000 tons of wheat to the state. But that July there were no celebrations for Kulakov. Instead there was a funeral.

Pravda and the other newspapers reported on July 18 that Kulakov had died suddenly after "his heart stopped beating." This bizarre formulation—a statement of the obvious, not a medical diagnosis—had never been used before in obituaries of Politburo members. Kulakov was given full honors in death, including a funeral conducted from atop Lenin's mausoleum in Red Square; Gorbachev was one of the speakers. But strangely, Brezhnev, Kosygin, and Suslov all failed to appear at the funeral—noteworthy absences in a political culture whose rituals are usually attended by all the senior leaders. Rumors soon spread in Moscow that Kulakov had killed himself by slitting his wrists.

What actually happened has never been explained. Gorbachev himself has never mentioned Kulakov since becoming leader in 1985. A senior official who has good sources in Moscow told me in 1990 that he had heard a report—impossible to confirm—that Kulakov had proposed radical economic reforms that summer, and that his colleagues had turned on him, accusing him of trying to take the Soviet Union "down the Yugoslav path," a reference to the relatively undisciplined and decentralized Yugoslav economic model. "He either had a heart attack from this episode, committed suicide, or they murdered him; anything is possible," my informant said.

Kulakov was hardly a liberal, but he was apparently a practical man, and some of his ideas may have been harbingers of Gorbachev's *perestroika*. A well-informed official told me this historical anecdote: In 1978, hundreds of Georgians demonstrated in the streets of Tbilisi, their capital, against a new constitution that would have ended the historic status of the Georgian language as the official tongue of the republic. Eduard Shevardnadze, then the Party's first secretary in Georgia (and later Gorbachev's foreign minister), reportedly telephoned to the Kremlin for instructions. Brezhnev was ill, and according to this account, Kulakov took the call—a sign of his rank at the time. Kulakov told Shevardnadze not to use the army to quell the demonstration; Shevardnadze then went before the crowd to announce that, "proceeding from the democratic nature of our society," the provision of a 1922 constitution making Georgian the state language would remain in effect. The demonstrators dispersed, and troops that had moved to the outskirts of Tbilisi were withdrawn. "It was an important liberal act by Kulakov," said my source, "one that foreshadowed everything that is happening now [in 1990]."

The success of the Ipatovsky experiment gave Gorbachev the best kind of national reputation; the untimely demise of Kulakov created a vacancy at the seat of power that suited the talents and training of the young first secretary from Stavropol. The connections he had made with senior leaders at the resort areas in his *krai* gave him needed friends in high places. With all those advantages, it still took four months after Kulakov's death before Gorbachev was appointed the new secretary of the Central Committee responsible for agriculture.

His promotion followed two meetings—job interviews, in effect—

with senior leaders who came to see him in Stavropol. In September 1978, Brezhnev, joined by his constant companion, Konstantin Chernenko, made a stopover in Mineralnye Vody, the Stavropol resort, on a train trip to Baku in Azerbaijan. Andropov, vacationing in the neighborhood, joined the meeting, where Gorbachev was able to announce that Stavropol would be delivering 750,000 tons of grain to the state above the 1.75 million tons called for in the plan. In October, Andrei Kirilenko, another senior member of the Brezhnev leadership group, made a more extensive visit to Stavropol, accompanied the entire time by Gorbachev. Evidently the young man—he would be the youngest member of the senior leadership by five years—passed muster. At the Central Committee plenum on November 27, his promotion to secretary was formalized.

• • •

It had been twenty-three years since Gorbachev and Raisa had come back to Stavropol from Moscow State University. In the capital he had received the best formal education of any modern Soviet leader; in the North Caucasus he added a splendid political education, thanks to his mentors in Stavropol and his exposure to the high politics of Moscow through his contacts with senior members of the national leadership. Perhaps he carried memories of the horrors of the uprising at Novocherkassk; he certainly had vivid images in his mind from his trips to France and Italy. He had learned a good deal about agriculture, both in his correspondence course and on the ground. He was famous among the peasants of Stavropol and the managers of local collective farms for his willingness to stretch the rules for higher production, and for his eagerness to give responsibility to individuals. His knowledge of industry was much more modest; there was little of it in Stavropol *krai,* and Gorbachev may not have known much about the country's manufacturing problems.

He had spent those twenty-three years as a first-rate politician and intellect surrounded by second- and third-rate comrades. This is one of the most interesting facts of Gorbachev's biography, though its significance is difficult to describe with precision. Anyone who has traveled widely in the Soviet Union in the last quarter century knows that men of Gorbachev's caliber are exceedingly rare in the Communist Party. After 1937–38, when Stalin obliterated the last of the veterans of the Bolshevik Revolution who he feared were independent-minded, resourceful, or courageous, the Party was never again known for the quality of its people. Those who got ahead were more often toadies than innovators. An unusually superior man like Gorbachev must have had to develop tactics for dealing with his comrades to avoid either intimidation or condescension. He also had to learn to bite his tongue in the presence of real stupidity or ignorance.

One way to stay out of trouble was to adapt to the prevailing political culture and adopt its rituals, and this Gorbachev did. In May of 1978, for example, just six months before he was promoted to Moscow, Gorbachev indulged in the sycophancy so characteristic of the late Brezhnev period. At an ideological conference in Stavropol (an account of which Zhores Medvedev discovered in the local newspaper), Gorbachev spoke of Brezhnev:

> L. I. Brezhnev has revealed a talent for leadership of the Leninist type. His titanic daily work is directed toward strengthening the might of our country, raising the well-being of workers and strengthening the peace and security of nations.
>
> And not long ago we opened the pages of Comrade L. I. Brezhnev's remarkable book, *Little Land,* in which the legendary heroes of the battles of the North Caucasus are portrayed in letters of gold. A short time has elapsed since its publication, but the memoirs have provoked wide, truly national interest. To meet the innumerable requests of the workers of Stavropol, in February the memoirs were reprinted . . . in our *krai* newspapers. . . .
>
> In number of pages the book *Little Land* is not very large, but in the depth of its ideological content, in the breadth of the author's generalizations and opinions, it has become a great event in public life. It has evoked a warm echo in the hearts of Soviet people, a delighted response from front-line soldiers at readers' conferences and in the press.
>
> Communists and all the workers of Stavropol are boundlessly grateful to Leonid Ilyich Brezhnev for this truly Party-spirited, literary work, in which the sources of the great feat of our heroic nation, its spiritual and moral strength, its steadfastness and courage are depicted with deep philosophical penetration.

A man who could pronounce those words with a straight face was truly a Party man. He had mastered the language and style of Party officials and knew the appropriate response in all situations. Just the year before Gorbachev's promotion to Moscow he had been in the capital to take part in the 25th Party Congress when he learned that his father, Sergei, had died suddenly in Privolnoye. "The Defense Ministry flew him down for the funeral, and he returned the same night," according to Giorgi Gorlov, an old family friend interviewed by Remnick of the *Post*. "He was very sad, obviously. But he was there [in the Palace of Congresses] the next morning. He never missed a minute of the congress." The story is reminiscent of Kosygin's response to the news that his wife had died, which reached him while he stood on Lenin's mausoleum, reviewing the traditional November 7 parade. He stayed right where he was until the end of the parade.

Gorbachev had learned to give a long, dull speech, write a boring article for the press, and put up with all the tedious rituals of Party life. It isn't easy for a Westerner to appreciate the significance of these talents. Many of Gorbachev's brightest contemporaries at Moscow State University had no patience whatsoever for Party life; many chose academic or creative careers to avoid the lies, hollow slogans, and exhausting formalities of their country's politics. For someone as intelligent as Gorbachev to put up with all of them was a rarity.

Only Gorbachev's combination of ambition, self-confidence, and faith could have given him the patience to survive in Party politics. The faith seems a critically important ingredient; the obvious fact that he was not guided by crude selfishness or a lust for power suggests his faith in a greater purpose. But what was it? His later rhetoric makes it clear that Gorbachev really did respect Vladimir Ilyich Lenin, and really believed in something called socialism, but was he in any conventional sense a Soviet Communist? In 1978, preparing to go to Moscow, he must have thought that he was such a Communist, and thought too that he was about to have his chance to put his mark on the system that had reared him, and improve it. But he was very different from most of his new comrades in the small circle of senior leaders—more honest, more intelligent, more flexible of mind, and more imaginative. He may have considered himself one of them, but subsequent events would show that he was not.

CHAPTER TWO

MOSCOW, AT LAST

Gorbachev had fulfilled the plan for loyally waiting his turn; only after twenty-three years in Stavropol did he get his chance to make a name for himself in the center. If in fact he had come to Moscow with ambitions to grapple creatively with his country's problems, he could not have come at a worse time. He took responsibility for agriculture at the beginning of a disastrous period for Soviet farming; and he joined a sclerotic leadership far past its prime that had long since lost interest in finding solutions to the country's many grave problems.

Brezhnev was beginning his fifteenth year in power, but he had only just completed the installation of his cronies in the dominant positions at the top of the Party. For fourteen years Brezhnev had presided over a true collective leadership; his voice had long been dominant, but never dictatorial; he had to compromise with other strong figures, including Kosygin, Suslov, and Nikolai Podgorny. But one by one those rivals were leaving the scene, replaced usually by reliable Brezhnev men.

The same Central Committee plenum that named Gorbachev a secretary made Konstantin Chernenko a full member of the Politburo and elevated another Brezhnev crony, Nikolai Tikhonov, to candidate membership. Chernenko's new status and duties made it clear that Brezhnev had chosen him as his successor, though Chernenko's only real preparation for the job was as his mentor's longtime companion and assistant. Tikhonov was now positioned to succeed the failing Alexei Kosygin as premier—though at seventy-three he too was no younger than other members of the Brezhnev inner circle.

Brezhnev finally had his team in place, but he no longer had his health. According to Georgi Arbatov, the Soviets' chief "Americanologist" and an adviser to Brezhnev and all successive leaders, from 1976 onward, Brezhnev was incapable of active participation in affairs of state. His illness in 1976 ushered in a disastrous period for the Soviet Union, one marked by rampant corruption, cronyism at all levels, deteriorating social and economic conditions, and increasing cynicism.

This was the nadir of what Gorbachev later dubbed "the time of stagnation," and it was the time of his own introduction to life at the top. Gorbachev came to Moscow as the junior member of the leadership. After the November plenum in 1978, the leadership group consisted of thirteen full members of the Politburo, nine nonvoting candidate members, and eleven secretaries of the Central Committee, five of whom were also members of the Politburo.

As secretary for agriculture Gorbachev had more responsibility than many of the members of the Politburo who had no comparable administrative authority, but he had considerably less stature. And because his area of responsibility was one of the most vulnerable—though also most critical—sectors of the economy, he occupied an exposed position. Under both Khrushchev and Brezhnev, a series of secretaries and Politburo members responsible for agriculture had been fired from the leadership as scapegoats for poor performance in the countryside, or even to take the blame for bad weather. Kulakov had been a rare exception; he was the first man responsible for agriculture to receive an honorable burial in Red Square.

Central Committee secretaries run departments of the Party bureaucracy, so each stands at the head of a uniquely Soviet institution that combines limited administrative control with great political power. Day-to-day affairs in Gorbachev's new realm were handled by the Ministry of Agriculture and other ministries responsible for transport, fertilizer, farm equipment, and so on. Each of the fifteen republics had its own governmental bureaucracy for agriculture. All these ministries reported upward to the premier, not directly to Gorbachev.

He presided directly over the immense Party apparatus devoted to agriculture, which stretched from Moscow to each provincial capital, then into each administrative district and every farm. The Party's *apparatchiks* were meant to organize, exhort, and lead.

Every participant in this vast enterprise—millions of bureaucrats and nearly forty million peasants—understood that the Party was the ultimate boss. The officials all knew that the Central Committee secretary for agriculture stood at the top of their pyramid. But the entire system was inherently unmanageable; it simply could not respond to most attempts to change course. The underlying facts of Soviet agriculture dictated the true nature of the situation: too few roads (for example, fewer miles of paved road in Stavropol *krai*—which is the size of South Carolina—than in one county in Iowa or Kansas); too little good equipment; appalling shortages of refrigerated facilities to store meat, fruits, and vegetables; inadequate transportation and storage facilities for grain; and worst of all, a peasantry long since bereft of energetic farmers who knew how to take responsibility for managing a piece of land. The Soviet system called for all this to be "administered" from Moscow; the facts of life made that impossible.

Gorbachev discovered this soon enough. Thanks principally to good weather, the harvest of 1978—completed before his promotion—was unusually successful. It produced 237 million tons of grain. But 1979, a year of poor weather conditions, was a disaster. The harvest fell to 179 million tons. In 1980 it was just slightly better—189 million tons.

Those bad numbers did not seem to affect Gorbachev's political career. In November 1979, after just a year in Moscow, he was named an alternate member of the Politburo; a year after that he was promoted to full member. Obviously there was more to judge him by than the size of the harvest; the youngest member of the leadership had apparently made a good impression on his elders.

Gorbachev left no real mark on agricultural policy during the four years that he was theoretically in charge. Agriculture got the most attention in the last year or so of his tenure, when Brezhnev's much-promoted Food Program for the Eighties was drawn up and released. Gorbachev would have been in charge of the paperwork for this exercise, which was of staggering proportions. The program was introduced at a Central Committee plenum in May 1982 (after another bad harvest in 1981), but curiously, Gorbachev did not even speak at the meeting. Perhaps he was content to let Brezhnev (who introduced the program and spoke for it at length) take full credit, since in fact the new policy statement contained little that was new—or that held out hope of improving the agricultural situation.

Gorbachev did defend the program in a long and dreary article for *Kommunist,* the Party's theoretical journal, and expressed hopes that its ambitious targets would be fulfilled. He must have been concerned about the potential consequences for himself of a fourth consecutive poor harvest, particularly as the political situation grew more complex toward the end of Brezhnev's life. Suslov had died in January 1982 after a stroke. In May 1982, at the same plenum that adopted the Food Program, Andropov was chosen to replace Suslov as secretary of the Central Committee responsible for ideology, a change that moved him from the KGB to Central Committee headquarters. Andropov and Chernenko were now in direct confrontation over the succession to Brezhnev, whose health was visibly failing as the year progressed. Gorbachev (it became clear later) was an Andropov man.

Food Program or no, the 1982 harvest was another bad one. (No statistics were published for '81 or '82, a sign that the numbers were so bad the leadership did not want to acknowledge them. Years later, when *glasnost* was in fashion, it was disclosed that the harvests for those two years were 158 and 187 million tons.) The fourth bad harvest might have had serious political repercussions for Gorbachev had not fate intervened; on November 10, 1982, Leonid Brezhnev finally died.

• • •

The next twenty-eight months were a critical period for Gorbachev. When it began he was the junior member of the Politburo, an ally of Yuri Andropov in a fierce power struggle against the old men who had surrounded Brezhnev. When it was over he was the leader of the Soviet Union.

While it was happening, Gorbachev's rise to the top seemed speedy but also logical. In fact it was far from inevitable. For—as the old men clearly understood—Gorbachev represented a great deal more than youth. His reputation for probity must have alarmed those who had grown comfortable with the corruption of the Brezhnev era; his intelligence was a threat to the many simple-minded yes-men who had survived their way to the highest reaches of power; his penchant for changing things was a challenge to the inherent conservatism of the entire Soviet system. There were strong arguments for avoiding the confrontation with the future that the selection of Gorbachev as leader would imply.

Andropov's brief tenure in power following Brezhnev's death sharpened those arguments. Yuri Andropov was one of the most interesting Soviet figures of the postwar era. Like Gorbachev, he was both more intelligent and better educated than most of those around him. Only the barest outline of his early biography can be recounted because few specifics have ever been revealed.

Born in Stavropol *krai* in 1914, Andropov attended a water-transport technical college and began his political career, like Gorbachev, in the Komsomol.* He benefited from the purges of 1937–38, when countless Komsomol officials were arrested, making room for Andropov to move quickly up the hierarchy. In 1940 he was first secretary of the Komsomol in Karelia on the Finnish border, a sensitive post for a twenty-six-year-old in the wake of the brief Soviet-Finnish war in 1940. The Germans, assisted by Finns, occupied much of Karelia in 1941, and Andropov was apparently active in the resistance to the occupation. After the war he moved into the Party apparatus, where he did so well that he was promoted to the Central Committee staff in Moscow. After Stalin's death in 1953 he was assigned to the Foreign Ministry, and was soon sent to Budapest as counselor in the Soviet embassy there. In 1954, just forty years old, Andropov was promoted to the position of ambassador in Budapest.

His coincidental participation in the Hungarian Revolution of 1956 put Andropov on a career path that led to high politics. He was not a central actor in the suppression of the revolution, which was handled by more senior figures sent from Moscow, but he was deeply involved; by one apparently reliable account, he was in the office of Imre Nagy, leader of the revolution, when Soviet troops broke through Hungarian defenses on the outskirts of Budapest. He must also have played a significant role in the subsequent purge of Hungarian officials (including Nagy, who was killed). Andropov's reward for his role in Hungary was promotion to a major post in the Central Committee, head of the department for relations with fraternal socialist countries. He was named a secretary of the Central Committee.

In this role Andropov gave the first discernible hint that he was an unusual Soviet politician. He gathered around himself a personal staff of bright young men who could all be called children of the 20th Party

---

* Whether their common Stavropol origins were a factor in the relationship between Andropov and Gorbachev has never been explained. Once in power, Gorbachev almost never mentioned Andropov.

Congress—relatively liberal, relatively free-thinking, and surprisingly intellectual for junior members of the Central Committee staff. After working for Andropov in the early and mid-1960s, members of the group went off in many different directions, but in the late eighties nearly all turned up in prominent roles working for Gorbachev, or supporting him from important positions in academic life or the press. The group included Georgi Arbatov, who for nearly a quarter century has run the Institute for the Study of the U.S.A. and Canada; Oleg Bogomolov, director of the Institute on Economics of the World Socialist System; Georgi Shakhnazarov, who had a reputation as a futurologist, and became a personal aide to Gorbachev; Alexander Bovin, an enormous man with an enormous personality, who became nationally famous as a columnist for *Izvestia,* the government newspaper; Fyodor Burlatsky, one of the country's best-known commentators and social scientists, who became editor of the influential weekly *Literaturnaya Gazeta* (Literary Gazette) in 1990; Nikolai Shishlin, a Central Committee official, who arranged many of Gorbachev's interviews with the foreign news media; and several others.

I have gotten to know most of these men, and can testify to their unusual qualities. They liked to discover for themselves what was going on in the world around them; they learned foreign languages and read books; they were much more likely than ordinary Soviet officials to question the conventional wisdom of any particular moment; they had some courage; and many ideas of their own. It is not a homogeneous group; its members made very different decisions about how much to cooperate with the Brezhnev regime, for example, and personal relations were strained in the process. But none of them could be described as a conventional Soviet *apparatchik.*

Andropov's close association with such people made him unique among senior members of the Khrushchev and Brezhnev leaderships. So did his proclivity for spending time alone reading serious books. Bovin once found him at home reading Plato's *Republic.* Andropov's special reputation was well known in the Moscow intelligentsia, the community of educated people—some officials, many more writers and scholars—who have given a special quality to the intellectual life of the Soviet capital since the earliest days of Bolshevik rule. So it came as a considerable surprise when, in 1967, Andropov was suddenly appointed chairman of the Committee for State Security, the notorious KGB. Some of his allies thought the appointment was intended to take him out of contention for higher office by sidetracking him in a policeman's career.

Andropov was to spend fifteen years in that difficult and powerful job. The KGB has extensive responsibilities; it acts to protect the "security of the state" at home and abroad—spying and buying information in foreign countries; spying, censoring, and harassing wayward citizens inside the Soviet Union. When Andropov was moved into the agency in 1967, Brezhnev and his colleagues were clearly worried about open displays of dissidence by Soviet intellectuals. Two years earlier, in 1965, the writers Andrei Sinyavski and Yuli Daniel had been arrested for publishing books of fiction abroad under pseudonyms; in 1966 they were tried, convicted, and sentenced to labor camps. Sinyavski was given a seven-year term; Daniel a five-year sentence. Hundreds of intellectuals signed letters of protest against this first example of jailing writers for what they had written. The signers then became the target of official reprisals; many lost jobs or opportunities for work in the arts. The KGB was responsible for those reprisals, which were continuing when Andropov took command at the Lubyanka, the famous dark-yellow building on Dzerzhinsky Square that housed the KGB's headquarters. The sequence of events that began with the Sinyavski-Daniel trial led to what later became known as the dissident movement.

Crushing it was perhaps Andropov's most important responsibility. Superficially, at least, he was successful. Using an inventive array of devices, he did away with virtually the entire group of activist dissidents. Some ended up in psychiatric hospitals, some in prison camps; many were forced to emigrate; many more were scared into abandoning their dissidence; the most famous of all, Andrei Sakharov, was internally exiled (a form of repression for which there was no legal basis) to the city of Gorki two hundred miles east of Moscow. Sakharov was exiled early in 1980, fifteen years after the arrests of Sinyavski and Daniel. That was how long it took to wipe out the activists who—in the spirit of the Thaw and out of a hunger for freedom—had dared to challenge the dreary orthodoxy of the Brezhnev years.

Andropov's role in these repressions did not endear him to the many intellectuals who sympathized with the dissidents. Many of Moscow's intellectuals thought Andropov was hostile to them as a class, an impression reinforced by the widely believed story that Andropov attributed the untoward events in Hungary in 1956 to a rowdy group of Hungarian intellectuals. Andropov developed a reputation as a kind of ruthless, shrewd hard hat who faithfully fulfilled his assignment from Brezhnev and his cronies to wipe out "those who think differently," which is the literal translation of the Russian word for dissidents.

But this rendering of Andropov's complex personality is much too stark. He certainly was a man capable of great cruelty; the KGB almost certainly took innocent lives—and ruined others—while he was running it. And yet it could have been much crueler. Exiling Alexander Solzhenitsyn to a comfortable life in the West cannot have been the first thought that came to the minds of the Soviet officials who decided (in 1973) that it was time to move against him. Similarly, many dissident activists were given the chance to leave the country to avoid more painful retribution, and countless citizens who sympathized with the dissidents and helped them on occasion were never punished. Andropov was not bloodthirsty, even if he could be ruthless in performing his official functions.

And he had several qualities that were exceedingly rare among members of the Brezhnev-era leadership. For one, he was apparently impeccably honest. There has never been any hint of corruption associated with his name. And he had unusual intellectual interests for a senior Communist official. He took an interest in the theater, including Moscow's most interesting and progressive theatrical company, Yuri Lyubimov's Taganka. Lyubimov (who left the Soviet Union by choice after Andropov died, but returned to stage plays again when Gorbachev was in power) was constantly stretching the rules, pushing the censors to the limits of their tolerance, or beyond. Andropov, whose daughter Irina was married to an actor, protected Lyubimov against hostile cultural bureaucrats. Most significant, at least for the purposes of this story, Andropov cared deeply about what was happening to his country while Brezhnev and his cronies dawdled over its worsening economic and social problems.

We have no record of how the startling events in Poland that began in July 1980 affected the leadership in Moscow, but they were certainly an important part of the backdrop to Andropov's rule. The Solidarity trade union had emerged spontaneously from a strike that July at the shipyard in Gdansk; an obscure electrician named Lech Walesa, leader of the new movement, soon became a national and international hero. The popular force he represented as a true representative of the workers in a state supposedly organized by and for the workers initially sent the Polish Communist party reeling. Its discredited leaders had to turn to a military man, General Wojciech Jaruzelski, to save them; he was the first military officer ever chosen to lead a

Communist party in the Soviet bloc, a sign of the party's desperation. After a major scare, Jaruzelski succeeded in December 1981 in imposing martial law on the country and suppressing Solidarity, at least for a time. But the images of the Polish uprising were powerful. They so terrified the Brezhnev regime that it restored jamming of foreign radio broadcasts in Russian, to prevent news of Solidarity's successes from reaching the Soviet public. (Jamming had been suspended in the flowering of détente, early in the 1970s. It wasn't stopped again until Gorbachev came to power.)

Solidarity's success grew out of poor economic conditions in Poland, but every Soviet political leader knew that Polish workers actually lived a good deal better than their Soviet comrades. Sixty years after the Bolshevik Revolution, the Soviet economy provided only the barest essentials for the citizens of the country. In the late 1970s, after a generation of steady if modest improvement, conditions in the Soviet Union were actually deteriorating.

Andropov was evidently worried about the economy. A senior official in Moscow well connected to the party hierarchy told me that he created a new, secret department in the KGB in the late 1970s or early 1980s to prepare critical evaluations of the economic situation. This was not a logical function for the state security agency, but according to my informant, "Andropov wanted to attract the attention of the ruling circles to the coming economic catastrophe."

Similarly, Andropov was apparently upset by the rampant corruption of the late Brezhnev years. The evidence of this was explicit; despite the obvious sensitivities involved, Andropov's KGB mounted serious investigations of Brezhnev cronies and even of the leader's own daughter in the last year or two of the old man's life.

The daughter's case became a sensation. Galina Brezhneva Churbanova was married to General Yuri Churbanov, the deputy minister of internal affairs. (The Ministry of Internal Affairs is the national police department.) She had many lovers, including a singer in the Bolshoi opera company named Boris Buryata, known as Boris the Gypsy. The scandal exposed by the KGB in the summer of 1982 involved a huge diamond-smuggling and foreign-currency operation, in which Boris the Gypsy and a number of prominent members of the Moscow Circus company were involved. The ring evidently dealt in valuable gems and hundreds of thousands of dollars in cash. When arrests were made, the repercussions were widespread. Churbanov lost his post at the Ministry of Internal Affairs, and another Brezhnev crony—his brother-in-law, General Semyon Tsvigun, who was a deputy chairman of the KGB and had helped cover up evidence of the diamond smuggling—died, apparently a suicide.

The same summer, another Brezhnev crony, S. F. Medunov, first secretary in Krasnodar Oblast, next door to Gorbachev's Stavropol, was put under house arrest and dismissed from his official posts on charges of corruption. Medunov was close to Brezhnev. He took care of the leader's palatial summer dacha on the Black Sea coast in Krasnodar. Moscow buzzed with rumors about who might be next. On November 9, two famous figures from Moscow's commercial underground were arrested—the manager of the capital's most famous food store, and his wife, an executive of GUM, the principal department store. Both were said to be friends of Brezhnev's daughter.

Where this campaign was headed is not clear. Before it could go any further, Brezhnev died on November 11.

His demise came a little too early for Chernenko, Tikhonov, and the other Brezhnev cronies who were plotting to try to retain control after their leader's death. They did not yet have the dominant position inside the Politburo that they sought. The key figure then was Dmitri Ustinov, the minister of defense and nominally a marshal of the army, though the title was an honorific, bestowed on this venerable Party politician and manager of the military-industrial complex when he became minister. Ustinov and the generals under him had little regard for Chernenko; they backed his more formidable rival, Andropov. The KGB, the second institutional pillar of Soviet national security, also backed its old boss. Neither institution plays a direct role in Soviet politics, but the influence of both, especially when they act in concert, is great. Chernenko had none of the qualifications traditionally associated with the top job, and none of the stature. Andropov had both.

•   •   •

Andropov's ascent to the leadership marked a sharp break with the past—or at least the beginning of such a break. Andropov had to accept power on the terms he was offered, which meant he had to accept collective decisions by the Politburo on major issues. At least initially he had to live with the Chernenko group of old men as his senior colleagues. And they had no interest in discrediting the Brezhnev period or turning on their mentor.

To fulfill his ambitions for reorienting national policies, Andropov needed allies at the top, and he began with very few reliable ones. Ustinov and Andrei Gromyko, the venerable foreign minister, were his staunch supporters, but both had narrow, defined roles. Gorbachev, the only younger man in the Politburo and probably the brightest (with Andropov) of the group, and the only one with an established personal relationship with the new leader, quickly became an important figure. Yegor Ligachev, the Party boss in the Siberian city of Tomsk, was brought to Moscow to head the Central Committee's department responsible for Party personnel, an important job, the more so after Andropov began (in the last months of his life) to make many changes in the regional Party bureaucracy. According to one knowledgeable Muscovite who told me about him in 1988, the KGB considered Ligachev one of a very few Party secretaries in major industrial centers who did not take bribes. Vitali Vorotnikov, another man with a reputation for honesty, whom Brezhnev had exiled by naming him ambassador to Cuba, was brought home, first to replace the corrupt Medunov in Krasnodar, then to join the leadership in Moscow.

Andropov's long association with the KGB gave him an asset that wasn't well appreciated at the time: information, particularly reliable information about the state of the Soviet Union. As would become explicitly clear several years later, when *glasnost* allowed for such revelations, the Party and state structure had been so corrupted during Brezhnev's eighteen years in power that official statistics were largely incredible inventions. Brezhnev had long ago declared that the Soviet Union had reached the stage of "advanced socialism," the last step before the achievement of true communism; it fell to Party propagandists and other officials to produce the facts and figures to prove the leader's contention. They cheerfully did so, often without regard for contradictory facts.

But Andropov knew those facts; many of them could have come from the new KGB department he created to study the Soviet economy. From KGB officials in every town and province of the country he knew which local officials were corrupt—and it was nearly all of them. He knew how serious social and medical problems had become, how much people were drinking, how poorly the Soviet economy was adapting to modern technologies. He was in a position to understand the degree to which his country was falling behind its capitalist rivals in nearly every category of modern industrial life.

We know little about what went on in Andropov's inner circle—

how its members talked to one another, how frankly they acknowledged the country's problems. But the available hints suggest that they were open and honest, especially by comparison with their predecessors.

Andropov set a new tone just days after assuming the leadership, when he gave a general report to a plenum of the Central Committee. Instead of the usual rosy scenario, he offered a blunt accounting of shortcomings in many sectors. ("The performance of railroads, regrettably, is deteriorating from one year to the next. . . . Setbacks in ferrous metallurgy have become more frequent.") He warned his comrades, "You cannot get things moving by slogans alone." He warned further that "some people just don't know how to set about doing the job." In subsequent public pronouncements Andropov seemed to be trying to signal his countrymen that he knew how bad things had gotten, and that he wanted to do something to improve conditions.

He reinforced that signal by authorizing publication of brief accounts of the regular meetings of the Politburo. One of the first was devoted to corruption; the report on the session published in the newspapers included an implicit invitation to the citizenry to report violations of "socialist legality" to the central authorities. Apparently, thousands of citizens did so.

Andropov also initiated what became known as his discipline campaign—a well-publicized attempt to combat the malingering that had become endemic in Soviet workplaces. Policemen were sent into the ornate though fading Sundonovsky Baths in downtown Moscow during ordinary working hours to challenge the customers' rights to be bathing when most people were at work. Some were arrested for shirking. Other policemen cross-examined women waiting in lines to buy food, sending those with jobs back to work.

Andropov took interesting though limited steps toward economic reform as well, launching experiments in several branches of industry and in selected sections of the country to see if individual enterprises would work more efficiently if they had greater independence from the central authorities. Like the discipline campaign, the experiments had more symbolic than practical utility.

The new, more open atmosphere that Andropov introduced must have suited the man from Privolnoye who liked Hegel's observation that "truth is always concrete." Gorbachev the reliable Party man had been compelled many times during his career to say things he knew were false—lying was part of his many jobs. So was sycophancy to leaders who he knew did not deserve his respect. How refreshing at last to have a leader who himself eschewed any kind of personal cult, and who seemed honestly interested in dealing with the country's problems.

Still more stimulating, no doubt, was the access to real power that Andropov gave Gorbachev. Soon after Andropov became leader he began to broaden Gorbachev's area of responsibility to include other sectors of the economy beyond agriculture. He encouraged Gorbachev to begin a serious examination of the country's situation and how to improve it, which led to the creation of "working groups" to study economic, political, and social issues. Gorbachev invited numerous intellectuals, including many who had never played much of a role in affairs of state, to join these groups, which were apparently first organized late in 1982. They laid the intellectual foundations for Gorbachev's reforms when he became leader in 1985. The intellectuals who got a chance to work with Gorbachev in this period were invigorated by the experience. He was smart; he listened to them; he asked provocative questions.

Evgeny Velikhov, a vice president of the Academy of Sciences, who has worked with Gorbachev for years, has spoken about what it is like to give him advice: "It is very easy to talk to him if you really have something to say. It is not easy if you have nothing to say. He demands that advisers be properly prepared so that there are results. In my case the subjects are usually nuclear issues, strategic weapons, and computers. As a rule, our meetings are long, serious, thoughtful conversations that last an hour to an hour and a half. Gorbachev doesn't like brief, formal, protocol-like meetings. He cares about substance, and you are in trouble if you have no substance. Gorbachev talks during meetings, but he also listens attentively. He is a good listener. That's a rare quality. It is easier to talk than to listen. Gorbachev is never formal or intimidating with me and other advisers, but he is businesslike. He wants to solve problems."

Gorbachev earned a reputation with the intellectuals he befriended as someone who would protect them when they got into trouble. Alexander Bovin told me that after a visit to Bulgaria he made in 1985, Todor Zhivkov, the longtime Bulgarian leader, was upset with him (Bovin did not explain why) and tried to get him fired from his job on *Izvestia*. Bovin wrote a personal note to Gorbachev asking for his help. "He intervened and saved me," Bovin recounted.

Georgi Arbatov of the Institute for the Study of the U.S.A. and

Canada had a similar experience. During Chernenko's brief tenure in the Kremlin, the German magazine *Stern* reported that Arbatov had referred to the general secretary as "an ignorant peasant." Arbatov told friends this was the work of enemies of his who were trying to get him fired. He went to Gorbachev and asked his advice. Gorbachev recommended that Arbatov find a good pretext for requesting a personal meeting with Chernenko—just for twenty minutes or so. Don't mention the *Stern* article, Gorbachev suggested—find some business to discuss. After the meeting, Gorbachev said, he would make sure that word got around in Moscow that Arbatov had met alone with Chernenko. That would confuse anyone who thought Arbatov might be in trouble. Arbatov did as Gorbachev suggested, and the gambit was a total success. Arbatov never heard any more about the *Stern* report.

• • •

Andropov's kidneys failed in March 1983, just four months after he became general secretary; in the remaining eleven months of his life he depended entirely on kidney dialysis, and for his last five months, after an operation to remove one kidney, he apparently never left a hospital bed. As Andropov's health waned, Gorbachev's role grew. In April 1983, Gorbachev gave the speech on Lenin's birthday, an honor and also a clear signal that he enjoyed the leader's patronage. In May he made an extended visit to Canada, ostensibly to study agriculture, but also to get needed experience in foreign affairs. (He had an extensive tour of the country—another chance to see a successful capitalist society at close range.) In June, judging by the Kremlinological clues, Andropov gave Gorbachev new responsibilities for Party personnel matters. In August, Andropov asked Gorbachev to preside over a meeting of Party Veterans, a society of old Bolsheviks. Andropov addressed the gathering—his last speech shown on Soviet television before his final illness.

He used the occasion to speak warmly of the younger generation, in terms that could be read as an endorsement of Gorbachev as his successor. "Young people will be our successors," he said. "This sounds trite, but in fact it is far from trite. Time works for youth. That's how it should be." And he cautioned the older generation not to be too critical of the young: "The younger generation is no worse than ours—it's just a different, new generation. New generations aren't reproduced like copies on an offset duplicator. . . . It must be recognized—though it isn't easy for everyone to do so—that each new generation is stronger in some ways than the previous one, that it knows more and sees farther."

Also that August, when Andropov went on vacation, he left Gorbachev in charge of the Party secretariat, which meant he was running day-to-day affairs. The assignment became important in September, when Soviet pilots shot down a Korean jumbo jet that had mistakenly violated Soviet air space in the Far East. Gorbachev apparently chaired the meeting where it was decided to respond to worldwide condemnation of the shootdown by sending Marshal Nikolai Ogarkov before television cameras to give an unprecedented news conference. The tall, imposing Ogarkov, then chief of the general staff, forcefully defended Soviet actions in the affair. Of course the story he told—that the Korean plane was on a spy mission—was an invention.

Andropov spent his last months in an apartment created for him in the Kremlin hospital in Kuntsevo, outside Moscow. Gorbachev was one of the few officials who saw him regularly there, and he became the agent of Andropov's policies in the Politburo and in the Central Committee secretariat.

By early 1984, Gorbachev appeared to be the fourth-ranking member of the Politburo.* Andropov, Chernenko, and Tikhonov, the aged premier, outranked him. A month later that ranking was confirmed when Andropov died, and Chernenko was named general secretary.

* * *

Where Andropov might have led the Soviet Union if he had lived longer is far from clear. He was feeling his way toward major changes. In that last televised speech in August, he had deplored the state of the economy and warned that "now we must make up for lost time. This will require . . . changes in planning and management and in the economic mechanism." Attentive *apparatchiks* would have read those words as a call for fundamental reform. But Andropov as leader proved to be a hard man, with no evident liberalizing bent. Alexander

---

* Traditionally, the rank of Politburo members could be determined each time candidates for a new Supreme Soviet were nominated, as they were in January 1984. The general secretary was always nominated by the largest number of constituencies; the second-ranking member by the second-largest number, and so on. The nominations had no other effect; each Politburo member chose one district to represent in the rubber-stamp Supreme Soviet, which met once or twice a year to ratify government decisions. Gorbachev got the fourth-highest number of nominations that January.

Bovin, his aide in the mid-1960s, told me that he and Georgi Arbatov, another veteran of that early Andropov staff, met with their old boss when he was still healthy in 1983 and complained bitterly to him about "his reactionary policy toward art and culture," which under Andropov remained tightly constricted by cultural bureaucrats and the censors. Andropov got angry, Bovin recalled, and refused to speak to him again for months. Bovin said he thought Andropov might have pursued reforms more like Deng Xiaoping's in China—putting economic decentralization and market-oriented changes ahead of political reforms.

But he did not live long enough even to ease the way for his chosen successor. The evidence is persuasive that Andropov wanted Gorbachev to get his job, but from the grave he had no direct influence on the choice. Gorbachev's closeness to Andropov was advertised for the world to see when Andropov's body was lying in state. Alone among Politburo members, Gorbachev approached Andropov's wife and family to express personal condolences.

For several months before Andropov's death, members of the old guard, most prominently Chernenko, had begun to assert themselves. At a Central Committee plenum in December the Andropov faction had its last chance to alter the membership of the Politburo; one new man, Vorotnikov, was elected a full member. Ligachev was elevated to the rank of secretary of the Central Committee. But Andropov's men had neither the numerical strength nor the experience to head off the election of Chernenko as the new general secretary. According to numerous knowledgeable Soviet officials, Gorbachev recognized the Andropov group's weakness, and moved to make the best of it by backing Chernenko himself, and even putting his name into nomination.

In return, the Brezhnevites appeared to yield to Gorbachev the second-ranking position in the Politburo. There may have been an explicit deal. Chernenko's health was frail; none of the participants in this round of Kremlin politics could have expected him to last very long. At least Gorbachev would be well positioned after the next state funeral. And Andropov's supporters appeared to have the influence to demand that Chernenko stay on the political course that Andropov had set. In his long address accepting the leadership, Chernenko never mentioned his patron Brezhnev, and pledged explicitly to carry out Andropov's policies. The understandings that surrounded Chernenko's elevation may have had the effect of freezing Kremlin politics; in the year he was in power, no one was promoted to or demoted from the senior leadership.

Chernenko's brief reign was not entirely uneventful, however. It was marked by an important change in Soviet foreign policy, one that was useful to Gorbachev when he came to power in 1985. Under Andropov Soviet-American relations had taken a nasty turn: President Reagan's intensely anti-Soviet rhetoric; his introduction of the Strategic Defense Initiative, suggesting the possibility of a new arms race in space; the successful NATO deployment of new intermediate-range Pershing II and cruise missiles in Europe; then the shooting down of the Korean airliner had all contributed to a sharp deterioration of relations. Soon after the KAL incident, which was followed by bitter American and West European denunciations of the Soviets, Andropov had gone so far as to declare: "Even if someone had any illusions about the possible evolution for the better in the policy of the present U.S. administration, the latest developments have finally dispelled them." He seemed to be shutting the door on further diplomacy.

Perhaps his years at Brezhnev's side convinced Chernenko that this kind of isolation was too dangerous. Whatever the reasons, while he was leader direct dealings with the Reagan administration were renewed. In the fall of 1984 Moscow simply accepted the American conditions for reopening arms-control talks (suspended by Andropov the previous year), and negotiations resumed in Geneva.

Chernenko made a change of a very different kind in the official position on Joseph Stalin. Attempts to rehabilitate Stalin, at least partially, recurred from time to time during the Brezhnev era, and over the years the dark image of him left by the 20th and 22nd Party Congresses had mellowed. Chernenko and his associates went further, allowing publication of favorable recollections of Stalin as a war leader. And in July 1984, Chernenko authorized the political rehabilitation and readmission to the Party of Vyacheslav Molotov, Stalin's premier and foreign minister and longtime comrade-in-arms. Molotov was ninety-four years old when he was rehabilitated. Party *apparatchiks* all over the country would have understood the move as a signal that Stalin had regained still more respectability.

I went back to Moscow a month after Molotov's rehabilitation, in August 1984. It was my first visit in ten years, and I was stunned by the change in atmosphere. I had left Moscow in July 1974, after a three-year tour as the *Washington Post*'s Moscow correspondent. The Soviet Union at that moment was an increasingly confident global power, enjoying what Brezhnev and his cronies had concluded was a fundamental shift in the international "correlation of forces" to their advantage. They saw the United States, weakened by the Vietnam

War, seeking their cooperation—that was the Soviet interpretation of Richard Nixon's détente policy. They saw their own role in the world growing quickly, as they demonstrated, soon after I left Moscow, by their aggressive decisions to use Cuban troops as their surrogates in a series of African conflicts, beginning in Angola and Ethiopia.

Ten years later, that ambitious optimism had disappeared. The country was in a genuine crisis: socially, economically, and politically. I had followed developments from afar, and knew a good deal about the deteriorating situation, but nothing had prepared me for the way Soviet citizens, even official apologists, spoke about the state of their country in the summer of 1984.

There was a certain logic to their candor. The country showed signs of social disintegration: dramatically declining life expectancy for men; rising infant mortality; increasing alcoholism affecting younger and younger age groups and, for the first time, a substantial number of women; increasing crime, corruption, and cynicism.

One old friend whom I had known for fifteen years reported that most of the clinics where babies are born in Moscow were contaminated with staph infections. Many newborns became infected, and the chronic shortage of antibiotics made curing those infections difficult. Another friend, recently hospitalized, said many Moscow hospitals had virtually no nursing staff, so patients had to depend on friends or family for nursing care.

I heard a new joke about two workmen with shovels walking along the edge of a city street, stopping every five yards so that one of them could dig a hole in the dirt. As soon as it was dug, his comrade filled the hole back up. Then they moved along another five yards and repeated the exercise.

A Soviet citizen observing this scene erupted angrily. "Comrades!" he shouted. "What kind of craziness is this? You dig a hole, then the other fellow fills it right up. You're accomplishing nothing at all! We're wasting good money paying you!"

"No, no," one of the workers replied, "you don't understand at all. Usually we work with a third lad, Volodya, but he's home drunk today. Volodya plants trees. I dig the hole, he sticks in the tree, and Ivan here fills the hole back in. Just because Volodya's off drunk, does that mean Ivan and I have to stop working?"

The nation of drunkards I had left ten years earlier had become a nation of staggering drunkards. My old friend Felix Uskov, who worked as an alcohol counselor in a huge Moscow factory, told me the situation was steadily getting worse. As many as 85 percent of the workers in ordinary Soviet factories regularly drink too much, he said —not because they are alcoholics but because getting drunk is part of their lives.

The official press was beginning to acknowledge that alcohol abuse was a worsening problem. According to a December 1983 article in the newspaper *Selskaya Zhizn* (Rural Life), "the average age of people suffering from alcoholism has fallen five to seven years in the last decade." The same article reported that "according to research on ill patients, 90 percent of them started drinking before the age of fifteen, and one-third of them started before the age of ten. In most cases, familiarity with alcohol begins with the cooperation of the parents."

An elderly couple recounted their experience that summer of walking into a village one hundred miles from Moscow at about five in the afternoon. "Everyone was drunk," the woman said. "The men, the women, the young people, they were all drunk as skunks. Many were laid out on the ground. It was an amazing sight."

Many Russians complained that summer about the new crime problem that was just becoming serious. This was something new and alarming. I found new locks on the entryways to Moscow apartment houses intended to keep "hooligans" from prowling the halls, and many friends had added multiple locks to their own doors. The authorities had begun to talk much more openly about crime, and to provide statistics on its occurrence. But the citizenry didn't need statistics, particularly on economic crimes against the state. Friends reported that government chauffeurs and truck drivers regularly sold the gas in the tanks of their state-owned vehicles to private motorists, while others sold all kinds of raw materials stolen from their workplaces. Thievery had become a factor in high-level policy debates. That summer officials discussed whether to authorize private repair garages to help service the country's new private cars—then numbering about 10 million. Some opponents of private garages argued that there weren't enough spare parts available to stock them. "If we have garages but no spare parts, then thievery will go way up," one official said, explaining that the new garages would have to get parts somehow.

Nearly every conversation I had in Russia that summer touched on some aspect of the economic failures that had come to haunt the Soviet system. When I had left the country ten years earlier it had been clear that the economy was backward and inefficient, and that it would never compete with the advanced economies of the West. But it seemed stable enough, and able to continue muddling through. That was too rosy a judgment. Throughout the 1970s economic performance had steadily deteriorated; Andropov's discipline campaign had improved the situation slightly, but the underlying weaknesses remained. What I had perceived as muddling through was really muddling downward.

In the summer of 1984 the officials I met were surprisingly unanimous in their view that significant economic changes would come. "The question," one said, "is whether the economic changes will be made deliberately, according to our plan, or only after we have cracked our heads against the wall once or twice."

It was on this trip that I discovered the reformist zeal of an outspoken economist from Novosibirsk, in Siberia, who would later become famous around the world as one of Gorbachev's early advisers—Abel Aganbegyan, director of the Institute of Economics and Management of the Siberian Department of the Soviet Academy of Sciences.

During the dog days of August, when many officials were on vacation, the newspaper *Trud* (Labor), published two startling articles by Aganbegyan, analyses of the country's economic problems that were unusually candid. In the previous five-year plan (1976–80), he noted, 11 million people reached working age, but in the current five-year plan (1981–85), only 3 million new workers would join the work force, 2.5 million of them residents of Central Asia. In the five-year plan beginning in 1986, "the increase in the working-age population will be still smaller."

Traditionally the central planners would have looked to increased capital investments in new plant and machinery to offset declining growth in the labor force, but Aganbegyan wrote that this would now be impossible. Though it has once been possible for investment to rise 50 percent in each new five-year plan, in the 1976–80 period, investment grew by just 32 percent; in the 1981–85 period, it would grow by 10 percent—"That's all!" Aganbegyan wrote. At the same time, raw materials and energy resources were disappearing from the European part of the country, where most industry was located. There had been a radical decline in new discoveries of energy resources and raw materials.

Only radical changes, Aganbegyan argued, could salvage economic performance: "For the economy's normal development, we must accelerate labor productivity growth rates at least 50 percent," while simultaneously forcing enterprises to use fewer raw materials, make better use of investment capital, "and effect a radical improvement in the quality of output." He supported decentralizing the economy, reducing Moscow's control, and encouraging enterprises to experiment on their own.

Aganbegyan's commentary was amazingly direct by the standards of 1984. His criticisms were frontal challenges to the system.

The most interesting thing I learned on the 1984 visit was that important people shared Aganbegyan's outlook. The most important, according to an old friend with excellent contacts in Moscow, was Mikhail Gorbachev. Gorbachev, I was told, had asked economists for briefings on the reforms designed by Pyotr Stolypin, Czar Nicholas II's enlightened prime minister, who encouraged entrepreneurship among the peasants, and on Lenin's New Economic Policy, or NEP, which revived some forms of free enterprise in the difficult years after the Bolsheviks consolidated their power. But according to one professor whose friends were helping draft papers for Gorbachev, the man who many hoped would be the country's next leader had privately wondered about the practicality of reform. How, Gorbachev had reportedly asked, would the vast "middle level"—the administrative bureaucracy in the ministries and enterprises that had always blocked reforms in the past—be persuaded to go along with really significant changes?

And if that middle level could be persuaded, would the workers who would ultimately be responsible for the success of reform be willing to work? That was an old question in the Soviet Union. My notes from that visit indicate that I was surprised to rediscover the degree to which Soviet workers avoided real work—I had forgotten their penchant for sloth in the ten years I had been away. A senior official I had known for years was very fatalistic about the future: "I think if you put the question to a referendum, and asked our people if they want the current system with some shortages and problems, but also guaranteed access to the necessities of life, or do they want another arrangement in which much more is available, but in which they might get fired if they don't really work hard, I have a feeling that our people would vote to keep things the way they are. Every society has to make a choice, according to its own values."

My friends in Russia were mostly intellectuals, an important but isolated segment of the population. They knew they were out of step with the great mass of their fellow citizens, but they also knew they were important to the country. There had always been a gulf between masses and intellectuals, but for two centuries at least the intellectuals had always played a significant part in the life of the country.

I was shaken that summer by the collective depression I found among intellectuals who had survived so much in the past without succumbing to despair. "Stalin died thirty years ago," one elderly Muscovite observed, "and our hopes soared." He raised his arm in an arc to demonstrate. "For a while things did change; there was excitement and creativity and we dreamed of a better future. But now," he went on, completing the arc he had drawn in the air so it became a circle, ending where it began, "we're back to here again."

Many intellectuals had succumbed to a wave of nostalgia for the time of the Thaw, when living conditions were worse but expectations were high and rising. "In the fifties a new generation was bursting into its own," as one member of that generation put it, "and we could feel the earth shaking under our feet. Older people saw it too, and seized on these youngsters as heralds of a new age. But the new age didn't come."

"We missed our chance," a man who was Gorbachev's age told me.

In 1984 there was a feeling of intense isolation in the intelligentsia, many of whose members had benefited from the détente of the 1970s by traveling abroad, befriending foreign colleagues, and gaining access to Western books and materials. Those opportunities had largely disappeared in the grim atmosphere that settled on the country after the invasion of Afghanistan in 1979. Censorship had grown much stricter. Jamming of foreign radio broadcasts was intense; many of my acquaintances had given up trying to listen. Everywhere I went I heard bitter complaints about harassment, arbitrary exercise of power, official stupidity.

One of the most interesting complaints, however, was directed not at the authorities but at the younger generation. People I knew in their forties, fifties, and sixties repeatedly expressed disappointment with the cynicism and careerism of the young. "Of course you can't generalize about all of them," one mother of a twenty-two-year-old said. "There are lots of wonderful ones, just as idealistic as we were. But most of them seem to be in it for themselves, for a comfortable life and career."

"Our young people believe in nothing," said another parent, "but they join the Party because they know it will advance their careers, and they do what they know is expected of them."

I found it easy to sympathize with the young people, who appeared to me to have little to be idealistic about. They could easily see that a few people enjoyed most of the privileges, and that only the élite could travel abroad—the greatest privilege of all. They understood that the government didn't trust them—to travel overseas, to hear foreign radio broadcasts, to know the truth. They realized how far the Soviet standard of living lagged behind that of the West, and even of Eastern Europe.

Fazil Iskander, one of the most talented writers of the post-Khrushchev era, described his own arrival at a Moscow railroad station in 1984. "Aren't you Iskander?" asked a young porter who helped him with his baggage; Iskander acknowledged he was. The porter then asked him detailed questions about each of his last two books. While the writer answered, the porter beckoned to a number of his colleagues in the station to join the conversation. Soon something like a literary press conference was under way, with young baggage porters cross-examining the famous writer.

"You find a lot of talented people working as porters these days," Iskander said. "They're former dissidents, or poets, or just honest men who can't put up with regular jobs where they have to be dishonest."

The young, of course, bore the brunt of the war in Afghanistan. That war had an eerie presence in Soviet life. The Soviet expeditionary force in Afghanistan was then rarely mentioned in the press and never fully described. But because of the war university students had lost their traditional draft deferments, and by 1984 everyone knew of someone who had been killed in the fighting.

I saw signs of a growing generation gap. The twenty-year-olds of 1984 were born in the year Khrushchev was ousted; they knew nothing firsthand about the forces that shaped their parents' lives: Stalin's dictatorship, World War II, the Khrushchev era. Compared to their parents they seemed cynical, but less afraid. "They take a lot for granted; they won't be pushed around," said a man in his late thirties. It struck me that the new generation would not easily fit into the roles played by its elders.

When I left Moscow in September 1984, I wrote, "The aspect of the new mood in Moscow that makes the strongest impression is the absence of any clear sense of the future. A blank horizon lies before this country, one that matches the geographical horizon visible from this great city on the vast Russian plain. Ask a Russian what things

might be like here five or ten years from now, and the response is a
shrug, a blank look, or a vague comment about the momentum of this
behemoth of a nation."

In an article for the *Post,* I quoted an editor I had known for fifteen
years: "You know, I have no idea what may happen. Maybe I'll be
visiting you in America in five years. And maybe I'll be shot."

CHAPTER THREE

STRUGGLE FOR POWER

Gorbachev's urge to reform the Soviet Union—and the support he found inside the Communist Party—can only be understood in the context of a demoralized and decaying country. The seriousness of the crisis and the fact that no senior leader could fail to perceive it were Gorbachev's greatest assets—apart from his personal qualities—in the power struggle that continued for the thirteen months that Chernenko survived as general secretary. Gorbachev had openly cultivated the image of reformer at least from the time that Andropov came to power. His work at Andropov's side, including the creation of his "working groups" to study the country's problems, made him the standard-bearer for those who were ready to change Soviet society. That group clearly included the most intelligent members of the leadership, but did it also include the most influential?

The Kremlinological clues during late 1984 were intriguing, but as usual not conclusive. Andropov's influence was still visible in the continuing anticorruption campaign, which brought down several more powerful figures while Chernenko was nominally in control. (In the summer he apparently suffered a heart attack, and never fully regained his strength.) In September the Politburo dismissed Marshal

Nikolai Ogarkov as the chief of the general staff and deputy defense minister, a startling turn of events that has never been fully explained. Ogarkov has a reputation for intelligence and forcefulness; his television appearance a year earlier to explain the shooting down of the Korean airliner had enhanced his stature. He appeared to be one of the most competent figures at the top of the Soviet government. But he had angered his political superiors somehow. Very likely it was his constant harping on the need to invest more in new military technology, a cause he pressed aggressively and openly. The defense budget already devoured an enormous portion of the national budget (fully 25 percent, Eduard Shevardnadze, the foreign minister, would reveal years later). At the time, the veteran minister of defense, Dmitri Ustinov, was in failing health, and his colleagues may have expected his death at any moment. There could easily have been a consensus in the Politburo that Ogarkov—an acerbic, sometimes condescending personality—should be moved aside before any question could arise of his becoming the new defense minister, a sensitive post for such a formidable figure.

In October 1984, the first strong hint appeared that Gorbachev would be challenged for the leadership by yet another old man, Viktor Grishin. Since 1967 Grishin had been the first secretary of the Moscow Party organization. He was a walking embodiment of the personal and political values of the Brezhnev era: ponderous, predictable, and— subsequent revelations would make clear—deeply involved in corruption. He observed his seventieth birthday that October, an occasion that Chernenko celebrated by awarding Grishin the Order of Lenin, one of the highest state honors. The citation was pregnant with political implication: Chernenko praised Grishin's "political and organizational abilities, his capacity to inspire and mobilize people in the solution of great and complicated tasks."

Gorbachev got a different sort of boost at the end of 1984. He made a triumphant official visit to Britain. The British press, always hungry for a story to pump up, fell for this new type of Soviet official and his attractive wife. Building on his experiences a year earlier in Canada —where his visit was barely noticed by the press—Gorbachev disarmed his hosts with his friendly, direct manner, his ability to speak forcefully with no notes, and his obvious purposefulness. For the theatrical Gorbachev, Britain provided a large stage and a huge audience; he seemed to love them both.

Gorbachev took no startling or liberal positions on his visit, staunchly defending the Soviet war in Afghanistan and the human-rights situation in his country, as a number-two man must. But there was no mistaking the dramatic difference between this energetic personality and his elders who had been ruling in the Kremlin for a generation. Shortly after the Gorbachev visit, I took part in a conference in Britain with several British officials who had met and talked with him, and their eyes fairly shone with enthusiasm when they discussed the Russian. They all agreed with Prime Minister Margaret Thatcher's famous dictum, pronounced that December: "I like Mr. Gorbachev. We can do business together." And they all assumed, as I did, that he was destined to be chosen the next leader.

No doubt to promote that idea, Gorbachev's visit was given extensive coverage on Soviet television. Gorbachev's position in the hierarchy gave him the power to order up this publicity. The coverage, including nightly items on the most popular Soviet television program, *Vremya* (Time), was unusual by Soviet standards. It showed Gorbachev's spontaneous interaction with the British, and—for the first time—introduced Soviet viewers to Raisa Gorbachev, the most presentable official wife they had ever seen. It was the first opportunity for Gorbachev to show off the television personality that was to become famous throughout the world. Soviet viewers did not miss the symbolic message. Their country might finally have a leader who could make a powerful impression on the outside world. The contrast with Brezhnev and Chernenko could not have been sharper.

Nevertheless, the success of Gorbachev's campaign to win the general secretaryship was not assured. It could easily have failed, especially in 1985. We still know very little about the terms of the debate inside the leadership—for example, about how Grishin's allies would have argued his case against Gorbachev's, and vice versa. But on one intriguing occasion just before his trip to Britain, Gorbachev himself made a public speech that could easily be interpreted as part of his campaign. Judging by the way it was censored, others in the leadership did not approve.

The occasion was a typical Soviet mouthful: "The 10th of December Session of the Moscow All-Union Scientific and Practical Conference on 'The Improvement of Developed Socialism and the Party's Ideological Work in Light of the Decisions of the June (1983) Plenum of the Communist Party of the Soviet Union's Central Committee Plenum': 'The People's Living Creativity.' " Gorbachev's speech was also a mouthful—it was buried in conventional Soviet boilerplate

("Once again it is necessary to check the pulse of ideological activity against the high social criteria of its effectiveness and against the country's general labor rhythm"). And it included numerous ritualistic passages on the importance of the "ideological struggle" with imperialism. But in a fascinating departure from past Soviet practice, the speech also contained rather direct references to every major aspect of Gorbachev's future reform program, including some that didn't show up in practice until he had been general secretary for several years.

Years after it was delivered I was alerted to this speech by a Moscow friend who remembered it vaguely as a reassuring "liberal" document —as a sign that the hope people like my friend had invested in Gorbachev was justified. Read in the sixth year of Gorbachev's rule, the speech appears to be much more than that. It has all the earmarks of a political platform.

At the outset Gorbachev declared himself a reformer with a mission: "Profound transformations must be carried out in the economy and in the entire system of social relations, and a qualitatively higher standard of living must be ensured for the Soviet people. . . . This, comrades, is a problem of truly huge scale. From it arises the main task of our time—the achievement of a palpable acceleration of social and economic progress." His strongest message was the need to improve economic performance: "Life sets us a task of tremendous political significance—to bring the national economy up to a qualitatively new scientific, technical, organizational, and economic level." Lest his audience miss the importance of fulfilling this task, Gorbachev spelled it out: "Only an intensive, fast-developing economy can ensure the strengthening of the country's position in the international arena, enabling it to enter the new millennium appropriately, as a great and prosperous power." Or, more bluntly, the Soviet Union's status as a superpower is at risk.

Gorbachev chastised Soviet economists for failing to point the way to necessary reforms: "The science of economics has not yet provided a detailed concept of how to make the transition to a dynamic, highly efficient economy." He offered the economists and planners advice: "Priority must be given to fundamentally new, truly revolutionary scientific and technical solutions capable of increasing labor productivity many times over. In other words, we need a profound breakthrough in the main direction of scientific-technical progress and an increase in the effectiveness of the economy." Each of these statements contained the same basic message: it is finally time for fundamental changes—sweeping reforms.

He referred bluntly to the economic slowdown of the late 1970s and early 1980s, and said the country had not yet "made the turn" toward economic efficiency. He suggested that the country was economically illiterate, and thus incapable of making necessary changes. He proposed educational reforms. "Without a basic knowledge of economics, without the ability to think and act with economic literacy, one cannot be a modern worker," he said.

He laid out a number of the details of what would later become his early economic policies as general secretary. For example, he mentioned the need to concentrate on modernizing the machine-tool industry. He spoke of the need to make use of economic levers like "prices, profit, credit, and others"—all exotic concepts at the time, which he returned to after 1985. Most radically, he described as a "main task" the need "to find methods for significantly increasing the rights and the economic independence of enterprises while simultaneously strengthening their responsibility for the final product"—in other words, the decentralization of economic power. Economists, he said, had to help find the best way to achieve a needed "restructuring of the management of the economy." The Russian word for restructuring is *perestroika*. This appears to have been Gorbachev's first use of the term in this context.*

Gorbachev introduced the subject of "the improvement of the Soviet political system." He noted approvingly the "founders of Marxism-Leninism's profound idea on self-government. Marx, Engels and Lenin developed the idea of a transfer to workers' self-management as a practical task for the proletariat from the moment it took power." He embraced the need for steps "to ensure real, practical participation by an increasingly large mass of working people in management, and in the elaboration, discussion, adoption and implementation of socioeconomic decisions," and said this could be done through elected soviets, or councils. He said it was "important to ensure the strict implementation of the constitutional principles of accountability of all executive organs" so citizens could monitor the government's actions. "We particularly need a serious study of the theoretical problems of the development of socialist self-government by the people," he said. In other words, Soviet society should be more democratic.

---

* At least it's the first time I have found him using it.

He proposed reliance on the same device he later formally introduced —stronger elected councils.

Gorbachev broached the need for *glasnost,* apparently for the first time. This is a particular Russian word that translates only imperfectly into English as "openness" or "publicity"—and which isn't translated at all now that Gorbachev has made the original Russian part of the world's vocabulary. Soviet intellectuals recognized it as a word from the time of Alexander II, the great reformer czar who liberated the serfs and experimented with *glasnost.* In his speech Gorbachev gave an intriguing description of a Soviet citizen in 1984: "Our contemporary is a person of developed culture and education, with a wide range of spiritual interests, who has seen and experienced a great deal," from the Bolshevik Revolution through the "complex postwar years." Such a citizen "won't accept simplified answers to his questions," and "is sensitive to falsehoods" resulting from attempts to cover up "the true contradictions of social development and the sources of the problems that worry him." So "we must speak to him only in the language of truth." Currently, Gorbachev said, both politicians and the news media talked formalistically to the public; many newspapers and radio and television broadcasts "still suffer from uniformity, anonymity, and superficiality."

"*Glasnost* is an integral part of socialist democracy," he continued. "Wide, prompt, and frank information is evidence of confidence in the people and respect for their intelligence and feelings, and for their ability to understand events for themselves. It enhances the resourcefulness of the working people. *Glasnost* in the work of Party and state organs is an effective means of combating bureaucratic distortions and obliges us to be more thoughtful in our approach to the adoption of decisions and . . . to the rectification of shortcomings and omissions." These are precisely the arguments Gorbachev and his allies used later when *glasnost* revolutionized Soviet life.

Gorbachev bluntly allied himself with Andropov's anticorruption campaign. "Our Party will become still more cohesive and authoritative if we continue to rid ourselves of those who do not value Party principles and Party honor, and of moral degenerates." He also spoke of the need for the rule of law: "The inescapable force of law must be placed in the path of those who are not susceptible to the arguments of reason or the voice of conscience and civic duty."

Another interesting aspect of the speech was a topic it did not cover at all: Soviet foreign and military policies. Gorbachev ignored them—

probably an accurate reflection of the emphasis he put on them in his private campaign for the leadership. His cause was saving the country, not the world.

This remarkable speech even included a passage that can be read as Gorbachev presenting an advertisement for himself. "The facts suggest that the ability—and sometimes the persistence—to organize things effectively isn't in plentiful supply everywhere, not by a long shot. Formalism is the powerful enemy of lively thought and deed; its manifestations are numerous. The essence of formalism is incompetence, indifference, and the substitution of a bureaucratic approach for a Party political approach; importance is attached not to getting things done but to looking good.

"Of course there are no ready-made formulas for combating formalism in every instance. But the Party has always followed an immutable Bolshevik principle: Judge people by their deeds, not their words, and judge work by results, not by 'measures' adopted."

In other words, vote for Gorbachev, a can-do guy, not for those old geezers who can barely talk a good game, let alone play one.

This speech has not been given the attention it deserves by Soviet commentators or Western Kremlinologists.* Here was Gorbachev publicly laying out his program for change months before there would be a vote on a successor to Chernenko. We now know that members of the leadership realized that Chernenko was soon to die; he was not responding to medical treatment. Other clues—especially Grishin's Order of Lenin citation—suggest that the succession contest had begun in earnest that fall. For Gorbachev to take his campaign into the public arena was a bold move and courageous, too, because Gorbachev gave no quarter to the conservative Brezhnevites. He would continue to prosecute corrupt officials; he would pursue sweeping political and economic reform; he would open up the news media and public discussion generally; he would make people in power accountable to the public. He would change the country to try to preserve its status as "a great and prosperous power."

The best evidence of the significance of this speech may be the way it was handled in the official news media, then still in the hands of conservative *apparatchiks*. No newspaper or magazine printed its full

---

* Archie Brown of Oxford University noted many interesting points in the speech in an article he published in the journal *Problems of Communism* just after Gorbachev came to power. But then it was too soon to realize how much of Gorbachev's future program the speech contained.

text. *Pravda* published much of it, but paraphrased key sections so that some of Gorbachev's most challenging language disappeared. References to shortcomings and past mistakes were excised. The intriguing description of "our contemporary" as someone who can't be trifled with or lied to was also censored. So was all the language emphasizing that he sought radical economic reform, not tinkering. The reference to prices and profits was cut.

But much of the language quoted here did appear in *Pravda,* including nearly everything cited that referred to democratization and *glasnost.* A close reader of *Pravda* in 1984 would have realized how boldly Gorbachev was speaking out.

Soviet television went farther to censor Gorbachev. It broadcast an excerpt from the speech on the evening news that contained none of its provocative passages. Viewers would have had the impression that Gorbachev said nothing at all new or interesting. George Orwell's Winston Smith would have been proud of the transformation of the speech into routine pap.

So someone important disliked Gorbachev's platform, and chose to censor it. The address was subsequently published in full as a forty-six-page pamphlet by the political literature publishing house in Moscow,* but the primary audience—members of the leadership—probably received copies directly from the speaker, or received the classified news digests prepared by Tass (the state news agency) to give senior officials a full account of foreign and domestic developments.

•   •   •

At the end of the year the country prepared for another round of unanimous voting for deputies of the Supreme Soviet. This time, the Kremlinologists' count of nominations showed that Grishin had moved up in the Politburo's pecking order; he was now fourth, right behind Gorbachev. (Tikhonov, the ancient premier and not a candidate for the succession, had the second-highest number of nominations.) In December Ustinov died; Chernenko was too ill to take part fully in his funeral. In February Grishin read Chernenko's election address to his constituents. A macabre drama was staged for Soviet television to show Chernenko casting his ballot; the film broadcast on the evening news showed him in a room that was clearly not a regular polling place (many surmised it was his hospital suite), barely manag-

---

* *Zhivoye Tvorchestvo Naroda,* Moscow, 1984.

ing to put his ballot paper into a box. Grishin was at his side. Four days later television showed the two of them again; this time Grishin was conveying congratulations to Chernenko for his victory, by unanimous vote, in the Kiubishev constituency in Moscow. These broadcasts appeared to signal that Grishin was Chernenko's chosen successor; a number of my acquaintances in Moscow thought they meant Grishin had displaced Gorbachev as the second-ranking member of the Politburo.

Chernenko finally succumbed on March 10. The Politburo was called into session that same day to discuss the succession. With Ustinov and Chernenko dead, just ten full members of the governing body remained. Five of them were obviously Brezhnevites who would be inclined to support Grishin; that left no more than four, besides Gorbachev, who might line up behind the young reformer.*

According to my best-informed source, one of the first members to speak was Grigori Romanov, the tough and nasty former first secretary in Leningrad, who had come to Moscow two years earlier to take responsibility for the military-industrial complex as a secretary of the Central Committee. Romanov, I was told, suggested that the group follow the advice of the founding father, Vladimir Ilyich Lenin, who —Romanov said—recommended that when the Party is split the first secretary of either the Moscow or the Leningrad Party organization should become leader. The Party clearly was split; Romanov reportedly noted that he might qualify under Lenin's guideline as a former Leningrad first secretary, but he proposed instead to nominate the Moscow first secretary, Grishin. Gorbachev was nominated by Andrei Gromyko, the venerable foreign minister.†

In his first bit of Machiavellian power politics, Gorbachev is said to have arranged to delay the return to Moscow of Vladimir Shcherbitsky, who was then leading a parliamentary delegation to the United States and was on the West Coast. I had met Shcherbitsky in Washington just days before, and had a lively but unproductive conversa-

---

* The Brezhnev men were Vladimir Shcherbitsky from the Ukraine; Grigori Romanov; Grishin; Premier Tikhonov; and Dinmukhamed Kunayev, first secretary in Kazakhstan. Gorbachev, Gaydar Aliev of Azerbaijan, Vitali Vorotnikov, and Mikhail Solomentsev were all identified as Andropov men. Andrei Gromyko, brought into the Politburo by Brezhnev, supported Gorbachev in 1985.

† I cannot attest to the accuracy of this information, only to the sobriety and reliability of my well-connected informants. Until the participants themselves were willing to recount what happens in these secret deliberations, we will have to rely on secondhand information, which can always be wrong.

tion with him. He was a Party man of the old school; he would give away nothing of interest in his talks with Americans, including any hint of his preference as successor to Chernenko. But he was a Brezhnev man (he continued to honor the former leader in the Ukraine, where he ruled as first secretary, long after Brezhnev had been disgraced in Moscow), and probably backed Grishin. He didn't reach Moscow until Gorbachev had been elected general secretary.

By some accounts Dinmukhamed Kunayev, like Shcherbitsky an old Brezhnev crony and likely Grishin supporter, also failed to get to Moscow from distant Kazakhstan in time to participate in the meeting. Vitali Vorotnikov, an Andropov protégé expected to support Gorbachev, was traveling in Yugoslavia when Chernenko died; some sources say he got back in time to join the Politburo's discussions; others say he did not.

But a simple head count is not enough to explain what happened on March 10. There were eleven candidate, or nonvoting, members of the Politburo entitled to participate in that meeting; the five secretaries of the Central Committee who were not also full or candidate members of the Politburo could also have been in attendance. Whether there was a formal vote isn't known.

It may not have been possible for all present to express their true preference. One of the candidate members of the Politburo, Viktor Chebrikov—an Andropov man who was chairman of the KGB—may have had a disproportionate influence on the proceedings. By some accounts he came with a dossier documenting Grishin's involvement in massive corruption in Moscow. Some believe that even Grishin's supporters would have realized that he was unsuitable as national leader. Zhores Medvedev suggests that Grishin could also have been disqualified because of his connection to Lavrenti Beria, Stalin's murderous henchman and head of the secret police, one of the most notorious thugs of the Stalin era. Beria's illegitimate daughter had been married to Grishin's son.

Ustinov's death less than three months earlier may have been the single most important event enabling Gorbachev to prevail. Ustinov had assured Andropov's selection in 1982 by playing the military card shrewdly; if he had played that card against Gorbachev in 1985, as he well might have, it is difficult to see how Gorbachev could have won. Ustinov was close to Romanov, who had large ambitions himself; some of my best-informed acquaintances in Moscow speculated that Ustinov, had he lived, might have tried to push Romanov into the top job when Chernenko died.*

One intriguing piece of concrete evidence about the selection of Gorbachev does exist: an official version of the nominating speech that Gromyko gave on his behalf to the entire Central Committee, which convened the next day, March 11. The speech was not printed in the press, but was published two months later in *Kommunist,* the Party's monthly theoretical journal, read by all Party activists but not by many ordinary citizens. It was clearly not a traditional, carefully prepared address; it has all the earmarks of impromptu remarks. As Mark Frankland of the *Observer* has pointed out, this may be a rare example of the way members of the leadership actually talk to one another about important matters. Most significant, the speech appears to show that the Party leadership was deeply divided over the choice of a new leader.

Gromyko confirmed that Gorbachev had indeed been the second-ranking Party official. "As is well known, he led the secretariat" of the Central Committee, Gromyko said, and "likewise, he chaired the meetings of the Politburo in the absence of Konstantin Ustinovich Chernenko." In those capacities, Gromyko said, "He demonstrated that he was brilliant, without any exaggeration. . . . This is a man of principles, a man of strong convictions. . . . During discussion of the question in the Politburo, it was said that Mikhail Sergeyevich is a man of sharp and deep intelligence, and anyone who knows him, who even meets with him just once, can confirm this. . . . [He] is a man of broad erudition, both by education and from his experience at work. . . . [He] has a great skill for organizing people, and for finding a common language with them."

Gromyko endorsed Gorbachev's ability to "grasp the essence of processes going on outside our country, in the international arena," and praised his concern for maintaining Soviet military strength while "keeping our powder dry." Gromyko, the country's senior statesman for a generation, seemed to intend these comments as reassurances.

And, in the most interesting passage of the speech, Gromyko talked about Party unity:

"We live in a world where, figuratively speaking, various telescopes are pointed at the Soviet Union—big ones and small ones, from a

---

* In his biography of Gorbachev, Zhores Medvedev describes Ustinov as a friend and supporter, but my best-informed sources say, on the contrary, that Ustinov did not support Gorbachev.

short distance and from a long distance. Possibly more of them are looking from a long distance. And they are looking to see if they can find, finally, some kind of splits in the Soviet leadership. I can assure you that we have seen evidence of this dozens and dozens of times, we've observed it. We have been witnesses, if you will, to conversations, to whispered and half-whispered conjectures: somewhere abroad they are thirsting to see disagreement in the Soviet leadership." On this occasion, Gromyko went on, "Let us not give our political opponents any satisfaction on this point." He expressed the hope that "the plenum of the Central Committee, like the Politburo, will unanimously support and greet" his nomination of Gorbachev.*

Of course the Politburo could only have been "unanimous" under traditional Party rules, which require all members to accept and endorse decisions once they are taken, however they may have felt before consensus was achieved. Gromyko's real message (which may have been dressed up a little before it was published) was to warn of the consequences of a split. There is no record of how his plea was received. Gorbachev certainly had support in the Central Committee, particularly from a group of younger first secretaries of provincial Party organizations who had known him from Stavropol, and shared his reformist outlook.

Ligachev was a member of that group when he was first secretary in Tomsk. When Andropov brought Ligachev to Moscow and named him a member of the Central Committee secretariat responsible for Party cadres, he was in a more influential position to help Gorbachev. Ligachev provided another glimpse of the way Gorbachev was selected when he spoke defensively about his role in the process more than three years later. Ligachev had then become a target of Party reformers, who accused him of opposing meaningful change; at the special Party Conference in July, 1988, he wanted to defend himself: "A completely different decision could have been made," Ligachev said then, and "quite different people could be sitting on this podium" had it not been for the efforts of himself, Gromyko, Chebrikov, and Solomentsev. But he gave no further details of what they had done.

Boris Yeltsin, the colorful former first secretary from the industrial center of Sverdlovsk, who will reappear often in this tale, has provided his own version of Gorbachev's election in the fascinating book of

---

* It has been widely reported that Gromyko also said of Gorbachev on this occasion, "Comrades, this man has a nice smile but he's got iron teeth," a colorful addition to his endorsement. This language is not in the published text, and I have been unable to find any independent confirmation that Gromyko used it. But he may have.

memoirs he published in 1990. Yeltsin writes, "There was, of course, a fight," adding the juicy tidbit that "Grishin's list of the Politburo members who would support him [for leader] had been found." The list "did not include Gorbachev among his supporters; nor were many other Politburo members included." Yeltsin doesn't explain how or when this list was found; Yeltsin succeeded Grishin as first secretary of the Moscow Party organization, and presumably inherited Grishin's files.

Yeltsin dismissed Ligachev's account as an insult to Gorbachev "and, indeed, everyone who took part in the election of the general secretary." He credits the Central Committee, not the Politburo, with the choice of Gorbachev. At the time Yeltsin was a member of the Central Committee, not of the Politburo, so his version may be self-serving, but it could be accurate:

> Practically all the participants in that [Central Committee] plenum [of March 11], including many senior, experienced first secretaries, considered that the Grishin platform was unacceptable, that it would have meant the immediate end of both the Party and the country. . . . Furthermore it was impossible to overlook the defects of Grishin's personality: his smugness, his blinkered self-assurance, his sense of his own infallibility, and his thirst for power.
>
> A large number of first secretaries agreed that of all the Politburo members, the man to be promoted to the post of general secretary had to be Gorbachev. He was the most energetic, the best-educated, and the most suitable from the point of view of age. We decided to put our weight behind him. We conferred with several Politburo members . . . [and with] Ligachev. Our position coincided with his, because he was as afraid of Grishin as we were. Once it had become clear that this was the majority view, we decided that if any other candidate was put forward—Grishin, Romanov, or anyone else—we would oppose him *en bloc*. And defeat him.
>
> Evidently the discussions within the Politburo itself followed along these lines. Those Politburo members who attended that session were aware of our firm intentions, and Gromyko, too, supported our point of view. . . . Grishin and his supporters did not dare risk making a move; they realized that their chances were slim (or rather, to be precise, zero), and therefore Gorbachev's candidacy was put forward without any complications or problems.

Gorbachev's elevation was announced to the nation that same day, March 11, 1985. A new Soviet era had begun.

•   •   •

That a younger generation would finally come to power and change the Soviet Union had long been predicted. Seweryn Bialer of Columbia University, perhaps the most insightful of all American students of the Soviet Union, published a brilliant book called *Stalin's Successors* in 1980 that foresaw a sharp increase in pressure on the Soviet system to change itself in the 1980s. Bialer saw precisely the economic crisis that was taking shape when he wrote his book in the late 1970s, and he realized that the old men then in charge were ill equipped to meet it. He used stark language: "By far the central problem, the key to the entire emergency, has to do with the need to reform the entire system of planning and management." He also wrote perceptively about the younger men who would eventually take over, noting that they were less insecure and more worldly than their elders, and more willing to acknowledge the shortcomings of Soviet society. But there were limits to Bialer's foresight; Gorbachev's name appeared just once in his book, in a list of four younger members of the leadership.

I had been back from my 1984 visit to Moscow for six months when Gorbachev became general secretary. I was excited that the man touted by my old friends the previous summer as a student of past Russian reforms, who was eager to invigorate his country, now had a chance to do just that. I had spent fifteen years following Soviet affairs, and my avocation had become depressing. At last there was the promise of something really new in Moscow.

I have a record of my own expectations for Gorbachev, because I wrote an article for *The Washington Post*'s Sunday Outlook section about him a few days after his elevation. I understood that "there will be change, both in domestic and foreign policies," and that the change might be very dramatic. I understood how much Gorbachev differed from his predecessors, and suggested that his worldliness and education were potentially important factors. But I also assured *Post* readers that a new Gorbachev era "does not mean a transformed Soviet Union. It will remain a relatively poor, technologically backward, insecure, overarmed, politically ambitious and troublesome world power. Its domestic economy will continue to be inefficient and cumbersome. Its political style will remain autocratic and arbitrary. There may be some loosening of controls, but the Soviet Union will not become a 'liberal' society, nor will it learn to respect human rights."

"The Soviet Union has been so badly run for so many years that a modicum of intelligent, practical change—far short of radical reform —could transform the public mood, and probably result in considerably improved economic performance," I wrote in 1985. "We should be ready to see Gorbachev try just such a course of action."

And I took a cautious view of possible changes in international relations: "Gorbachev retains a bristling arsenal and a great-power position; his country will continue to be America's most troublesome rival. He himself faces an intriguing personal and political challenge. After a long intermission, the drama of competitive international politics may soon begin anew."

I would have more to regret if I had written anything in that article about Communist ideology, censorship, and the role of the Party, which I then considered largely immutable, or about the Soviet empire in Eastern Europe, which I did not expect to disappear any time soon.

Nearly all—perhaps absolutely all—of the Westerners who studied the Soviet Union were unprepared for the most dramatic departures that Gorbachev was to cause, or to permit, in the next five years. We were mired in misconceptions about the status of reformist ideas in Soviet society; we thought the taboos and myths at the heart of Soviet power were too sacrosanct to be toyed with; we lacked imagination.

So did the Soviet citizens who took the time to think about their country's prospects. Not surprisingly, after living with the Stalinist system for more than half a century, they took it for granted and presumed its permanence. They, too, misunderstood the degree to which some senior Party officials would be prepared to reexamine first principles.

I failed to appreciate how ideas reborn in the Thaw—reformist, humanistic, pragmatic ideas about the need to make the post-Stalin Soviet Union a better society—had survived Brezhnev's "De-Khrushchevization," and then survived eighteen years of Brezhnev. I knew that the small band of dissident, liberal intellectuals held on to these ideas, but I didn't understand that they also lived on in the minds of many senior *apparatchiks,* academics, diplomats, scientists, and even some Party leaders.

It was the children of the 20th Party Congress who kept them alive. As they grew into mature adults they held on to an us-them mentality first developed in the 1950s. "We" were the sensible, practical, and decent Communists who wanted to bring what Khrushchev started to its natural conclusion: a truly de-Stalinized Soviet society freed from totalitarian control. "They" were the conventional Stalinist *apparat-chiks* who liked the old ways and were terrified of changing them.

"We always knew the Thaw would return," Roald Sagdeyev told me in 1990. Sagdeyev was a distinguished scientist who became director of the Moscow Institute of Space Research, making a successful career while guarding his personal views from all but his closest friends and relatives. Sagdeyev recalled the satisfaction that he shared privately with friends in 1963 when, for the first time, the Soviet Union imported foreign grain. That was confirmation of their belief that the economic system was doomed unless it was reformed and decentralized, Sagdeyev thought; eventually, economic crisis would force reform. Sagdeyev and many others perceived a direct relationship between economic decentralization and the general loosening of central controls—economic reform would have to mean a freer society.

There was a serious flirtation with reform later in the 1960s, when Alexei Kosygin, the premier, agreed to pursue the ideas of a number of economists for making prices more realistic and enterprises more independent. The economists involved were initially exhilarated that the government would listen to them and act; only later, when it became apparent that the opposition of officials at every level was sabotaging the changes, did the economists realize they had been too optimistic.

Mikhail Gorbachev agreed that decentralization was the key to real progress, according to his Czech roommate at the university, Zdenek Mlynar. In 1967, when Mlynar visited his friend in Stavropol, Gorbachev "expected greater autonomy and responsibility from Brezhnev [then in his third year in power] for lower-level leaders in the republics and various regions. He considered this necessary for real change in the system of economic and political management in a country so immense, and with such varied conditions."

In 1967–68 Mlynar and his colleagues in the reformist Czechoslovak leadership created a model for a new kind of communism, which became known as "socialism with a human face." They articulated specific plans for freeing the economy from many of its Stalinist central controls; they ended censorship; they spoke of individual freedoms; and they invited trouble. The Prague Spring of 1968 put the issue starkly to Brezhnev and his comrades: was it tolerable to liberalize communism and abandon Stalinist centralization? The men in charge voted No, and invaded Czechoslovakia to oust the Dubček government.

That invasion had a devastating effect on the morale of the children of the 20th Party Congress. Many were shocked by the decision to invade, then depressed when they contemplated the implications for them and for Russia. The new day the liberals dreamt of kept being postponed.

There was a second event in 1968 of great importance for progressives in the Soviet élite. Months before the invasion of Czechoslovakia, copies began circulating in Moscow of a typescript entitled "Reflections on Progress, Coexistence, and Intellectual Freedom." It was a bold statement of progressive principles written by an exemplary Soviet citizen, a man who had three times been named a Hero of Socialist Labor, the country's highest honor. This of course was Andrei Sakharov, father of the Soviet hydrogen bomb, once the youngest member of the Soviet Academy of Sciences (he was admitted at thirty-two), and a figure held in almost universal admiration. Khrushchev, in his memoirs, had called Sakharov "a crystal of morality among our scientists."

With this one essay, Sakharov declared himself a dissident ready to challenge the most basic tenets of the Soviet regime. "Intellectual freedom," he wrote, "is essential to human society—freedom to obtain and distribute information, freedom for open-minded and un-fearing debate, and freedom from pressure by officialdom and from prejudices. . . . Freedom of thought is the only guarantee of the feasibility of a scientific, democratic approach to politics, economy, and culture." He called for the creation of a multiparty political system in the Soviet Union, the end of censorship, and the completion of de-Stalinization: "The exposure of Stalin must be carried through to the end, to the complete truth."

At the time it appeared and for many years afterward, Sakharov's essay seemed little more than a visionary appeal from a disillusioned scientist who probably did not understand the facts of political life. I got to know Sakharov in the early 1970s. I felt then that he was one of the most noble people I would ever know, and also a man whose mission in life—to open up his country and make it free—was destined to fail. He had taken on too big an opponent: the entire Soviet system. Or so it seemed then.*

---

* Sakharov's essay included many prescriptions for the rest of the world that have long been forgotten, and that look considerably less prophetic than his recommendations for his own country. He called for "the victory of the leftist reformist wing of the bourgeoisie" in the capitalist countries, which could lead to the convergence of the capitalist and socialist systems. He proposed a 20 percent tax on the national incomes of all developed countries to finance development in the third world. And he foresaw the creation of a world government to oversee total disarmament by the end of the twentieth century.

His essay wasn't published in the Soviet Union, though it was smuggled out of the country and ultimately printed in many languages all over the world. But typescript copies circulated widely. It isn't known whether Gorbachev or any of his future allies in the Party actually read the document, but they certainly learned of its contents, either from foreign radio broadcasts, classified official documents, or word of mouth. One of the beauties of Sakharov's piece was its simplicity. But its greatest asset was the identity of its author. Party officials could dismiss many of the dissidents as kooks and misfits, but the father of the hydrogen bomb did not fit those categories.

It turned out that even during dark days in the Brezhnev era, progressive academics and officials had opportunities to try to push the leadership toward pragmatism or reform. These opportunities were mostly hidden at the time, but it was possible to learn about them years later, when *glasnost* was in fashion. Abel Aganbegyan, the clever economist who was an early member of Gorbachev's working groups when Andropov was leader, published a book in 1989 that recounts many frustrating encounters with political leaders who didn't understand economics, though the economists kept offering explanations—and recommending reforms.

In 1972–73 Aganbegyan was one of the experts consulted by officials who had been assigned to prepare a special Central Committee plenum devoted to the need for greater scientific and technological progress. Georgi Arbatov, director of the Institute for the Study of the U.S.A. and Canada, was one of the leaders of this effort. Months were spent interviewing experts and officials all over the country; according to Aganbegyan, sweeping plans were developed to redirect investment, integrate science and production, reform higher education, and more. Arbatov oversaw an effort to boil all this down into a 150-page document. It was presented to the senior leadership, which reacted by abandoning the idea of holding a special plenum. The document was found in a safe in Brezhnev's office when he died in 1982, according to one senior official.

In the mid-1970s, according to Alexander Bovin, one of Andropov's personal aides in the mid-1960s, reformers who understood its significance quietly promoted the Helsinki agreement on European security, a document signed in 1975 by the United States, the Soviet Union, and all the European nations. It declared "inviolable" the existing borders in Europe, but also committed the signatories to respect the sovereignty of each nation, renounce "the threat or use of force," and respect basic human rights, including "freedom of thought, conscience, religion or belief."

In 1975 Brezhnev's signature on the document seemed to be a typically cynical Soviet gesture with no practical significance, but this was wrong. The Helsinki agreement inspired many people throughout the Soviet bloc; it encouraged Solidarity in Poland, the most important democratic movement in the Communist world before Gorbachev. The Helsinki accords were "extremely important," Bovin told me in 1990. "We fought for them."

In the early 1980s economists and social scientists began to speak out with increasing boldness on the need for significant reforms. One of the boldest was a colleague of Aganbegyan's in Novosibirsk, Tatyana Zaslavskaya, a sociologist. She composed a devastating critique of the economic system and the unrealistic assumptions underlying it for presentation to a seminar sponsored by the Central Committee's economic department in 1983. Her paper caused a sensation in the West when it was leaked to Dusko Doder of *The Washington Post*. It was actually one of numerous studies, some of them openly published, that drew similarly damning conclusions about the economic situation in the early eighties. In 1984, Aganbegyan published in the popular press the grim analysis of the faltering economy that I quoted in the previous chapter.

So the reformist ideas that startled the world when Gorbachev made them official policy in the late 1980s actually had been nurtured since he and his contemporaries were young men. Alexander Yakovlev, Gorbachev's principal ally in the Politburo, confirmed this years later. "The ideas of *perestroika* were nourished in different fields for a long time, sometimes a very long time, even too long," Yakovlev said. "These ideas have been developed over the years by scholars, cultural figures, and people engaged in political activity. Such ideas have been discussed in the press and in private conversations. All this was the background to the growing understanding that it was impossible to live in the old way and many serious changes were necessary."

But there was a great difference between that "growing understanding" and the courage to act. Liberals like Yakovlev who made official careers had learned to endure the falsifications and procrastinations of the Brezhnev years. Many of them were just rationalizers who told themselves and their friends that they were eager to change things, but then found excuses to continue cooperating with the status quo. This is understandable. A man who began a Party career when Gorbachev did, in the hopeful years between the 20th and 22nd Party Congresses, and who—like Gorbachev—approved of the removal of Khrushchev in 1964, then found his country trapped in an eighteen-year period in which things ultimately seemed only to get worse. By the time the deterioration was too obvious to deny—in the late 1970s or early 1980s—that man was at least forty-five years old, and far advanced in his career. Unless he had the courage of a Sakharov—who was forty-seven when he circulated his essay on intellectual freedom, knowing it would end his official career—he had no appealing options.

But such people could, it turned out, make an important historical contribution. They could help preserve the values and ideas that ultimately would burst upon the Soviet Union and the world under the banners of *glasnost* and *perestroika*.

The Gorbachev revolution had roots that ran deep in Soviet society and even in the Communist Party. But they were hardly the only roots in those soils. Stalinism had strong roots, too; so did crass careerism and selfishness. In the nearly three decades since the 20th Party Congress, a huge state and Party bureaucracy had grown up, fattened on generous privileges and comfortable with the status quo.

Gorbachev personally was the best-educated, most articulate and forceful, most self-confident and independent-minded man to become the Soviet Union's leader since Lenin. By happenstance and good luck he had, from boyhood on, a series of opportunities to see for himself the huge gulf between his Party's propaganda and real life, at home and abroad. But he was still a Party man who had internalized Party rituals and beliefs, who respected Party discipline and "democratic centralism," which required all Party members to accept Party decisions, even those they bitterly disputed.

So on March 11, 1985, when Gorbachev began what would become the most dramatic display of political leadership seen anywhere in the world in the second half of the twentieth century, no die was cast. Gorbachev had ideas and enthusiasm, but he carried heavy burdens from the past—bad habits, fear, a deeply flawed economic system, and many more—that would hang over any attempt to begin change.

CHAPTER FOUR

SLOW BEGINNINGS

Gorbachev in power faced three immediate challenges. He had to consolidate his position, to ensure that those who thought of blocking his ascension this time would be in no position to oust him in the future. He had to decide what to do first to initiate the changes in Soviet society that he wanted, and to establish his own new political personality for his countrymen and the world. And he had to find competent allies and associates who could help him first formulate and then achieve his goals.

Looking back more than five years later, it is surprising to be reminded how very slowly Gorbachev began, and how many wrong steps he took. In domestic policy Gorbachev appeared to be a conservative, modest reformer and a typical Party man, more puritanical than the norm. In Party politics he was creative and tough but predictable, moving promptly to strengthen his situation. He relied heavily on Yegor Ligachev, whom he quickly promoted to be his number-two man, a move that nearly had disastrous consequences. His most notable early innovations involved his style as a leader. Gorbachev was most adventurous in foreign policy, signaling a desire to pull back from the contentiousness in Soviet-American relations that marked

Ronald Reagan's first term in Washington. In diplomacy his first year did have momentous consequences.

In 1985 and 1986 there was no hint of the great upheavals that would sweep away the old order in Eastern Europe and the Soviet Union in 1989–90. I think it was Gorbachev's failure to make more progress in those first two years that led to his much more radical departures beginning in 1988. "You must understand," Gorbachev's comrade-in-arms Alexander Yakovlev said later, "it wasn't until 1985 that we learned just how bad things really were, particularly in our economic and financial affairs."

•   •   •

At the Central Committee plenum in March 1985 that named him general secretary Gorbachev gave a brief speech that echoed his un-usual address of the previous December, when he first touched on so many of his plans. Using more diplomatic language this time, he told the Central Committee that he would implement "the strategic line" formulated by Andropov and Chernenko, giving emphasis to his men-tor's role in a way that could have surprised no one in the hall. This would mean persistent efforts "to improve the economic mechanism and the whole system of management," which would require "enhanc-ing the autonomy of enterprises"—and thus reducing central con-trols. He called for "the further perfection and development of democracy and the whole system of socialist self-government." He again used the word *glasnost,* saying, "We must continue to in-crease the *glasnost* given to the work of Party, administrative, state and public organizations." But no one (except perhaps Gorba-chev and a few close associates) understood that these formulations might actually lead to radical changes. On foreign-policy issues he was firm but also forthcoming, soliciting better relations with China and success in arms-control negotiations with the United States, which, by coincidence, were to resume the next day in Geneva.

Close readers of the Soviet press noticed that the papers were not making a great fuss over the new general secretary. No orchestrated outpouring of enthusiasm was evident in March—a contrast from the early weeks of Chernenko's tenure, when he was instantaneously glo-rified. Gorbachev seemed to adopt Andropov's more modest ap-proach. The first hint of new policies came on April 4, when Radio Moscow reported that the Politburo, meeting that day, had discussed plans for a new campaign against alcoholism and drunkenness. This set off a flood of rumors, including reports that the Soviet Union was about to adopt absolute prohibition of alcoholic beverages.

But nothing was announced right away. The first public statement from the new leader came in an interview with *Pravda* on international affairs, particularly Soviet-American relations. In it Gorbachev made clear his own eagerness for an early summit meeting with President Reagan. And he announced a unilateral moratorium on the deployment of SS-20 intermediate-range missiles in Europe—the missiles that had upset the European military balance and led to NATO's decision to deploy Pershing II and cruise missiles in response. The moratorium would last at least seven months. Gorbachev was trying to defang the principal source of East-West tension at the time.

Five weeks after assuming power, Gorbachev convened a special Central Committee plenum to introduce his new line. For years afterward this meeting was described in official shorthand as "The April Plenum," where *perestroika* and reform were born and officially blessed. But in fact no program was presented that day, only vague goals. Gorbachev embraced the Central Committee's support for those goals as a mandate, which he invoked repeatedly during the next several years. The speech he gave at the plenum must have required several hours to read; it broke little new ground. It was a speech of the old school, full of ritualistic genuflections to various totems of Party life. There is no description of this prose that can do it justice—to be appreciated it needs to be sampled, however briefly:

"Lenin taught communists to base everything they do on the interests of the working people, to scrutinize life deeply, to evaluate social phenomena realistically and from class positions, and to engage in a constant, creative search for the best ways to implement the ideals of communism. Today we are checking our deeds and plans against Lenin and his great ideas; we are living and working in accordance with Lenin's behests."

The speech repeated points Gorbachev had made already: the economy required a scientific and technological revolution, people had to work harder, the standard of living had to be improved. He introduced one concrete idea: more money had to be invested in the making of machine tools to modernize Soviet industry. (This led to a massive machine-tool initiative, which was much trumpeted and then—when it showed no signs of success—dropped.) The speech included a tough section attacking the United States for aggravating the arms race.*

Reading this tedious speech years after it was delivered, one nugget caught my eye in a section devoted to the special responsibilities of Party members. "The example here must be set by Communists," Gorbachev said. "It is necessary to intensify the demands made on every Party member regarding his attitude toward public duty, the fulfillment of Party decisions, and the honest and pure aspect of a Party member's character. A Communist is assessed according to his actions and deeds; there are no other criteria, nor can there be."

You can almost hear the pleading tone in his voice. By the time Gorbachev took control of the Communist Party of the Soviet Union, it was a tired and soiled instrument. Petty corruption was much more common in its ranks than the heroics Gorbachev hoped for; entrenched interests were more likely to be defensive and protective than adventurous or innovative. Gorbachev had somehow preserved his own enthusiasm and determination through thirty years of Komsomol and Party work, and he desperately sought the same qualities in his comrades now that he needed their help. But the odds of finding them were slim.

The situation was worst in the Party bureaucracy, what Russians called the *apparat*. It was populated by *apparatchiki*—millions of them—gray people with bureaucratic outlooks who had spent lifetimes obeying and giving orders. They obeyed what came to them from above, and expected the same behavior from those to whom they gave orders below. There were people in various corners of the *apparat* who could be described as bright and creative, but the standard-issue *apparatchik* was neither. "An intelligent, independent-minded official of the Central Committee," Boris Yeltsin wrote in his book, "is a combination of words so paradoxical that one's tongue cannot even utter them." As Gorbachev would soon discover, finding effective allies in these ranks would not be easy.

•   •   •

Gorbachev's speech attracted less public attention than the changes in the leadership announced at the same plenum. Three new full members of the Politburo were named—the first changes in the group

---

* One of my best-informed sources in Moscow told me the full—and unpublished—version of the speech was more interesting and included strong criticisms of certain government ministers.

since Andropov's death. All three were Andropov men. Ligachev was the most important; at the plenum Gorbachev invited Ligachev to sit next to him on the podium, a clear sign he was the new number-two man. Viktor Chebrikov, the head of the KGB and reportedly a Gorbachev ally (or at least a Grishin opponent) in the succession struggle, was also made a full member. So was Nikolai Ryzhkov, then a Central Committee secretary responsible for industry. Ligachev and Ryzhkov were vaulted into the Politburo without serving the traditional apprenticeship as candidate members.

None of these men proved to be effective allies. Because, like Gorbachev, they were all Andropov protégés, many Russians—and numerous Western commentators—assumed that Gorbachev had now added "his men" to the leadership. But this was not the case. He had added three tough-minded, independent, and relatively honest men, who agreed in 1985 that the country needed shaking up, but they were not Gorbachev's clients, and owed him no special allegiance. This would become clear in all three cases over the next several years.

Two weeks after the plenum Gorbachev addressed a huge crowd of five thousand guests invited to the Kremlin's Palace of Congresses for the fortieth anniversary celebration of victory in the Great Patriotic War.* The speech was a traditional recitation of familiar propagandistic formulations. But there was one electrifying moment that foretold troubles for the new leader. After a long section crediting every conceivable element of Soviet society for a share of the glory for winning the war, Gorbachev added this almost perfunctory sentence: "The gigantic work at the front and in the rear was guided by the Party, its Central Committee, and the State Defense Committee headed by the general secretary of the CPSU [Communist Party of the Soviet Union] Bolshevik Central Committee, Josef Vissarionovich Stalin." At the mention of Stalin's name the audience roared its approval, then gave a long ovation.

The symbolism of Gorbachev's winning such cheers for invoking the name of Stalin sent shivers down many spines in Moscow and elsewhere; it must also have made Gorbachev and his colleagues think harder about how they wanted to handle this delicate issue—on the

---

* Like so much else from the Stalinist past, this name was purposeful. In the war Stalin had fused the causes of Bolshevism and Russian patriotism; it was a critical accomplishment to assure the legitimacy of Bolshevik rule. In Party mythology, winning the war was the greatest single accomplishment since 1917.

face of it historical, but, as that spontaneous cheer revealed, still vividly contemporary.

•   •   •

It was mid-May 1985 when Gorbachev, with the help of Soviet television, first made a striking new impression on his people. The event was a three-day visit to Leningrad, the second city of the Soviet Union. It had dramatic quality from the moment Gorbachev stepped out of his airplane and was approached—in a traditional Soviet ritual —by a young girl offering him a bouquet of flowers. Gorbachev suggested that the flowers be distributed to the women present, then turned to the local first secretary, Lev Zaikov, and immediately proposed revising the schedule for his visit. Evidently he wanted to avoid seeing only the establishments that had preened and polished to prepare for him.

On the second day of his visit the main evening news program on Soviet television, *Vremya* (Time), devoted about twenty minutes to film of Gorbachev and Raisa in Leningrad. More than 100 million people are said to watch the news each evening. That night they saw something entirely new: the leader of the Soviet Union mixing freely and spontaneously with his fellow citizens. (The leader's wife was also a new sight.) It was the same Gorbachev who was to become familiar to the entire world in the years to come—animated, eager to touch and talk and even argue, comfortable in a spontaneous crowd. Television showed him visiting factories, war memorials, and various sights around the city, and broadcast snippets of his spontaneous conversations. At one point a woman in a crowd yelled, "You should be closer to the people." Gorbachev, surrounded by Leningraders as he spoke, replied: "How can I be any closer?" The crowd laughed appreciatively.

This one newscast evoked a powerful response from a Soviet public inured to the idea that its leaders were decrepit old men. Nothing remotely comparable to this performance had been seen in the television age (which began in the Soviet Union after Brezhnev came to power in 1964). Russians of my acquaintance remembered this broadcast and their delighted reaction to it years later.

On that visit to Leningrad Gorbachev for the first time used the verb *perestroit'*—to reconstruct, rebuild, or renew—the root of the noun *perestroika*. He used it in a long, unscripted speech to leading Party cadres in Leningrad gathered at the Smolny, the building where Lenin plotted the final scenes of the Bolshevik Revolution in 1917.

This speech also caused a sensation when large parts of it were broadcast four days later on Soviet television.* There was no explanation for the delay, or for the fact that no newspaper ever printed a full account of the speech. These were the first examples of a strange censorship of Gorbachev's public remarks that continued through his first two years in power, a sign of the strains in his new leadership group. Evidently some of his comrades didn't like what he was saying.

The speech attracted attention in part because Gorbachev delivered it instead of reading it, barely referring to his notes, an unprecedented departure for a modern Soviet leader. At the time the speech was widely described as a dynamic, honest, and heartfelt appeal to come to grips with the country's problems, and to prepare to reconstruct not just the economy but also the psychology of individuals. Reread five years later, it is a rather lifeless document, windy and full of traditional Soviet rhetoric, but punctuated by half a dozen vivid passages that explain why it seemed so unusual then.

"It is obvious," Gorbachev said after a long-winded prologue, "that all of us must restructure ourselves—all of us, I would say, from worker to minister to secretary of the Party Central Committee, to leaders of the government." Later he picked up this theme: "Overall this will require immense mobilization of creative forces and the ability to restructure, and conduct the country's business in a new way— not only in the economy, but in all spheres, social, cultural, ideological." He compared the task to the achievements of the older generation that prepared the country for war against Hitler's Germany; his audience would have understood the comparison as a signal that he meant business. "We must of course give all our cadres the chance to understand the demands of the moment and to reconstruct themselves. However, those who don't intend to reconstruct themselves and who are an obstacle to fulfilling our tasks must simply get out of the way—step aside, not be a hindrance. We cannot regard the interests of one person as being more important than the interests of society as a whole."

That kind of firm, direct talk implicitly threatening *apparatchiks* everywhere was utterly unlike anything that had escaped the lips of Brezhnev or Chernenko; it was also considerably stronger than Andropov's relative candor. The people loved it.

---

* A black-market videocassette of the speech sold at the time for 300 rubles—two months' pay for a Soviet physician.

Gorbachev's off-the-cuff use of statistics also impressed viewers. He spoke of the great waste of natural resources that typifies the Soviet economy. "We are awash with resources in the sense that we possess great natural wealth, but it has seduced us." The average oil-fired electric generator burned 320 grams of fuel to produce a kilowatt hour of electricity, but some generators needed as much as 600 grams of oil. "If all thermal power stations could now be made to reduce fuel use to 320 grams, savings of 20 to 22 million tons of fuel per year could be achieved." In agriculture, he noted, "the land may be plowed to great depth, or it may be tilled by blade cultivator with the same results, while also sparing the soil. And in the latter case, 35 percent less fuel is used.

"You squander countless resources in every industry, but nobody is going broke, comrades. In fact it only seems that way, because you don't feel it. In a family you do feel it, when it comes out of your own pocket. . . . We must arrange things so that it is felt."

It was the first example of what became one of Gorbachev's most disarming tactics: bluntly calling things by their right names. This was still the man who, as a university student, liked Hegel's aphorism that "truth is always concrete." Truth telling by a Soviet leader was essentially unprecedented—and very well received by the public. (Not that every Gorbachev utterance fell into this category; he continued also to repeat exhausted phrases from the Marxist-Leninist vocabulary in nearly all his public appearances.)

This speech provided the first example of another Gorbachev habit that was less popular than truth telling, and in time frustrated his countrymen. As he was to do time and again in the future, Gorbachev that day in Leningrad made it clear he could not yet say just what his policy of reconstruction might consist of. "We will reach our goal," he promised, "with a thoroughly elaborated, well-considered, integrated, mobilizing policy—a policy in the interests of the people, a peace-loving policy, an energetic policy, which should lend dynamism to our society."

The new leader made a concerted effort that day to put himself in the shoes of his countrymen—a new approach for a Kremlin leader. "You and I spend 75 percent, if not 80 percent, of our cash outlays on the acquisition of goods alone," he said in a passage bemoaning the insignificance of the service sector in the Soviet economy. "Try to get your apartment repaired. You will definitely have to find a moon-lighter to do it for you. He will steal the materials he needs from a construction site. They come from the state anyway." He was talking about recognizable facts of everyday life—something previous leaders almost never mentioned.

In Leningrad Gorbachev offered a formula for leadership that clearly was heartfelt. It was probably the most revealing passage in the speech. "The Soviet people," he said, "strongly condemn instances of immodesty, ostentation, and empty talk. . . . Our cadres must take this into account in their work. The closer one gets to the people, the greater their trust, but at the same time I should say that this certainly does not mean playing up to them. People don't like leaders who do that. People like strict, organized leaders who demonstrate by their personal example a conscientious attitude toward affairs of state— exacting, considerate people. The people always support such leaders."

• • •

The campaign against drinking unveiled on May 16 got the most attention from the public during Gorbachev's first months in office. The idea for an anti-alcohol crusade apparently came from Ligachev,* the former first secretary from Tomsk, whom Andropov had brought to Moscow when he was looking for honest men to help him dislodge the corrupt personalities of the Brezhnev era. It is easy to see why the idea might have appealed to Gorbachev and others in the new leadership. Alcohol was taking a terrible toll on the society. Consumption had skyrocketed during the Brezhnev era, and it was high at the beginning. According to Ligachev, revenues from the legal sales of alcoholic beverages were 15.5 billion rubles in 1965, and 53 billion rubles in 1984. Women and children were starting to drink heavily in large numbers. Alcohol was probably the largest single cause of a stunning increase in the Soviet Union's crude death rate; it rose from 6.9 deaths per 1,000 citizens in 1964 to 10.8 in 1985.

The May 16 decrees raised the legal drinking age from eighteen to twenty-one; ordinary food stores that had sold vodka, cognac, and wines would no longer stock them, and liquor stores could not open until 2 P.M.; restaurants could serve no alcohol until 2 P.M. either; production of alcoholic beverages was curtailed. Prosecution of those violating the regulation on drinking would be stepped up. To the

---

* At the 28th Party Congress, in July 1990, Ligachev acknowledged his authorship.

amazement of many officials, drinking at all official functions, including banquets and receptions that used to flow with vodka and wine, was banned.*

The impact of the new decrees was a reminder of the power authoritarian governments can wield. Overnight the habits of a vast nation were transformed. Huge lines blossomed outside the liquor stores—lines whose occupants were unlikely to join Gorbachev fan clubs. Entire enterprises previously devoted to the production of alcoholic drinks were ordered to make something else. In grape-growing areas of the South, vineyards were ripped up. Gorbachev, the general secretary (generalnyi sekretar), became known as Gorbachev, the mineral water secretary (mineralnyi sekretar).

At first the campaign seemed to have precisely the effect Gorbachev hoped for. It was a nice symbol of his seriousness of purpose; it put him on the side of decent, hard-working people; it got everyone's attention. But eventually it caused enormous disruptions without noticeably reducing the amount of drinking in the country. For Gorbachev, the anti-drinking campaign became a painful lesson in the laws of unintended consequences—laws that worked with dismaying efficiency to undermine his initiatives.

After an initial public reaction the authorities interpreted as proof of their success, contrary signs began to appear. Sugar disappeared from the stores—one basic commodity that never used to be rationed suddenly had to be. It was being used by home distillers, whose numbers multiplied as it became harder and harder to buy a legal bottle of vodka. Doctors began reporting alarming numbers of cases of people poisoned by industrial alcohol, paint solvent, and the like. A new black market in alcoholic beverages thrived.

In his memoir written in 1989, Boris Yeltsin (who was promoted into the leadership in July 1985) gave this account of what he called Ligachev's crusade:

> His entire campaign against alcoholism was ill-conceived and ridiculous. He [Ligachev] had taken neither the economic nor the social consequences into account. He simply plunged ahead without proper thought. I spoke about this to Gorbachev several times, but for some reason he adopted a wait-and-see attitude, although it was quite clear

---

* Perhaps in an effort to mitigate the impact of this decree, three days later the government announced it would raise pensions and other benefits for the poorest retirees and for single-parent families, a popular gesture.

to me that you could never conquer drunkenness, that centuries-old evil, by going at the problem with the tactics of a cavalry charge. . . . Statistics from various Soviet republics were quoted at me: In the Ukraine, for example, the sales of wine and spirits had fallen 46 percent. I suggested that we should be patient and take a second look in a few months' time. Sure enough, people were soon beginning to drink anything that was liquid and contained alcohol; they started sniffing solvents, and the number of illicit stills increased sharply.

Nobody was actually consuming less alcohol, but the income from the sale of spirits was being diverted back into the black market rather than going to the state. [Before the campaign began, revenue from the sale of alcohol provided as much as 20 percent of the national budget.] The number of cases of alcohol poisoning rose catastrophically; many were fatal. The situation was becoming critical, yet Ligachev was still issuing cheerful reports on the success of his campaign.

By the time the negative consequences were clear, Gorbachev was closely tied to the campaign in the public mind. Some drinkers surely never forgave him. Others did. When I visited Moscow in 1988 I found old friends who were great Gorbachev enthusiasts—and who had become distillers of their own *samogon* (self-distilled) vodka. It wasn't bad, either. In 1989, the whole campaign was quietly shelved; production of alcoholic beverages was increased.

• • •

Kremlin intrigues continued to preoccupy Gorbachev, as befitted a new Party leader who did not yet have full control. In July he took an important step by firing a rival for the first time. Grigori Romanov, the man who had reportedly proposed Grishin for the leadership when Chernenko died, was retired "for reasons of health" at age sixty-two. The official announcement omitted traditional expressions of gratitude for his past services.

From the early weeks of the Gorbachev regime Romanov was clearly out of favor. He was not invited to accompany the new leader to Leningrad, where Romanov had been the Party boss for thirteen years, and he was not present at the Central Committee conference on scientific and technological progress, though he was theoretically responsible for heavy industry in the Central Committee secretariat. Romanov was brought down with the help of the anti-alcohol campaign. He was a heavy drinker who often got drunk at official functions—as he did in March 1985, on a visit to Hungary.* Hungarian comrades, I was told by a well-informed official, wrote a letter protesting his behavior to the authorities in Moscow. It gave Gorbachev the pretext he needed to remove Romanov.

Also in July, Eduard Shevardnadze was promoted to full membership in the Politburo and named foreign minister. He replaced Gromyko, who was elevated to the ceremonial position of chairman of the presidium of the Supreme Soviet, the formal chief of state, but a powerless position. Shevardnadze was truly a Gorbachev man, the first to be brought into the Politburo. He was also an unusual Soviet politician.

Gorbachev and Shevardnadze apparently first met in the 1960s, when both were working in the Komsomol. Shevardnadze's native Georgia was next door to Gorbachev's Stavropol *krai*. Like Gorbachev he went from the Komsomol to Party work, then was named Georgia's minister of internal affairs in the 1960s. It was a wild and crazy time in Georgia, traditionally a free-wheeling corner of the Soviet empire, whose temperate climate and romantic people give it a Mediterranean flavor. The Georgian Party boss then was Vasily Mzhavanadze, a Brezhnev crony who was a member of the Politburo in Moscow. Mzhavanadze and his wife were in business in Georgia, protecting (and profiting from) elaborate illicit enterprises that manufactured and sold hard-to-find consumer goods. It was said that she also dealt extensively in furs and gold. It can't have been easy to be responsible, as Shevardnadze was, for the republican's police force while Mzhavanadze was the local potentate.

In 1972, in circumstances that have never been fully explained, Mzhavanadze was fired and Shevardnadze was promoted to replace him. He quickly established a reputation not only in Georgia but throughout the country. I was living in Moscow at the time, and soon picked up wonderful Shevardnadze anecdotes. Their reliability could never be confirmed, but they were told and retold by appreciative Muscovites, who were eager to believe them. According to one, Shevardnadze once dressed as a peasant, filled the trunk of a car with

---

* Tales of Romanov's excesses are legion. My favorite involves his daughter's wedding when he was still first secretary in Leningrad. For the occasion, it was said, Romanov instructed the Hermitage Museum to loan him chinaware that had been used by Catherine the Great in the eighteenth century; the museum staff reluctantly complied. The wedding turned raucous, and a number of the plates were broken. In 1990, Romanov, in retirement, denied the story but officials of the Hermitage have privately confirmed it.

tomatoes, and drove north toward Russia. He himself had recently ordered that no produce be exported from the republic; as he drove north he bribed each policeman who stopped him, or so the story went. A purge of the police then followed. On another occasion, Shevardnadze supposedly asked his colleagues in the Georgian leadership to vote on some question with their left hands. When they raised their hands to vote, he remarked on the fancy, foreign-made wristwatches they were wearing, and suggested they take them off at once, and go out and buy Soviet watches.

I met Shevardnadze in 1987 and had a chance to ask him if such stories about his personal crusade against Georgian corruption were true. He grinned appreciatively when I alluded to some of the more famous anecdotes. But were they true? He grinned some more.*

The decision to make Shevardnadze foreign minister was the first obvious display of Gorbachev's remarkable political creativity. It took both his countrymen and the world of Sovietologists utterly by surprise. Shevardnadze had absolutely no experience in foreign affairs. He wasn't Russian—he even spoke Russian with a strong Georgian accent. Following more conventional instincts, I had written in March about the possibility of Anatoli Dobrynin, the longtime Soviet ambassador in Washington, becoming foreign minister—that was the sort of person whom we experts expected to succeed Gromyko. But Gorbachev had his own idea, a much better one. In Shevardnadze he got a talented politician who could build personal relationships with foreign leaders while persuasively conveying the new spirit that Gorbachev wanted to promote. Gorbachev also got a friend at his right hand who proved to be a reliable comrade for the next five years.

Gorbachev named two new secretaries of the Central Committee in July as well, Boris Yeltsin and Lev Zaikov. Yeltsin had been first secretary in Sverdlovsk, in the Urals; Zaikov had succeeded Romanov in Leningrad. Both were seen then as technocrats promoted for their industrial expertise. Nothing was known in the West about Yeltsin's colorful personality. Two months later Gorbachev accepted the resignation of Tikhonov (then eighty) as premier, and named Ryzhkov to take his place.

---

* Shevardnadze went on to be an unusually successful first secretary in Georgia, improving the republic's agriculture and industry while conducting a quiet but effective liberalization campaign to loosen political controls. His successful intervention to prevent the forced adoption of Russian as the republic's official language added to his popularity. He was promoted to Moscow soon after that episode in 1978.

But probably the most significant personnel change made that summer wasn't announced publicly. It was the appointment of Alexander Yakovlev, the ambassador to Canada when Gorbachev had traveled across that country in 1983, to be head of the propaganda department of the Central Committee.

Yakovlev deserves to be better known outside Russia. He is the second great personality of the Gorbachev revolution, fully its co-author in many respects. Without his influence, events at many key junctures would have developed differently. From the outset he was Gorbachev's ambassador to the intellectuals, the new leader's first critical constituency. He was the architect of *glasnost* and the most important protector of the liberal editors who, beginning in the summer of 1986, began to give the Soviet Union its first critical and independent press. Yakovlev also helped create and cultivate the new Gorbachev image at home and abroad, and he was a co-author of Gorbachev's "new thinking" in foreign policy. Perhaps most important, he was a soul mate for Gorbachev, a lonely man on a lonely mission.

Yakovlev's life parallels Gorbachev's in several interesting ways, though he is the older of the two men by eight years. He too was born of peasant stock. His father had a fourth-grade education from a church school; his mother was illiterate. They farmed near the ancient city of Yaroslavl, the oldest Russian town on the Volga, north of Moscow. After fighting for the Reds in the civil war, Yakovlev's father —like Gorbachev's maternal grandfather—became the first chairman of one of the original collective farms.

Like so many of the liberals who emerged in the Gorbachev era, Yakovlev has vivid personal memories of Stalin's terror. In his case the memories are mitigated by an unusual happy ending. He has given a compelling account of his father's brush with Stalin's insane campaign against imaginary "enemies of the people."

> Chance saved my father in 1937. Our district military commissariat was headed by a man named Novikov. As it turned out, he had been the commander of my father's platoon in the civil war. He was an amazing person. He was the only one in the district leadership we knew. One day he came and knocked on the window with his whip handle. My father was not at home and Novikov said to mama: "Tell him that he must come to the conference, which—be sure to get this right—will last at least three days. I will come later."
>
> Mama didn't understand a thing. When she went to tell my father, he questioned her several times—especially about the last sentence, "I

will come later." My father put a few things in a bag and went to the neighboring district, to my mother's sister, Aunt Raya, "to the conference." He told mama where he could be found. Mama was a silent person, a peasant.

During that night there was a knock at the door and they asked where my father was. Mama said, "He went to a conference." "Which conference?" "I don't know, he didn't tell me," she said. They left. They came again the next night. . . . Three days later Novikov appeared—this is the meaning of friendship at the front. No, not everything was inhuman even then; some human qualities survived. . . . So Novikov came and told mama that it was time for her husband to come home, the conference was over! Mama sent me off to get him. . . . And after that nothing ever happened.

The elder Yakovlev was saved by the fact that even the political police in that paranoid time operated according to a plan that had to be fulfilled. "There was a plan for 'enemies,'" the son recalled, "in terms of numbers and time periods. During those nights they apparently seized others, and fulfilled their plan."

From a young age Yakovlev was a reader of books. His mother thought this was a waste of time, but his father encouraged him to study. "I missed out on part of my childhood because I didn't spend much time with other children. . . . I was more and more drawn to reading. Mama would get very upset with me. And my eyes were not very good. I had scrofula (tuberculosis of the lymph nodes) in childhood. Everyone was expecting me to die and they did not register my birth for two years, but I survived."

When the war broke out Yakovlev was seventeen. He was quickly drafted. At eighteen he was a lieutenant in the marines, assigned to the Baltic fleet. He had a traumatic war, seeing much action and losing many friends. "The Germans did not take prisoners," he recalled. "Neither did we." He was saved by the marine tradition of never leaving a wounded man on the battlefield. Fighting near Leningrad he was gravely wounded, and "five people dragged me back. Four of them were killed. And the fifth could see that things were bad so he jumped up and stopped dragging me along the ground and the swamp, but stood up and took me in his arms and ran. I stayed alive and was all right." But he spent a year in a military hospital and never fully recovered. Now a small man with a bald pate and thick hair above his ears, who wears oversized eyeglasses, Yakovlev still walks with a limp.

Yakovlev recalls that he happily joined his colleagues as they ran into battle in the most popular cry of those years, "For the Motherland! For Stalin!" As he put it, "I really did believe!" But right after the war he began to ask questions. "Even in my childish mind a real flaw appeared when, after the war, I saw how we treated our prisoners. Prisoners began to return from Germany, and we put them in prison camps.* There was no way I could reconcile myself to this. I was terribly ashamed—for I knew how they ended up as prisoners. I spoke openly about my feeling. I don't know why they didn't arrest me. Apparently I wasn't around anybody who would report it."

Yakovlev joined the Communist Party in 1944. He got a degree from a teachers' college in Yaroslavl in 1946 while he was working for a local newspaper, work he says he enjoyed enormously. The local Party organization sponsored his application to the Higher Party School in Moscow, a training ground for important *apparatchiks*. In 1953, the year Stalin died, Yakovlev joined the staff of the Central Committee's propaganda department. During the Thaw he spent his days not far from Moscow State University, where Gorbachev was studying.

In 1956, Yakovlev has said, he was invited "as an apparatus worker" to hear Nikita Khrushchev's report to the 20th Party Congress—the famous secret speech on Stalin's crimes. "I remember how we came down from the balcony and could not look one another in the eye— either from a feeling of surprise, or from a sense of shame or shock."

Soon after that dramatic moment Yakovlev had an opportunity, even better than Gorbachev's trips to France and Italy, to see the Western world. He took part in the first Soviet-American student exchange, spending the 1958–59 academic year at Columbia University in New York. Gorbachev has never said much about the impressions he took from his visits to the West in the mid-1960s, but Yakovlev has shared his views of America in articles, several books, and interviews. They all reveal a deep ambivalence about the United States. He was profoundly upset by the hatred and suspicion of Soviet communism that he encountered among ordinary Americans in that post-McCarthy era.

"When I studied at Columbia . . . students asked me questions that made my hair stand on end," he recalled in 1989. "Once I spent four days in Iowa living with a farmer's family, a very nice family. . . .

---

* In his paranoia Stalin concluded that Soviet soldiers who had been held prisoner in Nazi Germany could not be trusted when they came home; hundreds of thousands—perhaps millions —were thrown into prison camps.

When the farmer's wife watched me playing with their five children, she expressed surprise that I liked children. I said, 'Well, of course I love them. I have two of my own at home.' 'If you love children,' she asked, 'why do you have wives in common and communalized children in your country?' 'Lord be with you! Who told you that?' 'A priest,' she said. And in downtown New York, in a little store, they felt my head to see if it was true that we Soviets have horns."

One American graduate student who befriended Yakovlev at Columbia was Loren Graham, now a distinguished professor of the history of science at M.I.T. Graham told me he thought Yakovlev was "a frightened man when he arrived in New York in the fall of 1958. He was convinced that people would take advantage of him, that people hated him and all Soviets, and that the capitalist system was evil incarnate." But he learned a lot that year, Graham said, in part by exploring areas like Harlem where ideological clichés took on more complex, human form. "He saw it wasn't simple. He was discovering the nature of capitalism." But Graham also felt that Yakovlev remained "not far from being a Stalinist" when he left New York.

In later years Yakovlev has repeatedly expressed resentment at American moralizing and the presumption that the American way is inevitably best. In a book published in 1984, on the eve of his new career as a liberal reformer, Yakovlev wrote: "The U.S. is a nation governed more by deception and demagoguery than by conviction, more by force than by law, more by deadening habits and traditions than by respect for and interest in whatever is new, more by hatred, suspicion, and intolerance than by the ability to recognize there may be another way of life and thought." That last clause seems to be what really gnaws at Yakovlev—you Americans won't allow for the possibility that we Russians may have ways of living and thinking that we truly believe are better than yours!

At Columbia Yakovlev wrote a dissertation on Franklin D. Roosevelt and the New Deal. Graham recalled seeing him once as he was coming out of the stacks of the university library, looking excited. "Loren," he said, "I've been reading FDR's right-wing critics. They all said that Roosevelt was a traitor to his class, that he was destroying capitalism in America. But it's obvious to me that Roosevelt was not destroying capitalism at all. He was saving capitalism when it was on its knees." A reformer and savior, not a traitor—that proved to be a useful formulation nearly thirty years later.

After his year in New York Yakovlev came back to Moscow and

rejoined the propaganda department of the Central Committee. He moved steadily upward, becoming acting head of the department in the Brezhnev years. In that position he had considerable influence over the press, culture, science, and the academic establishment, so he became known to Moscow intellectuals. He had a reputation as rather liberal for an *apparatchik*. I heard about him late in 1972, when he published a long, convoluted, but at times outspoken critique of Russian nationalism in the weekly *Literaturnaya Gazeta* (Literary Gazette). Friends in Moscow told me at the time that the convoluted sections of the two-page article were just "window dressing." The real point was the sharp attacks on a number of writers who propagated romantic views of Russian village life, old churches, and other symbols of the prerevolutionary past. Yakovlev assailed his targets by name. He also criticized all manifestations of exclusive nationalism.

Six months after the article appeared, Yakovlev was exiled to Canada as the Soviet ambassador. I wrote an article for *The Washington Post* at the time suggesting that his dismissal from the Central Committee staff could have been connected to the *Literaturnaya Gazeta* article, or to other events about which nothing was known. Over the years it became an article of faith that Yakovlev had been fired for attacking the Russian nationalists. But in 1990 he revealed that this was not the case.

In an interview with the Komsomol newspaper *Komsomolskaya Pravda,* Yakovlev said he was forced out for reasons that were "more complicated" than the reaction to his article. The article was a "catalyst," he said, which gave his colleagues a pretext for criticizing him. The real reason he fell out of favor, Yakovlev said, was the questions he raised about the beginnings of a cult of Brezhnev's personality in 1971 and 1972. He objected to gestures that smacked of a Stalin-like cult, and was told that they had been approved in advance—in other words, they were what Brezhnev wanted. "I myself raised the question of leaving the Central Committee apparatus," Yakovlev said. "I asked about diplomatic work in one of the English-speaking countries, for example in Canada. The decision was made [to send him to Ottawa] that same day."

In the same interview Yakovlev described work in the *apparat* in terms that suggested why he might have been ready to give it up. "The *apparat* is a kind of rigid force. Like any other political institution it has its own rules. You can like it or not but there is no point in beating your head against the wall. But a knife cuts both ways. The apparatus gradually develops a unique kind of character in a person, a style of behavior. It's another question how much personal honor and decency survive."

Yakovlev was to spend ten years in Canada—"an immense term," as he put it. He did not enjoy living abroad for so long, and tried repeatedly to find a way to return to the Soviet Union. Once, I was told, he flew to Cuba, where an influential acquaintance from Moscow was visiting, to plead unsuccessfully that he be allowed to come home.

What Yakovlev missed while in Canada was the "time of stagnation," the last half of Brezhnev's reign, when conditions in the country only deteriorated. His involuntary exile gave him a chance to read and think, to absorb Canadian and American politics, to learn about modern news media, especially television, and to spend time with some interesting Canadians, beginning with Pierre Trudeau, the prime minister. Trudeau and Yakovlev used to eat lunch alone together from time to time.

Yakovlev has not said much about how those years in Canada may have changed his views of the world, but they must have had quite an effect. His year at Columbia already made him a rare figure among Central Committee *apparatchiks;* an additional decade living comfortably in North America, able to pursue his natural intellectual curiosity with only light official duties to distract him, gave him a unique experience. He came to Canada as the product of an ossified political culture that was still acting out the rituals—and respecting the taboos—of the Stalin era. In Ottawa he could master the intricacies of a parliamentary democracy and study modern, media-oriented electoral politics. No previous member of the Politburo in modern times (he became a full member in June 1987) had spent a prolonged period in the West.

In Ottawa Yakovlev had a reputation for being a patriotic Russian, a staunch Communist, but an unusually open and straightforward ambassador, especially for a Soviet ambassador. One of his closest Canadian friends was Ed Schreyer, then the country's governor general, or head of state, a largely symbolic office except in time of constitutional crisis. Schreyer was the former premier of rural Manitoba on the Canadian prairies, and he hit it off with the son of the peasant from Yaroslavl. Schreyer invited Yakovlev and his wife not only to formal state occasions, but also to family affairs, and picnics, and they were often pleased to come.

Schreyer told me that Yakovlev was usually discreet and did not try to advertise his differences with his own government, but that occasionally he could not hide them. For example, Schreyer said, Yakovlev considered the Soviet invasion of Afghanistan in 1979 "an horrendous error in strategic judgment," as well as a blow to his own diplomatic efforts over the previous six years. Yakovlev was proud of the friends he'd made and his success in cultivating better Soviet-Canadian relations. He felt that "to have it all go down the drain because of something like Afghanistan was tragic," Schreyer recalled.

Schreyer and other Canadians liked Yakovlev for his charm, his intelligence, and his openness, but none I could find thought he was any kind of closet liberal in Ottawa. Apart from that indiscretion on Afghanistan (a position shared by Soviet diplomats all over the world, and by many officials in Moscow), he did not openly dispute his government's line, or criticize its officials, although the Canadians knew that he was only in Ottawa because he had fallen out of favor in Moscow. Schreyer and several other Canadians who knew Yakovlev reasonably well all told me they have been surprised by the role he has played under Gorbachev. Schreyer said he was particularly struck by Yakovlev's ability "to turn his back on the [Soviet] past."

The high point of Yakovlev's diplomatic career came near the end of his tour—in May 1983, when Mikhail Gorbachev, then secretary of the Central Committee responsible for agriculture and a new member of the Politburo, came to Canada for a week's visit. The two men traveled together across Canada; they spent many hours in planes and cars, talking to each other. It was long thought that they had never previously met, but Yakovlev told an interviewer in 1990, "I knew him before," when he worked at the Central Committee. Yakovlev said he had supported an initiative Gorbachev had taken as first secretary in Stavropol that other officials in Moscow had disapproved of. (It involved hiring brigades of students on contract, presumably to do agricultural work.) In Canada they discovered how much they had in common, and how similarly they viewed their country's plight. "The main thing was, we couldn't go on living like that," Yakovlev recalled. "And that was two years before *perestroika*."

Schreyer missed the Gorbachev visit because a previous commitment took him out of the country, but he vividly remembers Yakovlev's reaction right after Gorbachev went home. "He seemed just tickled pink with the whole visit. He told me, sort of overbrimming with enthusiasm, how well it went and, oh, my, how many things he and Gorbachev had discussed!"

Two months later Yakovlev was back in Moscow as the newly named director of the Institute of World Economy and International Relations, a leading Soviet think tank. He loved that position, but was promoted out of it two years later when Gorbachev brought him back to the job he'd lost in 1973—head of the propaganda department in that "rigid force" that robbed men of their honor and decency, the Central Committee *apparat.* Yakovlev moved back into the stolid Central Committee headquarters on Staraya Ploshchad (Old Square) in the summer of 1985.

●   ●   ●

To reread now the speeches Gorbachev made as he moved around the country in 1985 is to be reminded of a traditional Soviet political culture that has since gone up in smoke. Gorbachev himself might cringe if he looked back at those early pronouncements. They were earnest, certainly; they almost reeked of determination. They were very long, in the tradition of speeches by Soviet leaders, and in most passages utterly predictable. Every one contained several references to or quotations from Lenin, and all of them were built around familiar clichés about the responsibilities of the Communist Party and its leaders to guide the country to new victories.

But there was one new theme in these speeches that was not ritualistic. In Dnepropetrovsk in late June, for example, discussing the need to "look at everything anew," Gorbachev told a meeting of metal workers that no amount of planning or analysis could solve the country's problems. "The central factor in all our plans is each person's attitude toward work, toward carrying out his obligations—that which we call the human factor." In Kiev on the same trip, he announced that everyone in the Ukraine "must work in a new way." He carried the message to Minsk, the capital of Belorussia, to Kazakhstan in Central Asia, to Tyumen, the oil-producing center in Siberia. At nearly every stop he met with local citizens, and the meetings were shown on television. He often asked people how they felt about the changes he was trying to make, and it became clear that he really cared about their answers. In Dnepropetrovsk he asked the metal workers if they thought "we are turning too sharply." A few replied that he was on the right course. "But are these just individual voices, or the general opinion?" Gorbachev asked. The workers got the message, and responded more enthusiastically. "I feel great satisfaction," Gorbachev said. In Tyumen he explained explicitly why he cared.

"Without workers' support no policy is worth anything," he said. "If it's not supported by the working class, by the working people, it isn't a policy, it's just something far-fetched." He seemed to be hoping that spontaneous enthusiasm for his reforms from the workers would somehow make them real.

A great part of Gorbachev's first year was devoted to preparing for the 27th Party Congress, scheduled to begin in February 1986. In modern times Party Congresses had met every five years to set down a policy line—and a five-year plan—for the country. The Congress was the highest political body in the land; its delegates would elect a new Party Central Committee, which in turn would choose a new ruling Politburo. The timing was fortunate for Gorbachev; he could present a new program to the Congress just eleven months after coming to power. The Congress would also give him an opportunity to put his own people into key Party positions.

Preparing for it meant devoting many hours to ritualistic ideological questions. The Party was committed to present a successor to the Third Party Program adopted under Khrushchev in 1961, and presumably in effect ever since. In fact the Third Party Program was a joke; it made numerous unfulfilled promises and predictions, foreseeing, for example, that Soviet industrial output would exceed America's by 1971, and promising "a comfortable flat" by 1980 to "every family, including newlyweds" in the Soviet Union. (Tens of millions of families were still waiting for a private flat of any kind in 1990.)

In October 1985, the Party published a draft version of a new program—more than thirty thousand words of Party jargon. Amid the familiar phrases about the glories of socialism and the crisis of imperialism, Gorbachev's men wove a gentle version of their reform program, emphasizing that the time had come for "acceleration" to help the Soviet system fulfill its vast potential. Like all Gorbachev's pronouncements that first year, the program was not specific. But—by omission—it was clear on one point: the Party was no longer promising that the Soviet Union would soon surpass the United States in industrial production, or anything of the kind. Its tone was more modest throughout. For example, on housing: "The Party deems it a matter of special social significance to accelerate the solution of the housing problem, to ensure that by the year 2000 practically every Soviet family is in possession of a housing unit—an apartment or individual house—all to itself."

It would soon turn out that this Party program had no more practical significance than Khrushchev's 1961 version, but at the time its preparation was a serious matter.

Another serious matter was the replacement of Party and government officials all over the country. In late December Gorbachev moved against Grishin, the man who had hoped to get the top job in March. Attentive newspaper readers realized Grishin was in trouble during the summer, when his leadership began to be criticized in the press. In the fall the criticism became stronger. But he was an entrenched figure, a member of the Politburo for nearly twenty years, who was protected by a giant political machine in the capital. Gorbachev himself attended the December 24th meeting of the Moscow Party organization, which had convened to elect its leader. Rumors circulated in Moscow—never confirmed, but certainly plausible— that Gorbachev came to instruct the delegates not to reelect Grishin. Some say there was a real fight. If there was, Gorbachev prevailed; Grishin was retired, and Yeltsin was named to take his place. The choice of Yeltsin for this highly visible and important position convinced Kremlinologists that Gorbachev considered him a trusted ally.

Without his own people, Gorbachev stood little chance of instilling the new attitudes he kept insisting on. There was high turnover in the first year he was in power: overall, about one-third of the Party secretaries with significant responsibilities were replaced in a year. Of the 307 voting members of the Central Committee elected near the end of Gorbachev's first year, 131 were new. But the high numbers disguised an important fact: Ligachev, the number-two man responsible for Party cadres, was picking most of the new men, and he was not picking Gorbachev enthusiasts or radical reformers. Events would show that the new appointees were often just as conservative and resistant to change as their predecessors.

•　　•　　•

During his first year as general secretary Gorbachev launched a new Soviet diplomacy that had momentous consequences—much more fateful than he could have expected then.

Sometime in 1985 Gorbachev and his colleagues, certainly including Shevardnadze and Yakovlev, decided to see if they could stop the arms race through diplomacy. It was an obvious gambit if they were serious about domestic reform. They knew (as Shevardnadze disclosed five years later) that the Soviet Union was effectively devoting a quarter or more of its national budget to military expenditures. If the United States now launched an entirely new competition in space-based weapons—the consequence Soviets feared most from President Reagan's Strategic Defense Initiative—how could the Russians keep up and still save their economy?

Gorbachev may have come to power with a secret hope that he could negotiate his way to large savings on armaments—or, more boldly, that he could use diplomacy to create benign international conditions that would enable him to pursue sweeping change in the Soviet Union. That would be the simplest explanation of his decision to begin his tenure by giving an interview to *Pravda* asking for a summit meeting with President Reagan, and announcing a unilateral suspension of deployments of SS-20 missiles in Europe.

But Gorbachev had a problem: Ronald Reagan. Over the previous four years, Soviet propaganda had transformed the American president into an all-purpose bogeyman. Soviet newspapers had compared Reagan to Hitler, portraying him as bent on establishing American hegemony across the globe. Soviet officials (Yakovlev in Ottawa was one of them) concluded that Reagan was really a madman who was prepared to risk nuclear war. Fear of a war, fanned by the propaganda, had become widespread in the Soviet Union. Could the new Soviet leadership now deal with this same Reagan?

In July Moscow and Washington announced that Gorbachev and Reagan would meet in Geneva in November for their first summit. With that encounter obviously in mind, Gorbachev invited editors of *Time* magazine to his office for an interview at the end of August. He used the occasion to appeal directly to *Time*'s readers for better relations and an end to the arms race:

"We are convinced that we [the U.S. and the U.S.S.R.] should look for a way out of the current difficult situation together." He pleaded with the Reagan administration to take seriously the Soviet desire to reach new arms-control agreements. He urged Washington to cease dismissing his every gesture as "propaganda" (as it had). Almost plaintively he observed that "Moscow is trying to practice restraint in its pronouncements about the U.S.; it is not resorting to anti-American campaigns, nor is it fomenting hatred for your country."

These were prepared comments responding to written questions; in conversation in his Kremlin office, Gorbachev was more explicit: "You ask what changes in the world economy could be of benefit to the Soviet Union. First of all . . . an end to the arms race." And: "I want to emphasize this: the attention we have recently devoted to the economy is not due to any intention to set new records in producing metals, oil, cement, machine tools, or other products. The main thing is to make life better for people. There is no goal more important to us."

He sprinkled the interview with not-very-subtle invitations to President Reagan to respond to his offer to end what Gorbachev referred to repeatedly as a very dangerous and discouraging period in Soviet-American relations. For example, when a *Time* editor mentioned Richard Nixon, Gorbachev responded: "Your mentioning Nixon certainly gives me some associations and some memories. . . . After all, it was in a very difficult period of our relationship that we managed to find, with Nixon when he was president, the solutions to some very important issues. I recall still further back in 1961 the meeting between Khrushchev and President Kennedy in Vienna. That was a difficult time as well. There was the Caribbean [i.e., the Cuban missile] crisis [in October 1962], yet in 1963 we saw the partial test-ban treaty. Even though that was again a time of crisis, the two sides and their leaders had enough wisdom and the boldness to take some very important decisions. History is very interesting in that way, when you attempt to draw lessons from it."

If anyone feared Gorbachev might bear Reagan a grudge for past insults against "the evil empire," Gorbachev was eager to dispel the anxiety: "I regard him as president of the U.S.A., a man elected to his high office by the American people, so our attitude toward President Reagan is prompted by our feeling of respect for the people of the U.S.A. We are therefore prepared to do business with him and to treat him with the respect that is befitting him."

And if by chance the message still wasn't clear, Gorbachev added these last words: "I would like to end by just saying a few words that are important to understanding what we have been talking about all along. I don't remember who, but somebody said that foreign policy is a continuation of domestic policy. If that is so, then I ask you to ponder one thing: If we in the Soviet Union are setting ourselves such truly grandiose plans in the domestic sphere [a reference to the 'restructuring' of the Soviet economy, which he discussed in the interview] then what are the external conditions that we need to be able to fulfill those domestic plans? I leave the answer to that question with you."

But he didn't leave his crusade there. He went considerably beyond that interview to try to enhance the atmosphere for the summit. During the summer and fall the Soviet Union announced a series of new steps on arms-control issues: a unilateral moratorium on underground nuclear tests and on testing of antisatellite weapons, and a formal proposal to cut Soviet and American arsenals of strategic weapons by roughly half. Shevardnadze and his American counterpart, Secretary of State George P. Shultz, held four meetings to prepare for the Geneva summit.

Before seeing Reagan, Gorbachev scheduled a preliminary round of summit diplomacy in Paris—his first trip to the West as leader. He used the Paris trip as an occasion to practice his new type of diplomacy, beginning, on the eve of his visit, with an interview on French television. It was the first time a Soviet leader had submitted himself to this kind of questioning with cameras rolling. Gorbachev clearly enjoyed the gladiatorial aspects of the encounter; he even spoke right up when questioned about human-rights abuses.

This was a difficult subject for him. The point of granting the interview was clearly to try to charm the French public, but Gorbachev was not prepared to give any satisfaction on human rights. "I could put it as follows," Gorbachev told his interviewers. "Let us in the Soviet Union manage our affairs ourselves, and you in France manage yours." (This was essentially what he said to members of Parliament in Canada and Britain who asked him about human rights in his 1983 and 1984 visits to those countries.) But he then did answer in more detail, saying he was ready to debate human rights in international forums, adding that the issue "is now being artificially played up by Western propaganda." He referred to dissidents as "people who by virtue of some logic or other have fallen out with the Soviet form of government, with socialism, and profess some different ideology." In their questions on human rights the Frenchmen mentioned Andrei Sakharov, by 1985 an international *cause célèbre*. Earlier in 1985, reports had reached the West that Sakharov was again on a hunger strike in Gorki. Gorbachev ignored Sakharov in his answer.

The trip to France was a successful diplomatic outing, and included a joint press conference with President François Mitterrand—another first for a Soviet leader. This time he faced a large international press corps. I was eager to see the performance, and learned that NBC had a tape of it at its Washington bureau. It was a stunning experience, still thoroughly unexpected, to watch this new general secretary fielding questions, including some tough ones, with aplomb. He got angry just once, when Dan Rather of CBS asked him about Jewish emigration and political prisoners. Gorbachev refused to answer the question.

But in private talks with the French—most explicitly, apparently, in a dinner conversation with Danielle Mitterrand, the president's wife—Gorbachev indicated that he might be forthcoming on the Sakharov question. Three weeks after he returned home from Paris, Elena Bonner, Sakharov's wife, was given permission to travel abroad for medical treatment. Sakharov had indeed gone on another hunger strike to try to persuade the authorities to grant Bonner this permission. Bonner was in the United States when Gorbachev flew to Geneva to meet President Reagan.

•   •   •

The Geneva summit marked a turning point in postwar history. In three days in Switzerland, Ronald Reagan effectively abandoned the anti-Communist crusade that had been a centerpiece of his political career. "I bet the hardliners in both our countries are bleeding when we shake hands," Reagan said to Gorbachev as they prepared to read closing statements at the end of the summit.* With that quip the president separated himself from his oldest supporters, and set off on a course that was to lead to four more meetings with Gorbachev, an unprecedented arms-control agreement, and a transformed international situation, before he left office thirty-eight months later.

Reagan's willingness to make that change in his own policy was precisely what Gorbachev must have been looking for. His expression at the end of the summit, and his jocular manner during the portions of the meetings that cameramen could witness, told his countrymen that something important had changed. Soviet television for the first time broadcast pictures of the friendly, smiling actor-president, reinforcing the message.

Not that the Geneva meeting resolved many practical issues. It did not. But in five hours of private meetings both men decided they could do business with each other. "I have to believe that . . . they share with us the desire to get something done, and to get things straightened out," Reagan told his cabinet the day after the summit ended. And he told a group of newspaper columnists the same day, "I think I'm some judge of acting, so I don't think he was acting. He, I

---

* At least Reagan told his senior aides that he'd made this quip; they quickly passed the quotation on to Lou Cannon of *The Washington Post*.

believe, is just as sincere as we are in wanting an answer." Curiously, Reagan had apparently resolved in his own mind a question that continued to perplex other Americans—including his successor, George Bush—for as much as four more years: Gorbachev was for real, Reagan had decided—different from all his predecessors, sincere in his desire to change course.

In his public statements Gorbachev conveyed a similar message about his assessment of Reagan. At a press conference after the last session in Geneva, he noted that "of course a great deal of time was spent in the private sessions," and "this enabled us to discuss a wide range of issues, looking one another straight in the eye. Our talks proceeded . . . in a very open way, a very straightforward manner, and I think that was not only of great significance, I would say it was decisive. . . . As a result of the Geneva meeting, I believe there is the possibility for very broad-based cooperation between our two countries and our peoples, and in saying this I'm not trying to simplify matters. I'm well aware of the deep differences that divide us, and I appreciate the realities of present Soviet-American relations, but I am convinced that this is possible.*

No attentive Soviet citizen could have misunderstood: Gorbachev had met the leading anti-Communist on the world stage, and found him reasonable. The deep anxieties that Reagan had evoked in the Soviet Union could now be eased—Gorbachev would ease them.

According to one of his senior advisers, Gorbachev was immensely relieved by that first encounter with Reagan; he had expected someone more formidable. According to my informant, Gorbachev and Shevardnadze—who by then had dealt extensively with the Americans —concluded after Geneva that these were not supermen. On the contrary, they decided that Reagan wasn't terribly bright or very knowledgeable about specific issues—they could handle him.

That judgment was a key link in the chain of events that led to the collapse of the Soviet empire in 1989—or so it seems to me in hindsight. Once Gorbachev and his associates had chosen the course of trying to negotiate a better international environment for their reform efforts, they were caught in a political web that would prevent them

---

* Gorbachev's military advisers were less sanguine. They left Geneva concerned that because no significant impediment had been put in the way of the Americans' Strategic Defense Initiative, no real progress had been made. *Krasnaya Zvezda* (Red Star), the armed forces' newspaper, published a postsummit editorial criticizing "the illusions of people who, despite facts to the contrary, still believe . . . that the U.S. administration is capable of heeding the voice of reason."

from exercising the nastier alternatives used by their predecessors to keep order in the empire. Gorbachev and Shevardnadze knew that the invasions of Czechoslovakia and Afghanistan had turned the outside world against the Soviet Union; both events caused ruptures in Soviet-American diplomacy and resulted in prolonged periods of Soviet isolation.

At Geneva Gorbachev and Reagan agreed to exchange visits to one another's countries. Gorbachev told his press conference, "I'm very optimistic when I look ahead to the future." In effect Gorbachev was signing up for a prolonged period of improved relations and negotiations.* That would require a prolonged period of Soviet restraint in international affairs.

Subsequent events demonstrated that Gorbachev understood this perfectly well. Over the next five years, he withdrew Soviet forces from Afghanistan, cut adrift the Sandinistas in Nicaragua, withdrew from Indochina, and pulled back in Africa. Most important, he did nothing to prevent the former Soviet satellites in Eastern Europe from asserting their independence and ending Communist Party domination. He actually did nothing to prevent this from 1985 onward, but it took years for the East Europeans to realize that they were really free to act as they wished. (It also took time for Gorbachev and his comrades to realize that, without the threat of invasion by the Red Army, nothing held the East Europeans inside the "socialist camp." They certainly did not expect their empire to unravel as quickly as it did.)

Gorbachev would undoubtedly argue that letting the East Europeans go was simply a moral deed, consistent with his approach to politics: "Our policies are open and honest and that's the way we act," as Gorbachev put it at his Geneva press conference. But this was a situation where *Realpolitik* required virtuous behavior, so separating the two motives is impossible. It is always easiest to do the right thing when one has no choice. Gorbachev might have cajoled, urged, even threatened the East Europeans to stay in line, but he could only have compelled them by taking action that would have blown up his new diplomatic relationship with the United States. As long as the Ameri-

---

* This was formally confirmed in January and February 1986, when the Central Committee and Gorbachev personally made new proposals for accelerating disarmament negotiations, and offered new Soviet concessions. However, the Reagan administration reacted warily, and the subsequent months were trying ones for Gorbachev, who repeatedly complained of American foot dragging. The negotiating process was restored at Reykjavík in October—about which more below.

cans and their allies pursued the new diplomacy, the Soviet Union would have to be on its best behavior. After Geneva Gorbachev was caught—and the Soviet empire in Eastern Europe was doomed.

•   •   •

In his first eleven months as leader Gorbachev had few concrete achievements, but he succeeded magnificently in building excitement, both in his own country and abroad. Much of that excitement was focused on the 27th Congress of the Communist Party of the Soviet Union, which convened in Moscow on February 24, 1986.

For eleven months Gorbachev had been punching away at the entrenched system he inherited from Brezhnev. He had established his own credentials as a new kind of leader, who was more honest, more open, and evidently more determined than his predecessors. He had harped on the need for everyone in the country to learn to do his or her job in "a new way." He had campaigned for "acceleration." But there was no concrete program. At the Congress, it was widely assumed, he would finally present one.

In a way he did. His opening "political report" to the Congress—which took him five hours to deliver—touched on every conceivable subject, and included scores, even hundreds of specific instructions to the Party faithful. Rhetorically it was a strong statement. Right at the outset, in the introductory passages traditionally used only to sing the praises of Soviet socialism and its accomplishments, Gorbachev began speaking of "lapses in our political and practical activities" and "unfavorable tendencies in the economy and the social and moral sphere." He said "signs of stagnation had begun to surface in the life of our society."

To fight these negative phenomena (and he spelled them out in more painful detail later in the report), Gorbachev called for "a radical reform" of the system of economic management. Using the term violated a taboo in Soviet politics, which previously had considered radical reforms unacceptable on their face, implicitly because they suggested something was seriously wrong with the status quo. Characteristically, Gorbachev found a reference in the works of Lenin to "radical reform," which he quoted to take the edge off his own use of the term. He reiterated his support for *glasnost,* for more "socialist democracy," for higher standards of moral and political rectitude. He attacked bureaucratism. He spoke warmly of cooperatives, and encouraged the creation of more of them, to provide services and even to build housing. He again endorsed "acceleration," and called on everyone to work harder and more efficiently.

But at the end of five hours it still wasn't clear where Gorbachev wanted to take the country. His problem was partly one of language. Fifty years of Stalinism had destroyed the meaning of most words in the standard political vocabulary, just as George Orwell predicted (or understood) in 1948, when he wrote *1984*. When Gorbachev spoke of *glasnost,* no one in his audience could be sure what he meant. When he used the term "socialist democracy," delegates had to wonder if he meant something new, or the same old authoritarian methods that had been called socialist democracy for years.

At the same time, Gorbachev's speech, the new Party program, and other documents and speeches at the Congress revealed a fundamental ambivalence about where the Party was headed. The authors of the Party program could not abandon much of the old rhetoric, so—for example—it had this to say about socialism:

"The experience of the U.S.S.R. and other socialist countries convincingly demonstrates the indisputable socioeconomic, political, ideological, and moral advantages of [our] new society as a stage in mankind's progress that is superior to capitalism and provides answers to questions that the bourgeois system cannot solve."

Other speakers at the Congress delivered conventional addresses that would have fit into any previous Party Congress. Nikolai Ryzhkov, Gorbachev's premier, didn't even mention reforms in his report on the economy. Many speakers at the Congress called for stronger central administration and controls to put things right in the country, even as Gorbachev seemed to be asking for more autonomy for enterprises and localities. The final resolution adopted by the Congress declared: "The Congress makes it incumbent on the Party, governmental, economic and social organizations strictly to enforce new measures to ensure the intensive development of the national economy." How could new strict measures and more autonomy be reconciled?

It was vastly easier to understand what Gorbachev was against than what he was for. Indeed, if you read his report from the perspective of a nervous senior official who could feel unwelcome winds of change blowing across his brow, it carried a lot of meaning. Gorbachev made clear his preference for taking administrative power away from most of the people who then exercised it, and giving it to others. "It is high time to put an end to the practice of ministries and departments exercising petty tutelage over enterprises," he said, though just such "tutelage" had been the norm for decades. Gorbachev wanted enterprises to make their own decisions—truly a radical reform. Party officials heard him speak of increasing the influence of local councils, or soviets, which would inevitably mean a smaller role for Party organs. They also heard him demand tougher self-criticism, more exposure of wrongdoing, and the like—more threats to entrenched Party officials.

There were other signs of changes in the air at the Congress that seemed to be aimed at incumbent officials. One was open discussion of the privileges of the Party élite, another traditional taboo that broke into the columns of *Pravda* a fortnight before the Congress began. *Pravda* printed an unusual attack on the special care and feeding provided to senior officials, and quoted a letter from a reader who complained of an "inert and sticky stratum" of officials who stand "between the Central Committee and the working class" and who "carry Party cards but have long ceased to be Communists." Boris Yeltsin picked up the same terminology in his outspoken speech to the Congress, asking: "Why even now is the demand for radical changes getting stuck in an inert stratum of timeservers with Party tickets?"

Conservatives responded to these jabs. Ligachev told the Congress that *Pravda* had gone too far in its criticisms—he did not say of what, but delegates understood him to be referring to the article on privileges. Vladimir Kalashnikov, the new first secretary in Volgograd, responded to Yeltsin and *Pravda:* "One should not for the sake of sensation or under the pretext of 'frank discussion' blacken the officials of a certain 'slow-moving, inert and sticky party and administrative stratum.' It is not difficult to understand whom such authors have in mind." Kalashnikov was applauded by the delegates.*

The Congress ended on a hopeful note with the adoption of the new Party program and endorsement of Gorbachev's report. A new Central Committee was elected, which, as I noted earlier, included 131 new members, or 43 percent of the total. Just before and just after the Congress a series of important changes were made in the senior leadership: Grishin was dropped from the Politburo, having been replaced by Yeltsin as Moscow first secretary two months before; Lev Zaikov from Leningrad was named a full Politburo member; Yeltsin

---

* In 1989 he was driven from office in Volgograd by an unprecedented wave of popular resentment.

and the new Leningrad first secretary, Yuri Solovev, became candidate members. So did Nikolai Slyunkov, former deputy director of the State Planning Commission, who in 1983 had become first secretary in Belorussia. Five new secretaries were appointed to help run the Central Committee *apparat,* while two holdovers from the Brezhnev era retired.

• • •

Then nothing happened. I've been told by several senior officials that in the aftermath of the Congress it became clear to Gorbachev's allies just how difficult a job lay ahead. Gorbachev's plans all depended on active cooperation from the Party *apparat* at every level. Alas, "life itself had shown," to borrow a favorite from the Soviet phrasebook, that this cooperation was not materializing. New tools had to be found to carry this great enterprise forward.

Fate then intervened dramatically. Just two months after the Party Congress, the Soviet Union endured by far the worst accident of the nuclear age. One of the four nuclear reactors at the Chernobyl power station near Kiev in the Ukraine exploded shortly after 1 A.M. on April 26. The explosion and subsequent fire sent huge quantities of radioactive material into the atmosphere, contaminating many parts of Europe and making the immediate area around Chernobyl uninhabitable. But the damage was even greater than that. The accident was also a grave blow to the new leader of the Soviet Union and to his efforts to reform his country.

The vigorous new general secretary, who had made such a powerful impression on his countrymen by meeting them in the streets and speaking their language, found no clever response to Chernobyl. Later, when natural disasters struck, Gorbachev rushed to the scene —in Armenia after the 1988 earthquake, for example. But he made no move to visit Chernobyl—he made no visible move of any kind in response to the accident for eighteen days.

The fire and meltdown at Chernobyl were not brought under control for nine days, and—as became clear only years later—the accident very nearly developed into a full-fledged catastrophe.* Only the heroic, and in some cases literally suicidal, efforts of emergency personnel prevented a much bigger disaster.

---

* Zhores Medvedev's 1990 book, *The Legacy of Chernobyl,* provides a hair-raising account based on much fuller information than was made available while Chernobyl was still a news story.

Initially the Soviet government followed old-fashioned rules for dealing with accidents and said nothing about it. Alarmed Europeans detected the radioactive cloud from Chernobyl with their own measuring devices, and demanded explanations. In the absence of official information, wild rumors spread; some got into print in the West, reporting hundreds of thousands of casualties. On the tenth day the Soviets called a press conference in Moscow, where officials gave an incomplete and partially misleading account of events thus far, and left numerous questions unanswered. The press conference was scantily reported inside the Soviet Union, adding to popular concern and confusion, but the full version had the same effect in neighboring countries.

Two days later the director general of the International Atomic Energy Authority, Hans Blix, was given a tour of Chernobyl by helicopter. He took along his own dosimeter, which measured a dangerously heavy dose of radiation four hundred meters above the power plant from inside the helicopter—and this after the emergency had been contained. Blix's visit resolved none of the outstanding questions about the accident, but it served another purpose: it demonstrated that the authorities were trying to cover up the seriousness of radioactive emissions. A *Pravda* reporter who accompanied Blix reported in his newspaper that the dosimeters registered a low level of radiation from the same helicopter—thirty-five times lower than Blix had already reported!

On May 14 Gorbachev finally made a television speech to the country on Chernobyl. It was an uninformative speech, but at the same time highly revealing. He offered no real explanation of why the accident occurred—"the reactor's capacity suddenly increased during a scheduled shutdown." * He sought to turn the accident to the service of his foreign policy, emphasizing what it revealed about the horrific potential of the atom, and thus illustrated the need to support his program for the total elimination of nuclear weapons. And he made a long attack on Western reaction to the accident, using language that could have come from the mouth of any one of Gorbachev's predecessors from Stalin to Chernenko.

---

* It took years to sort out the real causes. The accident happened during a botched experiment to test the reactor's turbine under low power. The experiment was conducted by an inexperienced crew, which made grave errors; why the experiment was necessary is still not clear, but it may have been needed to compensate for testing that was not done before the reactor came on line. It was subsequently concluded that the basic design of the reactor was faulty.

In hurt, angry terms, Gorbachev thrashed the outside world for its response to Chernobyl: "Political figures and the mass media of certain countries, especially the United States . . . used the Chernobyl accident as a jumping-off point for an unrestrained anti-Soviet campaign." He spoke about sensationalist news accounts in Western media that wildly exaggerated casualty figures as if they were official commentaries from Western governments—"a mountain of lies, the most virulent and malicious of lies." Gorbachev saw a conspiratorial purpose here, which he attributed to "certain Western politicians": "They needed a pretext to discredit the Soviet Union and its foreign policy, to lessen the impact of Soviet proposals for the cessation of nuclear tests and for the elimination of nuclear weapons . . . and to sow seeds of mistrust and suspicion toward the socialist countries. . . . [They] wanted to use Chernobyl as a pretext for distracting the attention of the world public from all the real problems that make them uncomfortable."

This was the unreconstructed *apparatchik* Gorbachev, slashing back defensively at threatening outsiders, knowing he had a weak hand and overplaying it badly. Gorbachev's natural supporters in the Soviet Union, particularly intellectuals but also many ordinary citizens eager for change, were discouraged by his performance. It was one of Gorbachev's worst moments, but characteristically he found a way—eventually—to use it creatively to his own advantage. Chernobyl was an important turning point in several respects.

The accident was a devastating blow to Gorbachev's hopes for building popular trust and enthusiasm. Chernobyl aggravated the Soviet public's deepest suspicions about its government by reminding people how little they trusted official reassurances or official information in general. The authorities gave good cause for such doubts, for example by evacuating children from Kiev long after they had suffered the worst radiation, while assuring the populace that this was just a precaution—there were no grounds for concern. Traditionally in the Soviet Union, when official information was obviously incomplete, unofficial information, often no better than rumor, filled the void; Chernobyl provoked countless rumors and unattributed inside information. The initial official silence, then Gorbachev's unsatisfactory speech, only exacerbated public suspicions.

Chernobyl reminded Gorbachev and his comrades how badly their system worked. The power plant that exploded had been rushed prematurely into service under pressure to fulfill the plan; various officials had lied about its readiness; safety violations and other shortcomings had been winked at. The reactor design was faulty, but no one wanted to face up to that, because there were dozens more of the same model in service, and more still planned for the future. Eventually, the design was shelved; no more have been built. Many officials were fired, several were tried and sentenced to jail. Eventually, I was told by a well-informed official, Gorbachev realized that he had been misled by local leaders. In the neighboring republic of Belorussia, for example, officials denied they had been seriously affected by the fallout, but in fact they may have suffered worse radiation damage than the Ukraine. In Kiev, the local potentate, Shcherbitsky, defied scientific advice and went ahead with the May Day parade, churning up dust that was full of radioactivity. There must have been great anger and frustration around the tables where Gorbachev and his colleagues met for honest discussion. Chernobyl was a scary and tragic accident, but it was also a painful reminder of the huge mess that was—and is—the Soviet economy.

The accident immediately undermined the five-year plan just approved at the Party Congress, which called for doubling the percentage of electricity generated by nuclear power (from 11 to 22 percent of all electricity consumed in the country). That target would now be unreachable, and billions of rubles would have to be spent to clean up from, and then compensate for, the losses at Chernobyl. The accident heightened suspicions of the Soviet Union among its neighbors, and just at a moment when Gorbachev was cultivating the opposite sentiment. More hopefully for the leadership, it also created deep new anxieties about nuclear energy, which Gorbachev quickly seized on to help him pursue nuclear-arms control.

Psychologically Chernobyl unhinged the Soviet Union. It became the only real topic of conversation that summer; citizens worried about their friends in the Ukraine, about their children, about the safety of the food they ate and the water they drank. Extensive press and television coverage of the accident and its aftermath was devoted largely to the heroics of those who responded to the crisis, especially in the first weeks. But in private conversations the accident became a source of great foreboding.

"Listen, this is incredible," a Russian writer said to Serge Schmemann of *The New York Times* that July. The writer had opened an old Bible to Revelation: " 'And the third angel sounded, and there fell a great star from heaven, burning as if it were a lamp, and it fell upon the third part of the rivers, and upon the fountains of waters: and the name of the star is called Wormwood: and the third part of the waters became wormwood; and many men died of the waters, because they were made bitter.' " The writer opened a Ukrainian dictionary, and pointed to the word for wormwood: *chernobyl.*

Word of this coincidence of Biblical prophecy and real life was passed from friend to friend across the entire country. It appealed to the romantic and spiritualistic streak common in many Russian intellectuals, so it joined the floodtide of rumors and anecdotes about Chernobyl that changed the nation's outlook, at least for a time. The accident took on the qualities of a parable of modern life, a sign of man's helplessness in the face of his own technological creations. This new mood was not hospitable to Gorbachev's original brand of reformism, which emphasized scientific and technological progress.

This was the first of many occasions when Gorbachev would be faced with an unexpected event that challenged his plans. His response was—it turned out—characteristic. He took the Chernobyl disaster as a prod to move farther and faster. The Party Congress, curiously, had seemed to slow things down; now there was a new impetus to speed them up. Soon after Chernobyl, Soviet information policy began to change dramatically. *Glasnost,* until then largely a slogan, began to take on a life of its own. This was first evident in stories about Chernobyl itself. In July, after many weeks in which the press played down radiation dangers, *Komsomolskaya Pravda* published a detailed description of the different types of radioactive elements and their possible effects, including their ability to cause various cancers. Then the newspapers began to report on frantic efforts to prevent contamination of the Dnieper River, which passed next to Chernobyl and flowed on to Kiev, which drew most of its drinking water from the river.

We have no concrete evidence that this fuller *glasnost* represented an official reaction to Chernobyl, but it must have. Gorbachev told a revealing anecdote in his book *Perestroika:* "I recall a meeting in June 1986 with the personnel of the apparatus of the Central Committee. It concerned *perestroika.* I had to ask them to adopt a new style of working with the intelligentsia. It is time to stop ordering it about, since this is harmful and inadmissible. The intelligentsia has wholeheartedly welcomed the program for the democratic renewal of society." Gorbachev was instructing the watchdogs to loosen up on the intellectuals—the group with the most immediate interest in more *glasnost.*

Yakovlev called a meeting of senior members of the journalists' union on June 6, apparently to discuss the lessons of Chernobyl. That summer there were further signs of a more aggressive policy of *glasnost*. The most dramatic came on August 31 when a Soviet ocean liner, the *Admiral Nakhimov,* sank after colliding with a freighter in the Black Sea. The official news media quickly gave gruesome details of the accident, in which 398 lives were lost.

During the summer of 1986 three new editors took control of publications in Moscow that were to become heralds of the new era. Vitali Korotich, a writer and poet living in Kiev, who was hardly known in Moscow, was invited to the capital by Yakovlev and offered the job of editor of *Ogonyok* (Little Flame), a weekly picture magazine in the style of the old *Paris Match* or *Life* that was part of the *Pravda* publishing empire. Korotich was reluctant to give up a comfortable and easy life in Kiev for this most uncertain prospect, but Yakovlev and Ligachev persuaded him to take the job.*

Also that summer an energetic seventy-two-year-old writer who was not a member of the Communist Party, Sergei Zalygin, was appointed editor of the country's most important literary journal, *Novy Mir* (New World). There is no American or British equivalent to *Novy Mir,* a monthly "thick journal" that was long considered the organ of the intelligentsia. Under its greatest modern editor, Alexander Tvardovsky, *Novy Mir* published Alexander Solzhenitsyn's *One Day in the Life of Ivan Denisovich* and many other ground-breaking works, when that was possible. It ceased being possible in 1970, when Tvardovsky was fired after sixteen years as editor. Zalygin would now revive the journal, at first by publishing banned works from the pre-Gorbachev past.

The third important *glasnost* editor was Yegor Yakovlev, who was invited by Valentin Falin, a former Soviet diplomat who was then director of the Novosti press agency, to take over an odd little weekly newspaper called *Moscow News,* then published in several languages primarily for tourists visiting the Soviet Union. According to Yakovlev (who is not related to Alexander Yakovlev, Gorbachev's close associate), Falin told him that *Moscow News* "should publish articles that other Soviet newspapers weren't publishing." Falin made the offer in August 1985, and Yakovlev—then living in Prague—took "a long

---

* One important consideration in Korotich's decision, he told me, was where he could live in Moscow. He had a large apartment in Kiev, big enough for his mother, wife, and two sons. His new patrons acquired for him a handsome flat of four or five rooms in a new building for employees of the Central Committee—and a separate flat nearby for his elderly mother.

time" to consider it. He finally agreed, and began work at the paper in August 1986. He and Korotich were soon in a kind of good-natured competition to see who could stretch the traditional rules farther.

As the press became bolder and franker, so did Gorbachev. At a Central Committee plenum in June, apparently called to try to reinvigorate the line adopted at the Party Congress, he observed that "in many places, everything still continues as before: initiative comes up against a wall of indifference, if not outright resistance." Soon after that plenum, he met with a group of writers and spoke about his frustrations. The speech was not published, but the resourceful Moscow correspondent of *L'Unità,* the Italian Communist newspaper, Giulietto Chiesa, acquired a copy of the text and printed it in his newspaper. "Every day that goes by," Gorbachev told the writers, "brings new facts, one worse than the other, that demonstrate the difficulties" facing those trying to implement his reforms.

Gorbachev returned to a debate that had electrified the Party Congress by telling the writers: "A ruling stratum lies between the leadership of the country and the people, who wish for change, who dream of change—the *apparat* of ministers, the *apparat* of the Party, which does not want transformations, which does not intend to lose certain rights tied to privileges." Gorbachev was taking Yeltsin's side in the debate, flatly contradicting his own number-two man, Ligachev, who had disputed Yeltsin on the question of the "inert stratum" at the Congress. Gorbachev told the writers about opposition to change in the state planning commission and other redoubts of reaction, and he pleaded for a new democracy: "If we do not involve the people, nothing will come out of this." He indicated impatience with his colleagues in the Politburo: "There are fights, arguments. We have been postponing for two, three years. Now we want to act. The society is ripe for change. If we withdrew, the society will not agree. We need to make the ongoing processes irreversible." Then Gorbachev invoked the famous words of the Talmud: "If not us, who? If not now, when?"

Gorbachev made several interesting speeches on trips inside the Soviet Union in the summer after Chernobyl. One was in Khabarovsk in the Soviet Far East, where he addressed Party activists on July 31: "We can in no way be satisfied with what has been achieved. . . . So far there have been no profound qualitative changes that would have consolidated the trend toward accelerated growth. . . . Let's be frank about it—the most important work is yet to be done."* He indicated that his own assessment of the country's situation had become more pessimistic. "The further we go along the road of restructuring, the more its complexity becomes obvious, and the more the tremendous scale of the work to be done is revealed. . . . We shall have to overcome, step by step, the problems that have built up in every area of public life, to get rid of whatever has outlived itself, and boldly adopt new solutions."

The previous February, a French Communist journalist had asked Gorbachev if the Soviet Union was beginning "a new revolution." Gorbachev replied: "Of course not. I think it would be wrong to formulate the question in those terms." In Khabarovsk just six months later, he said: "The current restructuring [perestroika] embraces not only the economy but all other facets of public life: social relations, the political system, the spiritual and ideological sphere, and the style and work methods of the party and all of our cadres. 'Restructuring' is a capacious word. I would equate the word 'restructuring' with the word 'revolution.' "

These examples of Gorbachev publicly changing his mind were still relatively rare; later they would become too numerous to count. After fifteen months in power Gorbachev had begun to demonstrate what would be his most important political attribute, his creative flexibility. One road didn't work? Take another. Someone else's idea, once apparently foolish, began to look attractive? Seize it. Most politicians live in dread of being caught contradicting themselves, but Gorbachev seemed to have no qualms about changing his mind.

His speech in Khabarovsk provided an ominous clue that intrigue continued in the Kremlin. It was censored before being published in *Pravda*. The transcript of the speech as delivered showed that Gorbachev had said this about the Party's cadre, or personnel policy: "We must guarantee a combination of experienced cadres and younger people. There must be a process of cadre promotion and growth, but a deserved one, without, so to speak, favoritism and chummy relations, but based on the job done. There must be a constant inflow of fresh forces [in other words, of new people]."

---

* In part Gorbachev was reacting to published statistics that showed a slight improvement in the economic situation since he had come to power. Those first-year figures were attributed primarily to greater discipline and more active direction from Moscow, and not to any reforms. "We should not allow our heads to be turned by success," Gorbachev said in Khabarovsk; he knew then how serious the situation was, regardless of what the statistics said.

Pravda published the "text" of the speech on August 3. In its version, that passage said: "We must ensure a combination of experienced and young cadres on the basis of a continuous process of growth and cadre promotion with due consideration for their political and professional qualities."

With Gorbachev out of town, Ligachev would have been the acting boss in Moscow when this change was made; it was probably his handiwork.

•   •   •

That Khabarovsk speech capped a year and a half of unusual candor from the new general secretary. Gorbachev had established a fundamentally new style of discourse—new for what it contained, and for what it omitted. I spent quite a while that summer reading Gorbachev and thinking about what he was saying. In October 1986, I wrote an article about this subject for *Foreign Affairs* under the title "The Soviet Pretense." Like the article I wrote when he first came to power, this one reveals the ungenerous limits of my own imagination. Here is part of what I wrote:

> Since the Bolshevik Revolution the ideology of Russian communism has had a haunting power outside Russia's borders, even at times when the country was desperately poor and backward. The central proposition of Marxism-Leninism—that a struggle between "socialism" and "imperialism" is inevitable and will inevitably result in the triumph of socialism—has long baffled and alarmed the West.
>
> Inside the Soviet Union the same oft-repeated faith in the inherent superiority of socialism has been a fundamental aspect of Soviet life. By its repetition, the country's leaders have sought to assure their people that hardships and sacrifices were worthwhile, even noble, because they all marched toward such a glorious end.
>
> Official confidence in the superiority of the Soviet system and in the certain victory of socialism over capitalism might be called the Soviet Pretense. It has been a crucial ingredient of the Soviet Union's national character, and an important tool for all of its leaders, from Lenin through Chernenko. But in the era of Mikhail Gorbachev, the Soviet Pretense is collapsing. This is a momentous change. . . .
>
> Gorbachev has abandoned the rhetorical style on which he himself and all his countrymen were reared. The traditional Soviet approach was to minimize bad news while repeating again and again how great is Soviet power, how glorious its many victories, how brilliant its future.
> Instead, Gorbachev emphasizes the bad news—the country's stagna-

tion—and dwells on the radical changes in individual citizens' attitudes necessary to put things right.

Initially, this change was refreshing. It won Gorbachev considerable sympathy among his countrymen. But in a deeply ideological society whose ideology has long been formulated in slogans, this new kind of rhetoric may eventually have serious political consequences. In effect Gorbachev has repealed the happy-ever-after promised by all his predecessors. He still holds out hope for a marvelous tomorrow, but only if his demands for sweeping changes in the status quo are met. . . .

Because [Gorbachev's public acknowledgments of the country's many shortcomings] sound ominously like admissions [of the failure of Soviet communism], they are politically risky. By tinkering with the promises of communism, Gorbachev is calling into question an important traditional source of the system's legitimacy. . . . It cannot be easy for an ideological society to prosper in the absence of persuasive doctrinal explanations for either current conditions or future prospects. . . .

What is in prospect now is the loss of the Soviet national ideal—the logical extension of the collapse of the pretense of Soviet superiority. The whole point of the Bolshevik Revolution was to put Russia on the curl of the wave of history, so its communism would triumph when the internal contradictions of capitalism brought down the traditional great powers in the West. That was the Leninist rosy scenario. Without it, new generations of Soviet leaders will have to reformulate both their private and the Party's public visions of their country and its place in the world. . . .

A stagnant or declining Soviet Union in a world of dynamic technological change and rapid growth in once-backward nations will surely suffer from further erosion of ideological confidence. It is not difficult to imagine the effective demise of Marxism-Leninism as anything but a legitimizing doctrine justifying the continued rule of the Party elite.

It has long been clear that communist ideology by itself is an insufficient source of legitimacy. Nationalism—really Russian nationalism, barely disguised to accommodate the multinational Soviet state—has been the most effective substitute for Marxist-Leninist zeal since Stalin put patriotism at the center of the war effort against Germany. Today Gorbachev usually tells his countrymen that their past efforts were worthwhile because they made the Soviet Union a great world power, and rarely because they advanced communism or world revolution.

But certain elements of Soviet ideology that have always troubled the West will survive as long as the system does. One is the mythology of the Party and its leading role, which justifies the elite's status. Another is the presumption that the struggle between socialism and "imperialism"—the West—will continue indefinitely, a formula for permanent struggle that gives the elite a useful tool to dominate the society. The idea of a permanently hostile outside world is so resonant with the deepest insecurities of the Russian national character that it is doomed to survive.

When I wrote that in 1986 I was obviously still resisting the idea that Gorbachev was headed toward profound and fundamental change, not just tinkering—even though I saw evidence that what he was doing would indeed be serious.* It was a typical failing among students of the Soviet Union. We assumed that certain fundamental aspects of the Stalinist system simply could not be changed, because changing them would risk the legitimacy of the entire structure of Party power. And that was unthinkable.

But it wasn't unthinkable. It is what happened. Gorbachev's approach to power was to challenge the Party to throw off its many bad habits and confront the crisis besetting the country. He challenged the Party by telling the truth, something it was not used to hearing. But he gave the Party the opportunity to seize control of the new situation. "The example here must be set by Communists," as he put it in his speech to the April 1985 Central Committee plenum. I believe that in the beginning he expected the Party to accept his challenges, and to help him lead the way.

Whatever he expected, he got a new situation. The legitimacy of the old system did crumble under the pressures Gorbachev's candor created.

When I lived in Moscow in the early 1970s I decided that the system really did enjoy the legitimate acceptance of the public, even though the formal claims it made to justify its rule were based on myths. The most basic of these were the myth of Lenin (transformed into a deity after his death); the myth of the October Revolution of 1917 (a coup d'état led by a tiny band of Bolsheviks, later portrayed as a massive popular uprising by workers and peasants); and the myth of the Great Patriotic War (the Soviet name for World War II, portrayed as the lonely triumph of Russia over Nazi Germany, with barely a reference to the other allies who fought Hitler, and no reference at all to Stalin's 1939 pact with Hitler, his devastating purges of the Red Army on the eve of the war, or other embarrassing details).

---

* I also insulted the "Russian national character," as events in 1989–90 would demonstrate. I will return to that subject later.

The official mythology in these three cases was built on lies; lies pervaded nearly all Soviet pronouncements on history, society, and politics. As Solzhenitsyn wrote bitterly but accurately, "The lie has become not simply a moral category, but a pillar of the state." I saw this, but I also saw that people accepted the lies, and often believed them. Therefore, I concluded that the system was stable—that it qualified for the political scientists' blessing, it was legitimate.

What I misunderstood was the fragility of that legitimacy. Much of it was based on fatalism—the popular fatalism that "they" would never relinquish control, that "they" had all the advantages, that their lies would never be effectively challenged. Gorbachev, one of "them," then introduced a revolutionary idea: Let's stop claiming the right to lead on the basis of myths, let's demonstrate that we have earned the right to lead by deeds. Let's offer the people a chance to say whether they agree with us. And let's start telling the truth.

Gorbachev made his message much more credible by separating himself from the time-serving petty tyrants whom many citizens knew as their local Party leaders. It was an entirely new psychology for a modern Soviet leader to adopt—I am on your side, he said to ordinary people, not on the side of the headstrong and entrenched *apparat*. He said this bluntly in Krasnodar, next door to his native Stavropol, in September, 1986. In a speech broadcast to the entire country on television, Gorbachev declared that "people who occupy leading positions" are among the enemies of democratization. These are the people who prefer "giving commands, issuing orders" to more open methods. And they don't want things to change: "They are capable people. Some are even resourceful. Their main concern is to preserve the old, obsolete ways, to preserve their own privileges, though this does not accord with our principles, laws, morality, or with our present policies. We can see them shouting about restructuring from every platform, and louder than anyone else, even as they apply the brakes to its implementation on all kinds of pretexts, including the most specious ones." The goal, he said, must be to end the habit of giving orders and create the conditions that will "allow each person to feel himself to be the master of his country."

The invitation to be truthful, to judge the Party by its deeds and to become the masters of their country proved irresistible, first to a relatively small group of intellectuals, later to millions of Soviet citizens.

• • •

In the second half of 1986 Gorbachev began to speak openly about the opponents of his reforms inside the Party and government—those capable and resourceful people who pretended to support *perestroika* while they worked to undermine it. At a conference of social scientists in Moscow in October, he admitted, "Quite obviously, a sharp, not always open and uncompromising struggle of ideas, psychological attitudes, mentalities and behavior is taking place in the course of *perestroika*. . . . The old does not give up without a fight. . . . Some attempts are being made to squeeze the concepts of 'acceleration' and *'perestroika'* into the framework of obsolete dogmas and stereotypes, emasculating their novelty and revolutionary essence in the process."

By then many of Gorbachev's most ardent supporters among the Moscow intellectuals feared for his survival, politically and physically. Physical threats had entered the political dialogue. At an amazing meeting of Party officials in Moscow in April, Yeltsin answered written questions from the floor. One, which he read aloud to the assemblage, said: "You have very grand plans; what are you meddling with? Gorbachev just needed a loyal man. Go back to Sverdlovsk [the Siberian city where Yeltsin had been first secretary] before it is too late." According to an account of the meeting published later in *Le Monde,* shouts of "Shame!" were heard in the hall. Yeltsin said: "Calm down, comrades. I do not think this question comes from the floor. It must have been received earlier and slipped into the bundle. The author is obviously sick." Even if there was no real physical danger, political peril lay around every corner. Gorbachev's acknowledgment that "a sharp, not always open struggle" was under way was not news to any member of the political élite.

In 1986 Western Kremlinologists thought Gorbachev probably had the KGB on his side, since its new boss, Chebrikov, was, like Gorbachev, a longtime protégé of Andropov. But an event in September 1986 raised doubts about that loyalty. It looked like a classic Russian *provokatsiya,* or provocation.

To be fair, the episode began with an event that the KGB undoubtedly interpreted as an American provocation—the arrest in New York of Gennadi Zakharov, a low-level official at the United Nations who had tried to buy technical documents on computers from an African student studying in the United States. Zakharov was charged with espionage, though he wasn't trying to acquire government documents or classified material. In Moscow Zakharov's arrest must have looked like a cheap shot.

The KGB responded a week later by picking up Nicholas Daniloff, the Moscow correspondent of *U.S. News & World Report* magazine. On September 7 Daniloff was charged with espionage and held in Moscow's notorious Lefortovo prison. It was the first time an American journalist had ever been put in a Soviet jail, and it caused a political uproar in the United States, the more so because the Soviets had no evidence that Daniloff had done anything worse than behave foolishly.*

This sequence of events left Gorbachev (then vacationing in the South) in a terrible quandary. He was struggling to revive the cooperative spirit of the Geneva summit to make further progress with the United States on arms control. All year he had continued offering new proposals, while renewing the unilateral Soviet moratorium on nuclear testing. He reiterated his appeal for progress in the negotiations in an interview with a Czechoslovak newspaper two days after Daniloff was charged with espionage, pleading with the Reagan administration to credit his sincerity.

Shevardnadze was scheduled to come to Washington in connection with his annual visit to the September session of the General Assembly in New York. He and Gorbachev planned to use the visit to invite Reagan to a preliminary summit outside either of their countries to try to reinvigorate the arms talks. But the uproar over Daniloff in the United States jeopardized their plan, as Gorbachev acknowledged on September 19 in a speech in Krasnodar.

Gorbachev spoke of the enemies of arms control in the United States. "Now they have raised the Daniloff affair, a spy who has been caught red-handed, who engaged in espionage matters. . . . But they want to call this a run-of-the-mill affair. Espionage is no run-of-the-mill business. Nevertheless, in comparison with all international relations, this whole complicated business, this, of course, is a common event, but they have turned it around in such a way as to again damage and sow doubt in the Soviet Union's policy, to damage its image, the image which people—especially in the United States—were beginning to understand, and simply reap a harvest of hatred toward us."

---

* He had delivered a letter to the U.S. embassy from a man who claimed to be a dissident, and in fact was a KGB agent. This violated the Moscow correspondent's code of sensible behavior, but not the law.

Was Gorbachev really complaining about Americans—or about his own KGB? Subsequent events suggest that at the very least it was both. Shevardnadze came to the U.S. as scheduled, and quickly began intensive negotiations to find a way out of this crisis. The Reagan administration said it would not swap Zakharov for Daniloff, since that would ratify the Soviets' false claim that the two cases were comparable. Shevardnadze offered to swap Zakharov for Yuri Orlov, a famous Soviet dissident jailed under Brezhnev in 1977, and to release Daniloff at the same time. This face-saving arrangement was accepted by the United States.

Shevardnadze simultaneously pressed the Americans to accept the suggestion for a mini-summit on neutral ground, and once the Daniloff matter was resolved, the Americans agreed. The meeting was scheduled for Reykjavík, in Iceland, in October.

Reykjavík became one of the most bizarre meetings of the Cold War era. Before it was over, Gorbachev and Reagan were talking about the elimination of all nuclear weapons and all ballistic missiles —previously unimaginable options for the Soviet and American leaders to consider. Gorbachev made yet another concession, agreeing to Reagan's proposal to eliminate all of the intermediate-range missiles in Europe, but only in conjunction with other agreements. He pressed for 50 percent reductions in intercontinental, strategic weapons. But he also demanded that the United States agree to confine its research on a missile defense system (the Star Wars idea) to laboratories, and not test any devices in space. On this point Reagan would not budge, and the meeting broke up. After toying with the most sweeping ideas ever considered at such a meeting, Reagan and Gorbachev parted empty-handed.

But Gorbachev would not take no for an answer. He went immediately from his farewells with Reagan to a press conference, where he gave a remarkable performance. First he briefed the reporters on how the talks had gone, giving them a detailed account fully consistent with the best American description of the meeting.* Then, answering questions, he surprised many in the crowd by emphasizing his continued determination to reach agreements with Reagan. A Czech reporter asked when there would be another chance to make progress on the arms issues. "You know that I would give an optimistic answer to that because much has already been done, both on the eve of the meeting and at the meeting itself. If we, from realistic positions both

---

* See Strobe Talbott's *The Master of the Game*, New York, 1989.

in the United States . . . and in our country . . . think through everything once again and show realism and responsibility, then the opportunity to resolve these issues is not yet lost."

Many commentators thought Gorbachev was wildly overoptimistic.
Subsequent events would prove them wrong. Reykjavík helped establish the idea in Western capitals that Gorbachev was genuinely different from his predecessors, not just a cosmetic change. It would take
more time still for this notion to be fully accepted, but Reykjavík
promoted it effectively. It also established a standard for the Soviet-
American arms-control talks that would survive—a standard that
would require sweeping actual reductions of existing weapons to justify a new arms-control treaty. Reagan had sought to establish this
principle from the beginning; now, with Gorbachev's eager assistance,
it had been accepted.

·   ·   ·

In arms control as in so many other realms, Gorbachev was haunted
by—and constricted by—the past. He said he wanted to turn a new
page, but he was dealing with a thick book. Earlier pages kept pressing
in on his.

The past had vastly different meaning for different segments of
Gorbachev's domestic audience. For the *apparatchiks* in his Communist Party—the people on whom he depended to implement his first
reforms—the past included years of deep anxiety under Stalin, the
unpredictable vagaries of Khrushchev, and the comforts of the eighteen-year Brezhnev era. Pampering the cadres was Brezhnev's leadership style; he bought support and stability by extending power,
privileges, and job security to an ever-widening group of *apparatchiks*.
They came to see their status and privileges as entitlements. They
certainly saw no reason to give them up.

But for millions of Soviet citizens, including the technical and
intellectual élites whose support Gorbachev needed, the past was a
time of lies, a false time in which pompous, ignorant Party *apparatchiks* conducted hollow ceremonies of power, pretending to know
what they were doing and where they were leading the country. There
had been a profound falseness to Soviet life for many decades; it had
bred the darkest kind of cynicism and disrespect for authority. That
cynicism actually worked to Gorbachev's advantage, because it left
thoughtful citizens with absolutely no expectation that a figure like
him could ever emerge from the Communist Party. They were thus
all the more thrilled and astounded when he did appear.

Curiously, the *apparatchiks* would not challenge the legitimacy of Gorbachev's authority. He had been elected general secretary according to the rituals and procedures they all recognized—he was the boss, fair and square. (This of course did not prevent intrigues against him —they were fair and square, too, and utterly traditional.) But the more independent-minded, thoughtful body of opinion quite instinctively questioned Gorbachev's authority, as it had questioned all Soviet authority since Stalin's. In effect, he had little to prove to the *apparatchiks,* but everything to prove to the élites outside the Party *apparat* that were so important to his efforts to reinvigorate the society.

Winning their respect would be complicated. It would have to begin with two basic ingredients, freedom and honesty.

In the Soviet context, the most basic unrespected freedom was the freedom to say what one thought. For years it was dangerous to do so —unless of course one thought precisely what *Pravda*'s editorials said, as many pretended to do, and quite a few did. Gorbachev began to speak about the need for people to say what they thought with increasing bluntness. Touring Krasnodar in September 1986, he told collective farmers that it was time to stop "giving one another rose-colored spectacles" and uttering only "fine words . . . and mutual compliments.

"We want our people . . . to say what they think," he said. "When we come to know how things really are—when we stop telling each other niceties and begin to discuss things in a businesslike and open way and try to get to the bottom of things—then we will undoubtedly find answers to all your questions." It was a simple enough formula, but a lot of the most intelligent, best-educated people in the country weren't sure they believed it.

Gorbachev spoke about creating a new outlook, a new psychology, but such things only develop in a congenial atmosphere. *Glasnost* had the power to create such an atmosphere, especially through the mass media. If officially controlled organs, from *Izvestia* (the government paper) to state television to plays and movies, could speak in new, more honest and truthful voices, then perhaps a new atmosphere would follow.

·　　·　　·

Russia has been susceptible to the impact of individual works of art in a way few other societies are. Pushkin's epic poem *Eugene Onegin* is the best example; it defined modern Russian culture, even the modern Russian sensibility. In more recent times Solzhenitsyn's *Onc Day in the Life of Ivan Denisovich,* first published in 1962, became a critical part of the shared experience of every intellectual alive when it came out. At the end of 1986, a great work of art appeared that played a momentous role in the evolution of *glasnost,* and in the creation of that new atmosphere Gorbachev sought.

Ironically, it was a work that was completed—and relegated to the shelf where censored works often lay for years or decades—in 1984, a year before Gorbachev became general secretary. And it wasn't a Russian work of art but a great example of the culture of Georgia in the Soviet South. And—befitting the reign of the first Soviet leader of the video age—it was not a poem or a book, but a movie called *Repentance,* by Tengiz Abuladze.

Abuladze made *Repentance* in just five months after working on a script for several years. He began writing it in 1981 after consulting with the local Party boss in Georgia at the time—Eduard Shevardnadze. Shevardnadze blessed the project then, and apparently helped win approval for its release at the end of 1986—interesting evidence that he shared the values of Gorbachev's revolution long before he joined it.

I cannot do the film justice in words. It is a stunning accomplishment, combining—in Abuladze's word—phantasmagoric imagery, uncompromising morality, and gut-wrenching, realistic emotion. I have never before been so affected by a movie.

Abuladze tells the story of Keti, who appears in the film both as an adorable young girl and a handsome middle-aged woman. She is the daughter of Sandro, a talented artist, and Nino; they live in an unnamed city of an unnamed country in the time of Varlam, the omnipotent mayor. (In Georgian his name means "no one.") Brilliantly played by Avtandil Makharadze, Varlam is a composite tyrant. He has high leather boots like Stalin's, a black shirt like Mussolini's, a mustache like Hitler's, and a pince-nez and general manner strongly reminiscent of Lavrenti Beria, Stalin's murderous comrade. Varlam is charming, and crazy. Soon he is conducting a mad campaign against his own people, aided by secret policemen who wear medieval armor as they go about their business of arresting innocent citizens. Keti's parents are eventually included among Varlam's countless victims. Varlam dies and is succeeded as tyrant by his son, Avel. At the end of the film, Avel's son, Tornike, turns on his father in a moral rage. But the sequence of these events is often jumbled, and the events are regularly overwhelmed by the power of Abuladze's images.

The middle-aged Keti is introduced at the time of Varlam's death (which comes near the beginning of the movie, but no matter). After a bizarre funeral and burial, his corpse reappears the next day, propped up against a tree in his son's backyard. He is buried again, and reappears again, and again. Finally the police set an ambush at the cemetery and catch the grave robber—an elegant woman in a white dress. It's Keti. To let him lie peacefully under the earth is to bury his crimes, she declares; she won't permit it. She is put on trial, and her trial provides an occasion for flashbacks and dreams.

The story then recommences with Varlam's inauguration as mayor. The beautiful eight-year-old Keti appears, blowing soap bubbles out the window of her family's flat. Her beautiful parents (some critics have seen her father, Sandro, as a Christlike figure) are initially admired by Varlam; Sandro uses his connection to the mayor to try to save a church that he is using for some kind of electrical experiment, but to no avail. (Later the church is blown to smithereens.) Soon Varlam's madness is increasingly evident, and the inhabitants of Keti's family's world begin to disappear, carried off by the strange armored figures of Varlam's political police force.

One night Varlam himself comes to the apartment of Keti's parents to admire Sandro's paintings, and to philosophize. "Sometimes the flight from reality signifies an even greater reality," he proclaims. "The people need a great reality. . . . We must enlighten the people." But Sandro disagrees: "The people will only be enlightened by their spiritual pastor, their moral hero." Soon the men in armor are knocking at Sandro's door; they take away both him and his paintings, leaving mother and daughter behind. Nino, his wife, runs to an influential older friend for help, but is told that he has been arrested. She goes then to her old friend Yelena—also arrested. Her desperate loneliness is haunting.

Abuladze shows mother and daughter standing with many other women outside a window; whoever is inside is not visible. The women are asking about the fate of their menfolk, and the authoritative voice inside is barking out the ominous phrases made famous in the thirties: "Sentenced to ten years, no right of correspondence!" Then they hear that logs that were cut by prisoners have been brought to the sawmill; some of the men managed to carve their names and locations into the logs. Mother and daughter rush to the scene (this is based, Abuladze has said, on a true story), where other women are grasping at the logs, some hugging them in delight. "I found him, I found him, Mama! Mama!" shouts a little boy. Keti and her mother search the logs but find no hint of their Sandro. It is a searing scene.

Abuladze shows the interrogation of Sandro. It turns out the older family friend to whom his wife fled when he was arrested has told the police that Sandro is an enemy. At first Sandro refuses to believe it: "It's immoral to defame an honest man to get false testimony out of me." One of his captors replies, "What's moral is what's useful to the common cause." Then the family friend is produced, and confirms that he has confessed to being a spy whose assignment was "to dig a tunnel from Bombay to London." He then tries to explain to Sandro that he has confessed to "carry everything to the point of absurdity." The system will be overwhelmed, he explains, if "we accuse as many people as possible"—the authorities won't be able to prosecute them all.

There are other scenes of madness. The tyrant Varlam declares at one point, "We must not trust people, neither their deeds nor their words. . . . Of every three people, four are enemies. Yes, yes, don't be surprised: one enemy is greater in quantity than one friend." One of his loyalists, told to arrest a certain man, arrests thirty-five people who have the same last name. "I've brought you a truckload of enemies!" he proudly declares.

As this story unfolds at Keti's grave-robbing trial, Varlam's grandson, Tornike, is appalled. "Did you know all this?" he asks his father, Avel, who took up the tyranny when Varlam died.

"Those were difficult times," Avel replies, using language familiar to every Soviet citizen who ever heard the rationalizations of one of Stalin's collaborators. "The question of 'to be or not to be' was being decided, we were surrounded by enemies. . . . I'm not saying we didn't make mistakes. But what does the life of one or two people mean when it's a question of the happiness of millions?"

"And if grandfather had ordered the destruction of the whole world?" Tornike challenges his father. "You justify grandfather, you're following in his footsteps. I hate you. I hate you!"

Later, at home, Tornike turns on both his parents, who have concluded that Keti must be insane to be repeatedly digging up Varlam's corpse. "She's not insane, no. Aren't you sick of endlessly lying? All you care about is preserving your own well-being, and for the sake of that you'll gnaw through anyone's throat. You declare an innocent person a criminal, and a normal person insane. Don't you hold anything sacred? Doesn't your conscience torment you? . . . This isn't a house, it's a grave." Tornike takes his own life with a gun.

The film was first shown in October to large audiences at Moscow's House of Film, the headquarters of the Cinematographers' Union. The cinematographers' was the first of the giant creative unions to elect new, liberal leaders after Gorbachev came to power. The union's new secretary, Elem Klimov, himself the director of many movies that lay unseen "on the shelf" for years, helped promote Abuladze's film, but it needed higher-level support than he could give it. Shevardnadze, Yakovlev, and, according to widely-believed rumors in Moscow, Ligachev all blessed it for general showing, which began in Tbilisi, the Georgian capital, in November. *Repentance* was shown all over the country in the next few months.

It was seen by tens of millions of people. Roy Medvedev, the dissident historian who had spent years studying Stalin and his crimes, called the movie "the most important event in Soviet cultural life in at least a decade." It was as important as Solzhenitsyn's *Ivan Denisovich,* he said, and even more universal. "After all, 'One Day' was about just one man, his experience. This goes deeper. It shows the impact on the whole of society."

A reviewer in *Izvestia* ended her rapturous praise for the film with this paragraph:

> Go see the film *Repentance.* If you don't consider it a shortcoming that the film will make you think and perhaps judge yourself, go, go to the movie theater today! Your prospects for the future will improve, your hopes will gain strength, your dreams will grow wings. This is the art of a powerful voice, of true optimism, art that affirms faith in man, in his ability to be renewed and to renew social relations. The film leads viewers through suffering, through serious trials by truth, to repentance, to purification, to the light.

Purification may be the key word in that passage. Stalinism was a giant pile of filthy linen in the closet of Soviet life; the closet was bigger than the rest of the house. The linen gave off a stench that no breeze could carry off. The closet door had to be opened; the linen had to be laundered, almost piece by piece. People could only begin to believe that truthfulness had become a real value in Soviet life when the lying from the past was totally discredited. *Repentance* was released barely a year and a half after a Party audience gave Gorbachev an ovation for mentioning Stalin's name, a sign that Keti was right—the tyrant was dead, but somehow he lived on. Or, as Avel put it to his wife when they were discussing whether his constant reappearances meant that Varlam really hadn't died, "The medical conclusion is one thing, but a fact is something else."

• • •

The release of *Repentance* was an apt prelude to the final drama of the first phase of Gorbachev's rule. That was an exciting fall in Moscow; *Ogonyok* and *Moscow News* had begun to publish bold material under their new editors; *Repentance* was in the theaters; change was in the air. But Ligachev was in charge of ideology in the Politburo, and the Moscow intellectuals were deeply suspicious of him. Foreigners too were arguing about how liberal Gorbachev would prove to be. The handling of Chernobyl, particularly the lies and the long initial silence, had provoked strong, negative reactions that were played back to the Soviet Union on short-wave radio broadcasts. Many of the people whose support Gorbachev wanted and needed were withholding it still, unsure that they could really trust this new man to be different from his predecessors. One of my friends said, "We were waiting for him to release Sakharov and get out of Afghanistan—then we would be willing to take him seriously."

The two were related. Sakharov was still living in Moscow when Soviet forces invaded Afghanistan at the end of 1979, and he protested bitterly against the invasion. Until then Brezhnev had continued to tolerate Sakharov's presence—and dissidence—in Moscow, probably out of fear of foreign retaliation if he was blatantly mistreated. But after Afghanistan relations with the West were ruptured anyhow; the leadership no longer felt restrained. Sakharov was bundled off to Gorki without any trial or other legal proceeding. His involuntary exile was a punishment not provided for in any Soviet law—it was just an exercise of raw power.

Gorbachev made no move to free Sakharov in his first twenty-one months in power. He did allow Elena Bonner, Sakharov's wife, to travel to the West for medical treatment after his visit to France in 1985, but his only public utterance about Sakharov was a harsh one. "It is well known that illegal acts were committed on his part," Gorbachev told the French Communist newspaper *L'Humanité* in February 1986. "This has been reported in the press on many occasions.

Measures corresponding with our laws have been applied with regard to him." Gorbachev was wrong on all points: Sakharov had never been accused of illegal acts, and his punishment was not in accordance with any Soviet law.

I've been told by a senior scientist who was close to the authorities at the time that Alexander Yakovlev had advised Gorbachev that he would win important support from the intelligentsia by freeing Sakharov. Gorbachev himself had begun to speak of the need for "new thinking," a phrase he borrowed from the title of a Soviet book on nuclear arms and first used in his press conference at Reykjavík. Another senior official told me Gorbachev had obviously sympathized with Sakharov for years—perhaps since the appearance of his reformist essay in 1968. This official noted that Gorbachev agreed entirely with Sakharov about Afghanistan (as subsequent events appeared to confirm), and would naturally have been drawn to the older man, whose values seem so close to Gorbachev's own. Others in Moscow took a more cynical view of Gorbachev's motives. Yuri Afanasyev, one of the first liberals to break with the Party in 1990, told me he thought Gorbachev had no choice but to act on Sakharov—he could not proceed as a progressive reformer while Sakharov languished in Gorki. However it happened, Gorbachev in December decided to make one of the most dramatic political gestures of modern times.

Sakharov has described what happened in his memoirs. He and Elena Bonner were watching television as usual on the evening of December 15, when someone knocked at their door. It was ten or ten-thirty, and they were surprised. A KGB search? They opened the door. It was two electricians and a KGB agent. They said they'd been ordered to install a telephone—a convenience the Sakharovs had not enjoyed in their seven years in Gorki. When the telephone was hooked up, the KGB man said, "You'll get a call around ten tomorrow morning," and they left. Sakharov recounts:

> On December 16 we stayed at home until three in the afternoon, waiting for a call. I was just getting ready to go out for bread when the phone rang, and I answered. A woman's voice: "Mikhail Sergeyevich will speak with you."
> "I'm listening."
> I told Lucya [Elena Bonner], "It's Gorbachev." She opened the door to the hallway, where the usual chatter was going on around the policeman on duty, and shouted, "Quiet, Gorbachev's on the phone." There was an immediate silence.

"Hello, this is Gorbachev."

"Hello, I'm listening."

"I received your letter [Sakharov had written Gorbachev demanding the release of a long list of political prisoners]. We've reviewed it and discussed it." I don't remember his exact words about the other participants in the decision process, but he didn't mention names or positions. "You can return to Moscow. The decree of the Presidium of the Supreme Soviet will be rescinded. A decision has also been made about Elena Bonnaire."

I broke in sharply, "That's my wife!" It was an emotional reaction, not so much to his mispronunciation of her name Bonner as to its tone. I'm glad I interrupted his speech.

Gorbachev continued: "You can return to Moscow together. You have an apartment there. Marchuk [Guri Marchuk, president of the Academy of Sciences, of which Sakharov was still a member] is coming to see you. Go back to your patriotic work!"

I said, "Thank you! But I must tell you that a few days ago my friend [Anatoli] Marchenko [a famous dissident, author of *My Testimony*] was killed in prison. He was the first person I mentioned in my letter to you, requesting the release of prisoners of conscience—people persecuted for their beliefs."

Gorbachev: "Yes, I received your letter early this year. We've released many, and improved the situation of others. But there are all sorts of people on your list."

I said, "Everyone sentenced under those articles has been sentenced illegally, unjustly. They ought to be freed!"

Gorbachev: "I don't agree with you."

I said, "I urge you to look one more time at the question of releasing persons convicted for their beliefs. It's a matter of justice. It's vitally important for our country, for international trust, for peace, and for you and the success of your program."

Gorbachev made a noncommittal reply.

I said, "Thank you again. Goodbye." (Contrary to the demands of protocol, I brought the conversation to a close, not Gorbachev. I must have felt under stress and perhaps feared subconsciously that I might say too much.) Gorbachev had little choice, so he said, "Goodbye."

The conversation was brief, but this may have been the most important telephone call made in Russia in the twentieth century. Andrei Sakharov embodied the crushed liberal spirit of the Russian intelligentsia—the spirit that reappeared first in modern times after Stalin's death, and survived despite ferocious official efforts to snuff it out for three decades before Gorbachev placed that call. The call was an act of conciliation, forgiveness, and even repentance. There was no way to welcome Sakharov back to Moscow without acknowledging the correctness of his past positions, and the injustice of his persecution. Gorbachev had to understand this.

At the same time, there was no way to acknowledge the correctness of Sakharov's positions without discrediting the Party. The Party had made Sakharov a pariah. Its leaders and agents had attacked him viciously, literally almost killed him. Gorbachev had opened up what a well-trained Marxist like himself would quickly recognize as a glaring contradiction. It was so fundamental that he would have to find some way to resolve it.

CHAPTER FIVE

REAL POLITICS,
AND REAL CHANGE

As 1986 ended Gorbachev found himself in a tense and difficult position. He was trying to persuade recalcitrant comrades to go along with his plan for the next phase of *perestroika,* a sweeping political reform. There was no mystery about what he wanted to do—he had laid out his goals in the December 1984 speech, before he became leader. He wanted to democratize the Party and the state to encourage ordinary people to take part in rebuilding their country, and to "ensure . . . the accountability" of those who held power in society. But the specific steps he had in mind represented a direct attack on the powers of the conservative Party *apparatchiks* who were already most nervous about reform.

The call to Sakharov cannot have made it any simpler for Gorbachev to carry the argument. It was a reminder of how profoundly the rules of Soviet politics had changed in twenty-one months—and none of those changes would have struck a conservative Party official as personally beneficial to him. Another sign of disturbing change was the first ethnic rioting of the Gorbachev era, in Kazakhstan. On the very day that Gorbachev telephoned Sakharov, the Party announced the retirement of Dinmukhamed Kunayev, a member of the Politburo and first secretary of the Party organization in Kazakhstan, in Central Asia. According to tradition, an ethnic Kazakh would have been appointed to succeed Kunayev, but in this case tradition was ignored. Moscow announced that Gennadi Kolbin, a member of the Chuvash minority, whom the Kazakhs considered a Russian, would be the new first secretary in Alma Ata.* Young Kazakhs immediately took to the streets of the capital city to protest.

Kunayev was one of the most corrupt local potentates of the Brezhnev era. He ran his republic for two decades through a giant clan of associates, all of whom exploited their Party or state positions for personal gain. He was also a symbol of the fast-disappearing old status quo; after his departure, the only Brezhnev man running an important republic was Shcherbitsky in the Ukraine. Kunayev's allies in Alma Ata, realizing their own vulnerability, helped to organize the protests, which ultimately involved scores of thousands of demonstrators and considerable violence. Both police and demonstrators were killed—how many has never been disclosed.

In this atmosphere the Soviet Union began to experience real politics, something it had not known in any recognizable form since Stalin consolidated his power in the late 1920s. The orderly, ritualized patterns that Stalin had established and all his successors had respected were beginning to break down. The most startling evidence of this was the January 1987 plenum of the Central Committee.

Great struggles surrounded the preparation of that meeting. Gorbachev subsequently disclosed that "we postponed the beginning of the plenum three times, because we couldn't hold it without having a clear idea of the main issues." According to Dusko Doder and Louise Branson,† Gorbachev met with members of the Central Committee one at a time that December and January at his dacha outside Moscow, trying to persuade each to follow him into the next stage of his reconstruction of Soviet society. That would have been characteristic; Gorbachev has always put great stock in his ability to change people's minds. During December *Pravda* editorialized about the operations of Party organs, criticizing resistance to change and the tendency of Party officials to make unilateral decisions overriding economic enterprises and the opinions of the workers—a hint of what the argument

---

* Kazakhs actually constitute a minority of the population in their huge but sparsely populated republic. Russians and other Slavs who have migrated to the republic since the early nineteenth century now constitute a majority of its residents.

† *Gorbachev, Heretic in the Kremlin*, New York, 1990.

was about. According to Giulietto Chiesa* of *L'Unità* who had good sources in Moscow at the time, at one meeting of the senior leadership Gorbachev was given a selection of letters sent by Party members to the Central Committee complaining of the disruptive consequences of *perestroika* thus far. Someone—Chiesa does not say who—made "a peremptory request [to Gorbachev] to drastically review the tendencies thus far followed, or alternatively, to acknowledge the impossibility of the situation and resign 'for health reasons' if need be. Gorbachev turned down the request; my health 'is excellent,' he replied sharply; there are 'no alternatives' to the line taken."

When the plenum finally took place at the end of January, the reason for the postponements was clear. Gorbachev's intention was to escalate his criticism of the Party's contribution to the stagnation of the country while demanding sweeping structural changes, almost all of them at the expense of the power of Party officials. How much, if at all, he tempered his report after the debates with comrades preceding the plenum is not known; as delivered, the report shows little sign of tempering.

Despite the Party's decision to face up to past shortcomings and turn the country in a new direction, Gorbachev said at the beginning of his report, "The further we go with our reorganization work . . . more and more unresolved problems inherited from the past appear." They could only be dealt with by a commitment to further restructuring, but "there is still some misunderstanding in society and in the Party about the complexity of the situation in which the country finds itself." Evidence of this were the questions "from some comrades" about whether "we are not making too sharp a turn." No, the turn was not too sharp, he insisted.

He then launched into an unprecedented attack on the Party itself for the trouble the country was in: "The main cause [of the current problems]—and the Politburo considers it necessary to say so with utmost frankness at this plenary meeting—was that the Central Committee and the leadership of the country failed, primarily for subjective reasons [i.e., because of their own mistakes], to see in time and in full the need for change and the danger of the intensification of crisis phenomena in society, and to formulate a clear policy for overcoming them. . . . Comrades, it is the leading bodies of the Party and the state that bear responsibility for this."

---

* In his book with Roy Medvedev, *Time of Change,* New York, 1990.

He went on to attack the system he inherited—the Stalinist system of rigid central control and inflexible orthodoxy. Gorbachev called it authoritarian and "absolutized," based on "ossified" concepts and simplistic interpretations of Lenin's ideas of socialism. "Spurious notions of communism" gained currency, he said—"such ideas were actually equated with the essential characteristics of socialism."

As a result of these errors, the economy faltered, the society suffered a moral decline, corruption flourished, and ordinary Communists were denied the opportunity to voice their opinions, or suggestions for improving things. All that was deplorable, Gorbachev said, and left the Soviet Union in a grave state. His analysis showed "how serious the situation was . . . and how urgent was the need for deep changes." He reminded his audience, which must have found this entire presentation deeply disquieting, that the Party had already "found within itself the strength and courage to take a sober view of the situation" and "to admit the need for drastic changes." There was no turning back now: "We need to make this decisive turn because we just don't have the choice of another way. We must not retreat—we have nowhere to retreat to."

This was an early public view of the basic Gorbachev political personality that would emerge in this new period of real politics. When others lost stomach for the crusade, he would be there to press ahead —even at times when he could not have known just where he was going. That is probably the essence of leadership in a revolutionary situation—the willingness to push forward even in dark moments, when the objective is only vaguely visible, because the consequences of giving up seem too painful. At this difficult juncture, twenty-two months after coming to power, Gorbachev found himself battling against the very people who had made him general secretary, telling them the country's woes were their fault, insisting that they help him put things right by relinquishing their own power. "Some Party leaders . . . cannot yet give up the control functions," he said ominously. "They want to decide all questions for everyone and keep a tight grip on things."

"The further democratization of Soviet society is the Party's urgent task," Gorbachev announced—and he meant giving people a serious voice in their own affairs, from shop floor to central government and Communist Party bureaucracy. "Some comrades apparently find it hard to understand that democratization is not just a slogan but the essence of perestroika." This meant multicandidate elections for state and Party offices, and for management positions in enterprises. In Party elections, Gorbachev said, "comrades suggest that secretaries, including first secretaries, could be elected by secret ballot at the plenary sessions of the Party committees. In that case members of the Party committee would have a right to propose any number of candidates." His use of the phrase "comrades suggest" indicated that there was no consensus yet on this radical point, but Gorbachev pushed it nevertheless.

Why this emphasis on democracy? Gorbachev offered "a simple and lucid thought" to explain: "A house can be put in order only by a person who feels that he owns the house." It is the same point Gorbachev made in December, 1984, when he called for *glasnost,* democracy, and "socialist self-government by the people." This may be Gorbachev's one essential idea. It is also his solution to the problem of legitimacy. If the old ways produced results as bad as those he described, then they *deserved* to lose the support of the people. Only revitalized state and Party organs based on the expressed consent of citizens and Party members could legitimately reclaim the right to lead the country.

In his long report to that plenum Gorbachev had lots more to say to annoy his audience. He defended the need for more *glasnost* as an important part of "normalizing the atmosphere in society," and said there should be more criticism of abuses of power, not less. "There should be no zones closed to criticism." The time had come to make personnel changes that had been put off in some cases "for decades." Now "the top echelons of state and Party leadership should be open to an influx of fresh forces." People who were not members of the Party should have greater opportunities to fill important positions. Some officials would have to be removed from high posts and given jobs "that would correspond to their abilities." Many in the hall could have assumed—no doubt correctly—that Gorbachev was talking about them.

Having failed to win approval for all the changes he was ready to make, Gorbachev told the plenum he had a new idea—to convene a "Party Conference," a sort of mini-Congress, to evaluate conditions midway through the five-year plan that was approved at the 27th Party Congress in February 1986. This was an attempt to go over the Central Committee's head by convening a larger body of Party activists. In an astounding display of real politics—which seemed at the time to be an ominous sign of Gorbachev's weakness—the plenum ignored this proposal; the final resolution didn't mention it. Nor did the resolution pick up Gorbachev's ideas for secret ballots and multicandidate elections in Party bodies. But it did include a long passage echoing Gorbachev's report that blamed the Party itself for the country's shortcomings—a painful portion of humble pie.

Meetings of the Central Committee were traditionally closed affairs. In the past it was common for ordinary citizens to be given only the briefest account of what went on inside a plenum. But on this occasion Gorbachev ignored all precedent and put his closing speech to the gathering on national television. The documents of this plenum, including his report and the final resolution, would also be published, but the televised closing speech would reach vastly more people. Gorbachev used it to provide his own version of what had happened.

He began by declaring a success. The plenum had advanced the cause of *perestroika.* To be truly successful, its decisions would have to be put into effect by the people, but it offered new opportunities. *"Perestroika* is no stroll on a well-beaten path. It is an ascent, often through untrodden paths." But there can be no turning back—the fate of the country is now "linked to *perestroika."*

Then he blithely ignored the hesitancy of the Central Committee to adopt all his proposals, pretending that they had fully endorsed them: "The people need the whole truth. . . . The Communist Party is firmly of the opinion that the people should know everything. Openness, criticism and self-criticism, and control exercised by the masses are guarantees of the healthy development of Soviet society." Using vague language, he implied that the plenum supported his suggestion for a Party Conference: "Members of the Central Committee have spoken in favor" of such an event, he said—not noting that a majority declined to support the proposal.

The most vivid passage of the speech was devoted to the idea he cared most about: "We need democracy like air. If we fail to realize this, or if we do realize it but take no serious steps to . . . draw the country's working people into the process of *perestroika,* our policy will get choked, and *perestroika* will fade away, comrades."

•   •   •

In hindsight, 1987 looks like a period of political guerrilla war. Gorbachev was still outnumbered in the Central Committee and in the Politburo when it came to his most radical plans. But majorities in both bodies had endorsed the idea of reform, and he seemed determined to make them define the term as he did. Until he could do that, he would advance on other fronts, exploiting the power available to the general secretary and his closest comrades.

From the beginning, Gorbachev, Yakovlev, Shevardnadze, and their helpers were more resourceful and inventive than their conservative opponents. In this guerrilla phase, they operated on the understanding that they might not yet control all the levers of political power, but they could control the political environment. This was traditionally a key aspect of Soviet power. The myths that had sustained the system from Stalin through Chernenko were propped up by the enormous state propaganda machine, which chose the ideas—and plays, books, movies, television shows, and so on—that would reach the public. So for decades the political environment was stultifying. The rigid prevailing orthodoxy set the tone of public life; the predictability of official ritual reflected the predictability of the environment. The taboos of the official culture, strictly enforced by the propaganda apparatus, preserved the orthodoxy.

Gorbachev began to challenge the inherited orthodoxy as soon as he came into office, abandoning long-cherished prohibitions against any serious criticism of Party rule. By late 1986 and early 1987, he and his allies in the Party and in the intelligentsia were behaving a little like mischievous boys set loose in a giant china closet, shattering taboos while obviously relishing the sound of the breakage. The release of *Repentance* was perhaps the single biggest contribution to this effort, but there were many, many more. Literary breakthroughs occurred almost weekly. In January the writers' union—still dominated by conservatives, but no longer monolithic—announced creation of a commission to oversee the publication of Boris Pasternak's *Doctor Zhivago*. Announcing this, Moscow Radio for the first time reported the news that Pasternak had won the Nobel Prize for Literature in 1958 in recognition of *Zhivago*, a novel about the Bolshevik Revolution and its impact on the country that was a literary event all over the world when it first appeared—but not in the Soviet Union. Two long-suppressed anti-Stalinist poems were published, Alexander Tvardovsky's "By Right of Memory" and Anna Ahkmatova's "Requiem." A powerful novel of the 1930s, Anatoli Rybakov's *Children of the Arbat,* was published in three installments between April and June, twenty-one years after it was first scheduled to be published in *Novy Mir*—and then rejected by the censor. It was the first modern novel published in the Soviet Union to draw a detailed portrait of

Stalin as a manipulative and paranoid human being, not a political icon. The novel meant more to older people who remembered the thirties than to the young, but it was the talk of the intelligentsia for months.

Novy Mir published two outspoken articles on economics early in the year, both of which caused sensations. The first, by Vasili Selyunin and Grigori Khanin, documented the way official economic statistics had been manipulated and even invented for five decades, so that they were now utterly unreliable. The authors urged that official figures not be used as the basis for planning economic reform. Their article made it clear that the economy was in much worse shape than even Gorbachev-era statistics might suggest.

The second article, by Nikolai Shmelyov, was even more devastating. "I understand what kind of reproaches I am inviting," Shmelyov wrote, "but the question is far too serious and vitally important for me to soften my language and resort to silence." The Soviet economy has been operating "in defiance . . . of the laws of economic life" since the 1920s, with this result:

> Today we have an economy in deficit, unbalanced in practically all respects and unmanageable in many, and—if we are to be completely honest—we have an unyielding planned economy that still does not accept technological progress. Industry today rejects up to 80 percent of newly approved technical solutions and inventions! Our labor productivity is among the lowest of all industrialized countries, especially in agriculture and construction. During the years of stagnation the working masses displayed a nearly complete lack of interest in full-blooded, honest labor. . . . Apathy and indifference, stealing and disrespect for honest work have all become commonplace, along with aggressive envy of those who earn a lot, even if they earn it honestly. Indications of an almost physical degradation have appeared in a significant part of the nation because of drunkenness and idleness. . . . We must call things by their true names: stupidity is stupidity, incompetence is incompetence, and active Stalinism is active Stalinism."

The solution, Shmelyov wrote, can only be found in reliance on market forces and price reform that will create a meaningful relationship between costs, supply and demand, and the prices of goods.*

---

* Shmelyov is a well-connected member of the élite. His first wife was Nikita Khrushchev's granddaughter, and he had many friends in high places. Before publishing this article in *Novy Mir*, I was told by a reliable informant, he showed a draft personally to a number of members of

Early 1987 also saw the beginnings of an intense debate about Soviet history. The playwright Mikhail Shatrov played an important part here; he wrote a number of plays set in the early years of the Revolution that tried to come to grips with distorted chapters in official history. One, *The Dictatorship of Conscience,* was being performed at the Vakhtangov Theater at the beginning of the year.

Shatrov was one of the founders of a new theatrical union, and addressed an opening conference of the organization in December 1986. This interesting session was attended by the entire top Party leadership, who heard Shatrov say: "We realized the truth about [the corrupting influence of power] when deviations from the ideals of the October Revolution had to be paid for in millions of human lives, in moral devastation, the spread of slavish psychology, and the onset of social and political apathy." Shatrov quoted Tolstoy to the effect that those who are reluctant to examine the past must still be infected by it. And he recalled, "In the mid-1970s my students often asked me: 'Why didn't everything change in 1956 [at the time of the 20th Party Congress]? Where were you? What did you write then? How did you help the Party?' Let us now, without further delay, do everything in our power to exclude the necessity of asking anybody such questions ever again," he concluded.

Also at the turn of the year Yuri Afanasyev became rector of the Moscow State Institute of Historian-Archivists. He gave a tough inaugural address attacking the "servile cowardice" of official historians in the past and their "regrettably too slow" reaction to change in the Gorbachev era. Historical textbooks, he said, "present a one-sided, crippled picture of many events in the actual history of the Communist Party of the Soviet Union, while they pass over many other things simply in silence." In an interview soon after giving that speech, Afanasyev told the newspaper *Sovetskaya Kultura* (Soviet Culture) that it was time for Soviet historians to begin looking at Stalin's crimes. "It is hard to believe the statement that the mass repressions against honest Soviet people in the 1930s were some kind of mistake or shortcoming," he said. In the spring of 1987 Afanasyev's institute held a series of public lectures on Soviet history that attracted large audiences and intense interest. The lectures included electrifying details of the horrors of the Soviet past.

the Politburo. According to my informant, Gorbachev, Yakovlev, and Ligachev all reacted positively to it. This was an indication of Ligachev's own complex views. He shared Gorbachev's evaluation of the economic crisis, and favored strong action to ease it. It was on cultural and political issues that he was markedly more conservative.

Mass media aimed at much broader audiences were also shattering old taboos by describing real problems besetting Soviet society. *Pravda* and *Izvestia* both published statistics on drug addiction in the Soviet Union. (The number of "frequent users" of narcotics rose from 75,000 in 1984 to 123,000 in early 1987, *Izvestia* reported.) *Ogonyok* published articles on gangs of young toughs roaming the streets of Moscow, beating up people whose looks they didn't like; on police brutality and torture; and on homelessness. *Sovetskaya Rossiya* (Soviet Russia) reported that there were 3,500 prostitutes working in Moscow. Several major papers began writing about AIDS in the Soviet Union. All of this was unprecedented for readers of the Soviet press.

Even more startling were criticisms of the privileges of the powerful that were published that spring. *Sovetskaya Rossiya* criticized special schools in Moscow that, it said, had become havens for the children of the élite. It reported that only 6 percent of the students in special schools were the children of workers, and said the parents who sent their children to them were breeding feelings of superiority. Many of the children became arrogant and succumbed to a "money-grubbing spirit," the paper said. *Moskovskaya Pravda,* organ of the Moscow Party committee, then headed by Boris Yeltsin, attacked the misuse of limousines by officials to whom they were allocated, saying those who abused the privilege of a car and driver should lose it.

Television also started to become interesting. New programs presented realistic discussions of emotional issues—something never seen before. Programs like *Twelfth Floor* and later *View,* mixing interviews, filmed news reports, rock music, and more, attracted tens of millions of viewers and were the talk of the country.

And there was political ferment. In February the government announced that 140 political prisoners would be released, and the cases of 140 more would be reexamined. Sakharov, playing his traditional role as a kind of national ombudsman, confirmed that large numbers of prisoners held for political reasons were being freed, though he could cite others who still languished in captivity. New informal groups and new publications began to appear as well. Not all of them were liberal. The most vocal new group, Pamyat (Memory), had a reactionary, nationalistic platform, and many in its ranks were rabidly anti-Semitic. In May the group organized a march of about six hundred people in central Moscow. To the amazement of many Muscovites, Yeltsin and the mayor of Moscow received the demonstrators and discussed their demands.

Mao Zedong taught guerrillas the importance of taking away the countryside from their city-bound enemies, so they could then squeeze the citadels of power. The guerrillas of *glasnost* and *perestroika* were doing something comparable by depriving orthodox Communists of the political and intellectual surroundings in which they had grown up, and which they had so long taken for granted. They had thrived in a sea of lies; their power grew from myths. Now even the official newspapers were exposing the myths. The Soviet past, it turned out, was not a succession of glorious triumphs; the Party did not always embody the people's interests; the society it ruled was not egalitarian or even moral in many instances; the great socialist economy was far from great—was in fact a mess. The guerrillas scored great successes—more significant, I believe, than they realized—by laying all these unpleasant truths on the record. They changed the vocabulary of political discussion, throwing the conservatives on the defensive while depriving them of their most reliable arguments.

The sheer quantity of new information was as powerful as its quality. Westerners cannot easily appreciate how quiet Soviet life had become in the long period of stagnation. Even when interesting things happened, they came slowly, one at a time. Suddenly the entire political culture was overloaded with new information and new opinions. It was a struggle to keep up, even for intellectuals who were used to reading a great deal. In the old days there might have been half a dozen interesting things to read in all the Soviet newspapers in the course of a week. By the first months of 1987 there were often dozens of interesting items every day—plus good movies to see, and plays, and television programs. All of this was very exciting, but exhausting. Not since the years right after the Revolution had Russia seen anything like it.

•   •   •

Real politics were ambiguous, a fact that made many Russians uncomfortable. Lenin had written of political struggle, of two steps forward and one step back, but contemporary Russians had no experience with such uncertainty. They were used to politics held under control, politics guided from the center.

Gorbachev was walking a precarious path—sticking to it would be his preoccupation for the next four years. He was trying to reorganize his country at the expense of the Party's powers; none of his goals was more important than taking Party officials out of decision-making roles in governmental and economic institutions, replacing their control with democratic procedures. But he was trying to accomplish this in a society still ruled by the Party, as a leader whose authority came from his position as Party general secretary! It was almost a circus trick, as Evgeny Velikhov, vice president of the Academy of Sciences, put it later. He wanted to jump from the driver's seat of one cart (the Party) to the driver's seat of another (his new, democratic state), while both careered along at full speed. And both were pulled by the same horse—Russia.

Scholars will debate for years to come whether Gorbachev acted as a revolutionary who knew the system had to be transformed, or as a reformer who thought it could be perfected. It may be an irresoluble debate. It was clear from at least the December 1984 speech onward that Gorbachev planned to make fundamental changes—changes that would inevitably bring the transformation of Soviet society. But I think he has always considered himself a good Communist and a faithful Leninist—I'm sure he considers himself a better Communist than the orthodox Party men he had to push out of the way to achieve his goals. He has never stopped quoting Lenin, or defending Lenin's vision. Nor has he ever lost confidence in his own ability to persuade others to follow him and adopt his point of view—what one senior official calls Gorbachev's "missionary quality."

If you believed, as the historian Yuri Afanasyev was arguing publicly in early 1987, that the entire Soviet enterprise got off on the wrong track when Stalin abandoned Lenin's New Economic Policy (NEP) * and organized a new system based on total central control, then you could consider yourself a good Communist even as you tried to destroy everything Stalin had built. And that, roughly speaking, really was everything—every significant structure in Soviet society was an invention of the Stalinist years, from the state planning commission to the collective farm.

Gorbachev never acknowledged that his goals were so grand. On the contrary, in 1987, though he had taken the plunge for democratization at the January plenum despite fierce Party opposition, Gorbachev was also trying to reassure the Party by showing respect for its concerns. He was playing a double game: encouraging the guerrilla war, but simultaneously trying to persuade its victims that he remained on their side of the barricades.

There was a hint of this in February, when Gorbachev, Yakovlev

---

* The NEP was Lenin's attempt to merge market stimuli with socialism, and it was having considerable success when Stalin abruptly replaced it with a highly centralized system of controls and the first five-year plan.

and Ligachev met with senior editors of Soviet newspapers—a forum Gorbachev would use repeatedly in the years to come. The atmosphere in Moscow was nervous; rumors circulated about the opposition Gorbachev faced before and during the January plenum; the guerrilla warriors of *glasnost* lived with constant anxiety that they might be sent back to their barracks peremptorily at any moment. The calling of this meeting for February 12 raised the liberals' anxieties.

The full text of Gorbachev's fifty-minute talk at the beginning of the session wasn't published, though a long account was broadcast on radio. Yegor Yakovlev, the editor of *Moscow News,* published a description of the session in his newspaper. Both accounts demonstrate the cautious line Gorbachev followed, trying simultaneously to reassure the liberals fighting for reform and the conservatives who were so afraid of it. He firmly reiterated that there was no other course but his, that *glasnost,* including criticism of both past and present, were indispensable. But much more of what he said seemed to be intended to reassure Party officials that Gorbachev would continue to admire and to protect them, and to respect what they cared about.

Don't cast certain people as enemies, Gorbachev said: "There aren't that many direct and open opponents of *perestroika.* There are a certain number of people who don't know how to work in the new way. . . . They must be taught. . . . Our whole society is on one side of the barricades." And don't make ad hominem criticisms that aren't relevant, Gorbachev said, citing the example of a television program that had singled out a collective farm chairman, not for running the farm poorly but for repairing the roof of his house (presumably with the farm's supplies). "Well," said Gorbachev, "is the chairman supposed to live without a roof?" He cautioned the editors that it wouldn't be fair only to blame Party officials for shortcomings in society—under *perestroika,* the Party should no longer be held responsible for every shortage of railroad ties or every puddle in the road; there were relevant government officials responsible for such things.

Yegor Yakovlev added two intriguing details in his account of the meeting. First—this must have been an "authorized leak"—he quoted Gorbachev as saying that if the January plenum had come to the conclusion that *perestroika* had failed and should be rejected, "I would have said: I cannot work any other way." In other words, he would have threatened—or perhaps he did threaten?—to resign. This would have been proof to the assembled editors that the battle preceding the plenum was deadly serious. Second, Yakovlev quoted an un-named participant, presumably a conservative editor, as saying, "We must heighten exactingness with an iron hand." Gorbachev replied, "Not with an iron hand—with an intelligent one." These anecdotes would have reassured the liberal readers of *Moscow News*.

Gorbachev was conducting this balancing act at the same time he was trying to put himself near the ever-shifting center of a new polit-ical spectrum—or so it seems in retrospect. Later he made almost a fetish of finding a compromise course between extremes; this inclina-tion first appeared in 1987, when he may have felt that keeping a visible part of the political culture to his left helped make his own position look more reasonable and responsible.

Boris Yeltsin was Gorbachev's left wing, at least in the Politburo. There was no shortage of intellectuals, journalists, and writers whom Gorbachev could portray as more liberal than himself, but Yeltsin was the only senior politician in that category. It was widely assumed—wrongly, judging by the book Yeltsin published in 1990—that he and Gorbachev were personally close.* When he became Moscow Party secretary late in 1985, Muscovites (and Kremlinologists) assumed that Gorbachev had installed his own man to run the capital for him. Yeltsin quickly established himself as an ardent proponent of both *perestroika* and *glasnost,* and as a populist. He did this by riding the subway to work, visiting Muscovites in their homes and workplaces, and making clear his disdain for old-line *apparatchiks.*

Yeltsin was by far the most colorful political figure of the Gorbachev era. A towering hulk of a man with thick white hair, his good looks and dominating manner quickly set him apart. But he was a man of humble origins, which he had not forgotten, and could quickly convey an empathy for ordinary people that they readily understood.

Yeltsin was born in 1931 in a village near Sverdlovsk, nine hundred miles east of Moscow. In his early years his family lived in a large dormitory while his father worked as a construction laborer; they never had their own home, and Yeltsin remembered those years as extremely difficult. He did well in school, but often got into trouble. When he was eleven, soon after the war broke out, he sneaked through barbed-wire barriers into a local church that had been converted into

---

* Yeltsin describes many contacts with Gorbachev dating back to the late seventies which suggest that they were never intimate. He writes that Gorbachev always addressed him as *ty,* or "thou," the familiar form of "you" that Russians use for family members and close friends, but that this always made Yeltsin uncomfortable.

an armory and stole two hand grenades. He and several friends took the grenades into the forest, where young Boris volunteered to take them apart. He struck one with a hammer; it exploded, and the thumb and little finger of his left hand were mangled by the blast. They later had to be removed.

Graduating from the Soviet equivalent of primary school at thirteen or fourteen, Yeltsin—an all-A student—asked if he could say a few words. Permission was granted, and, by his account, he launched into an attack on the cruel and manipulative woman who had been his home room teacher. His unexpected assault broke up the graduation ceremony; soon afterward Boris's parents were notified that his diploma had been rescinded. Yeltsin refused to accept that punishment, and appealed to the local authorities, including the Party committee, which set up an inquiry. The teacher was fired, and Yeltsin got his diploma.

He later won a place at the Urals Polytechnic Institute, where he studied engineering and played volleyball. The volleyball was the most important part of his student life—it took up six hours a day. After graduating with a degree in engineering, he was offered a job as a construction foreman, but decided it would be "a great mistake to go straight into a job that put me in charge of men and construction work without my having acquired direct experience. I was certain I would find life very difficult if any work-team leader could—deliberately or not—twist me around his little finger, since his practical knowledge of the job would be so much greater than mine."

As Yeltsin tells the story in his book, he decided he should spend his first year mastering the twelve basic construction trades, from bricklaying to carpentry to plumbing—a month for each. Then he agreed to become a foreman. He spent the next thirteen years as a construction engineer building things in Sverdlovsk. Only in his mid-thirties was he recruited into Party work, first to head the section of the local Party committee responsible for construction.

Yeltsin obviously had a natural politician's personality, but this biography also helped him enormously. He had grown up in the Soviet version of the real world, not in the cocoon of the Party. He knew how to build with his own hands. He had a good athlete's self-confidence. All of this set him apart from the standard-issue *apparatchik* in ways that ordinary people sensed at once. There is something earthy and real about Boris Yeltsin that draws people to him.

Yeltsin lived up to his radical reputation in the early months of

1987. For example, he gave *Moskovskaya Pravda,* his local paper, an outspoken interview in April, laying into the *apparatchiks* who stood in the way of reform. He ridiculed "Party ceremonial," saying: "In recent years many leaders have outdone even the clergy in ritualism. They know at what point to clap, when to say what, how to greet the authorities, and what décor to put up for an event. This is the invention of wheeler-dealers and toadies who are trying to keep afloat." Any Soviet citizen could recognize the type, and many must have loved Yeltsin for deflating it.

In the same interview the unnamed journalist questioning Yeltsin read from a letter he said the newspaper had received from "an elderly Muscovite, the wife of a *nomenklatura* [senior] official."* It was quite a letter. "Don't snipe at us," she wrote. "Surely it's clear that this is futile. We are the élite, and you cannot halt the stratification of society. You are not strong enough. We will rip up the puny sails of your *perestroika* and you will be unable to reach your destination. So moderate your ardor." Printing this anonymous threat was calculated to evoke popular anger. Yeltsin barely deigned to acknowledge the woman's comments. "She's talking about privileges," he said, then went on to assure readers that he was fighting for "social justice."

If Yeltsin was on the left, Ligachev was emerging more and more clearly as a man of the right—so much so that many Gorbachev supporters among Moscow intellectuals wondered why Gorbachev relied on him. In March Ligachev was in Saratov, speaking to local intellectuals on his view of *glasnost* and democracy. His remarks, broadcast on national television, included praise for the effects of *glasnost* and democratization, but Ligachev also used terms that never came from Gorbachev's mouth. For example, he criticized "attempts to reduce the leading role of state management in the cultural sphere." He said "wholesale disparagement of everything is impermissible," since even in the time of stagnation, "there were splendid works of literature and art that truthfully reflected glorious pages in our motherland's history." He decried the appearance of "elements of mass bourgeois culture" in Soviet art, and said Soviet classics should not be denigrated just because "many works that previously were unknown to the broad public for one reason or another recently have been published and shown." Conservative literary bureaucrats on the secretariat of

---

* Traditionally, all senior state and Party positions were part of the *nomenklatura;* anyone occupying one of those posts had to be appointed by Party organs.

the Russian Republic's Union of Writers reacted enthusiastically to Ligachev's signal a fortnight later, denouncing *Ogonyok,* the publication of Pasternak, and "opportunists" who were using reform to advance themselves.

To keep yet another of his political balls in play, Gorbachev authorized the arrest in February of Yuri Churbanov, Brezhnev's former son-in-law, who had been deputy minister of the Interior. He was charged with embezzlement and abuse of power. This too was a signal to local Party organs, warning that the crackdown on corruption would continue.

With all this going on around him, Gorbachev stuck to his diplomatic offensive. In February he made yet another major concession to the United States, agreeing to separate completely the issue of intermediate-range missiles (Soviet SS-20s and U.S. Pershing IIs and cruise missiles) from negotiations on longer-range weapons. Since both sides had already said they wanted an agreement banning these weapons entirely from Europe, the way seemed clear to reach an agreement. (It was signed in December when Gorbachev went to Washington for the first time.) In May, visiting Prague, Gorbachev put short-range nuclear weapons on the table, and urged accelerating talks on reduction in conventional forces in Europe. For the first time, he acknowledged that the Warsaw Pact had a numerical advantage in troop strength.

•　　•　　•

The untoward event in the spring of 1986 had been Chernobyl—hardly welcome, though Gorbachev had found ways to turn it to his advantage. The unexpected occurrence of spring 1987 created a more straightforward opportunity, and Gorbachev exploited it so effectively that you might have thought he had planned the whole thing.

May 28 is a minor holiday in the Soviet Union: Border Guards' Day, in honor of the considerable force—a branch of the KGB—that stands guard along the nation's long borders. It isn't clear whether young Mathias Rust knew of this holiday in advance, but it was a nice ironic touch that he picked it for his amazing flight from Helsinki, Finland, to Red Square. The nineteen-year-old pilot, flying a rented Cessna 172, a single-engine plane not designed for international missions of surpassing geopolitical significance, performed one of the great debunking acts of the Cold War epoch. No early-warning radars or interceptor forces deterred his craft, which flew across the Soviet border with Estonia, just south of Leningrad, and proceeded 420 miles farther into the center of Moscow. After buzzing the astounded crowds in Red Square three times and passing very close to the green dome of the Old Senate building inside the Kremlin walls—where Gorbachev had an office—Rust landed his tiny craft on cobblestones at the edge of the Square, next to St. Basil's Cathedral.

The Soviet government would say later that radar did pick up Rust's Cessna, and Soviet interceptors did check him out in the sky, but then inexplicably did nothing, allowing him to proceed to the capital. No official word of the plane's landing was forthcoming for twenty-four hours after Rust was taken into police custody. Gorbachev was in East Berlin when the plane landed, meeting with his allies from the Warsaw Pact. He hurried home, and two days after the incident convened an emergency meeting of the Politburo. That night viewers of *Vremya,* the evening news broadcast, were stunned by unusually strong language: the Politburo had accused the Defense Ministry of "a major dereliction of duty," and fired both the minister of defense, Marshal Sergei Sokolov, and the commander of the air defense forces, Marshal Alexander Koldunov. (Eventually, about two hundred more officers would lose their jobs or be expelled from the Party because of the incident.) Dmitri Yazov, an obscure Soviet general recently transferred from the Far East to headquarters in Moscow, was promoted over at least twenty more senior officers to become the new defense minister.

Until then Gorbachev had made no significant changes in the military establishment he inherited. The status of the armed services was clearly diminished; unlike his recent predecessors, Sokolov was never made a full member of the Politburo. (He was a nonvoting candidate member at the time he was fired.) As I noted earlier, there were signs that senior officers were not pleased with Gorbachev's continuing arms-control offensive. Now—because of a genuine bolt from the blue —the military establishment had been publicly humiliated. Gorbachev was able to bring in a man—Yazov—who had to realize that he owed his new exalted status entirely to Gorbachev. The two had apparently met on a recent Gorbachev trip to the Soviet Far East; they were not close associates. This bit of speedy improvisation proved enormously useful in the next few years, as Gorbachev took a series of steps that undoubtedly upset many senior officers, but which they were helpless to prevent. As time passed, however, Yazov's mediocre qualities undermined his credibility, and in 1989 Gorbachev had to

intervene personally to prevent the new Supreme Soviet from rejecting his nomination as minister of defense.

The new czar was tough—no Russian would have missed that message from the Rust affair. It was the kind of decisive political gesture
that has gone out of fashion among the world's statesmen, which made
it all the more noteworthy. Gorbachev built his reputation steadily,
one surprise at a time, and different audiences reacted at different
speeds to the idea that there was a qualitatively new type of Soviet
leader in Moscow. But this was one of the turning points no one would
forget.

It came at an opportune moment. After more than two years of
discussion, Gorbachev and his team were finally ready to introduce
what they considered a concrete plan for economic reform. At the
June 1987 plenum of the Central Committee, the general secretary
made another of his roundhouse speeches, confronting his opponents
and those who refused to take *perestroika* seriously with a barrage of
arguments and statistics. We're not stopping, he told them all fear-
lessly—we're going farther than ever before.

This audacity was Gorbachev's largest contribution to the real politics of 1987 and afterward. For generations Soviet politics had been
governed by an unspoken system of constraints: such-and-such just
isn't done, words like that just aren't used, some problems are better
left unmentioned, and so on. The old political culture was powerful;
nearly every one of its members knew and respected the rules. Not
Gorbachev. As a Russian friend of mine put it, he was "the Bobby
Fischer of politics," as disrespectful of Soviet political tradition as the
eccentric American boy genius was heretical about the accepted truths
of chess. The members of the Central Committee must have been
amazed each time they were summoned to another of Gorbachev's
truth-telling performances. Each time he had a new wrinkle to attract
their attention.

At the June 1987 plenum, he started to criticize the failures of his
own tenure. The effects of *perestroika* on the economy thus far were
"insignificant," he declared. In some cases, "positions gained earlier
are even being abandoned"—early improvements have been reversed.
"Take the work to improve discipline and order, for example. It is a
fact that in many places enthusiasm has flagged, and work is being
done in an extremely sluggish fashion. Cases of drunkenness have
become frequent again. Loafers, spongers and pilferers—people who
live at the expense of others—are feeling at ease again."

He also perceived "an alarming tendency" in the failure of some

Party organs to keep up with the pace of reform. "A number of Party organizations are out of touch with the dominant moods, and lagging behind the dynamic moods and the dominant processes now developing in society." Some of this was willful: "The behavior of those who for the sake of their personal advantage impede social transformations and stand in the way of the drive for renewal is particularly unseemly." He named names, too, citing officials who had failed to fulfill their responsibilities, from the head of the State Planning Commission to regional Party secretaries. For example: "Few marked changes for the better have been occurring in the major Gorki Region's Party organization. Many vitally important issues are being tackled there in an unsatisfactory way. . . . It may be presumed that the regional Party committee headed by Comrade Y. N. Khristoradnov . . . will draw conclusions from the criticism and put things right." This had more in common with old-fashioned methods of Party discipline than with the new decentralizing and democratizing Gorbachev also preached about. But Comrade Khristoradnov and the others—aware of the recent fate of Marshal Sokolov, whose performance Gorbachev again criticized at the plenum—surely got the message.

Gorbachev also announced that he had won approval for the convening of a Party Conference the following year—the idea he had tried to bulldoze through the January plenum without success. This time he announced blithely that "the January plenary meeting supported the proposal"—which it hadn't—and now "the Politburo is proposing that the 19th All-Union Conference of the Communist Party" be called on June 28, 1988. Well-informed officials indicated that Gorbachev got his way on this issue after promising not to try to use the conference to make personnel changes. He kept the promise when the Conference took place the next year.

But the most important business of this plenum was economic reform, adopted by the Central Committee and, several days later, by the Supreme Soviet, then still operating in its traditional, rubber-stamp mode. The economists who had worked with senior officials to prepare the reform documents convinced themselves that they had finally gotten a grip on the problem. Abel Aganbegyan, the economist whose candid evaluation of the economic crisis had seemed so radical in 1984—and who had become an important adviser to Gorbachev— said on the day the plenum closed that by approving the reform the Central Committee had initiated "a truly new period of *perestroika,* a period of cardinal breakthroughs."

The idea of the reforms was to break down the centrally planned economy by making every enterprise self-financing, and by replacing the command system of planning with contracts between enterprises and the state, and between enterprises independent of the state. Enterprises would be allowed to decide themselves how to allocate their profits. A new, rational price structure would be introduced. Systems of finance and credit would give enterprises new opportunities to borrow money for investment. Reform would proceed in an orderly manner—"stage by stage," Aganbegyan said—until an entirely new system, with a new, rational price structure, would be in place by 1991. It all looked and sounded neat and tidy.

In his report to the plenum Gorbachev gave a vivid description of the current situation: "An enterprise is given production quotas and is allocated resources [by central authorities]. . . . Virtually all its costs are reimbursed [by the state]. The marketing of the enterprise's output is guaranteed. . . . There is an inadequate link between workers' incomes and the products produced by their enterprise. . . . With the present [economic] mechanism, manufacturers find it disadvantageous to use cheap raw materials and inexpensive products, they find it disadvantageous to improve the quality of their output, they find it disadvantageous to introduce technological innovations. Under such a mechanism, the line between efficient enterprises and those that systematically lag behind is virtually erased."

This was precisely the critique Westerners had been making for years. In the Soviet economy, all that mattered was fulfilling the plan. The planning mechanism offered no effective way to require modernization, to induce efficiency, to heighten product quality. And because shortages were endemic—as Gorbachev put it in his speech to that plenum, "There has been and remains a shortage of everything: metal, fuel, cement, machinery, and consumer goods"—any factory manager knew that he had to use whatever raw materials he could get his hands on, and that he would have no trouble disposing of whatever he produced. As Gorbachev said in that speech, "Our economic mechanism, whether we like it or not, is geared to mediocre or even substandard work."

These were not Gorbachev's first economic reforms. Earlier, new laws had been adopted authorizing "individual work activities" and cooperatives—the first legalized private enterprise in modern times. They went into effect just two months before the plenum, and their impact would prove to be substantial. However, local authorities fought tooth and nail against cooperative enterprises, with a dismaying degree of success. The manager of the first private restaurant in Moscow held an audience of writers at the House of Literature spellbound one evening in the spring of 1987 with an account of the obstacles thrown in his path by city officials. His enterprise at least survived. Many others were simply closed down—most often because they were too successful. Roy Medvedev told the story of a cooperative formed in a seaside town "to manufacture footwear for the beach. . . . A huge demand was discovered, since no one produced this type of article. The cooperative's earnings quickly reached dizzying heights. But the local authorities and part of the populace counterattacked, and the cooperative was closed . . . [because it] earned 'too much.' " Such stories were repeated all over the country.

From January 1, 1987, many enterprises were subjected to a new form of discipline, imposed in the name of reform, known by its Soviet acronym, *Gospryomka,* or "state acceptance." Affected enterprises had to submit their production to independent quality-control inspectors, who were empowered to reject products that didn't meet their standards—and who were held responsible if products shipped by the factory turned out to be poorly made. This of course was the opposite of decentralization, and it caused enormous disruptions when implemented, because production rejected by the new state inspectors could not be counted toward plan fulfillment. Initially the inspectors rejected 15 to 20 percent of everything produced at the first 1,500 enterprises covered by the procedure, but by the end of the year only 10 percent was being rejected.

As Gorbachev said at the June 1987 plenum, only insignificant changes had been made by then. The real work, as he kept saying, lay ahead. But after the plenum, at least, there was a blueprint to follow. At the time, Western specialists were surprised by its boldness. Assurances from Soviets like Aganbegyan, who had a reputation for honesty, convinced many of us that something of real significance had begun.

At the same time, three new full members were added to the Politburo. One of them was Alexander Yakovlev, so we assumed that Gorbachev had gained a clear upper hand, and that the other two new members—Viktor Nikonov and Nikolai Slyunkov—were also Gorbachev loyalists, who helped give him firm control of the ruling body. As it turned out, that was a misreading—Nikonov and Slyunkov may both have been closer to Ryzhkov than to Gorbachev, and they were both technocrats who could not be counted on as supporters of the most radical political reforms. But western Kremlinologists didn't realize that at the time; nor did most Soviets who paid attention to such matters. The June plenum looked like an unqualified triumph for Gorbachev when it ended on June 26.

•   •   •

The excitement of the June plenum could not be sustained; when it ended, Gorbachev once again fell silent, or nearly so. This was now a recurring pattern—periods of intense, creative activity, followed by lulls, sometimes accompanied by a sense of lost momentum. One of my acquaintances who has participated in the exciting events of these years speculated that this is a reflection of Gorbachev's personality, which he called "somewhat manic-depressive." I would not offer this as a psychological diagnosis, but it is a good description of the way Gorbachev has behaved: "manic" periods of remarkable drama, often accompanied by surprising innovations, followed by longer phases of relative calm and apparent withdrawal. That was certainly the case in the summer of 1987, when Gorbachev withdrew from most public activities, and his conservative rivals seized the moment to press a case that was clearly at odds with his platform.

The opponents of reform did what they could that summer to remind Gorbachev—and everyone else—of their strength. For example, when the Supreme Soviet—the old rubber-stamp legislature, now emboldened by the new spirit of the times—met right after the June plenum, the *apparatchiks* were able to water down two legal reforms that seemed to offer the promise of significant change. One was a law on public opinion and governmental decision, originally envisioned as a vehicle to create the possibility for national referenda on major issues. The word "referendum" disappeared from the act as passed. The second was a law to enable citizens to bring lawsuits against officials for abuse of power, which was watered down to the point that it was probably meaningless before finally being approved.

In early July Ligachev, still responsible for ideology, although Yakovlev's elevation to the Politburo was seen as a challenge to his authority, visited the editorial offices of *Sovetskaya Kultura,* one of the leading organs of reform. After a two-day "inspection" he issued a report criticizing the editors, and instructing the paper's writers to remain "profoundly faithful to Party ideology."

Perhaps to reassure his supporters, Gorbachev, accompanied by Yakovlev, called another meeting of editors two days later, and reiterated his carefully drawn middle line. He cautioned the editors not to show "a disrespectful attitude" toward Party officials, but then said there is no room for "callous, insensitive people" in important jobs. He said his economic reforms should not be interpreted as renouncing a centrally planned economy. His most noteworthy comments involved history, then a topical subject because of preparations underway for celebrations of the seventieth anniversary of the Revolution the following November. "I think we will never be able to forgive or justify what happened in 1937–38," he said, speaking of the worst years of Stalin's purges, "and we never should. Never!" But he tempered that remark with assurances that what happened then "does not detract from all we have today" or from "the enormous strength that is to be found in socialism."

In retrospect, the most interesting—and the most accurate—observation Gorbachev made that day involved the style of debate in the newly liberalized environment. "We are now, as it were, going through the school of democracy afresh," he said. "We are learning. Our political culture is still inadequate. Our standard of debate is inadequate. Our ability to respect the point of view of even our friend and comrade—that too is inadequate. We are an emotional people, but we'll get over it. We will grow up."

As if eager to prove Gorbachev's point, the conservatives then launched an offensive against the liberals that was not polite. The deputy editor of one of the right-wing literary journals, *Moladaya Gvardia* (Young Guard), attacked Korotich and *Ogonyok*, Yegor Yakovlev and *Moscow News*, and several others, charging that the editors of the liberal journals were encouraging "shabby tastes" and were toying with "the amorality and the consumerism of Western mass culture." He warned that *glasnost* was "a double-edged sword" that could come back to "hurt the person using it"—the sort of vague threat that was characteristic of the bad old days. He even defended Stalin, quoting approvingly the idea that he was more a victim than a criminal. He criticized historians who don't really explain history, but just demonstrate that "they don't want to forgive Stalin."

In August, when Gorbachev was on vacation and Ligachev was in charge in Moscow, *Pravda*—the most official Party organ—published a full-page article attacking the reopening of old historical issues. *Pravda* suggested that the preoccupation with revelations about Stalin's repressions raised the danger that "we are discrediting the history of the motherland," and declared: "We are proud of every day we have lived." Several days later, speaking in the provincial city of Elektrostal, Ligachev echoed the same line, but more forcefully, denouncing those who "through their talk of unjustified repressions . . . end up overshadowing the achievements of the people who consolidated socialist power in the U.S.S.R." That was simply a defense of Stalinism —far removed from what Gorbachev had been saying on historical subjects.

Viktor Chebrikov, the Andropov man who was running the KGB, finally showed his true colors. In September, in a speech marking the birthday of Felix Dzerzhinsky, Lenin's first political police chief, Chebrikov said: "There are among us carriers of ideas with viewpoints alien to and even openly hostile to socialism," including people "under the influence of the Western secret service." He decried "representatives of the artistic intelligentsia" who were captivated by "hyper-criticism, demagogy and nihilism, and the denigration of certain stages of the historical development of our society." These remarks, too, smacked of ugly periods from the past, when unconventional ideas were inevitably attributed to Western spies and traitors.

Then Ligachev called another meeting of editors in Moscow. According to Giulietto Chiesa, the Moscow correspondent of L'Unità, it was an ominous session.* Part of what Ligachev said was published in Pravda, including criticism of those who were "showing a disrespectful attitude toward the generations who constructed socialism." In his unpublished remarks, Ligachev denounced Korotich, Yegor Yakovlev, Sovetskaya Kultura, and other individuals and publications. Echoing Chebrikov, he said Moscow News, particularly, was providing a voice for "enemies from abroad." Some journalists had "exceeded the limits of the trust given to them." Yegor Yakovlev replied by saying he disagreed with Ligachev's opinions, but adding: "If you ask me to leave, I will." Apparently, this meeting led Yakovlev to write a letter to Gorbachev, on vacation, offering his resignation. Gorbachev urged him to stay on as editor, which he did.

At about the same time, in mid-September, Boris Yeltsin wrote to Gorbachev too, complaining of the treatment he was receiving from Ligachev, and bemoaning the failure of the Party apparat to reform

---

* I have drawn heavily here on Chiesa's excellent book Time of Change, written with Roy Medvedev, the dissident historian who became a member of the Congress of People's Deputies and, in 1990, the Central Committee.

itself. Yeltsin proposed that he resign from the Politburo. Gorbachev did not reply to his suggestion.

Because this was a time of real politics, there were also events that summer that pleased the reformers. Neither conservatives nor liberals could establish a dominant position. In June, Shmelyov, the economist who wrote so outspokenly about the economy in *Novy Mir,* gave a lecture that included statistics never heard before on the number of prisoners held in labor camps from 1937 to 1953 (seventeen million!) and the number of peasants forced off their land during collectivization (five million). *Ogonyok* published details of Stalin's purge of the officer corps on the eve of the Great Patriotic War. Other publications carried accounts of the rehabilitations of a number of Stalin's victims. In June it was announced that new regulations had been adopted that would permit most Soviet citizens to travel abroad with relative ease—something many had been aching to do for decades. A new magazine, cheekily named *Glasnost* but without any official sanction or backing, began to appear in June. In July, Crimean Tatars staged several days of protests on Red Square, and were received cordially by senior government officials. The first exhibit of paintings by the Russian Jewish master Marc Chagall was announced. And this is just a partial listing.

*   *   *   *

Gorbachev had left Moscow in early August for what turned out to be a seven-week vacation. The unusual length of his holiday coupled with the increasing boldness of Ligachev and his allies while it continued eventually provoked a wave of anxious rumors that something terrible had happened to the leader. But the truth turned out to be more interesting than the rumors. Gorbachev had decided to do something no other modern statesman had ever attempted: he would write a book while still in office, explaining his policies. And by all indication he really wrote it himself. No doubt aides contributed, and some of the material was borrowed from his earlier pronouncements, but the book is written in Gorbachev's own unmistakable voice.

The book was *Perestroika: New Thinking for the Country and the World.* Officials acting on Gorbachev's behalf first indicated to Western publishers in October 1986 that he might write a book, and in the spring of 1987 the message was stronger—he planned to write. In September, a manuscript was delivered to Harper & Row, the American publisher that handled world rights to the book outside the Soviet bloc.*

The book is a fascinating document, particularly now that it has been thoroughly overtaken by events—a process that took less than three years. The book is actually more useful as a glimpse of Gorbachev's state of mind and—by implication—his political situation that summer than it is a guide to his strategic thinking. On most points, the rationalizations and explanations in the book were quickly outdated, and in many cases transparently insincere or incomplete.

Perestroika has a surprisingly defensive tone. Gorbachev seems preoccupied with skeptics and critics at home and abroad; he constantly addresses both groups. "There is a view," he writes, "that [perestroika] has been necessitated by the disastrous state of the Soviet economy and that it signifies disenchantment with socialism and a crisis for its ideals and ultimate goals. Nothing could be further from the truth." But Gorbachev the truth teller could not be suppressed. A few pages later, he is describing the crisis facing the Soviet Union in compelling terms: "Any delay in beginning *perestroika* could have led to an exacerbated internal situation in the near future which, to put it bluntly, would have been fraught with serious social, economic and political crises."

When I first read the book in 1987, I felt it was directed first at foreign readers, and that Gorbachev intended it as a primer explaining what he was trying to accomplish. Reading it again three years later—and understanding better the political pressure he was under in 1987—I now think it was primarily intended for a domestic audience. This makes more sense logically. Gorbachev may have known more about the outside world than any previous Soviet leader, but he still knew relatively little, and could hardly have kept an image of American or West European public opinion in his mind as he wrote the book. In fact, the book reads as an extension of his speeches and other public statements in 1987—as part of the political campaign he was conducting to move ahead with reforms that could only come at the expense of the Party *apparat*'s power, but without alienating the Party.

The book is filled with fuzzy formulations obviously intended to reassure comrades that he remained a good Party man who thought good Party thoughts. So Gorbachev writes spirited defenses of Stalin's

---

* *Perestroika* was a publishing sensation. It ultimately sold well over two million copies in forty-odd countries.

forced industrialization and the collectivization of agriculture (both were "indispensable"), but a few pages later declares that "Lenin's ideas were not always adhered to in the years after his death"—meaning during the time of forced industrialization and collectivization. He even repeats the justification for Khrushchev's ouster in 1964 that he gave to his Czech friend Mlynar in 1967: that it was necessary to take "a line toward stabilization" to counter the "extremes" of Khrushchev's rule. He indulges in wishful thinking, writing: "The prestige of and trust in the Party have been growing," and "The Revolution and socialism have done away with national oppression and inequality [among the ethnic groups of the U.S.S.R.] and ensured economic, intellectual and cultural progress for all nations and nationalities."

But there is also outspoken candor from an author who by mid-1987 appeared committed to certain basic principles, even if they did offend some comrades. "Politics is undoubtedly the most important thing in any revolutionary process. This is equally true of *perestroika*. Therefore we attach priority to political measures, broad and genuine democratization, the resolute struggle against red tape and violations of law, and the active involvement of the masses in managing the country's affairs. All this is directly linked with the main question of any revolution, the question of power."

That is a most revealing passage. For years many in the West—and many Russians—accepted the conventional wisdom that Gorbachev's reforms consisted of *perestroika* and *glasnost,* or economic restructuring and openness, truth telling and criticism. Gorbachev understood otherwise, and subsequent events proved him correct. The issue was political power. As he formulated it, the question was whether power would be wielded by an entrenched *apparat,* or democratically, by officials held accountable to the public. At the time, we didn't understand what he was saying—or we weren't ready to believe what he was saying.

The same could be said of two important passages on foreign policy in the book. Gorbachev wrote that "the time is ripe for abandoning views on foreign policy which are influenced by an imperial standpoint. Neither the Soviet Union nor the United States is able to force its will on others. It is possible to suppress, compel, bribe, break, or blast, but only for a certain period. From the point of view of long-term, big-time politics, no one will be able to subordinate others." There in four sentences was Gorbachev's East European policy, and the rationale for it. But when they first appeared we still expected Soviet leaders to use words without any concern for their real meaning; wasn't this passage—as the Soviets might say—just window dressing?

Similarly, in a brief sentence Gorbachev seemed to obliterate the traditional Soviet explanation for East-West tensions—the inevitable confrontation between the working class, represented by Soviet power, and imperialism. Yes, Gorbachev acknowledges, traditionally Marxist philosophy "was dominated . . . by a class-motivated approach," but then thermonuclear weapons appeared, creating "an objective limit for class confrontation in the international arena," because neither capitalists nor workers could risk "universal destruction." Was that an epitaph for the cold war—or more window dressing?

•   •   •

Gorbachev reappeared in public at the end of September. He hadn't been seen for fifty-two days. It still isn't clear whether he was just working on the book, and perhaps also his speech for the forthcoming celebration of the seventieth anniversary of the Revolution, or if some other factor contributed to his absence. Whatever the full explanation, he looked just fine on television on September 29, greeting a large group of visiting Frenchmen. "Some people think I took too long a vacation, but I can tell you that I've earned it," he quipped. If there was a great power struggle going on, it was certainly well hidden. But this was the beginning of the worst period of Gorbachev's first five years; it would last for seven months.

His troubles began in mid-October with another of the unexpected events that were so important in the Gorbachev years. This one began routinely enough as a plenum of the Central Committee devoted to the report Gorbachev would give at the seventieth anniversary celebration. The report was eagerly awaited; intellectuals assumed that Gorbachev would use the occasion to lay down a definitive new Party line on the country's history. Rumors were rife that he would use the occasion to attack Stalin and rehabilitate some of his most prominent victims, beginning with Nikolai Bukharin, the man Lenin had called "the darling of the Party" and who was a candidate to succeed Lenin, when Stalin claimed the mantle. Bukharin had been shot after his conviction in one of the most notorious show trials of 1938.

At that time a Central Committee plenum was an entirely closed affair; no details of such a meeting ever appeared in print. But a year and a half after the event, as part of radically new policies of *glasnost,* a transcript of the October 1987 plenum was published in a new journal called *News of the Central Committee.* There are indications that this transcript is incomplete, but it nevertheless provides a rare glimpse of a spontaneous political event under the traditional rules of Soviet politics. Of course Gorbachev had begun to modify those rules considerably, but basic rituals were still respected, as this transcript shows.

Gorbachev's report to the plenum included frank acknowledgments of Stalin's crimes. He disclosed the number of members of the Politburo and Central Committee, the number of delegates to Party Congresses, and the number of senior military officers who were arrested or killed in the purges. This was obviously a selective enumeration of Stalin's victims, but one well chosen for this audience. Stalin could not be excused on the grounds that he didn't realize what was happening, Gorbachev said, because he knew: "Stalin and his immediate circle are guilty before the Party and the people." Gorbachev implicitly rehabilitated Bukharin by giving a rather detailed description of his true role, and mentioned several other "nonpersons" whose names had been obliterated in all official histories, including Trotsky, Stalin's hated rival. The rest of his long report is much less interesting. But then there was real drama.

As Gorbachev wound up his report, Boris Yeltsin made clear his desire to speak. Ligachev was in the chair, and he tried to deny Yeltsin the floor, but Gorbachev intervened: "Comrade Yeltsin has some kind of announcement to make." Ligachev then allowed Yeltsin to speak.

What followed was brief, disjointed, and historic. Yeltsin had decided to create a sensation. He began by saying he had no comment on Gorbachev's report, but wanted to raise some other matters.

The June plenum, Yeltsin said, was a signal to all Party organizations, beginning with the secretariat of the Central Committee, to "reconstruct" their work, but "I cannot help remarking that although five months have passed since then, nothing has changed in the style of work of either the secretariat of the Central Committee or of Comrade Ligachev. Despite the fact that [Gorbachev] said here today that bullying reprimands are not permissible at any level, they are still used" by Party bosses. "Despite what was said at the Party Congress [twenty months earlier] about what *perestroika* was to achieve in two or three years, two years, or nearly two years, have already passed, and now we are again told that it needs an additional two or three years. This greatly confuses people, the Party and the population as a whole, since we, who are aware of the people's mood, can now sense the tidal wave of their attitudes toward *perestroika.* At first there was a tremendous surge of enthusiasm. . . . Then, after the June plenum of the Central Committee, people's faith began to ebb, and that worries us very much indeed."

The Central Committee busily churns out new orders and instructions, Yeltsin continued, but they are not taken seriously. Efforts to remake the Party have gotten nowhere, and even if they were begun in earnest now, "after [another] two years we may well find that in the eyes of the people, the Party's authority has drastically fallen."

And—most dramatically—he complained that "recently there has been a noticeable increase in what I can only call adulation of the general secretary by certain full members of the Politburo. I consider this to be impermissible, particularly now when we are introducing properly democratic forms of relations among one another, truly comradely relationships. The tendency to adulation is absolutely unacceptable. To criticize to people's faces—yes, that is necessary—but not to develop a taste for adulation, which can become the norm again, can become a 'cult of personality.' We cannot permit this."*

"I am clearly out of place as a member of the Politburo," Yeltsin said in closing. "For various reasons. There is my lack of experience, as well as other factors. Perhaps it is simply the absence of support from certain quarters, especially from Comrade Ligachev." So, Yeltsin continued, "I must put before you the question of my release from the duties and obligations of a candidate member of the Politburo."

As one of the members would point out a few minutes later, there had never been a speech like this one in the Central Committee that any of them could remember. In all likelihood, no one in the hall had ever heard a comparable interjection at any Party meetings. Yeltsin had shattered the ritualized decorum of the occasion. His remarks epitomized the one quality that had been missing from Party occa-

---

* This translation of Yeltsin's speech is taken from his 1990 book. Yeltsin writes that he had no transcript of the speech himself, and used the one published by the Central Committee eighteen months later. But in the original, Russian-language published version, the inflammatory phrase "cult of personality" does not appear. It was by far Yeltsin's harshest criticism, implying that Gorbachev was slipping into a Stalinist pattern of allowing himself to be praised constantly. I think it is most likely that Yeltsin did use the phrase, despite its absence from the official transcript, since later in the same meeting—according to the official transcript—Gorbachev himself ridiculed Yeltsin for not understanding "what a cult of personality is."

sions for many years—spontaneity. Now he and his comrades would learn how they would behave in a truly spontaneous situation in this new era of democratization, openness, and candor.

As soon as Yeltsin had finished, Gorbachev took the chair from Ligachev. He had made notes during Yeltsin's speech, and he was ready to talk about it. "Comrade Yeltsin has made a serious speech. I didn't want to start a debate, but we must discuss what has been said." Gorbachev gave a point-by-point review of Yeltsin's remarks, which was reasonably fair and thorough until the last point, when he accused Yeltsin of wanting "to fight the Central Committee" by implying that it lacked the authority to consider his resignation as Moscow Party secretary—that the Moscow Party Committee should do that. It was a small point, based on something Yeltsin had indeed said, but Gorbachev had twisted it to put Yeltsin in a corner, as an outsider who had come to challenge the authority of the Central Committee. With that signal, Gorbachev told the 307 members of the Committee where he stood.

Ligachev spoke next. He said Yeltsin's suggestion that the two of them had bad relations was "a slander"—they got along just fine. He denied that anyone in the Politburo was flattering Gorbachev unduly. He declared that Yeltsin's assessment of the public's loss of faith in *perestroika* was "a fundamental political error. It raises doubts about our entire policy." And he used the occasion to reiterate his own unyielding support for "radical reform and democratization of the country."

There followed two dozen speakers. Nearly every one denounced Yeltsin, sometimes in harsh personal terms. Many questioned whether he had the abilities needed to run Moscow. He was called "a deserter," politically "ambitious," and "self-serving," "an embarrassment," "immature," "a political nihilist," "a publicity hound," "irresponsible," "a wrecker of Party unity," "a coward," "a demagogue," "a slanderer," and more. Numerous speakers denounced the timing of his remarks, which they said spoiled the atmosphere leading up to the celebration of the seventieth anniversary of the Revolution. The opportunity to attack Yeltsin—a symbol of Party liberalism and the most visible critic of the privileges enjoyed by Party officials—was clearly irresistible to many Central Committee members.

Yeltsin wrote in his book that he was particularly wounded by the remarks of Premier Ryzhkov, with whom he had worked earlier in Sverdlovsk, and Alexander Yakovlev, whom he obviously considered an ally on the Politburo. Ryzhkov said Yeltsin's accusations were "too serious," and not justified. In his opinion, Ryzhkov continued, "the main mistake of the Central Committee secretariat was giving you too much support." He added: "In my view, as soon as he moved over to the Moscow Party organization, he began to develop political nihilism."

Yakovlev was harsher. "Comrades," he began, "Boris Nikolayevich probably thinks that he spoke here today to the plenum with courage and principle. In fact, in my view, he showed neither the first nor the second. In fact, his speech was politically wrong and morally wrong. Politically wrong because he proceeded from an incorrect evaluation of the situation in the country. . . . And immoral because, in my view, he put his personal ambitions and personal interests ahead of the general interests of the Party." Yeltsin wasn't up to his job, Yakovlev said: "Of course, it's very sad that one of the leaders collapsed in simple panic." He attributed Yeltsin's panic to "petty-bourgeois feelings, which have a place in society. But we can only regret and be puzzled by the fact that such feelings appeared in the leaders of the Moscow [Party] organization."

Many comrades at the meeting came to Ligachev's defense. One of the most eloquent was Eduard Shevardnadze. "Who in this hall doubts that Comrade Ligachev is a most pure man? A man of the highest moral principles, committed, as they say, body and soul to the business of *perestroika?* I don't think you could find such a person here."

As for Yeltsin, Shevardnadze said: "I didn't want to use this word, and perhaps my speech is a bit too emotional, but to some extent this [Yeltsin speech] is a betrayal of the Party."

There were only a handful of friendly or supportive expressions toward Yeltsin in the entire session, which went on for several hours. One came from Georgi Arbatov, the director of the Institute of the U.S.A. and Canada, an adviser to every leader from Brezhnev to Gorbachev. Arbatov began his brief remarks by observing that "the very fact of Boris Nikolayevich Yeltsin's speech from this tribune is evidence of *perestroika,* of the great changes that have occurred." Arbatov said he couldn't assess Yeltsin's remarks on the operations of the secretariat, since he had never seen this secretariat at work. And he declined to stand in judgment of Yeltsin now, and list all his past errors. "We're still used to that style," he admitted, "but there's no need to return to it." (In fact, most of Arbatov's comrades were doing just that.) "And by the way, don't ignore his courage. This wasn't such a simple step." Then he criticized Yeltsin for risking the unity of the Central Committee at a delicate moment. Others pounced on Arbatov's remarks. Ryzhkov specifically disputed his assertion that Yeltsin had shown courage.

When the barrage had ended, Gorbachev offered Yeltsin another chance to speak. "This was a harsh school for me today, of course," Yeltsin began. He retracted none of his remarks, but said several had been misinterpreted. Regarding undue praise for Gorbachev, he said he was only referring to two or three comrades in the Politburo who he thought paid insincere tribute to the general secretary. Gorbachev interrupted him several times, and said he thought Yeltsin had spoken out in an attempt to get attention.

"You had to go to such a level of vanity, of self-regard, to put your ambitions higher than the interests of the Party, than the interests of our work!" Gorbachev said. "And that at a moment when we find ourselves at such an important stage of *perestroika* . . . I consider this an irresponsible action."

But Gorbachev seemed unprepared to deliver a coup de grace. He asked Yeltsin, "Do you have enough strength to carry on?"

According to the official transcript, "a voice" then said, "He can't —you can't leave him in such a post."

"Wait a second, wait a second," Gorbachev replied to that voice. "I asked him a question. Let's approach the matter democratically. We all need an answer before we make a decision."

Yeltsin stuck to his guns. He had "let down" the Party, and judging by the day's speeches, everyone had a similar opinion of him. He repeated his request to be relieved of his duties.

Again Gorbachev ducked the issue, and returned briefly to the subject of his original report on the seventieth-anniversary celebration. Then he came back to Yeltsin, and told the Central Committee that, in fact, Yeltsin had sent him a letter while he was on vacation expressing his desire to step down. He said they had spoken and agreed to put off the question until after the seventieth anniversary, so he had been taken aback when Yeltsin suddenly raised the subject. Gorbachev said he interpreted Yeltsin's decision to bring the matter up that day as a display of disrespect for the general secretary. He defended *perestroika* as the right course for the country, spoke of the need for unity, sharply denied the "hollow" reports of "foreign radio stations" about some kind of split between him and Ligachev, and concluded: "Apparently, Comrade Yeltsin wasn't prepared, theoretically or politically, for his present job, and now he's having difficulty."

But Gorbachev added, "I wouldn't say that this assignment is not within his powers in the future, if he can draw conclusions." And he noted that Yeltsin hadn't directly answered his question about whether he could find the strength to carry on, and he asked the Central Committee to postpone a final decision on Yeltsin's fate. The Politburo and the Moscow Party Committee could decide it after the anniversary celebration, Gorbachev proposed. No one disagreed.

In his own remarkable book published in 1990, Yeltsin reprints the letter he had written to Gorbachev. It was dated September 12, 1987, or two days after a Politburo meeting chaired by Ligachev at which he and Yeltsin got into a fight of some kind. It too is a first—the first internal communication between members of the Politburo that I can remember seeing. Yeltsin informed Gorbachev that "there has been a discernible change from an attitude of friendly support to one of indifference toward matters concerning Moscow and coldness toward me personally, especially in several members of the Politburo and some secretaries of the Central Committee." He noted that he previously wrote or spoke to Gorbachev about several personnel questions, but now wanted to mention several other matters.

"First, there is the style of work favored by Comrade Yegor Kuzmich Ligachev." He didn't spell out his complaint, but implied that Ligachev was peremptory and condescending. "Certain secretaries . . . copy him unthinkingly, but the real point is that it is the Party as a whole which suffers. Great harm will be done to the Party if all this were to be said publicly. Only you personally can change this state of affairs, in the interests of the Party."

Yeltsin went on to criticize the Party *apparat* for its failure to reform itself. "*Perestroika* has been devised and formulated in revolutionary terms. But putting it into effect, particularly in the Party, has come down to the same old approach—a lot of inflated language for public consumption, while in reality the implementation has been self-serving and bureaucratic." Ordinary Party members are afraid to complain, he added.

Then, clumsily, he returned to Ligachev. "In my view, Yegor Kuzmich Ligachev works in a way that is altogether unsystematic and crude. . . . I cannot describe his behavior toward me after the June plenum . . . and his attacks on me at the Politburo meeting of September 10 as anything but systematic persecution." He urged Gorbachev to cut the Party *apparat* by 50 percent and to reorganize it, so it could not hamper reform. Yeltsin wrote that he was "personally distressed" by the insincerity of several Politburo members who claimed to be strong supporters of *perestroika,* but in fact were not. "This suits them and, if you will forgive my saying so, Mikhail Sergeyevich, I believe it also suits you. I sense that they frequently feel the need to remain silent, when in fact they disagree, so that the agreement expressed by some of them is insincere."

Yeltsin conceded, "I am an awkward person," and said he would no doubt cause more difficulties for Gorbachev in the future if he stayed in his job. Those difficulties could "hamper you in your work. And that I most sincerely do not want to happen . . . because, despite the incredible efforts you are making, the struggle to maintain political stability can lead to stagnation, to the state of affairs (or something very like it) that we reached before, under Brezhnev. And that must not happen." So he asked to be relieved of his duties.

That final warning about the excessive cost of maintaining political stability is the best clue about the real substantive content of Yeltsin's complaint. Since March 1985, Ligachev had been Gorbachev's emissary to the traditional Party *apparatchiks.* The Party had accepted the idea of Gorbachev as general secretary—after all, he was one of them, a lifelong *apparatchik* himself. But he was clearly different from the others—more self-confident and outspoken, an innovator, a man who did his own thinking, and who was prepared to depart from established rituals and beliefs. Yes, they needed a vigorous leader to try to get the country moving again, but the princes of the Party remained somewhat uneasy with Gorbachev, and Gorbachev knew it. That is why he had reached so far outside normal channels to put a man like Yakovlev next to him in the leadership, and why he had picked Shevardnadze to be his foreign minister. The usual run of Party officials couldn't give Gorbachev the help he needed—except perhaps to reassure the other *apparatchiks* that Gorbachev was not a threat to their vital interests. Ligachev was meant to provide those reassurances.

But he was doing more than that, Yeltsin warned Gorbachev—he was contributing to the effective opposition to reform. If Ligachev and the people he represented were allowed to stifle *perestroika* by embracing it so firmly that it choked, there would be no reform, and no success for Gorbachev. That was Yeltsin's message in that extraordinary letter of September 12.

• • •

Not until nine days after the Central Committee meeting did anything appear in the press about Yeltsin's apostasy—in the Western press, not in Moscow. Official spokesmen acknowledged that a disagreement had broken out in the leadership. They tried to minimize it. At once, rumors began flying in great profusion. But there would be no immediate *glasnost* on this matter; whatever was said in the Central Committee meeting would remain secret.

On November 2, Gorbachev delivered his long-awaited speech to the seventieth-anniversary jubilee. It was a great disappointment to many who participated in drafting it, and to all who hoped that Gorbachev would give a clear new anti-Stalinist line. Its passages on the contemporary situation reassured liberals, because they showed no sign that Gorbachev had been forced to make serious compromises of his reform policies. But the historical sections were wooden, cautious, and weighted down by convoluted language. The speech read as though it were written by a committee—which, I was told later, it was. By one informed account, every member of the Politburo was invited to make editing changes before it was delivered.

Dissecting the speech now is like trying to parse a medieval church document. It contains only praise for Lenin, then tries to explain what happened after Lenin as, first, a rise of petty-bourgeois divisiveness ("this applies above all to L. D. Trotsky, who after Lenin's death displayed inordinate claims to leadership in the Party"), then a recreation of unity when "the Party spoke out in favor of the Central Committee's line and against the opposition, which was ideologically and organizationally routed. Thus the Party's leadership nucleus, headed by J. V. Stalin, upheld Leninism in the ideological struggle."

Gorbachev's tortured analysis continued with an explanation of the necessity for forced industrialization in the first five-year plans. Those who took part in the heroism of the industrialization (when the Stalinist system of central control was born)—"our grandfathers and fathers"—"made it possible to save the homeland from mortal danger, and to save socialism for the future, for you and me, comrades. . . . Their labor and selfless dedication were not in vain. . . . Glory to them, and hallowed be their memory!" However, Gorbachev continued, "the period we are talking about also brought losses. They had a certain connection with the very success about which I have spoken. People at that time came to believe in the universal effectiveness of rigid centralization." Bureaucratism, "whose dangers Lenin once warned about," appeared. Good results were achieved in industry, but "such a rigid system of centralization and command was impermissible in tackling the tasks of transforming the countryside." So the collectivization of agriculture was based on "a deviation from Leninist policy," and grave errors were committed. But wait—"in the final analysis, [collectivization] was a turning point of great importance."

And so on. Gorbachev and his colleagues were not just struggling with the horrors of Soviet history; they were putting at risk myths that propped up the very foundations of the Soviet regime. Their goal was to be more truthful about the past without being so truthful that their words might undermine the legitimacy of the Party's claim to power. The passages on Stalin revealed the tension in their position most clearly of all.

Things went wrong, Gorbachev said, when "an atmosphere of intolerance" was created in the country at a time when the class enemy had actually been routed, and there was little to fear. This led to the "cult of personality"—a bizarre term, whose coiners must have thought it somehow separated the Party from its support for Stalin— and "real crimes stemming from an abuse of power." Then the sentence that most disappointed intellectuals in Moscow waiting for a cathartic confession: "Many thousands of Party members and non-Party people were subjected to mass repressions." Little hint there of the tens of millions of victims of Stalin's dictatorship.

"Keeping to positions of historical truth," Gorbachev said, "we must see both Stalin's indisputable contribution to the struggle for socialism . . . and the flagrant political mistakes and arbitrary actions committed by him and his entourage." He then repeated the formulation he had first used at the Central Committee plenum several weeks earlier, that Stalin did know about the crimes, and that his guilt before Party and people "is enormous and unforgivable." But he went on to defend Stalin's secret pact with Hitler, which included a secret protocol in which the two dictators divided up Poland and the Baltic states, and to praise Stalin's contribution as a war leader, while giving principal credit for victory to "the ordinary Soviet soldier."

As a practical matter, none of this rhetorical ballet mattered very much. The most important element in the speech turned out to be the acknowledgment that further study of the past was needed. Gorbachev announced that the Central Committee had created a commission to conduct a study on which future actions could be based. "Even now one still encounters attempts to turn away from painful questions in our history, to hush them up or to pretend that nothing special happened," Gorbachev said—a nice summation of the campaign waged by Ligachev and his allies while Gorbachev was on vacation the previous summer. "We cannot agree with this. This would show disregard for the historical truth and disrespect for the memory of those who were the innocent victims of lawlessness and arbitrary rule. We also cannot agree with it because a truthful analysis should help us solve our current problems of democratization, legality, *glasnost,* and the overcoming of bureaucratism—in short, the vital problems of *perestroika.*" That was a firm rebuff to the conservatives, and an invitation to the country's intellectuals and historians to continue to dig into the past. It was all they needed. Disappointment in Gorbachev's speech gave way, after some months, to the appreciative realization that it had protected the process of de-Stalinization that was already well under way in society at large.

Now came the worst aspect of the Yeltsin affair—his public lynching. On November 11, just nine days after the seventieth-anniversary speech, Gorbachev himself led the hanging party at a special meeting of the Gorkom, or City Party Committee. This was the ugliest event of Gorbachev's first five years in power—and if Yeltsin's subsequent account in his book is accurate, then it was even uglier than it looked at the time.

How much confidence to put in Yeltsin's account is not clear to me. This is an unusual man. He is emotional, proud, extremely vain, and mercurial. Friends of mine who knew something about his tenure as first secretary in Moscow agree that his record was mixed. By all accounts he was not a great administrator, nor very effective at following through on his own decisions and policies. There was astounding turnover of Party officials in the Moscow organization during his twenty-three months in office. But he could not claim credit for noticeable improvements in living conditions or economic performance in the capital, and he knew it.

Yeltsin had worked himself into a state of physical and emotional exhaustion that fall. He complained to many, including some foreign ambassadors, that he was at a loss as to how to improve conditions in the city. He did attack corruption and privileges, and he certainly won the affections of Muscovites with his populist gestures and his ability to talk to ordinary people. But he made the intelligentsia nervous. Many intellectuals considered him a demagogue and a fraud. Many also thought he really was planning to challenge Gorbachev for power. Yeltsin's is the first kiss-and-tell account ever written by a Soviet leader. (Khrushchev's dictated memoirs, though fascinating, were discreet by comparison.) I quote from it here without certain knowledge of its reliability.

According to Yeltsin, the lynching began with a telephone call from Gorbachev to him in the Kremlin hospital on the morning of November 11. Yeltsin had been admitted to the hospital two days earlier—"I had suffered a physical breakdown," in his words. "I was pumped full of medicines, mostly tranquilizers, which relaxed my nerves and muscles. The doctors forbade me to get out of bed." He was in great discomfort, he wrote.

> Suddenly . . . the telephone rang on my special Kremlin line. . . . It was Gorbachev, and he spoke as if he were calling me not in the hospital but at my dacha. In a calm voice he said, "You must come and see me for a short while, Boris Nikolayevich. After that, perhaps we will go and attend the plenum of the Moscow City Committee together." I said I couldn't come because I was in bed and the doctors wouldn't let me get up. "Don't worry," he said cheerfully. "The doctors will help you get up."

The meeting was attended not only by members of the Moscow committee, but by most of the senior leadership too. Gorbachev opened it with a tendentious description of the Central Committee plenum where Yeltsin spoke out. His remarks were "politically immature and extremely confused and contradictory," Gorbachev said. "Comrade Yeltsin basically tried to call into question the party's work on *perestroika* since the April [1985] Plenum . . . and went so far as to say that *perestroika* effectively does nothing for the people."

Perhaps realizing that what was happening to Yeltsin might not appear consistent with his proclaimed policy of encouraging people to criticize whatever they disagreed with, Gorbachev reiterated that criticism was "normal," and said, "in the Party there should be no zones closed to criticism or workers protected from it." But "in this case what happened was something entirely different. At a critical moment, when the Central Committee's attention was focused on fundamental questions of theory and practice of our development, Comrade Yeltsin tried to lead the plenum's work in a different direction, declaring his own special position on a number of questions." In other words, criticism was fine provided one didn't disagree with his comrades. Gorbachev declared that the Central Committee had "displayed complete unanimity" in rejecting Yeltsin's speech; "not one of those who spoke supported Comrade Yeltsin," he said, erroneously. He then gave a quite defensive review of the many accomplishments of *perestroika* so far, before turning the meeting over to members of the Moscow committee.

Then began a stream of invective markedly harsher than the denunciations delivered at the Central Committee plenum. "Such a man must not be involved in political work at all," said the first speaker. Yeltsin's conduct amounted to "political adventurism, a treacherous stab in the back for the Party," said the second. The third speaker disclosed that Yeltsin had been "making ultra left-wing and overtly radical statements from the outset of his activity" as Moscow Party secretary. The fourth speaker said Yeltsin had "gone astray and he must not lead the Moscow Party organization." And on it went, for several hours. Several of Yeltsin's colleagues took the occasion to settle scores for past slights. One courageous member of the committee, A. S. Yeliseyev, a former cosmonaut and rector of a large technical college, had the decency to observe that blaming Yeltsin alone for all these shortcomings might not be entirely fair. "I would not fully dissociate myself from his guilt," Yeliseyev said. "I take part in the work of the Party Committee's plenums, and I have never heard speeches like today's even half as sharp, even one-third as sharp. There is a point at which we start to lose our principledness." He was alone in expressing such sentiments.

When his comrades were finished, Yeltsin gave a brief, contrite reply to their denunciations. He acknowledged that his own ambition was largely to blame for his errors. "I tried to combat it but, unfortunately, not successfully." And he said he bore "a great burden of guilt . . . I bear a great burden of guilt personally before Mikhail Sergeyevich Gorbachev, whose prestige is so high in our organization, in our country, and throughout the world."

•　•　•　•

The way the Yeltsin affair was handled seemed to prove one of the points Yeltsin made in that extraordinary letter to Gorbachev: the Party still handled matters with "the same old approach." Many Muscovites compared that meeting of the Moscow Party Committee to events under Stalin—a "show trial" *à la perestroika*. When the transcript of the session was published in *Moscow Pravda,* it became the talk of the town for days. But because this was a time of real politics, and not just Party-controlled ritual, the consequences of the Yeltsin affair turned out to be very different than traditional Soviet practices might have suggested.

One surprise came six days after the Moscow City plenum. Yeltsin, back in the Kremlin hospital (where he would remain for weeks), received another telephone call from Gorbachev. The general secretary proposed that he become first deputy chairman of the state construction trust, a job that carried the rank of minister in the government. This was an unprecedented gesture to a man who had suffered the punishment Yeltsin had just survived. It was also evidence that Gorbachev would not allow his conservative comrades the satisfaction of thinking they had destroyed Yeltsin. In his book Yeltsin wrote that when Gorbachev offered him the job, "I accepted it without a moment's reflection." Many Muscovites were amazed to hear the news.

A second surprise probably had something to do with the first. The people of Moscow did not accept Yeltsin's dismissal passively. For the fist time since Trotsky was expelled from the Party in 1927, a personnel change in the Politburo provoked a spontaneous and strong public outcry. Yeltsin wrote, "When I was dismissed, the Central Committee, *Pravda* and indeed all the national newspapers and journals were flooded with letters protesting the decisions of the Central Committee and the City Committee."

That was apparently true. One of my friends in Moscow, a professor, recalled the unusual atmosphere on the day *Moscow Pravda* published its report of the City Party Committee meeting: "The reaction was amazing. That was the first time we realized that we were living in a changed country—that the people had woken up, or at least were starting to wake up. I came to a publishing house on business that morning and found the people there reading *Moscow Pravda* together, and complaining about Gorbachev! A friend of ours was walking on the street that day and ran into a demonstration in support of Yeltsin, where people were collecting signatures on a protest petition. I then went up to the university to give a lecture, and found student meetings under way in defense of Yeltsin. The whole city was talking about nothing else. There had been thousands of such cases in the past, thousands of people fired, thousands of stupid speeches, but no one reacted. This time they did. 'Hey, we have woken up, we're free people, what kind of a way is this to do business?' And of course, this was a result of Gorbachev's policies, which—for the first time—had been turned against him."

The Yeltsin affair marked a genuine turning point in the evolution of Gorbachev's revolution. Yeltsin correctly described his speech as "the first piece of criticism aimed at Gorbachev, the first attempt— not over the kitchen table but in a party forum—to discuss openly why *perestroika* was making no progress. It was the first expression of the pluralism that had been declared to be so desirable." Well, the first such expression from a member of the Politburo, anyhow.

The Party's reaction to the affair did not build public confidence. The initial decision not to publish Yeltsin's offending speech to the Central Committee became the focus of discontent. Withholding it seemed a flat contradiction of the principles of *glasnost*. The fact that it wasn't published also led to a rich harvest of rumors in the capital about what Yeltsin really had said. According to some, he had attacked Raisa Maximovna Gorbacheva; others said he had personally insulted the general secretary. Foreign reporters also pressed for publication or release of the speech, to the embarrassment of officials, who could not provide it.

It isn't easy to dissect all of Gorbachev's motivations in this episode. Part of his reaction seemed personal; he is, as one of his colleagues put it, a man who "takes offense"—he remembers insults and can react to them heatedly. Part of it was a reflection of thirty years' experience as a Party man. The ugly methods used against Yeltsin were Party methods, learned almost like reflexes in such a long Party career. At the same time, Yeltsin did rain on Gorbachev's parade at that Central Committee plenum. And it was a delicate moment, given the narrow path Gorbachev was trying to follow between conservatives and modernizers on the historical issues he had to confront at the seventieth-anniversary jubilee. He must have seen a political threat as well, though I am not sure how he would have formulated it. Did Gorbachev believe—as some of my best-informed acquaintances in Moscow do—that Yeltsin was preparing to attack him frontally, perhaps challenge him for power? Or was he angry that Yeltsin wouldn't cooperate with the balancing act he had constructed?

"It is my belief," Yeltsin wrote,

> that if Gorbachev didn't have a Yeltsin he would have had to invent one. . . . He realizes that he needs someone like me—prickly, sharp-

tongued, the scourge of the overbureaucratized Party *apparat*—and for this reason he keeps me near at hand. In this real-life production, the parts have been appropriately cast, as in a well-directed play. There is the conservative Ligachev, who plays the villain; there is Yeltsin, the bully boy, the madcap radical; and the wise, omniscient hero is Gorbachev himself. That, evidently, is how he sees it.

Whatever the correct explanation—and this seems to be one of those complex human situations where no simple answer is satisfactory—the immediate consequences for Gorbachev were bad. The Yeltsin affair cast the general secretary as a bully whose sincerity about *glasnost* was now suspect; in Moscow and elsewhere, many ordinary people felt that a true friend of the working class had been unfairly persecuted. Gorbachev acknowledged that there were negative reactions two months later when he told newspaper editors: "We shall not conceal the fact that the Party's rebuff [to Yeltsin] was viewed by a certain part of the intelligentsia, especially young people, as a blow to *perestroika.*"

But it is important to keep in mind that the affair ended ambiguously—more ambiguously than many of the most alarmed liberals thought at the time. Gorbachev had kept Yeltsin in a visible job in Moscow. He had opened the door to further de-Stalinization. He had denied the conservatives a clear-cut victory. (He sought to emphasize this point in a speech on November 17, when he reformulated his middle way, criticizing both "conservatism and artificial avant-gardism.") He continued to assert the importance of further democratization as the next stage of reform. Yes, it was also true that Gorbachev had pandered to the traditionalists, and had turned on a man regarded as a crusader for reform. But this was real politics—outcomes were inevitably somewhat ambiguous. Many Russians—and many of us who followed these events through foreign eyes—were so used to the idea that one or another clear "Party line" would prevail that we misinterpreted what we were seeing. In fact, Soviet politics was no longer a zero-sum game, in which any advance by the conservatives inevitably came at the expense of the reformers. Now it was more recognizable, more normal politics, in which all contestants balanced victories and defeats.

Utlimately the Yeltsin affair hurt the conservatives. They came out of it looking like stubborn protectors of the old ways and values, which at that moment were being broadly challenged in Soviet society. Yeltsin wrote—self-servingly, but also accurately—that for "unprejudiced people," the publication of the proceedings of his lynching party at the Moscow City Committee "was a severe blow [to the conservatives]. It plainly revealed the attitudes of fear, cowardice and subservience that prevailed in the upper echelons of the Party."

I also think the Yeltsin affair had an enduring significance for Gorbachev personally. It ended the initial phase of his career as a reformer —the period one friend in Moscow called "reform in the hands of the Party." He had worked hard to hold the Party together on the line he had set, despite the threat that line posed to Party power and privilege. Popular reaction to the Yeltsin affair demonstrated that his loyalty to the Party was beginning to jeopardize his reputation in the country. "The Party was going right when the country was going left," as Andrei Sakharov put it at the time to friends.* In 1988, Gorbachev would demonstrate that he had learned a lesson; he would side with the people against the entrenched "inert stratum" that separated him from the country, with the most dramatic consequences.

---

* Sakharov's analysis was supported at year end by the results of the annual subscription drives by newspapers and magazines. *Pravda* lost one million subscribers; *Izvestia,* an increasingly bold supporter of reform, gained two million. All the liberal magazines registered huge gains.

CHAPTER SIX

BREAKING WITH
THE PAST

Nineteen eighty-seven ended on a high note for Gorbachev with his visit to Washington in December. Initially he had hoped to make that trip a year earlier; Reykjavík and its aftermath in the fall of 1986 threw off the schedule of diplomacy he and President Reagan had adopted in Geneva in 1985. He preceded the trip, as was now his custom, with an interview, this time with Tom Brokaw of NBC News. That prime-time hour gave Americans their best chance yet to get to know this lively Russian with his intense eyes and forceful, controlled gestures. It was a defensive performance. Brokaw made Gorbachev answer for his government's arbitrary controls on travel and emigration, for the Berlin Wall, for the war in Afghanistan. Within two years all three would be gone, but at the end of 1987 the general secretary still had to take responsibility for them. He didn't enjoy it.

One question Brokaw posed caused a stir in the Soviet Union. He asked about Raisa Maximovna: "Do you go home in the evening and discuss with her national policies, political difficulties, and so on in this country?" Gorbachev replied, "We discuss everything." Brokaw pressed on: "Including Soviet affairs, at the highest level?" Gorbachev: "I think I have answered your question in toto. We discuss everything." That exchange was removed from the transcript of the interview published and broadcast in the Soviet Union, but Russians heard about it on foreign radio broadcasts. It added to Raisa Maximovna's reputation among Russians as a pushy woman who did not know her place.

In Washington Gorbachev put on quite a show. He displayed enormous energy and a great appetite for meeting and talking with—or at least to—Americans, including a battalion of prominent citizens invited to meet him in a series of meetings at the Soviet embassy. These sessions, like nearly every event on his schedule, were broadcast at home on Soviet television. It was obvious from the outset that Gorbachev was playing simultaneously to two audiences: an American one that he hoped to impress, and a Soviet one that he hoped would be impressed by his American reception.

I was fortunate to be able to meet him and see him in action at the White House state dinner on the second night of his visit. The Soviet Embassy in Washington obviously had not briefed him on who the Reagans' guests were, so Gorbachev and his wife had to ask what each one did. They were so attentive to the guests' answers that dinner started more than half an hour late. Gorbachev consumed every morsel of food put before him, and spent considerable time admiring Nancy Mehta, wife of conductor Zubin Mehta, a handsome woman wearing a low-cut gown who sat two chairs from him. The conversation at his table was lively. At dinner he told Dick Cheney, then the congressman from Wyoming, that either his attempts to reform Russia would succeed, or Russia would never be reformed.

Gorbachev and the members of his entourage were thrilled with the admiring reception he received from the Americans he met. They had taken the visit very seriously. A large group of academics, journalists, and officials had preceded Gorbachev to Washington and canvassed the city for clues to the Reagan administration's plans or any other tidbit that might be useful to the general secretary. There was a characteristic meeting between this group and Gorbachev on the night he arrived, when he went around the room asking what they knew that he ought to know. I've known some of the members of this group for nearly twenty years, and it was striking how exhilarating they found this opportunity to conduct a serious, lively discussion with the leader of their country. None of them had ever had an experience like it before Gorbachev came to power.

Historians of the arcane details of arms control will record that the treaty signed in Washington, eliminating intermediate-range ballistic and land-based cruise missiles, was based on a series of unilateral Soviet concessions. Indeed, the whole issue came up in the first place because the Soviets, when Brezhnev was leader, deployed a powerful new intermediate-range missile, the SS-20, aimed at Europe; it provoked the deployment of American Pershing II and cruise missiles. The 1987 treaty eliminated them all. It also created a new kind of on-site inspection to verify its terms, including the permanent stationing of Soviet and American inspectors on each other's territory. The elimination of an entire class of weapons gave Gorbachev a palpable psychological lift. He had validated the course he had first taken in Geneva in 1985, and had proven that he could do constructive business with the arch-anti-Communist of the Cold War era, Ronald Reagan. It was no use telling Soviet officials that winter that Reagan needed the deal as much in his way as Gorbachev did, to wipe off some of the stain from the Iran-Contra affair. They preferred to see a case of the taming of a wild beast by a shrewd new Soviet leader. A prominent Moscow editor told me in Washington that Gorbachev's visit was "the first success for *perestroika.*"

The Soviet news media provided lavish coverage of the trip, describing it as a historic event as well as a personal triumph for the general secretary. The television pictures of Gorbachev surrounded by smiling Americans made the most important point: the Soviet Union had a formidable statesman at the helm. This spectacle must have frustrated the Party men who secretly detested what he was doing to their country. Gorbachev had become a great national asset as a diplomat. The conservatives had no candidate to offer who remotely compared.

•   •   •   •

But they still had an agenda, and determination to pursue it. No doubt the Yeltsin affair emboldened the conservatives. So did their perception of what was going on around them. The country was changing before their eyes. Not only was the liberals' guerrilla war succeeding in destroying the old orthodoxies, now ordinary citizens were also challenging established conventions. This was most noticeable in the proliferation of new clubs, associations, and organizations —"informal groups," in the new argot of *perestroika*. The realization that it was now possible to form such groups was sweeping across the Soviet Union. By late 1987 there were perhaps four or five thousand of them around the country (by mid-1988 there would be at least thirty thousand, according to Roy Medvedev). Many of the new groups had obviously political agendas, from rabid, anti-Semitic Russian nationalism to environmentalism and religious revival. Many began to produce their own publications on mimeograph machines and personal computers, though this violation of the official press monopoly was not formally permitted by any new regulations. These manifestations of real politics unnerved the traditionalists, who saw their world crumbling.

Gorbachev and Yakovlev were able to maintain an upper hand from week to week, but they could not crush their conservative opposition, or quell its efforts to preserve what it could of the old ways and values. The conservatives' stubbornness must have forced Gorbachev repeatedly to confront the basic contradiction of his policy—that he wanted the Party to support reforms that would inevitably undermine the Party.

Before their departure to Washington in early December, Yakovlev, for the first time taking advantage of his new status as a full Politburo member, called his own meeting of editors and cultural figures to reiterate that "*glasnost* is our firm line, and the Central Committee has no intention of turning away from it," regardless of the Yeltsin affair. He told his audience to pay "enormous attention" to Gorbachev's November 2 warnings against "conservatism, which has the capacity to take revenge." Ligachev called what amounted to a counter-meeting of a similar audience a fortnight later, disputing Yakovlev on a number of points and reformulating his own more conservative line. (Yakovlev's speech was reported in some detail, Ligachev's was only mentioned in the press.) Editors were confused, understandably. Gorbachev called a third meeting on January 8, obviously to assert the primacy of his and Yakovlev's line.

"If *perestroika* is indeed the continuation of the revolution, if we are currently pursuing a revolutionary policy, then struggle is inevitable," he said, clearly referring to the Yakovlev-Ligachev disagreements. He acknowledged an absence so far of "tangible positive results" from reform, but insisted this was no reason to turn back. "If we stop the emerging processes, get frightened by them, this would have most serious consequences, for we will not be able to mobilize our people for an undertaking of this scope one more time." (This is just what Gorbachev had told Dick Cheney at the White House a few weeks before.) He chastised the conservatives who criticized reform as people who feared giving more power to the people. He took an important step on historical issues by saying explicitly that his pronouncements on the seventieth anniversary were not dogma, but rather a starting point for continued research. "The deepening knowledge and understanding of history and drawing lessons from the past" had "enriched the entire political, ideological, and spiritual sphere."

But he also cast himself as a moderate, noting that "we are frequently criticized, by some on the right, some on the left." And he warned the editors not to be irresponsible. "No one is outside control in our country," he said, letting the old *apparatchik* inside him shine through for a moment. "This applies to the mass media. The Soviet press is not a private shop."

From the Yeltsin affair onward, many of Gorbachev's staunchest supporters remained on edge. He was not decisively in control, and they could feel it—particularly the editors and journalists in the front lines of the guerrilla war. In November the state censor at *Ogonyok* killed a piece critical of the police in Uzbekistan, the first time an article had been censored out of the magazine in many months. The journalists sensed a power struggle above them, saw Ligachev on one side and Yakovlev, with Gorbachev, on the other, but had no feel for the dynamics of the situation. Unsure where things were headed, they got nervous, even as they tried to forge ahead with both historical and contemporary revelations. Some editors became rigorous self-censors. A characteristic example involved Nikolai Bukharin's "testament," a bitter letter to future generations of Communists composed several days before his arrest in 1937, when he sensed what was about to happen to him. Bukharin wrote of the "terrible crimes" Stalin was committing, defended his own innocence forcefully, and concluded: "You should know, comrades, that there is also my drop of blood on the banner that you will carry on your triumphant march to communism." *Ogonyok* printed an interview in November with Bukharin's widow, who had memorized the testament and preserved it in her head for many years before she felt it was safe to write it down. But the editors of the magazine were afraid to print the testament, since by the widow's admission it could not be documented—she had memorized it. A month later, *Moscow News,* which was in a continuing competition with *Ogonyok* to see who could be boldest in print, published Bukharin's testament. In this case anxiety was misplaced. Bukharin was formally rehabilitated by the Supreme Court early in February 1988.

One of the most interesting reformist journalists was Fyodor Mikhailovich Burlatsky, a columnist for *Literaturnaya Gazeta* (he became the paper's editor in 1990). Burlatsky, a contemporary of Gorbachev, had been one of the bright young men on Andropov's personal staff in the mid-1960s. Though discouraged by the politics of the Brezhnev era, he looked for interesting academic or journalistic work that would keep him inside the system—he was no dissident. I first met him in the spring of 1972, when he was deputy director of the Institute for Concrete Social Research in Moscow, the country's first sociological think tank. Burlatsky, with a handful of others, was trying to propel Soviet social science into the modern age. But his effort failed; Party elders were not prepared to accept the challenges to conventional Marxism-Leninism posed by modern sociology. The institute was disbanded within a year or two.

Before working with Andropov in the Central Committee *apparat,* Burlatsky had been an aide to Nikita Khrushchev, writing speeches and documents. Like so many members of his generation, Burlatsky had warm but also ambivalent feelings about Khrushchev. Also like many others his age, he saw numerous parallels between Khrushchev and Gorbachev, whom he also knew. Some parallels were obvious: both men took on the entrenched system they inherited; both were de-Stalinizers; both were sincere reformers, who seemed truly to care about the welfare of their citizens; both fancied themselves peacemakers in foreign affairs. But Burlatsky saw more than that.

In early February 1988, when he—like many Gorbachev supporters among Moscow writers and intellectuals—worried intensely that the moment was being lost, Burlatsky published an article in *Literaturnaya Gazeta* ostensibly to rehabilitate Khrushchev, who had been a nonperson throughout the time of stagnation. His long piece did fill in many blanks in the Khrushchev story, including a gripping account of the decision to arrest and shoot Beria soon after Stalin died. But the article was also an open letter to Mikhail Gorbachev (whose name it never mentioned). I read it as a warning to Gorbachev that he was vulnerable to some of Khrushchev's flaws and errors, but also as a piece of cheerleading, urging Gorbachev to stick to the path he had chosen.

Burlatsky's first parallel involved the way Khrushchev came to power—"there was a large element of chance." If Georgi Malenkov and Beria had made a deal in 1953, for example, Khrushchev never would have made it—his ascent was (like Gorbachev's elevation thirty-two years later) a close call. "But history made the right choice,"

Burlatsky wrote, because the Soviet Union needed a reformer to deal with its poverty, its technological backwardness, the housing crisis, and the country's isolation in the world. "All this demanded a new policy and radical changes," and Khrushchev came "as the hope of the people and the precursor of a new time."

Burlatsky described Khrushchev's courage, manifested best at the 20th Party Congress. "How had Khrushchev dared deliver a report about Stalin, knowing that the overwhelming majority of delegates would be against the disclosures? . . . This is one of those extremely rare instances in history when a political leader risked his personal power and even his life in the name of higher public goals." Burlatsky then quoted Khrushchev's own explanation, given to "foreign guests": "Since I had been elected first secretary,* I had to, I was obligated to tell the truth . . . about the past, no matter what it would cost me. . . . Lenin taught us that a Party that is not afraid to tell the truth will never perish."

Burlatsky noted that Khrushchev's career as a truth-teller was hobbled: "From the start, Khrushchev was brought up short by the problem of personal responsibility, since many people in the Party knew about the role that he himself had played in persecuting cadres in the Ukraine and in the Moscow Party organization. Without telling the truth about himself, he couldn't tell the whole truth about others." Clearly, Gorbachev did not have this problem, so he could go on telling the truth.

"Economic policy remained one of the most vulnerable spots in his activity," Burlatsky wrote diplomatically of Khrushchev—as it did, obviously, for Gorbachev, who was admitting publicly at the time that no tangible benefits had yet been seen from his economic reforms. Khrushchev's problem was that he thought the economy could be fixed by changing the administrative apparatus in Moscow—he didn't understand the importance of "thoroughgoing structural reforms." Burlatsky wrote that Palmiro Togliatti, the Italian Communist, had warned Khrushchev that the entire Soviet system was flawed, but Khrushchev couldn't see it. Burlatsky quoted Mao Zedong on Khrushchev: He "walked with two feet—one stepped boldly into a new era, while the other was inextricably stuck in the mire of the past." To make the same point in another way. Burlatsky noted admiringly the

---

* From Khrushchev's time to Gorbachev's, the leader's title had changed from first to general secretary, and what had been the presidium had become the Politburo.

bust of Khrushchev on his grave, done by Ernst Neizvestny, a talented modernist sculptor whom Khrushchev denounced when he was alive. Burlatsky described the bust of Khrushchev in front of black and white marble slabs that "aptly symbolize the contradictory nature" of the man. Part of his dark side, Burlatsky wrote, was his susceptibility to flattery, his vanity.

Khrushchev failed because "the conservative forces were able to gain the upper hand over the reformers." More concretely, he said, Khrushchev did not rely on the best specialists to draw up his economic reform—he depended too much on the Party *apparat*. Also he failed to democratize society and convince ordinary people that reform was their cause, too. Finally, he let sycophants delude him: "Bootlickers drowned him in a sea of flattery." On all points, these were cautions to Gorbachev, too.

I've been told by several of my best-informed acquaintances in Moscow that Gorbachev has been painfully conscious of the Khrushchev parallel since he became general secretary—and particularly of the fate that befell Nikita Sergeyevich. "The way Khrushchev was removed [by a secret plot of his colleagues in the leadership] is a trauma for Gorbachev" one reformer in the new Supreme Soviet told me in mid-1990. According to this man and others, avoiding Khrushchev's fate has been a preoccupation of Gorbachev's since 1985. "I've heard him talk about it," another acquaintance told me.

•   •   •

Gorbachev and Yakovlev planned to use the 19th Party Conference, now scheduled for late June 1988, to strengthen their hand against the conservatives, but the rush of intervening events hindered preparations for the conference. First Afghanistan, another of the international problems that—it soon became clear—Gorbachev was eager to dispose of. In early February Gorbachev announced that he was ready to withdraw all Soviet forces over a ten-month period starting in May. This began a period of intense diplomacy, including an early-April Gorbachev meeting with Najibullah, the Afghan leader, and then a formal decision to pull out. It was as amazing a departure as any of Gorbachev's earlier surprises. The well-established axiom that "the forces of socialism march only in one direction" had convinced nearly all of us who studied the Soviet Union that withdrawal simply wasn't possible—that it would amount to the kind of admission of error that no Soviet leader would make. It would also be an invitation to other countries occupied involuntarily by Soviet forces to begin to hope that perhaps their occupation was not permanent—another reason why withdrawal seemed impossible.

The second distraction that spring was a tragic crisis in Armenia and Azerbaijan, the beginnings of a bitter ethnic conflict that may be beyond peaceful resolution for many years to come. The rioting in Kazakhstan after Kunayev was fired was alarming, but the bloody conflict between these two Transcaucasian peoples, the Christian Armenians and Moslem Azerbaijanis, was much more ominous. The trouble began in Nagorno-Karabakh, a predominantly Armenian enclave within Azerbaijani territory. In February the regional Party committee there voted to ask that the territory be united with Armenia. The vote set off huge demonstrations of support in Yerevan, the capital of Armenia, and other Armenian towns, and produced violence in Nagorno-Karabakh itself, killing two and wounding dozens. Four members of the senior leadership were dispatched from Moscow to Yerevan and Stepanakert, the capital of Nagorno-Karabakh; a personal appeal from Gorbachev was read on television; some order was restored.

But it lasted only briefly. One of the most brazen provocations of the Gorbachev era brutally ended the relative calm on February 28. Azerbaijanis, apparently encouraged by local authorities, launched a violent pogrom against the Armenian residents of the town of Sumgait on the Caspian Sea, about twenty-five miles from Baku, Azerbaijan's capital. Armenians were dragged from their homes and beaten brutally; thirty-one were killed, and hundreds wounded. It later became clear that preparations for the pogrom had been conducted openly for days before it occurred, and that local authorities did nothing to inform Moscow of what was happening for a long time after the events began. When they finally did, the army was sent in to restore order.

Here was evidence that even officials of the Soviet regime would put ethnic sentiment ahead of any political or legal responsibility— precisely what Moscow would fear most. The hundreds of thousands of Armenian residents of Azerbaijan feared it too—tens of thousands of them immediately abandoned their jobs and homes and set off for Armenia. Thousands of Azerbaijanis made similar voyages in the opposite direction. As the situation deteriorated, so did the authorities' commitment to *glasnost*. The national news media carried almost no information about these events, aggravating tensions and encouraging rumors. In Moscow rumors were rife that the pogrom in Sumgait was an anti-Gorbachev provocation, intended to undermine his authority. Tens of thousands of Armenians demonstrated daily in the main square of Yerevan. New committees led by prominent Armenian intellectuals became spokesmen for the rights of Nagorno-Karabakh. The central authorities looked for ways to impose discipline, finally arresting three Armenian activists late in March. It was a grim period.

Gorbachev himself had no helpful contribution to make. This kind of ethnic explosion was not on his agenda. He neither expected it nor knew how to deal with it. Like most Party officials of his generation, Gorbachev seemed truly to believe that the multinational Soviet state was a viable political entity—that the many ethnic groups which populated the land had learned to live together and could continue to coexist to mutual benefit. Gorbachev seemed to shy away from situations which challenged that optimism.

• • •

While that crisis bubbled, the conservatives made their move. In characteristic Russian fashion, its first step was a piece of writing. On March 13, while Alexander Yakovlev was preparing to leave on a trip to Mongolia and Gorbachev was preparing to depart for Yugoslavia on an official visit, the newspaper *Sovetskaya Rossiya,* a national daily, published an article that filled its second page, under the provocative headline "I Cannot Deny My Principles."

The article was long and disjointed; it was written without a hint of literary flair, and was burdened by extensive use of Marxist-Leninist jargon. But its purpose was nevertheless clear: its author, a Leningrad chemistry teacher named Nina Andreyeva, was trying to formulate a manifesto against *glasnost.*

She began by complaining that the open debate over the Soviet past had confused her students: "[With all the] talk about 'terrorism,' 'the people's political servility,' 'spiritual slavery,' 'universal fear' . . . it isn't surprising that nihilistic sentiments are intensifying among some students and there are cases of ideological confusion, loss of political bearings, and even ideological omnivorousness [!]." She wrote that she had "read and reread the much-talked-about articles," and concluded that they only sowed doubt and confusion. She accused the authors of famous anti-Stalinist works of borrowing their historical ideas from foreigners and émigrés. She fiercely defended Stalin personally and Stalinism, crediting them with "bringing our country into the ranks of the great world powers," decrying those who only see evil in the Stalin era. "Things have reached a point where insistent demands for 'repentance' [a reference to Abuladze's film] are being made of 'Stalinists.' . . . Praise is being lavished on novels and films that lynch the era of tempestuous changes [her euphemism for the Stalin period]." She quoted what she said was Winston Churchill's assessment of Stalin—that he was "a man of extraordinary energy, erudition, and inflexible will, blunt, tough, and merciless in both action and conversation, whom even I . . . was at a loss to counter."

She quoted Ligachev approvingly on the importance of teaching young people "the class vision of the world," and she contradicted Gorbachev on several points, including the need for further study of the dark periods of Soviet history (she saw no need) and his assertion that the individual and his development should be the center of the state's attention. Andreyeva preferred "proletarian collectivism." She decried "left-liberal socialism," part of a "militant cosmopolitanism" that was the work of Jews.* She accused Jews who sought to emigrate from the Soviet Union of "class and nationality betrayal." She attacked the new, informal groups as a threat to "the leading role of the Party and the working class," and denounced the tendency to criticize past leaders for their shortcomings. "Where did we get this passion for squandering the prestige and dignity of the leaders of the world's first socialist country?" she asked.

Even by the standards of Soviet political rhetoric, this was a crude and clumsy document. It was not unlike many other articles that had appeared since the guerrilla war began in 1987. But this one, it turned out, was the opening shot of a serious offensive against Gorbachev's reforms, and therefore much more important than the others.

I arrived in Moscow two months after the publication of Andreyeva's article for my first visit in four years. I knew a little about the article and the events it provoked, but realized after my first conversations in Moscow that it was much more important than I had appreciated from afar. Over the next three weeks I was able to compile a detailed account of the incident—a story unlike any I had ever written from the Soviet Union. It was the first time I had actually succeeded in discovering what in other world capitals is a routine part of journalism—inside information. In the Moscow I had known previously, it simply wasn't possible for a Western journalist to uncover details of Kremlin intrigue. In the spring of 1988 I found that knowledgeable officials were prepared to discuss subjects that had remained far off

---

* Jews were often described as "rootless cosmopolites" in the propaganda surrounding Stalin's postwar campaign against them.

limits in previous years. It also seemed to me that the people I knew
—not Politburo members or Central Committee secretaries, but mid-
level officials, academics, and journalists—were much more knowledgeable than they used to be.

I learned that Ligachev had used the occasion of Gorbachev's and
Yakovlev's absence from Moscow to launch what one Soviet official
later called "an uprising against Gorbachev and *perestroika.*" Gorbachev "felt fear for the first time" in the days after Andreyeva's letter
was published, according to one of his associates. "It was a moment of
panic" among Gorbachev supporters, another Soviet official said.

Not everything I was told could be categorized as firsthand information. My sources were not the key participants, but people with
access to some of them. Their information was incomplete, and could
have been wrong in some details. But the facts I used then—and here
—were confirmed by at least two knowledgeable Soviet sources.

Ligachev was not an obvious candidate for leadership of an uprising. He considered himself a reformer, too. He obviously believed
that the Soviet Union had to be overhauled to avoid its demise as a
great power. But he was also a strait-laced Communist puritan, a
believer in the contributions of earlier leaders from Stalin to Brezhnev. At age sixty-seven he was a proud Russian, who cringed at the
Western influences he saw creeping into Soviet society.

Ligachev had become a national political figure only in 1983, when
Andropov brought him to Moscow from the Siberian city of Tomsk,
to which Brezhnev had exiled him eighteen years before. By one account, the KGB told Andropov that Ligachev was the only first secretary of a major Party organization in the country who was not taking
bribes. Gorbachev indicated his choice of Ligachev as his number-two
man with a public gesture at the Central Committee plenum that
elected Gorbachev general secretary, by inviting Ligachev to sit next
to him on the dais. A month later Ligachev was named a full member
of the Politburo. But I was told that Ligachev considers Gorbachev an
accidental leader whose experience was considerably narrower than
his own—and that he saw himself as an alternative.

That the two men were at odds had become obvious the previous
summer, when Gorbachev took his mysterious fifty-two day vacation
from Moscow. Ligachev served as acting general secretary during that
period, and he apparently used the opportunity to try to bend the
Party line in a more conservative direction. He publicly defended
Soviet accomplishments both under Stalin and Brezhnev, jarring Gorbachev supporters.

Yeltsin had formalized Ligachev's status as a leading conservative enemy of reform by attacking him by name at the Central Committee plenum the previous October, in the secret speech that led to his ouster as Moscow Party leader. Gorbachev's eager contributions to the subsequent campaign against Yeltsin emboldened the conservatives, and there was a subtle but unmistakable shift in the political atmosphere. It was during the fall of 1987 that several of the most liberal publications, including *Ogonyok* and *Moscow News,* found they were again being actively censored. Nevertheless, numerous editors and writers pressed ahead with material that broke new ground for *glasnost.* It wasn't at all clear which way the wind was blowing.

While Gorbachev was in Washington in December, Ligachev again used the powers of acting general secretary, this time to set aside plans for the formal rehabilitation of Nikolai Bukharin, who had become a symbol for the reformers. A formal announcement of his rehabilitation had been prepared for early in 1988, but Ligachev called off this plan in December. Gorbachev was able to reinstate it on his return from Washington.

Why Ligachev decided to make a serious run at Gorbachev and his policies in March remains unclear. The conservatives may have been emboldened by the unexpected appearance of blood in the water—a surprise vote against Gorbachev in the Politburo sometime early in the year. The vote reportedly came on a new law on cooperatives (finally enacted in May 1988) that would legalize limited forms of private enterprise. Initially, it is said, a majority in the Politburo expressed opposition to the act. Though Gorbachev eventually prevailed, the early majority against him may have suggested that he was vulnerable.

Soon after the Andreyeva article appeared on March 13, Ligachev called a meeting of leading newspaper editors. He pointedly excluded Korotich of *Ogonyok* and Yegor Yakovlev of *Moscow News.* At the meeting, Ligachev praised the Andreyeva letter as something others should emulate, indicating that it was the new Party line.

Ivan Laptev, the chief editor of *Izvestia,* returned to his newspaper from the meeting and assembled his senior staff. Under Laptev, *Izvestia* had become a staunch promoter of reform, so the editors knew that Ligachev's offensive was directed in part at them. Comrades, Laptev said, the time has come for each of us to decide with whom we will march. He would stick with Gorbachev to the end, he said; but he was near retirement age, and would understand if younger colleagues made a different decision.

Viktor Afanasyev, the chief editor at *Pravda,* took a different tack. Afanasyev was a Brezhnev man, who was considered closer to Ligachev than to Gorbachev. He reportedly chastised his staff for allowing such an important piece as the Andreyeva letter to appear not in *Pravda* but in a secondary paper like *Sovetskaya Rossiya.*

(In fact, Andreyeva did send her letter to *Pravda* and other papers, according to knowledgeable sources, but none of them printed it. I could not find out how and why *Sovetskaya Rossiya* seized on it. The published version was considerably expanded from her original—with the help of Ligachev himself, according to several officials.)

Tass, the official news agency, sent a message to regional newspapers advising them to pay attention to the Andreyeva letter. According to one Moscow editor, the message said local papers were "authorized" to reprint it. Another editor said it amounted to an instruction. In fact, numerous papers around the country did reprint it, though a few, including one in the northern city of Tambov, refused to print, and even criticized, Andreyeva's piece.

The "uprising" then moved to a more ominous stage. Party lecturers began speaking positively about the Andreyeva letter in closed meetings of Communist activists, a traditional and confidential channel through which shifts in the Party line were often transmitted. In one such lecture to employees of Leningrad Television, the lecturer criticized Gorbachev by name, saying the leader was partly to blame for the rioting in Armenia and Azerbaijan because of his relationship with reformist economist Abel Aganbegyan. Aganbegyan, an Armenian, was said to have made nationalistic comments that encouraged Armenian protests.

Party lecturers in the army also took up the Andreyeva message. The Moscow party committee reportedly made numerous photocopies of her letter.

Gorbachev and his traveling party learned of the publication of Andreyeva's article in Ljubljana, the capital of Slovenia. Word of it was brought to him by Georgi Shakhnazarov, one of his closest aides. Shakhnazarov, I was reliably informed, was in an agitated state, and said it was necessary to draft a reply to Andreyeva at once. Gorbachev calmly disagreed. "Let's think it over," he said. The Gorbachev party was hampered by the fact that Yakovlev was also out of Moscow—its members felt cut off from critical information.

In Moscow, the atmosphere was tense. The new turn of events emboldened conservatives who had privately opposed Gorbachev, and in many offices there were knowing grins and more hostile gestures to those known to sympathize with liberalization.

"We found out who was with whom," one editor said.

After Gorbachev and Yakovlev returned to Moscow on March 18 and 19, they set about learning what had happened and planning their response. At first they had only sketchy information. Their aides turned to allies in intellectual circles to learn just what the Party lecturers in Leningrad, for example, had said about the Andreyeva letter and Gorbachev. "It's a sign of how the old system has broken down," said a participant in this intelligence gathering. "Gorbachev couldn't even rely on the KGB to tell him what was happening in the country on an issue as important as this. Central control doesn't work the way it used to."

Gorbachev moved to reassert his authority when Ligachev took a trip on March 27 to the Vologda region north of Moscow. Gorbachev called yet another meeting of editors to reassert his liberalizing line. He told the editors that Ligachev was an impediment to *perestroika,* a powerful signal given the traditional disinclination of senior leaders ever to discuss their differences.

Several editors asked Yakovlev if they could print answers to Andreyeva, but he discouraged them, saying an authoritative response would soon appear in *Pravda.* Yakovlev himself was drafting it. On Thursday, March 31, the long reply was delivered to *Pravda*'s offices.

Word quickly leaked to pro-Gorbachev elements that a strong denunciation of Andreyeva's letter would appear in *Pravda* the next day. But there was nothing in *Pravda* on Friday, or on Saturday, or on Sunday or Monday. The small circle of Gorbachev supporters who knew what was going on became intensely concerned that their leader's bold new policies had indeed been crushed by conservative opponents. At some point during those first days of April the Politburo considered the issue. Gorbachev had reportedly been lobbying members one by one.

According to an unconfirmed, dramatic report, Gorbachev left the Politburo alone to debate the issue—announcing that he was going home to his dacha to await their verdict. I later met well-informed sources who doubted the accuracy of this detail.

Whatever happened inside the Politburo, a clear majority agreed to back Gorbachev. One well-placed official said there were initial rumors of a sharp split, but later reports suggested that in the end even

Ligachev may have agreed with the others to support the general secretary.

On Tuesday, April 5, five days after it had arrived in *Pravda*'s editorial offices, Yakovlev's reply to Andreyeva was published. Under the headline "Principles of Restructuring: Revolutionary Nature of Thinking and Acting," it forcefully reasserted the need to press ahead with *glasnost* and *perestroika*. It called the Andreyeva article a reflection of the feelings of those "who bluntly propose stopping or else turning back altogether."

> We are all learning to live under conditions of broadening democracy and *glasnost* and undergoing a great learning process. It is no easy learning process. It has proved harder than we presumed to rid ourselves of old thoughts and actions, but . . . there is no going back.
>
> Some people have become confused and perplexed. The launching of democratization, the rejection of edict-based and command-based methods of management and leadership, the expansion of *glasnost* and the lifting of all manner of prohibitions and restrictions have caused concern. Aren't we shaking the very foundations of socialism and revising the principles of Marxism-Leninism?
>
> "Don't rock the boat," others say intimidatingly. There are also those who bluntly propose stopping or else turning back altogether. The article [in *Sovetskaya Rossiya*] was a reflection of such feelings.
>
> The article is dominated by an essentially fatalistic perception of history, which is totally removed from a genuinely scientific perception of it, by a tendency to justify everything that has happened in history in terms of historical necessity.
>
> But the cult [i.e., Stalin's dictatorship] was not inevitable. It is alien to the nature of socialism and only became possible because of deviations from fundamental socialist principles.
>
> The article expresses concern about the well-known spread of nihilism among a section of our young people. This disease is rooted in the past. It is the consequence of the spiritual diet that we fed to young people for decades and of the discrepancies between what was said on rostrums and what actually happened in real life. There are no prohibited topics today. Journals, publishing houses, and studios decide for themselves what to publish. But the appearance of the [*Sovetskaya Rossiya*] article is an attempt little by little to revise Party decisions.

After April 5, the Soviet press blossomed with attacks on Andreyeva's letter. Even *Sovetskaya Rossiya* had to reprint *Pravda*'s attack on it. Then—but only then—many Gorbachev backers expressed chagrin at their behavior during the twenty-three grim days between the appearances of the two articles. "We were all cowards," said one. "There we were again—waiting for a new line to be handed down from above," complained another.

According to one senior official, an aide to Ligachev was fired as the scapegoat for the Andreyeva affair. According to another source close to Gorbachev, Ligachev apologized to the general secretary for making a serious mistake. He lost direct influence over both Soviet television and *Pravda,* and according to Georgi Arbatov, a member of the Central Committee with ties to Gorbachev, Yakovlev had assumed control over ideological matters.

Gorbachev supporters took heart from the fact that Ligachev and his allies had no coherent plan for forcing a change in the Party line or for removing Gorbachev. They considered Ligachev foolish for taking a stand on a pro-Stalin platform—"no basis for a counterrevolution," as one official put it. But I could learn no explanation for how the campaign of Party lectures on the heels of the Andreyeva letter was organized, or by whom.

A number of sources sympathetic to Gorbachev spoke fearfully of the possibility of "an accident" befalling the leader. "So much rests in the hands of just one or two people," said one official, referring to Gorbachev and Yakovlev.

I was told that Gorbachev had assembled a special corps of personal security men who were only nominally in the chain of command of the KGB. "They are Gorbachev's own guard," according to one knowledgeable Muscovite. Yakovlev, according to an official, acquiesced to the preferences of his security men and no longer slept in his Moscow apartment. "He's been told it is safer to stay at his dacha" outside of town.

It is difficult to imagine that the conservatives had a concrete plan for removing Gorbachev from power. Ousting him in March 1988 would have traumatized both the Soviet Union and the rest of the world. A coup would have provoked a reaction in the West of exactly the kind the Soviets could least afford to confront—more military spending, more active support for rebels in Afghanistan, more pressure everywhere. At home too the reaction against the perpetrators of a coup would have been strong, led by the intellectuals who had become such enthusiasts for reform. Controlling them would have required ugly repressive measures; none of the putative conservative leaders showed any enthusiasm for that.

Gorbachev's cool reaction to the Andreyeva letter suggests that he saw it more as a power play than a personal threat. Gorbachev understood his own revolution better than virtually anyone else affected by it. The Moscow intellectuals, Party officials, and foreign hangers-on like me were all waiting for a new Party line to be set. This was the way things had been done since the time of Lenin. Factions battled, one prevailed, and it laid down the new line. That was the old politics. But Gorbachev's real politics were different; they left room for continuing disagreements and debates. There would be no victorious new line that everyone would have to adopt. Gorbachev was prepared to battle the conservatives on the ground they had chosen—he was probably eager for a fight over their attempt to restore Stalin's reputation. By March 1988, after many months of hair-raising disclosures of Stalin's crimes, defending the dictator was hardly a popular platform. Gorbachev could wage that fight with confidence.

Which isn't to say that Gorbachev had no personal anxieties. On the contrary, as the story of his new personal bodyguard indicates, he and his immediate entourage have worried often about their physical safety. As I noted earlier, Gorbachev has frequently spoken to his associates about the fate of Khrushchev, convincing many of them that he feared something like it might await him. But the Andreyeva affair was not conducted like a coup d'état; it was a political offensive. Ligachev's behavior, especially his statements to meetings of editors when he was trying to promote the Andreyeva line as the Party's own, suggest the true nature of this fight.

My informants thought the episode had ended with the publication of *Pravda*'s refutation of Andreyeva's article on April 5. But Giulietto Chiesa, the Moscow correspondent of *L'Unità,* subsequently acquired new information about the affair suggesting it continued after that.* According to Chiesa's account, when Gorbachev and Shevardnadze flew to Tashkent on April 6 for critical talks with Najibullah, the Afghan leader, Ligachev again took advantage of his status as Gorbachev's number two to convene a Politburo meeting. At it he requested a full Central Committee plenum to debate the issues raised by the Andreyeva affair. Ligachev must have believed that his views would prevail at a Central Committee plenum. He had good reason for such confidence, since, with Gorbachev's blessing, he had picked so many members of the Central Committee himself.

---

* I recount Chiesa's version here without any independent confirmation of its details, but with considerable confidence in Chiesa himself as a well-connected and reliable journalist.

As he ended his visit to Tashkent on April 8, Gorbachev gave a speech to Party activists there that seemed to contain an attack on Ligachev. "The destiny of our country and of socialism are in question," he said. Some comrades were scared or confused, and "there is only a short step from here to sounding the retreat." He noted that ideology—Ligachev's responsibility in the Politburo—had "a crucial significance," but "without definite, revolutionary breaks in our way of thinking, we cannot achieve radical transformations." This sounded like criticism of Ligachev.

When he returned to Moscow Gorbachev evaded the suggestion to call a Central Committee plenum. Instead, according to Chiesa, he met separately with three different groups of Central Committee members on April 11, 14, and 18; none of these groups was invited to cast any votes. Later, several of Chiesa's sources told him, the commanders of the military districts into which the Soviet Union is divided were summoned to Moscow to meet individually with Gorbachev. If true, this story suggests that Gorbachev was shoring up his personal position with the commanders—a hint that he feared his continued leadership might indeed be at risk.

The final showdown, Chiesa wrote, came at a Politburo meeting that lasted for two days, April 15 and 16. Gorbachev reported that he had asked a personal assistant to investigate the Andreyeva article, and had determined that it was inspired from within the Politburo itself.* A tense debate ensued. At the end of the meeting Ligachev was isolated. The Politburo curtailed his duties; many of his responsibilities for ideological matters were transferred to Yakovlev. According to Chiesa, Yakovlev told a friend at the time, "We have crossed the Rubicon."

This was a turning point for Gorbachev. Sometime during that spring of 1988 he completed an important psychological break with the conservative Party *apparat,* and thus with his own past. How exactly the Andreyeva affair affected that break remains a mystery, but the circumstantial evidence is compelling that Ligachev had finally gone too far, forcing Gorbachev to make a choice that he had previously ducked. Until that spring Gorbachev continued to try to placate the *apparat* and to persuade it to embrace his reforms as the best course for the country and the Party. But he was on the verge of

---

* One of the telling points made by critics of Andreyeva was based on her purported quotation of Winston Churchill. Churchill's entire oeuvre had been searched; he never used those words about Stalin.

a sharp turn away from that approach. In six weeks, he would be ready to launch the real Gorbachev revolution by finally laying out a plan for political changes that would explicitly take power away from the Party.

In mid-May, a month after the resolution of the Andreyeva affair, I arrived in Moscow for a three-week visit. Just twenty-one years earlier, when Gorbachev's roommate Mlynar and his comrades were opening up Czechoslovakia with the most creative reforms yet seen in the Communist world, someone named that new season the Prague Spring. After several days back in Moscow, I felt I had landed in something very similar—Gorbachev's Moscow Spring.

It took several days to adjust to the new atmosphere, which was exhilarating but also disorienting because it was so different from the Moscow I had known previously. I was living in old Moscow, in a big room in the National Hotel, a structure of mock-Parisian elegance built in the last century, where Lenin once lived in a suite facing the Kremlin. But from the moment one of my oldest friends instructed me to "call right from the telephone in your hotel room, nobody worries about that anymore," I realized that this was a very new Moscow—Moscow without fear.

It would never have occurred to me to use the telephone in my room. It was certain to be closely monitored by the KGB, and using it to call a friend could only raise the prospect of trouble for that friend. Better to call from a public phone on the street. That was one of a thousand reflexes developed after years of living under surveillance, reflexes that were no longer needed—or so everyone kept saying. Where were those legions of KGB agents who used to follow us around, listen to our phone calls and to the tapes made by microphones buried in our walls? No one was sure—perhaps they were still on the job, still listening. So what? "They can't do anything now—at least not right now," one friend said reassuringly—well, somewhat reassuringly. This is our moment, the Moscow intellectuals all said in one way or another. It may not last, but for now we are seizing it.

That visit began with one surprise right after another. I had come with Katharine Graham, the chairman of The Washington Post Company, and a group of editors from the *Post* and *Newsweek;* our mission was to interview Gorbachev on the eve of Ronald Reagan's first visit to Moscow. The first night there we ate dinner at a brand-new Georgian cooperative restaurant, built on the ground floor of a typical gray brick Moscow apartment house. The proprietors had acquired rustic

wood paneling somewhere, and had decorated with cast-iron orna-
ments. It was like nothing I had ever seen in Moscow, and the food
was excellent. (This sort of private enterprise was very new in 1988;
dozens of restaurants have sprung up since, and dozens have also
failed and gone out of business.)

The next day we spent an hour with Valentin Falin, an interesting
figure who had served as Soviet ambassador to West Germany and as
a senior *apparatchik* in the Central Committee, and in 1988 was chairman of the Novosti press agency. In a conversation that lasted several
hours in 1984, Falin had regaled me with an anti-American diatribe,
explaining how every aspect of the Cold War had been the fault of the
United States.

So it came as quite a surprise to hear him in 1988 deliver a devastating denunciation of Joseph Stalin. He said it was clear that "the
Leninist and Stalinist versions of socialism were mutually exclusive"
—that Stalin had taken the country far off course, and now Gorbachev
was trying to steer it back. He said evidence had been found in official
archives that showed that Stalin personally had ordered certain political rivals to be arrested and killed. But he acknowledged that a considerable portion of the Soviet public still considered Stalin a great
hero. "That is a reality we'll have to deal with for a long time to come,"
Falin said. He boasted of the material then being published and
broadcast that was introducing the masses to Stalin's crimes, recommending a new documentary that would be broadcast the next night.
He said, "One hundred forty million people will probably see that
film."

I did watch the next evening. The film was called *Protsess,* which is
the Russian word for "process," and also for "trial." It described and
depicted many of the great events of Soviet history, interspersing old
film clips that had never been shown before on television with interviews with old people who took part in the events described. There
were vivid pictures of peasants being driven off their land during the
collectivization of agriculture, of the show trials of the thirties, and
much more. The comments from survivors were amazing. "Stalin took
a perfectly good agricultural system and—with no war or other difficulty—he put us all on food rationing," said one old man in a matter-
of-fact tone. Others described killings and arrests of their comrades
that still upset them after fifty years. Just as Falin had said, the film
was made for ordinary citizens, not intellectuals. Its effect was to
shred the mythology that used to prop up the Party's rule.

Those first impressions were followed in the days ahead by a series of amazing occurrences. The exhilaration of discovering a liberated Russia where people could say—or shout—what they thought, read the truth, debate all the once-taboo subjects of politics and history produced in me a kind of euphoria. The most fun was seeing old friends, people I had known as disaffected intellectuals who had little or nothing to do with official matters, who in the 1970s and early 1980s could go for months without glancing at *Pravda* or worrying about affairs of state. Now all that had changed. One family I'd known for years whose bookish members were always strapped for money had worked out a system in their apartment house for sharing the daily papers, weeklies, and monthly journals that everyone was suddenly eager to devour. The people on the second floor subscribed to *Izvestia;* my friends got *Ogonyok* and *Novy Mir,* upstairs they got *Komsomolskaya Pravda* and *Yunost* (Youth), a literary journal. Everyone marked the good pieces and passed them back and forth.

There was an excitement in the air that no one had ever expected to experience. I met a painter who had just returned from his first trip abroad—three weeks in Paris. His head was still spinning from the experience. A gallery there had offered to sell his works; émigré friends had urged him to give up Russia and come to France. "I thought about it," he said, but decided to come home, especially after he realized that everyone in France wanted to talk about what was going on in the Soviet Union, and not about France. "I had no idea this could happen in my lifetime—to live in truly interesting times in Moscow!"

Not that all the news was good. The city hummed with rumors of right-wing plots to undo Gorbachev, and not everyone exploiting the new freedom shared a liberal outlook. The Pamyat society had become one of the strongest of the new unofficial associations, and it was blatantly anti-Semitic and reactionary. Reports of impending pogroms against Jews were persistent; some named the dates and places where violence would occur. (One of the named dates passed uneventfully while I was still there.) Zoya Bogaslavskaya, a writer married to Andrei Voznesensky, the poet, described a new club called "Stalin's Eagles," which she said had attracted a following among young men. To become a member, one had to steal from a public library a copy of one of the new anti-Stalin books—Rybakov's *Children of the Arbat,* for example—and take the book to Gori, Stalin's birthplace in the Georgian mountains. There the new initiate would burn the book in some kind of ritual. Members pledged to wear only foreign-made clothes. I found no further confirmation of this tale, but many in Moscow had heard and believed it.

Perhaps the single most interesting conversation I had during those weeks in Moscow was with a man I'd known since the mid-1970s, a former KGB officer who had become an academic expert on international relations. Like many others I saw on that visit, he wanted to convince me that he was truly a man of the new spirit, now prepared to disavow not only his country's past but his own. "You know what I'm ashamed of?" he asked, looking across the crowded desk in his office. "I'm ashamed of the fact that for all those years I stood up and defended it! You know, after a while it became difficult to sleep at night. I mean, if you have no conscience, well, it's easy to sleep. But if you are cursed with a conscience—it can be difficult."

"We have never lived normal lives, or had a normal country," he said, hoping that both would now be possible. He said it was absolutely necessary to establish the rule of law—"the law must be above the Party." And "we have to get rid of our secrecy fetish." He deplored the "crazy fact" that the economic system actively discouraged people from working hard. He said it was time to admit that the ideological view of the outside world that he and so many others had propagated was ridiculous. "We have to admit that we just don't know the rest of the world." The time had come for the Soviet Union to become a full member of the community of nations.

"I don't think our country is worse than others," he said near the end of this burst of candor. "We have the same number of talented people, of smart people. But they haven't been given any chance to show what they can do!"

He talked this way for two hours. I could not believe my ears. To see this man, nearly sixty years old, push himself through this painful confession left me shaken. What amazing things were happening in Russia!

•   •   •

The opportunity to interview Gorbachev at this critical moment in his crusade seemed like almost miraculous good luck. Katharine Graham had been pressing for a chance to interview the Soviet leader since Andropov was in power; finally her perseverance had paid off. We had only learned officially that the interview was on a few weeks before, when two emissaries from the Soviet leader showed up in

Graham's Washington office with the news. They came late in the day, and she offered them a drink. They joked about the antidrinking campaign still going on in their country, and poured themselves enormous glasses of Scotch. Yes, they assured Graham, the interview was on; she could conduct it eleven days before President Reagan arrived in Moscow.

Graham had interviewed many statesmen, often with Meg Greenfield, the editor of the *Post*'s editorial page, and Jim Hoagland, for years the paper's editor in charge of foreign news, and then its chief foreign correspondent and a columnist. It was my good fortune to be invited to join them and Rick Smith, the editor-in-chief of *Newsweek,* to prepare and conduct the Gorbachev interview.

We worked hard to educate ourselves, and then to formulate questions. We held the final discussion of what to ask on benches in Gorki Park, where no microphones could eavesdrop. I think this was my idea, a sign that I still wasn't used to Moscow without fear. We wanted to preserve an element of surprise—no good having the KGB brief Gorbachev on the questions we planned to ask before we even got to his office. We had already delivered a list of written questions, and expected written answers to them. This was a pattern Gorbachev had established with earlier interviewers. But it was the verbal give-and-take that would be the most fun—and, we hoped, the most revealing.

Our list of questions settled, we set off to Staraya Ploshchad, or Old Square, the site of the office building housing the Central Committee. When I was a Moscow correspondent no American journalist got into that building; it was a remote fortress. But it turned out to have doors like any building, and we walked right in.

It was the finest office building I'd ever seen in Moscow, a city not known for its architectural finery. There were carpet runners in every corridor, which are found in other buildings, but these runners had carpet pads beneath them—something I had never experienced in Moscow before. Brass lamps with glass shades lit the corridors. Gorbachev's office was perhaps fifty feet long, with a fifteen-foot ceiling. The same greenish carpet runner connected the most-used spots in the office, but most of the bleached wood parquet was bare. We sat at the long table famous from many photos of Gorbachev's meetings with visitors, he and an aide on one side, our group of five facing him.

We stayed for ninety minutes. I have never seen a politician work as hard as Gorbachev did during that hour and a half. His intensity was palpable; you could almost hear his mind whir. It was flattering to be taken so seriously. He seemed determined to charm us, but more determined to convince us of his seriousness. The fervent brown eyes worked us over; when forced to slow down for the interpreter to convey his words in English, he drummed the table with his fingertips. In informal moments before and after the interview, I caught him studying his guests individually, taking them in as human beings. Altogether, an entirely serious person.

The interview fit neatly into a stream of public statements he was making that spring, which is not surprising, since he intended to print the text of the interview in *Pravda* the following week (it did appear, with a photograph of our delegation facing Gorbachev across the ubiquitous table in his office, and covered nearly the entire front page). "You know," he told us, "it may be paradoxical, but now I am more confident in the political line we have chosen for *perestroika,* for the renewal of our society, than at the beginning of this road, although we have more difficulties than before. What is the explanation for that? I think that we do know better now what we want, and how to do it. Therefore we have more confidence." That sounded like the voice of the man who had just come through the Andreyeva affair. So did this remark: "This is a turbulent time, a turbulent sea in which it is not easy to sail the ship, but we have a compass and we have a crew to guide that ship. And the ship itself is strong." He was a little defensive about his ability to solve his country's problems: "Jesus Christ alone knew answers to all the questions, and knew how to feed twenty thousand Jews with five loaves of bread. We don't possess that skill, we have no ready prescription to solve all our problems quickly." But he expressed satisfaction that so many people were debating possible solutions. "The whole country is now an enormous debating society."

It is difficult to recreate now a sense of the skepticism that pervaded our view of Gorbachev that spring, but it was powerful. The real Gorbachev revolution was just beginning. Nothing had changed yet in Eastern Europe; there had been no real elections in the Soviet Union; the Party was still in firm control. Like so many from the West, we were dubious about the ultimate significance of Gorbachev's more liberal policies; we wanted to be convinced. He felt our doubts, which was one reason, I'm sure, why he worked so hard to prove that he was serious. Like many others who had questioned him over the previous three years, we demanded that he answer for those aspects of the situation that fed our doubts. As he had in the past, Gorbachev gave testy replies that were not entirely reassuring.

For example, we asked about Eastern Europe. He had said publicly that every nation had the right to choose its own path, but it wasn't clear what that meant. Would it be "tolerable to you" if Poland adopted "a pluralistic system in which the Communist Party might not play the leading role"?

He ducked the question. "I am confident," he said, "that an overwhelming majority of people in Poland favor continuing along the path on which the country started after the war [World War II]." In other words, Poles didn't want a pluralistic system of that kind.

We asked about the sincerity of his advocacy of freedom of speech, and noted that at that time there was an Armenian nationalist, Paruir Arikyan, and a Moscow dissident, Sergei Grigoryants, who had recently been detained by the authorities for what looked to us like exercising freedom of speech. Did that mean some authorities did not understand his "new thinking"? Or had Arikyan and Grigoryants done something that he did not regard as exercising freedom of speech?

This question provoked an unpleasant appearance by the *apparatchik* Gorbachev. He skipped over Arikyan, a participant in the tense drama then still unfolding in Armenia, but he spoke nastily of Grigoryants, the editor of an unofficial journal in Moscow. "People know that Grigoryants's 'organization,' is tied not only organizationally but also financially to the West, that his constant visitors and guests are Western correspondents. Therefore people think of him as some kind of alien phenomenon in our society, sponging on the democratic process, sponging on the positive aspects of *perestroika*. This happens— it happens in nature, too. There are such parasites living off healthy organisms and attempting to harm them. But we are sure that our country is strong enough to overcome such a thing." His use of the word "overcome" seemed particularly unpleasant; it would have been more reassuring if he had used "tolerate" instead.

The most interesting moment of the interview came when Rick Smith of *Newsweek* asked Gorbachev directly about the Andreyeva affair. He noted that several Soviet editors had told us that Andreyeva's letter had been endorsed by Ligachev, and that *Pravda*'s reply had Gorbachev's personal imprimatur. "Does this exchange suggest that there is a serious difference of opinion in the leadership?"

This was not a question Gorbachev wanted to deal with, as his strained body language instantly made clear. First he rejected the idea that Soviet editors were the source of reports about a division in the leadership—that was the work of "the Western media," he said. Such reports are "systematically tossed up" abroad, then broadcast into the Soviet Union on hostile radio stations. Of course there was "lively and constant discussion" within the leadership, but "to present these discussions—which are a normal part of the democratic process—as division within the leadership would be a great mistake." Again the *apparatchik* came to the fore, and tried to fib his way out of an awkward moment.

Smith pressed on. Some of your strongest supporters are worried about political divisions, he told Gorbachev. And he quoted from a recent letter to the newspaper *Sovetskaya Kultura,* whose author speculated on the possibility of a Central Committee plenum "at which M. S. Gorbachev could be ousted." Had Gorbachev heard about that letter?

"That letter's not the only thing I've heard about," he said, laughing with his aide, Anatoli Chernayev, the only person who accompanied him during the interview. But he insisted that the fact that such a letter had been written and published was "entirely positive." He saw it as proof that "people have become involved in the political process. They want to participate, to express their opinions. . . . And that is wonderful. It may be the most important product of *perestroika."* But he insisted that the letter writer's anxieties had no basis in fact. "I mean, there is no such thing that promises any kind of split in the leadership."

The interview took place on May 18, a Wednesday. At five that afternoon, one of the Central Committee officials who had helped arrange the interview—one of the two men who had poured themselves generous Scotches in Kay Graham's office—called the Moscow bureau of *The Washington Post.* I spoke with him. He said there was a problem to discuss. The general secretary had told him not once, not twice, but three times after the interview that he did not want to be quoted mentioning any of his colleagues in the Politburo. He didn't even want any of them mentioned by name in the transcript of questions asked of him. Tomorrow, the caller said, he would deliver an official Soviet transcript of the interview to us, and we would see how they proposed to reformulate Rick Smith's question about Ligachev —without mentioning Ligachev's name.

And you would like us to use your formulation? I asked. Yes, he replied. "In the spirit of mutual cooperation," the caller said he hoped we would agree not to mention Ligachev at all. "Let's play this by Moscow rules," he said in Russian, using the phrase made famous in spy novels. I told him that only Mrs. Graham could make a decision of that kind—we would discuss it when he delivered the transcript in the morning.

In the excitement of that heady day, I concluded that we had stumbled into a major power struggle, some kind of extension of the Andreyeva affair, and our interview had suddenly become a pawn in the game. Our group discussed the request I'd received for an hour or more; we all agreed that there was no honorable way we could censor our own question in the transcript of the interview.

The next morning our contact at the Central Committee came as promised with his transcript. It was surprisingly honest; it did not put words in Smith's mouth, but paraphrased his question instead: "R. Smith asked a question the point of which was, did the appearance of the famous articles in *Sovetskaya Rossiya* and *Pravda* indicate the existence of serious differences in the Politburo?" Any attentive Soviet reader would realize that the question had been censored, since this was the only paraphrase of a question in the transcript.* But the offending reference to Ligachev had disappeared.

Well, what about it, the man from the Central Committee asked—can you do as the general secretary requests? No, we told him, we just couldn't do it. It was the sort of request we would not grant even from the president of the United States. (The man from the Central Committee gave a disbelieving grimace when I said that.) Why not, he proposed, use the suggested paraphrase and add a footnote, explaining that the question obviously referred to Ligachev? No, we would have to stick to the real transcript, we said; it was a point of principle, no doubt incomprehensible to Russians, but we could not abandon it.

He left, chagrined. Perhaps twenty minutes later the phone in the bureau rang again. Him again. He wanted to know where Mrs. Graham was at that moment. In the Moscow bureau chief's apartment, I told him. The general secretary had a message for her; he wanted the message delivered by Mr. ——, the second official who had helped arrange the interview, who outranked the man from the Central Committee. Mrs. Graham agreed to meet ——, who appeared at the apartment within fifteen minutes, as did I. "I have a personal message for you," he said as he arrived, sweeping her into the dining room of the four-room apartment and leaving the rest of us in the living room.

---

* This was just how the question appeared a few days later when *Pravda, Izvestia,* and all the major papers printed the full interview.

The apartment is small and we could easily overhear the discussion. Mr. —— pleaded eloquently that we should respect Gorbachev's request in return for the great favor he had done us by granting the interview. Mrs. Graham would not be budged—we didn't censor ourselves for anyone. It was a cardinal rule at *The Washington Post,* and we couldn't do it for Gorbachev, either. She apologized more than once, but remained firm. They rejoined the rest of the group, and —— repeated his arguments. We became convinced that neither of these men knew why Gorbachev was so sensitive about mentioning Ligachev's name. Mr. —— suggested that his concern must have been based on some understanding between the two men, but he couldn't explain it. After an hour or more they realized we really wouldn't budge, and they rose to leave. "Don't worry," —— said to Mrs. Graham, "you won't be arrested!" I walked them both to their car, reminding them that this was the same Katharine Graham who had stood up to the threats of the Nixon crowd when she thought they might try to take her television licenses away from her. They shouldn't be surprised that she stood her ground with Gorbachev, too. They nodded glumly.

We never did get an explanation for Gorbachev's sensitivity about mentioning Ligachev. I decided that he must have made a deal with his rival after defeating him in the Andreyeva affair, perhaps a bargain that both of them would preserve the appearance of Party unity at all costs, and Gorbachev would preserve Ligachev's status as an important member of the Politburo. It was just a guess. A friend in Moscow with close ties to senior officials said he interpreted this episode as a sign of Gorbachev's great sensitivity to any suggestion that he might be splitting the Party—a cardinal sin by its traditional standards. It is true that Gorbachev has often gone to great lengths to cater to the conservatives, who he knew distrusted him. But it isn't clear how printing Rick Smith's question would have contributed to accusations of Party splitting. Shortly afterward, at a televised news conference during the summit when Reagan was in Moscow, Gorbachev willingly answered a question about his relations with Ligachev, with no sign of sensitivity. A mystery.

* * *

Six days after our interview, Gorbachev sprang yet another surprise on his countrymen. The newspapers on the morning of May 24 all carried front-page reports that a special Central Committee plenum the day before had approved "theses" for the 19th Party Conference, then just a month off. The theses described what were called the Central Committee's plans for the conference, though it was obvious that they were Gorbachev's and Yakovlev's plans, and probably would have been defeated (or substantially modified) if put to a free vote of the Central Committee. They contained radical propositions, the likes of which the Party had never before endorsed.

The selection of delegates to the Party Conference had gone badly for the reformers. Although Gorbachev had explicitly instructed local Party organizations that they were to pick only staunch supporters of *perestroika* as delegates, the Party committees reverted to form, and chose reliable *apparatchiks* for a large majority of the seats. Some of the most famous public figures associated with reform, including Tatyana Zaslavskaya, the reformist sociologist, Gavril Popov of Moscow State University (the future mayor of Moscow), and economist Nikolai Shmelyov, were denied seats, most of them after being recommended by the Party organizations of large institutions.

The elections of delegates were the first events in the modern history of the Party that did not have a foreordained result—in other words, the Party's first flirtation with real politics. As such they attracted intense public interest, another first for any Party endeavor in decades. Unprecedented protest rallies were held in many towns and cities; petitions were signed, and thousands of letters were sent to newspapers all over the country objecting to the arbitrary selection of conservative *apparatchiks* over real reformers. "Bah! All the faces are familiar," complained V. Severgin in a letter to *Izvestia.* "The bureau of the province Party committee narrowed down our 70 candidates to 48. . . . There were 48 slots—so they voted for 48. What sort of election is that?" asked P. Pyanov from Odessa. "If the delegates don't see any violation of democratic principles in the procedure by which they were elected, will they be able to defend these principles at the conference itself?" asked twenty-five physicists who wrote a letter of protest from Gorki.

Gorbachev, Yakovlev, and their associates must have realized that they had lost control of the elections process, and would face another conservative gathering at the conference. But they were not intimidated by that realization. Using their control over the Party secretariat, which planned the conference, and the device of the theses, they set a radical agenda anyhow. Gorbachev understood that the natural inclination of the *apparatchiks* to accept guidance blindly from above —a powerful instinct, no matter how often Gorbachev deplored it—

could be used to his advantage. He used it repeatedly, right up to the 28th Party Congress in the summer of 1990, when he persuaded the Party to vote to remove itself from the levers of state power.

The critical antecedents for that historic turn were the theses of May 1988. They were the most coherent formulation of the Gorbachev revolution yet. They began with a declaration that *"Perestroika* has created a fundamentally new . . . situation in society" featuring "real pluralism of opinions, an open comparison of ideas and interests." At the same time, "the advocates of dogmatic notions about socialism are surrendering their positions slowly. Attempts are being made to preserve the old, pressure methods of managing the economy and other spheres of life." But these reactionary forces will be defeated. "The Party will consistently conduct a policy of candor and openness and of free discussion of problems about the past and the present, because only such a policy facilitates the moral improvement of Soviet society and its liberation from everything that is alien to its humane nature."

The theses included a long section on economic reform and the benefits it would bring, but they admitted that little had yet been accomplished. "Of course, two or three years [it was thirty-eight months since Gorbachev had come to power] is an insufficient time for fundamental economic transformations. We are in the initial stage of such transformations, in a kind of transitional period."

And then a key passage: "An objective analysis of what has been achieved during the past three years in the economy, the social sphere, and culture, and an effort to comprehend the problems that have arisen in the course of *perestroika* have led to the conclusion that a reform of the political system . . . is necessary. Its goal is to truly include the broad masses of the working people in the management of all state and public affairs, and to complete the creation of a socialist state based on the rule of law."

Gorbachev had first introduced the idea that political reforms were needed in January 1987; now he spelled out what he meant in startling detail. First, "all Party organizations must act within the framework of the U.S.S.R. Constitution and state laws. The adoption by Party committees of resolutions that contain direct instructions to state and economic agencies and public organizations should be ruled out." In Soviet terms, this was a prescription for rewriting the power arrangements that governed society. Party committees—starting with the Politburo—had always given orders to everyone else. That was how the system worked.

At the same time the Party had to be truly democratized. Secret ballots and multiple candidates should become "the norm" for select-ing all officials. Tenure in Party offices should be limited to two terms, or three in extraordinary circumstances. The *nomenklatura* system that allowed the Party to appoint all important officials had to be changed.

To replace Party power, the theses declared, the time had come for "full restoration of the role and authority of the Soviets [councils] of People's Deputies as sovereign bodies of popular representation." Though Lenin had first promoted the soviets and understood their importance, "as a result of well-known deformations, the rights and powers of the representative bodies have been curtailed, and Party committees continue to exercise unwarranted tutelage over them." Now it was time for "the transfer to the soviets of the full range of powers, from top to bottom." Under the new arrangements, a demo-cratically elected Supreme Soviet would be "the country's supreme body of power."

Here was Gorbachev's revolutionary answer to the legitimacy crisis he had helped precipitate during his first three years in power. He spelled it out more clearly a month later in his opening speech to the Party Conference, which was an elaboration of the theses. A truly legitimate new state power would be built on a Congress of People's Deputies, most of whose members would be elected by the public in contested elections, by secret ballot. The theses included a proposal that this new form of power be limited by a rule setting a two-term limit for all elected deputies, local and national.

One of the most startling passages in the theses concerned the need to establish "a socialist state based on the rule of law." Here, perhaps, were the fruits of Gorbachev's legal education thirty years earlier. The "fundamental feature" of this new socialist state "is the supremacy and triumph of law. . . . State and party agencies, public organiza-tions, labor collectives, and all officials and citizens should operate on a strictly legal basis." This would mean "creating the material and legal conditions for the realization of constitutional freedoms (free-dom of speech, freedom of the press, freedom to assemble and hold rallies, street processions, and demonstrations, freedom of con-science, and others). It also has to do with strengthening guarantees of the citizen's personal rights (the inviolability of the individual and of the home, the right to privacy in correspondence and telephone conversations and others)." Suddenly the Communist Party had em-braced the American Bill of Rights! A new legal system, the theses said, would adopt "an adversary system with equality for all the parties at law, openness, and the presumption of innocence." Many new laws must be written, but the new system must give "strict adherence" to "the principle that everything not forbidden by law is permitted."

This was a blueprint for turning Soviet society upside down. Gorbachev could not ensure the selection of loyal reformers as delegates to the Party Conference, but he could ram his radical reforms through the Central Committee—that was the irony of his position in 1988. He was imposing change on the Party by exploiting the Party's traditional deference to power. The Central Committee was not enthusiastic about these changes, but it was not prepared to block Gorbachev either. Again, his success grew out of his willingness to lead, to press ahead when others were anxious or scared or simply opposed to the changes he sought, but unable to block them.

•   •   •

On the eve of the Party Conference Gorbachev had a visit from one of the men who had helped him establish his dominant position as a leader, Ronald Reagan. This was Reagan's first exposure to the "evil empire," but he came as a pussycat, not a tiger. Reagan seemed to like Moscow, and to enjoy his encounters with Russians, including spontaneous ones on the street and in Red Square with Gorbachev. The Soviets were still edgy about this American who had hated them so fiercely; they did not televise his most pointed and interesting speeches to the writers' union and to an audience of students and faculty at Moscow State University. They bridled a little when he insisted on meeting with a group of Jews who were trying unsuccessfully to emigrate, but no one objected when Reagan invited Andrei Sakharov to the official dinner he hosted.

Nothing of great significance was decided at this summit; after successful completion of the treaty eliminating missiles in Europe, the arms-control negotiations had reached an impasse, at least temporarily. But the atmosphere was positive, and the picture of a grinning Reagan moving around the capital of the Soviet Union was, in Soviet eyes, testimony to Gorbachev's greatest success—the taming of the American reactionaries. The meeting ended with extraordinary statements of friendship and confidence between the two leaders. I watched the farewell ceremonies in St. Catherine's Hall in the Kremlin with a sense that this really might be a historical turning point, the end of the Cold War. Reagan said he and Gorbachev had "slayed a

228   WHY GORBACHEV HAPPENED

few dragons" as allies fighting together against "threats to peace and
to liberty," an extraordinary formulation suggesting both a common
purpose and common values. The Reagans and Gorbachevs parted
warmly, like old friends. The president told Gorbachev that he and
Mrs. Reagan had been "truly moved" by their reception in Moscow.

• • •

I left Moscow right after the Reagans did. I came home feeling
gloomy about Gorbachev's prospects for turning the Soviet Union into
a prosperous and humane society.

This gloom seemed almost unfair. The visit had been exciting; the
obvious changes were dramatic. But the Stalinist system had done
profound damage to Russia—so much damage that a decade or two
of reform seemed unlikely to put things right. Of all the Communist
countries, Russia will have the most difficulty finding a new path to
real progress, because the foundation on which the future must be
built is so rotten. No other Communist system is even half a century
old; the Soviet model has had three or four generations to reach its
present dismal condition.

We in the West have little firsthand experience with societies that
are structurally unsound. "Our model failed," one official in Moscow
told me during my visit. "It took us nowhere." Yuri Afanasyev, who
was emerging as one of the most outspoken liberals, offered an ironic
elaboration of that judgment. "We have made one important contribution," he said. "We have taught the world what *not* to do."

Nikolai Shmelyov, a novelist and economist, wrote in a similar
spirit in *Novy Mir* in the spring of 1988: "It is important that we all
recognize the degree to which we have gotten out of the habit of doing
everything that is economically normal and healthy, and into the habit
of doing everything that is economically abnormal and unhealthy. . . .
We are now like a seriously ill man who, after a long time in bed,
takes his first step with the greatest difficulty and finds, to his horror,
that he has almost forgotten how to walk."

That notion of forgotten skills came up in many of my conversations
about the prospects for reform. Millions of Soviet workers had no idea
of the difference between careful, high-quality work and what has
traditionally been acceptable in their country. Soviet citizens have
long had an utterly contemptuous view of Soviet workmanship. "It's
ours, it's bad," *The Washington Post*'s chauffeur in Moscow told me,
as though the two adjectives were synonyms.

The Soviet Union did not keep up with the rapid technological change of the last generation—it has missed out almost entirely on the computer revolution—and has no infrastructure to enable it to catch up. For example, the primitive telephone system, which still reaches only a fraction of the population, is largely incapable of transmitting computer data.

Some Moscow intellectuals spoke hopefully about at least finding a way to produce more food. At first blush there seems a certain logic here; farmers have been tied to a hopelessly inefficient structure of state and collective farms, forced to fulfill orders from far-off bureaucrats who know nothing of farming, while managing, almost as a hobby, to produce more than a quarter of the nation's food on their tiny, legal private plots. Give that private initiative freer reign, many argued, and the food problem could be solved.

But this was too optimistic. The ineradicable consequences of a half century of misrule were just too great to be speedily overcome. There is no tradition of entrepreneurial farming in the Soviet countryside, and no living farmers who ever practiced it. The successful entrepreneurs of old, who made prerevolutionary Russia an exporter of grain, were wiped out as unwanted kulaks in the ugly first stages of collectivization. A new rural élite then arose—tractor drivers, who had the best jobs and the highest status. The mechanics who cared for the machinery were also better off than the ordinary farm workers. In many areas the bulk of the manual labor on the land is performed by women, who fall at the very bottom of the rural pecking order. Tractor drivers and mechanics know little if anything about managing farm acreage, protecting its vitality from season to season, planting and harvesting to get the most out of it. A tiny private plot was easy to manage; fifty acres was another problem altogether.

The smothering of initiative and responsibility is one of the most discouraging but also most palpable consequences of the Stalinist epoch. Soviet citizens at every level instinctively look upward for guidance and instruction. "We are trying," said one Moscow scholar, "to squeeze the slave out of us."

Part of the slave mentality was the widespread belief that everyone should receive about the same rewards, no matter what his contribution—the "leveling mentality," Gorbachev called it. This instinct runs deep in the national character, in part because it grows from a peasant reflex much older than Bolshevism. Georgi Arbatov, the survivor who is director of the Institute for the Study of the U.S.A. and Canada, described this peasant outlook: "Okay, maybe I'll have to go hungry, but just don't let my neighbor prosper!"

During my visit to Moscow in 1988 I asked Felix Uskov, the alcohol-abuse counselor who worked in the giant ZIL automobile factory in Moscow, what the men on the shop floor thought of Gorbachev's reforms. "They don't believe in anything," he replied, "and they especially don't believe that things will get better."

It occurred to me during the summer of 1988 that the Russians were coming to terms with the failure of their system, and that we should do the same. Stalin's goal was to create an empire tied together by Communist ideology, fueled by Communist efficiency, and dominated by Great Russian ambitions. The ideology had failed, the efficiency had proven illusory, and the ambitions were anachronistic in the modern world. What was left was a brontosaurus empire, one unfit for survival.

This metaphor was suggested by Lev Kopelev, an extraordinary Russian who was born in Kiev five years before the Bolshevik Revolution and participated in many of the most exciting phases of the Soviet experiment. He was driven from his homeland in 1981 because of his own brand of *glasnost,* then not in favor. After the Soviet government stripped him of his citizenship, Kopelev settled in West Germany, where I saw him on my way to Moscow in 1988. In his own lifetime, Kopelev observed, he had seen the demise of the German, French, British, Austro-Hungarian, Portuguese, Dutch, Italian, and Japanese empires—the twentieth century has not been hospitable to such enterprises. Now it was the Russians' turn, he said—more than a year before the dramatic events of 1989 made him a prophet. There was no more adhesive to hold the Russian empire together, Kopelev argued. It had all worn out.

•   •   •

The 19th Party Conference was a great event for a simple reason: it was the first modern gathering of the Communist Party that was not fully scripted from first to last. Instead the country saw something unique: real politics in a formal Party setting. In place of the deadening unanimity of the past, suddenly there were anger, repartee, and genuine debate. The delegates sensed the newness of the situation from the outset. One of the first speakers, a Moscow Party secretary named V. K. Belyaninov, was interrupted by rhythmic handclapping when he lapsed into traditional claptrap. The delegates' reaction was described with evident satisfaction by two *Pravda* reporters, who wrote: "When Belyaninov . . . began to stray from the point, people in the audience began clapping. No, not in support of the speech, of course—it was a distinctive protest against boring blather. And since the speaker could not get back into a businesslike key, the applause grew until he left the rostrum. Finally, the presiding officer read out a note that had come up from the presidium: 'Don't get caught up in self-congratulation or laudatory talk—it takes up too much time for no purpose.'

"Yes," *Pravda* continued, "speakers will now have to think twice— as they should—before mounting the rostrum. The delegates to the 19th All-Union Party Conference will not accept twaddle and general, fine-sounding phrases!"

Initially it had been decided not to broadcast the conference, perhaps because of uncertainty about how the *apparatchiks* elected as delegates by many Party organizations would respond to the radical proposals of the theses, which Gorbachev elaborated on in his initial report. But after several days the news media's coverage had become quite freewheeling, and Soviet television had begun to broadcast long excerpts from the proceedings each evening.

The conservatives participated cautiously in the debate; many bit their tongues. But occasionally one of them spoke out bluntly and won rapturous applause. The most outspoken was Yuri Bondarev, a reactionary writer and an official of the writers' union of the Russian Republic. He denounced the press organs in the vanguard of *glasnost* —"this press of ours which destroys, belittles and throws into the trash heap our experiences and our past, things sacred to our nation"—and said: "We are betraying our young people . . . we are devastating their souls with the scalpel of anarchistic twaddle, empty sensationalism, all sorts of alien fashions and cheap, demagogic flirtations." The crowd loved it. "Could our *perestroika* be compared to an airplane that has taken off without knowing if there is a landing strip at its destination?" Bondarev asked.

Gorbachev did not respond directly to Bondarev, though on many occasions he, as presiding officer, entered into banter and debate with individual speakers. On the third day he returned to the podium to address the gathering. His announced purpose was to talk about the proposed division of responsibilities between Party and state, and to defend the need for the sweeping political changes he had proposed. His speech included a dramatic moment. He noted that an earlier speaker had called for firm action—"he urged that we bang our fists on the table," Gorbachev said. "Well, that can be done, comrades. If you agree with this, then let's start doing it." And he banged the podium. The delegates burst into applause. And then he reproached them: "But you know that this isn't what we need. In accomplishing the tasks of the renewal of the Party and of society as a whole, we must refrain from the old methods, which are exactly what brought our society to its grave condition." More applause!

Gorbachev had exposed the yearning in the hall for decisive leadership that would take all responsibility away from people like those who were in the audience as delegates, and turn it over to a tough leader who would bang his fist on the table. But Gorbachev refused to be that kind of leader. "I will never agree with that approach, I take my stand on that, and I tell you honestly and bluntly: This position of mine is firm. If we do not include the people in the processes of management, no administrative apparatus (and ours consists of eighteen million people, and we spend forty billion rubles a year to support it) will be able to cope with it."

In other words, Gorbachev was telling the *apparatchiks* in the hall, they were incapable of running a modern country, despite the staggering size of their *apparat* and the money spent on it. He could have found a blunter formulation, but the intelligent members of the audience certainly understood the message: the Party would be losing its responsibility for running everything because it had run everything so badly in the past.

A strong current of truth telling ran through the conference. Gorbachev set the tone in his opening report: "It must be said frankly, comrades—we underestimated the depth and gravity of the distortions and stagnation of the past. There was a lot we just didn't know, and are seeing only now. It turned out that neglect was more serious than we thought." As if to fill in the details, others picked up the theme.

Evgeny Chazov, the minister of health, spoke bluntly on subjects once considered taboo in public discourse: "In the past . . . we kept quiet about the fact that we were in fiftieth place in the world for infant mortality, after Mauritius and Barbados. . . . We kept quiet about the fact that our life expectancy ranks thirty-second in the world." He listed the per capita expenditure on health care in a number of Soviet republics—from 70 rubles a year in Latvia down to 42 in Tadzhikistan. (In the United States, per capita spending on health care in 1987 was just less than $2,000.)

G. A. Yagodin, chairman of the State Committee on Public Education, told the conference that *half* the schools in the Soviet Union "do not have central heating, running water, or a sewerage system." A quarter of all students attended school in split shifts; 53 percent of all schoolchildren were not in good health, and "during their education, the number of healthy children drops by a factor of three or four. This is a calamity."

D. K. Motorny, chairman of a collective farm in Kherson Oblast, acknowledged that in his rural area the authorities had failed "to resolve the three most important tasks: providing heat, constructing roads, and providing running water and sewerage." As a result, he said, "people are simply leaving for the cities."

A. A. Logunov, rector of Moscow State University and a conservative who was hardly a Gorbachev ally, gave a blunt evaluation of Soviet science. "The situation," he said, "is altogether unfavorable. . . . Essentially, science has been a hollow word in our country. We have talked about it a great deal, we have allegedly done everything scientifically, but we have done very little for its development. . . . It is simply amazing that in a number of fields, especially theoretical fields, we can still keep up." This of the society that launched Sputnik!

Ivan D. Laptev, the editor of *Izvestia,* said the Soviet system had "created an astonishing, unique situation: the person who makes the decisions [an official of the Communist Party] bears no legal or material responsibility for its consequences, and the person who bears that responsibility [e.g., a factory director, a school administrator, or the like] does not make the decisions."

For senior members of the old establishment, these were astounding confessions. They and other revelations like them were the most important contributions of *glasnost.* In the West we were fascinated by Soviet truth telling about historical figures like Stalin, Bukharin, and Trotsky, but they were all dead. The confessions of the failure of the system were alive, and once made they could not effectively be retracted. Gorbachev could be ousted by conservatives who restored Stalin's halo or reexpelled Bukharin from the Party, but they could not restore the myths about the supposedly great triumphs of Soviet socialism. The myths were shattered.

The highest drama of the Party Conference was provided, aptly, by Boris Yeltsin, who had been elected a delegate from Sverdlovsk, the city where he had been a successful first secretary before coming to Moscow. Yeltsin was much discussed during the debates. He was denounced for giving an interview to Western television networks during the recent summit meeting (he had baldly demanded Ligachev's ouster from the leadership). The "Yeltsin affair" was a popular topic, with some liberal delegates demanding to know what had really gone on the previous October and November, when Yeltsin was fired as Moscow first secretary. Conservatives criticized his inarticulate defense of himself at the Moscow Party Committee meeting.

When Yeltsin was given the podium he began by answering those points, explaining that the television interview had been arranged through official channels, and disclosing that he had been brought to the Moscow Party Committee meeting from his hospital bed. He boldly repeated what he had said in the television interview: that *perestroika* would move more quickly if Ligachev were not an important official. Then he launched into the most outspoken speech delivered at a Party meeting since the death of Lenin. He denounced members of the current Politburo who had been part of the leadership under Brezhnev, who voted for what Brezhnev wanted "every time," and "kept silent" while the country fell into a crisis. "Why did they promote the sick Chernenko?" Why were Party authorities "afraid to bring charges against major leaders of republics and provinces for taking bribes"? They should be fired, Yeltsin said.* He criticized the ineffectual progress of *perestroika,* and attacked the party for squandering huge sums for "luxurious private residences, dachas and sanatoriums on such a scale that it's embarrassing."

Then Yeltsin electrified the hall by raising the issue of "my personal political rehabilitation." At those words there was "noise in the hall," as *Pravda* put it. Yeltsin said, "If you think that time no longer permits, then that's all," but Gorbachev intervened: "Speak, Boris Nikolayevich," he said, "they're asking you to."

Yeltsin plunged ahead. He noted that he had been punished by the Moscow Party Committee because his speech at the October Central Committee plenum was judged "politically erroneous." But this Party Conference was dedicated to the idea that all points of view were welcome, debate was needed, no single point of view could be dismissed as wrong. He noted that the traditional method of granting political rehabilitation was to provide it "after fifty years," but "I am personally asking for political rehabilitation during my lifetime. I

---

* At the time, Shcherbitsky, Solomentsev, Gromyko, and Gorbachev were the members of the Politburo who had been members while Brezhnev was alive. Yeltsin's recommendation of dismissals presumably applied to the first three.

consider this question fundamental and appropriate in light of the socialist pluralism of opinions, freedom of criticism, and tolerance of one's opponent that are proclaimed in the report [that is, Gorbachev's opening report to the conference] and in the speeches."

Altogether a remarkable performance. Yeltsin now had a regular role in the politics of the country; it fell to him to shatter the smugness of the moment, and challenge the latest variation of the *apparat*'s continuing effort to block meaningful changes. He was a scold from the left, a reminder to Gorbachev that the reformer side of his some-times-split personality had grander ideas than were yet being imple-mented.

Ligachev apparently sensed the power of Yeltsin's speech, and felt constrained to reply to it. He said it wasn't easy for him to talk about Yeltsin, "because I recommended him for a seat in the secretariat of the Central Committee, and later for one in the Politburo." But he now believed that Yeltsin had only "destructive energy," and attacked his criticisms of *perestroika* as attempts "to sow doubt—and this is just what our foes abroad expect from us."

Ligachev defended his own role during the Brezhnev years, using language that soon became a source of ridicule among Moscow intel-lectuals. "I am frequently asked, what was I doing during that time [of stagnation]? I answer proudly: I was building socialism. And there were millions like me."

Defensively, Ligachev sought to convince the delegates that he was a progressive himself. He disclosed that he had been personally touched by Stalin's terror. "In our family, too, there were those who were shot, and others who were expelled from the Party." He recalled the "anxious days" when Chernenko died and it was not clear who would succeed him. "I happened to be at the center of those events, so I have an opportunity to judge. Totally different decisions could have been made. There was a real danger of that. I want to tell you that thanks to the firm position taken by the Politburo members Chebrikov, Solomentsev and Gromyko and a large group of first sec-retaries of province Party committees, the March [1985] plenum of the Central Committee [which selected Gorbachev general secretary] adopted the only correct decision." In other words, he was telling the delegates that without his help for Gorbachev someone like Grishin or Romanov might have become their general secretary.

Ligachev boasted of his power. "I have been instructed to manage day-to-day activities in the secretariat of the Central Committee," he said. "This is an instruction from the Politburo." He defended Party members against accusations that they enjoyed excessive privileges. He flatly denied that there was any split in the leadership. He denounced Yeltsin for violating Party discipline by making direct appeals "to the bourgeois press."

In the hall Ligachev's speech was warmly received. He was often interrupted by applause. But the speech was a serious miscalculation. The harshness of the tone, the defensiveness, the boasting all undermined his position—not with the delegates, perhaps, but with Gorbachev and other members of the leadership.

Gorbachev ended the conference with a final speech of his own. He struck a liberal note. He actually apologized indirectly for the harsh, Stalinist punishment that had been meted out to Yeltsin the previous fall. The nasty meeting of the Moscow City Committee was "a lesson not only for Comrade Yeltsin, it is a lesson for the Politburo, for the general secretary . . . for all of us. . . . We cannot accomplish the great tasks of *perestroika* which we have set for ourselves by resorting to old methods that have been condemned not only by the Party but by all of society." Then he warned the delegates that "we must not allow a repetition of what happened with the January [1987] plenum of the Central Committee," his first great reforming plenum, whose decisions were never implemented, but "ended up 'hanging in midair,' as it were. . . . Under no circumstances should we doom the decisions of our Party Conference to the same fate." This was a clear warning to the conservative *apparatchiks;* so was his closing endorsement of the proposal to build a monument in Moscow "to the victims of [Stalinist] repression." Gorbachev said he was "sure" that building a monument "will be supported by the entire Soviet people."

The Party Conference completed Gorbachev's first important course correction. Changing national policy had proven enormously difficult. He had begun to try to alter his course at the January 1987 plenum; he'd had more success at the June 1987 plenum; but the momentum evaporated, and in the spring of 1988 he had to begin anew. Until the conference Gorbachev's program could be described in terms that smacked of continuity—reform, and especially the oft-used "acceleration." The plans outlined in the conference resolutions were qualitatively different. They envisioned new departures, fundamental changes.

The conference approved every proposal Gorbachev had put before it, effectively embracing all the radical theses that were published before the delegates convened. Gorbachev was able to advance his vision of democracy by imposing it autocratically.* The most important conference resolution called for elections the following spring to the new Congress of People's Deputies—"the country's supreme body of power." An unspecified portion of the seats in this new Congress [one third, it was later agreed] would be reserved for representatives of the Party and other "social organizations," but many members would be chosen in democratic elections to represent geographic sections of the country—the first legitimate, elected institution in the history of the Soviet Union.

•   •   •

The selection of delegates to the conference and the event itself, coming on the heels of the Andreyeva affair, seem finally to have convinced Gorbachev and Yakovlev that they were not going to win over the *apparat.* Of course conclusions of that kind are rarely clear-cut. They had known for years already that the Party bureaucrats were reluctant to change their ways. But that spring and summer, as the next episodes of this melodrama will make clear, Gorbachev apparently made a fundamental decision to stop trying to court his right wing.

Milovan Djilas, the Yugoslav who had served at Josip Broz Tito's side in the Yugoslav party and then turned against communism, had popularized the idea that the ruling Party *apparat* in Stalinist societies had become a "new class" whose members would fight to protect its special interests. Djilas's book *The New Class* was published in 1954. Traditional Marxists rejected this idea, arguing that a class could only be defined by an economic interest, so the group Djilas had identified could not be considered a class. This was never much of an argument, but after eighteen years of Leonid Brezhnev's generous rule, it was no argument at all.

Brezhnev had made sure that an enormous Communist Party élite enjoyed comforts and privileges simply unknown to ordinary Soviet citizens. Controversy over these privileges had been part of the Gorbachev era at least since the 1986 Party Congress. The controversy involved more than the existence of special stores and special oppor-

---

* He had made one compromise that distressed liberal delegates, proposing that local Party first secretaries be designated the chairmen of the new, more powerful local councils, or soviets. This was clearly a sop to local Party princes, whose support Gorbachev obviously still sought. Later, after the councils were elected and took office, this idea was abandoned.

tunities for the lucky members of the *nomenklatura*. Criticism of privileges was actually criticism of the distribution of power in society.

Gorbachev surely understood this, and so did the privileged Party officials who stood to lose their comforts and their power if the rhetoric of *perestroika* was ever translated into real change. The traditional defense of privileges was well known—Gorbachev had invoked it himself in his 1987 interview with *L'Unità:* those who worked the hardest and made the greatest contribution to society deserved the greatest rewards. But by the time of this Party Conference Gorbachev —and much of the country—had abandoned the implausible contention that Party officials made the most valuable contributions to social well-being. On the contrary, it was increasingly clear that they were obstacles to increased well-being. So why should they continue to lead lives so much more comfortable than their countrymen's?

In the 1970s I spent months trying to learn details of the actual privileges enjoyed by the élite. I could see one of them out the window of my Moscow office—a tailor shop visited regularly by the long black limousines used by government ministers. According to neighborhood lore, it was the tailor shop of the Council of Ministers. In other parts of town I found clinics, food stores, and other facilities reserved for the powerful. But I never got a full picture until Boris Yeltsin published his book *Against the Grain* in 1990.

Finally, Yeltsin laid out in detail just what the Party *apparat* was fighting so hard to keep. His is the first betrayal of these secrets by a former member of the inner circle. In earlier years it would have caused an international sensation, but when published in the United States in the spring of 1990 Yeltsin's book was barely noticed.

> The Kremlin ration [he wrote], a special allocation of normally unobtainable products, is paid for by the top echelon at half its normal price, and it consists of the highest-quality foods. In Moscow, a total of some forty thousand people enjoy the privilege of these special rations, in various categories of quantity and quality. There are whole sections of GUM—the huge department store that faces the Kremlin across Red Square—closed to the public and specially reserved for the highest of the elite, while for officials a rung or two lower on the ladder there are other special shops. And so on down the scale, all organized by rank. All are called "special": special workshops, special dry cleaners [a particularly poor service in the Soviet Union], special polyclinics, special hospitals, special houses, special services. What a cynical use of the word!

Most sensational are Yeltsin's revelations about the privileges enjoyed at the very top, by secretaries of the Central Committee and Politburo members.

Every Central Committee secretary, every member or candidate member of the Politburo, is assigned an officer in charge of his bodyguard; this man is his aide-de-camp and organizes his life. . . .

Do you want a new suit? Precisely at the appointed hour comes a discreet knock on the door of your office. In walks a tailor, who takes your measurements and returns the next day for a fitting. Soon you have an elegant new suit.

Do you need a present for your wife on March 8, International Women's Day in the USSR? No problem: You are brought a catalog with a choice of gifts to satisfy even the most sophisticated taste. . . . The attitude toward families is most considerate. There is a Volga [the Soviet Chevrolet] for their use, bearing prestigious Kremlin license plates, with drivers working in shifts, taking your wife to work or the children to and from the dacha. The big ZIL [a copy of an old Lincoln Continental], of course, is reserved for the father of the family. . . .

The ZIL . . . was with me around the clock. Wherever I might be, the car and its radio were always near. If I drove out of town to spend the night at the dacha, the driver was put up in a special lodge so as to be ready to drive away at any moment. The dacha is a story in itself. . . . Before it was assigned to me, it had been occupied by Gorbachev, who had moved into another, specially built for him.

When I drove up to the dacha for the first time, I was met at the door by the commander of the bodyguard, who introduced me to the domestic staff. Then we began our inspection of the house. . . . I entered a hall measuring about thirty by fifteen feet, with an enormous fireplace, marble paneling, parquet floor, large carpets, chandeliers, and luxurious furniture. We went on, passing through first one room, then a second, a third, and a fourth, each of which sported a television set. Also on the ground floor was an enormous veranda with a glass roof and a small movie theater-cum-billiard room. I lost count of the number of bathrooms and lavatories. There was a dining room with an incredible thirty-foot-long table and behind it a kitchen big enough to feed an army, with a refrigerator that constituted a separate underground room. We went up the steps of a broad staircase to the second floor. Again there was a vast hallway with an open fireplace, and a door opened into the solarium, furnished with rocking chairs and chaise longues. After that came the study, the bedrooms, two more rooms,

intended for I know not what, more lavatories and bathrooms. Everywhere was crystal, antique and modern chandeliers, oak and parquet
floors.

His personal staff as a candidate member of the Politburo, Yeltsin
wrote, consisted of "three cooks, three waitresses, a housemaid, and a
gardener with his own team of assistant gardeners."

For ordinary Soviet citizens, who consider themselves lucky to have
one- or two-room flats of their own and struggle for every small comfort that comes their way, this is a devastating description of opulence.
From the other end of the telescope, those who shared some or all of
these luxuries understood how vast was the gulf between them and the
masses. Life in the Soviet Union is hard; even well-known and successful people must devote many hours of every week to the most basic
chores, particularly the never-ending hunt for something good to eat.
The senior officials who could avoid all that, who could live in well-
supplied comfort thanks to their official status, have never shown the
slightest inclination to give up their advantages.

It seems cynical—or perhaps excessively Marxist—to attribute the
opposition to genuine reform among "senior cadres" to questions of
cheese, salami, and summer cottages, but much of it is just that simple. According to Yeltsin, one of the senior officials who is most
susceptible to the charms of luxury is Gorbachev himself.

"I believe the fault lies in his basic cast of character," Yeltsin wrote.
"He likes to live well, in comfort and luxury." By Yeltsin's account
Gorbachev has "built a new house for himself on the Lenin Hills [in
Moscow] and a new dacha outside Moscow," had his dacha on the
Crimean coast rebuilt and then put up an "ultramodern" new one.
He wears suits made by a tailor in Rome. Perhaps this is Gorbachev's
revenge for all those years he had to spend in Stavropol.

•   •   •

In the weeks after the Party Conference adjourned in early July,
1988, Gorbachev finally took action to try to resolve the political
uncertainty that had hovered over his efforts since the Central Committee plenum in January 1987. The preparations for that plenum had
marked the beginning of real politics. From that time onward, traditionalists represented by Ligachev had fought a rear-guard action
against Gorbachev's policies. He had indulged them, even as he struggled against them, probably because he understood their power within

the Party and saw no way to survive an open break. His ambivalence was reinforced by his own split personality—the *apparatchik* Gorbachev could empathize with those who stood in the way of the reformer Gorbachev's plans. But now the conflict had become acute.

A serious political reform was under way; by early 1989 the country would have an elected Congress of People's Deputies that would represent the first expression of genuine popular sentiment in the modern era. Through that Congress Gorbachev could claim an entirely new kind of legitimacy, one disconnected from the Communist Party. The realization that this change was coming may have emboldened Gorbachev that summer. Or perhaps he was pushed by Ligachev's refusal to give up, even after he was repeatedly defeated inside the Politburo. Whatever the reason, it was finally time—three and a half years after he became general secretary—for Gorbachev to establish a clearly dominant position. He moved to do so in September, as soon as he had finished his annual vacation in the South.

The mood in Moscow was uneasy, in part because so little had been done to support the reforms supposedly adopted by the Party Conference. During Gorbachev's August vacation, Ligachev had once again made conservative public statements that alarmed the liberals. Andrei Sakharov spoke of the uneasiness after a ceremony on September 9 at the home of the American ambassador, where Sakharov was inducted into the American Academy of Arts and Sciences. Sakharov said he was worried by the signs that the Politburo was undermining some of the latest democratic reforms. He perceived a "political compromise" between progressives and conservatives in the leadership that was impeding reform. He called Ligachev "a very dangerous reactionary force."

But Gorbachev's aides insisted that he would press ahead, and so he did. He visited the Siberian city of Krasnoyarsk in mid-September, and the television film of that four-day trip filled the evening news each night. It showed Gorbachev at his outspoken best, bantering with citizens who raised serious complaints about the meager benefits from *perestroika,* and directly attacking the *apparat* for failing to make improvements. In an interview with a television correspondent at the end of the trip, Gorbachev noted that many people blamed *apparatchiks* ("cadres") for "mistakes and difficulties." He went on, "Yes, they are largely to blame, both in the past and today. Not all of them have joined in our endeavor in the proper way." He defended his reforms, including controversial aspects like the new economic cooperatives, whose expensive products and higher wages were disrupting people's sense of normalcy. And he insisted on democratization. "People keep coming to me and saying, 'Mikhail Sergeyevich, do something.' But it is time to abandon czars and dictators."

When Gorbachev returned to Moscow a new political drama began. It lasted a fortnight; many of its scenes were (and remain) hidden from view. The first that was visible came on September 23, at another meeting between Gorbachev, Yakovlev, and leading figures in the media. Gorbachev gave a blunt speech that amounted to a prediction of imminent personnel changes, presumably at the top.

"We are still moving slowly and wasting time. Hence, we are losing. In short, there is a gap between the goals and slogans we have put forward, and our work. . . . Now we must act. The present stage of restructuring requires a change in approaches, and in methods of work, and new people must come forth, too." And then a confession: "This is a transitional period, in which all methods, all ways of working—the old and the new—will coexist. We see that some problems cannot be solved now unless someone intervenes in the old way, as used to happen. But what can you do? That's real life." In other words, the changes he was predicting would not be voted democratically—he would be imposing them.

What exactly was he talking about? Gorbachev only gave hints. "There have been some requests for retirement. Some of our comrades perceive this as a dramatic occurrence, but I think a natural process is taking place. Yes, people are retiring, but only those who are not prepared to work in the new conditions or who feel they don't have the strength for it. We must not be afraid of this." He also confided that the leadership was moving to "reform the Party apparatus on the basis of the principles formulated at the 19th Party Conference." The Politburo had already "adopted a decision," he disclosed, without revealing its contents in any detail. He did say that "the apparatus will be reduced in size."

Gorbachev gave that speech on September 23; on the 25th it was reported in *Pravda*. According to Giulietto Chiesa of *L'Unità*, there was one and perhaps two secret meetings of the Politburo on the 26th and 27th. "On those same days," Chiesa wrote, "the Moscow military district was placed on alert. Airplanes and helicopters flew over the downtown area, an absolutely unusual sight in the capital." On the 28th the world learned that an emergency plenum of the Central

Committee had been called for the 30th. Word of the meeting came from New York, where Shevardnadze was making his annual appearance at the fall session of the United Nations General Assembly. Shevardnadze obviously had no advance warning of the meeting in Moscow, and had to cancel two days of appointments he had already made in New York to fly home at once. On the night of the 28th Gorbachev entertained Erich Honecker, the East German leader, at a state banquet. He appeared calm and jovial. In a toast, he defended *perestroika* and said the country had to make a sharp break with its past.

Most members of the Politburo attended that dinner; Ligachev did not. He had left for vacation in early September and was evidently still out of the city. Once again, plotting had proceeded in the absence of a key player.

Two days later the emergency plenum was held. It lasted just one hour, and when it was over Ligachev had been pushed aside. Instead of being the number-two man, in charge of ideology, he would henceforth head up a new Politburo commission responsible for agriculture. Gromyko—who had just made plans for an official visit to North Korea in late October—"retired" from the Politburo.* So did Mikhail Solomentsev, another Brezhnev survivor, and two Brezhnev-era candidate members. The KGB chief, Viktor Chebrikov, clearly a Ligachev ally, was also moved aside, to head another new commission on legal affairs.

The next day the rubber-stamp Supreme Soviet met to complete the shake-up. Gromyko resigned his ceremonial post as chairman of the presidium of the Supreme Soviet—the Soviet "presidency" at the time. Chebrikov gave up his KGB job, replaced by Vladimir Kryuchkov. And a new president was elected by unanimous vote—Mikhail Gorbachev.

Now it was clear what Gorbachev had meant when he told the media officials on September 23 that some problems could only be solved if "someone intervenes in the old way." These two meetings, each tightly controlled and quickly completed, were classic Soviet events of the old type. Both assemblies did the czar's bidding, nothing more. The

---

* Gromyko's trip to North Korea was announced after Gorbachev had disclosed publicly that "there have been some requests for retirement." This suggested either that Gromyko had fought against the suggestion that he retire, or that on September 23, when Gorbachev spoke to media representatives about retirements, Gromyko's was not one he had in mind. There must have been quite a battle that week.

road to democratization was paved with authoritarian gestures of this kind. It was easy to wonder if the old ways would ever really change.

• • •

The Supreme Soviet had added the title "president" to Gorbachev's general secretaryship; he had displaced his conservative rivals; he was firmly in the driver's seat. And yet, as had happened so often before, victory for Gorbachev in this latest power struggle in the autumn of 1988 was just a prelude to more frustration. The years of his leadership had now established a recurring pattern: breakthrough, followed by loss of momentum, then crisis, then breakthrough again. Each round did leave Gorbachev stronger politically; each round left the country more open, more democratic, more like the "normal" country so many Soviet citizens craved. But this was a perverse kind of progress, because it offered so few tangible benefits. The food situation did not get better—it got steadily worse. Economic performance did not improve—it deteriorated. Local nationalisms flourished, exacerbating divisions within the country.

Even from his new position of strength, Gorbachev was obliged to continue his balancing act. He could defeat the conservatives, but he could not rout them. So Ligachev remained a full member of the Politburo, even if he had been sentenced to responsibility for the least-successful sector of the Soviet economy, agriculture. Gorbachev apparently dared not pick Yakovlev, his closest ally, as Ligachev's successor, perhaps because the traditionalists would not accept such a liberal figure in the sensitive role of chief ideologist. So he chose an inconsequential economist named Vadim Medvedev to assume the ideological portfolio; Yakovlev was given responsibility for foreign policy. (In fact, as Gorbachev's closest ally, he retained a loud voice in all policy discussions.) Almost as soon as Gorbachev had left for vacation in August, liberals thought they had perceived a right-wing "provocation." New rules were announced that would have radically limited the number of subscriptions that could be sold by the popular liberal journals in the avant garde of *glasnost*. (This ruling was subsequently reversed.) Sugar disappeared from state stores in many parts of the country that August and September—another provocation, many reformers believed.

In October the authorities published draft laws and constitutional changes intended to implement the political reforms approved at the Party Congress. The Congress of People's Deputies, Gorbachev's new "supreme body of power," was to consist of 2,250 members, but 750 of them would be elected by "social organizations" like the Communist Party, the Young Communists' League, the Academy of Sciences, and so on. Everyone assumed that the Party would decide who got these seats. The remaining two-thirds would be elected individually in constituencies around the country. The Congress would be a sort of people's assembly, meeting no more than a few times a year. It would elect a 542-member Supreme Soviet that would remain in session year round. This upper house would elect a chairman with powers that would make him, in effect, president of the country. The Supreme Soviet appeared to be the more powerful legislative body under Gorbachev's proposals, though its members would not face direct popular election.

Publication of the legislation initiated a month of public discussion on the country's new political structure. The proposals for the new political structure alarmed many liberals. Sakharov, who had returned to full respectability (he was elected a member of the governing presidium of the Academy of Sciences on October 21), became a leading critic. Until then he had been a staunch Gorbachev supporter, but the new proposals smacked of a "dangerous" return to overcentralization, he said. The idea of allowing one man to lead the government and the Communist Party simultaneously was "just insanity," he declared. Permitting one person to hold both jobs gives him "practically boundless power."

"Today it is Gorbachev, but tomorrow it could be somebody else. There are no guarantees that some Stalinist will not succeed him. Once more, everything boils down to one person, and that is extremely dangerous for *perestroika* as a whole and for Gorbachev personally. This is an extremely important question, on which the fate of our country depends." Nor did Sakharov like the proposal to elect a two-tier legislature. "This is *perestroika* only from above," Sakharov complained.

Several of the most controversial provisions involved the rights of the non-Russian Soviet republics, which were strictly subordinated to the new Congress of People's Deputies in the draft legislation. Debate on these points was aggravated by new turmoil in the Transcaucasus and in the Baltics.

The crisis in Armenia and Azerbaijan had waned somewhat during the summer, but returned with a vengeance in the fall. Violence flared, setting off a flood of tens of thousands of refuges in both directions—Armenians fleeing Azerbaijan to return to a homeland many of them had never known, Azerbaijanis who had lived in Armenia fleeing in the opposite direction. More than thirty people were killed.

In the Baltic republics a new surge of nationalist sentiment had enlivened local politics. Reformers in Estonia, Latvia, and Lithuania formed "popular fronts," ostensibly to support Gorbachev and *perestroika,* but obviously to provide a vehicle for local nationalists as well. In mid-November the Estonian Supreme Soviet declared "the supremacy of its laws over the laws of the U.S.S.R." Gorbachev personally rejected this unilateral assertion of Estonian "sovereignty." He said the Estonians had provoked a constitutional crisis with moves he called "totally unacceptable." The question of the future of the Union itself was now on the table, much to Gorbachev's dismay.

On November 28 a plenum of the Central Committee approved the legislation on political changes after accepting some modifications of the original draft. On the 30th the old Supreme Soviet approved the package of changes to institute a new system. Five members from the Baltics voted against final approval; twenty-seven more abstained—dissent that symbolized the end of the era of a rubber-stamp legislative body, which the old Supreme Soviet had always been. Gorbachev acknowledged that this first effort to create democratic institutions had not been a total success, but promised that the system could be refined and improved in the future. He hailed the beginning of "a new era" for the country.

Many of his strongest supporters were not convinced. The mood was sour in Moscow at the end of November, especially among the liberal intellectuals. The debate over the new political structure had aggravated the ambivalence they felt toward their reformer czar. He kept insisting that the goal was genuine democratization, but he kept behaving like a dictator, not a democrat. The violence in Armenia and Azerbaijan, the turmoil in Estonia, Latvia, and Lithuania, the deteriorating economic situation, all conspired to reinforce the bad mood.

●   ●   ●

It was another difficult moment: the danger in Armenia and Azerbaijan was palpable, the compromises inherent in Gorbachev's reform package were undeniable, the new instability signaled by the restless Baltic states was entirely real. But these few generalizations could not do justice to the complex situation that fall. Other forces were at work that would make the first half of 1989 the most amazing period yet in the Gorbachev revolution. Within a few months, many of the liberals who were victims of the sour mood of late November would be euphoric about the true democratization that blossomed in the spring.

Mood swings have been a constant feature of the Gorbachev period. They are something new for the Soviet public, whose politics had been drained of all emotion for decades. The sudden ups and downs could be dizzying. But beneath an emotional surface, *glasnost* continued to do its work. Gorbachev had compared democratization to oxygen for this starved political culture; to extend the metaphor, truthful information could be as important as water. As truthful information washed over the entire society, providing new understanding of both past and present, a new political reality was born.

The success of the Gorbachev revolution would depend largely on the society's ability to come to grips with its own past. What the liberals feared most was Stalin's ghost, which could reappear in a thousand different forms. Sakharov said it bluntly: what if a Stalinist succeeded Gorbachev? People his age, particularly—those who had experienced Stalin as adults and remembered the horrors—worried constantly that the Stalinist strain in Soviet history would reemerge and sweep Gorbachev's fragile experiment away. But I think they misunderstood what was going on then all around them.

Gorbachev had delivered his hesitant speech on Soviet history a year before, on the seventieth anniversary of the Bolshevik Revolution. He had disappointed the liberals by hedging on Stalin's crimes, referring only to "thousands" of victims, and giving a positive account of some of Stalin's contributions. But the speech also invited further study of the past, and blessed continued efforts to learn and describe the truth. That invitation had been accepted, not only by scholars and journalists, but by countless ordinary citizens.

The Memorial Society, formed initially to support construction of a monument in Moscow to Stalin's victims, had become a thriving new organization, devoted in part to assembling the memories of survivors and the families of victims. The artistic outpouring that began with *Repentance* and *Children of the Arbat* had become a torrent. Newspapers, literary journals, movies, and television had been full of revelations of Stalin's horrors for more than a year. Even knowledgeable experts had been surprised by some of the new disclosures. Roy Medvedev, who had labored for years to produce his masterpiece on Stalin's crimes, *Let History Judge*, told me in June 1988 that he was learning new facts he had never dreamed of. (His book still had not been published in the Soviet Union; it was in 1990.) Denouncing Stalin became so commonplace that some worried it could become another meaningless political ritual. "Everyone is rushing to criticize Stalin, even those who previously used to glorify him," observed Anatoli Rybakov, author of *Children of the Arbat*.

No doubt there were cynical contributions to the anti-Stalin outpouring, but they could not diminish its importance. By the end of 1988, and probably earlier, the cumulative impact of more than two years of revelations had changed political reality. The horrors had come alive—brought back by literature and art and most powerfully by the memories of simple people who at last had a chance to tell their stories. New physical evidence was uncovered, including mass burial sites, where the victims were dumped in open pits. Five of them were identified around Minsk, the capital of Belorussia. Zenon Poznyak, an archeologist, described one such site in *Moscow News:* "The shootings took place every day, in the afternoon, toward evening and throughout the night. The doomed people were brought in closed vehicles, shot in groups and thrown into large pits. The murderers wore NKVD uniforms." The NKVD was Stalin's political police force, precursor to the KGB.

It had become impossible to defend the traditional Stalinist rationalization: Of course mistakes were made, many in Stalin's name but without his knowledge, yet look at all he accomplished! Gorbachev and others repeatedly explained that those accomplishments were actually grave distortions of socialism—and not really accomplishments at all, or (as in the case of victory in the war) not accomplishments for which Stalin deserved the credit. The truth about the "mistakes" became unavoidable in the barrage of new information. Even Gorbachev, in his nervous speech a year earlier, had declared flatly that the historical record proved Stalin knew what was being done in his name. There is no recognized method for assessing a nation's historical memory, but surely Russia's has changed. Fyodor Burlatsky, the editor of *Literaturnaya Gazeta*, a member of Gorbachev's generation, put it this way: "We have destroyed the spiritual and practical foundations of Stalinism. . . . No one can restore them. It's all gone."

That was a great accomplishment—more important than the provisions of the laws creating the new Congress of People's Deputies and Supreme Soviet. In the heat of battle, alarmed by signs of continued conservative strength and by events in Armenia, Azerbaijan, and the Baltics, the liberals understandably worried about where Gorbachev was headed at the beginning of December 1988. But they underestimated what had already been accomplished. The myths that might have propped up a traditionalist alternative to Gorbachev had been destroyed. The conservatives would only realize this two years later, but it was already true. They were exposed and vulnerable, and only Gorbachev himself could give them any useful protection.

• • •

Gorbachev did know where he was headed in early December—to New York, to speak to the United Nations. His performance there gave compelling affirmation of his extraordinary capacity for leadership. Despite all the difficulties that beset him at home, he had obviously found many hours to prepare for one of his most dramatic moments on the world stage.

In the excitement of 1989, the year the Berlin Wall came down and the postwar era ended, many forgot Gorbachev's United Nations speech of December 7, 1988. Rereading it now makes clear that it was a preface to those events, and perhaps an invitation to them. It was one of the most remarkable speeches by an international statesman in many decades.

Gorbachev came to the podium in the General Assembly with something very close to an apology for his country's past outlook and behavior. He implicitly acknowledged that the Soviet Union had been a closed society, but observed that "Nowadays, it is virtually impossible for any society to be 'closed,' " and he offered to participate in a new world order based on cooperation and openness. Amazingly, he spoke about "an end to the jamming of broadcasts by foreign radio stations . . . to the Soviet Union," and announced: "People [in the Soviet Union] are no longer kept in prison for their personal and religious views." He promised to resolve disputes about the right to emigrate "in a humane way."

Gorbachev seemed to admit that the Soviet Union had been blinded in the past by ideology: "Life is forcing us to abandon traditional stereotypes and outdated views, and free ourselves from illusions." He assigned the Bolshevik Revolution to remote history, coupling it with the French Revolution and describing them both as events that had "radically changed the course of world developments. . . . But today a new world is emerging, and we must look for a different road to the future." Tossing aside Communist prescriptions for a class struggle, he said: "We are entering an era in which progress will be based on the common interests of the whole of humankind. The realization of this fact demands that the common values of humanity must be the determining priority in international politics. . . . This new stage requires the freeing of international relations from ideology."

These passages implied a revolutionary transformation of the Soviet world view. Other portions of the speech had more concrete implications. "It is evident," Gorbachev said, "that force or the threat of force neither can nor should be instruments of foreign policy. . . . All of us, and first of all the stronger of us, must exercise self-restraint and renounce the use of force in the international arena." Was that the death knell for imposed discipline in the Soviet bloc? "The principle of freedom of choice is mandatory. Refusal to recognize this principle will have serious consequences for world peace. To deny a nation the freedom of choice, regardless of the pretext or the verbal guise in which it is cloaked, is to upset the unstable balance that has been achieved. . . . Freedom of choice is a universal principle. It knows no exceptions." This sounded like a new guarantee to the East Europeans that they could go their own way. Did he mean that? Two paragraphs later he seemed to answer the question: "The multioptional nature of social development" is a feature "of both the capitalist and socialist systems."

The passages that attracted the most attention at the time were still to come. Gorbachev declared "a new historic reality: The principle of excessive stockpiling of arms is giving way to the principle of reasonable sufficiency for defense." To prove his point, he announced that "the Soviet Union has decided to reduce its armed forces . . . by 500,000 men" over the next two years, and to do so unilaterally, without new international agreements. Fifty thousand Soviet soldiers would be withdrawn from Eastern Europe, and five thousand tanks.

Gorbachev even addressed a question that his speech must have provoked in the minds of many hearing or reading it: Is this guy serious? Yes, he said, some might consider his goal of a new kind of humanistic international relations "a little too romantic," but "I am convinced that we are not floating above reality."

Gorbachev was offering the world a fresh start after four decades of cold war. His offer was accompanied by such an unusual combination of candor and concrete concessions that the international audience had to take it seriously. One important target of Gorbachev's message was the newly elected American president, George Bush, whom Gorbachev would meet briefly during his visit to New York. Bush proved more resistant than many other Western statesmen to Gorbachev's offer to start afresh, though before the end of his first year as president he too had signed up.

The immediate international reaction to Gorbachev's speech was enthusiastic, but before he could bask in the acclaim, another great catastrophe struck the Soviet Union. On the very day Gorbachev was addressing the UN, a severe earthquake shook Soviet Armenia, destroying the town of Spitak and much of the city of Leninakan, killing tens of thousands of people and leaving at least 400,000 homeless.

Like the accident at Chernobyl thirty-two months earlier, the earthquake was both a disaster and a revelation. The disaster was tragic. Almost none of the buildings in the stricken region were built to withstand a serious quake. There were many reports that the steel rods that should have been used to reinforce concrete structures had been stolen and sold before the concrete was poured, leaving those buildings as brittle as plaster. Most of the victims were buried in rubble. Many of the affected villages were in remote areas, difficult to reach even before the quake. The weather was cold and harsh. Many thousands suffered.

The revelation was just as sad—the authorities were utterly unprepared to cope with this disaster. They had neither the equipment nor the necessary combination of will and competence to respond effectively. Some devastated villages received no help at all; others were given a few tents, nothing more. Troops were rushed into the affected area, but once on the scene they stood around uselessly for days, or patrolled with rifles, as though the Armenian mountains were about to be invaded. There was virtually no suitable equipment for lifting large hunks of rubble; medical workers were scarce, medicine and supplies even rarer.

For the first time since Hitler invaded the country, the Soviet Union welcomed foreign assistance. When emergency teams from many nations responded generously, officials in Armenia didn't know what to do with them, or how to use the help they offered. One of the most poignant moments in the aftermath of the earthquake was a tableau shown on the main television news program. Nikolai Ryzhkov, the premier, who led rescue efforts on the scene, was shown dressing down an official from the Ministry of Foreign Affairs in Moscow for failing to give foreign volunteers the basic help they needed—

beginning with translators—to contribute to the rescue effort. "Some of the foreign groups are leaving now with heavy hearts," Ryzhkov told the official, "and not because of what they have seen, but because of the treatment they received here." Aid and supplies worth tens of millions of dollars were sent into Armenia. Months later it was learned that much of this material never got beyond the airport in the republic's capital, Yerevan, where it was stolen.

The earthquake and its aftermath were a vivid reminder of the weaknesses of Soviet society. After six decades, the system invented by Joseph Stalin had created a third world superpower. Its intercontinental ballistic missiles may have been impressive, but the most basic human services were appallingly inadequate. The infrastructure was feeble. The organization of society, especially to deal with a crisis, was pathetic. *Glasnost* allowed open discussion of all this, and the self-examination in the Soviet press was vivid, even painful.

The earthquake was a bad moment for Gorbachev. He flew directly from New York to Yerevan, made a tour of the stricken region, then returned to Moscow and disappeared from view for several weeks. Ryzhkov, who stayed on the scene for days, became something of a hero for his straightforward efforts to cope with the mess. Gorbachev made a serious political error on his brief visit, a misstep that revealed his emotions but not his wisdom. He was interviewed for television while touring the earthquake zone, and spoke warmly of the heroic efforts of rescuers, and of his determination to rebuild the area within two years. The interviewer then asked a question about the continuing conflict between Armenians and Azerbaijanis over Nagorno-Karabakh, the isolated, predominantly Armenian enclave inside Azerbaijan whose fate had sparked months of demonstrations, riots, and violence. The question seemed out of place under the circumstances, and many Armenians assumed Gorbachev had instigated it.

Gorbachev responded angrily, denouncing the so-called Karabakh Committee, a group of Armenian nationalists who had organized the demonstrations in Yerevan that had continued for many months. He claimed that "the grass roots" of Armenia supported his policy of leaving Nagorno-Karabakh under Azerbaijani control, and denounced those who fought his policy as "demagogues" and "adventurists." He added, "Political gamblers must be stigmatized and the public should know this." Soon afterward, five members of the Karabakh committee were arrested and detained.

It was a nasty outburst, inappropriate to the circumstances and certain to anger Armenians. As the Nagorno-Karabakh crisis had dragged on, Gorbachev had become increasingly unpopular in Armenia. At first the Armenians considered him sympathetic to their cause—and at first he may have been. But he could not bring himself to try to alter the political alignment in the Transcaucasus, a region of numerous ethnic groups living in enclaves, many of them coinciding with republic boundaries, but many not. The recurring mass demonstrations in Armenia against Moscow's policy were a thorn in Gorbachev's side; he had no idea how to end them. Now the earthquake would inevitably build sympathy for Armenia, perhaps complicating his problems. Whatever the explanation, Gorbachev's outburst served no good purpose.

But it did reveal a trait of Gorbachev's character that would soon become more visible. In 1989, the Soviet Union would discover real politics on an entirely new level—competitive electoral politics, featuring aggressive challenges to the Party and the status quo. The democratization Gorbachev had been saying he wanted since 1984 would become a reality. The Karabakh committee of Armenian nationalists was a precursor of the kind of opponents Gorbachev would soon be facing in large numbers. They were stubborn and determined; he could yell at them, but they refused to shut up. As much as Gorbachev liked the idea of democratization, he found the reality of it aggravating. The aggravation again revealed a human weakness. "He takes offense," as one of Gorbachev's early, enthusiastic allies had put it. This reformer czar found it difficult to give up the czar's prerogatives.

CHAPTER SEVEN

THE BIRTH OF
A NEW RUSSIA

Decades, even centuries from now, 1989 will be remembered as one of the most amazing years in the history of nations, but it began quietly and not very auspiciously in the Union of Soviet Socialist Republics. Six prominent liberals* marked the turn of the year by writing an open letter to Gorbachev, published in *Moscow News*. Reflecting the sour mood that still prevailed, they assured Gorbachev of their own support, but warned him that progress was being undermined by "a kind of dictatorship of mediocrities"—talentless people who continued to occupy powerful positions from which they could block reform. They accused "Party functionaries" of refusing to implement Party policies, and declared that the decisions taken at the Party Conference and other important meetings "must be implemented with a firm hand, not permitting any sabotage. . . . Whoever disagrees with the new course must resign and leave the Party."

Pravda, still edited by Viktor Afanasyev, a Brezhnev protégé, who

---

* The six included Roald Sagdeyev, director of the Institute of Space Research; Mikhail Ulyanov, a famous actor; Elem Klimov, head of the filmmakers' union; Grigori Baklanov, an editor; Alexander Gelman, a playwright; and Daniel Granin, a novelist.

was closer to Ligachev than Gorbachev, rarely endorsed views promoted by *Moscow News,* but on this occasion the Party organ did just that. A sharply worded editorial in early January echoed the six liberals' letter, accusing many Party officials of "illegally" frustrating reforms. It attacked those who insisted on issuing orders "in the old style," and said some ministries were sabotaging efforts to reduce the size of the bureaucracy, while other officials put "illegal obstacles" in the path of those trying to launch new cooperatives.

A string of dismaying statistics was published in January. The 1988 harvest had come in far below the planned level—195 million metric tons of grain, compared to 211 million tons a year earlier. More grain would have to be imported, draining scarce hard currency. According to year-end figures the economy had grown somewhat, but half as much as planned. The Ministry of Internal Affairs revealed crime statistics for the first time; reported crimes went up 16.9 percent in 1988; street crimes rose by 40 percent.

"Why are we downcast?" wrote Yegor Yakovlev, the editor of *Moscow News,* in January. "There are many reasons for this . . . as many frustrations as hopes." He cited the slow progress of *perestroika,* the endless talking and bickering, the sniping of critics afraid of change. Gorbachev himself gave a defensive performance at a meeting with scientists and cultural figures. Critics' charges that he was conducting *perestroika* "without a fully worked-out program, and that we don't know what we are striving for or what we want" were "groundless," Gorbachev insisted. But he also said something that sounded quite a lot like those critics: "I am not going to try to convince you that we have a theory and policy of *perestroika* that is fully worked out in all its details or that we have made the necessary decisions in all practical areas, much less assert that we have a complete picture of the society toward which we are moving."

The main business of the new year was the elections of members of the new Congress of People's Deputies. The entire procedure was new, and no one was certain how it would work. The authorities had created numerous hurdles to prevent spontaneous democracy from sweeping away the established order. Many liberals feared that this new experiment would produce little more real democracy than the ritualized procedures it was replacing.

One early election meeting produced a distressing result. A Moscow electoral district was to nominate candidates; Vitali Korotich, the liberal editor of *Ogonyok,* was a favorite to win nomination. Several

dozen members of Pamyat, the reactionary Russian-nationalist organization, showed up carrying anti-Semitic banners and shouting, "Korotich, you Jew, give back your silver coins." (Korotich is not Jewish,
adding absurdity to the ugliness of the moment.) Korotich supporters
in the hall got into fights with the Pamyat demonstrators, breaking up
the meeting.

Gorbachev formally initiated the campaign at the Central Committee plenum on January 10. It was another discouraging moment. Gorbachev's speech had a distinctly old-school flavor. This "highly
important political campaign" must proceed in the spirit of *perestroika,* he said. "But, while noting the growth of *glasnost . . .* we
should nevertheless approach the election campaign not as some kind
of spontaneous process, but as a highly important mass campaign, the
success of which can be ensured by a high degree of organization and
responsibility." In other words, comrades, don't let go of the process
—organize. He warned that in the campaign's early phases there were
already signs of "negative phenomena" like "manifestations of group
selfishness, arrogance, and political careerism. . . . Party organizations must take clear-cut, principled positions on all these questions."

It was announced at the plenum that the Communist Party would
propose a list of one hundred candidates to run for the number of
seats in the new Congress allocated to it under the complex electoral
law—one hundred seats. Most Politburo members and other senior
Party representatives would be included in this list. In other words,
neither Gorbachev nor most other senior Party officials were going to
risk a competitive election; they would get their seats in the new
"supreme body of power" automatically.

With signals like these coming from the center, it is no wonder that
outlying Party organizations didn't all get into the democratic spirit.
A welder named N. Belous gave a vivid account of one kind of provincial reality in a letter that month to *Izvestia.* Belous wrote that in his
hometown of Strezhevoi, in Tomsk Oblast, Siberia, "my comrades
nominated me as a candidate" for the Congress. "However, the bureau of the city Party Committee decided that I am unworthy of such
an honor."

By Belous's account—which *Izvestia* implicitly credited when it
published his letter—he was an outspoken fellow who had criticized
local Party and judicial authorities. He was nominated to run for the
Congress at a meeting of workers at his plant, a petroleum enterprise
where he had worked for twenty years. Someone nominated Gor-

bachev as a candidate as well, but Belous got more votes. His letter
picks up the story:

> A week later I was told right on the job that I was being urgently
> summoned to an expanded meeting of the city Party committee. As
> soon as I got there I discovered the reason why I had been summoned
> in such a hurry: my candidacy was to be discussed. . . .
> One after another, as if by prearrangement, the floor was taken by
> the people I had quite recently criticized from the rostrum of the city
> Party conference: the head of a mobile mechanized column, the direc-
> tor of a state farm, the general director of an association. City prose-
> cutor N. Fedko . . . threatened to bring criminal charges against me.
> I was dumbfounded. For what? It turned out that it was "for the
> slander" I had allegedly committed when I spoke at that Party con-
> ference!

"Everyone whom I had criticized had been invited to the bureau's
meeting, but not one of those I had defended," Belous wrote. He
quoted the chairman of the meeting's description of it as "socialist
pluralism in action." The Party committee offered Belous a chance to
withdraw his candidacy. "I refused," he wrote, "because I'm no good
at wagging my tail. . . .

"It's bitter to realize that today, in the decisive stage of *perestroika,*
my candidacy was 'axed' precisely for the uncompromising nature of
my statements against dodgers, hypocrites, lovers of report padding
and bureaucrats," he concluded.

The election rules created numerous obstacles for candidates like
Belous. Each had to be recommended by a meeting of no fewer than
five hundred residents of his district, a considerable number in a
society whose citizens had no experience of attending political meetings. A candidate could only be approved if a majority at the voters'
meeting backed him or her, so the Party could try to stack the crowd
with loyalists when such meetings took place. Even candidates approved in this matter had to be formally put on the ballot by an
electoral commission the Party could manipulate. (When election day
came, there was only one name on the ballot in 384 of the 1,500
districts.)

The spectacle of Party officials once again standing in the breach,
blocking real reform, sent a shudder through the liberal intelligentsia.
The reactionaries and *apparatchiks* simply would not give up, no

matter how often Gorbachev outmaneuvered them, no matter how often they lost specific fights with the leadership. It was less than half a year since Gorbachev had bumped Ligachev out of his path, but that triumph had lost its luster. The conservatives would not roll over. In late January seven of them published a nasty letter in *Pravda* attacking Korotich and *Ogonyok* as "a dirty foam on the new wave" of *glasnost*. *Ogonyok* published "slanders," they charged, adding, "Culture and values are being falsified." Ten liberal writers, led by the poets Andrei Voznesensky and Yevgeny Yevtushenko, wrote a spirited reply to *Pravda*, but Viktor Afanasyev, *Pravda*'s editor, refused to print it. (*Moscow News* did publish the reply.)

Once again, rumors circulated that Gorbachev's days were numbered. At a neighborhood election meeting in Moscow, historian Yuri Karyakin, a defender of reform, was asked: "When they throw out Gorbachev, will you still fight for reform?" Karyakin did not challenge the questioner's fatalistic prognosis, but promised that he and his fellow liberals would "fight to the end." After being reported in Western newspapers, the new rumors—and commentaries on them by Western specialists—were broadcast back to the Soviet Union by foreign radio stations, no longer jammed and avidly followed by millions of Soviet listeners. Gorbachev felt constrained to respond, which he did to a gathering of workers in remarks that were broadcast on television on February 16. "If you listen to Western radio talk . . . they say that the longest we can give Gorbachev is a year, as if that were the issue," Gorbachev said. "They have been trying to pin everything on one personality. Of course personnel is important. We need personnel, but that is not the issue. The issue is, the entire country has adopted the policy of reforms, and the people will not allow it all to be thrown to the wind."

Ever the balancer, Gorbachev used the same occasion to reassure conservatives. Talk of a multiparty system for the Soviet Union was "rubbish . . . thrown up at us by irresponsible people."

•　　•　　•

The BBC and the Voice of America could speculate about Gorbachev's future; Soviet publications and broadcasters could not. For years he had urged the elimination of all "forbidden zones" to allow criticism and discussion of every aspect of Soviet life, but Gorbachev had never invited or permitted the Soviet news media to write speculatively or interpretively about him. The country was being transformed by a political movement authored by this one man, but he was not a permissible subject for analysis.

This fact contributed to Gorbachev's isolation. For all his man-of-the-people routines, he remained a remote figure. A man who knew Gorbachev well told a friend of mine, "You can't imagine how lonely he is!" Apart from his wife, Alexander Yakovlev, and a handful of loyal aides, Gorbachev had no intimates.

He still seemed to be popular in the country—though less popular as the standard of living continued to decline. But he avoided exploiting that popularity by seeking some kind of popular mandate; he remained content to rely on the Party to legitimize his authority. On the face of it this was a strange choice for a man whose policies were calculated to diminish the Party's influence in the society—and whose policies were enjoying palpable success. But it may have been a shrewd choice nevertheless. If Gorbachev had tried before 1989 to win a popular mandate at the expense of the Party, he would have invited his comrades to dump him. And he could see a new situation coming: once elected and installed, the Congress of People's Deputies would elect the president of the country in the name of the people, not the Party. Gorbachev certainly expected to win that vote when it came. Perhaps his vision of this future was clearer than his supporters', who worried that winter about whether he could survive until the Congress was chosen.

Whatever he was thinking, he kept all his balls in the air, defying the laws of political gravity. While launching this first somewhat-free election campaign at home with his right hand, Gorbachev completed the Soviet withdrawal from Afghanistan with his left. Minor last-minute glitches did not disrupt the timetable; on the 15th of February, the last troops left Afghanistan, ending the Soviets' costliest foreign adventure of the cold war era. It had taken the lives of fifteen thousand young Soviet citizens—and many times more Afghans.

By the time the withdrawal was completed, its impact both inside the Soviet Union and abroad was less dramatic than it might have been, since the world had had nearly a year to get used to the idea. Gorbachev deserved more of a celebration. When he first floated the idea of a total withdrawal ten months earlier, it had stunned the world. Gorbachev had broken every Kremlinological rule of thumb, undermined the confidence of every student of Soviet affairs (including me), by abandoning Afghanistan—a neighboring country, ruled by a "fraternal" socialist party. Nothing he could have done made a stronger statement than that decision—it proved that he meant what he said about "new thinking."

•   •   •

Sometime in February those following or participating in the election campaign for the new Congress began to realize that democracy was infectious, even in the Soviet Union. The political wind changed. What had seemed remote was suddenly at hand—ordinary citizens were taking sides, making commitments. The telltale was Boris Yeltsin's campaign, which started to take off.

Yeltsin was nominated in nearly two hundred constituencies around the country—testimony to the symbolic status he achieved after his brutal firing in November 1987. Gorbachev, of course, had kept him in the game by giving him a ministerial job in the government's construction trust—an interesting fact to keep in mind as we watch Gorbachev go after Yeltsin through the rest of 1989 and 1990. As he writes in his book, Yeltsin realized that he would run for the Congress as soon as he understood that the electoral procedures might give him the chance to do so. Soon after the electoral calendar was approved in November he began making campaign-style appearances, honing his stump style. At first he wasn't sure where he ought to run, so he tried to line up constituencies in various parts of the country. Then he discovered that his popularity had spread far and wide; offers to back his candidacy flooded in from many directions. By February he had decided to try to run from the single largest constituency in the country, a special district covering the entire city of Moscow.*

His campaign in February and March was a tumultuous succession of boisterous meetings punctuated by clumsy official attempts to discredit him. The high point of Yeltsin's preelection-day maneuvering came on February 21, when he was officially certified as one of two candidates in the Moscow-wide National-Territorial District Number One. The preelection meeting held in Moscow's Hall of Columns that day lasted thirteen hours. Yeltsin assumed it was rigged against him. Less than a hundred of the thousand citizens in the hall were his supporters, and the Party clearly favored two other candidates, the director of an auto factory that made the leadership's ZIL limousines, and a highly decorated former cosmonaut.

---

* The complex election rules provided both for smaller districts consisting of a fixed number of voters and larger ones covering traditional geographical areas, like the city of Moscow. Yeltsin could have run from any one of several Moscow neighborhoods, too.

Demonstrators outside the Hall of Columns carried signs demanding that all the candidates who had been properly nominated by the requisite number of voters or large organizations be put on the ballot —the populist position that was put forward in many electoral districts, but rarely met success.* Yeltsin got the two officially blessed candidates to join in signing a letter requesting that all of them be put on the ballot so the voters could make the choice. More important, he learned from the cosmonaut, Georgi Grechko, that Grechko planned to withdraw his candidacy. In his memoir Yeltsin writes that he urged him not to do so until the speechmaking and question answering were over.

In Yeltsin's own account of what followed he casts himself as an ingenious David up against the Goliath of the Party *apparat.* He takes the toughest questions first, and disarms his critics with clever answers. Then, just as voting is to begin, Grechko announces that he has decided not to run. The crowd, well briefed to vote for the two officially blessed candidates, is thrown into disarray. When the secret ballots are counted, Yeltsin has won a majority; at 3 A.M. he is formally nominated.

David Remnick of *The Washington Post* reported that Yeltsin actually had a few bad moments during the questioning, particularly when asked why his granddaughter attended a special school, emphasizing English-language training, that is a favorite of the Party élite. Yeltsin replied that this was the school closest to his granddaughter's home, and boos were heard in the hall. According to an account of the meeting in the weekly *Nedelya,* the cosmonaut, Grechko, when he withdrew, threw his support to Yeltsin, a critical boost. No matter. Yeltsin was now an official candidate in the most prestigious constituency in the country, poised to humiliate the Party establishment by proving his own popularity at its expense. "I represented to them a collapse of faith in the unshakability of the established order," Yeltsin wrote, correctly I think. "The fact that the established order had long since turned rotten did not worry them. The main thing for them was to keep Yeltsin out."

Yeltsin's platform was straightforward. He called for an end to special privileges for the élite, a direct popular election of the new president (under the new procedures, the Congress would elect a president), and a nationwide debate on a multiparty system—that is,

---

* In one-fourth of the electoral districts, only one candidate was nominated—a hint of how many local areas were still controlled by thoroughly unreconstructed *apparatchiks.*

on ending the Communist Party's constitutionally mandated "leading role." But the public reacted at least as strongly to his personality and to his reputation as the victim of harassment by the Party *apparat*. To be for Yeltsin was to be against the power structure—and that was more than enough for many citizens. "You must understand," a Muscovite named Mikhail Erlich told Remnick of the *Post* at an election meeting filled with enthusiastic Yeltsin supporters, "our people have been waiting decades for something like these elections. It's like they have been bursting, just waiting to make their feelings known."

That was the energy behind the miracle of 1989—in Russia, and also throughout Eastern Europe. Know-it-alls like me had assumed that the Soviet people were so downtrodden and demoralized by half a century of Stalinist rule that they were numb to politics and instinctively passive. We knew they had inherited this passivity from Russian ancestors, most of whom had been serfs. How magnificently wrong we were!

The surge of popular feeling alarmed the Party establishment, and not just because of its anxiety about manifestations of opposition. This is a society which, under both czars and commissars, had almost no experience with spontaneous political events. The last time large crowds had been seen in the streets was during the Bolshevik Revolution. Many Russians share a dread of anarchy that surprises a Westerner; it is a national trait.

Anxieties produced by Yeltsin's obvious popularity led the authorities into a series of political blunders. They published attacks on him in the press, spread rumors intended to undermine him, and finally went so far as to create a special commission of the Central Committee to investigate whether, in his campaign statements, Yeltsin (still a Central Committee member) had violated "the Central Committee's political directives, Party ethics and the Communist Party's statutory norms." The issue was raised by a machine-tool operator named V. P. Tikhomirov, one of the worker members of the Central Committee who never spoke up, it was widely assumed, unless instructed to do so. Tikhomirov's principal complaint concerned Yeltsin's endorsement of discussion of a multiparty system. According to Yeltsin, Gorbachev personally proposed creating a commission of inquiry.

These efforts to undermine Yeltsin's support could not have been more foolhardy. They were based on the implicit assumption that if the Party explained Yeltsin's shortcomings to the public, the public would turn against him. In fact, every time the Party criticized Yeltsin, it reminded the public why it supported him—because of his independence, because he made *them* mad. So every official criticism probably won him more votes.

Several days after the Central Committee meeting an article signed by Tikhomirov appeared in *Moskovskaya Pravda*. It is a wonderful example of the *apparatchik*'s mentality. He wrote that he considered it his "Party and civic duty to explain why, without beating around the bush, [he] and a number of comrades" proposed an inquiry into Yeltsin. First, he had been appalled to discover, during a recent visit to Yeltsin's office at the state construction trust, that everyone on his staff was busy working on his political campaign, not state business. Yeltsin only reluctantly met with him, and responded to a request for help by issuing a peremptory order to an underling. Then, "several days later, at an openly provocative assemblage in the center of Moscow, under the flag of the so-called Democratic Union [one of the new liberal informal groups], leaflets were distributed containing filthy attacks against the October Revolution and Soviet power. . . . Leaflets urging people to vote for Yeltsin were also distributed there. It was a strange, inconceivable combination."

On top of these outrages, Tikhomirov wrote, Yeltsin was a hypocrite. He criticizes Party policies, but doesn't acknowledge his own responsibility for helping shape those policies in his twenty years as a Party official. He attacks the privileges enjoyed by senior officials, but he has happily taken advantage of them himself. For example, Tikhomirov said, he had received "official information" from the Moscow city government showing that Yeltsin's daughter had traded on her father's influence to move into a large apartment to which she was not entitled. Yeltsin himself used a big government limousine and the special health-care services available to senior officials. Though he was famous for traveling around Moscow by public transportation when he was the city's first secretary, Tikhomirov could testify that on one occasion, when Yeltsin arrived at a certain factory by streetcar, he had actually driven to a streetcar stop a block away in his official car, then boarded the public conveyance. "What is one to make of this?"

"Politics demands honesty from a person, above all else. That is why I submitted the proposal" to create a commission of inquiry into Yeltsin's statements, Tikhomirov concluded.

Publication of Tikhomirov's article gave Yeltsin a chance to reply, which he did with gusto. *Moskovskaya Pravda* printed his letter, which ridiculed Tikhomirov, did not deign to respond to his specific charges of abuse of privileges, but laid out his own case that "the [Party] apparatus is using methods that are far from democratic in this campaign. They include pressure on the labor collectives that nominated me as their candidate, difficulties in organizing meetings with voters, disallowing nomination documents, picking the participants in election-district meetings, and distributing within neighborhood Party committees an anonymous 'compromising letter,' and even a special appeal from a session of a borough soviet advising residents whom to vote for and against. . . . This is a policy that . . . will lead ultimately to a rift between the Party and the people and to the loss of the Party's prestige among the masses." He turned out to be absolutely right.

One of the most exciting moments of the campaign came on Sunday, March 19, when a crowd of more than five thousand—a huge gathering by Soviet standards—marched through the streets of Moscow to the headquarters of the city government to cheer for Yeltsin and protest a decision to ban a pro-Yeltsin rally. It began when policemen told citizens gathering for an authorized rally in Gorki Park that the authorities had withdrawn their approval for the event. Someone suggested a march on city hall to protest that decision, and a crowd set off for the city center a mile and a half away. En route the crowd swelled; it paused at the modern office building that houses Tass, the government news agency, to shout "Shame! Shame!" then went on to City Hall on Gorki Street, the main thoroughfare of the capital. Traffic was blocked for hours as speakers harangued the Central Committee for setting up its Yeltsin inquiry. Many speakers expressed fear that the authorities would rig the outcome of the election, then just a week away.

Three days later *Moskovskaya Pravda* printed a cautionary interview with Moscow's chief of police under the headline "Don't Confuse Democracy with Anarchy." The chief criticized speakers at the Sunday rally, noting that "appeals were made inciting people to ill-considered actions and kindling unhealthy emotions. There were attempts at abusive actions against representatives of legitimate authority."

Pravda, reporting on the same rally, noted that "some of the speeches were antisocial in nature, a lack of self-control was shown, attempts to inflame the situation occurred, and inflammatory statements were made."

Because it was taking place in the capital, where all the foreign correspondents were based, and because he had become such a personal symbol, Yeltsin's campaign got the lion's share of publicity and attention. But it was hardly the only interesting contest. Amazingly, populist candidates had sprung up all over the country. In some places, new democratic organizations even waged impressive campaigns on behalf of no candidate at all. Under the rules, even an unopposed candidate had to win more than half the votes cast, and citizens had the option of voting No—a tempting alternative in many communities where the authorities had successfully headed off competitive elections. The attention Yeltsin received—described in foreign journalists' dispatches, then played back into the Soviet Union by shortwave radio—emboldened opposition groups all over the country.

In the city of Yaroslavl northeast of Moscow, the officially backed candidate was General Boris Snetkov, the sixty-four-year-old commander of Soviet forces in East Germany, who ran on a status quo platform. He was challenged by a forty-four-year-old Lieutenant Colonel, Viktor Podziruk, who was scathingly critical of the military establishment. Podziruk advocated radical military reforms, including ending the draft of college-educated young men and gradually creating an all-volunteer, professional force. In Zhitomir Territory in the Ukraine, a local journalist who had dared criticize authorities in her area by name in articles she wrote for *Izvestia* and *Pravda* in 1987, Lydia Grafova, ran against a Komsomol official with strong official backing. Grafova was viciously attacked by the local press, including the paper she worked for. Ilya Zaslavski, a textile research scientist who was crippled as a child because of a doctor's error, ran on a platform of giving more help to the disabled and other needy citizens, and won the hearts of the residents of Mikhail Gorbachev's own Moscow neighborhood, the Oktyabrski region. His opponent was a handsome television commentator who enjoyed strong backing from the Party.

When the votes were counted they added up to a humiliating defeat for the conservative establishment. Yeltsin received 5,118,745 votes in Moscow; his opponent got 392,633. Virtually wherever there was a real contest between a reformer and a representative of the entrenched élite, the reformer won. All three of the candidates mentioned in the previous paragraph were elected, for example. So were large numbers of deputies from the new popular fronts in the three Baltic states, who handily defeated Party regulars. Among the official losers were the commander in chief of the Moscow military region, the chairman of the Moscow city council, the prime minister of Lithuania, the mayor of Kiev, the chief of the KGB in Estonia, and thirty-five Party first secretaries from around the country.

The most striking results were in districts where no one was elected —where voters deliberately defeated the single candidates running, members of the local ruling establishment. This is how most of the losing first secretaries were beaten. One of them was Yuri Solovev, first secretary in Leningrad and a candidate member of the Politburo, who received about 110,000 votes in his Leningrad district, while 130,000 cast ballots explicitly opposing him. In an interview after the election, Solovev blamed the outcome on the fact that "these elections took place in a special psychological and emotional atmosphere evoked by the social discontent of a significant portion of the population." He said he had to take the blame for all the shortages and frustrations of everyday life. Did the results indicate that the Party's prestige had fallen? Not at all, he insisted feebly: "Because the Party . . . deliberately put itself under the fire of criticism during the election campaign, its prestige only grew."

Five thousand miles to the East, in Khabarovsk, the local first secretary, Viktor Pasternak, was defeated by the director of a state farm, Yuri Chichik. Pasternak also gave an interview after the voting; his was considerably more candid and interesting than Solovev's. This is how he explained his defeat to an *Izvestia* correspondent:

> In the first place, I was up to my ears in work in the Party committee. In the second place, I thought: Is it right and proper to bring forceful pressure to bear on voters, to squeeze my rival? After all, I'm the first secretary of the Party committee, which means that I have to behave more modestly, not push myself forward. Besides, I'll say honestly that I'm not used to fighting for a deputy's seat. Take any Party official at the province or republic level, and he'll say the same thing. . . . None of us has learned how to win the general public's political or ordinary human sympathy, and there has been no need for it. Look at how we Party officials frequently appear to people—pompous, sullen, unsmiling. But the campaign struggle—yes, struggle!—for victory requires not only competence and a clear-cut political position, but also tactical know-how, oratorical skills, delicate diplomacy and, finally, human charm.

What advantages did his opponent enjoy?

> He had not been in charge of a territory with its many difficult problems. . . . I am certain that people voted not so much for him as

against me. . . . I now understand that my publicity agents from the executive ranks didn't do me any great service, although they canvassed for me very conscientiously. . . . They are worthy people, but such a concentration of bigwigs . . . doesn't elicit trust in a candidate; rather the opposite. . . .

In general I sensed a kind of—I almost said "unhealthy," but no, it's probably perfectly natural—interest in my private life. In our country, it isn't customary, after all, to ask a high-level Party official what books he reads, what he values in people, whether he likes sports, what kind of music he prefers, etc. And we don't like questions of that sort. This perpetual inner stiffness, keeping all one's buttons buttoned, seems to have come into fashion with Stalin's service jacket, but the bureaucratically formal style of the executive is provoking a cruel revenge today. People want to see your living, human face, and if you hide it, they are offended and turn away.

What question had voters asked him most often?

Almost everywhere, especially after the March plenum of the Central Committee [where the commission was appointed to investigate Yeltsin] I was asked if I knew Yeltsin and what my attitude toward him was.

His answer was that Yeltsin had some good qualities, but tried to go too far. He expressed regret that Yeltsin's original speech to the October 1987 plenum hadn't been published at once "in order to stop rumors and idle talk."

Pasternak had only been first secretary in Khabarovsk for six months, which may help explain his extraordinary candor. He acknowledged that he felt he had carried a heavy burden from the past.

I must say frankly that Brezhnev, Rashidov, Kunayev, Medunov, and the hundreds of "endowment princelings" who ruled provinces and districts as if they were their own private domains* all had a hand in the current election results. Communist arrogance, bureaucratism, bribery, links with the criminal world—I'll say honestly that these "merits" marked certain Party figures, including some in our own territory. But it's not just a matter of abuses. People are fed up with commands and shouts, sick of the *diktat* of the apparatus, and dis-

---

* Pasternak was referring to notorious first secretaries of the Brezhnev era who were famous for their corruption.

gusted with officials who put private interests, frequently their own
selfish interests, above the political interests of the Party. . . . As the
leader of the Party organization . . . I sometimes find it very difficult
to establish normal contact with people—there is wariness, distrust,
sometimes even hostility. "You're all tarred with the same brush," they
say. The people have seen so much that now an immense effort is
required from each of us to regain their trust.

That extraordinary account came from an unknown Party official
named Viktor Pasternak, but it was spoken in the voice of Mikhail
Gorbachev. Pasternak saw exactly what Gorbachev had seen years
earlier—that the people were alienated; that corruption, arrogance,
and the arbitrary use of power had set back both the Party and the
country; that a new approach and a new style were required to put
things right. This is just what Gorbachev had been saying since December 1984, but many of his comrades did not want to hear the
message. Now he had orchestrated the first real elections in the history
of the Soviet Union, which had allowed the great mass of citizens to
bring that message home with brutal clarity. What an astounding
event!

• • •

The elections produced intriguing revelations about the state of
affairs at the beginning of the fifth year of Gorbachev. The country
and its institutions were beginning to show the consequences of the
collapse of fear.

Fear is a grim companion—and a persuasive teacher. The fear
created by a cruel authoritarian government—especially one supported by a mammoth secret police force equipped with modern technology—can be all-embracing. During the years I lived in Moscow I
learned the awful feeling that there was no place to hide. If the KGB
wanted to find you, listen to you, harass you, follow you wherever you
went, it could easily do so. Of course I was just there temporarily—
three years and home to a different world. Soviet citizens were there
for the duration; they had to weigh all the big and small decisions in
their lives against the possible repercussions from the system of control so ably represented by that KGB.

It was that process of weighing that led nearly every Soviet citizen
to learn to live with lies. If you didn't learn that skill, you were in a
special kind of danger every day of your life. One wrong statement
and a career could be destroyed; one truth uttered where a lie was

required and your life could be transformed—and not for the better. Fear taught nearly everyone what not to say or do. In other words, fear enforced all the taboos that preserved the Soviet orthodoxy, which survived for nearly sixty years.

Gorbachev ended the fear. The KGB withdrew from aggressive surveillance of the population (though many assumed it was still performing its historic function, but quietly). The authorities stopped enforcing rigid orthodoxy—indeed, some officials encouraged open debate about subjects that had long been off limits. The publication of long-banned books, the end of jamming of foreign radio broadcasts, the radical transformation of the Soviet news media, all contributed to a general relaxation of tension in the society.

But by ending the fear Gorbachev pulled a rug out from under millions of Soviet citizens—perhaps it should be called a security blanket. Most people who signed up for the old reality—who learned to repeat the lies and in many cases ultimately to believe them—assumed that in return they were guaranteed a basic peace of mind. They were on the side of the bosses; they belonged to the official church; the system would work for them. For many years that was a safe assumption. Gorbachev shattered it.

Generally speaking, Soviet citizens reacted much more positively to this startling change than might have been predicted—than I had predicted. I had assumed that the basic social contract in Soviet society was stronger than it turned out to be. The contract provided that the state and Party would provide food, shelter, health care, education, recreation, and so on—none of them in lavish amounts, but all more or less adequately—and the masses would respond with their fundamental allegiance. They would play ball.

The election for deputies to the new Congress showed that the contract had lapsed. As Gorbachev realized years earlier, the authorities had not kept up their part of the bargain. Living conditions had improved steadily from the end of World War II until the mid-1970s, but then they faltered. By the early eighties the situation was deteriorating sharply. At the same time, the Party put on an appalling demonstration of loss of control by placing one dying old man after another at the helm. It was logical to think that the Party might pay a price for this history, but only if the people saw a safe way to exact that price. More than two years of official *glasnost* gave them the confidence to act on their convictions. Truth telling was infectious.

Millions of votes cast against the Party and its leaders were the most powerful evidence that the society had changed, but not the only evidence. Even the Central Committee, which shied away from a direct democratic challenge by assuring the election of its favored 100 candidates, showed a new openness. It published the results of the vote taken by 641 full and candidate members on the 100 candidates the Central Committee proposed for election to the Congress.

The results showed that the least-popular candidate on the list among Central Committee members was Ligachev; 78 members voted against him. But the second least-popular candidate was Gorbachev's ally Alexander Yakovlev, who received 59 No votes. Another liberal, actor Mikhail Ulyanov, received 47. Fourth on the list of No's, with 38, was another conservative, Viktor Afanasyev, editor of *Pravda*. Twelve members had voted against Gorbachev himself.

Another institution jolted by the elections was the Academy of Sciences. There is no Western equivalent of the Soviet Academy, a huge bureaucracy that controls most of the research institutes and allocation of resources for research in the country. It has long had a split personality, because its membership has included many of the greatest intellectuals in the country—Sakharov symbolized this category of academicians—but its leadership has been conservative and obeisant to the authorities. The leadership has maintained discipline among scientists by carefully doling out funds and privileges.

The electoral law allocated 20 seats to the Academy from the 750 reserved for representatives of "social organizations." The governing presidium of the Academy, controlled by scientific bureaucrats and politically reliable figures, met in January and nominated 23 candidates for those 20 places. Sakharov had been proposed as a candidate by 55 scientific institutions, far more sponsors than any of the other potential candidates. But the presidium ignored those recommendations to pick its own reliable personalities.

An outcry ensued. Two weeks after the presidium's vote, several thousand scientists staged an angry demonstration outside the elegant Academy headquarters on Leninsky Prospekt. They chanted democratic slogans, called for the resignation of senior Academy officials, and demanded that Sakharov be nominated.

A group of scientists determined to try to reverse the decision of the presidium then began an intense campaign to organize institutes and individuals all over the country. One of the leaders of the effort was Roald Sagdeyev, director of the Institute of Space Research, who had also been proposed as a candidate for the Congress by numerous scientific institutions. The revolt succeeded. A special meeting of the members of the Academy plus about 1,000 representatives of research institutes around the country met in late March, several days before the popular vote, and rejected all but eight of the candidates originally recommended by the presidium. That left twelve vacancies, all of which were subsequently filled by progressives, including Sakharov and Sagdeyev.

•   •   •

The election had altered the country; it could never again be what it had been before. Not that reform and liberalization were now irreversible—too many uncertainties stood in the way of that prediction. But a new national sensibility had been created; the seeds of popular sovereignty had sprouted. Future historians may well consider the election and the first session of the Congress it elected as the turning points that marked the final collapse of the old order.

For several days after the ballots were counted, the Soviet news media was largely silent on the results. No paper reported on Yeltsin's triumph, for example, or on the humiliation of Party first secretaries in Leningrad, Kiev, and elsewhere. Editors apparently did not know how to react to real democracy. Gorbachev called a meeting of editors on the third day after the voting, as if to put his imprimatur on what had happened. He called the results a natural democratic occurrence that should not cause alarm. The people had picked the candidates they considered the strongest allies of radical reform, Gorbachev said.

The meeting was not officially reported, but what transpired was conveyed to Western journalists by participants. Vitali Korotich of *Ogonyok,* for example, gave an account of Gorbachev's comments to Michael Dobbs of *The Washington Post.* Gorbachev "said that we needed democracy," Korotich reported, "and that pluralism gives people the possibility to go their own way. The people, he said, supported candidates who wanted to do something and work for change. . . . When we dreamed about building a democratic society, it meant that there would be winners and losers in elections—that is natural—but that when it was over we all have to work together."

The senior Party officials defeated in the elections must have been stunned to hear that this was their general secretary's reaction. Forced to choose between standing with the electorate and soothing the Party, Gorbachev picked the people.

The papers then began to report on the results, printing interviews with many of the losers, including the ones I quoted earlier. Yeltsin was not given much publicity, but he didn't need it. Every ordinary citizen could understand the significance of his triumph: it was a big finger in the eye of the bosses.

*   *   *

No sooner had the progressives won their stunning victory at the polls than the conservatives again flexed their muscles. It is intriguing, looking back, how often this pattern recurred. This time the reaction was ugly. Gorbachev was out of the country again, making the visits to Cuba and Britain that he had postponed at the time of the Armenian earthquake. Large crowds of Georgians, mostly young people, met for several successive evenings on Rustavelli Avenue, the handsome, tree-lined main street in Tbilisi, the capital of Georgia. They spoke and demonstrated for increased autonomy from Moscow. At times the crowds exceeded ten thousand people. On April 7 and 8 the Politburo held meetings to discuss what was going on there. The Party first secretary in Georgia, Dzhumber Patiashvili, requested permission from Moscow to use army troops to disperse the crowds. Viktor Chebrikov was the Politburo's "duty officer" at the time; Ligachev also participated in the discussions; they and the defense minister, General Dmitri Yazov, approved the use of troops that Patiashvili requested. Early on the morning of April 9, soldiers moved against the demonstrators, clubbing many of them and firing poison gas into the crowd. Nineteen people were killed, most of them women, and many scores were injured.

Except for the death toll and the fact that gas had been used, none of these details was known at the time. (They were assembled by commissions of the Georgian Supreme Soviet and the Congress of People's Deputies, which reported on the incident later in the year.) Tass published the official version of the event, which blamed "extremist-minded groups for whipping up unhealthy feelings" in the crowd; the army acted against "antisocial forces" that had gone "out of control," the government news agency said. The incident bore all the hallmarks of the kind of provocation many liberals feared would someday be used to bring an abrupt halt to Gorbachev's reforms—an open display of opposition, countered by an excessive use of military force, producing a siege mentality in the leadership and an excuse for a general clampdown. The incident also marked a symbolic turning point; it was the first time in the Gorbachev era that the government had deliberately used lethal force against the population. There was a great outpouring of protests. A group of six newly elected deputies wrote an open letter to *Moscow News,* which said the events in Tbilisi "could be seen as a kind of model on how *perestroika* could be cut short."

Just one day after the killings in Georgia, the presidium of the soon-to-be superseded Supreme Soviet published a new decree changing the laws on "state crimes." The changes were advertised as improvements in vague statutes that formerly allowed prosecutions of dissidents for "anti-Soviet" activities. But the new provisions carried criminal penalties of up to three years in prison for "arousing national enmity or discord," "undermining the political and economic systems of the U.S.S.R.," and for insulting or "discrediting" government officials.

And at the same time, the editors of liberal journals reported a sudden toughening of censorship on a wide range of subjects, from Alexander Solzhenitsyn to the KGB.

This congruence of events sent liberal intellectuals in Moscow into another emotional tailspin. Their anxieties were heightened by reports that, contrary to Gorbachev's own wishes, the Central Committee would hold an emergency plenum on April 25. Rumors spread that the Central Committee members who had been humiliated at the polls, led by Leningrad's Solovev, were pressing for some kind of redress of their grievances. Then two days before that session, Moscow police roughed up demonstrators who had gathered in Pushkin Square to honor the victims of the Tbilisi violence; forty-seven were detained.

Once again, Gorbachev had prepared a stunning surprise—both for the worriers and for his conservative critics. For years he had sought a way to fire the older members of the Central Committee, who were, at best, reluctant comrades in the cause of *perestroika,* and often outright opponents. This was one of the original reasons for calling a special Party Conference in 1988, but the conservatives blocked the idea of using the conference for high-level personnel changes. The conservatives knew that in a showdown the Central Committee would be closer to them than to Gorbachev, provided its members had an opportunity to express their true sentiments. Gorbachev and Yakovlev knew this too.

Now, in the wake of election returns that had shattered the confidence of the old guard, Gorbachev opened this plenum by presenting a petition signed by seventy-four elderly members and twenty-four candidate members of the Central Committee in which they "requested" that their retirements be accepted. The petition said in part: "We believe that at present, when intense activity as regards participation in *perestroika* is required of all comrades who make up the Central Committee . . . it is necessary for us, in the interests of the cause, to relinquish our authority." At the same time, Gorbachev proposed elevating twenty-four candidate members of the Central Committee—nearly all identifiable as his allies, including some of his closest comrades—to full membership.

What a delicious bit of political theater! As if to rub in the irony, Gorbachev told the plenum that despite the tradition that major changes in Central Committee membership be made only at Party Congresses, it would actually be perfectly acceptable to grant the request of these men to retire at once: "There are no statutory obstacles on this score. It does not require a vote by secret ballot, since, according to the statutes, such a vote is taken only in cases in which it is necessary . . . to remove someone from membership in the Central Committee. But in this case what is involved is that people are themselves resigning their authority for objective and weighty reasons, and we should take an understanding approach to their request."

Deprived of a secret ballot, there was no way for a Central Committee member to challenge this ploy without risking his own neck. The idea that this was a voluntary act by the affected elderly members was quickly laid to rest by one of the first speakers, himself a putative retiree, A. P. Nochevkin. He recommended that, before the resignations were accepted, Party organizations around the country should be thoroughly consulted. "From my viewpoint, this is the most appropriate option," Nochevkin declared—in vain. At the end of the day he was officially retired, with all the others.

But this wasn't Gorbachev's best trick of the day. That was saved for later. A discussion was conducted in which a number of conservatives spoke their minds—no doubt assuming that the traditional confidentiality of Central Committee meetings would be preserved. The groans and complaints came one after another, many directed at *glasnost* and its consequences, barely disguised as attacks on the liberal press. Some of the comments were almost plaintive. No one loves us any longer, one member complained—"a psychological stereotype" had become common that casts "apparatus officials and Party and economic executives as the main brakes on *perestroika,* and as total bureaucrats." We read, he said, about "the praise that leaders of bourgeois parties are giving to *perestroika*" without remembering Lenin's caution, "Think hard every time your class enemy praises you" (R. S. Bobovikov, first secretary in Vladimir). Members of the Party now "speak out openly against the Party and against its vanguard role in society . . . and are calling for the Party of action to be turned into a Party of debating clubs" (Yuri Solovev, first secretary in Leningrad).

Some called for firm action. "We could lose a great deal if . . . we do not take immediate steps against these unofficial associations, and especially the Democratic Union, which has its own program" (V. I. Melnikov, first secretary in Komi).

And at one dramatic moment the same Melnikov revealed the emotion that was clearly just below the surface in the hall: raw fear. He noted that new elections were scheduled for local soviets, or councils. "The [Party] secretaries are saying that they will not take part in these elections, because there is a 100 percent guarantee that they won't be elected." When Melnikov said that, voices in the hall chimed in, "That's right!"

"That's right?!" Gorbachev interjected. "You mean that the Party is supposed to avoid participation in leadership and in the elections?"

Melnikov replied: "A way must be found for the secretaries of the city and district Party committees to stand in the elections, along with alternative candidates, of course, but on an equal footing with them, with no prejudice stemming from their membership in the Party apparatus, which is seen now only in a negative light." In other words, a "level" playing field must be invented so that profoundly unpopular Party officials can be assured of victory.

After all this spleen had been vented, Gorbachev sprang his best surprise. "There is a proposal to publish in full everything that has been said at this plenum," he announced from the rostrum. "Let the Party and the people know, so that everything will be clear." The only voices heard agreed with him. For the first time since the 1920s, the transcript of a Central Committee plenum would appear in the newspapers.

When it did, a few days later, the country was given unique exposure to the fear and anger of senior Party conservatives. There could be no hiding now; everything was clear. So was Gorbachev's own eloquent defense of the elections and his policies generally, which he delivered in closing remarks to end the plenum.

The fact that thirty-five first secretaries had been defeated by the voters caused no apparent concern in Gorbachev's mind. He declared the elections a great success: "The Soviet people spoke out unequivocally in favor of *perestroika*, reaffirmed their allegiance to socialism, and supported the Party's line aimed at the further renewal of society.

"Some people," Gorbachev said, obviously referring to some of the earlier speakers, "are already going so far as to say that, don't you see, democracy and *glasnost* are all but a disaster. They perceive the fact that the people have begun to act—the fact that they refuse to remain silent, and are making demands—as a price exacted by *perestroika*.

"Comrades, I see this as the *success* of *perestroika*. . . . We are moving toward rule by the people, we are including the working person in all economic and social processes. We are doing this by restoring him to his place as master on the job, through democratic procedures and new methods of economic management, through the election campaign, through the revival of soviets [elected councils]. This is precisely what we need. This is why we started everything in the first place—so a human being can feel normal, can feel good, in a socialist state. So that he will feel above all like a human being."

That was as clear and strong a statement as Gorbachev had ever made to distinguish his outlook from his conservative critics'. They feared what he applauded; the world they'd lost and wanted to restore was, in his opinion, an abnormal and inhuman world. The new organizations and associations that had sprung up reflected legitimate views in society, they were a healthy development, not a threat to the Party—even though many comrades, even members of the Politburo, "have proven to be unprepared for this turning point in the development of democratic processes."

"Some people are beginning to panic," Gorbachev said, again obviously referring to earlier speakers, "all but seeing a threat to socialism from this development . . . of democratic processes." Not he. "The dialogue between the Party and the working people is not a weakness, not a transformation of the Party into a debating club. If it is a weakness to conduct a dialogue with all strata of society, then I do not know what courage is."

Soon after that plenum Gorbachev made a momentous decision that would result in further erosion of the conservatives' position. After meeting several times with Sakharov and other representatives of a group of liberal Moscow deputies to the new Congress who were urging him to do so, Gorbachev agreed that the first session of the

Congress should be broadcast live on television. He did not agree at once; according to a Moscow deputy who told me this story, others in Gorbachev's entourage disapproved of the idea. "This was the subject of long discussions," according to my informant. The liberals were convinced that public opinion would coalesce behind the radical reformers—the election results showed that, as did the reaction to publication of the April plenum.

In a busy spring schedule, Gorbachev next made time for a long-awaited visit to China, another target of his diplomatic campaign to normalize Soviet relations with the rest of the world. In fact, normalization had been achieved. Some Soviet troops had already been withdrawn from the overmilitarized Sino-Soviet border, and many more would be. There was no longer any serious disagreement between Beijing and Moscow, no dispute worth energy or resources on either side. Gorbachev's visit was meant to ratify the new situation, and to crown Deng Xiaoping's career as a world statesman.

But the world discovered that Gorbachev's symbolic power had reached into China, too. In mid-May, when the trip began, the serious excitement of 1989 was still yet to begin in Eastern Europe; so, in a curious way, China was the first Communist country that Gorbachev inspired to seek freedom that year. The students who comprised the Chinese "Democracy Movement" were emboldened by the prospect of his presence in their country. And Gorbachev did not shy away from the drama of the moment; he spoke out forcefully in Beijing for more democracy, saying, "Economic reform will not work unless supported by a radical transformation of the political system." He also acknowledged that the public's appetite for reform and change often outpaced the ability of the authorities to provide it, implicitly urging China's students to be patient. At the end of his visit, he said he hoped differences between the Chinese government and the protesters could be resolved through "dialogue." He left Beijing a fortnight before the tanks moved into Tiananmen Square.

•   •   •

On the 25th of May, the new Congress of People's Deputies convened in Moscow. For the 2,250 new deputies and for the nation watching them, this was an entirely new experience. It was as if the entire population of the Soviet Union was learning to ride a bicycle or to ice skate—all at the same time.

The Congress was to be a special event for many different reasons, but two of them were obvious from its first day. Soviet television would broadcast the proceedings, gavel to gavel. This would be the first great political event in the history of the country in which every citizen could take part. And it would be worth taking part in, because the newly elected deputies, enjoying the confidence that only a majority of the ballots cast can give, had found the courage of their convictions. They would speak their minds.

This was evident literally from the first moment. No sooner had the presiding officer declared the session open than V. F. Tolpezhnikov, a delegate from Latvia, walked up to the microphone on the podium and proposed: "Before we begin our meeting, I ask that we honor the memory of those who died in Tbilisi." Every delegate in the hall stood for a minute of silence. As they sat down Tolpezhnikov continued: "On instructions from my constituents, I demand that it be announced publicly and right now, at the Congress, who gave the order for the beating of peaceful demonstrators in Tbilisi."

The main business of the first day was to be the election of a new chairman of the Supreme Soviet, the new Soviet presidency. But there was emotion in the hall that wouldn't be deferred. A delegate from Georgia immediately sought the floor to pursue the question of the killings of demonstrators in Tbilisi—"military punitive action, I can find no other words for it." The delegate, Eldar N. Shengelaya, denounced a fellow delegate, General I. N. Rodionov, who was the military commander in Tbilisi when the killings occurred. "I don't think it becomes our Congress to have such a deputy in our ranks," he declared, to applause. Obviously by prearrangement, the presiding officer, with Gorbachev's encouragement, quickly proposed that the Congress establish a commission of inquiry to discover what really happened in Tbilisi.

Once the debate turned to Gorbachev's candidacy for chairman, the vast audience began to hear things said that they had never dreamed might be broadcast on Soviet television. L. I. Sukhov, a Kharkov truck driver, quoted from a telegram he said he had sent Gorbachev during the Party Conference the previous summer: "I compare you not with Lenin and Stalin but with the great Napoleon, who, fearing neither bullets nor death, led his people to victories. But thanks to yes-men and his wife, he went from a republic to an empire. . . . Apparently, you too are unable to avoid the adulation and influence of your wife."

A. A. Shchelkanov, a teamster from Leningrad, said: "In 1987 and 1988 there was a great deal of talk about construction of a dacha in the Crimea [for Gorbachev]. Today I would like to receive either a refutation of this or a statement from you on this matter."

Yuri Solovev, chairman of the national union of designers, said he had "complaints to make to Mikhail Sergeyevich. I must say that recently we have had no successes inside the country to rank with the brilliant successes in the international arena. . . . And I have noticed that recently Mikhail Sergeyevich's speeches have lacked the clarity and boldness that used to characterize him."

Several delegates debated whether Gorbachev should be required to give up either the leadership of the government or the Party general secretaryship; others thought he should be required to hold on to both. A liberal delegate shouted from the auditorium: "During the campaign, those of you who were undesirable candidates in the eyes of the *apparat* experienced all the might, strength, craftiness, cruelty, and treachery of the Party bureaucracy." Therefore, concluded this man, who was not identified in the published transcript, it would be crazy to remove Gorbachev from his position atop that *apparat*. "I'm not at all sure that he controls it himself, but he participates in some way." If Gorbachev gave up his Party job, the delegate went on, "this mighty Party bureaucracy, which has immense power—the only real power in the country—will quickly crush him and disperse all of us here."

Gorbachev responded with a remarkable speech that was both contrite and hopeful, and on some points painfully candid, almost confessional. "Many questions have been raised here," he said, "including some to the effect that there have been major miscalculations and that we have suffered some misfortunes. Some of these misfortunes did not have to happen. That's right, they did not have to happen. And I am deeply upset about that." He admitted that he knew he wasn't popular with everyone in the country. He'd heard of a group of veterans, he said, who ride "the last bus in Moscow [and] carry with them some 'visual aids'—Brezhnev's portrait covered with medals [Brezhnev loved to wear all his state honors] and Gorbachev's portrait covered with ration coupons."

He acknowledged that dachas had been built in the Crimea, adding that many of them had been turned over to public organizations for their use. But he also said there was "a limited circle of people who must be given the use of state-owned dachas for their term of office" in high government posts.

On loftier political subjects Gorbachev cautioned that "we are still learning democracy, we are all learning. We are still forming our political culture." He endorsed the view that for now, at least, he could not give up the Party. "Without the Party's position—without, so to speak, leaning on the Party for support—this process [of political reform] will not go well. . . . There is simply no other way."

An unknown engineer from the Leningrad region, Alexander Obolensky, had the cheek to nominate himself to run against Gorbachev for chairman, an unexpected event that astounded the crowd. Obolensky gave a brief, progressive speech on the need for creating a true legal state in which the rule of law prevailed, then said he had no expectation of beating Gorbachev, but wanted to set "a precedent for holding elections." The Congress voted not to put his name on the ballot. A secret vote followed. Gorbachev won 2,123 votes; 87 deputies cast ballots against him.

As chairman, Gorbachev was now the permanent presiding officer. He conducted the Congress as a scoutmaster, then as a law professor, then as a preacher, then as a scold. It was a tour de force from the former boy actor, one that set the tone for the twelve-day session.

"To his credit, Gorbachev is showing amazing flexibility and wisdom in this situation, so unfamiliar to us," said Chingiz Aitmatov, one of the country's finest writers, who had nominated Gorbachev for chairman. Aitmatov noted that in the Congress "a young deputy can shout fervent disagreement with him [Gorbachev] from the balcony as equal to equal," and Gorbachev didn't seem to mind. He had "taken upon himself all responsibility for the fate of the endeavor we have begun," Aitmatov said, and "he realizes, as no one else, the full price of the people's rebirth, and himself serves as the generator and lightning rod of this highly complex process." It was flowery prose, but it was also the truth.

Not that the Congress was a textbook example of democracy in action. Gorbachev was feeling his way; he became a more effective and more flexible chairman as time went on. He freely inserted his own view, knowing the weight it would carry, whenever he felt the urge. Ironically, the Congress was clearly in the hands of a large majority of deputies who would respond to the wishes of the leadership, and who weren't at all beguiled by the outspoken liberals—most of whom represented Moscow, Leningrad, and the Baltic republics. Initially there were about three hundred deputies who openly identified themselves as progressive reformers. Many members of the majority were appalled by the irreverence of the liberals; on the first day they began making their feelings known, booing Andrei Sakharov when he complained about procedural arrangements, then razzing many of the liberal speakers.

Commentators had made much of the fact that more than 85 percent of the deputies were members of the Communist Party, but the statistic was misleading. Many of those Communists did not work in the Party *apparat,* and acted independently of it. There were deep divisions in the hall between reformers and reactionaries, between ethnic groups, between intellectuals and less-educated deputies. The old slogan that "Party and people are one," a mainstay of the Brezhnev years, was obviously a laughable anachronism.

The second principal item of business was the election of the Supreme Soviet, a bicameral body whose 542 members were to be selected from the membership of the Congress. Under the reform plan approved the previous fall, the new Supreme Soviet (with the same name as the old, rubber-stamp parliament, but in the new version endowed with real powers) would be the functioning legislature of the country, meeting for as much as eight months of the year, setting up committees not unlike the American Congress's and so on. An entire day was spent debating how this election should take place—a great exploration of theory and practice and democracy. The method chosen gave little chance to the candidates favored by the liberals, and when the votes were cast, only a handful of obvious progressives were chosen. One of those passed over was Boris Yeltsin, who had been elected to the Congress with several million more popular votes than any other member (because he represented by far the largest district in the country, and won nearly all its votes).

On the day after the voting for members of the Supreme Soviet, historian Yuri Afanasyev, rector of the Moscow State Institute of Historical-Archivists, provoked an uproar with his commentary from the podium on the people they had elected. "We have put together a Stalinist-Brezhnevite Supreme Soviet," he declared. This comment met "noise in the hall," as *Izvestia* put it, and also some applause. Gorbachev, presiding, at first wanted to cut Afanasyev off. "Your three minutes are up," he said, though there was no three-minute rule for speeches.

But Afanasyev insisted on continuing: "There is something else depressing that I wanted to mention. I am talking directly to you, to this aggressive-obedient majority, as I would call it, which yesterday blocked all the Congress decisions that the people are expecting from us."

There was more "noise in the hall," but now Gorbachev had

changed his view of Afanasyev's contribution. "Quiet, comrades," he said. "I think a serious discussion is under way."

"I am almost finished," Afanasyev said. "But I want to ask you not to clap and shout, because that is precisely what I came here to talk about. So here is this respected aggressive-obedient majority, and you, Mikhail Sergeyevich, either are listening very closely to this majority or are influencing it skillfully. We can continue to work like this. We can be obedient. . . . We can be agreeable. . . . But let's not forget for a single minute about those who sent us to this Congress. They sent us here not so we would behave agreeably, but so that we would make a decisive change in the state of affairs in the country."

In just a few days the deputies realized that they were acting in a drama that had transfixed their countrymen. In countless towns and cities, citizens who had watched the proceedings all day on television gathered in public places to discuss what they had seen. In Moscow, the authorities reserved Luzhniki Park for these gatherings, which went on every evening, sometimes involving thousands of people. By all accounts almost no one in the Soviet Union was doing his or her regular job—nearly everybody was glued to a television set. Those who couldn't watch during the day saw the reruns and excerpts at night, or read the transcript in the next day's papers.

Citizens caught on quickly to the fact that the people they were seeing on television were their representatives; deputies began to receive phone calls and telegrams from constituents. One effect of this was to create larger votes in support of liberal proposals—sometimes as many as eight hundred. Another was the creation of new personalities. Sakharov, for example, who had been known to the public for years primarily as an outcast and even outlaw, suddenly became a real human being. So did a number of younger deputies who were soon to emerge as a new political force in their own right.

The scene in the Palace of Congresses was not the only attraction. There was also a constant spectacle in the lobbies around the hall, where Soviet and foreign reporters could mingle with all sorts of people who had never been accessible to them before, particularly senior Party officials. Early in the Congress Raisa Maximovna Gorbacheva showed up in the lobby and talked with reporters. It was soon after she had been compared to Josephine by the deputy who feared Gorbachev's vulnerability to his wife's flattery. What did she think of that? No big deal, she replied—"everyone speaks as he perceives the world. Others were for me. Men. That's the men. But the women are all for me. It doesn't matter. You know, in the end, everyone's different. Everyone wants to express an opinion." Not exactly a Marxist-Leninist viewpoint from the first lady.

In the course of a fortnight, the Congress rewrote the rules and definitions of Soviet politics. Things that just weren't said—or had been legally unmentionable—for decades were suddenly in common parlance, and on television. The fundamental relationship between government and people was altered. "The people in the country have always been afraid of power," said Vitali Korotich, the editor of *Ogonyok,* remarking on the astounding outspokenness of the deputies. "Now, maybe, the powerful are becoming a little afraid of the people."

The most outspoken speech of the entire session was delivered by Yuri Vlasov, a well-known former weightlifting champion. When he stood up to speak he said, "No one arranged my speech"—he prepared it himself:

"One of the richest countries in the world is, during peacetime, making ends meet with coupons, which are the same as ration cards. Elementary foodstuffs are unavailable. Our ruble is pitiful compared to other currencies. There is a great deal of corruption, lawlessness, and high-handedness in the country, and the country is drowning in irresponsible decisions. A great country has been brought low. It cannot fall any further, because the next step is collapse. The individuals responsible for such a turn of affairs usually resign, and not alone but with their entire staffs, as people who have made a mess of things." ("Applause," recorded *Izvestia.)*

Vlasov's principal topic was not resignation, but the most sacrosanct institution in Soviet society:

"When the first steps are being taken on the path of democratization, and at the same time some hope to crush it, a force such as the KGB takes on special meaning. After all, the KGB is subordinate only to the [Party] apparatus, the KGB has been removed from the control of the people. This is the most closed, the most clandestine of all state institutions. . . . Its actions are sometimes quite dubious. . . . [But] it is impossible to find the truth [about its activities]. It is dangerous to look for it. To this day, manipulations involving alleged psychological abnormality can threaten people who are dangerous to the apparatus.

"The democratic renewal of the country has not changed the place of the KGB in the political system. This committee exercises all-encompassing control over society and over each person individually.

. . . The KGB is not a service but a real underground empire that has still not yielded its secrets, except for the graves [of Stalin's victims slain by precursors of the modern KGB] that have been discovered. And, despite such a past, this service retains its special, exceptional position. It is the most powerful of all the existing tools of the apparatus."

Vlasov urged his fellow delegates to put the secret police under the strict control of a new oversight committee of the Supreme Soviet that would know its budget and the scope of its activities. "One hundred fifty years ago," he concluded, "Pyotr Chaadayev, an original Russian thinker and friend of Pushkin, wrote about Russia: 'We are an exceptional people; we are among those nations that, as it were, are not members of mankind but exist to give the world some terrible lesson.' There should be no more of this 'terrible lesson.' "

That was an electric moment. There were others. One came when General Rodionov took the podium to defend the decision to use force against the demonstrators in Tbilisi, whom he accused of "subversive, anti-state actions." They were political enemies, Rodionov said, who had to be dealt with. Many in the hall were appalled, and made that clear with groans and catcalls. "Don't prevent me from speaking!" the general snapped at one point, as though the deputies were his recruits. Rodionov was gravely undermined by D. I. Patiashvili, who had already been removed as first secretary in Georgia for his role in the killings. Patiashvili took responsibility for the decision to use the army, but insisted that the operation had gone out of control; demonstrators were "brutally beaten" with shovels by soldiers who chased them up and down the main avenue of Tbilisi; "more than three thousand people were poisoned" by chemicals. But when it was discovered that people had been killed, Patiashvili said, General Rodionov first denied that his troops had used shovels or gas. Later he had to acknowledge both.

Sakharov became a lightning rod for many conservative representatives of the *apparat* in the Congress. During one session he was attacked bitterly for comments in an interview critical of Soviet atrocities in Afghanistan. "You have insulted the entire army, the entire nation, all our war dead," shouted Tursun Kazakova, a teacher from Uzbekistan. "I despise you."

But Sakharov stood his ground. He was not criticizing individual soldiers, Sakharov said. "I am talking about the fact that the war in Afghanistan was in itself criminal, a criminal adventure taken on, undertaken by who knows who, and who knows who bears the responsibility for this enormous crime of our Motherland. This crime cost the lives of almost a million Afghans; a war of destruction was waged against an entire people. . . . And that is what lies on us as a terrible sin, a terrible reproach. We must cleanse ourselves of this shame that lies on our leadership." Conservative delegates jeered at Sakharov and shouted, "Shame!"

Another historical event seen by some deputies as a terrible sin was the Ribbentrop-Molotov pact of 1939, the Soviet-German nonaggression pact that carved up Poland and the Baltic states, allocating the latter to Stalin. The Soviet government had never acknowledged the existence of the secret protocols to the treaty providing for this division of territories. They had become a major issue in Estonia, Latvia, and Lithuania, because those secret protocols were the basis of Stalin's forcible absorption of the three republics in 1940. At the Congress Gorbachev repeated the rather tired official line that extensive searches of the archives had never produced original copies of the protocols, so perhaps they weren't genuine, but under pressure he also agreed to form a commission to investigate—a fateful step, since there was no way a serious commission could avoid concluding that the protocols were genuine.

As if the drama of the Congress were insufficient, two tragedies occurred outside Moscow during the days of that first session that suddenly distracted the entire country. The first was a horrific explosion of butane gas that had leaked from a pipeline in Siberia. Tragically, it was ignited by a passing train; more than 450 passengers were killed in a blast described as the equivalent of 10,000 tons of TNT. Gorbachev flew to Ufa to see the scene of the accident, where trees were leveled for two and a half miles in all directions. Then he reported to the Congress. He blamed the explosion on "incompetence, irresponsibility, and mismanagement," adding: "There will be no progress in the country if we have such laxness."

The second tragedy had a more explicit political content—an uprising in the Uzbek region of Fergana. Young Uzbeks armed with bars and axes hunted down, beat, and killed dozens of Meskhets, members of a Moslem minority whom Stalin had forcibly removed from Georgia to Uzbekistan at the end of World War II. It was a violent pogrom against the Meskhets, and because it occurred in Uzbekistan, where Gorbachev was openly at war with a corrupt local establishment that had prospered for years under the Communist Party banner, many liberal delegates in Moscow again smelled a provocation—an attempt by anti-Gorbachev forces to provoke violence and a crackdown, hoping to derail reform.

On this occasion Gorbachev called an unpublicized, closed session of the Congress to discuss what had happened. Amazingly, word of this meeting did not leak out; I only heard about it a year later from a deputy who had been there. According to my acquaintance, it was a telling—and discouraging—moment. "The Uzbek deputies, including the Moslems, wanted martial law. They wanted the *Russian* army to move in. It was a completely colonial mentality." But Gorbachev opposed that suggestion. Instead troops from the Ministry of Internal Affairs were sent, though the violence continued for days.

The gas explosion and the pogrom in Uzbekistan contributed to a sense of confusion, even chaos during the Congress. The Soviet world had come slightly unhinged, or so it seemed to many who took part in or watched these amazing events. "The fact that there is chaos is not a tragedy," observed Roald Sagdeyev, the progressive space scientist, who, with Sakharov, finally won a seat in the Congress from the Academy of Sciences. "In the beginning, as the Bible says, there was chaos. This chaos is better than the order that existed before."

With their outspokenness and courage, the progressives changed their country at the Congress, yet they lost every vote they contested. Their only "victory" grew from a compromise that gave Yeltsin a seat on the Supreme Soviet. In the complex balloting procedure, he had finished twelfth on a list of Moscow candidates for the permanent legislature, but there were only eleven seats for the Muscovites. One of those who finished ahead of Yeltsin volunteered to step aside in Yeltsin's favor; Gorbachev endorsed the idea (he may have been its original author) and it was accepted by the Congress. In practical terms it was a small concession to Yeltsin's enormous popularity in the country, but symbolically it was significant. The powerful *were* becoming a little afraid of the people.

As the first session of the Congress drew to a close, Sakharov made another bitter speech. The session was a "failure," he declared. The new Supreme Soviet would contain too many "idle functionaries," and too many important questions had been passed over. Many jeered him as he spoke, and Gorbachev cut him off at the end: "I'm asking you to finish. That's all! Take your seat, please! I ask you to sit down." It was an ugly moment. And yet Gorbachev had arranged to include Sakharov on the new commission, set up by the Congress, to rewrite the Soviet constitution—a considerable honor, one the Congress itself would not have bestowed if given a chance to vote on the proposal.

Gorbachev delivered closing remarks in which he rejected accusations that he was taking too much power into his own hands. "This is alien to my views, to my philosophy, and to my character," he declared. And he took the extraordinary step of denying that there was any danger of a Party coup against him. "I assure you that there is no danger here of any coup or anything of that kind. Let's put an end to all kinds of rumors . . . let's not heed the twaddle that some people try to palm off on us."

Gorbachev spoke at the end of twelve days that had shaken the Communist Party to its foundations, explicitly challenging (and implicitly negating) its "leading role" in society, yet he spoke up strongly in the Party's defense. "Some people," he said, were trying to peddle the idea of political pluralism and constructive opposition (Gavril Popov, a leading liberal deputy, had indeed suggested that the progressives band together). But the Congress showed that there can be debate and compromise "within the framework of the Soviet political system," Gorbachev said. In other words, the Party should retain its monopoly position: "I am confident that the twenty million Communists [total Party membership at the time] and the Central Committee will be able to prove through *perestroika* that they are equal to the difficult tasks of the times, that they are capable of continuing to perform the role of the political vanguard of Soviet society."

Did he still believe that, after all the stonewalling by Party officials, the open expressions of hostility to his reforms, the scheming by Ligachev and others? I doubt it. But this was a struggle—I also doubt Gorbachev allowed himself to indulge in much philosophical reflection. The key point was the one Gorbachev made in his first speech to the Congress. Without "leaning on the Party for support" and taking advantage of its national influence and organization, "this process [of political reform] will not go well. . . . There is simply no other way."

•   •   •

Everyone who shared in the excitement of the Congress was changed by it. Yeltsin gave this commentary:

> Gorbachev made the important decision that the entire session should be broadcast, live, on national television. Those ten days [actually twelve], in which almost the whole country watched the desper-

ate debates of the Congress, unable to tear themselves away from their television sets, gave the people more of a political education than seventy years of stereotyped Marxist-Leninist lectures multiplied a millionfold and flung at the Soviet people in order to turn them into dummies. On the day the Congress opened, they were one sort of people; on the day that it closed, they were different people. . . . Almost the entire population was awakened from its state of lethargy.

Arguably this was the first revolutionary experience of the television age—one that could be shared by 200 million people. It will probably never be possible to fully sort out its impact; it certainly isn't possible now. Yuri Karyakin, one of the liberal delegates, a Moscow intellectual and a historian, gave perhaps the best brief assessment. "The main achievement here," he said, "was the demystification of Soviet power."

CHAPTER EIGHT

THE MAGICIAN RUNS OUT OF TRICKS

There was an unexpected whiff of popular sovereignty in the air at the end of June 1989, when Premier Nikolai Ryzhkov had to submit to the Supreme Soviet his nominations for the ministerial positions in his new government. This was an entirely new idea for the Soviet Union, and it produced surprising results.

The Supreme Soviet had settled down into something like a routine of legislative business. Live television coverage had abruptly been abandoned on the first day of the new session. That day's papers had listed gavel-to-gavel coverage in their television schedules, so it was obviously a last-minute decision, announced by Anatoli Lukyanov, the Gorbachev protégé who had been chosen vice chairman and permanent presiding officer. Lukyanov told the legislators that industrial output had fallen 20 percent during the just-closed session of the Congress of People's Deputies, because so many workers had abandoned their jobs to watch the proceedings on television. Liberals complained that the real purpose was to give the conservatives and the *apparat* a freer hand to try to manipulate the Supreme Soviet out of public view, but the sessions were taped and rebroadcast each evening.

Loss of their live audience did not diminish the deputies' indepen-

dence. Ryzhkov found himself trying to defend his choices as ministers against blistering criticism. In the first days of the session he
withdrew six of his nominees, admitting sheepishly that he never
should have proposed the six in the first place. After hearing deputies'
criticisms of the men he had proposed—much of it focused on their
poor performance in earlier assignments—Ryzhkov told reporters, "I
could not see any substantial reasons that would allow me to defend
them."

The most interesting debates involved the chief of the KGB, Vladimir Kryuchkov, and General Dimitri Yazov, minister of defense.
Kryuchkov won confirmation easily, but only after he was subjected to
extensive questioning and criticism by a range of delegates. Yeltsin
said that the KGB had not been significantly touched by reform, and
that it was still engaged in illegal snooping on Soviet citizens. He said
the agency's staff was growing at an alarming pace, and warned that it
had too much power. Anatoli Sobchak of Leningrad complained that
local Party bosses misused local branches of the KGB to harass political opponents. An Estonian delegate complained that the KGB in
her republic recruited student informers by promising that they would
pass all their exams automatically if they cooperated. Kryuchkov said
he was pleased to have the unique opportunity to present himself for
confirmation, ignored all the criticisms, and promised to run an efficient intelligence agency.

Yazov had a harder time. He was criticized from right and left—
for cutting the military too quickly and not quickly enough, for being
too old (sixty-six), for tolerating too much bureaucratism and window
dressing in the ranks. Listening to all this, the general looked pained,
and for a time his confirmation was in serious trouble. But Gorbachev
came to the podium to defend him, assuring deputies that he was a
"progressive" working closely with the government. Gorbachev also
urged the delegates to approve a change in the voting procedure that
would allow Yazov to be confirmed by a simple majority of the deputies present, instead of a majority of the membership. The change was
adopted, which saved the minister of defense from humiliation. He
got 256 votes, 16 less an absolute majority. By saving Yazov's job,
Gorbachev appeared to create a special bond with his senior military
commander. Liberals who feared the possibility of a military coup
took some comfort from the new power relationship, though few had
much confidence in the pedestrian Yazov.

A more interesting struggle involving the military was conducted
out of view, and was never publicized. It involved the creation of a

Supreme Soviet committee on "Questions of Defense and State Security." Progressives had hoped to create a strong committee that would be able to challenge the vast military-industrial complex and the KGB, two of the country's most sacred cows. Participants in this effort described it to me later. They hoped that the committee's chairman would be Evgeny Velikhov, a progressive nuclear physicist, who was vice president of the Academy of Sciences and a national hero after playing a large part in the emergency response to the Chernobyl disaster. Velikhov, who had long advised the Soviet leadership on arms-control issues and had long enjoyed good personal relations with Gorbachev, was clearly interested in the job. He even spoke to several other liberal members about the possibility of their joining him on the committee, suggesting to them that he had been encouraged from above. But when the membership of the committee was announced, the chairman was an engineer who had worked for years inside the military-industrial complex; the committee was heavy with senior military officers and others with vested interests in preserving the status quo. Velikhov and his allies concluded that officials of the Central Committee and the Ministry of Defense had managed to block his appointment precisely because it threatened to create an independent power center that might limit their influence and their claim on the country's resources.

In mid-July Gorbachev flew to Leningrad for a revealing show of his personal power. The time had come to replace Yuri Solovev, the Leningrad first secretary, who had been defeated in the congressional elections even though no one ran against him. Solovev, a candidate member of the Politburo, was one of the most outspoken conservatives at the April Central Committee plenum, whose transcript Gorbachev had unexpectedly published; his demise had been expected for some time. The Leningrad Party organization was in disarray; Solovev was one of the six senior officials defeated in the election.* Numerous informal groups were active in the city, which also had the country's most lively television broadcasts. *The Fifth Wheel,* a regular news and interview show, had become an independent voice challenging the establishment. Party leaders blamed the program for contributing to its humiliation at the polls.

Gorbachev attended the meeting of the city's Party Committee,

---

* Solovev was also involved in the Andreyeva affair, though I cannot say exactly how. The flurry of pro-Andreyeva activity in Leningrad immediately after the publication of her letter must have been sanctioned by local Party officials.

where Solovev's resignation was accepted and his successor named. According to a well-informed acquaintance of mine, it was a brief meeting. Gorbachev made clear his support for Boris Gidaspov, a chemical engineer and corresponding member of the Academy of Sciences, who ran a major enterprise in Leningrad. He had been elected to the Congress in March, and had a reputation as a moderate. According to my informant, Gorbachev was drawn to Gidaspov as a representative of a new kind of Soviet "scientist-businessman," a technocrat for a new era—not a typical *apparatchik*. At the meeting where Gidaspov was chosen, the writer Daniel Granin, a leading liberal, stood up to ask why Gidaspov was being selected without any debate or any consideration of alternatives. The answer, of course, was that Gorbachev wanted him.

It was a relatively small but telling example of Gorbachev's own difficulties in adapting to the new situation he himself had created. He had repeatedly lectured the Party on the need to reform itself, adopt democratic procedures, and open up its affairs to public scrutiny, but when it came time to fill the important job of first secretary in Leningrad, he set all that aside and acted arbitrarily. Granin's mild protest was unusual; most still took it for granted that a general secretary would act in this way. But such arbitrary behavior did not necessarily aid Gorbachev's cause. Gidaspov proved to be something other than the ally Gorbachev obviously expected. He became a clever and resourceful critic from the right. It was yet another example of Gorbachev's making a speedy personnel decision that turned out badly. He'd done the same in choosing Ligachev as number two in 1985, and in promoting Yazov to defense minister immediately after Mathias Rust's dramatic landing in Red Square.

• • •

It was inevitable that the country's workers would eventually take advantage of the new freedoms Gorbachev had offered. Since Novocherkassk, spontaneous labor actions had been rare, but in July 1989 a new phenomenon appeared. The coal miners of Siberia went on strike. They were angry not at any particular boss or provocation—they were angry at everything: food shortages, bad pay, long hours, terrible working conditions, chronic housing shortages. One of the original demands of the first group of strikers was that they be assured a regular supply of soap to wash at the end of their shifts. As Valentina Alisovna, a member of the Party committee at one Siberian mine, put it, "We live like pigs."

As the strike spread from the Kuznetsk Basin in Siberia to the

Donbass in the Ukraine, to the mines of southern Russia, then Cen
tral Asia and the Arctic North, it became clear that the passive Soviet
worker, so patient with appalling conditions for so many years, was
finally starting to fight back. This display of workers' determination
and organization stunned the entire nation. Visions of Poland's Solidarity were in many minds—the more vividly since Solidarity's candidates had humiliated the Polish Communist Party in parliamentary
elections in Poland the month before.

Gorbachev and his colleagues reacted quickly and cleverly to the
walkouts by trying to ally themselves with the miners. Gorbachev sent
Politburo member Nikolai Slyunkov to Siberia, where he praised the
strike committee's high-mindedness, and said, "We understand you,
and we shall not limit ourselves to half-measures." Food and soap
were flown in to the mining region, and miners' salaries and benefits
were quickly improved.

Gorbachev clearly saw the opportunity the miners offered him. He
had asked the country to become active, to help him reform the system
with a revolution from below, and the miners were doing just that.
But it would not be easy to turn their protest to a good purpose—
significant reform of the system of management, for instance—and it
would be all too easy for the miners' example to become infectious,
causing massive economic disruptions. Gorbachev alternated between
encouragement and caution. He spoke of the "acute" political and
economic dangers posed by the strikes, even as he tried to ally himself
with the strikers and satisfy at least some of their demands.

Barely a week after the strike began Gorbachev assembled a meeting
of senior Party officials in Moscow and delivered them a stern lecture.
The Party was in trouble, he told them, because it was lagging behind
the changes in society. It simply had to move faster. It had to bring in
new blood, from the lowest Party committees to the Central Committee and the Politburo. "The most important thing now is to extricate
the Party from what I would call a state of siege and to impart dynamism to it," Gorbachev said.

But the conservatives had their own, different diagnoses of the
problem. "One gets the impression," said A. M. Masaliyev, the
Kirghiz first secretary, "that someone is skillfully directing popular
dissatisfaction with the Party. [Gorbachev himself, perhaps?] Certain
expressions are commonly used: 'Party functionaries,' 'bureaucrats,'
and so on. There continues to be writing and talk about special privileges for Party personnel." Imagine!

Bobykin of Sverdlovsk, now a regular naysayer at these events, declared: "It is time to draw a line between a healthy pluralism of opinions and tastes and the propaganda of an alien ideology that is openly corrupting society."

Ligachev, the true conservative, spoke of people's fear for their own safety. "Naturally, people are asking, what sort of socialist state is this if it cannot provide its citizens with personal security and a tranquil life? Why is all this happening, and where are we going?"

"The prestige of the Party cannot be decreed," Gorbachev warned them at the end of the meeting. "There will not be any return to the 'good old days,' although some people still have twinges of nostalgia." No one should be surprised, he added, by the tumultuous changes in society—"we brought them into being through our policy. . . . Revolutionary times are not a comfortable situation."

Miners had started to return to work after winning major concessions, though they remained on strike in some areas. The crisis atmosphere did not quickly subside. A few days after that Central Committee meeting, Gorbachev spoke to the Supreme Soviet. He called the coal strikes "a very serious crisis, the biggest test during the four years of *perestroika.*" He announced that he was withdrawing the one significant concession he had given the Party *apparat* in May, when it was reeling from its electoral defeats. Then Gorbachev had announced a postponement of the second round of elections foreseen in the new electoral laws—elections for local officials in the nation's towns, cities, and provinces. Party officials feared that in the wake of their disastrous performance in the congressional voting, they would be obliterated in local contests, and Gorbachev agreed to put off those elections from the fall of 1989 to the spring of 1990 to give them a chance to regroup. Now he reversed himself again, telling local authorities to proceed with the elections whenever they were ready to do so. "We won't succeed commanding things from here," he said. Again taking the miners' side, he invited voters to hold the authorities responsible for the strike. "The latest conflict, which spread across the nation and assumed the nature of a political crisis, was possible only because the center of government and the local authorities failed to react adequately to the issues that were raised," Gorbachev said.

At the end of July, 260 liberal deputies to the Congress formally joined the Inter-Regional Group, a new alliance of like-minded legislators committed to more openness, more reform and more freedom. The group chose five leaders: Sakharov, Yeltsin, Yuri Afanasyev, economist Gavril Popov, and Viktor Palm, an Estonian deputy. In two

days of speeches and discussions the members spoke hopefully of radicalizing the Supreme Soviet and building an alliance between intellectuals and the newly assertive working class. The group even
produced an issue of its own newspaper. This was the first formal
opposition group to appear, and though its initial proclamations were
relatively cautious, everyone involved understood the symbolic significance of their new creation. They also talked openly about the tense
situation in the country, newly aggravated the weekend they were
meeting by reports of a possible strike by railway workers. "This is a
dangerous situation," said Sergei Stankevich, a boyish political scientist from Moscow, who was a leading member of the Inter-Regional
Group. "If strikes spread to crucial industries like the railways—
Moscow can't survive without the railways for more than a few days—
this could be a pretext for putting a stop to the democratic process."
Liberals shared a chronic fear of a provocation that would prompt a
crackdown and end reform.

The summer session of the Supreme Soviet adjourned on August 4.
The railroad strike had been averted, and the leadership was hoping
for a respite. "The country has not had a single calm day throughout
the past one and a half months," Gorbachev said in a closing speech,
referring to both the ethnic violence that began in Uzbekistan and the
labor unrest.

The new legislature had comported itself respectably. It had rejected nine of Ryzhkov's fifty-seven proposed ministers, and exacted
many promises from others it approved. It had instructed the Ministry
of Defense to exempt college-level students from the draft, restoring
a policy that had prevailed before the Afghan war. And it had passed
numerous pieces of legislation. "I'm satisfied," said Anatoli Sobchak,
a Leningrad law professor who was one of the more liberal members
of the legislature. "We've taken some very serious steps. The fate of
perestroika is no longer just in the hands of a few leaders. It is also in
the hands of the representatives of the people."

Sobchak was referring to a great change in the politics of the country, one just beginning to become obvious that summer. There really
were significant new people outside the traditional seats of Soviet
power who were starting to have a palpable influence on the life of the
country. Sobchak was one of them. (Nine months later, he would be
elected, in effect, mayor of Leningrad.) Yeltsin was obviously another.
Sakharov was an important third. Gavril Popov, the Moscow State
University economics professor who was one of the co-chairmen of

the Inter-Regional Group, was another. (He would be elected mayor of Moscow in 1990.)

Those men had all become well known through their active participation in the Congress of People's Deputies—the Soviet Union's first political television stars. But there were many other new people whose names were not yet famous, including deputies, who had taken Gorbachev at his word and signed up for a life in politics.

I discovered this in Washington during the month of August 1989, when I met three of them: Nikolai Fyodorov, Konstantin Lubenchenko, and Andrei Sebentsov, names I had never previously heard. They had come to Washington to study the operations of the United States Congress, looking for ideas on how best to organize their own new legislature in Moscow. Over lunch, they talked about their hopes and ambitions for changing their country, about their relations with constituents who paid close attention to their work, about the need for new laws to guarantee basic freedoms, starting with freedom of the press. It was a social occasion and I took no notes, alas, but I cannot forget the exhilaration those three young men evoked. They were the products of a brand-new politics—they'd only been elected deputies five months earlier—but they spoke with the authority and confidence of well-established legislators. I left the lunch table thinking to myself, These are just politicians! Smart, responsible ones, too. I thought of how often I had heard Russians speak longingly of creating a normal country. These three were the avant-garde of normalcy, or so it struck me that August afternoon—human monuments to Gorbachev's success in actually changing his country.

•   •   •

One of the great questions about the historic events of 1989 will be something like this: Did Mikhail Gorbachev cause the collapse of the Soviet empire in Eastern Europe, or was it a historical inevitability that he was smart and agile enough to step out of the way of?

There is evidence that supports both answers, and I am not going to attempt a definitive reply here; we still have much to learn about the course of events in Poland, Czechoslovakia, East Germany, and the others during 1989, and much more to find out about how these events were discussed privately by Gorbachev, Shevardnadze, Yakovlev, and their colleagues. But it does seem clear that what happened in 1989 was not something Gorbachev foresaw when he became the Soviet leader in 1985.

One interesting piece of evidence is a speech Gorbachev made to the 10th Congress of the Polish United Workers' Party (the Polish Communist party) on June 30, 1986. At the time Solidarity was an illegal organization, and the Polish political situation was relatively calm. Gorbachev declared that the experience of the Polish crisis of the early 1980s, when Solidarity rose up and then was crushed, "confirmed in full measure that socialism now manifests itself as an international reality, as an alliance of states closely linked by political, economic, cultural, and defense interests. To threaten the socialist system, to try to undermine it from outside and wrench a country away from the socialist community, means to encroach not only on the will of the people, but on the entire postwar arrangement, and in the last analysis, on peace."

That was Gorbachev the *apparatchik,* of course, but there is no reason to doubt that it was also what he thought—or hoped—at the time. In the summer of 1986 Gorbachev was just starting to come to grips with the need for more radical changes in his own country; he could not have been hoping then for simultaneous disruptions in Eastern Europe.

Reformers in Eastern Europe were enthusiastic about Gorbachev from the start. They saw him as a welcome change from his predecessors, more modern and more flexible. As he became more radical, they became more hopeful. In Hungary, particularly, reformist Communists began to stretch their own notions of what might be possible. In 1988 they edged aside János Kádár, the party leader since 1956, and began implementing significant changes. In January 1989, the Hungarian parliament legalized freedom of assembly and freedom of association. In February the Hungarian Communist party's central committee embraced the idea of a multiparty system. These liberalizing steps evoked a popular response. On March 15, the anniversary of the 1848 revolt against Austrian rule, eighty thousand Hungarians marched peacefully through Budapest. At a giant rally, speakers called for free elections and the withdrawal of Soviet troops from Hungary. This was the first mass demonstration of the year in Eastern Europe. On May 2, Hungarian soldiers began dismantling the barbed-wire section of the Iron Curtain that divided Hungary from Austria, creating the first open border between an East Bloc country and the West.

But Poland was the main engine of change. General Wojciech Jaruzelski had failed to revive his country after the imposition of martial law and banning of Solidarity, and by the end of 1988 he was ready to acknowledge that failure. He authorized the beginning, in February 1989, of "round table" talks with Solidarity to try to persuade the union to accept a minority position in new political institutions in return for legalization. Solidarity's leaders weren't interested, but they eventually did agree to a more forthcoming offer of truly free elections for an upper house in a new, bicameral parliament. That election, on June 4, produced a triumphant result for Solidarity—and a disaster for Jaruzelski's Communists. Solidarity won ninety-nine of the hundred seats in the new Senate, and also every seat it was allowed to contest in the Sejm, or parliament. Suddenly the balance of power in Poland had shifted dramatically against the Communists.

The Polish campaign was going on during the first sessions of the Soviet Congress of People's Deputies and Supreme Soviet; election day, June 4, was also the day of the murderous pogrom against Meskhet Turks in Uzbekistan. (June 3 was the day Chinese troops and tanks crushed the student demonstrations in and around Tiananmen Square—an assertion of old-style Communist discipline whose relevance was obvious throughout the Communist world.)

A week later Gorbachev began a visit to West Germany, where the Polish election result was a compelling topic of discussion. At a press conference in Bonn, Gorbachev was asked if the Berlin Wall might someday come down. "Nothing is eternal in this world," he replied enigmatically, adding that the wall was built under certain conditions, which would not last forever.

These issues had domestic implications for Gorbachev, obviously. The bitter struggle between Armenia and Azerbaijan was also about the control Moscow exerted over both of them. The uprising that had led to tragedy in Tbilisi was explicitly about Georgian aspirations for independence. The independence movements in the Baltic states were continuously growing in strength, encouraged most recently by the strong showings of "popular front" candidates in the elections for the Congress. Even the Communist parties of Latvia, Lithuania, and Estonia were infected by yearnings for greater freedom from Moscow. In May the legislatures of both Lithuania and Estonia adopted legislative declarations of "sovereignty," declaring the precedence of local laws over those of the Soviet Union. In July Latvia's republican Supreme Soviet did the same. Gorbachev was juggling with volatile, nationalistic emotions, both within his country and in its satellites.

In August the revolution gathered speed. The key event, at least symbolically, was another telephone call—from Gorbachev to Mieczyslaw Rakowski, leader of the Polish Communist party, on August 22. Ever since the elections in June, Polish politicians had been jockeying over the makeup of a new government. Having lost control of the voting, the Communists sought desperately to retain control of the levers of power. They were forced into a corner by the Peasant and Democratic parties, longtime allies of the Communists, which decided in August that they could save themselves politically only by agreeing to join a Solidarity-led government. The Communists then had to choose between entering such a government (Solidarity was willing to leave Communists in charge of the Defense and Interior ministries), or taking responsibility for shattering the political process they had initiated early in the year. The Polish Communists were sharply divided when Gorbachev telephoned Rakowski. The two men talked for forty minutes. Gorbachev apparently urged his Polish comrades to join a coalition government to be headed by Tadeusz Mazowiecki, and Rakowski agreed.

At the time, Gorbachev may have seen a choice between this outcome and some Polish version of the recent events in China. "The political and moral choice that we faced," said Andrei Grachev, a Soviet Party official interviewed by Michael Dobbs of the *Post* at the end of the year, "was formulated after Tiananmen Square." Six months before that, Gorbachev had told the United Nations that the time had come to renounce the use of force, and that every country had the right to freedom of choice. And Gorbachev's entire foreign policy was based on continued good relations with all the Soviet Union's neighbors, the West Europeans, and the United States. He had already implemented substantial unilateral cuts in the military establishment. This was no time to take or support harsh action that could rekindle the Cold War.

The Polish Communists voluntarily relinquished power to Solidarity, the forerunner of all the popular movements that were to transform Eastern and Central Europe before the year was out. No serious person in the region—*apparatchik* or dissident—could have missed the significance of Gorbachev's telephone call to Rakowski. For the first time, a Soviet-sponsored Communist party had voluntarily given up power. Moscow was no longer on the side of enforced Communist discipline. It would bow to palpable popular will.

So a tentative answer emerges to the question with which I began. Gorbachev did cause the revolution in Eastern Europe—with a series of practical and symbolic steps, culminating in that telephone call, which informed the East Europeans that he had abandoned the old rule book that had required them to submit to Moscow's discipline. But the telephone call amounted to a sensible recognition of a new reality. Not making that call—not pushing the Polish Communists into that coalition government—would have implied a radical and expensive change in Gorbachev's own course. Realistically, he could not have made such a change that summer; making it would have meant abandoning both his domestic and foreign policies. So he caused the revolution, but revolution was inevitable.

• • •

In August 1989, the situation in the Baltic republics got more complicated in a way that illustrated Gorbachev's difficulties. Yakovlev, as chairman of the committee set up by the Congress to investigate the secret protocols to the nonaggression pact with Nazi Germany, admitted in an interview with *Pravda* that a secret protocol did exist that gave the Soviet Union the right to annex Estonia, Latvia, and Lithuania, which had been independent from the time of the Versailles Treaty until Stalin brutally absorbed them in 1940. Yakovlev "unequivocally" condemned the secret agreement. But in a political pas de deux that illustrated the touchiness of the issue, Yakovlev added: "It is far-fetched to see some kind of connection between the present status of the three republics and the nonaggression treaty." Claims that the treaty made the absorption of the three into the Union illegal were "unfounded," he insisted. He based his interpretation on "requests" made under the heel of the Red Army by the three little republics to be admitted to the Soviet Union in 1940. This was traditional official doubletalk: yes, there was a secret treaty; yes, it led to Stalin's brutal annexation of the three republics; but no, this history raised no relevant question about the three republics' current status.

Not surprisingly, Baltic activists were not impressed with Yakovlev's reasoning. Several days after his interview the Lithuanian Supreme Soviet announced the results of its own investigation: the secret treaty was illegal and invalid, and so was the subsequent absorption of Lithuania into the Soviet Union. Then activists in all three republics staged the biggest protest demonstrations in the history of the country on August 23, the fiftieth anniversary of the Nazi-Soviet Pact. Hundreds of thousands of people—perhaps a million, there was no way to count—locked arms to create a human chain for 430 miles from Vilnius, the Lithuanian capital, to Tallinn, the Hanseatic port that is the capital of Estonia. The population of the three republics is only seven million, and about a third of them are ethnic Russians, so the rate of participation in the demonstration was remarkable. Many of the protesters carried banners demanding complete independence from Moscow.

The combination of events in Poland and the Baltic republics apparently traumatized Party officials in Moscow. In late August, while Gorbachev was on vacation (but with his expressed approval, officials insisted), the Central Committee issued one of the nastiest public statements of the Gorbachev years, a bitter denunciation of the independence movements in the Baltic republics.

"Anti-socialist, anti-Soviet" opposition will not be tolerated, the statement said, comparing the nationalist groups of the Baltic republics to "political formations dating from the bourgeois period and the time of fascist occupation." Organizers of the human-chain demonstration "tried to work people up into a mood of genuine nationalistic hysteria," and self-anointed leaders were trying to "rupture long-established, organic ties" with the rest of the Soviet Union. "Things have gone too far," the Central Committee document declared. "The fate of the Baltic peoples is in serious danger. People should know toward what abyss the nationalistic leaders are pushing them. If those leaders were to succeed in achieving their goals, the consequences could be catastrophic for the peoples. Their very viability could be called into question."

The Baltic activists turned the other cheek, and Moscow took no action to follow through on the implicit threats in the statement. Gorbachev came back from vacation, and on September 9 went on television to give a speech intended to reassure the public. "Everything has become tied together in a tight knot," he said, "the critical state of the consumer market, conflicts in relations between nationalities, and the difficult, sometimes even painful, processes" of perestroika. "One can hear attempts at intimidation by predicting impending chaos and talk about the threat of a coup, or even civil war," he went on. He criticized conservatives who call "for a return to the old, command methods of management" to avoid chaos, and attacked "ultra-leftists" for wanting to go too fast. He urged that everyone "show restraint," "not fall into confusion," and stick to the course of reform, which he elaborated in some detail with a long list of legislative projects that faced the next session of the Supreme Soviet.

A Central Committee plenum was held on September 19–20 in part to consider the country's ethnic tensions. Gorbachev introduced a plan for a "radical transformation" of the Union, including increased autonomy for individual republics, but he ruled out any discussion of secession. At the same plenum he renewed his offensive against the conservatives, ousting Shcherbitsky of the Ukraine (the last Brezhnev-era survivor) and Chebrikov, the former KGB director, from the Politburo. He also announced that the next Party Congress would occur six months ahead of schedule, in October 1990, to consider an entirely new Party platform for the future.

Then he was off to East Germany for a fateful state visit to the faltering Erich Honecker. The occasion was the fortieth anniversary of the establishment of the German Democratic Republic, a ceremonial event that Gorbachev probably felt he had to attend. It was not a good time for a visit. East Germany was tense. Since September nearly fifty thousand East Germans had left the country through Czechoslovakia and Hungary, bound for West Germany. On October 3, four days before Gorbachev was to arrive, Honecker made a desperate attempt to reassert control by closing East Germany's border with Czechoslovakia, a move that only increased tensions. Large crowds of protesters gathered to try to use Gorbachev's presence to their advantage. Some shouted, "Freedom! Freedom!" but more chanted, "Gorby! Gorby! Help us!" Gorbachev avoided any inflammatory statements, but made one subtle pronouncement (conveyed to reporters by his spokesman) that was widely taken as a warning to Honecker: "Life itself punishes those who delay." There were also reports— credible but not confirmed—that he warned Honecker that the Soviet garrison in East Germany could not be used to quell civil disorders.

West German intelligence officials believe that Gorbachev actively pushed for Honecker's ouster and encouraged other East German Communists to remove him from power. According to a West German official with access to his government's best intelligence information, Gorbachev understood that Honecker intended to see *perestroika* fail and to survive him in power. According to this official, Gorbachev sent Ligachev to East Berlin later in September to discuss "the leadership question" with Honecker, on the theory that Ligachev's reputation as a conservative would make him more credible to the East German. I have not been able to confirm any of this West German information from Soviet officials, though it sounds plausible.

The day after Gorbachev returned home to Moscow, the biggest crowd in the history of East Germany—well over 50,000 souls—joined what had become a weekly, Monday-evening protest in Leipzig. Honecker reportedly ordered that force be used to disperse the demonstration, but intervention by conductor Kurt Masur and other prominent figures in Leipzig headed off any violence. A week later the Monday-night crowd swelled to perhaps 150,000, and two days after that, on October 18, Honecker was out of office. (The Wall was opened on November 9.)

• • •

The frenetic activity, the deteriorating economic situation, the ethnic tension, and the absence of a sense of where things were going conspired to create a heavy cloud of gloom in Moscow that fall. Gorbachev was clearly feeling the strain himself, and let it show at another of his regular meetings with editors on October 13. No *glasnost* on this occasion; the only available accounts of the session were provided to Western correspondents by participants. They described a leader at the end of his tether.

An "angry, almost hysterical" Gorbachev spent two hours ripping into liberal editors and deputies for aggravating what he called "a dangerous period" in the country's history. (The quotations are from participants in the meeting.) He accused the journalists of publishing "inflammatory," "irresponsible," and "provocative" material. According to Vitali Korotich, Gorbachev condemned factional fighting between liberals and conservatives, and compared those who insisted on making irresponsible statements to a man standing in a pool of gasoline and lighting a match.

Gorbachev picked on several individuals by name, including Popov and Afanasyev of the Inter-Regional Group—"a gangster group," he called it. He questioned whether Afanasyev had a right to remain a member of the Communist Party in light of his public statements, which Gorbachev described as "anti-socialist."

His harshest comments were directed at Vladislav Starkov, the editor of *Argumenti i Fakti* (Arguments and Facts), which had become the country's single most popular publication (with twenty-two million subscribers) by exploiting *glasnost* to publish straightforward, factual material, much of it in response to readers' questions. Starkov's weekly had published the results of a "poll" (in fact it was not a scientific opinion survey, but a tabulation of readers' letters) which concluded that Sakharov, Popov, Yeltsin, and Afanasyev were the most popular members of the Congress of People's Deputies. The magazine also indicated that Gorbachev's support appeared to be declining, though it discreetly gave no numbers. Gorbachev denounced this survey as "divisive," and said that if he were in Starkov's position, he would resign as editor of the paper.

The lecture had an immediate impact. Producers of *Vzglyad* (View), one of the country's most popular television shows (despite the fact that it was shown in the middle of the night), were ordered to disinvite Sakharov from a scheduled appearance on the program that night. Sakharov said he got their call at home just hours after Gorbachev's talk. In the days that followed, Starkov was called repeatedly to the Central Committee for criticism; he was pressured to take several other jobs. But he declined them all, and his staff threatened a strike if he was removed. Editors of the paper were amazed to receive a telephone call expressing support for Starkov from Yegor Ligachev. More than forty deputies signed a petition criticizing Gorbachev's threat to fire the editor.

It was an extraordinary moment—the father of *glasnost* threatening to devour his children. The offspring were wounded and alarmed. Starkov urged foreigners, particularly Americans, to take Gorbachev's outburst as "an important, indicative signal." He added: "In the United States there has been great euphoria. There has been the feeling that so long as Mikhail Gorbachev stays in office we will have democracy and *glasnost*. That is a big mistake. Look at the course he is taking."

Starkov also embraced the two-Gorbachevs theory. "It's Gorbachev battling Gorbachev. . . . He cooked the kasha [cereal] and it didn't turn out the way he expected."

It was another case of Gorbachev's taking offense. One of the editors who witnessed the tantrum offered this explanation: "I have the feeling that all of the positive attention he has gotten for several years has produced in his soul the self-image of a completely good and unerring leader. A few Central Committee meetings ago, he began to hear more direct criticism of his policies, and then a great deal more criticism started to appear in the press and in the legislature. I think he can't stand this personal criticism. He isn't used to it."

Afanasyev had a similar but broader interpretation: "Things are not working out the way he thought they would. Nothing has gotten better. The economy, interethnic conflicts, the psychological mood of the people, all of it has deteriorated. I think Gorbachev feels a sense of his own powerlessness to change things sometimes, and that is an unpleasant feeling for any head of state. I think that is what is causing the inconsistency in his behavior and causing him to ignore, and even shut off, the constructive voices around him."

It was the end of the era of Gorbachev the Magician. Some of Gorbachev's strongest supporters in Congress had suggested the previous June that he offer himself to the entire country then, in a popular election for president, instead of accepting the office on a vote from the Congress of People's Deputies. They theorized, as one of them explained later, that the country was then in a euphoric state, Gorbachev was at the height of his popularity, and his election was assured. A clear popular mandate would have vastly enhanced his position vis-à-vis the Party and the entrenched bureaucracy. But Gorbachev rejected this suggestion, and now, barely four months later, it no longer looked like a good idea. His popularity had fallen considerably—real polls, like Starkov's reader survey, showed the decline. He became the butt of jokes. People started referring to him as "Baltoon" —the chatterbox—for his many long speeches. It was four and a half years—longer than an American president's term, Yeltsin noted— since Gorbachev had taken the helm, and he had precious little to brag about.

Not that he was short of accomplishments. As he himself often pointed out, strong expressions of popular discontent were actually a sign of success—proof that the sleeping *narod* or mass of citizens had finally awakened. *Glasnost* was real; the restoration of history was real; the beginnings of popular sovereignty through the new Congress were real; the end of the Cold War and the transformation of Eastern Europe were real. But in a country where sugar was rationed, meat impossible to find in most state stores, even potatoes beginning to disappear in some communities, nothing on that list sounded very good to the citizenry.

Playing the role of the first Soviet leader subject to open criticism cannot have been easy for Gorbachev. No matter how well he could intellectualize the part, living it was no fun. Consider how poorly Western statesmen—who have usually spent entire careers absorbing criticism—react to sustained periods of sniping. Until he was fifty-four years old, Gorbachev had never had to endure a single public criticism. The political culture that reared him was utterly reliable in protecting its senior people from any form of popular hostility. Citizens who challenged the system of protection went to jail.

Even when he could overcome the simple pique of being a target of other people's second guesses, Gorbachev had to cope with the simultaneous loss of power and control. He had discovered the limits of his ability to invigorate the country. It just wouldn't respond to his exhortations or his policy changes; the economic situation only got worse. That was the loss of power. The loss of control was more subtle; he could ask for things to happen that clearly were within his *power,* but they didn't happen anyway. Starkov did not resign as editor of *Argumenti i Fakti,* for example.* Conservative Party officials would not stop speaking wistfully of good old days. Unless he abandoned his nonviolent principles, Gorbachev would have to endure such insubordination. This realization must have eaten away at him.

And now a curiosity: just when the morale of the liberals had fallen to this low ebb, Gorbachev fired Viktor Afanasyev, the conservative editor of *Pravda,* who had held on to his job, obviously with significant conservative patronage, for all these years. Viktor Afanasyev had been a leading apologist for Brezhnev, then an ally of Ligachev. Under his guidance *Pravda* had lost millions of subscribers. Gorbachev named Ivan Frolov, an old acquaintance who had worked for him in the Central Committee, as the new editor. Then a few days after that, Shevardnadze denounced Brezhnev's invasion of Afghanistan as "the most serious violation of our own legislation, of Party and civic norms and ethical standards of the time." These gestures did not placate the progressives, whose concerns had passed far beyond *Pravda* and Afghanistan, but they were reminders that Gorbachev and his group could keep their eyes on the ball they were playing with.†

•   •   •

At the end of November Gorbachev again took his show on the road. The Wall in Berlin had been breached; the old-line regimes in Bulgaria and Czechoslovakia ‡ had collapsed; and Gorbachev was off

---

* Some liberals in Moscow thought this was a sign that the entire episode was a piece of acting by Gorbachev—that he was never really angry with Starkov, but wanted to put on a show for the conservatives.

† Another sign of the same type: In November, I was told by a deputy, Gorbachev won approval for a 40 percent pay raise for members of the Party apparatus. The raise was never announced, but must have been appreciated.

‡ Miloš Jakeš and his clique in Prague also got a direct shove from Gorbachev. After sending numerous signals that they would not support any effort by Jakeš to suppress dissent, the Soviets summoned the ideologist of the Czechoslovak Party, Jon Fojtik, to Moscow on November 16. Fojtik was told that the Soviet Union was about to repudiate the 1968 invasion of Czechoslovakia

to Rome and the Vatican for a historic meeting with the Polish Pope, and then on to Malta for a brief summit meeting with President Bush.

The Italian part of the trip had a confessional quality. In a speech in Rome, Gorbachev explicitly relinquished the traditional Marxist-Leninist claim to superiority: "We no longer think that we are the best and that we are always right, that those who disagree with us are our enemies. We have now decided, firmly and irrevocably, to base our policy on the freedom of choice, to build our economy on the principle of mutual advantage, and to develop our culture and ideology through dialogue." He quickly added that no one should confuse this with a decision to "abandon socialism," which had not been made, he insisted.

Gorbachev acknowledged that the Soviet regime had been mistaken in its hostility to religion in the past. "We have changed our attitude. . . . We proceed not only from the assumption that faith is a matter of conscience for each person and something in which no one should interfere, but also from the assumption that the moral values that religion has developed and embodied over the centuries can serve and already serve the cause of renewal in our country."

To prepare for the meeting with the Pope, the Soviet government had finally legalized the Ukrainian Catholic Church, also known as the Uniate Church, which had been persecuted for forty years, since Stalin brutally destroyed it after World War II. This was announced in Kiev shortly before Gorbachev and the Pope sat down for their eighty-minute meeting. After the meeting Gorbachev declared that all Soviet citizens had the right to "satisfy their spiritual needs," and promised that the Supreme Soviet would soon enact new legislation to guarantee freedom of conscience.

The summit at Malta was Bush's idea, perhaps a realization that he had lost useful time conducting a fruitless "policy review" of Soviet-American relations that took up most of the first year of his presidency. It had ended with the realization in the new administration that it should take up where Ronald Reagan had left off, and resume the search for new agreements and understandings with Moscow. The Soviets welcomed this shift, and after initial wariness toward Bush they expressed considerable satisfaction with the president's careful

---

—the underpinning of any claim to legitimacy Jakeš could make. At the same time, Soviet military officers in Czechoslovakia conveyed hints to their Czech counterparts that they might block any attempt by Jakeš to employ the army to defend his regime. On November 24 Jakeš resigned.

and correct responses to the crumbling of Communist regimes in East Europe. At Malta they hoped for a clear signal that Bush was eager to help Gorbachev succeed.

They got that and more. The Americans volunteered a list of initiatives they were ready to take to help the Soviets economically. None of them amounted to a great deal, but the symbolism was better than Gorbachev could have hoped for. Bush was in his corner. There was also an agreement to try to accelerate the completion of new arms-control agreements covering both conventional armaments in Europe and strategic nuclear weapons. The meeting was marred by terrible weather, which actually shortened the hours the two leaders could spend together on board ship, but it was a great success for Gorbachev nevertheless.

His meeting with Bush gave Gorbachev a visible lift. He went from Malta to a summit of the Warsaw Pact—by then not even a shadow of its former self—where it was formally agreed that the 1968 invasion of Czechoslovakia had been an illegal error. "History has shown how important it is, even in the most complex international situations, to use political means for the solution of any problems, and to observe strictly the principles of sovereignty, independence, and noninterference," the pact's statement said. It was the formalization of a new reality—Moscow had abandoned its empire.

•   •   •

In early December Gorbachev reentered the political fray in Moscow. The mood was still tense. A Central Committee plenum held on the eve of the second session of the Congress of People's Deputies issued an appeal to the citizenry to remain calm. Debate in the plenum was heated. No transcript was published, but Daniel Granin, the Leningrad writer and a deputy, was Gorbachev's guest at the plenum (he was not a member of the Central Committee). Granin gave a brief but alarming account of it in an article for *Moscow News*. After seeing the Central Committee debate, Granin wrote, "I know for sure that there is a struggle" between Gorbachev and "a Party and bureaucratic clique" of conservatives, "and it is fierce." Granin made it clear that a number of members directly attacked Gorbachev (another source later told me there were four or five), saying that "his line is wrong and 'it's about time we all got back on the right track.' . . . One speaker stated that if capitalists and the Pope praise us, that means we are moving in the wrong direction. . . . Some speeches sounded oppressive for their political dependence and recollection of every fault in order to belittle what has been achieved and to peddle the idea that we need to turn back."

According to Granin these speeches "touched Gorbachev to the quick. So much so that he said if that was their assessment of what had been done over the years, he was ready to resign. It was a tough moment."

No member of the Central Committee took Gorbachev up on his offer to step aside. And he had strong defenders—"their voices rang clearly during the plenum," Granin wrote. But it was an alarming episode for supporters of reform. Granin advised his fellow liberals to stand up and be counted with Gorbachev, even if they weren't always delighted with his actions. "This is a moment of choice," Granin wrote. Georgi Arbatov, the Americanologist, spoke to the deputies elected by the Academy of Sciences soon afterward (according to one of them) and said it was time to drop their petty disagreements with Gorbachev and come forcefully to his defense, because he was under siege from the Party's conservatives.

One of the issues discussed at that plenum was the status of Article 6 of the Soviet constitution, the provision that assured the "leading role" of the Communist Party. All over Eastern Europe the new regimes had formally renounced the idea of a leading role for the Party, and many Soviet activists had begun to press for a similar decision in Moscow. The Baltic Communist Parties were particularly active in this effort, as were members of the Inter-Regional Group. The provision clearly was at odds with Gorbachev's policy of turning power over to elected councils, or soviets, and taking the Party out of day-to-day administration of the country. Article 6 also seemed to guarantee the Party a significance the electorate—judging by the voting for people's deputies—did not feel it deserved.

This was the key paragraph of Article 6: "The leading and guiding force of Soviet society and the nucleus of its political system, of all state organizations and public organizations, is the Communist Party of the Soviet Union."

Gorbachev looked for a way to temporize on this sensitive point. He told the Central Committee that Article 6, like any provision in the constitution, could be changed when the entire document was rewritten, but he criticized those who urged its immediate elimination for trying to "demoralize Communists." His position was apparently dictated by the fact that a majority of the Central Committee opposed any early change in Article 6.

A few days later he spoke to an unpublicized, preparatory gathering of deputies on the eve of the opening of the Congress's second session. Sakharov, among others, pressed the issue of removing Article 6. (A plurality—but not the legally required majority—of the Supreme Soviet had voted earlier to put Article 6 on the Congress's agenda.) A deputy who was present recounted what happened. Gorbachev gave an eloquent speech, clearly implying that he personally favored changing Article 6—and making many other changes too—which the Party wasn't yet ready for. In a remark that startled his audience Gorbachev said he was constantly being harangued by critics who ask why he is moving so slowly. He wanted to go faster, Gorbachev said, but he could not: "More than many of you I want to go faster." Any change in Article 6, he said, should begin with the Party, since it affected the Party. "It was a good speech," according to my informant, more sincere and persuasive than the ones Gorbachev allowed himself to make on television. In public, this deputy said, Gorbachev is speaking first of all "for Ligachev and Chebrikov"—in other words, for the benefit of the Party's conservatives, the people he was most afraid of.

One of my most thoughtful and best-informed acquaintances in Moscow, a deputy and active participant in these affairs, said Gorbachev's behavior at this moment made most sense if seen as a product of his "Khrushchev trauma." This was ironic, my friend said; "the country doesn't care anymore about what happened to Khrushchev, but Gorbachev thinks about it all the time." It was still the Party hierarchy that could separate Gorbachev physically from the levers of power—the fledgling new Congress and Supreme Soviet could not protect him. Or so he felt. Or so my friend theorized.

When the new session of the Congress formally convened, it debated whether to put Article 6 on its agenda. Gorbachev, the Party loyalist, defended the view that Article 6 should not be changed. He noted that it was only added to the Brezhnev version of the constitution in the 1970s; "it was not even included in the three previous constitutions," and removing it would not make "everything . . . clear and fine." Baltic deputies and Moscow liberals favored the idea. The proposal was defeated, but by a surprisingly narrow margin: 1,138 to 839, with 56 abstentions. This result suggested that since the first session adjourned in June more than 300 deputies had moved from the loyalist to the reformist camp. It was a striking demonstration of the real power of public opinion on the legislators.

Three days after that vote Andrei Sakharov collapsed and died. He had suffered a massive heart attack at age sixty-eight. His wife found his body near his study, where he had been working on a speech for the next day's session of the Congress. His last words to her had been, "There will be a battle tomorrow!" He died just two days before the third anniversary of Gorbachev's dramatic telephone call to Gorki.

The response to his death was a revealing snapshot of the state of Soviet politics at the end of 1989. The official reaction was correct but exceedingly cautious. Though foreign correspondents in Moscow learned of Sakharov's death in the early hours of December 15, the Soviet media remained silent for hours, obviously awaiting instructions on how to handle this delicate matter. A day later *Pravda* printed an official obituary, signed by Gorbachev and other members of the leadership, which described Sakharov as "a major scientist of our time, a well-known public figure, U.S.S.R. people's deputy, member of the presidium of the Academy of Sciences, and winner of the Nobel Peace Prize." When he had won the Nobel in 1975, he had been the subject of vicious attacks by the Brezhnev regime.

The obituary did not describe Sakharov's dissident activities or the 1968 essay that contained so many of the ideas that Gorbachev had come to embrace, but it referred to his "political confrontation," which "took much of his strength." It credited him with pressing the idea of limiting nuclear tests at a time when "his calls were ignored" by the Soviet government. "But he continued to uphold these positions."

"A gross injustice was done," *Pravda* said, when Sakharov "was banished from Moscow to the city of Gorki," though there was no explanation of what prompted the banishment, or when it occurred.

On the morning after he died Vitali Vorotnikov, a Politburo member, opened the Congress with an announcement of Sakharov's death. All deputies, including Gorbachev, stood for a moment of silence. Dmitri Likachev of Leningrad, a distinguished scholar in his eighties, who was close to both Sakharov and Gorbachev, went to the podium to say, "A part of our heart is gone."

Soon normal business resumed—discussion of the state economic program. But not everyone was satisfied with the tribute to Sakharov. Ilya Zaslavski, twenty-nine, the Moscow deputy who had lost the use of his legs as a child, carried himself up to the podium on crutches. He stood by the microphone patiently. Gorbachev, understanding his mission, leaned toward him and instructed him to "sit down!" Zaslavski held his ground. Someone else offered to help him back to his seat. He refused. Finally he was able to speak. He called for a full day of mourning for Sakharov.

Later Zaslavski told Remnick of the *Post* that he had sought out

Gorbachev before the session began to ask him to call for a period of national mourning for Sakharov. "He said he probably could not do that because it would defy tradition. We have a procedure, it seems, for this: a general secretary gets three days of mourning, a Politburo member one, and none for an academician [Sakharov's official status]." No official day of mourning was declared.

Gorbachev spoke warmly of Sakharov. "I feel this misfortune with all my heart, with enormous pain," he told a *Moscow News* reporter. His memory "will remain in our history forever." Gorbachev recalled their own relations: "Starting with our first conversation, the conversation when I telephoned Gorki so that Andrei Dmitrievich could return from exile, from that first conversation the debates between us began. . . . I always valued him as an open, direct, and sincere person. . . . even when I didn't agree with him."

An acquaintance of mine who was close to Sakharov theorized that that first conversation had won over Gorbachev. The call had come out of the blue, as did Gorbachev's offer of freedom. Despite the emotion of the moment Sakharov had found the presence of mind to plead for the release of several political prisoners. "If Sakharov had just said 'thank you' and hung up," my acquaintance speculated, "the two men might not have had such a good relationship later." According to this man, the two had closer relations than was generally understood. They met privately for serious discussions on several occasions. They often glanced knowingly at one another during sessions of the Congress, and in private Gorbachev agreed with nearly all of Sakharov's opinions, according to my acquaintance. In public of course Gorbachev was much more cautious, but Sakharov seemed to understand why, and held firmly to the role of leader of the loyal opposition. He knew it was his function to keep pressuring Gorbachev to move faster, and more radically.

Several hours before he died, Sakharov spoke at a caucus of the Inter-Regional Group. As usual, he made it exceedingly clear what was on his mind. "By stretching out the restructuring process over many years," Sakharov said, Gorbachev and his colleagues "are leading the country toward catastrophe." Delay would mean disillusion in the populace; "disillusionment is making an evolutionary path of development in our country impossible. The only path, the only possibility for an evolutionary path is the radicalization of *perestroika*." Evidently, that was the message of the speech he was working on when he died.

Sakharov's body lay in state in an open coffin; more than 100,000 people came to pay last respects. Many stood in line in bitter cold for three hours. Memorial services were held in numerous cities and towns around the country. On the day of the funeral, the 19th, Gorbachev and seven other members of the leadership came to the Academy of Sciences to pay their last respects. Tens of thousands joined the funeral procession in a dank and cold December rain, which turned to snow. But at the Congress of People's Deputies, a proposal to declare a formal day of national mourning was shouted down crudely by the same deputies who had often booed and harassed Sakharov when he spoke from the podium.

"Every revolution has its saint, and Andrei Dmitrievich is the saint and martyr of *perestroika,*" observed Vitali Korotich, the editor of *Ogonyok.* "If God sent Jesus to pay for the sins of humankind, then a Marxist God somewhere sent Andrei Sakharov to pay for the sins of our system."

•   •   •

Another death of a very different kind transfixed Moscow before 1989 had ended. The last shoe was dropping in Eastern Europe— Romanians had found the courage to rise up against Nicolae Ceauşescu. After Sakharov's funeral on the 19th the news from Bucharest was tense; first the security forces were killing citizens, then Ceauşescu and his wife fled the city, but were caught and put on trial before a makeshift military tribunal. On the 25th they were shot by firing squad.

The Congress of People's Deputies was in session during these days, and Gorbachev began each morning's meeting with a briefing on the overnight news from Romania. When they learned on the 22nd that the Ceauşescus had been toppled, deputies cheered. Gorbachev and Shevardnadze showed their extreme satisfaction with the outcome. Ceauşescu had openly criticized Gorbachev's reforms as a repudiation of socialism; he ruled in the Stalinist manner himself. So his demise was a parable—or so the Soviet reformers hoped.

CHAPTER NINE

THE END OF
THE PARTY

One morning in about 1972, according to a much-loved anecdote told in the Brezhnev years, Lenin woke up in his mausoleum on Red Square. The father of the revolution made his way up to the street and started to look around. He spent all day walking and talking to people, reading the newspapers, even watching this new-fangled television. At the end of the day he was seen in the Kiev Railroad Station —the station for trains to Poland and the West. "Vladimir Ilyich," someone asked, "where are you going?"

"Back to Zürich," he replied, "to start over again." *

If, at the beginning of 1990, Leonid Brezhnev could have arisen from his place of honor a few paces from Lenin's mausoleum (virtually the last honor he still retained) and taken a look around Mikhail Gorbachev's Soviet Union, he would have had a similar shock. After nearly five years in power, after so many amazing events and changes, Gorbachev's country and its empire were in many respects unrecognizable. But Gorbachev's most radical achievement was still to come.

Gorbachev had to devote the first month of the new year to ethnic politics. The centrifugal forces created by three years of *glasnost* were

---

* Lenin spent the years prior to his return to Russia in 1917 in exile in Zürich.

much stronger than he, Yakovlev, and their immediate circle had expected. This was an area where a lifetime of propaganda had taken a toll; Communists of the Gorbachev generation, reared on a strict diet of "Leninist internationalism," seemed incapable of grasping the strength of nationalist sentiment, and the lack of regard for the idea of a multinational Soviet Union, in the non-Russian republics.

For Gorbachev this was largely a practical matter: the Soviet Union existed, it was a fact; its component parts were tied to each other by extensive economic and human connections. Rupturing those ties would cause all kinds of practical problems, some of them gravely serious—didn't everyone see that? Of course there was a powerful psychological factor at work too; he did not want to preside over the dissolution of his country. Watching him dodge and maneuver in the long-running melodrama over Lithuania's claim to independence, it seemed that Gorbachev had simply ruled out the idea of letting Lithuania go—he just wasn't going to do it. But for a long time he seemed unprepared to use force, at least in any crude or conventional way, in order to prevail. It was a great test.

In December the Lithuanian Communist Party had taken the remarkable step of declaring its independence from the Soviet Party headquartered in Moscow. For Russian Communists this was a contradiction in terms; their Party—known to them by its initials, CPSU, the Communist Party *of the Soviet Union*—was a disciplined, centralized organization, not some kind of confederation. But the Lithuanian Communists understood that their only hope of surviving as a significant political force was to align themselves with the powerful pro-independence sentiment in their republic. Already, the Lithuanian Supreme Soviet—not yet even reconstituted by free elections, so a product of the old method of Party selection of deputies—had declared Lithuania a sovereign state, beyond the reach of Soviet laws. (Estonia and Latvia had done the same.) Now elections were coming in February, and strong, independent nationalists could win control of the republican government.

Gorbachev decided to beard the lion in its den—he would go to Lithuania, meet the people himself, explain to them their errors. It was a dramatic example of his boundless self-confidence, particularly in his ability to convince people. The same confidence had persuaded him, in his first years in power, that he could bring the Party apparatus along as he made radical reforms. It was a stubborn confidence, not dissuaded by experience.

Whatever else it accomplished, Gorbachev's stubbornness in Lithuania made great television. He arrived in Vilnius on January 11, 1990, and went right from the airport to Lenin Square in the center of the city, where a crowd was waiting. Earlier in the day 250,000 Lithuanians had rallied outside the Catholic cathedral in Vilnius to demonstrate their support for independence. Gorbachev spent an hour in conversation on the square. He began on a conciliatory note. "We shall decide everything together. If someone succeeds in pitting us against each other, and it comes to a clash, there will be a tragedy. We cannot allow this."

But wherever he went, he found the Lithuanians all but united in favor of independence, and willing to say so bluntly. "At present no republic can live without the other republics," he insisted to one group of factory workers. "We're all tied together now." He was right about that on some practical level, but the Lithuanians were not in a practical frame of mind, as he discovered a moment later. Gorbachev said that troublemakers had "palmed off seditious thoughts" on Russian residents of the Russian Republic, allegedly based on scholars' "findings," to the effect that "if Russia detaches itself from the Union, in four years it will be the most prosperous state in the world." Before Gorbachev could deflate that false claim he was interrupted—by applause! This crowd loved the idea of Russia breaking off from the Union. "There is no need to applaud," Gorbachev chided them. "It's better to listen. In general, I don't want us to stomp our feet and clap our hands. I want us to listen."

At a meeting of intellectuals he chastised them for trying to "impose a professorial pattern on real life, on the entire people, regardless of the realities," an inclination he compared to Stalin's totalitarianism. If "society is made to fit the required pattern," he said, then "heads fly . . . I'm afraid that is a pattern which has formed here, too," he said, clearly frustrated that no one was buying his arguments. "You are tilting at windmills," he told them. "You are battling the past."

Which of course they were—a past that included violent usurpation of their country by Stalin, the execution of tens of thousands, and forced expatriation to Siberia and elsewhere of hundreds of thousands more, and long years of active repression of Catholicism and Lithuanian culture. Gorbachev could fairly complain that he had nothing to do with any of that, but in Lithuania, as the current occupant of the Kremlin he had to accept full responsibility for it all.

For three nights Gorbachev's personal confrontation with Lithuania played on national television. The entire country saw their leader make his arguments, and saw his arguments rejected. Now everyone would realize what he was up against. Not that this helped advance his cause in Lithuania.

The only hint of compromise Gorbachev offered involved the possibility of a multiparty system in the future (something we now know he had already decided was desirable). "We should not be afraid of a multiparty system the way the devil is afraid of incense," Gorbachev said in Lithuania. "I don't see a tragedy in a multiparty system if it serves the people."

Even the local Communist leader, Algirdas Brazauskas, talked back to the general secretary. When Gorbachev complained bitterly to Party activists that their break from Moscow undermined his entire reform effort, Brazauskas replied with some common sense of his own: "We did comprehensive analyses in the republic," he said, "and the report showed that only an independent Communist Party had any chance to win the trust of the Lithuanian people and remain a serious political force." This was just as much a fact as Gorbachev's assertion of economic interdependence. The confrontation was a stand-off.

As soon as he returned to Moscow Gorbachev was challenged by a more immediate and more gruesome ethnic problem. New anti-Armenian riots broke out in Baku, the capital of Azerbaijan, and the violence quickly spread. Armed bands in both republics started shooting at each other. Two weeks earlier Azerbaijanis had rioted near their border with Iran, prompting the central authorities to send troops into the border area. In this new outbreak more than forty people were killed, and there was no sign of the violence's diminishing. Gorbachev had to confront the question he had been able to avoid until then: whether to send his troops into a conflict between two of the country's ethnic groups. In this case the Azerbaijanis would inevitably interpret sending in troops as taking Armenia's side; but no firm action could mean hundreds or thousands of casualties. One of Gorbachev's personal assistants told an acquaintance of mine that Gorbachev decided, changed his mind, decided, and changed his mind again before finally sending in the army, the navy, and troops of the KGB.

A decree of the presidium of the Supreme Soviet justified the dispatch of troops as a response to "murders, robberies, and attempts at armed overthrow of Soviet power." In the days that followed there was appalling carnage in both republics. The full toll will never be known, but hundreds died. According to Soviet press reports, Azerbaijanis looted many hundreds of Armenian homes in Baku; fighting broke out again in Nagorno-Karabakh, the predominantly Armenian enclave inside Azerbaijan that had been the initial cause of violence in 1988. There were reports of pitched battles involving machine guns and hand grenades. According to the Interior Ministry, armed bands even commandeered helicopters to take fighters to the scene of battle. Gorbachev added more troops, bringing the total to sixteen thousand. Armed Azerbaijanis fired on the troops, inflicting casualties.

Gorbachev was feeling great strain. With the situation still worsening three days after the first troops were sent in, he told a public meeting in Moscow that the government was only trying to prevent conditions from deteriorating further. And he leaped to the defense of *perestroika* against his conservative critics—"the rabble," he called them. "We are getting results, and this must be seen. We can't get frustrated and say everything is going to pieces. What is really falling apart are the old ways."

On the night of January 19, 1990, Soviet troops had to fight their way into Baku against armed members of the Azerbaijani Popular Front, the nationalist organization that was becoming more popular every day the crisis continued. At least sixty more people were killed. On the 20th a tired, drawn Gorbachev went on television. In an unusually halting voice, he defended the use of force and appealed for "wisdom and reason." He said it was "the duty of the state" to preserve order and fight outlaws, "who are ready to sacrifice others for the sake of their personal ambitions and profiteering for power." Boris Yeltsin warned publicly that Gorbachev's government "might collapse within several months."

Another political crisis was at hand. The Central Committee was due to meet on January 29, a session originally scheduled to consider the Lithuanian Party's declaration of independence. Gorbachev's own defensiveness about reform and predictions like Yeltsin's fed speculation that another showdown could be looming. In a front-page commentary, *Izvestia* urged Gorbachev to "take action" to defend democracy by speedily introducing "a state based on law."

The situation only got worse. The Azerbaijani Supreme Soviet openly took the side of the Popular Front, even threatening to hold a referendum on Azerbaijani independence if Moscow did not withdraw its troops. Popular anger there grew as it became clear that many innocent civilians had been killed when the Soviet army shot its way into Baku. The authorities in Moscow realized that they had to acknowledge the strength of the Front, and did so openly on the television news, implicitly offering to negotiate. General Yazov, in Baku, told reporters that the Front had tried to seize power by force, and said forty thousand Azerbaijani militants were armed. Gorbachev dropped from public view, and rumors circulated in Moscow that he and Yakovlev were working hurriedly to prepare a new version of the Communist Party program—finally, a blueprint for truly radical reform that would be presented to the Central Committee as a working document for the Party Congress later that year. The scheduled plenum was postponed for a week.

Two weeks after the troops were sent in, the situation began to calm down. Revealingly, the Azerbaijani Popular Front and its Armenian counterpart, the National Movement, agreed to peace talks proposed by the Baltic authorities. The talks would take place in Riga, capital of Latvia, led by representatives of the popular fronts of all three Baltic republics. This arrangement amounted to an acknowledgment by all concerned that they shared a common interest in circumventing Moscow while eliminating any pretext for Moscow's intervention.

In the capital Gorbachev's allies began to drop clues about his next surprise, using code that was easily understood. Wasn't it time, *Pravda* asked, for the Soviet leader to have more power—to be more like a real president? Several senior officials told reporters in Moscow that the time was right to enhance Gorbachev's authority, so he could carry on with real reform. As the Central Committee meeting drew closer, the official press blossomed with criticisms of the Party as the principal obstacle to *perestroika*. Men-on-the-street interviewed on television made the same point.

The danger of a putsch from the right had mobilized pro-reform activists in Moscow, who quietly organized the biggest demonstration the capital had seen. One of the organizers was summoned to meet with Anatoli Lukyanov, a close associate of Gorbachev's. Will this be an anti-Gorbachev demonstration? Lukyanov asked, according to an account of their meeting from a reliable informant. Quite the contrary, the organizer said, we want to defend him. All right, Lukyanov said, then we will permit it.

On Sunday, February 4, perhaps 200,000 citizens* took part in a parade and rally to demand more democracy and an end to the Com-

---

* Moscow's police estimated nearly 200,000; Moscow Radio said perhaps 300,000.

munist Party's political monopoly. The Central Committee was to convene the next morning, and the event was obviously aimed at its conservative members, who might try to push Gorbachev in the opposite direction. "This is the last chance for the Party," Yeltsin told the crowd. "When they all show up at the Kremlin Monday morning, they had better have in mind the image of the hundreds of thousands of people you see out here today," said Vladimir Tikhonov, a deputy. Yuri Afanasyev called for "a peaceful February revolution of 1990," a formulation calculated to alarm Party officials. The February Revolution of 1917 toppled Czar Nicholas II and created a short-lived democratic regime that the Bolsheviks in turn toppled in November. The czar was killed after the November revolution.

The evening news on television included extensive coverage of this unprecedented demonstration. Its reportage emphasized demands from the crowd for accelerated reforms of the Party. There were many other slogans. "Party bureaucrats: remember Romania!" and "Soviet Army—don't fire at your own people," among others. Anarchists, monarchists, and even Hare Krishnas joined in.

It is difficult to know how the specter of crowd vengeance affected the conservatives, who must have been terrified by what they saw all around them. There had been cases already where angry citizens had turned on local Party authorities and forced them to step down. This had happened in Volgograd (the former Stalingrad), a city of a million on the Volga, and in Tyumen in the oil-producing area of northern Siberia, and in Chernigov in the northern Ukraine. I suspect the example of Ceauşescu was a telling one. Many of the older Central Committee members who were most hostile to Gorbachev had no real defense against accusations that they had helped bring the country to its present, ruinous state. Yeltsin, as we will see, used the threat of revenge to great effect at a later dramatic moment.

When the Central Committee convened, Gorbachev unveiled his latest makeover of Party policies. Henceforth the Party would favor changing Article 6 of the constitution to eliminate its own privileged position before the law. The Party would favor a multiparty system in which it would have to compete for influence. The Party must "cleanse itself of everything that linked it with the authoritarian-bureaucratic system." Now, "Our ideal is a humane, democratic socialism." The new Party platform, said Gorbachev, "clearly indicates what we must renounce: The ideological dogmatism that became entrenched over decades. . . . Everything that led to the socialist countries' isolation from the mainstream of world civilization. . . . The idea that it is possible to build socialism according to a predesigned pattern."

Why was it necessary once again to change course? Gorbachev trotted out his now-familiar explanation: "We have seen that the crisis that has struck the country is much deeper and more serious than might have been supposed."

And yet this was still Gorbachev the well-trained Leninist speaking; he neither abandoned the idea of communism nor relinquished the style of a Soviet Communist politician. "Needless to say, the Communist Party of the Soviet Union intends to struggle for the position of ruling party" in the new, multiparty democracy it foresaw, he said. As usual, he spoke at egregious length—a seven-thousand-word speech. Trying to reassure nervous comrades that he would not abandon the Party, he spoke dismissively of a mood of "liquidationism," an obscure reference to a small group of Mensheviks who in the years before the Revolution opposed conspiratorial, revolutionary tactics, favoring instead proselytizing openly in legal institutions. Gorbachev was not abandoning the revolution, he assured them: "We remain committed to the choice made in October * 1917."

Gorbachev's report ignited an outpouring of hostility from the left (Yeltsin alone) and right (numerous members). "One gets the impression," said Yeltsin of Gorbachev's report, "that it was written with two hands: the right and the left." Compromises would no longer work: "Today the Party is on the brink of a crisis to which it has been brought by, among others, the current membership of the Central Committee."

The conservatives aggressively disagreed. V. I. Brovikov, the Soviet ambassador to Poland and a former mayor of Minsk, hurled his disapproval in Gorbachev's face. The proposed new Party platform "is hardly acceptable . . . and is in serious need of additional work." The leadership had brought the country "face to face with a rampage of anarchy, the degradation of the economy, the grimace of general ruin, and a decline in morals. . . . Our country, the mother of us all, has been reduced to a sorry state; it has been turned from a power that was admired in the world into a state with a mistake-filled past, a joyless present, and an uncertain future."

---

* The "Great October Revolution" occurred on November 7 by the modern calendar, but on October 25 on the old-style calendar then used in Russia.

Gidaspov, the man Gorbachev had traveled to Leningrad to install as first secretary, called for a U-turn in economic policies to return to old methods, and demanded that the Party find a way "to increase its prestige and its mobilizing role in our society." If it does not, he added, "we will be leading our society toward complete chaos; I wouldn't want to use the word 'collapse.' "

V. G. Anufriyev, second secretary in Kazakhstan, implied that the forthcoming Congress should replace Gorbachev and his allies in the leadership. "Someone should answer, comrades, for the breakdown of Party unity and for ideological failures; someone should answer, comrades, for the events in Eastern Europe. . . . They have destroyed our buffer zone, but just forget about it, let them live as they want."

Yakovlev and Shevardnadze defended Gorbachev eloquently, and in the end everything he asked for was approved. Yeltsin cast the only No vote. "We have taken a step of exceptional magnitude," Yakovlev said after the plenum, which lasted an unusually long three days. But the published transcript of the session left the strong impression that this group of Central Committee members was now riven beyond mending. Either the conservatives would find some way to restore the world they had lost, or they would be swept out themselves. There was no longer any room for compromise.

Right after the plenum, Ivan Frolov, the new editor of *Pravda,* disclosed the details of the leadership's plan for disposing of the obstructionist Central Committee members. They would sink along with the power of the Party. At the Congress less than five months later the Politburo would be replaced by a presidium composed of senior members of the leadership, the heads of the fifteen republican Communist Parties and representatives of rank-and-file Party organizations. There was no prospect that such a large and diffuse committee could act as a governing body, as the Politburo did. The inclusion of regional leaders assured a wide diversity of views. This would obviously be a toothless institution. A new, smaller Central Committee would be elected; the permanent apparatus of the Party would be sharply curtailed. The Party could obviously get by with less, since, as Yakovlev put it after the plenum, "power is being transferred from the Party to the soviets."

The important new political institution would be outside the Party altogether—a much stronger Soviet presidency. Two weeks after the plenum, members of the Congress began to learn what Gorbachev had in mind: a president to be elected initially by the Congress of People's

Deputies (and subsequently by universal suffrage), with the power to rule by decree, veto all legislation passed by the Supreme Soviet, and cancel legislation passed by republican legislatures. Sergei Stankevich, a Moscow deputy and a political scientist who was a student of the American presidency, spoke for many of the liberals when he said, "I don't think this new legislation will be acceptable to anyone who believes in a constitutional system of checks and balances." The liberals asked their supporters to join in mass demonstrations all over the country on February 25 to press for more democracy and the removal of conservatives—beginning with Ligachev—from the leadership. Some liberals spoke of compelling the government to enter "round-table negotiations"—the term made famous in Poland when Solidarity was relegalized—with the opposition forces.

The idea of a presidency outside the Party's domain was not a new one. According to one knowledgeable informant, Yakovlev developed a proposal for a strong presidency as early as 1985. It was an obvious device to circumvent the Party, which is why many of the liberal legislators, including Sakharov, had also urged the idea on Gorbachev in 1989 (though the powers of the presidency the liberals had in mind would have been extensively checked and balanced). Until early 1990 Gorbachev had shown no interest in the idea. His reaction was generally interpreted as another sign of his anxiety about splitting the Party. But Gorbachev now seemed willing to accept a split. Under the overwhelming pressures created by escalating conservative criticism, ethnic unrest, economic collapse, and the failure of all previous initiatives in agriculture, trade and industry, he was ready finally to make "a sharp turn," as he called it.

But, fittingly, a measured sharp turn—he still would not turn against the Party, or deny his own Party ties. Nor would he turn the country over to mass democracy; control would still be exercised. The caution inherent even in this most radical phase of Gorbachev's reforms was evident in the official propaganda campaign against the February 25 demonstrations called by the progressives. Television and the newspapers were filled with alarmist reports about the dangers of "mob rule." A typical one in *Izvestia* betrayed a characteristic Russian anxiety about anarchy: "The thousands-strong human sea . . . erupts into the street to defend *perestroika,* but once in the street it forgets about the constitution and the law. . . . It is almost getting beyond all control, beyond the influence of even its favorite orators. Or is someone striving for just that—for it to get out of control? What happens after that we already know, unfortunately." In the week before February 25 Soviet television broadcast regular appeals urging citizens to stay at home. Some warned that reactionary Communists wanted to exploit the rallies to impose harsh discipline and sabotage reforms. On February 21 a statement was issued in the name of the Supreme Soviet, noting, "Many Soviet people are expressing alarm over the prospect that extremists and even criminal elements. . . . may join the mass rallies and processions."

The threats were successful, at least partially. In Moscow organizers had hoped for a crowd of up to half a million; they got no more than 100,000. Around the country crowds did turn out, but also in smaller numbers than hoped—about twenty thousand each in Kiev, Tbilisi, Minsk, and Tashkent, for example. Speakers criticized the proposed legislation on the presidency, especially for failing to require direct popular election of the first president; called for disbanding the KGB; called for the resignation of senior Party conservatives. There were virtually no untoward incidents. Organizers claimed a "half success," and blamed government intimidation for the other half. *Izvestia* published a sheepish account of the uneventful rallies all over the country, acknowledging that the pre-demonstration alarm had been unjustified.

There was additional excitement on the night of the 25th that has never been explained satisfactorily. Soviet army and KGB units were seen near the capital, and according to credible accounts, KGB men with machine guns surrounded Gorbachev's new dacha near the village of Zhukovka outside of Moscow. "It may have been some kind of a probe by the KGB and the army, a show of strength of some kind," one deputy told me later. Weeks later, rumors circulated among NATO officers that Soviet army units had staged some kind of anti-Gorbachev protest that night. Yakovlev later denied this. The episode was a reminder that despite all the changes the system could still keep important secrets. Perhaps Kryuchkov and Yazov had taken seriously Afanasyev's threat of a new February revolution? I hope we will someday find out what happened.

The 25th was election day in Lithuania, the first republic to vote for local councils and a republican supreme soviet. Sajudis, the Lithuanian popular front, which ran on a staunchly pro-independence platform, won an overwhelming victory—72 of the supreme soviet's 141 seats in the first round of voting. (It would win 18 more in runoffs.) Communist Party candidates won 29 seats. Brazauskas, the Lithuanian Party leader, was philosophical: "Look, what happened to us is the future. It's inevitable that you are going to see this [kind of defeat of the Party] in other republics as well." He was absolutely right. Two weeks after Lithuanians voted there were elections all over Russia, the Ukraine, and Belorussia. Many Party *apparatchiks* were trounced; they ran especially poorly in bigger cities. They were beaten by democratic reformers, ecologists, former political prisoners, local nationalists (particularly in the western Ukraine), even an occasional television personality. In Leningrad reformers won 60 percent of the seats on the new city soviet. In Moscow they had a clear majority and would organize an independent city government. In Minsk, both the mayor and the Party secretary were defeated.

Here was tangible evidence of the collapse of public support for the Communist Party. It could not be called a surprise; opinion polls had shown what was happening. Even Gorbachev had fallen to a 43 percent approval rating in a poll published by *Ogonyok* in February.* And yet the election results were startling. They seemed to confirm that voters who felt free to express their true sentiments would hold the Party responsible for the country's past and for the mess it was in—and not give it credit for Gorbachev personally or for the changes he had wrought.

The country's politics had come alive. *Nedelya,* a weekly magazine, published a detailed article in February on the parties, fronts, clubs, and associations that were then functioning. It showed popular fronts or movements in every republic, front groups for specific purposes in many cities (the Lake Baikal Front in Irkutsk, Siberia, for example): the United Working People's Front of Russia and dozens of other labor organizations; a Christian Patriotic Alliance and a Nikolai Bukharin Political Club. The author identified 350 political clubs and citizens' initiative associations and a long list of political parties, though they had not yet been formally legalized: the Democratic Party, the Democratic Union, the Confederation of Anarcho-Syndicalists, the Party of the Dictatorship of the Proletariat, the Christian Democratic Union of Russia, and more. Two or three years earlier none of these existed. It was a dizzying list. And almost none of it had any connection with what had been the country's only political organization for generations—the Communist Party of the Soviet Union.

---

* Polling was another offspring of *glasnost;* before Gorbachev there had been almost no polling of the Soviet public, and what was done was never published in the press.

At the end of February the legislation on a strengthened presidency was debated by the national Supreme Soviet. It was the most emotional debate in the brief history of the new legislature. Critics questioned why Gorbachev should be given so much power, why the people could not vote for their president, why the legislation presumed that the Soviet Union was one country like France or the United States instead of a union of sovereign republics.

Gorbachev took many of the critical comments personally, or so it seemed to many in the hall. Again, he appeared to take offense. His own contribution to the debate was heated and pointed. "We have run into some very serious opposition here from representatives of a large part of the Inter-Regional Group. They want to tell us that we're being hasty, and they even hint that 'everybody is falling in line with Gorbachev.' This can only be evaluated as cheap demagoguery. Let's think about it. Those who just a few months ago were calling for the institution of a presidency are trying to suggest to us the thought that doing this means opening the way to dictatorship and choking off democracy."

Sergei Stankevich, the political scientist from Moscow, who was a leading spokesman for the liberals, took the floor to ask that henceforth Gorbachev please "show more respect for others in such discussions." Emotions were running so high that at the lunch break some Gorbachev allies thought the legislation was in trouble; in the end it passed easily, 306–65, with 38 abstentions. The vote was not binding —the full Congress still had to approve the measure.

On the eve of the special session of the Congress the Central Committee met again, and again heard outspoken criticism of Gorbachev. Still threading a narrow path through treacherous political territory, Gorbachev took the occasion to denounce the idea—advanced by some progressives—that the Communist Party should react to its unpopularity by changing its name or its stated objectives. This would be "a serious blow to the Party's ideological foundation, and would disappoint many Party members and non-Party people who support the Communist Party as a party of lofty ideals," he said.

In the Congress of People's Deputies the next day, the proposed legislation and constitutional changes to create a strong presidency ran into fierce opposition. Members of the Inter-Regional Group— there were now nearly four hundred members—spoke against the concentration of power the legislation permitted, while delegates from the independence-minded republics, now including Georgia, Azerbaijan, and Armenia, as well as the Baltic states—denounced the provisions limiting their potential sovereignty.

After the first day's debate Gorbachev agreed to send a drafting commission to work overnight on changes that might mollify the republics. Changes were made limiting the president's ability to declare a state of emergency in outlying republics and diluting his veto power. In a deft parliamentary move, Gorbachev combined all the pending constitutional changes—legalizing new political parties, allowing for private ownership of land and enterprises, and creating the new presidency—into a single motion, forcing deputies to accept the entire package or lose all of it. Gorbachev needed a two-thirds majority; he got 270 votes more than that, winning by 1,771 to 164, with 74 abstentions.

One question remained: should the first president be chosen by the people or by the Congress? Soviet television had broadcast an opinion poll that same week which found that 84 percent of the public favored a direct election. Gorbachev's allies argued that this would take too much time—the president was needed at once. The argument was not as disingenuous as it may sound. Gorbachev obviously wanted to be the president well in advance of the Party Congress now scheduled to begin at the end of June—the conservatives' last chance to somehow restore their dominance. Again a two-thirds majority was required; this time Gorbachev won narrowly, with just 49 votes to spare. Directly afterward he was nominated for president. No opponent was nominated. Gorbachev received 1,329 votes; 495 voted against him, and 420 did not vote. He had gotten what he said he wanted in two different respects: he was the president, and he was president of a country that had real politics, with real and open disagreement about the most fundamental questions.

Lithuanian independence, for example. On March 11, the day before the Congress began debating the constitutional changes, the new Lithuanian Supreme Soviet, controlled by Sajudis deputies, voted to declare the republic independent of the Soviet Union. Then it elected a new president of the republic—Vytautas Landsbergis, a professor of musicology and one of the founders of Sajudis. Landsbergis was not a Communist—indeed, by personal disposition he was an anti-Communist. The legislators formally requested that Moscow withdraw its army and KGB from Lithuanian territory. They quickly adopted their own flag, and removed or covered up all symbols of Soviet power in their meeting hall.

Two days later, Gorbachev told the Congress of People's Deputies in Moscow that the declaration of independence was "illegitimate and invalid," and said there would be no negotiations on the issue. "We hold negotiations only with foreign states," he explained.

Thus began a war of nerves that would continue until the eve of Gorbachev's trip to America at the end of May. Gorbachev demanded a formal retraction of the independence declaration "within three days"; he authorized military maneuvers in Lithuania, and a convoy of tanks and armored personnel carriers drove through Vilnius, the Lithuanian capital; he rushed additional KGB troops into the republic, and disarmed its national guard; he issued an executive order instructing all Lithuanian citizens to hand over their private arms "for temporary storage"; he ordered Soviet troops to seize the property of the Lithuanian Communist Party and to occupy a printing plant where republican newspapers were published; he sent Soviet soldiers to find and detain Lithuanian deserters from Soviet units; he warned of "grave consequences." Through all of this the Lithuanians stood their ground, refusing to reconsider. In early April Landsbergis did offer to talk about an extended transition period to Lithuanian independence, which opened the way to a meeting between Lithuanian leaders and Alexander Yakovlev. But the meeting was unproductive; instead of compromise, Gorbachev imposed economic sanctions, including cutting off oil and natural gas. Here was the logic of the situation he had tried to explain to the Lithuanians in January—they couldn't survive without Soviet energy supplies, didn't they realize that?

Yes, but no, was their answer. The embargo did not compel a quick capitulation. The Lithuanians did seize on a proposal made by France and Germany that they consider postponing implementation of their independence declaration. Their willingness to entertain that idea apparently persuaded Gorbachev to meet with the Lithuanian premier, Kazemiere Prunskiene, who called their conversation "a big step forward." A week later he met a delegation of Lithuanian legislators and told them they might achieve independence in two or three years, provided they suspended their March 11 declaration of independence. The Lithuanians were relieved, though nothing was finally resolved, and the oil remained turned off.

•   •   •

The frenetic pace had continued, unabated, for many months. By the time the leaves came out in May the Azerbaijan crisis was all but forgotten, at least in Moscow. Eastern Europe no longer got much attention. The coal miners? What coal miners? The new crises of every week were sufficient to fill each one. Gorbachev's stamina was surely one of his greatest assets. I haven't a clue how he coped.

He was juggling grenades. None of the problems he confronted really seemed soluble: there was no apparent way to fix the economy or provide food; no apparent way to quell the new nationalism being felt in nearly every republic and autonomous region; no satisfactory way to placate both Party conservatives and the ever-bolder liberals. Most painful of all, there was no understandable method for transforming a damaged society that was used to taking orders into a thriving, responsible, disciplined, civil, and humane democracy. All that was possible was to juggle the grenades, hoping desperately that none would explode, while doggedly pushing forward on the political front, counting on good luck and good instincts to carry the day.

It wasn't clear to me in January 1987 that Gorbachev knew what he was doing when he declared the primacy of political reform. Would it really be possible to teach politics to a politically illiterate country? Was this really the best way to begin to modernize and civilize that country? Three years and a few months later the results were starting to come in, and they were astounding. The country was learning politics with a vengeance; through politics, energies were being released that many Russians had doubted still existed inside their countrymen. And no group had an obvious advantage in real politics: the reactionary members of the Central Committee were as ill prepared as the most radical Lithuanian nationalists.

This odd type of equality was easy to see in the spring of 1990. The conservatives, thrashing about for some way to get at Gorbachev and restrain him before he destroyed their game, came up with a clumsy ploy. From some unidentified corner of the *apparat* came the idea of an "open letter" to all Communists, which was drawn up under the title "For Consolidation on a Principled Foundation." Initially, according to a Central Committee official who resigned in protest over the letter, it was to include instructions on purging undesirable (liberal) elements from the Party before the upcoming Congress, but that proposal did not survive the process of consultations among Central Committee members that had to precede the issuing of the letter. Even so the final version was a primitive document, full of old-fashioned exhortations to toe the line and "brook no conciliatory attitude toward ideological vacillations." Its appearance in April seemed anachronistic—or ominous. The official who resigned in protest,

Georgi Khastsenkov, a consultant to the Central Committee's Department of Party Organizational Work, said he interpreted the letter as an attempt "to carry out an anti*perestroika* coup on the eve of the 28th Party Congress."

Yuri Afanasyev, the outspoken historian and leader of the Inter-Regional Group, said the letter was an outrage, and announced his resignation from the Party. His announcement invigorated a debate among liberals about whether it was best to stay in the Party and fight, or break away and start afresh.

Real politics and his own declining popularity affected Gorbachev in a new way. He began to demonstrate palpable anxiety about public opinion. One of his strongest arguments for speedily creating a strong presidency was that he needed additional powers to deal forcefully with the economic crisis. Once he had those powers Gorbachev launched an intensive policy review to come up with more radical ideas. The country got the message; rumors spread of various draconian measures that might soon be taken. But Gorbachev blinked. After consultations with his new "presidential council," a body of sixteen politicians, academics, and writers, which he appointed at the end of March and quickly began to use as a kind of personal politburo, he announced in late April that there would be no "shock therapy." That was the term made famous in Poland, which had freed its economy from central controls at a stroke in January with tumultuous consequences. "Your cries of alarm are reaching us," Gorbachev told an audience of workers in Sverdlovsk, the industrial city where Yeltsin had been first secretary. There would be no dramatic price increases, he promised. He constructed a sentence that managed to capture both his policy and his political personality: "What we have in mind is a sharp turn, but we cannot do this all in one move." The difference between what he had in mind and what was doable largely defined his leadership.

Gorbachev's anxieties about public opinion were validated on May Day, the annual workers' holiday. As always, it was marked by a parade through Red Square under the approving eyes of the leadership, perched atop Lenin's mausoleum. But the leadership this year included Gavril Popov, the Moscow State University economist and leader of the Inter-Regional Group, with whom Gorbachev had often quarreled in the Congress. Popov had just been elected chairman of the new Moscow city soviet, which made him the capital's new mayor. (Stankevich was chosen as his deputy.) The traditional, tightly organized and thoroughly unspontaneous May Day parade was to be replaced by a free event. Anyone who wished to was invited to take part.

There was still a modicum of organization; the first hour of the parade was filled with official trade-union groups and others following the usual pattern of artificial enthusiasm and respect for the men on the mausoleum. With this group in the square, leaders of the official trade unions gave conventional speeches. After an hour the free parade began, and the mood change could not have been more abrupt. The crowd came alive with jeers and catcalls, many addressed to the leadership. Some looked Gorbachev right in the eye as they raised their fists. The signs carried by paraders made an amazing display: COMMUNISTS: HAVE NO ILLUSIONS. YOU ARE BANKRUPT; MARXISM-LENINISM IS ON THE RUBBISH HEAP OF HISTORY; THE BLOCKADE OF LITHUANIA IS THE PRESIDENT'S SHAME!; CEAUŞESCUS OF THE POLITBURO: OUT OF YOUR ARMCHAIRS AND INTO PRISON BUNKS!; DOWN WITH THE CULT OF LENIN!; LET THE COMMUNIST PARTY LIVE IN CHERNOBYL!; and more. In the old days marchers carried portraits of the leaders; in this parade many carried pictures of Sakharov and Yeltsin. A Russian Orthodox priest carried a crucifix taller than he was and shouted, "Mikhail Sergeyevich, Christ is risen!"

Gorbachev and his comrades stayed on the mausoleum and watched this surreal spectacle for twenty-five minutes. Then they marched off the monument and into the Kremlin, leaving the parade to continue without them. There was no precedent for this moment in Soviet history—tens of thousands of citizens joyfully giving the bird to the leadership in the holiest spot of all, right in front of the waxen mummy that is "the living Lenin." It was one of those political symbols made for television—but not Soviet television. Viewers all over the world saw the scene, but Soviet television interrupted its coverage of the parade when the rowdies first appeared. The next day the official press was filled with reproaches for the rudeness of the display. "It's hardly possible that the authorities in the capital of any country that considers itself civilized could allow such a demonstration," said *Izvestia.*

An *Izvestia* commentator writing a week later observed that "some people want to burst out angrily at Gorbachev with everything that has accumulated genetically for generations, everything that our grandfathers, fathers, and, of course, we ourselves did not dare to say to Stalin, Khrushchev, and Brezhnev." This was certainly true. It was Gorbachev's fate, having released his countrymen from their silence, to bear the brunt of what naturally followed. But he didn't like it! Alexander Yakovlev gave a press conference five days after the parade to denounce the protesters as right-wing provocateurs. "I saw flags from monarchists, anarchists, pictures of Czar Nicholas II and Stalin," Yakovlev complained. It was clever politics, but inaccurate reporting. As their leaders acknowledged, most in the crowd were anti-Communist progressives, not reactionaries. A week after Yakovlev spoke the government introduced a draft bill in the Supreme Soviet that would set a penalty of up to six years in prison for slandering the president of the country.

Oleg Rumyantsev, a leader of the new Social Democratic Party, suggested that Gorbachev and Yakovlev were going to have to adjust to the fact that the Communist Party was destined to be a minority opposition group. Gorbachev "has to change his basis of support," Rumyantsev said. "He cannot continue to turn his back on the very people who have walked through the door he opened."

* * *

At the end of May, as he prepared for a trip to Canada and Washington, Gorbachev was confronted again by an unwelcome presence from the past—Boris Yeltsin. There was a curious chemistry to this relationship. Gorbachev had advanced Yeltsin's career, then cut it short with a cruel display of authoritarian revenge in November 1987. But he had not delivered a *coup de grâce*—on the contrary, he went out of his way to preserve Yeltsin's official status by giving him a senior government job. It was clearly true, as Yeltsin wrote in his memoir, that Gorbachev looked on him with deep ambivalence—"if Gorbachev didn't have a Yeltsin, he would have had to invent one," as Yeltsin put it.

By May 1990, Yeltsin's giant Siberian frame was looming larger than Gorbachev could have liked. He was outgrowing the modest role Gorbachev had designed for him. Gorbachev and his colleagues had sought to hold Yeltsin back by exploiting his quirks and erratic behavior to try to diminish his popularity. Hence the attempt to persuade Muscovites not to vote for Yeltsin as their people's deputy—an attempt that backfired badly. Hence also the stink made in the official media over Yeltsin's trip to America in 1989, when he put on a raucous show that some Russians considered inappropriate. There were press reports, most of them exaggerated, that Yeltsin was drinking heavily on the trip. An Italian journalist wrote a fanciful account of a purportedly drunken Yeltsin touring the U.S., which *Pravda* printed in full. When the story was exposed as an invention, *Pravda* had to apologize—another dart directed at Yeltsin that turned into a boomerang.

The result of all this was a growing sense that Boris Yeltsin had become the most popular politician in the country. He decided he would try to become the president of the new government of the Russian Republic, a post of potentially enormous power, since Russia proper contains most of the Soviet Union's population, natural resources, and industry. Yeltsin had been elected to the new Russian parliament from his home base, Sverdlovsk, and he was the favored candidate of the large bloc of reform activists who had won seats. But there was a roughly equal bloc of Party-backed deputies, and fully a third of the new deputies seemed genuinely independent. The contest would clearly be close. As the vote approached, Gorbachev decided to contribute to the debate. He spoke to the new Russian Congress about Yeltsin's platform, which called for a sovereign Russian Republic that would conduct its own economic and foreign policies and demand businesslike relations, based on treaties and "world prices," with the other Soviet republics.

Gorbachev accused Yeltsin of trying to "excommunicate Russia from socialism" by proposing to drop the word "Socialist" from the republic's name. He accused him of trying to break up the Union by "rejecting the principles Lenin formulated" when the Soviet Union was first formed in 1922. It would be a tragedy, Gorbachev told the Russian congress, if its first session became not "a step forward [that would] advance restructuring in all areas," but instead "a corrosive acid." In other words, don't vote for Yeltsin.

That speech marked the beginning of a terrible week for Gorbachev. On the day he gave it, his premier, Nikolai Ryzhkov, was introducing his government's latest package of economic reforms, advertised as a truly serious attempt—at last—to dismantle the economic bureaucracy in Moscow and create a new market economy. Gorbachev's presidential council had endorsed the plan, which was lambasted at once by opposition deputies and many others. There was an amazingly easy target for criticism in Ryzhkov's proposal to triple the price of bread in phases beginning on July 1. This was the politically most sensitive of numerous price increases his plan envisaged. It promised full compensation for many of the increases, but with no clear explanation of where the money would come from.

The politics could not have been worse. When the outcry began, Ryzhkov quickly made known his idea to put the whole plan to a national referendum, a new notion that Gorbachev would soon back away from. The Inter-Regional Group announced plans to try to force a vote of no confidence in Ryzhkov's government. Citizens reacted with panic buying all over the country. Bread, flour, and pasta products disappeared from the stores over the next several days. The new Moscow city government announced that it would allow only residents of the capital with appropriate identification to shop in Moscow stores. Ordinarily, a million or more people from the provinces come to Moscow every day to shop.

Alarmed, an obviously edgy Gorbachev went on television on Sunday night, May 27, two days before he was to leave for North America. "I appeal to you not to give way to panic," he said. "Let's look at this soberly, and we will resolve the problem." He gave an overlong and underpersuasive speech; it lasted forty-eight minutes, and had no apparent impact on the country.

Voting had begun for the job of chairman of the new Supreme Soviet of the Russian Republic—in effect, the president of Russia. Gorbachev's chosen challenger to Yeltsin was Alexander Vlasov, a candidate member of the Politburo who was the premier of the Russian Republic's government under the old structure. Vlasov was a bland figure who created no excitement, and on the eve of the first ballot he dropped out of the race, apparently to avoid certain defeat. That left Ivan Polozkov as Yeltsin's only serious rival. Polozkov, first secretary in Krasnodar, was one of Gorbachev's most outspoken conservative critics in the Central Committee, a virulent opponent of the new cooperatives and an obvious skeptic about reform generally. He, too, enjoyed Gorbachev's endorsement against Yeltsin, indicating that the leader was prepared to back anyone to block his old nemesis. On the first ballot Yeltsin finished first, but without enough votes to win a majority; the second ballot produced a similar result. Polozkov then dropped out, and Vlasov reentered the race. The third-ballot votes were counted overnight and the result was announced just hours after Gorbachev took off for Ottawa. Yeltsin had won a majority with four votes to spare; he would be Russia's new leader.

•   •   •

The symbolism of Yeltsin's victory despite Gorbachev's attempt to block him was hardly what Gorbachev needed as he began his first visit to Washington in two and a half years. Yeltsin's triumph was icing on a new cake—a Gorbachev-is-faltering cake that the world's news media baked in many varieties on the eve of the summit. Gorbachev contributed to the gloomy analysis by leaving Alexander Yakovlev in Moscow; it was the first time he had failed to accompany Gorbachev to a major summit meeting, and a sign of their anxiety about the situation at home. *Newsweek* summarized the tenor of the commentary in its cover story: "Why Gorbachev Is Failing." Correspondents in Moscow reported the feeling there that events were moving beyond Gorbachev's ability to control them. The contrast could not have been sharper between the gloomy atmosphere of this summit and the euphoria that surrounded Gorbachev's first Washington meeting with Ronald Reagan.

But Washington suited Gorbachev; within twenty-four hours his spirits, even his body language, had palpably revived. His celebrity status had not been diminished in the United States, even if it had disappeared at home. Crowds responded to him wherever he went, and his American interlocutors declared themselves still impressed with his intelligence, vigor, and forcefulness. President Bush did his part to boost Gorbachev's morale, particularly by taking him to Camp David in the Catoctin Mountains outside Washington for informal talk and a game of horseshoes. Gorbachev threw a ringer on his first toss—or so the White House said later. The president also went out of his way to give Gorbachev the appearance of a victory on a new trade agreement—virtually meaningless in practical effect, but politically significant at home, members of the Soviet delegation said.

Gorbachev responded to suggestions that both he and his country had been weakened by economic failure and political turmoil. At nearly every appearance he addressed the issue, insisting that the turmoil was not weakness. "Please don't be frightened," he said to a group of congressional leaders in a moment of candor, "because if you get frightened, that can frighten us, too." The divisions in Moscow politics erupted in Washington in an unprecedented manner. Several key Gorbachev aides used the summit to attack Premier Ryzhkov and his latest package of economic reforms. Georgi Arbatov of the Institute for the Study of the U.S.A. and Canada, a Central Committee member, openly suggested that Ryzhkov had to be replaced.

After a whirlwind trip through Minnesota and northern California, a reinvigorated Gorbachev left for home.

•   •   •

The chaos Gorbachev had fled to travel to Washington was waiting for him, in a new version, when he returned. In Kirghizia in Central Asia, ethnic riots had taken at least 115 lives; as Gorbachev traveled home, army units were sent in to try to separate warring gangs of Kirghiz and Uzbeks. Two days later the new Russian legislature enacted a declaration of Russian sovereignty, asserting that the republic's laws took precedence over the Soviet Union's. This was an important bargaining chip for Yeltsin; he hoped to use the declaration to persuade Gorbachev to accept a looser federation of quasi-independent republics.

Gorbachev's reaction to the vote revealed a transformation in his attitude toward Yeltsin, whom he had accused of "destructive" politics in a Washington press conference. Now he was all reasonableness. Asked about the sovereignty question, Gorbachev said he couldn't believe the Russians wanted to destroy the Union. He was ready, he said, for "normal, businesslike relations" with Yeltsin. "We have common goals and tasks," he disclosed.

He then entered negotiations with the leaders of the Baltic states, signaling a more relaxed attitude than he had taken with the Lithuanians during the spring. He called a meeting of the new Federation Council, consisting of the leaders of all fifteen republics, and offered an olive branch. "We met each other halfway," Yeltsin said later of that session, at which he represented the Russian Republic. While Gorbachev had been in America, Yeltsin had been cultivating relations with the Baltic leaders, a fact that encouraged the harmony at this meeting.

The Supreme Soviet decided to postpone action on Ryzhkov's controversial reform package for at least two months, relieving a potential political problem. The legislature also passed decrees enhancing Gorbachev's authority by authorizing him to begin an early changeover to a market economy. Suddenly Gorbachev seemed back on top again, as if his trip to Washington had given him a second wind. He needed it.

The main business of the summer would be two Party congresses. First was a gathering of Communists of the Russian Republic, who had decided they needed a republican Party organization comparable to those in all the non-Russian republics. Then, right afterward, came the 28th Party Congress, whose opening had been urgently moved up at the Central Committee's April plenum. Now that these meetings were imminent, the political community was gripped by a combination of excitement and dread. In these events, everyone seemed to agree, lay the conservatives' best and perhaps last chance to reassert control before the country sped off in a new, democratic direction.

"The conservatives have a lot to lose," Alexander Yakovlev told a group of students and professors at Moscow State University in early June. It was a closed meeting, and Yakovlev spoke frankly. "It's a fact that the conservatives refuse to leave the scene. And you can hardly blame them for that. . . . Imagine a person who for forty years has been serving his ideal and who has grown accustomed to his position, his lifestyle, his living standards, who has grown used to wielding power—history's most corrupting habit. Now that the change has come, they find it difficult, in their human way, to accept it."

The goals of the conservatives remained vague, as they had from 1987 onward. They knew what they *didn't* like about the current situation; their list of dislikes had grown long. They didn't like freedom of speech and assembly, or a semi-independent press, or the new television programs, or the collapse of communism in Eastern Europe, or the end of the Party's leading role, or Boris Yeltsin. They hated the loss of their own power. On many and perhaps most days, they didn't really like Mikhail Gorbachev, though many remained impressed by him, sometimes awed. They regretted the passing of the old order, though many of them insisted that they realized the country had to be reformed. They wanted the new and the old together, in a reassuring combination that left them on top, where they felt they belonged.

Adversity revealed the true qualities of the men who had risen to the top of the Party bureaucracy under Brezhnev, Andropov, Chernenko, and Gorbachev. They proved to be small men of limited intelligence and imagination, men with little talent for real politics, men who were afraid. Fear easily breeds anger. Anger was obvious as the delegates gathered in Moscow for the founding congress of the Communist Party of the Russian Republic.

Perhaps because it was a new kind of meeting of a new organization with no established power or role, the delegates to the Russian Congress seemed to feel free to express themselves. This made the anger more obvious. Ligachev led the way. He spoke grimly of "the collapse of the socialist commonwealth," observing that "the positions of imperialism have strengthened incredibly." General Albert Makashov spoke bitterly of the "so-called victories of our diplomacy" that had led to the withdrawals of Soviet troops from nations in Eastern Europe "that our fathers liberated from fascism." He attacked, by name, many leading liberals for believing that "we don't need the army." But, to great applause, he assured the delegates that "the army and the navy will yet be of use to both the Soviet Union and Russia." Some liberals heard the threat of a military coup in those words.

A delegate named Ivan Osadchy won applause when he criticized the leadership for leaving the Party "crouching unarmed in the trenches under massive shelling by anti-socialist forces." Alexander Melnikov, well known for his criticisms of Gorbachev in Central Committee plenums, said "a cult of personality" had grown up around the leader. Viktor Tiulkin of Leningrad said *perestroika* had "given nothing to the people over the past five years."

Gorbachev reacted with spirited defenses of his reforms, describing the changes in the country since 1985 as "comparable to the most radical events in world history." He denied charges (Ligachev had made them on the eve of the Congress) that his policies were leading back to capitalism: "Nothing could be more absurd." But on the second day of the meeting, after enduring extensive direct criticism from the floor, Gorbachev hinted that he might give up the job of Party general secretary to concentrate entirely on the presidency. He also showed his pique. "I think that comrades are treating the general secretary, and the country's president, rather lightly. It's not a matter of me personally. Tomorrow, or maybe in ten or twelve days [at the end of the 28th Party Congress], it's possible that there will be another general secretary." Critics of senior leaders should not "speak off the top of one's head," Gorbachev said; if they did, those in senior positions would give them up; "we won't move anywhere except toward chaos."

The choice of a leader of this new organization gave the conservatives their best chance to show their feelings. A large majority of the delegates were full-time Party employees and officials—*apparatchiks.* (There was also a small group of liberals representing Democratic Platform, the strongest reform element in the Party, but it was numerically overwhelmed.) The favorite in the hall was the same Ivan Polozkov who had tried unsuccessfully to stop Yeltsin from winning the Russian presidency. Polozkov was the first secretary in Krasnodar, in the South. His thick features, heavy eyebrows, and deep, slow voice hardly conveyed an impression of strength, but Polozkov was much beloved by the staunchest right wingers. The published transcripts of Central Committee meetings at which Polozkov had criticized Gorbachev and *perestroika* contributed to his popularity. Nina Andreyeva, the author of record of the famous letter to *Sovetskaya Rossiya,* who had become a heroine to the right wing, praised Polozkov as a true defender of "classic" Marxism-Leninism and as "a rare genius."

In a campaign speech at the Congress, Polozkov attacked the Gorbachev leadership for "inconsistency and concessions," said there was a crisis in the leadership organs, and called for a return to orthodox Marxism. He denounced what he called "organized action to pull down the Communist Party from within." He said the decision to take responsibility for managing the economy away from the Party had contributed to the economic crisis.

Polozkov was elected leader of the Russian Party. He received 1,396 votes to 1,066 for his more moderate opponent, Oleg Lobov. He moved quickly to moderate his image, denying to reporters that he was a conservative. He suggested that Gorbachev should remain as general secretary, and described himself as a supporter of *perestroika* who just had a few "reservations."

But the public got a different message. There were reports from around the country of Party members handing in their cards and resigning in protest against the Russian Congress. In Moscow, twenty thousand people quit the Party on the first Monday and Tuesday after the Congress. The more liberal official newspapers were unusually critical. A commentary in *Komsomolskaya Pravda* denounced the new Russian Party organization as one that obviously "hates restructuring, hates . . . Gorbachev, will never agree to a market economy, is irate about *glasnost* and a democratic news media, is prepared to destroy those who think differently." *Izvestia* called the congress a rehearsal for the 28th Party Congress that was about to begin—"a rehearsal with a bad script." Yeltsin, expressing an alarm shared by many of the liberals, said it might be a good idea to postpone the 28th Congress, and he revealed that this possibility was being discussed inside the Central Committee. The success of the conservatives had caused panic in some quarters.

For several days the situation remained uncertain. Shevardnadze gave an outspoken interview to *Pravda,* lambasting those who criticized Soviet policy toward Eastern Europe—clearly a reply to Ligachev, General Makashov, and others who did so at the Russian Congress. "McCarthyite" questions about "who lost Eastern Europe" were offensive, he said. Shevardnadze accused the critics of really asking why tanks hadn't been used to impose traditional Soviet discipline, a policy, he said, that had been abandoned.

A special Central Committee plenum held on Friday, June 29, reaffirmed that the Congress would begin on Monday. On the 30th, Moscow responded to the Lithuanian parliament's suspension of its declaration of independence by lifting the economic embargo—an upbeat signal for the eve of the Congress. Gorbachev's aides spread the word that the situation was now in hand; the leadership would prevail at the Congress—would successfully dilute the power of the Politburo and the Central Committee and give new impetus to the reform process.

Whether that confidence reflected certain knowledge or just fervent hope is unclear. Gorbachev had come to the end of a crusade begun three and a half years earlier, in the preparations for the plenum of January 1987. Though it seemed at times to be confused or contradictory, in retrospect it was a remarkably consistent—though often improvised—crusade. Its objective was to break apart the monolithic bloc—the combination of state and Party *apparats*—that had crushed Soviet society while supposedly governing it for more than half a century. This Congress was to complete the job by restructuring the Party in such a way that it simply could not try to maintain administrative control over society. In effect, the Party Congress had been convened—a year ahead of the traditional schedule, which called for a Congress every five years—so that the Party could voluntarily withdraw from running the country.

Delegates to the Congress were supposed to be elected in the new spirit of democracy; Gorbachev and his allies had once hoped that genuine adherents of *perestroika* would be chosen. But the *apparat* understood that its power and status were at stake, so its members left little to chance. The largest group of delegates consisted of Party officials—about half of the total of 4,683. A large bloc of military officers, mostly political officers, augmented their number. There were just token numbers of workers and peasants, groups which, in the old days, would have been guaranteed much larger representation. More than half the delegates, about 2,800, had participated the week before in the Russian Party Congress, where they had been part of a right-wing triumph. Some liberals expressed the fear that the conservatives, emboldened by the Russian Congress, would seek to modify Gorbachev's reorganization plan so that a strong Politburo and Central Committee could keep him under control, and thus limit the scope of reform.

A second opportunity some conservatives perceived was in the new job of deputy general secretary of the Party. Gorbachev intended to be reelected general secretary, but in light of his new duties as president, he planned to turn over much of the day-to-day responsibility for running the Party to this new deputy. It could be a powerful job, and before the Congress began there was no public indication who might get it.

The Congress began with another of Gorbachev's protracted speeches—two and a half hours long. He quickly and forcefully took up his own case: "Revolutionary changes really have occurred in the country. . . . In place of the Stalinist model of socialism we are becoming a citizens' society of free people. The political system is being transformed radically, genuine democracy with free elections, the existence of many parties, and human rights is being established, and real people's power is being revived. . . . We told people the truth, we rejected false conceit, and have acknowledged that we have not in fact been able to provide them with a worthy life. . . . *Perestroika* has revived people's sense of their own dignity but has also . . . given rise to great expectations of rapid change for the better."

But almost at once he became defensive, and began responding to the criticism that things were actually better before 1985. "We have inherited an extremely difficult legacy," he said, enumerating the disastrous state of affairs that his predecessors left him. It was a vivid accounting of industrial, agricultural, and managerial chaos. "We cannot carry on like this," he said. "The issue today is this: either Soviet society will go forward along the path of the profound changes that have been begun, ensuring a worthy future for our great multinational state, or else forces opposed to *perestroika* will gain the upper hand. In that case—let's face the facts squarely—dismal times would be in store for the country and the people."

Gorbachev seemed to address his remarks first of all to the moderate element in his audience—Communists who might well be uncomfortable with the chaos and tumult in society, but who were susceptible to the argument that without reform and without Gorbachev's leadership, things would actually be much worse. He acknowledged that there were many Party officials, including some "leading cadres," who preferred the old methods of command and discipline, and couldn't accept the need for reform "politically or psychologically," but he sought to isolate them from the mainstream, emphasizing how much better it was to deal openly and honestly with the country's problems than to try to hide them as before.

To the criticism that he had "lost" Eastern Europe, Gorbachev replied forcefully that his critics really wanted him to use "the methods we used in the past"—invasion—to prop up regimes built on "the Stalinist authoritarian and bureaucratic system that we ourselves have abandoned." He made repeated references to his own Communist convictions, as if to reassure the delegates that he would remain true to their faith. One should not "close one's eyes to the fact that forces have been revealed in society that are pushing us toward a bourgeois system . . . [and] transferring the country onto a capitalist track," Gorbachev said, but he rejected that path. He also explicitly rejected the suggestion, made by many liberal reformers, that Communist Party cells in factories, the KGB, and the army be abolished. That would violate freedom of association, he insisted. In sum, Gorbachev spoke as a Party man—a modern, reforming Party man—to a giant hall full of Party men. He obviously hoped to convince them that sticking with him was better than all the available alternatives.

Gorbachev's attempt to set the tone for the Congress was undermined almost as soon as he was finished when a delegate named Vladimir Bludov came to the microphone with a proposal. "I am Bludov, a delegate from Magadan Oblast," he began. "Please do not switch off my microphone. I ask you to accept this proposal." He suggested that the Congress "take all Party powers into its hands," fire the existing Politburo and Central Committee, "guarantee the immunity of delegates, and extend their credentials until the 29th Party Congress." In other words, turn the Party over to the *apparatchiks* in the hall, and guarantee them control for five years. There was a stir in the Palace of Congresses, but Gorbachev quickly took the situation in hand. "We will return to this question," he said. "Now we will continue working in accordance with the program. Do you agree, comrades? Good."

But the nervous conservatives would not be dismissed that easily. The Congress agenda, drafted under conservative influence, called for members of the Politburo to "report back" to the delegates on their activities—in effect, to defend themselves against conservative criticisms. The first to speak was Nikolai Ryzhkov, the premier, newly unpopular because of his recent reform proposals that would triple the price of bread. He was jeered and razzed as he spoke. So was Vadim Medvedev, the Politburo member responsible for ideology, who spoke next.

Third came Alexander Yakovlev, a particular *bête noire* for the conservatives, who opened his speech with an acknowledgment: "It seems I am in for a difficult time, too." He made clear his distaste for the situation: "The demand for a report . . . frankly speaking, evokes an ambiguous response." At least it "gives everyone a chance to clarify his position once again," which Yakovlev proceeded to do.

His speech was one of the two most interesting delivered to the Congress. It amounted to a statement of principles and beliefs from the acknowledged co-author of the Gorbachev reforms. "The time has come for truth—to speak of nobility, charity, honor, and conscience, even at a Congress of Communists who are shaking from our feet the mud of enmity and suspicion that has built up over decades." It was not an agenda that many in the hall would be comfortable with, but Yakovlev proceeded confidently. He was, he said, absolutely convinced "of the historic correctness of the decision we made in 1985, and of its profound morality. Without a comprehensive renewal, neither the country nor the Party has a future or a worthy place in the world."

Yakovlev gave his view of where the Party had gotten off the track. "A misfortune happened; a Party based on a revolutionary idea has turned into a Party of power. . . . They have always coexisted: a Party serving the people, and a Party of unquestioning obedience, Communist arrogance and Communist lordliness. It was the Party of ideas that started *perestroika* in order to save the motherland from ruin."

The reform movement "cannot be halted. It will develop with or without the Party." He attributed the "conservative moods and trends that have expressively manifested themselves recently" to the "fact that the Party remains enslaved by the system of social stagnation brought about by the regime of personal power. It is precisely this backbone of the authoritarian organism that *perestroika* is trying to break; for the same reason, it provokes seething hatred among certain strata."

Yakovlev spoke movingly of his work on the special commission to investigate Stalin's crimes. "I will tell you honestly, it is heavy, spiritually exhausting work when the ashes of millions of people constantly haunt you. . . . The tragedy that befell the people at that time is astonishing both for its scale and its senseless cruelty."

In an astonishing passage defending the introduction of a free market, Yakovlev invoked the authority of the Vatican: "As is known, Christ once chased the Pharisees—merchants and moneylenders—out of the Temple, intending his religion for the poor. This took place over two thousand years ago. And only a year and a half ago, several centuries after the Reformation, the Vatican publicly recognized that only wealth that is earned helps to purify the soul and leads to heaven —that enterprise should be supported because it eases man's situation in this world and provides him with the means for raising himself. Surely, comrades, we are not going to match these records for lagging behind with our academic arguments over the market?" Just as astoundingly, delegates applauded the passage.*

"Let us remember," he cautioned the delegates, "that not only empty shelves but also empty souls brought about *perestroika* and demanded revolutionary changes." The renewal of souls was the accomplishment of which Yakovlev was most proud. "I regard myself— forgive this slight sentimentality—as a happy man, because I have been alive during, and have participated in, a great renovation of a great country and its historic crusade into the world of freedom."

There was no jeering of Yakovlev. The direct language and raw emotion of his speech reached even the most hardened *apparatchiks* in the hall. They listened with obvious respect, and applauded when he finished.

On the second day Ligachev, the hero of the right, got his chance to speak. It was a shrewd performance by a man who—like many of the conservatives—obviously believed what he said. His unhappiness with the anarchy and confusion in society was not artificial; nor was his anxiety about the cost of abandoning seventy years of history for something experimental and unknown. He was sincerely conservative in a way Gorbachev obviously understood, even appreciated. It was the honest sincerity of his position that made it so difficult to overcome.

Ligachev distanced himself from the last two years of reform, noting that when he was responsible for the work of the Central Committee secretariat it "worked at full force," but after his removal and assignment to the Commission on Agriculture in September 1988, the secretariat lost influence and he was shunted aside. These two years were "a time of lost opportunities," he said.

"I don't see an alternative to *perestroika*," he said, but he defined it differently than Gorbachev and Yakovlev. "All manner of rash radicalism, improvisation, and swinging from side to side haven't given us

---

* Yakovlev mistold the story. In the Bible, Jesus drives moneychangers and merchants from the Temple. The Pharisees have no part in this story.

much in the five years of *perestroika*," he said. He rejected the idea
of private property and the selling off of state assets. "Nor is it right
to cast the class approach into oblivion," he added, using the code
word that symbolized his oft-repeated desire to continue to conduct a
class struggle with the capitalist world. He gently but firmly separated
himself from Yakovlev by playing off a phrase in Yakovlev's speech the
previous day: "Recently people have started saying that, with the Party
or without the Party, *perestroika* will go on. I think differently. With
the Party and only in a vanguard Party can we move forward along the
road of socialist renewal." And in conclusion he made clear his own
availability for future service, notwithstanding the fact that he was
sixty-nine years old. "I am deeply convinced that the Party will become a Marxist-Leninist Party, a viable political force, profoundly
democratic," he said—a construction clearly revealing his assessment
that it wasn't such a Party at the moment. "With such a party, in any
of its ranks. I am ready to continue to go through life." The crowd
loved it. Ligachev got perhaps the warmest ovation they had yet given.

Shevardnadze spoke afterward, giving a passionate defense of Gorbachev's policies, bemoaning the waste of billions of rubles on a fruitless arms race. He defended putting "universal human values" over
the class interests Ligachev trumpeted—only universal values could
bring enduring peace and security. He was applauded also, but the
difference between the two ovations was telling. About two-thirds of
the delegates joined in the cheering for Ligachev, according to Michael Dobbs of the *Post,* who was in the hall; about one-third applauded Shevardnadze.

The rawest demonstration of conservative anger during the Congress occurred after the third day's session, on July 4, at a closed
meeting between Gorbachev and secretaries from city and regional
Party committees. No detailed account of the meeting has been published, but the brief reports that did appear give a clear enough sense
of what must have gone on. They appeared in a small newspaper called
Rabochaya Tribuna (Worker's Tribune) and in *Izvestia. Rabochaya
Tribuna*'s chief editor, Anatoli Yurkov, was a participant, though he
admitted somewhat sheepishly in his report that he had stayed in the
room after the secretaries had made clear their desire to remove all
"outsiders." This is how Yurkov began his account:

"Unless you remove the television cameras from the auditorium, our
discussion is off!"

The ultimatum stunned everyone who had assembled in the Grand Kremlin Palace. The voice of the general secretary struggled to make itself heard over the hubbub of voices expressing approval or anger.

"What about *glasnost?*"

But the hubbub in the auditorium became even louder. . . . The microphone in the auditorium added another thunderclap to the ultimatum: "Remove all outsiders from the auditorium!"

After that beginning, members of the audience began to vent their emotions. In Yurkov's diplomatic language, "a segment of the audience . . . had inflamed itself with grievances," asked hostile questions, and heckled Gorbachev's replies. He quoted an unnamed secretary who spoke up when Gorbachev was trying to explain how power would henceforth be divided between local soviets and local Party secretaries —the men in the room. "You did a stupid thing," the man said, interrupting Gorbachev. "You legitimized an artificial structure [the soviets], and now we're in a mess—no one will listen to us."

Another referred to the fact that although Gorbachev could be both president and general secretary it had been decided that local Party secretaries could not lead the soviets: "So, it's okay for you to hold two posts, but not for us?"

"Why don't you defend the Party?" asked another secretary. "*Perestroika* has gone far enough," said another. Others called for "closing ranks" and "issuing orders." According to Yurkov, one secretary stood up in the middle of this onslaught and said: "I protest at the attitude that the people sitting alongside me are displaying. Mikhail Sergeyevich, believe me, not everyone thinks this way. I feel ashamed, and I'm walking out." And he did.

Politically sophisticated Soviet readers certainly understood from Yurkov's account what had gone on, but he stepped gingerly around the substance of the discussion. A much shorter account in *Izvestia* in reporter Pavel Gutionov's "Political Diary" was blunter. Gutionov was not in the hall, but cited a participant in the meeting from Leningrad as his source—a delegate named Andrei Gorbachev, no relation to the general secretary.

According to him [Gutionov wrote], the policy of *perestroika* was given a real beating at the meeting; total rejection of the policy of change was demonstrated; and they openly demanded that Gorbachev abandon it, "finally instill order," and return, as someone put it, "to

Andropov's course." A sharp confrontation between the audience and the president was obvious. We are not going the same way, M. S. Gorbachev declared, if we do not agree on assessments of the political course. He emphasized that this course will not be changed as long as he remains at the helm.

Yurkov elaborated on the sharp confrontation: "I will confess, I felt uncomfortable. Because the general secretary ostentatiously left the chairman's seat under pressure of the emotions that rained upon him from the audience." Remarkably, the editor even reproached the general secretary for taking offense and walking out so abruptly. "He ought to have understood them and listened patiently while they got things off their chests," Yurkov wrote. Then he could have conducted a "constructive dialogue, which Mikhail Sergeyevich knows how to conduct so masterfully with any audience—first captivating them, then winning them over with the charm of his personality."

It doesn't sound as though this group was vulnerable to anyone's charm. These were the men who stood to lose the most from the political reforms. Previously they had been emperors in their own domains—just as Gorbachev had been in Stavropol as recently as ten years earlier. Gorbachev had created a new power structure, the elected local soviets, that deprived them all of their lordly authority. That was his "stupid" mistake. Why would any of these secretaries have liked it?

The alarming aspect of that meeting was not the opinions it revealed—they cannot have been a secret from Gorbachev, Yakovlev, and their associates. It was the nerve of these first secretaries that must have worried the general secretary—their willingness to speak out so bluntly right to his face. From the beginning Gorbachev had operated on the assumption that he could ultimately bring the Party cadres along. They might groan, even resist, but they would follow him. Partly this was his confidence in his own abilities to convince; even more, I suspect, it was a reflexive confidence that good Party men would continue to respect Party discipline, which meant following the leader. Time and again Gorbachev had persuaded Party conclaves to approve changes that the members might privately oppose but were unwilling to challenge publicly. He was planning to do just that at the 28th Party Congress. He would get these delegates to reelect him general secretary, pick his chosen number two as deputy general secretary, and adopt a program that would finally take the Party out of administering the country—or would he?

•   •   •

There was considerable anxiety among Gorbachev supporters as the first week of the Congress drew to a close. For the first time in the history of the modern Party, a Congress was under way whose ending remained uncertain. Gorbachev was helped immensely—as he had been since 1985—by the absence of a charismatic and resourceful leader of the right. Ligachev, earnest and plodding, was not such a figure. He had no flare for leadership. But if as many as two-thirds of the delegates really opposed his line, could Gorbachev continue to prevail?

On the fifth day Boris Yeltsin made his move—the most dramatic move of the Congress. A week before it began he had signaled his desire to restore cooperative relations with Gorbachev. "I have extended a hand to Gorbachev, and now he too has taken a step," Yeltsin said. "Now our collaboration must continue to develop." Gorbachev had gone out of his way to speak of Yeltsin in a friendly and hopeful manner. What—if anything—went on between them in private isn't known, but there is no question that Yeltsin's speech on July 6 was the best help Gorbachev received during the entire 28th Party Congress.

It was the speech of a man who knew he was the most popular politician in the country, who knew that his audience understood his popularity, and who knew how that audience feared its own fate. By upbringing Yeltsin was one of them; but because he had become the first hero of the new revolution, he was now far beyond them. So they hated him, and admired him, and worried what he might do to them.

No doubt Yeltsin had some professional help with his text. It was wonderfully written—blunt, eloquent, devoid of the traditional Party man's vocabulary, and brief. It took less than ten minutes to deliver. Yeltsin spoke as a wise elder statesman who had come to explain the facts of life to the delegates. But his tone was not condescending, just authoritative.

He began with an implicit rebuke to Gorbachev. The conservative forces had "gone over to the offensive," and "it has not proved possible to neutralize their activity." Paraphrasing—but not naming—Gorbachev, Yeltsin criticized the oft-heard argument that all Communists are "in the same boat, on the same side of the barricades"—one of the rhetorical devices Gorbachev had used to try to convince his comrades that they remained comrades. "This position has discredited those Communists who are sincere and consistent supporters of change," Yeltsin said. "This position has created a form of security for the conservative forces in the Party, and has strengthened their conviction that it is possible to gain revenge." They showed this, he continued, at the recent Russian Party Congress.

He noted that if the Party had held open, democratic elections of delegates to the Congress, there would have been a different crowd in the hall. Instead they were mostly *apparatchiks.* "For this reason, during discussions at this Congress, the main issue has not been *perestroika* in the country and the best ways for it to develop. This issue is being tackled by people outside this building, and it is being tackled in the soviets of people's deputies. The question facing this Congress is the fate of the Party itself. To be more precise, the only question being tackled here is the fate of the apparatus of the upper echelons of the Party."

Now he was talking about them, and the audience was rapt. No jeering of Boris Yeltsin. "The question is an acute one: Will the Party apparatus . . . take advantage of this last chance that the Congress offers it? It is either yes or no. Either the Party apparatus decides on the radical restructuring of the Party under the pressures of political reality or it will clutch to doomed arrangements and remain in opposition to the people, in opposition to *perestroika.* In that case the representatives of the apparatus will inevitably be squeezed out of all bodies of legitimate authority."

It was a direct threat. The Party will not only lose its leading role if it fails to reform itself, it will lose any meaningful role, Yeltsin predicted. Then "a nationwide struggle will begin for the total nationalization of the Party's property [worth many billions]," on the grounds that "as a Party that has gone bankrupt it is obliged to make good—if only by dint of its property—on its debts to the people."

And then the rudest threat of all: "It can be assumed that a struggle will begin to put Party leaders at all levels on trial for the damage that they personally have inflicted upon the country and the people. I can mention just one of these cases—the damage inflicted by the anti-alcohol campaign. [In his speech three days earlier, Ligachev had taken responsibility for that campaign.] The people will hold them responsible for everything else, too—for the failure in foreign trade, agriculture, for the nationalities policy, for policy toward the army, and so on and so on. The country should know what inheritance the Party has left it.

"Such is the possible outlook for the apparatus and the Party. Whoever is thinking about any other variants may look at the fate of the Communist parties in the East European countries. They separated themselves from the people, they did not understand their role, and they were left on the sidelines."

There was another alternative, much more pleasant to contemplate, Yeltsin continued. If the Party changed its name to "the Party of Democratic Socialism," democratized itself, abolished its organizations inside state bodies, including the army and the KGB, and in factories and enterprises, and made creative alliances with other democratic socialists in society, then it could prosper.

"We are no longer living in the old society," he concluded. "It will no longer go in single formation where it is told to. The country can no longer be commanded. It will not be held by demagogy, or frightened by threats. The people can dismiss any political force, however influential it has been in the past. They will only support a political organization that calls not to the distant Communist horizons beyond the clouds, but which every day, by deed, defends the interests of every person, and helps make him and all of our country progressive, wealthy, and happy."

This was a speech few of those present wanted to hear, but which none of them could dismiss. The audience listened, silent and attentive, to the end. There was a smattering of applause. Yeltsin had put the issue in the simplest, bluntest terms—down where the goats could get it. Those May Day demonstrators invoking the fate of Ceauşescu weren't kidding, Yeltsin was saying—they are my people now, and I know how they think. He spoke as an ambassador from the new world, a place where many of the men in the hall felt like strangers, a place Boris Yeltsin had mastered.

•   •   •

When the Congress reconvened Monday morning, there was a different atmosphere. The important business of the day was a change in Party rules to reconstitute the Politburo. The leadership proposed that henceforth the leaders of each of the fifteen republican Party organizations automatically be Politburo members, along with eight or nine senior officials of the national Party organization. The proposal was calculated to appeal to the majority of delegates, who represented non-Russian republics, all of whom could see benefit in diluting Russia's traditionally predominant role. (In the outgoing Politburo, only two of twelve full members were not ethnic Russians.) But the same provision meant that the Party *apparat* in Moscow could not control the Politburo—just what Gorbachev wanted. If those holding important government jobs were also excluded—which Gorbachev intended, except in the case of himself—then the Politburo could no longer run the country. The rules change was approved by a vote of 3,325 to 839.

The session of Tuesday, July 10, began with Gorbachev's second speech in eight days, which he used to try to take control of the Congress, at least rhetorically. He began by admitting that "these have been very tense days." He acknowledged that his meetings with different groups of delegates, including the city and regional Party secretaries, had "brought a great deal to the surface," not all of it positive. "It should be said that much in this discussion was alien, casual, was conducted in temper from an excess of anxiety or simply from bitterness, or else from an inability to conduct an argument." But he would not join petty debates about the marginal benefits of this or that policy, this or that approach—such small-mindedness was not for him. "Those who truly understand that *perestroika* is necessary, those who truly know that *perestroika* is a revolution, and not just a repainting of the façade, they understand that we still have a lot to face in the future and we must overcome it." He would argue his case on an elevated plane.

There followed a speech of a little more than an hour—curt by Gorbachev's standards—that cleverly wove together and elaborated on the themes introduced by Yakovlev and Yeltsin. It is tempting to see the three speeches as a joint undertaking, though I have no evidence of Yeltsin's complicity.

"The main overall positive aspect of what has been achieved . . . is freedom," Gorbachev declared. "Society has received freedom. This has unleashed the energy of the people. . . . This is what a revolution is for—to give . . . the people freedom." As a result of this "spiritual rebirth," he said, "society has become different, and all of us have become different." And "believe me, the Party's success depends on understanding that society is already different. Otherwise the Party will be squeezed out by other forces and we will lose our positions." This meant facing the fact that "everything that took place in the past has already, and to a significant degree, become obsolete and is unacceptable.

"How accustomed we have become to things being simple and clear, black or white, for or against," Gorbachev said. But that kind of simplification would no longer suffice; if we can't get beyond such formulas, "we will lose even what we have today." Future success, he told them, will be measured by "the extent to which we will help people in the country be fed, provided for, civilized, spiritually rich, free and happy, and to the extent that we assimilate new universal human values."

Gorbachev found a way to humiliate the audience—just a little, but just enough to remind them of his own intellectual superiority, still one of his strongest cards. It happened when he quoted one of the delegates saying to him during the Congress, "Why don't you stop traveling abroad and concern yourself with the country?" At that there were laughter, loud noise, and even applause in the hall.

"That's right, is it?" Gorbachev asked them, angered. "Here, then, is what our Congress is like, with all its achievements and problems as they really are! Why do we go abroad? Why do we go there? . . . We go there so that reliable, peaceful conditions can exist, so that favorable conditions are created, to prevent war, to carry out *perestroika* in normal conditions, and finally, to release resources and to channel them toward what is needed, toward the solution of these problems. Are we really on this level of thinking? And are there really such people, even among the delegates? It is a calamity, comrades! If this is the case, then it is our calamity! Let's assume you have your say, and you've said that there is no need to travel anywhere, and a decision like that is taken, and we don't travel. That would be tantamount to being entirely under the thumb of people who are incompetent in politics, who are unable to analyze processes, and it will be a disaster."

Still the actor, still quick to pick up a cue.

The time of absolute rule by the Communist Party is over, Gorbachev told them, and they had to adjust to that fact. "Ossified ideological clichés . . . must be renounced. The Party will not be able to restructure itself until we all understand that the end has come to the Party's monopoly on power and government. Even if we manage to win a majority at the elections, and we can and must act to do this . . . it makes sense to cooperate with non-Party deputies" and build alliances. "We must cooperate!"

"We cannot bring back yesterday in any way, and no dictatorship—in case there is such a delirious idea fermenting in someone's brain—will solve anything."

Finally, an exhortation that may have sounded to some like a threat:

"Comrades, I don't see a path other than the resolute and purposeful continuation of all that we have been doing . . . to implement the profound transformation of our multinational state. Let's get to work. We have begun the most crucial phase of *perestroika*. Major reforms await us." In other words, he wasn't turning back, so they had better come along.

After finishing his speech Gorbachev was nominated to stand again for the post of general secretary. (For the first time, there would be a secret ballot to choose the Party's leader.) He then answered questions from the delegates, two of which reflected the anxieties that Yeltsin had aggravated on Friday, and that Gorbachev had pricked again in his speech—anxieties about their own fates.

A delegate named Krylov asked Gorbachev to explain which Communists he was referring to when he spoke of those who were unprepared for the new conditions created by *perestroika,* and "how should we bring these Communists into the fold, or is that unrealistic?"

Gorbachev gave a brilliant answer, calculated to convey his empathy: "I believe that all of us are still unprepared, and that the process of *perestroika* is still going on inside all of us. We are children of our time, we are people whose character is already formed, we are overburdened with stereotypes. . . . We are accustomed to certain ways of life, a certain structure, and it isn't so simple to change this. That's real life. And so I am for change, and fundamental, revolutionary change, but using methods that will not break people on the wheel of their fate . . . so that we don't get drawn into bloody affairs again—confrontations and fratricide. We have already had a lot of pernicious politicians appear in our country."

Then Delegate Svobodkin asked about Yeltsin's speech. What did Gorbachev think of his proposals for changing the Party, and how did he evaluate Yeltsin's threat that if the Party does not reform itself, "then Party property will be nationalized and court prosecutions will be started against Communists"?

In this case the answer was clever for what it omitted. "When Comrade Yeltsin says that the Party has to reform itself, renew itself, here, I think, we are all united." Gorbachev wasn't sure exactly what Yeltsin had in mind on some points, and he opposed the proposal that party cells in state organizations be banned. The threat of trials? Gorbachev didn't mention it. He let it hang in the air. He went on to the next question.

•   •   •

That afternoon Gorbachev was reelected general secretary. The vote was 3,411 in favor, 1,116 against.* Party officials asked by reporters why Gorbachev won so handily responded that delegates were afraid to vote against him—they were concerned about splitting the Party, provoking mass resignations and destroying its influence. The greater fear, surely, involved themselves. The Congress had reminded them that they no longer enjoyed special protection; real politics applied to them, too.

They needed Gorbachev. Every new election result advertised the Party's unpopularity. The bigger the name or title of the Party man running for office, the bigger his margin of defeat was likely to be. If Gorbachev was prepared to remain a Communist—if they could continue to function in a Party led by a man with the reputation and standing of Gorbachev—that looked like the best available option. The absence of a plausible alternative was a critical factor. A Party leader like Polozkov, for example, who said and believed the "right" things but could attract no popular following, would be worse for them than Gorbachev—would leave them exposed and vulnerable to Yeltsin's threats.

The truth had come home to Gorbachev's comrades. Their Party was over. Not that Lenin's Communist Party of the Soviet Union would disappear—Gorbachev and many others seemed determined that it survive. But it would not exist as it had, as the only real source of power in the society, and as a guarantor of great comfort and security for many thousands of its officials.

Only Ligachev failed to get the message. In the wake of Gorbachev's thumping victory, the general secretary announced his candidate for the job of deputy—Vladimir Ivashko, the first secretary of the Ukraine. Ligachev decided to challenge Ivashko. The possibility that he might win clearly alarmed Gorbachev, who tried to have Ligachev's name removed from the ballot. At first the Congress agreed to do this, but then loud protests of unfair procedures convinced Gorbachev he should change his mind, and the Congress reversed itself, restoring Ligachev's nomination. Gorbachev's edginess was understandable: the delegates now had a chance to humiliate him in a secret ballot, whose result would be considerably less consequential than defeating Gor-

---

* Only one other candidate ran—Teimuraz Avaliani, a leader of the 1989 coal miners' strike in Siberia. Under the rules, delegates had to vote for or against each candidate individually. Avaliani got 501 affirmative votes; 4,020 delegates voted against him.

bachev for general secretary. Theoretically, at least, it gave the conservatives a tempting target.

Gorbachev supported Ivashko, an ethnic Ukrainian, by arguing that a non-Russian ought to have the number-two job. He added, "It's important that these two people [the general secretary and his deputy] should be close." Ligachev offered himself as a supporter of *perestroika* but also a protector of venerable values. "Either the Soviet Union ceases to exist as a socialist, multinational country, or it continues to occupy a worthy place among the powers that lead human civilization," he said in a nomination speech. In an open pitch for votes, he reminded the delegates that he had always been "a fervent supporter of continuity . . . in cadre policy," which they would have understood as a promise not to fire people.

It didn't work. Ligachev got just 776 votes; Ivashko got 3,109. At the beginning of the Congress there were probably 3,000 delegates who would have liked to see Ligachev win an important place in the Party hierarchy; by the end, barely a quarter of that number would vote for him. Suddenly the scourge of the reformers was a has-been. Ligachev was not nominated to sit on the new Central Committee, which Gorbachev successfully packed with liberals * and centrists. Ligachev announced his retirement from politics; he would write his memoirs.

Yeltsin used the next to last day of the Congress to announce his resignation from the Party. He could not be president of the Russian Republic, and fairly serve all Russians, if he remained subject to Communist Party discipline, Yeltsin said. He did it with wonderful theatricality from the podium of the giant Palace of Congresses, then strode out of the hall while his stunned former comrades watched in silence. Numerous other prominent progressives followed suit; soon it was clear that the split would occur despite Gorbachev's great victories.

•   •   •

Gorbachev now appeared to be a free man—free of the Party apparatus, free of a contentious Politburo. He enjoyed a mandate from

---

* One of them was Roy Medvedev, whom I had met nearly twenty years earlier when he was an active dissident, dodging the KGB as he worked to compile a true history of his country, then propagandize to reform it. For years he had been mercilessly harassed by the authorities; his twin brother, Zhores, a close friend of mine in Moscow, had been driven into exile in Britain. The idea that Roy Medvedev was now a member of the Central Committee left me a little breathless.

both the Party and the new parliament (though not directly from the people). He could act on his own.

Gorbachev lost no time in demonstrating his new independence. He quickly settled the German question, which had been bubbling uncomfortably on a diplomatic back burner since late in 1989, when it became clear that Germany would soon be reunified. For months the Soviets had insisted that the new Germany could not belong to the NATO alliance—they could not accept this outcome of their Great Patriotic War, when they paid such a high price to defeat Hitler. This argument had never made a great deal of sense; others with anxieties about Germany, particularly the British and French, reasoned that the Germans were a lot safer tied into a strong alliance structure than out on their own in some kind of neutral status, as the Soviets claimed to prefer. Domestic politics, Shevardnadze explained quietly to his Western colleagues; Gorbachev couldn't sell a Germany in NATO to his conservative countrymen.

But just three days after the Party Congress ended Gorbachev and Helmut Kohl announced a solution to the German problem. The new unified Germany would belong to NATO. The strong Soviet concerns expressed earlier evaporated.

CHAPTER TEN

A TIME OF
TROUBLES

Solving the German problem—the great unresolved issue of World War II, which threatened for decades to ignite World War III—turned out to be amazingly easy. Solving the Soviet problem was vastly more difficult. The 28th Party Congress was a triumphant turning point for Gorbachev, but the triumph proved narrow, and short lived. Removing the Party from direct responsibility for governing the country was critically important, but by itself this change could not resolve any of the society's most pressing crises. The Party Congress could not create an effective new economic mechanism, or bring food to market, or teach workers to work and managers to manage. Gorbachev had put political reform first, and he had accomplished it. As soon as the achievement was secure, its significance seemed to diminish rapidly.

There had always been a hole at the center of Gorbachev's strategy, because political reform created nothing that Soviet citizens could eat or wear or splurge on. The need to create such things had long been obvious, but the will—or the willingness—to try to change the system to produce them had never been found. For all the talk of reform and all the formalistic changes in the status of enterprises, ministries, the state planning commission, and so on, there had been no significant improvements in economic performance since 1985.

Agriculture, the area Gorbachev should have known best, provided a vivid if grim illustration of the difficulty of making improvements. Attempts to create entrepreneurial farming from the chaos and devastation of the Stalinist system of collective and state farms were repeatedly frustrated. Michael Dobbs of *The Washington Post* found a stark example in Rybinsk, about two hundred miles northeast of Moscow. There an engineer named Alexander Bozhko, the grandson of a successful farmer whose lands had been expropriated by Stalin, decided to take advantage of the new "leasehold" system Gorbachev introduced with great fanfare in 1988. "When we were offered the chance to farm our own land we seized it eagerly," he said.

A state farm allocated him about thirty acres, but the lease he signed involved much more than tenure and rent. He had to agree to raise steers and sell them to the state farm at half their market value. He had to get equipment and supplies from the state farm. "I was not allowed to hire any workers. I was unable to buy animal feed, fertilizer and farm equipment because all that is in chronically short supply. And I did not have the right to sell my produce on the open market," Bozhko explained. At one point the state farm failed to provide the feed it had promised; Bozhko and his wife persuaded a friend who worked in a state grocery store to sell them large quantities of low-grade kasha, which Galina Bozhko cooked for the steers. Farmers who worked on the state farm were hostile to the Bozhkos' efforts. They slashed the tires of Bozhko's tractor, and once drove a harvester through his wheat field, flattening the crop. "People are prepared to put up with not living well," he explained, "as long as their neighbor does not live any better. The fact that he works harder doesn't make any difference. When people see someone earn more money than they do, they start getting envious."

Frustrated by the terms of their lease, the Bozhkos began raising their own animals on the side to try to make a profit. When the chairman of the state farm discovered this, he accused them of violating the lease and demanded they give the land back. Bozhko could fight no farther. He gave up the thirty acres and went back to work as an engineer. "I used to believe in Gorbachev," he told Dobbs in the summer of 1990. "Now I've understood that all he does is talk."

•   •   •

After the Party Congress and Kohl's visit to the Soviet Union to settle the German problem, economics moved to the forefront. There was little choice. The dramatic worsening of economic conditions, most obvious in the declining availability of food, threatened to unhinge public confidence. The immolation of the Ryzhkov plan on the eve of Gorbachev's departure to Washington—brought on in part by a mass uprising of shoppers, who cleared the nation's shelves of nonperishable foods almost overnight after Ryzhkov proposed substantial price increases—left the government with no meaningful economic program.

At the end of July, as he prepared to depart for the Crimea for his annual vacation, Gorbachev met with a group of reformist economists. He convinced those present that he had finally decided to cast his lot with the radical reformers, though he acknowledged the dangers implicit in attempting a sudden transformation of the system. "My impression," said one of those present, Anatoli Strelyani, "was that [Gorbachev] understands that there are even, or perhaps slightly better than even, odds of everything ending disastrously in the country." Strelyani also reported that Gorbachev deplored the habits of a nation too willing to "obey orders unquestioningly, to shun responsibility or risks, to put up meekly with hardships." But his last words were more affirmative. "We must prevent a split of the center-left, friends," he told them.

Several days later Gorbachev and Yeltsin met to agree formally on a new working arrangement. They would jointly appoint a committee of experts to draw up a sweeping plan for fundamental reform. Gorbachev, it seemed, understood his need for the political support that Yeltsin could bring to this endeavor. With his own popularity drastically diminished, Gorbachev alone could not risk imposing economic changes that would certainly disrupt ordinary people's lives. But with the help of the country's most popular politician, Yeltsin, perhaps he could sell a painful dose of change to a wary nation. That, at least, seemed to be the rationale for the Gorbachev-Yeltsin pact, which they announced on August 3, 1990.

An alliance with Yeltsin could serve Gorbachev in another important respect. The various Soviet republics, beginning with Russia, were increasingly outspoken in claiming their own sovereignty. In June the new Russian parliament that Yeltsin headed formally declared the primacy of Russia's laws over those of the Soviet Union. In the weeks that followed a series of Soviet republics had formally declared their "sovereignty": the Ukraine in July, then Armenia, Turkmenia, and Tadzhikistan. Gorbachev explicitly acknowledged the significance of the cooperation of the individual republics when he and Yeltsin invited their representatives to join the effort to draft the new plan for overhauling the economic system. Both agreed that there had to be a new Union treaty setting out the rights and obligations of the republics and the central government. Gorbachev must have hoped that Yeltsin would help him temper local nationalisms, and keep them under control.

Gorbachev left for his vacation in early August, leaving behind a working group headed by Stanislav Shatalin, a member of the new Presidential Council and an economist who had spent a lifetime wondering if his country would ever come to its senses. On three occasions during the eighteen-year rule of Leonid Brezhnev, Shatalin had been thrown out of the Communist Party for ideological heresies; each time he was readmitted, no doubt in part because of his intellectual abilities. But he was tired and frail by the summer of 1990, and suffered from a heart condition. When Gorbachev asked him to head the committee that would draft the new reform plan, he was skeptical. "Look," he told Gorbachev (at least this is how he recalled it to Remnick of *The Washington Post*), "is this just another case of 'improving socialism' or creating a 'controlled market'? Because if it is, I'm a sick man and I don't have time left for such follies. But if you are serious now, I'm ready." Gorbachev convinced Shatalin of his seriousness. The new committee began marathon meetings in a dacha just outside Moscow.

I later met Shatalin, who described the committee's work, and recounted how Gorbachev joined its last phases. The president began to take part almost the moment he returned to Moscow from the Crimea. He asked for the group's working documents, and seemed to stay up all night to read them, Shatalin said. Ultimately Gorbachev appeared satisfied with a radical program whose first goal was to induce citizens to give up millions, even billions, of their rubles to buy assets traditionally owned by the state, from the corner bread store to shares in giant industrial enterprises. Shatalin and his colleagues understood that the billions of unspent rubles that lay under the mattresses or in the savings accounts of millions of Soviet citizens were a constant threat to economic stability. Because savings were so high, there was strong inflationary pressure in the economy—all those rubles chasing far too few consumer goods tended to push prices up. The plan foresaw a double benefit from selling off state enterprises: the creation of a sense of responsibility among the new owners, and the soaking up of those extra rubles. The plan also called for drastic reductions in government spending.

On the streets of the capital events conspired to remind the drafters of the new plan just how serious a problem they faced. In the first days of September, for the first time since the grim years after World War II, bread disappeared from Moscow's shops. Bread remains the most important staple in the Russian diet, and its ready availability has always been a psychological safety net as well as a nutritional one. Why it disappeared in early September was never explained; there was no shortage of grain, but the distribution system could have collapsed at any one of many stages. Or there might have been organized sabotage. Many of the liberals who had taken over big city governments, including Moscow's, suspected that their opponents in the Party, the army, and the KGB were actively trying to humiliate them by creating disruptions. The disappearance of bread stunned Muscovites.

Work on the new plan was completed in the first ten days of September. Shatalin and his allies were struggling against Ryzhkov and other traditionalists, and much of their fight was conducted in the open. Shatalin threatened to resign if his plan was compromised; it was widely assumed that Ryzhkov would depart if Shatalin's plan was adopted. The Supreme Soviet was in session, and its members eagerly awaited word from the government on its decision. On September 10 they were confused by an announcement from Gorbachev's loyal lieutenant, Anatoli Lukyanov, the presiding officer of the Supreme Soviet, that the government would introduce a plan that combined elements of Ryzhkov's discredited proposals and the Shatalin plan. Shatalin himself was clearly surprised and dismayed by Lukyanov's statement. His plan and Ryzhkov's, Shatalin told reporters that day, were "essentially incompatible."

The next day the Supreme Soviet was in rowdy disarray. Ryzhkov opened the session with a speech reasserting his own modest plans for reform, and expressed doubts about more radical steps. Was this the "unified" plan Lukyanov had promised the previous day? Many delegates expressed anger. One mocked the government and Gorbachev, "that great master of improvisation." The president watched from the dais, then finally joined the debate. In a theatrical performance combining solemnity, anger, gesticulation, moments of pregnant silence, and loud declamation, he announced that he supported the Shatalin plan. It was, he said, a break with the past; previously, "our brains just could not handle this idea of a market." But the time had come to try it.

Though he seemed to reject his policies, Gorbachev went out of his way to defend Ryzhkov, and to criticize those who were demanding his resignation. "This smells very bad, this is not what the political process is about," Gorbachev said, signaling his unwillingness to dump the premier who had been with him since the earliest stages of *perestroika*. Despite this effort to defend him, Ryzhkov was obviously shaken by Gorbachev's speech. "Until now," he told reporters afterward, "I didn't know that Gorbachev was in favor of the Shatalin program." And he warned that the plan would disrupt life in the country. "If market forces are just given free rein," Ryzhkov said, "then there will be a sharp decline in living standards." Shatalin and Gorbachev did not disagree. "No matter what program we choose for a market economy, we are in for hard times," Gorbachev told reporters and legislators after he spoke.

The Shatalin plan was genuinely bold—and probably unrealistic too. It foresaw a massive fire sale of state enterprises; 46,000 industrial firms and 760,000 firms engaged in wholesale and retail trade were to be sold off to the public, to individuals and to groups—all within six months. Ultimately, it foresaw the sale into private hands of 80 percent of the national economy.

The plan called for the dissolution of money-losing state and collective farms, giving their land to individuals or groups of farmers who wanted to go into business for themselves. It foresaw the early creation of 150,000 new peasant farms. And it required vast reductions in government spending, including a 10 percent cut in military budgets and a 20 percent reduction in spending for the KGB. The cuts in subsidies for failing factories and enterprises that the plan proposed would force many of them out of business, leaving their workers unemployed. Currency reform would begin at once, moving toward a new ruble that would be convertible with the hard currencies of the capitalist world. A new banking system would be created (the Soviet Union had nothing comparable to the capitalist world's banks) as Moscow relinquished control over economic activity. In the ideal world described by the plan, all this would occur in just five hundred days, though Shatalin privately admitted that this timetable was more hortatory than predictive.

Some radicals seized on Gorbachev's September 11 speech as the signal they had all been waiting for—finally, a presidential decision to take the giant steps they had urged toward freeing the economy. Their euphoria, which lasted only briefly, may have marked the high-water mark of liberals' hopes for Gorbachev's *perestroika*. It came too late for many of the early radicals, who had already concluded that Gorbachev was too cautious, too hesitant to carry reform to a truly radical conclusion. But others, and particularly those who participated in its drafting, felt that fulfilling the Shatalin plan would have meant finally destroying the structure of Soviet power that they had grown up with.

This is just what a great many people wanted. One of them was Nikolai Petrakov, an adviser to Gorbachev and an economist who had worked on the Shatalin plan. Asked by a reporter if Gorbachev's September 11 speech meant the Soviet Union was abandoning socialism, Petrakov replied: "If it's the socialism that Stalin created, we certainly want to get rid of that socialism. We don't want to have anything to do with it." The new parliament of the Russian Republic hurriedly embraced the plan with just one dissenting vote.

But the moment was lost. Nothing happened after September 11 to bring the Shatalin plan into force. Gorbachev showed his own uncertainty a week later when he called for a nationwide referendum on whether to allow private ownership of land, a key provision of the plan. Shatalin himself was openly critical of this suggestion, saying it would take months to organize a referendum when it was urgent to begin implementing reforms at once. Gorbachev also continued to defend Ryzhkov. And he avoided committing himself to any of the specific provisions of Shatalin's plan as the Supreme Soviet continued to debate the issue.

This was a critical test for Gorbachev, and he failed it. The country and its new, elected leaders were ready to choose a new course, or thought they were; Gorbachev was not. He had initiated the idea of finally producing a concrete plan for radical change, but once confronted with it, he wavered. His refusal to take the lead caused general confusion. To be sure, he was following the pattern that had served him well until then, looking for a middle path that would allow him to claim that he had established a consensus. But as Shatalin had said, there could be no consensus position embracing both him and Ryzhkov; Gorbachev had to make a choice.

The prospect of radical reforms had evoked strenuous opposition from powerful quarters. Many of the most entrenched institutions and individuals in Soviet society were threatened by the five-hundred-day plan, including the entire state planning apparatus, the powerful ministries that had run Soviet industry for generations, the military industries that had always claimed the best and the most resources, local Party barons who remained powerful in their own domains, and the huge administrative apparatus that sat atop Soviet agriculture. By many accounts the lobbying against the five-hundred-day plan was intense. Many of the opponents warned Gorbachev that implementing the plan would result in the crumbling of the Soviet Union—thus depriving Gorbachev of his own role as the Union's leader.

Petrakov, coauthor of the plan with Shatalin and also a personal adviser to Gorbachev at the time, described the strength of the opposition to Peter Gumbel of *The Wall Street Journal:* "Their blackmail was impressive because men under arms were behind them, five million workers from the military-industrial complex were behind them, and the producers of grain were behind them."

Izvestia published an extraordinary political commentary in mid-September under the headline "The Crisis of Power." The government newspaper wrote: "Our leader has attempted all these years to preserve a centrist position, steering between left and right. There have been times when such a political course has allowed us to avoid dangerous confrontations, but the end result is that the president is criticized by both sides." Now, *Izvestia* said, "the moment of truth has arrived."

When the moment of truth came, it was revealing but anticlimactic. Gorbachev never took a clear position during the Supreme Soviet debate, which lasted a fortnight. Toward the end he did announce that he might have to impose direct presidential rule in some parts of the country and use other emergency powers to prevent economic collapse and a breakdown in law and order. He asked the deputies to give him still more direct powers to act in emergencies and to ease the coming transition to a "market economy." (This term, never really explained, became a terrifying slogan in Soviet society that fall, invoked in public discussion almost as if it were a specter of disruptions and tribulations to come.)

In a boisterous session on September 24, the Supreme Soviet enacted legislation giving the president new powers to smooth the path to a free market. The new law empowered Gorbachev to issue decrees on all kinds of economic issues from prices to the national budget without direct parliamentary support. But the deputies could reach no conclusion on a reform plan; they voted to postpone making a decision.

"The system refused to give birth to a plan that could kill it," observed Grigory Yavlinsky, a young economist whose work inspired the five-hundred-day plan drafted by Shatalin and Petrakov.

Gorbachev used his new power three days after it was granted. He issued a decree ordering state-run enterprises to fulfill the plan for deliveries of raw materials to the state. In other words, powers granted supposedly to help achieve a freer market were first used to reinforce the old administrative-command system that had nothing to do with a market.

•   •   •

That first use of his new power was more than ironic. Concerns about his own position must have played an important part in Gorbachev's thinking during September. He may have been too worried about surviving in power—and with power—to seize that moment to act forcefully. Indeed, his personal concerns may have led him away from the Shatalin plan even as he claimed to support it.

If implemented, the plan would profoundly diminish the role of the government in Moscow. No longer would the central authority be able to guide the national economy, order enterprises about, require rural provinces to deliver food to the cities, and require the cities to produce goods according to a central plan. Combined with the new assertiveness of the local governments in the fifteen republics, the Shatalin plan would have undercut Gorbachev's own power dramatically.

Gorbachev seemed to have this on his mind when he criticized the idea of dismantling the administrative system during the Supreme Soviet debate on economic reform. "If we begin to overhaul the entire system across the land, this will be a gift to all manner of claimants of public office, an ambitious crowd prepared to exploit the country," he said—an odd way to describe the prospective fruits of a new, democratic system. But the speaker was a man who had never been popularly elected to any office.

The country, and particularly Moscow, buzzed with rumors during September that a military coup was imminent. During a debate in the Russian parliament, Yeltsin told his fellow deputies that paratroopers were heading for the capital. He expressed "strong doubts" about official explanations that these maneuvers were part of the preparations for the Revolution Day parade on November 7. Later, Defense Minister Yazov and other officials explained unusual maneuvers around the capital as part of the army's effort to bring in the potato harvest before the crop rotted in the fields. It would not be surprising if the man who had worried so much about the fate of Nikita Khrushchev was worrying in September about his own survival.

But even without such personal anxieties, Gorbachev had reason to hesitate. During the fall of 1990, I think, Gorbachev and many other Soviet politicians looked closely at the practical implications of radical reform, and flinched. Economists and politicians sitting around a conference table could come up with all sorts of beguiling plans, but the reality of dismantling the economic ministries in Moscow, privatization, market prices, truly autonomous enterprises, dissolution of the existing agricultural system, and more, was utterly daunting. Where to begin? By auctioning off the corner bread store? Who would bid? By freeing the factories to forage for raw materials where they might? How would they do it? And what if they failed to find what they needed? And until the country had a system of independent farms, private wholesalers and independent retailers, how would the people be fed? The fundamental question was how to take the country from here to there—from a status quo that, however bad, was at least familiar, to the uncharted world of freer economic life. The fundamental problem was a lack of preparation for survival in a relatively free marketplace. Most Soviet citizens were no better prepared for it than they would be prepared to play the viola in the orchestra of the Bolshoi Ballet. During the fall of 1990 the political leadership began to absorb the true dimensions of the economic dilemma; the growing realization of its enormity paralyzed the men who were trying to run the country.

The mood was grim; no afterglow survived from Gorbachev's great triumph at the Party Congress in July. Continuing ethnic tensions, separatist activism in many republics, and the obvious, continuing deterioration of economic conditions, especially food supplies, all contributed to the new gloom. So did a crime wave that made city streets feel unsafe for the first time in modern history. Newspapers reported on the elaborate criminal schemes of "mafias" that had exploited the breakdown of traditional discipline to get rich at the expense of ordinary citizens. The machinations of criminal elements were widely blamed for aggravating shortages and increasing prices.

Agricultural officials reported a huge harvest, but also huge problems in bringing it in from the fields. Wheat and potatoes in great quantities were rotting where they had ripened. In the old days students, workers, and other ordinary citizens would have been pressed into duty to bring in the harvest, but that custom had died with many other aspects of the old dictatorial system. Only soldiers could be ordered into the fields now, and they were, in large numbers.

During October and November the tide of affairs began to run strongly against Gorbachev. His popularity had fallen to below 20 percent in opinion polls (it got no boost from the announcement in mid-October that Gorbachev had won the Nobel Peace Prize), and outside of his immediate entourage, almost no one was speaking up in his defense. On October 16 he introduced his own economic reform plan, a watered-down compromise between Shatalin and Ryzhkov which, he claimed, offered the possibility of a relatively quick adoption of some sort of market economy. The radical economists disagreed. Yeltsin was furious that Gorbachev had walked away from the understanding the two men had achieved at the end of the summer; he called the Gorbachev plan "a deceit of the people" that would lead to "catastrophe."

Nevertheless, the Supreme Soviet endorsed the Gorbachev plan overwhelmingly. Speaking about it to the Supreme Soviet, Gorbachev accused Yeltsin of "playing political games." He also acknowledged that the economic situation was grave: "The situation in the consumer market has worsened catastrophically. The reason is clear. . . . We have begun to print money at several times the rate of previous years. We have lost control of the financial situation in the country." Despite that devastating criticism of his policies, Ryzhkov was delighted with the outcome, and jauntily told reporters that his "principled position" had carried the day.

In effect, Gorbachev was prepared to abandon his effort to build a close alliance with Yeltsin—the most popular political leader in the country—so he could remain loyal to Ryzhkov, who had become perhaps the most unpopular Soviet politician. Gorbachev's jealousy of Yeltsin's popularity must have been a factor in this choice, but there was a practical reason for it. If Gorbachev forced Ryzhkov out of office or humiliated him into resigning, he would have to name a new premier, who in turn would have to form a new government whose ministers would face confirmation in the Supreme Soviet. That opened the possibility of humiliating rejections of the minister of defense and head of the KGB—two allies whom Gorbachev obviously felt he could not alienate or lose. They controlled the only reliable forces that Gorbachev could call in in emergencies, and as conditions deteriorated, he must have considered them increasingly important.

There was another reason why Gorbachev may have been losing interest in an alliance with Yeltsin. Yeltsin was determined to enhance the powers of the individual republics, beginning with his own. He held firmly to his view that Russia and the other republics should have primary control over their own economic resources, a position that Gorbachev rightly understood was intended to undercut the national government and him personally. Yeltsin stuck to this position during a five-hour meeting with Gorbachev on November 10, a session that aides to both men described as another effort to find a common position. Yeltsin said he would not sign any new Union treaty that failed to spell out in detail the political and economic rights of the republics. The legitimacy he enjoyed as the man who had received more votes than any other Soviet politician no doubt emboldened Yeltsin—and worried Gorbachev. Of course, the psychological complexity of the two men's relationship provided a rich background to all of their maneuvering—one that outsiders could not penetrate.

Yeltsin's proud defense of the rights of Russia was just one manifestation of a sudden intensification of nationalistic sentiment that was palpable during the last months of 1990. In the Ukraine, tens of thousands took to the streets on October 1 to demonstrate against control of their republic by the authorities in Moscow and the Communist Party. The Russian Republic's parliament voted overwhelmingly—if unrealistically—to proceed with the original five-hundred-day Shatalin plan within Russia itself, regardless of what the Soviet authorities decided to do. In late October the parliaments in the Ukraine and Russia formally insisted that no Soviet legislation be applied on their territory without their approval. The actions of these rebellious legislatures became known as part of a "war of laws" that the country's many new parliaments were waging that fall.

In Moldavia, whose native population is Romanian, violence erupted when local authorities tried to crush a rebellion by a Turkish minority called the Gagauz that had declared its sovereign independence. Moscow sent Soviet troops into the republic to try to maintain order. Then at the end of the month pro-independence nationalists in Georgia won a landslide victory in the first multiparty election held in the Soviet Union since the Communist Party lost its formal political monopoly. Georgia's new leader was Zviad Gamsakhurdia, a former dissident and son of Georgia's greatest writer, a charismatic leader determined to establish a free, capitalist Georgia, though one with close economic ties to the Soviet Union. Many republics had begun negotiating economic agreements with one another, beyond Moscow's control. Several had begun to interfere with the call-up of army draftees.

Gorbachev displayed his anxiety about these developments in a remarkable meeting on November 13 with eleven hundred military men, all of them deputies to the national or republican legislatures. During the course of many hours, Gorbachev listened to a hair-curling litany of horror stories from these officers, many of them conservative political officers who were openly hostile to his policies. Their statements added up to a portrait of a military establishment that was crumbling.

For example, Colonel V. G. Suvadevidze from Tbilisi, the Georgian capital, said two thousand army deserters were at large in that republic alone. A new law passed in Georgia offering young men the chance to serve at home instead of in the army "is virtually halting the fall draft of young people into the army."*

Major A. Sokorchuk, a political officer stationed in the Western Ukraine, where Ukrainian nationalist sentiment is strongest, told the meeting that "antipeople, antisocialist and separatist forces" who enjoyed "overwhelming representation on local soviets" were openly trying to frustrate the army and terrorize its members. "There are cases of servicemen being directly threatened and beaten up. . . . The situation . . . is such that immediate, resolute action is required. Delay is tantamount to death. The orgy of reaction and the flouting of human rights must be stopped! . . ."

In Armenia, reported Lieutenant Colonel V. Y. Mizov, local authorities had promised to cut off food rations for the military. They had not allocated any apartments to military families for two years, he said. Nearly all the Russian-language schools in Yerevan, the Armenian capital, had been closed, so Russian-speaking military families had no place to send their children to school. Mizov turned ominously to Gorbachev to inform him that an emergency decree he had issued based on his enhanced presidential powers ordering Armenian nationalists to turn in their weapons "is not being implemented, Mikhail Sergeyevich. As of today not one weapon had been handed in."

That day Gorbachev heard dozens of stories of harassment of mili-

---

* The Soviet army inducts draftees twice a year, in spring and fall.

tary men and their families, grim living conditions for officers and men, food shortages, widespread desecration of monuments to Lenin, and more. A recurring theme was the disrespect of local populations and officials for the national government. "When is all this going to stop?" asked Major Sokorchuk. "When is our country's leadership going to defend us and our honor and dignity?" I've been told that some officers made more direct threats against Gorbachev during that tumultuous meeting.

In response, Gorbachev gave a speech that I believe revealed his own core belief about his role in the national crisis. Any attempt to separate peoples "who have lived side by side for centuries" could "turn into a bloodbath," he said. He had repeatedly invoked this idea that the multinational Russian state was already a long-established reality—as indeed it was. Most of the non-Russian peoples now part of the Soviet Union were brought into Russia in the nineteenth century or before. The country had "a unitary state economy," he said, and if it were broken up, "a situation could arise that would be worse than during the Cultural Revolution in China."

"To use a military expression," Gorbachev continued, "the union of sovereign republics [his formulation for the arrangement to be created by a new Union treaty] represents our last trench line. Beyond this lies the disintegration of the state." Gorbachev would not be the Russian leader recorded in history as the czar who lost his country— that was his bottom line.

Some senior army officers agreed. Marshal Sergei Akhromeyev, the retired chief of staff who served as a special assistant to Gorbachev, wrote in a newspaper article in mid-November that the armed forces were ready to act "to ensure the unity of our motherland and preserve the social system in line with the constitution. . . . The time has come to protect our federal socialist state vigorously and decisively. . . ."

A sense that events were spinning out of control brought a new mood to the country in November. Intellectuals began to speculate gloomily on parallels between November 1990 and November 1917. Then, Lenin's Bolsheviks, exploiting popular impatience with the ineffectual democratic government installed the previous February after the overthrow of Czar Nicholas II, were able to seize power in a coup d'état that became known as the Bolshevik Revolution. A philosopher named Nikolai Mikhailov wrote in *Izvestia*:

> The similarities are striking: the same, almost boundless *glasnost;* the same intoxication with democracy and soapbox oratory; the same

hasty emergence of all kinds of parties and movements; the same chaos of economic mismanagement . . .; blazing hotbeds of nationalism in the outlying regions of the former empire; rising crime . . . It is time to say bluntly and honestly: We are heading for a disaster.

Stanislav Kondrashov, a well-known commentator for *Izvestia* who had become an ardent supporter of Gorbachev's reforms after a long career as a reliable official journalist, described the new mood: "Disappointed by the fruitlessness of democracy, the people are rapidly becoming fertile ground for a 'strong arm.' . . . The Romans used to talk about bread and circuses [as diversions to preoccupy the masses]. But when bread rations are rapidly declining, people are ready to sacrifice the parliamentary circuses." A strong arm* is an ancient Russian notion, traceable at least as far back in the country's history as the reign of Ivan the Terrible in the sixteenth century. A leader with a strong arm might not respect the niceties, but he would get the job done, get the country in order. The yearning for such a figure was growing, Kondrashov warned.

He and many other self-styled "democrats" who were early enthusiasts for the new political institutions Gorbachev created were increasingly nervous that the public was losing patience with democratic procedures. The Congress and Supreme Soviet had been transformed in the public imagination from exciting new forums for truth telling into dreary debating societies whose members talked endlessly, but accomplished nothing. Even progressive members of the parliament began to despair that it was useless. Similarly, the newly elected non-Communist governments running Moscow, Leningrad, and other cities were quickly being discredited, though they had been in office less than a year. They had promised better conditions, but conditions only got worse. (Many of the new officials in these cities suspected that Party *apparatchiks* and the KGB were conspiring to withhold food from them to aggravate the situation.)

"There is no surer way to destroy democracy," wrote the filmmaker Stanislav Govorukhin in *Sovetskaya Kultura,* "than to plunge the country into chaos and anarchy. There is no surer way to discredit the democratic idea than to give the population grounds to think that changes for the worse in the country are connected to democratic changes."

The Supreme Soviet was not yet out of business, however. Like

---

* Arm, or hand—Russians use the same word, *ruka,* for both.

parliamentarians everywhere, its members took advantage of the November 7 holiday to visit their constituents at home, where many of them were bombarded with voters' complaints. They came back to work in a new frame of mind, and quickly voted to reject the agenda put forward by the leadership and demand a special debate on the worsening situation in the country. Gorbachev had to agree to open an emergency debate with a special report on the economic crisis. (At the same moment the new city government in Leningrad announced it would impose food rationing for the first time since World War II.)

The report Gorbachev gave on November 16 was ineffectual. He promised to reshuffle the government, but announced no new initiatives to deal with the crisis. He complained—almost whined—about a lack of respect for his previous orders. "For some reason, every decree that I issue is first discussed to see whether it should be carried out or not. For heaven's sake, if they are not carried out, nothing is going to get done. I think those officials who block my decrees should simply be fired!" Members were openly critical of the speech. Genrikh Igitian, a member from Armenia, took the floor to say: "Mikhail Sergeyevich, after listening to your speech, it seems to me that you have been abroad for a long period of time and have suddenly returned to see what is happening in the country." Yeltsin declared that the country was in "a crisis of a totalitarian state, which is reflected in the paralysis of power. . . . The people's patience is ending and an explosion could occur at any time."

One passage in that speech deserves note—it may be a clue to subsequent events. When he announced his intention to reshuffle the government, Gorbachev also promised "personnel changes at the highest level of command in the armed forces." Soon afterward he did indeed shuffle and reshuffle the government, but no "personnel changes at the highest level of command" occurred in the aftermath of that speech. One new deputy minister of defense was added, but that change didn't fit Gorbachev's description. I was struck the day he made that speech that he would advertise what might be a very sensitive change at the top of the army before he could announce the details; it seemed an odd thing to do when the army was so clearly a delicate part of the balance he was trying to maintain. Might he have been engaged in some kind of struggle with his top brass at that very moment? Might he have lost the struggle? This is one of the many mysteries in the events of late 1990.

The next day Gorbachev returned to the parliament with a plan to overhaul the country's executive structure. He had not lost his talent for improvisation under pressure. Members listened in surprised silence as Gorbachev outlined his plan: the position of premier would be abolished (finally, a solution to the Ryzhkov problem—no job, no problem); the Federation Council, composed of the leaders of the fifteen republics, would become a new kind of presidential cabinet, and would have the authority to approve or reject any proposal "affecting the whole country," in Gorbachev's words. He proposed a new governmental body to help fight crime and black marketeering, phenomena that were growing rapidly and alarming the country. He proposed dissolving the Presidential Council that was created with the new office of president and creating a national security council to oversee the ministries of Defense, Foreign Affairs, the Interior, and the KGB. He promised a new food program that would get the country through the winter. The Supreme Soviet quickly gave the plan its overwhelming support; final enactment would await action by the larger Congress of People's Deputies, scheduled to meet in December.

The new plan appeared to be a concession to Yeltsin, who had previously demanded a new way to give the leaders of the republics a share of national power. It was also a clear response to cries for stronger leadership, and was positively received by politicians from all sides of the new political spectrum. "This was the calming tonic the Supreme Soviet has been awaiting for so long," said Yuri Afanasyev, one of Gorbachev's most outspoken critics from the left.

But the initial reaction was short lived. Two days later, Yeltsin—visiting Kiev, the Ukrainian capital, to sign an unprecedented treaty on political, cultural, and economic relations between Russia and the Ukraine—said he didn't like the new Gorbachev plan. "One senses mainly an attempt to restore [Moscow's] supreme power," he said. A day later the chairman of the right-wing Soyuz (Union) faction in the parliament, a forty-year-old lieutenant colonel in the army named Viktor Alksnis, described the continuing efforts by individual republics to assert their sovereignty as civil war, and promised to push for Gorbachev's ouster unless he "finally begins to fulfill his promises" by ending "the collapse of the country."

Several days later Gorbachev began to circulate a draft of his proposed new Union treaty. While offering the republics considerable autonomy, including the right to choose their own economic and social systems, it retained great power for the central government in Moscow. The center would retain control over key natural resources, transportation and communications, the financial system, and all the security organs. In a symbolic gesture to the liberals (it would prove to be his last for a long time), Gorbachev proposed renaming the country the Union of Sovereign Soviet Republics, dropping the word "Socialist." He said the draft should be the starting point for future discussions, and welcomed proposals for improving it. Many Soviet and foreign commentators observed that if Gorbachev had offered such a proposal a year or two earlier, it would have caused a sensation —thrilling the independence-minded republics and angering Communist Party traditionalists. Now the reaction was approximately the opposite, a sign of how quickly the country had changed, and how Gorbachev's own position had shifted.

•   •   •

By late November 1990, the sense of danger in the country had infected Mikhail Gorbachev. He admitted as much in the remarkable extemporaneous speech he gave to a meeting of intellectuals and "cultural workers" in the Kremlin on November 28. This was the speech in which Gorbachev first disclosed that both of his grandfathers had been arrested in the 1930s—a story he seemed to tell to bolster his own credentials as a liberal before this intellectual audience. "We can speak of a certain danger that the great cause which we embarked on in April 1985 faces today," Gorbachev said. "This is a time of decisive events in our country, events that will determine what it will be like both in the years ahead and for decades to come."

He recalled the origins of *perestroika,* recounting how he and Shevardnadze had agreed in 1985 that "we cannot live like this," that the country had to change. They were vacationing together in Pitsunda, on the sea, Gorbachev recalled. They compared their experiences in Stavropol and Georgia, where they had been Party bosses, and Shevardnadze observed that "everything had gone rotten." So, continued Gorbachev, "we began looking for ways in which we might live. A concept came into being for the country and the world. In regard to internal affairs we called it *perestroika,* and we put forward a simple formula: more democracy, more *glasnost,* more humanity. Everything must be developed so that the individual in this society can feel like a human being. This is a simple formula. We used precisely the kind of language that people would understand."

But now, he complained, the formulas being advanced were getting more complicated—"formulas in which often you don't understand what's what, particularly for the ordinary person." Demagogues were confusing ordinary people with fancy terminology, "showing off in front of each other as to who uses more of these unclear words." But he remembers that "we agreed that we wanted genuine socialism."

But what was that? "I, for example, am a convinced socialist, in this sense. I am deeply attached [to the idea]. I do not just believe; this is not just religious; it is my knowledge and my thinking," Gorbachev said. But he acknowledged the uncertainty of what socialism means, noting that he had recently spoken about the subject with Felipe Gonzalez, the "socialist" (but pro-capitalist) prime minister of Spain, who also called himself a convinced socialist. Gorbachev ruminated: "If this is socialism, then it means first and foremost democracy. If it is democracy, then it means freedom, or perhaps even first and foremost freedom, and thereafter democracy, too, and political freedom, human and spiritual freedom, economic freedom, greater justice, the quality of life of the people, culture. The central character in the drama is the worker.

"I have always spoken in favor of the market," Gorbachev said, but not without reservation. "I, for example, do not accept private ownership of land. Do with me what you will, I do not accept it. Leasing, yes, even for a hundred years, even with the right to sell leasing rights, or to leave them as an inheritance. But I do not accept private property."

Nor would he accept suggestions to turn on the entire Soviet past, and renounce what his father and grandfathers had accomplished. Not everything had gone well, but a country had been built and defended against Hitler, and Gorbachev was proud of it. He would save it. "We are one country, a single people." But "it is clear that nothing decent will come out of our Union . . . if we do not allow every nationality to breathe freely, irrespective of whether the group is big or small. . . . We must make it possible for these people to independently expand their potential economically, and in the sphere of self-government. . . ." That is why he put forth the idea of "a union of sovereign states," he said. But "we must not split up. . . . Whether we like it or not, this is the way things have turned out for us. If we begin to split up, there will be a war, a terrible war, conflict will follow. . . . We cannot split up, nor can we split the army, or the nuclear weapons . . . [or] this may result in a disaster not just for the country, but for the whole world. . . . We have to provide the maximum freedom and independence, and at the center, to preserve the center. . . ."

Gorbachev perceived a great danger in the confusion of the present moment—"the legislative war, the legal confusion, the anarchy. It is —I will be frank with you—a quiet counterrevolution. . . . We have pushed the 'on' button but have forgotten about safety mechanisms. We have started the engine but have not adjusted the brakes. . . ." So now, "the most important thing for us is stabilization—economic stabilization, legal stabilization, political stabilization."

He knew that some people thought his push for stronger executive power meant he wanted to be a dictator, but Gorbachev disagreed. "I already had that in my hands," he recalled. "The general secretary of the Central Committee of the Communist Party of the Soviet Union was a dictator with no equal in the world. Nobody had more power than he. . . . So what did I want to start all this for? . . . The thing is, comrades, it was impossible to live. Indeed, everything has rotted, and the people have been humiliated. An enormous country, with such intellectual potential, such attachment to the land, such resources and wealth, is in such a state! We cannot go on like this any longer."

•   •   •

Those remarks signaled a profound change in Gorbachev's attitudes. In approximately one hundred days from August to the end of November, he had decided to make a radical course correction. There had been similar shifts over the previous five and a half years, but they had always been shifts in a more liberal direction. This time he had decided instead on an about-face. Despite his disclaimers and his insistence that dictatorship was not his objective, Gorbachev was about to push the country back toward authoritarian rule. The evidence of this decision would begin to appear a few days after that speech.

As I write in early 1991, it isn't difficult to identify the powerful forces that pushed Gorbachev in this direction. But it isn't at all clear which of them were most important in his own mind. The most obvious is crude ambition. Gorbachev had seen for months that his own power was at risk; he may simply have decided that he had to act to preserve it. Another possibility is power politics. The reactionary forces in the army, the military-industrial complex, the KGB, the police and the Party may have combined to threaten Gorbachev personally or politically in a way he found too plausible to ignore. His unfulfilled promise on November 16 to reshuffle the top command might support this proposition. A third source of pressure was the condition of the country, which was truly precarious. If Gorbachev has a chance to write the self-serving memoirs typical of politicians, I suspect he will tell us that he changed course at the end of 1990 to prevent the country from falling apart—that a firmer line was the only way to avoid the "disaster not just for the country, but for the whole world" that he mentioned to the intellectuals he addressed on November 28. In the messy manner of real human events, all these factors probably played a part in Gorbachev's reversal. Alas, his decision to embrace a new authoritarianism was reached in the old way, after backstage maneuverings conducted out of public view. The audience had no good explanation for the sudden change in the plot.

I do think Gorbachev was sincerely alarmed by the prospect of losing his country. He had come face to face with the strength of the forces his reforms had unleashed. A moderate, rational man, he was never comfortable with the immoderate emotionalism of so many of his countrymen, but he had to recognize what was happening. His reforms made it possible for citizens to form opinions freely, and then to express them freely. The result was a great flowering of many nationalisms, from Lithuania in the northwest to Kirghizia in the southeast. Freedom also allowed for the expression of ancient national rivalries and hatreds. Gorbachev could insist all he wanted to that the "multinational Soviet state" was a legitimate political entity that had grown up over centuries, but its constituent peoples weren't buying that line. The Soviet Union, like the imperial Russian state that preceded it, was always a vehicle to allow Russia to dominate the smaller peoples on its periphery. Those peoples understood this, even if Gorbachev insisted otherwise. They understood it better than ever because Gorbachev's policies had freed them to openly discuss their histories and their aspirations.

From Gorbachev's point of view the strongest arguments for preserving the country were practical, not historical or philosophical. Some argued that the Union could survive without the Baltic republics, Georgia and Armenia, and perhaps Moldavia, but Gorbachev must have feared—the fear was certainly justified—that once any part of the whole was allowed to secede, a general unraveling would follow. And he understood how, over seventy years, the Soviet system had made the country's parts dependent on one another. Cotton was grown only in Central Asia. Light bulbs weren't made in Central Asia, but in Armenia and Russia. In many cases a single factory provided the entire country's supply of a critical product. For example, the only source of the vaccine for tuberculosis was in Uzbekistan—where local authorities closed it as an environmental hazard. The transportation system was interdependent too. If the country fell apart, economic difficulties would be compounded many times over—Gorbachev was right about that.

Economic difficulties were grave enough already—another factor that must have pushed Gorbachev toward retrenchment at the end of 1990. There was no longer any hiding the depth of the crisis. Food shortages were endemic, and the Soviet Union was openly begging the West for help. Gorbachev himself took the astounding step of signing a "Dear Friends" letter to the German people that was published in the mass-circulation *Stern* magazine asking Russia's former arch-enemy for specific help—500,000 tons of meat, 500,000 tons of vegetable oil, 100,000 tons of noodles. (When foreign aid started to arrive in the Soviet Union in large quantities, many Russians said they were humiliated to have to receive it.) The ruble was fast losing all value as inflation on the free market reached a rate of perhaps 80 percent. Industrial production was falling. Because of declining production, oil exports, once the major source of Soviet foreign currency, were tumbling: from 127 million metric tons in 1989 to about 100 million tons in 1990 to a projected 60 million tons in 1991. The finance minister, Valentin Pavlov, told the Supreme Soviet in late November that without radical measures to control it, the state budget deficit could go up 400 percent in 1991, rising from an already disastrous level to an untenable 20 percent of national income. This would mean "the complete collapse of the consumer market and galloping inflation," Pavlov said. Gorbachev's curt public remarks on the subject made clear his own realization that there would be no avoiding a serious further reduction in the standard of living. The resulting public discontent would give Gorbachev additional reasons for turning to the right.

Gorbachev chose a characteristically practical path toward his new goals. There were four institutions in Soviet society capable of contributing adhesive that would help hold the country together on Gorbachev's terms: the army, the police of the Ministry of the Interior, the KGB and the Communist Party. At the end of November Gorbachev began a concerted campaign to strengthen the allegiance to him of all four.

On November 27 Gorbachev issued a package of decrees whose

main purpose was to offer new protection to the military. These measures were needed, he said, to respond to a "massive outburst" of hostility to Soviet troops around the country, particularly in Latvia, where local officials had recently tried to cut off electricity, water, and food to troops stationed there. The minister of defense, Dmitri Yazov, went on the main television news program to read the decrees—an unusual method of announcing a presidential decision. The decrees authorized soldiers to defend themselves and their interests "with their weapons" against harassment by local nationalists.

Then on December 2 Gorbachev announced that he had fired one of the leading progressives in the government, Vadim Bakatin, the interior minister. He was replaced by Boris Pugo, a Communist Party official who had previously been KGB chief, then Party first secretary in Latvia. Pugo's new deputy would be General Boris Gromov, the last Soviet commander in Afghanistan and an outspoken conservative member of the Congress.

These changes were ominous. Bakatin had been a surprise choice to run the ministry, which controls the country's 700,000 policemen and 400,000 of its own troops, which have been used to enforce order and put down open rebellion. A favorite among progressive intellectuals, Bakatin had begun earnestly to try to create the "rule-of-law state" that Gorbachev spoke about so often. He had become a target of bitter conservative criticism for his failure to control ethnic disorders around the country.

Pugo, by contrast, was an enforcer and *apparatchik,* a protégé of Yuri Andropov. Gromov was regarded by many of my friends in Moscow as a dangerous figure, a putative Napoleon, someone who might even try to lead a military coup one day. A small man who actually does like to stick his hand into the front of his jacket, Napoleon fashion, Gromov was a leader of the military group in the Congress that had been most hostile to progressive reform.

The following week Vladimir Kryuchkov, the KGB chairman, gave a startling speech on television. "A danger has developed that the Soviet Union might disintegrate," he declared. "National chauvinism is being encouraged, and mass rioting and violence have been provoked." But the KGB would fight "with all the means at their disposal" against "anti-Communist" elements inside the country and abroad that threaten the state. "To be or not to be, that is the choice for our great state," Kryuchkov said.

Several days later, Gorbachev issued another decree nullifying all decisions by local governments and republics that had disrupted the flow of food and other goods around the country. Another decree ordered all enterprises to honor their contracts through the first three months of 1991 for the delivery of goods and supplies to other state enterprises.

"I think we are seeing a creeping, militarized coup—not military, but militarized," said Yuri Leavada, a commentator in *Moscow News.* A senior Communist Party official told Remnick of *The Washington Post* that Gorbachev had taken a temporary rightward tack "to get us through the winter," but others were worried. "This is not merely a matter of getting through the winter," said Andrannik Migranyan, a prominent political scientist. "There is an open conflict now between the republics and the center, between the democrats who are trying to gain power and the traditional institutions of the centralized state which are trying to hold on to theirs. . . . Gorbachev knows that the KGB, the military and the party are still in place, and he must satisfy some of their grievances, make alliance with them, in order to rely on them."

Alexander Yakovlev, no longer seen on the public stage and apparently reduced to a minor role as an occasional personal adviser to Gorbachev, told the newspaper *Moskovsky Komsomolets:* "An offensive is under way by conservative and reactionary forces which are vengeful and merciless. I am very worried by the inertia, exhaustion, dejection, and preoccupation with petty matters which characterize the democratic forces."

Tatyana Zaslavskaya, the sociologist who was one of the early architects of reform, offered an intriguing analysis in an interview published in *Izvestia* in mid-December. "The situation is indeed exceptionally complex," she said, "but it is difficult to imagine that it could be anything else. In my view, everything that's happening is logical." Zaslavskaya explained that the first three or four years of Gorbachev's rule had seen "the breakup of mass consciousness," or the collapse of orthodoxy. Now the society was gripped by multiple struggles for power—"Gorbachev and Yeltsin, soviets and Party committees, center and republics, republics and regions." One important struggle was a fight over who would form the new "class of entrepreneurs" that would dominate the future economic life of the country. Its members could be "picked from the *nomenklatura,*" the Party-approved list of senior officials whose monopoly on political power was unchallenged before Gorbachev's reforms. "But there is another, democratic approach," Zaslavskaya continued, which would allow the new class of entrepreneurs to be created "from the most vigorous, talented people, irrespective of their social group." In other words, the old order was fighting against the new for the spoils of a freer economy. "Behind the scenes," said this shrewd woman, "a struggle is raging . . . a life-and-death struggle at that."

Real politics had evolved into real life. Disconnected from the orthodoxy that organized the society and its thoughts for so many years, freed to pursue self-interest however defined, able to experiment and to make egregious mistakes, and still crippled by the damage caused by seventy years of misrule, Soviet society had entered a time of troubles. The most unhappy aspect of this period was the total absence of appealing alternatives. Yes, Gorbachev had botched the chance to take a dramatic leap toward a freer economy. But he could justify his hesitancy. I suspect he was convinced that the leap would cause enormous suffering in the society. *Every* option seemed to offer suffering first, uncertainty later. Political paralysis was not the result of mysterious forces, but rather of deliberate choice. Paralysis seemed better than all the other possibilities.

•   •   •

In this grim atmosphere the Congress of People's Deputies convened on December 17. The various caucuses reorganized for the new session, and the membership of the principal ones was revealing. The Inter-Regional Group, the liberal bloc first organized by Sakharov, had shrunk to just 229 members. Soyuz, the conservative bloc that was openly hostile to Gorbachev, had 561 members. Some members actually moved from the liberal group to the conservative one. This alignment seemed to reflect the changing tone of the country's politics.

Gorbachev gave a sort of state of the union address to begin the session. He acknowledged a crisis, and took much of the blame for it: "The country's leadership has made major errors and miscalculations in the course of *perestroika*. We underestimated the depth of our society's crisis. Insufficiently grounded and hasty decisions were taken. . . ." However, he also bragged of the achievements of the previous sixty-nine months: "*Perestroika* has given society freedom and democracy. . . . We have destroyed the mainstays of the totalitarian, administer-by-command system that hobbled society for decades. . . . We have done away with the unitary approach to developing the multinational state, and paved the way to the healthy ethnic rebirth of all peoples. We have never known such freedom of thought. No one is persecuted for dissidence. . . . Our foreign policies have decisively helped improve the international situation. . . .

"The only sensible policy now," Gorbachev continued, "is to act together to stem the crisis, overcome our weak points, defeat negative trends in society and steer the country, in twelve to eighteen months, toward normal, healthy development along the path of renewal." There, evidently, was his plan: twelve to eighteen months of firmer discipline and control to put things on a healthy path. "If we have strong government, tight discipline, and control over the fulfillment of decisions, then we shall be able to ensure normal food supplies, rein in crime, and stop interethnic strife. If we fail to achieve this, a greater discord, the rampage of dark forces, and the breakup of our state will be inevitable."

He outlined his proposals for restructuring executive power to make it stronger and more efficient, and repeated his arguments for a new Union treaty. He proposed a national referendum on the treaty, a potential means of imposing it without the approval of the legislatures of the fifteen republics. He said the Union must stay together, but added that "our republics' sovereignty is a historically irreversible stage in the development of our multinational state." He criticized republican governments and himself for being too tolerant of separatist activity in the past; "resolute measures are needed." He criticized intellectuals for being argumentative and inconsistent supporters of reform. In all these respects his speech pleased conservatives. Ligachev, back from his retirement to take part in the Congress (he was still a member), was delighted: "Our views are coming together," he beamed after the speech.

But Gorbachev also declared emphatically that the time had come to create new "land relations" in the countryside, providing for individuals and groups to take over farms and run them independent of the authorities (something Ligachev had vehemently opposed). On the still touchy issue of private ownership of land Gorbachev called for a referendum in each republic, but said local governments should proceed at once to grant long-term leaseholds to farmers who wanted them.

He also promised to introduce key elements of the Shatalin reform, including a new "network of commercial, joint-stock, cooperative, and other nonstate banks," and an energetic effort to sell off some state enterprises to private interests. He pledged to terminate "the printing of money to cover the budget deficit," and to make sharp cuts in capital investments, spending on the state bureaucracy, subsidies for unprofitable enterprises and the military budget. Altogether, the initiatives he promised would constitute a sweeping economic turnabout if they were implemented.

And he promised to respect the law, and not to abuse the new powers he hoped the Congress would give him. "I see the tasks of presidential power as the defense of rights of citizens and the honor and dignity of every person, and in the normal functioning of the constitutional system and state institutions," he said.

That was the first day of the new session of the Congress. On the second day, after being pummeled for hours from the podium by members complaining about his policies or the state of the country or countless other problems, Gorbachev came out into the corridor outside the Palace of Congresses to make a little news. The first reporter to spot him asked, "Is it fair to say you are moving to the right?" Gorbachev quipped, "Actually, I'm going around in circles." When the television cameras were on, he said:

"Over these past six years I feel I've lived several decades, several lives. I feel like the man in our legend of Nasreddin who lived in Bukhara. He saddles up his jackass and goes down the road and everyone around him is saying, 'Look at that fool, why is he tormenting himself and his beast in such terrible heat?' So he gets off and puts the jackass on his back and walks on that way."

He had decided not to give another speech on the history, "the inferiority complexes and the problems" of his country, Gorbachev explained, because people would just have said, "Ach, there's Gorbachev on his hobbyhorse again, he loves to talk." But he did speak of the effects of history during this walk in the foyer: "Unfortunately, our society is not ready for the procedures of a law-based state. We don't have that level of political culture, those traditions. All that will come in the future, but the important thing in the meantime is not to smash each other's bones. . . .

"The problem is that our power has been torn to shreds," he said. "The chain of command is broken. The electrical current is switched off and the economy is grinding to a halt. . . . We're already in a state of chaos. People think I don't see what's happening, but I do."

"That's right!" shouted a deputy who was watching. "That's why we need the iron fist!"

"No, not quite," Gorbachev replied. "Everyone knows I will not be a dictator. . . . For once in our history, let's try to do things without bloodshed, without dividing society into Reds and Whites, or black and blue. . . ."

The next day Yeltsin gave a different interpretation of the situation in a pointed speech to the Congress. "One must frankly acknowledge," he said, speaking of Gorbachev, "that the Union's leadership does not have a precise political course directed toward the country's revival. Its external action bears the hallmarks of improvisation. . . . But there is a harsh political logic behind these maneuvers aimed at disrupting the sovereignty of the republics and sabotaging radical reforms. As a result, today we have a Union center of popular no confidence. The so-called revolution from above has ended. The Kremlin has ceased to be the initiator of the renewal of the country. . . .

"Russia will not agree to the restoration of the Kremlin's *diktat*," Yeltsin said. "The way out of the crisis requires honest dialogue, with equal rights, between the center and the republics. This does not mean the disintegration of the Union. On the contrary, this is the only way to save it."

Two days after Gorbachev joked that he was running around in circles, the true dimensions of the changes he was making suddenly became clear. It wasn't Gorbachev who made them clear, but his comrade-in-arms from the earliest days of *perestroika*, Eduard Shevardnadze.

In his speech to intellectuals on November 28, Gorbachev had spoken of Shevardnadze's important part in the first stages of reform. In 1985 the two of them had talked frankly on the beach at Pitsunda, on the Black Sea coast, Gorbachev recalled. Shevardnadze had said everything was rotten; they had both agreed that the country could no longer go on as it had.

Now it was Shevardnadze who had decided that he could no longer go on with Gorbachev down the new path the president had chosen. He announced this decision in a sensational speech to the Congress of People's Deputies—a speech that caught Gorbachev and the entire body by complete surprise.

It was a curious speech, largely ad-libbed from notes, and betraying hurt pride. The foreign policies associated with Shevardnadze's name had long been criticized by conservatives; they considered him too eager to dissolve the East European empire, too quick to make agreements with the Americans and others in the West. Lately the criticism had become bitter, especially after Shevardnadze had suggested at the United Nations in New York that Soviet forces might join in U.N.-sanctioned military action against Iraq, a longtime Soviet ally before its invasion of Kuwait in August. Later Shevardnadze had retracted this threat, after officials in Moscow made clear their unwillingness to fight Iraq. Shevardnadze commented on these criticisms, and called them part of a campaign against him. "Things went as far as personal insults. I endured that, too. Comrades, a hounding is taking place." He bemoaned the fact that no one had stood up to defend him, or to criticize those "boys in colonels' epaulets"—Lieutenant Colonel Alksnis and other military officers in the Soyuz faction, though Shevardnadze used no names—for attacking him.

After reviewing the evidence of his own mistreatment, Shevardnadze came bluntly to the real point of his speech. "Democrats," Shevardnadze warned the proreform members, "I'll put it bluntly. Comrade democrats! In the broadest meaning of this word: you have scattered. The reformers have gone into hiding. A dictatorship is approaching—I tell you this with full responsibility. No one knows what this dictatorship will be like, what kind of dictator will come to power and what order will be established.

"I want to make the following statement. I am resigning. Let this be—and do not react, and do not curse me—let this be my contribution, if you like, my protest against the onset of dictatorship.

"I would like to express sincere gratitude to Mikhail Sergeyevich Gorbachev. I am his friend. I am a fellow thinker of his. I have always supported, and will support to the end of my days, the ideas of *perestroika,* the ideas of renewal, the ideas of democracy, of democratization.

"We did great work in international affairs. But I think that it is my duty [to resign]. As a man, as a citizen, as a Communist, I can not reconcile myself with what is happening in my country and to the trials which await our people.

"I nevertheless believe that the dictatorship will not succeed, that the future belongs to democracy and freedom. Thank you very much."

That was it. A bombshell in fifteen hundred words. Many deputies thought the resignation was some sort of ploy; at first few seemed to believe that he meant what he said. Two hours after Shevardnadze spoke, Gorbachev came to the podium, and made it clear that the resignation was serious.

They had spoken twice on the telephone since Shevardnadze's speech, Gorbachev reported, and those conversations convinced the president that his foreign minister hoped to thwart "those who are trying to take advantage of the [current] difficulties and question the course toward *perestroika*. . . .

"I share his position in the sense that we must defend *perestroika*," Gorbachev continued, but he disputed Shevardnadze's analysis of the situation. "I reject Comrade Shevardnadze's thesis, because it smacks a little of panic." Yes, the country might turn to a dictatorship of some kind if his efforts failed, Gorbachev said, but not yet. ". . . The president now does not have information—and I get extensive information—that someone, somewhere is preparing a junta or some similar dictatorship."

And he admitted to personal pique. "Personally, I condemn Comrade Shevardnadze for doing this without consulting the president—even more, I will tell you directly, because it had come to this: My plans included recommending Comrade Shevardnadze for vice president." And a little later: "It is unforgivable to leave at such a moment. This must be condemned."

In the vestibule off the floor of the Congress, a liberal deputy approached Gorbachev to ask about Shevardnadze's departure. The president had only a brief reply, but it spoke volumes: "Everything humane is being forgotten," he said.

A few steps away he was accosted by Genrikh Borovikh, a playwright and journalist famous in the Brezhnev years as an apologist for the regime, but now associated with the Moscow liberals. "The leadership is moving to the right," Borovikh said.

Gorbachev replied, "The leadership is moving to the right with the society."

The same afternoon, Shevardnadze's spokesman at the Foreign Ministry, Vitali Churkin, released a statement to reporters elaborating on Shevardnadze's reasons for resigning. "The minister is profoundly convinced that at this stage, when the danger of reactionary forces entering the arena is a reality, he must make this sacrifice for the sake of salvaging the democratic gains [that have been made]. . . . The minister considers that this step, which has been taken by a man of importance and prestige, will be a serious warning to everyone, and that people will look at themselves and at the situation more soberly and calmly. If people do not rise up in defense of democratic gains, Eduard Shevardnadze believes, then dictatorship will be very close."

And one more point—this was not a hurried decision. "Eduard Shevardnadze's decision was made after much suffering and many sleepless nights."

That last comment rang true with me. I had seen Shevardnadze when he was in Washington eight days earlier; he looked awful. His complexion was ashen, and bags hung deep under his eyes. Of course he had been leading a mad existence, moving from capital to capital across the globe, dealing simultaneously with the Persian Gulf crisis, arms-control negotiations, European diplomacy, and more. I had wondered when he was in Washington if he could keep up the pace; he looked like a man who could collapse at any moment.

What did Shevardnadze know that the rest of the world did not? Had Gorbachev already sold out to reactionary forces in some secret deal? Speculation was intense. Perhaps Gorbachev's revelation that he intended to ask Shevardnadze to be vice president was a clue. The foreign minister had already said publicly he didn't want that job. He was an attractive candidate for it because he was a Georgian, not a Russian, and Gorbachev needed help in his desperate struggle to hold the Union together. But there were strong rumors at the time that force would soon be used in Georgia itself to bring that rebellious republic into line. Was it possible that Gorbachev had insisted that Shevardnadze accept the vice presidency, and that he wanted none of it?

In early January Shevardnadze gave an interview to Yegor Yakovlev, still the editor of *Moscow News*. He resigned, Shevardnadze explained, because he would be unable to defend the use of force to impose discipline on the country, and he feared that force would soon be used. "These days," he told Yakovlev, "we often hear it repeated that discipline and order are indispensable. [This had been Gorbachev's message for weeks.] They are absolutely indispensable. But unfortunately, in the minds of many, discipline and order are associated with the use of force."

And if force were used, he continued, that would undermine the basis of his foreign policy—the assurance that the Soviet Union was no longer a belligerent or dangerous nation, but had adopted "new thinking" in foreign affairs. "In the end it became clear to me that if destabilization of the country continues, and the process of democratization is halted, it will be impossible to follow the current course in foreign policy. . . . The development of events might lead to a repeat of what happened in Tbilisi or Baku [the sites of the two bloodiest interventions with force during the Gorbachev years]. What 'new thinking' will be worth talking about then?"

Shevardnadze did not explain why he came to this conclusion at that time, or why he failed to discuss it with Gorbachev before resigning. He did make clear that his warning about the impending return of dictatorship applied to his friend and patron the president, as well as to other, unnamed forces. He indicated that dictatorship could begin with the exercise of direct presidential rule, a power Gorbachev had held in reserve since it was granted him months earlier, but which he had threatened might be needed to quell ethnic violence in outlying republics. "I'm not sure that presidential rule or any other punitive measures, regardless of where they come from, can be a means to solve our current problems," Shevardnadze said. The formulation was diplomatic, but the warning to Gorbachev was unmistakable.

Shevardnadze's resignation was a shock to the liberals in Moscow. Suddenly Gorbachev seemed to have abandoned them. Bakatin had left the Ministry of Interior. Now Shevardnadze was quitting the Foreign Ministry. Alexander Yakovlev, the original progressive at Gorbachev's side, had all but disappeared from the stage soon after the previous summer's Party Congress, after he had given up his seat on the Politburo. He was seen regularly in public, occasionally gave interviews, remained loyal to Gorbachev, but also lost all influence, or so it appeared.

"There is a creeping coup d'état," Vladimir Chernyak, a Ukrainian economist, told the Congress. "The victims are Yakovlev, Bakatin and Shevardnadze. . . . At the head of this coup d'état is Gorbachev. Maybe he doesn't know that. But by demanding ever greater powers, he creates the legal basis for a dictatorship."

"Gorbachev is organizing his team to hold together the Union," said Nikolai Fyodorov, the minister of justice in Yeltsin's Russian Republic government. "Men like Shevardnadze, Yakovlev, Bakatin— men who study and analyze the situation and say honestly what they think—he doesn't need such people now."

Ales Adamovich, a filmmaker and liberal deputy, told the Congress he wanted to "rebuke Comrade Gorbachev," and then, looking at him, he did so. "We all remember how Khrushchev was unseated by depriving him of his most staunch allies, most committed to reform. By losing such allies as Shevardnadze, you are losing your own strength, your prestige, you are losing face. If this process goes on, the president will soon be surrounded by colonels and generals. They will surround the president, making him a hostage. Gorbachev is the only leader in Soviet history who has not stained his hands with blood, and we would like to remember him for that. But a moment will come when they will instigate a bloodbath, and later they will wipe their bloodstained hands against your suit, and you will be to blame for everything. . . ."

The days following Shevardnadze's resignation brought the progressives no reassurance. On the contrary. First Kryuchkov of the KGB returned to the podium of the Congress to make a speech that sounded, in some passages, like a document from the Brezhnev era. He attacked foreign intelligence agencies for aggravating the country's troubles and intensifying their spying on the Soviet Union. He said foreigners were delivering tainted goods to the Soviet Union, including grain with "above-average radioactivity" and a high content of weeds. He said some foreigners were trying to organize "a 'brain drain' from our country." This sounded like old-fashioned Soviet xenophobia and Slavophile paranoia about the West.

Kryuchkov also seemed to confirm Adamovich's concerns. "Fears are being voiced," Kryuchkov said, "that if today one is to embark on decisive actions to establish order, one must wittingly agree that blood will be shed. Esteemed comrade deputies! Really, isn't blood being shed already? Really, turning on the television and opening the newspapers, do we not learn almost every day of new human fatalities, of the deaths of innocent people, including women and children? I do not wish to frighten anyone, but the Committee on State Security [the KGB] is convinced that if the situation in our country continues to develop along the present lines, we will not be able to escape sociopolitical shocks more serious and grave in their consequences. What is at issue is moving away from fatalities, and averting new ones."

Gorbachev then picked his first target for a crackdown. On December 23 he issued a decree ordering the rebellious government of Moldavia to abandon a new language law that favored Romanian over Russian, to give up plans to form an independent military force and to make other concessions. The Moldavians apparently decided that Gorbachev was serious; within a week they had satisfied his principal demands.

The Congress gave Gorbachev the new powers he sought, and authorized a nationwide referendum on the future of the Union. It even voted to put the word "Socialist" back into the name of the country under a new Union treaty. On one important point, however, it denied Gorbachev's wishes. The president asked for power to create a new state body, the Supreme State Inspectorate, that would enforce presidential decrees around the country. This the Congress narrowly rejected, an interesting indication that even in the new, conservative mood, it could exert some restraint.

Before the Congress adjourned on the eve of the New Year, there was one more disappointment for the progressives. Gorbachev chose as his new vice president Gennadi Yanayev, fifty-three, a colorless Party *apparatchik* who had spent his career in Komsomol, trade union and Party positions. "I am a Communist to the depths of my soul," Yanayev told the Congress after Gorbachev nominated him. "My principal fight will be against political bacchanalia and vandalism—but through democratic means, not by repression."

After making offerings to the army, the Interior Ministry, and the KGB, Gorbachev had picked a vice president whose only real credential was the reassurance he would give to Communist Party traditionalists. "It's a great choice," Ligachev said with another big grin. At first the Congress was unconvinced; in a vote that embarrassed Gorbachev, Yanayev was first denied confirmation. But Gorbachev pleaded successfully for a second ballot, and this time Yanayev got the needed 50 percent of the vote.

•   •   •

The successful threat to Moldavia to step back in line proved to be a harbinger. It soon became obvious that Shevardnadze's warning was more than rhetorical. Out of sight, in a forum whose existence was not publicly known, Gorbachev and his new group of principal associates had agreed on a harsh course of action to reimpose central domination of the outlying republics. On December 18 Gorbachev had said, "The important thing . . . is not to smash each other's bones," the latest of many occasions when he had publicly insisted on the importance of avoiding violence. But as events would soon show, he had actually abandoned this central tenet of his reform politics.

Lithuania was an appropriate setting for the collapse of Gorbachev's humane approach. It had long been the most outspokenly hostile of all the republics to Moscow's rule. Vytautus Landsbergis, the single-minded, impolitic, and utterly devoted nationalist who had been elected president of "independent" Lithuania, had no patience for protocol or diplomacy. The stubborn purposefulness of this professor of musicology and founder of the Sajudis popular front had helped bring on the crisis of early 1990. That March, the newly elected republican legislature voted, 124–0, to declare independence. Then Moscow turned off the oil and gas in its first effort to force Lithuania back into line. That disagreement had been patched over, but Landsbergis's government had pledged vehemently never to sign a new Union treaty, and continued to insist on Lithuanian independence. Judging by public opinion polls and all outward indications, Landsbergis enjoyed overwhelming support from the ethnic Lithuanian population, and considerable backing as well from non-Lithuanians living in the republic.

The first hint of the impending crisis came in December 1990, when a small faction of the old Lithuanian Communist Party still loyal to Moscow organized a protest against the pro-independence government. (The bulk of the republic's Party organization had earlier declared its independence from the center and become a pro-independence faction in the parliament.) The Moscow loyalists convened a "congress of democratic forces of Lithuania" and set up a steering committee to lead a struggle against Landsbergis and his policies. This group spoke for a small fraction of the republic's population that vehemently opposed independence. Most of them were non-Lithuanians living in the larger towns and cities. Forty percent of the population of Vilnius, the capital, were Russians, Poles, or other non-Lithuanians. Lithuanians suspected that this Party group was firmly under the control of the powers in Moscow.

On January 7 the Ministry of Defense in Moscow announced that it was dispatching thousands of paratroopers to seven republics where nationalistic sentiment was strong. Their mission, the ministry said, was to enforce presidential decrees against draft dodging and to help find deserters from the army. The republics properly doubted that the mission was so narrow. In the Baltics the local army commander telephoned the premiers of the pro-independence governments in Lithuania, Latvia, and Estonia to inform them that a brigade of about six thousand paratroopers would be added to the already substantial garrisons in each of their territories. (Troops were also sent to Georgia, Armenia, Moldavia, and the Western Ukraine.)

In Lithuania the deployment coincided with a proposal from Landsbergis's premier, Kazimiera Prunskiene, a pragmatic economist, to sharply raise consumer prices in the republic—part of a local economic reform that she hoped would help build a stronger foundation for Lithuanian self-reliance.

The next day, January 8, Prunskiene was in Moscow meeting with Gorbachev, trying to persuade him that Moscow's disagreements with Lithuania could be resolved through negotiations. Gorbachev told her, she recalled later, to "go back home and restore order. Otherwise I will be obliged to do the job myself." She asked him if she could assure her countrymen that force would not be used against them. "You cannot give them any assurances that I have not given you," Gorbachev replied.

The price increases Prunskiene had announced were extremely unpopular, and the Lithuanian legislature, led by Landsbergis, quickly voted to rescind them. Prunskiene took this as a repudiation of her authority, and resigned on January 9.

Prunskiene's resignation created a political crisis; Lithuanians quickly grasped its significance. The independent newspaper *Respublika* published an editorial predicting that the crisis would be an invitation to Moscow to crack down. The timing was good, *Respublika* noted, because the world's attention was fixed on events in the Persian Gulf, where war might break out as early as January 15.

On January 10, Gorbachev sent a threatening message to the Lithuanian government and released it simultaneously to the press. It was a document written in the doublespeak of pre-Gorbachev Soviet rhetoric. It accused the Lithuanian government of "flagrant violations and deviations from the U.S.S.R. constitution and the Lithuanian Soviet Socialist Republic's constitution, the flouting of the political and social rights of citizens, and the desire to use the slogans of democracy as a cover for implementing a policy aimed at restoring a bourgeois system. . . .

"The need to escape from the present situation dictates that urgent measures be adopted," Gorbachev went on, citing the complaints of many Lithuanian citizens. "The people demand the restoration of constitutional order, reliable guarantees of security, and normal living conditions. Bereft of confidence in the policy being pursued by the current leadership, they are demanding the imposition of presidential rule."

The next morning, paratroopers accompanied by tanks and firing live ammunition seized control of the main printing plant in the republic, where all its newspapers had been printed. Troops also seized the training center of a 140-member antiterrorist squad, part of the Lithuanian police. A local Russian organization called Yedinstvo, or Unity, closely allied with the pro-Moscow Party group, forced the closure of Vilnius airport, and army troops stopped trains from entering or leaving the city. At the headquarters of the Communist Party faction loyal to Moscow, Juozas Jarmalavicius, a Party official, announced creation of a "national salvation committee" whose membership, he said, would remain secret. The new committee had been appointed, Jarmalavicius said, by the five leaders of the "congress of democratic forces" formed by his splinter group in December.

On Saturday, Jarmalavicius, speaking for the national salvation committee, said, "The process of the transfer of power in controlling the republics is under way. . . . It will not be long." That morning, Algirdas Brazauskas, a longtime Party boss who had led the Lithuanian Party's break with the center and had become a vice premier of the Lithuanian government, tried to call some of his old comrades in Moscow to head off further violence. He reached Kryuchkov, the KGB chief, who promised to convey a message to Gorbachev. No one in Moscow ever called back. The local military commandant told Brazauskas that he knew nothing about the use of troops to interrupt railroad traffic.

In Moscow on Saturday afternoon, Gorbachev's new Federation Council met. Pugo, the new minister of the interior, and Kryuchkov both condemned the Lithuanians. The meeting broke up with a call to resolve the dispute through political means.

Late Saturday night two delegations of self-described workers appeared at a Lithuanian government building and at the republic's television station. The first group carried a petition declaring that factory workers in the republic were fed up with "permanent terror [and] uncertainty about the future" and demanded that the parliament step down in favor of the national salvation committee. Members of this group smelled strongly of alcohol, according to a Lithuanian policeman who was present. Lithuanians on the scene, apparently anxious about a possible provocation, hauled off this group to interrogate its members in the parliament building. The second group wanted to complain about nationalist programming on television; it was turned away.

Just before 2:00 A.M. Sunday, a column of paratroopers accompanied by tanks attacked the television tower, firing assault rifles and clubbing Lithuanians who were trying to protect the tower. A tank broke through a human chain of about thirty people, rolling right over at least one person, who was crushed to death. Lithuanians fought back and taunted the soldiers, calling them fascists and occupiers.

Videotape made by courageous cameramen showed paratroopers both firing at civilians and clubbing them ferociously with the butts of their AK-47s. A second group of paratroopers assaulted the television studio, shooting and clubbing more Lithuanians. At both locations loudspeakers repeated a prerecorded message which declared that "all power in Lithuania" had passed to the national salvation committee. By the time the violence ended, at least fourteen Lithuanians had been killed, dozens more injured. At Vilnius's Clinical Hospital Number One, reporters saw horrific scenes: victims with crushed legs, bullet wounds, beaten faces. "My hair stood on end with some of the things I have seen tonight," said Dalia Steibliene, a doctor on duty at the hospital. At the Vilnius city morgue, Dr. Sergei Kazlovsky expressed astonishment at the number of corpses and the condition they were in. "I've seen airplane crashes, but nothing like this," he said.

Sunday night Pugo appeared on *Vremya,* the main national television news program. Suddenly, the spokesman for Gorbachev's government was a policeman with a bald pate and a round, flat, unexpressive face. He blamed Lithuanians for causing the violence, and said the army had only used its weapons after being fired upon—a contention contradicted by numerous Western reporters who witnessed the paratroopers' assaults. Pugo asserted that the incident began when those two workers' delegations were turned away by Lithuanians "with real bayonets." That led the national salvation committee to ask the military for help, Pugo said.

Tass, central television, and the principal official newspapers immediately spread the same account of the affair: Lithuania was flying out of control because the nationalists were trying to seize power; a new, legitimate authority had arisen to protect the interests of the working class—the salvation committee. Three days after the assault, central television quoted national government officials as saying they had intercepted secret, coded instructions for a Lithuanian military plot against Communist and Soviet authorities.

These were ridiculous rationalizations, reminiscent of attempts by earlier Soviet regimes to justify brutal repressions of the Hungarian and Czechoslovak revolutions in 1956 and 1968. No attempt was made to explain why the popularly elected government of Lithuania had suddenly lost its legitimacy, or to say who had recognized the mysterious members of the anonymous salvation committee as the legal authority in the republic. Gorbachev's "rule-of-law state" was in tatters.

The entire operation was a familiar Communist enterprise. Create a false pretext, arrange for a phony "invitation" to intervene, then lie profusely to obfuscate what really happened; these were all tricks from the Bolshevik handbook. At first, many shocked politicians in Moscow asked whether Gorbachev had been part of the chain of command— whether these horrible events could have occurred without his approval. But that was almost certainly wishful thinking. An operation of this magnitude, preceded by a crude warning from Gorbachev personally, executed by the army, the Ministry of the Interior, the Communist Party, and the KGB, purportedly intended to fulfill presidential decrees—this was not the work of free-lancers.

Gorbachev himself was silent until Monday, when he finally spoke publicly about the incident. First in remarks to reporters, then in a speech to the Supreme Soviet, he said he had known nothing about the violence until after it was over, "when they woke me up." The local commander had ordered the action, he explained, with full authority from the commander of the Baltic Military District. The commander acted after the national salvation committee had appealed for "protection," Gorbachev said. But he made no attempt to show disapproval of the operation or sympathy for the victims or their families. The closest he came to an apology was to remark, "We didn't want this to happen." In his speech he spoke of the "rights" and "grievances" of the national salvation committee, though he made no effort to explain its legal status, or its membership. He blamed the turmoil in Lithuania on the local government. And he refused to answer any questions from members, which infuriated a number of them.

The country did not wait to hear from Gorbachev. On the day after the violence, hundreds of thousands of citizens poured into the streets of major cities all over the country to protest. Five thousand Muscovites marched through the city calling for Gorbachev's resignation, some carrying astounding signs of protest: "Gorbachev Is the Saddam Hussein of the Baltics!" and "Down with the Executioner!" and "Down with Gorbachev the Bloody One!" Sergei Stankevich, the progressive deputy mayor of the capital, joined the march, and told Western television cameras in his excellent English that Gorbachev's reforms were now in mortal danger. He carried a banner that said, "Freedom Will Die with Us!" Yuri Afanasyev, who had found unusual words of praise for Gorbachev barely two months earlier when the president had tried to seize control of the deteriorating situation, now despaired: The killings in Vilnius "are the work of a dictatorship of reactionary circles—the generals, the KGB, the military-industrial complex, and the Communist Party chiefs," he said. "And at the head of that Party dictatorship stands the initiator of *perestroika,* Mikhail Sergeyevich Gorbachev."

Many agreed. None of Gorbachev's early progressive supporters tried to defend him. The only apologists for the killings in Vilnius were conservatives. In the days that followed Gorbachev discovered the strength of the democratic forces he had created. They fought back, led by Boris Yeltsin, who immediately flew to Riga, the capital of Latvia, where a national salvation committee had also been announced. Yeltsin denounced Gorbachev and the decision to use force. He rallied the leaders of other republics to band together and protect their rights. Within twenty-four hours of the killings, he had signed mutual assistance agreements between Russia and the three Baltic republics. He urged Soviet soldiers not to take up arms against their countrymen, and said it might be necessary to create an independent Russian army. (A furious Gorbachev dismissed that idea in an angry outburst to the Supreme Soviet.)

A week after the killings more than 100,000 people marched in Moscow in the snow to demand Gorbachev's resignation. Yeltsin decided not to attend the march out of fear for his own security, but an aide read a speech he had prepared for the occasion. It accused Gorbachev of violating his oath of office by supporting legally meaningless committees of national salvation over the elected leaders of republics. "The goals proclaimed to all the world have been cast aside," Yeltsin said. "Economic reforms are blocked, democracy is betrayed, *glasnost* is trampled. Lawlessness and *diktat* are being restored." But he remained optimistic. "It is within our power to stop the reaction. We have enough power to stop the slide of the Union government into lawlessness and the use of force, and to show that democracy is irreversible." And despite his harsh criticism, Yeltsin took care to hold out a hand to Gorbachev. "We are ready at any moment to open negotiations with the Union leaders to work out coordinated and joint actions," he said.

The independent news media also rallied to the democratic banner. Leningrad television broadcast a vivid documentary on the violence in Vilnius, including gory scenes of the beating and killing, which flatly contradicted official accounts; Leningrad's TV signal can be seen from the Baltics across northwest Russia to Moscow. *Literaturnaya Gazeta,* which had been edited for less than a year by Gorbachev's protégé Fyodor M. Burlatsky, printed the names of the fourteen victims of the Vilnius assaults on its front page, and asked in an angry editorial if the army was now running the Soviet Union. *Komsomolskaya Pravda,* the liveliest of the dailies, printed outspoken coverage and bloody photographs of the victims. The paper interviewed Vadim Bakatin, who had been replaced by Pugo as interior minister at the beginning of December. Bakatin said "the generals had no right to send in the tanks on the call of any committee, no matter how loudly it screams," and he called the events in Vilnius "an overnight putsch."

The strongest statements of disgust came from Gorbachev's earliest allies. The first appeared in *Moscow News* on the front page of the issue of the weekly devoted to the killings. The newspaper's board of directors, including some of the earliest crusaders for *glasnost* and *perestroika,* published this statement surrounded by a heavy black border:

> A regime in its death throes has taken a last-ditch stand; economic reform has been blocked, censorship of the media reinstated, brazen demagogy revived, and an open war on the republics declared. . . . The events in Lithuania can be unambiguously classified as CRIMINAL [emphasis in original]. It is a crime against one's own people to push them towards civil war. There is no need to turn the Union of fraternal nations into a fraternal cemetery to keep them together. . . . After the bloody Sunday in Vilnius, what is left of our president's favorite topics of "humane socialism," "new thinking," and "a common European home"? Virtually nothing. Lithuania is more than a tragic page in the history of the Soviet Union's internal affairs. The events in Lithuania have undermined the hopes that the entire world community cherished with respect to the Soviet Union, and violated the international accords signed on behalf of the Soviet people.
>
> The Lithuanian tragedy, however, must not fill our hearts with despair. While opposing the onslaught of dictatorship and totalitarianism, we are pinning our hopes on the leadership of other Union republics.
>
> We appeal to reporters and journalists: If you lack courage or opportunity to tell the truth, at least abstain from telling lies! Lies will fool no one anymore. They are evident today.
>
> We are counting on mass protests against the antidemocratic wave inundating the Baltic region and threatening the entire country. . . .

This extraordinary document was signed by names that have appeared often in this book, including Tengiz Abuladze, the filmmaker who created *Repentance;* Tatyana Zaslavskaya, the sociologist; Gavril Popov, the mayor of Moscow, and Sergei Stankevich, the deputy mayor; Nikolai Petrakov and Stanislav Shatalin, the two liberal economists who led the inventors of the five-hundred-day plan; Nikolai Shmelyov, the economist and novelist; Alexander Bovin, the former Andropov aide and *Izvestia* columnist; and many other famous academics, writers, and representatives of the performing arts.

Equally extraordinary was an open letter to Gorbachev from Shatalin, published in *Komsomolskaya Pravda.* Shatalin began the letter by reviewing his own biography, the trouble he had had in the Party before Gorbachev, the thrill he had felt when Gorbachev came to power, the hard work to produce the five-hundred-day plan, the exhilaration of working it out personally with Gorbachev, then his sense of devastation when it was ultimately abandoned. Shatalin wrote that "economic catastrophe is approaching, and nothing practical has been done to avoid it." And he expressed bafflement: "You, Mikhail Sergeyevich, with your intellectual potential and your comrades-in-arms beside you, were free to take the right course," but did not. "Why do you not want to take the right course—you are able to, but you don't. Why not? I will consider two possibilities. First, you do not want your people's happiness. Second, you want your people's happiness, but you are afraid that you will lose your power in the struggle to attain this goal." He opted for the second explanation: "You are afraid of losing power." This was understandable, Shatalin acknowledged: "Fear of losing power . . . is a natural instinct in a normal politician."

But Gorbachev's move to the right was the wrong way to preserve his power, Shatalin cautioned. "You are much stronger relying on the center-left bloc than you are in alliance with the right-wingers," he said—if Gorbachev could find a way to "overcome your mystically suspicious attitude toward democrats" on the left.

"It must also be kept in mind," he warned, "that we will never create an effective market economy or solve the problems . . . of our economic development without large-scale cooperation with the West," and that cooperation was jeopardized by Gorbachev's move to the right.

"Your current policy is making the West increasingly concerned."

Shatalin then gave Gorbachev a set of marching orders: He should return to the five-hundred-day plan, abandon the idea of a new Union treaty, and just let the republics cooperate as they saw fit; allow genuine republican sovereignty; give up the job of general secretary of the Communist Party, allowing the Party to break up into factions; and create a government of national reconciliation consisting of representatives from all ethnic groups and classes, with intelligent technocrats to run it. "If, Mikhail Sergeyevich, you fail to understand all this, then it is your duty to the people to resign at once. . . . A politician should not stay on beyond the point when people have pity for him."

Gorbachev's own children were ready to devour him—and he appeared ready to devour them. In the days after Bloody Sunday he lost his temper several times, most dramatically and pathetically in a speech to the Supreme Soviet less than a week after the killings. His angry remarks suggested that the *Moscow News* statement had provoked him. He sharply criticized that newspaper, then suggested that "in connection with the period we're in, a period of important decisions, we need constructive dialogue and cooperation. . . . We could take a decision to suspend the press law for these months and the Supreme Soviet could assure full objectivity" by assuming direct responsibility for all of the news media. This suggestion to suspend the relatively new law guaranteeing freedom of the press evoked a furious response from liberal members, and Gorbachev retreated from his proposal. Instead he offered a vague resolution suggesting that the leadership of the parliament examine "measures on ensuring objectivity" in the press, which carried easily.

Whether that was a sign of significant independence in the relatively conservative Supreme Soviet or just a bump on the road to a new dictatorship remained to be seen. A struggle had begun between the traditional powers in Soviet society—now, ironically, represented by Gorbachev—and the new democratic forces he had earlier unleashed. Both were testing their strength in the revolutionary new circumstances that nearly six years of *perestroika* had created.

Obviously Gorbachev was a changed man. Some thought he had been intimidated by the right-wingers in the army, KGB, and police. "They just terrified him," one deputy told me in January. "They made him fear for his own life." I was more convinced by Shatalin's analysis —that Gorbachev had confronted the possibility of losing his own power to the reformers he had created, and decided he didn't want to let this happen. "There was always a question of which he wanted more—to put a program into effect, or to hold power," one of my wisest Moscow informants observed in January 1991. The same man had made a very similar remark in the spring of 1988. "Now [in 1991] it appears he is most interested in personal power," he said. Of course, Gorbachev's conviction that he had to hold the entire Union together clearly limited his freedom of action.

Judging by his drawn appearance, his public temper tantrums, and his inability to take responsibility or apologize for the violence in Vilnius and then, on January 20, in Riga, where four more citizens were killed by troops, Gorbachev was under enormous strain. There were persistent rumors that he had serious health problems; diabetes, some said, or arteriosclerosis.

He was truly alone now. On January 21, the anniversary of Lenin's death, Gorbachev joined Pugo, Kryuchkov, and Yazov to lay a wreath at Lenin's mausoleum on Red Square. In that grim company, on that rather sad mission, Gorbachev began a new phase of his leadership that held none of the promise of the first years of his revolution.

CHAPTER ELEVEN

THE FINAL ACT

Later Gorbachev would acknowledge that he saw a constant need to keep maneuvering, to zig to the left and zag to the right repeatedly in order to keep his own balance atop the rickety structure of Soviet power. "I wanted to gain time by making tactical moves," he wrote in September 1991. "I had to outmaneuver them," he told an interviewer in December of the same year. But the early months of 1991 were no time for such candor. In those difficult days Gorbachev was saying little, and what he did say was calculated to please his new allies among the hardliners on his right.

In hindsight it is obvious that the protests at home and abroad against the crackdown in Lithuania and Latvia had moved Gorbachev. Outwardly he stuck with his new conservative allies, but he did not make good on the implicit logic of the Baltic repressions. The national salvation committees in whose name the crackdowns had been conducted quietly disappeared. The elected governments in Lithuania and Latvia remained in power (though they remained terrorized for months afterward). No new salvation committees appeared elsewhere in the country, although the hardliners had expected to see more of them.

The significance of these non-events was not so clear at the time, however. And in the wake of the crackdown in the Baltic states, it was easy to accept an ominous interpretation of events that did occur, including the announcement on January 25 that the army and police would soon begin joint patrols on the streets of major Soviet cities to insure public order. The parliament of the Russian Republic called on Gorbachev to rescind this order, which smacked of the militarization of the country. The joint patrols were actively opposed by the governments in five other republics, but they began anyway on February 1 in Moscow and many other cities.

Though Gorbachev did not give them all they were hoping for, the hardliners were emboldened by the new atmosphere. "Even the way they walked had changed," recalled Alexander Yakovlev later. "They were strong, arrogant, with smiles on their faces. They looked like victors." At the end of January, Ivan Polozkov, the leader of the new Russian Communist Party, told a Central Committee plenum: "Now is it clear to everyone that the *perestroika* reforms designed in 1985 and begun by the Party and the people to renew socialism . . . have failed?" Other conservatives openly denounced Gorbachev's foreign policies, accusing him of squandering the Soviet empire and strengthening the Western powers. In a bizarre interview published on February 12, Valentin Pavlov, a conservative whom Gorbachev had named his new premier a month earlier, said he had successfully foiled a conspiracy involving Western and Soviet banks to oust Gorbachev and restore capitalism in the Soviet Union. The conservatives' new outspokenness provided a kind of political background noise that added to the unease among reformers.

Neither reformers nor conservatives were making any headway. Sensing the stalemate, Gorbachev decided to seek a fresh source of legitimacy for his policies and himself. On February 6 he announced that a national referendum would be held March 17 and urged citizens to vote Yes on this ballot question: "Do you consider it necessary to preserve the Union of Soviet Socialist Republics as a renewed federation of equal Soviet republics, in which the rights and freedoms of people of any nationality will be fully guaranteed?" The wording of the question implied a test of sentiment on whether the republics and nationalities should have more independence, but Gorbachev's real purpose was to win support for the continued existence of a Soviet Union. A Yes vote was needed, Gorbachev said, to preserve the country's status as a superpower.

The liberals were critical of the referendum, but both its vague wording and the traditional Russian fear of anarchy helped Gorbachev sell the idea, as even the critics acknowledged. Yeltsin and his allies decided to try to use the referendum for their own purposes by adding several questions to the ballot in the Russian Republic. The most important of these offered Russians a chance to support the direct election of a president of Russia. If such an election were held, Yeltsin would be the overwhelming favorite to win it.

With this prospect in the offing, Yeltsin decided to sharpen the political struggle. In a rare appearance on Soviet television on February 19 (the conservatives running television did not want to give him publicity), Yeltsin called on Gorbachev to resign. Gorbachev had "deceived the people," Yeltsin declared, by trying to hold on to power and preserve the old centralized system. He should step aside and turn over power to the Federation Council composed of the leaders of the republics. "I've taken my stand," Yeltsin said. "Now you must all choose," he continued, speaking to the television audience. "Whom will you follow?"

This was a bold, perhaps intemperate move, but it did mobilize the country's politicians. Conservatives responded furiously. The Supreme Soviet of the Union censured Yeltsin for his remarks. Hardliners accused Yeltsin of calling for a civil war, of "criminal" behavior, and of pursuing uncontrolled personal ambition. In the Russian parliament, hardline Communists called for Yeltsin's impeachment. An "emergency session" of the Russian Republic's Congress of People's Deputies was called for March 28 to consider Yeltsin's fate. All this brought Yeltsin's supporters into the streets. Another huge rally— 100,000 people at least—was staged in Moscow to support reform and denounce the conservatives.

At the end of February Gorbachev responded to Yeltsin's call for his resignation by accusing his rival of trying to seize power unconstitutionally. Gorbachev said he and Yeltsin were following "two different political lines," and he aligned himself with the old establishment. "In fact, all these 'democrats' are anti-Communist in nature," Gorbachev said. "They reject all propositions by the Communist Party. They want to call the Party a criminal organization and put it on trial. It's ridiculous to try to put on trial more than sixteen million people [Party members]."

Ten days later Yeltsin replied. "Let's declare war on the leadership of the country, which has led us into a quagmire," he told a Moscow gathering of reformers. He accused Gorbachev of deceiving the country with promises of economic and political reform. "Now we must open our eyes wide and realize it was a lie. And we must take our own path, not the path of *perestroika* of recent years." Yeltsin predicted, prophetically, that 1991 would be a decisive year. "Either they [the Communist hardliners] will strangle the democrats, or we will survive and win."

In the same speech Yeltsin made clear his own opposition to the referendum on preserving the Union. Gorbachev's decision to publish a draft of a new Union treaty reinforced Yeltsin's view. The draft treaty did give added autonomy to the republics, but it also retained ultimate central control, which was anathema to Yeltsin as to most of the new republican leaders.

Huge pro-Yeltsin rallies were held all over Russia the day after that speech. A crowd of more than 300,000 turned out in Moscow, chanting its desire for Gorbachev to "Resign! Resign!" Speakers at the rallies urged a No vote in the union referendum scheduled for a week later on March 17, coupled with a Yes to the proposition that Russia elect a president by popular vote.

When the votes were counted, both national leaders could claim a victory. Gorbachev's ambiguous proposal to preserve a Union carried with about three-fourths of the vote, though in the big cities about 50 percent opposed it. Yeltsin won a huge victory on the issue of a direct election for the Russian presidency. The stage was now set for a confrontation.

•   •   •

The occasion for confrontation had already been scheduled—the March 28 emergency session of the Congress of People's Deputies of the Russian Republic, called by Party hardliners to remove Yeltsin from his post as chairman of the Congress, the basis of his power as leader of Russia. On March 25 the Soviet government announced a three-week ban on demonstrations in Moscow, an obvious attempt to keep Yeltsin's supporters out of the streets during the emergency meeting of the Congress. Gorbachev raised the ante by putting the Moscow city police under the command of the national Ministry of Internal Affairs, not pro-Yeltsin Moscow city officials. But the democrats proceeded with plans for a massive demonstration in Moscow on the 28th.

One minister in the Pavlov government told an acquaintance of mine in Moscow that the original plan was to use force to prevent the demonstration from occurring. Only when General Boris Gromov, the deputy minister of interior, told the council of ministers that he had no intention of ordering the use of force was that idea abandoned, according to this account. If true, this story would make the conservative Gromov a genuine hero of the events that followed.

On the eve of the demonstration Vladimir Kryuchkov, the head of the KGB, Interior Minister Boris Pugo, and Gennadi Yanayev, Gorbachev's vice president, personally warned leaders of Democratic Russia, the opposition group organizing the rally, that they would be held responsible for any disorder on the 28th. Gorbachev received information that the democrats planned violence. "I had a report," Gorbachev said, "about a meeting of the democrats. They were shouting, 'Out! Out! Storm the Kremlin!' . . . I had it on paper."

Alexander Yakovlev, still in touch with Gorbachev but much less influential than he once was, later recalled his efforts to convince the president not to overreact. Yakovlev suspected that Gorbachev's conservative aides were feeding him disinformation. "I tried to reason with Gorbachev, but he said, 'They've got ropes and hooks to scale the Kremlin walls.' " It was, Yakovlev said, "just like in some English film about the Middle Ages! You throw up hooks and climb!" Yakovlev warned Gorbachev of the consequences if violence did occur. "What if someone gets killed?" he recalled asking the president. "Just imagine the funeral. All Moscow will turn out. Every factory will stop work."

But Gorbachev went ahead with a massive deployment of soldiers and police—50,000 men, according to Pugo. Their mission was to prevent demonstrators from reaching the center of Moscow and the neighborhood of the Kremlin, where the Russian Congress would meet.

The 28th began well for Yeltsin when the Congress voted (by a majority of just one vote) to suspend Gorbachev's decree putting the Moscow police under Pugo's command. The Congress sent one of Yeltsin's key aides to Gorbachev to negotiate withdrawal of the troops from the center of Moscow. Meanwhile, at least 100,000 pro-Yeltsin demonstrators (and perhaps many more—it was impossible to make any systematic count) succeeded in gathering in two of the city's squares, each about half a mile from the Kremlin. One group did break through police lines and move toward the Kremlin, but they were pushed back forcibly. For the most part the demonstrations remained good-natured and peaceful. It was a powerful display of public sentiment, not least because all the participants had overcome great personal anxiety to take part in the show of support for Yeltsin. On the morning of the 28th many doubted that bloodshed could be avoided; by that evening there was great celebrating that the democrats had sent their message, and at no cost in blood.

Gorbachev told the envoy sent by the Congress that he would order the troops withdrawn, but only after the demonstrators had dispersed voluntarily. They did disperse that night, and the next day the troops and police who had occupied the center of the city were nearly all gone.

• • •

March 28 was a critical turning point. Gorbachev, foolishly, had let his hardline associates persuade him to make a show of force to try to intimidate Yeltsin's supporters. Instead the president made a spectacle of his own impotence. Yet he had further alienated the reformers. Questioned about this eight months later, Gorbachev had no explanation for his choice: "Well, what can I say? Perhaps my feelings got in the way. I took the wrong decision. I can see that now."

It was a wrong decision that emboldened Yeltsin and his followers. The very next day Yeltsin called on Gorbachev to convene a round-table conference of Communists and leaders of other parties to agree on a new political structure for the country. Several days after that the Russian Congress not only rejected hardliners' proposals to remove Yeltsin but voted him extensive new executive powers to cope with the continuing economic crisis. Worsening labor troubles, especially a growing coal miners' strike by at least 300,000 men, had worked to Yeltsin's advantage among delegates who thought he could persuade workers to stay on their jobs. The Congress scheduled the first popular election for president of Russia for June 12. Yeltsin added about fifty votes to his base of support during the two-week session, several dozen of them from a new faction that called itself Communists for Democracy—former Party loyalists who decided to vote with Yeltsin at key moments.

Demonstrating the political intuition that served him so well, Yeltsin quickly understood that he had bested Gorbachev and moved at once to extend a hand to the president. In place of his previous demands that Gorbachev resign and his suggestion that the country wage war on its government, Yeltsin suddenly adopted a more reasonable line. Closing the emergency session of the Congress, he said,

"There are no obstacles now that can get in the way of cooperation between Russia and the Union." Now the issue was renegotiating the legal relationship between the center and the republics. New structures of power became the democrats' rallying cry.

Yeltsin's triumph left the political situation tense and confused. He had led the reformers back from the depths of their January depression, but they were still in a decidedly weakened position. Gorbachev's unsteady flirtation with the conservatives had satisfied neither them nor him. The president had behaved appallingly in January, permitting the ugly crackdown in Lithuania and Latvia, but now he would not abandon what he seemed to regard as bedrock positions. Speaking to a gathering of hardline Party men in the military in early April, Gorbachev rejected calls for "decisive measures" to protect the state against radical reformers. "If 'decisiveness' is intended to mean a return to old methods, to suppression and violence, then I must tell you firmly, I won't resort to that," he said. It was just that attitude which infuriated the conservatives. Which side was the president on anyway?

Over the next several weeks Gorbachev offered an unexpected answer to that question. As always, he was not content to ride with events. He wanted to reclaim his position as a genuine leader, even as spokesmen for left and right called on him to give up and resign. He undertook a series of ploys directed both at the conservatives on his right and the reformers on his left.

First he announced plans to introduce a new "anticrisis program." Ostensibly this was a conservative plan. Gorbachev called for a ban on all strikes and demanded that the republics meet their economic commitments to the center and to each other. "Our statehood and federation are endangered," Gorbachev said in a speech to republican leaders. "The economy is coming apart. The institutions of power are paralyzed. The very foundations of our lives are endangered. . . . We must put aside our feuds and prevent the country from sliding into catastrophe." Initially the plan appeared to calm hardliners, persuading some members of the conservative Soyuz faction of parliamentarians to abandon their call for a special Congress of People's Deputies session to remove Gorbachev from power.

But labor unrest intensified, and Gorbachev showed no sign of actually cracking down. By late April Soyuz deputies were circulating a proposal to call a special Congress, not to oust Gorbachev but to impose a state of emergency on the country. The conservatives had been talking about a state of emergency for months; it smacked of tough discipline and enhanced power for the authorities to control the country, although the specifics were always vague.

Gorbachev stuck by the anticrisis plan a little longer. Valentin Pavlov introduced the specifics on April 22. He called for maintenance of central authority to guide the economy toward the free market but was vague on most key issues. The plan was immediately criticized from all points on the political spectrum. Nursultan Nazarbayev, the leader of the Republic of Kazakhstan and a moderate, said such an "incompetent and vague" scheme "will only prolong the tortures of the people."

But Gorbachev was playing a double game. Even as Pavlov presented the anticrisis package, Gorbachev was organizing a secret meeting of the leaders of nine republics (only nine would agree to participate) to discuss a redistribution of power in the country—in other words, to discuss the new political structures Yeltsin had been urging. Gorbachev organized that secret meeting knowing that he faced another rebellion from Party conservatives, some of whom spoke openly of removing him from the Party leadership at a Central Committee plenum on April 24 and 25. This must have been one of the most nerve-racking moments of Gorbachev's years in power.

In those tense days Gorbachev acknowledged to his aides that it was again time to change course. "Gorbachev said he could no longer preserve the old Soviet Union," recalled Georgi Shakhnazarov, one of his assistants. "He had introduced democracy. Now democracy required a new relationship between the center and the republics."

This was a far cry from the thinking that had swayed Gorbachev during the previous fall and winter. Then he had talked himself into the view that the country was moving to the right. He had accepted the arguments of the old-line Party men around him that there had to be a show of force to bring the more rebellious republics back into line. By spring he must have realized that he had been wrong on both counts.

The country was not moving to the right, at least not if that meant it wanted a crackdown from the center to restore order and the old ways of doing business. That was obvious by April from the ongoing strikes by workers all over the country, and from the continued political vitality of the reformers led by Yeltsin. Gorbachev had allowed (or encouraged, it was never clear which) a crackdown on the news media, including a purge of liberals from Soviet television, but this had not silenced the liberal journalists, who continued to press their causes. The most popular of the liberal television shows, "Vzglyad," or "View," had been taken off the air in Moscow, but its producers continued to make programs on videotape, and many provincial broadcast centers continued to show this underground version of the program.

The proponents of the turn to the right at the end of 1990 had convinced themselves that a show of strength would bring the country up short, restore discipline, and rout the democrats. But the subsequent months showed quite a different result. A society that had been transformed by five years of *glasnost* simply could not revert to its former self. By April the country was in turmoil, with no prospect of settling down. As Gorbachev put it later, "We felt the earth shake and the roof give way. We had to save the whole building."

The nine republican leaders who were willing to negotiate secretly on the future of the Union came to a villa in Novo-Ogarevo outside Moscow on April 23. The last to agree to participate was Yeltsin, who was on holiday at the time and thought he would be perceived as caving in to Gorbachev if he took part. Aides convinced him otherwise.

After ten long hours of haggling, the nine republican leaders plus Gorbachev—the "nine plus one," as they became known—agreed to sign a statement "on urgent measures to stabilize the situation in the country and overcome the crisis." It was published, to the astonishment of nearly everyone, in the newspapers of April 24, the very day the Central Committee was to convene to hear calls for Gorbachev's ouster. The document called for completion of "a new [Union] treaty among sovereign states" and the drafting of a new constitution, to be followed by popular elections. Meanwhile the nine participating republics agreed to take steps to improve the economic situation, including making promised deliveries and enforcing law and order. Later it was revealed that the participants also agreed secretly to allow the laws of the republics to supersede Soviet law on all internal matters, and to allow the republics to come up with their own economic reform programs.

For Yeltsin and the other republican leaders who took part, the most important line in the published document was the very last, which said, "The meeting's participants realize that all these measures to stabilize the situation and overcome the crisis are inconceivable without a fundamental enhancement of the role of the Union republics."

The most significant passage in this agreement lay elsewhere, however. It was the acknowledgment of "the right of Latvia, Lithuania, Estonia, Moldavia, Georgia, and Armenia to decide for themselves" whether to sign the new Union treaty. Gorbachev had finally abandoned his crusade to hold together the country he had inherited. This was a historic turn.

The nine-plus-one agreement was signed late Tuesday, April 23; on Wednesday morning Gorbachev faced his irate critics in the Central Committee. He acknowledged that a number of Party committees had passed resolutions "demanding the resignation of the general secretary" and said these critics deserved an answer. He gave them an emotional one. Revealingly, he compared himself to Lenin at the time the New Economic Policy (NEP) was introduced in 1921. Deteriorating economic conditions had pushed Lenin to adopt the NEP, a partial return to free enterprise, and many Bolshevik purists responded angrily. Some quit the Party. Gorbachev recounted this story, noting that "unfortunately, Lenin's ideas about a . . . new approach to socialism were not successfully implemented at that time." Instead Stalin's dictatorship arose, "with all the well-known consequences."

It had taken six years, but the Party's reactionaries had finally abandoned all pretext of supporting either Gorbachev or his *perestroika*. The huge Moscow City Party Committee called on Gorbachev to resign. Ivan Polozkov, general secretary of the Russian Party organization, said, "Mikhail Sergeyevich, you have simply taken your hands off the wheel. The whole government machine is effectively leaderless."

"It was an open attack on me," Gorbachev recalled later, "to remove me as president." He lost his temper.

The speech that set Gorbachev off was delivered by an obscure figure named A. P. Snigach, first secretary of the Kakhovka City Party Committee in the Ukraine. The excerpts of his remarks published in *Pravda* probably do not do them justice. "Communists and working people . . . are troubled by the great number of mistakes, and by the indecisiveness and halfheartedness of the actions of authorities at all levels, particularly the president," Snigach said. "We appeal to the president to do his duty and establish order."

Vladimir Shcherbakov, the deputy premier, described what happened to television producer Norma Percy in a later interview: "Gorbachev lost his temper and demanded the floor. The chairman said, 'Later.' Gorbachev said, 'No, now.' It was the shortest speech I'd heard from Gorbachev—less than a minute."

Moscow News subsequently published Gorbachev's remarks:

> Okay, that's enough, now I'll answer everyone. I have to admit that about 70 percent of those who have taken the floor have declared that the popularity and authority of the general secretary have dropped to almost nil. I think that neither the man nor the Party can remain in such a situation. This would be criminal.
>
> I suggest that debate cease and that the problem of the general secretary be dealt with—as well as who will take his place until the next [Party] Congress. Also, who would suit the two, three, or four parties in this hall. [This was a sarcastic reference to the many disagreeing factions into which the Party had divided.]
>
> For my part I want to say that the interests of the Party and state are no less dear to me than they are to those who have appeared in the political arena in the last two weeks. I resign.

By *Pravda*'s account "there was confusion in the hall." A recess was called. Gorbachev's allies on the Central Committee quickly regrouped. They drafted a petition accusing the president's critics of plotting a coup and threatened to leave the Party if Gorbachev was allowed to resign. This document was signed by seventy-two members, including many of those recognized as most intelligent and competent. Finally the conservatives had to confront the prospect of trying to preserve the Party and survive personally without Gorbachev's leadership and protection. Gorbachev himself stayed outside the hall.

"He was pacing alone up and down the corridor," Shcherbakov remembered. " 'Just look what they're doing,' he said with emotion. 'How dare they?' "

In the end they didn't dare. After hurried consultations, a motion was offered removing the question of Gorbachev's resignation from the agenda. It carried by a vote of 322 to 13, with 14 abstentions.

•   •   •

Yet again Gorbachev had routed the conservatives. He was buoyed by the experience. Six weeks of relative calm followed that Central Committee plenum—a welcome break after months of frenzied activity. Western journalists in Moscow began to write that the father of *glasnost* and *perestroika* had returned to the path of reform. The anxieties of Western governments that Gorbachev was turning away from his own policies began to subside.

Yeltsin did his part to foster the improved mood. He and Gorbachev worked out a deal to turn over control of the coal mines on Russian territory to Yeltsin's republican government, a gesture that helped Yeltsin settle the long-festering miners' strike in May. The two men spoke supportively of each other in public. A new television station under the control of the Russian government—and thus beyond the reach of the conservatives, who had taken over Soviet television late in 1990—began broadcasting for six hours every day. Gorbachev and Yeltsin together attended a memorial ceremony for Andrei Sakharov.

In early June Gorbachev finally got to Oslo to accept the Nobel Prize he had been awarded the previous October. The ceremony had initially been scheduled for December, a tense time in Soviet politics. Gorbachev had decided not to go to Norway to avoid an angry reaction at home—where the awarding of the prize provoked as much puzzlement as praise—and perhaps also to avoid a hostile reception that could have awaited him in Oslo after his turn to the right that fall. But by June the Yeltsin-Gorbachev rapprochement and attendant revival of reform put Gorbachev back in an appropriate position to accept the Nobel Prize.

He gave a long and thoughtful speech in Oslo on June 5. It was candid in some respects, though he offered no real explanation of his flirtation with repression in the months just past. But he confessed his distress. "Our democracy is being born in pain," he said. "For centuries, all the country's problems were finally resolved by violent means. All this has left an almost indelible mark on our entire 'political culture,' if the term is at all appropriate in this case. . . . When our society was given freedom it could not recognize itself, for it had lived too long, as it were, 'behind the looking glass.' Contradictions and vices rose to the surface, and even blood has been shed, although we have been able to avoid a bloodbath." And he confessed some of his own shortcomings. "In the beginning we imprudently generated great expectations, without taking into account the fact that it takes time for people to realize that all have to live and work differently, to stop habitually expecting that a new life would be given from above. . . . I did not imagine how immense were our problems and difficulties. I believe no one at that time [1985, when he came to power] could foresee or predict them."

* * *

By the time he gave that speech, Gorbachev was something of a sideshow in his own country. The center ring was occupied by Yeltsin and his spirited campaign for the presidency of Russia. By now Yeltsin was an accomplished performer on the stump. He traveled across much of the country, promising voters at huge rallies that he would improve their standard of living and fight for the sovereignty of Russia in a looser Union. It was a crowd-pleasing campaign; Yeltsin never dwelled on the difficulties that lay ahead. He particularly courted soldiers and their families—his running mate was an army general, Alexander Rutskoi—and he sought repeatedly to reassure men in uniform that as president he would protect their interests.

His principal opponent was Nikolai Ryzhkov, the former premier, who was the favorite of the Party establishment. Vadim Bakatin, the moderate whom Gorbachev had fired the previous fall from his job as minister of interior to please the conservatives, ran as a Gorbachev loyalist with Party blessing. Party activists encouraged all comers to run, calculating that a proliferation of candidates had a better chance of depriving Yeltsin of the 50 percent vote he needed to avoid a runoff election. Some of the Party's organs, especially *Pravda,* campaigned heavy-handedly against Yeltsin, but this time Gorbachev himself stayed out of the fray. When the votes were counted Yeltsin had won an easy victory. He received more than 57 percent of the votes cast; Ryzhkov got less than 18 percent. Vladimir Zhirinovsky, a rabid Russian nationalist who had no national reputation before the election, came third with 7 percent, or about six million votes. For the first time in its history of more than a thousand years, Russia had a leader chosen freely by her people.

Gorbachev quickly acknowledged the significance of the event by telephoning his congratulations to Yeltsin. It was more than a personal triumph. The election results suggested that the people of Russia were ready to put the Communist experiment behind them. This was most obvious in Leningrad, whose citizens voted overwhelmingly to restore the city's prerevolutionary name, St. Petersburg. Gorbachev's salute to Yeltsin's victory was self-interested. Now that there was one truly legitimate national leader—a man whose name was Yeltsin, not Gorbachev—the creator of the new Soviet order had no choice but to turn for support to the man of the hour. If Gorbachev was to have any future, he had to find ways to use Yeltsin's legitimacy for his own purposes.

Gorbachev had signaled his new intent when he invited the republican leaders to the nine-plus-one negotiations. These had continued even during the Russian presidential campaign. The participants had agreed in early June to drop the word "Socialist" from the name of their country, creating a new Union of Sovereign States in place of the old U.S.S.R. Just five days after Yeltsin's election, the nine plus one initialed a nearly complete draft of a Union treaty that vastly enhanced the powers of the republics, and markedly diminished the importance of the central government and its institutions.

The traditionalists who led those institutions understood what was happening. One of the most outspoken was Anatoli Lukyanov, Gorbachev's comrade since Moscow State University, who was chairman of the Supreme Soviet. He complained openly that the nine-plus-one talks were undermining the authority of his parliament, since the republican leaders and Gorbachev were deciding matters that should fall into the purview of the Supreme Soviet.

Lukyanov's anxieties were shared by all the leaders of the traditional power centers to whom Gorbachev had turned for support in the fall of 1990. Yazov, Kryuchkov, Pugo, Pavlov, and the rest were dependent for their power on the preservation of the old-style Union and its state and Party institutions. The vast military-industrial complex of factories, laboratories, and military institutions understood that its claim on the country's resources would be unlikely to survive if the individual republics got control of the national budget—one of their principal aims in the nine-plus-one talks. The conservatives tipped their hand on the morning of June 17, the very day the nine plus one would later initial a draft of a new Union treaty that undercut their position drastically.

Lukyanov told his deputy before the session convened at 10:00 A.M. that Premier Pavlov would be making an unusual request for new, emergency powers. When the premier reached the podium, he told the legislators that Gorbachev was simply overworked and had too many responsibilities. "If we push all questions onto him, he simply would not be in any condition to attend to them all, even if there were forty-eight hours in his working day," Pavlov said. "In my opinion, there is a lot the president simply cannot do. . . . Some matters are none of the president's business." This was the rationale for his request that the premier and his ministers be given control over the state bank, the fall harvest, and most other economic decisions. Reformers in the Supreme Soviet quickly understood what was afoot. "This is an attempt at a constitutional coup," said Ella Pamfilova, a member of the legislature.

It was well orchestrated. Hardline members of the Soyuz faction of deputies lined up to endorse Pavlov's proposal. "We must support the premier's request for powers," said Colonel Viktor Alksnis, one of the most notorious anti-Gorbachev conservatives. "He and his cabinet will stop the breakup of the Soviet Union." Questioned from the floor, Pavlov acknowledged that he was operating independently of Gorbachev. Asked if the president had endorsed the idea of giving him new powers, Pavlov replied, "I'll be completely honest. We've never discussed it."

On the second day of debate Soyuz deputies suggested holding a secret session, closed to the press and public, to give Yazov, Pugo, and Kryuchkov an opportunity to address the Supreme Soviet confidentially. All three spoke in alarmist terms. According to a partial transcript later published by the conservative newspaper *Sovetskaya Rossiya,* Yazov described the collapse of the military draft and other difficulties, and said, "Soon we will not have any armed forces." Pugo described deteriorating conditions in the country and the spread of arms through the population. Then Kryuchkov played the CIA card:

"The KGB has reliable information of a CIA plot," he told the deputies. "They [the CIA] have been subverting senior officials of the Soviet state. . . . Their agents now occupy key posts in the economy and government of the U.S.S.R." His information, he said, was based on a hitherto secret document describing American intelligence activities transmitted in 1977 by Yuri Andropov, then head of the KGB, to the Party's Central Committee. "Our fatherland is on the brink of catastrophe," Kryuchkov told the Supreme Soviet. "Unless urgent measures are taken our worst fears will become reality."

The conservatives pressed for a speedy vote on Pavlov's proposal after the closed session, but Gorbachev requested a delay. Finally on Friday, the 21st, he came to the hall himself to criticize Pavlov's plan. "Comrade Pavlov should have explained himself," Gorbachev said. "What he said was muddled, and I told him so." Gorbachev gave a staunch defense of himself and his plans for the future, to which Pavlov could offer only a limp response. During a break Gorbachev came into the lobby with a big grin, surrounded by Yazov, Kryuchkov, and Pugo. "The coup is over!" he said, laughing. The others neither spoke nor smiled.

Gorbachev's grin was for public consumption. Back stage, in Lukyanov's rooms off the floor of the Supreme Soviet, Gorbachev vented his anger. Ivan Laptev, the former editor of *Izvestia* who was deputy chairman of the Supreme Soviet, later recalled what happened when he walked into a meeting of Gorbachev, Yazov, Pugo, Kryuchkov, Pavlov, and Lukyanov:

"I could see that Gorbachev had raked them over the coals. They looked uncomfortable and kept trying to change the subject. Gorbachev kept at them. He told Pavlov and Lukyanov, 'Don't you dare try such tricks again behind my back.' "

Once again Gorbachev carried the day. After he spoke, the Supreme Soviet voted 262–24 to drop all further discussion of Pavlov's proposals for transferring power. It was another humiliation for the conservatives.

•   •   •

Pavlov's ploy was a distraction for Gorbachev. The negotiations for a new Union treaty had become his main game. The treaty offered a way to preserve a role for himself in the face of Yeltsin's powerful popular mandate and the strengthening local nationalisms that were splitting the country apart. The nine-plus-one negotiations had distracted Gorbachev from the intrigues of his own government and of the Party.

Nevertheless the intrigues continued. Shevardnadze quit the Communist Party in July after the Party's disciplinary control commission began investigations of both him and Yakovlev. They and others announced plans to create a new social democratic party, the Movement for Democratic Reforms, clearly an alternative to the Communist Party. Gorbachev welcomed its creation.

On July 10 Yeltsin was installed as Russia's president. It was a grand occasion, held in the Palace of Congresses, the architectural horror that Khrushchev had built on the grounds of the Kremlin. This is the familiar auditorium whose stage had long been dominated by a gigantic Lenin portrait—until now. For Yeltsin's inauguration Lenin and all the trappings of communism were removed. Russian Orthodox priests, rabbis, and other religious leaders took part in the ceremony. "Great Russia is rising from its knees," Yeltsin proclaimed. "We will turn it into a prosperous, democratic, peaceful, genuinely sovereign, law-abiding state." Mikhail Gorbachev, the man who had created Yeltsin as a national figure, then feuded with him, and finally been bested by him (not that he yet acknowledged this), was a guest in the hall. He offered the new president warm congratulations.

A week later Gorbachev was in London meeting with the leaders of the Group of Seven, or G-7 industrial powers. He had spent weeks maneuvering his way into that meeting; the United States and Britain at first had both opposed inviting him, but the Germans and French pressed his case, finally successfully. Winning new economic help from the West was Gorbachev's latest idea for addressing his overriding domestic crisis. The meeting in London was only a partial success. It led to special associate membership in the International Monetary Fund for the Soviet Union, which seemed only to mean that I.M.F. experts would make recommendations for improving the Soviet economy. No new aid was promised.

But the meeting was substantive enough to alarm some of Gorbachev's colleagues in Moscow. General Dmitri Yazov, the defense minister, later said that he and other conservative officials were upset that Gorbachev hadn't told them what he would say or propose at the London meetings, as if he had something to hide.

Soon after the G-7 meeting Yeltsin signed a decree forbidding "political activity" in all offices and enterprises in Russia—effectively a ban on Communist Party cells in the workplace, a frontal challenge to the Party's role in society.

This was provocative timing. The Central Committee was about to meet to consider Gorbachev's latest effort to persuade the Party to adopt a liberal new program for the new era. Yeltsin was deliberately outraging Party officials five days before this gathering. But he did it on purpose, or so he said in an interview at the end of July. His decree "was meant to thwart the plans of the reactionary forces who were planning a vicious attack on Mikhail Gorbachev" when the Central Committee met, he said. "I opened a second front, so to speak, and forestalled the blow."

Three days after Yeltsin's decree, on July 23, the conservative newspaper *Sovetskaya Rossiya*—the paper that printed Nina Andreyeva's article in the spring of 1988—published an extraordinary document called "A Word to the People." It actually consisted of about two thousand angry words denouncing the Gorbachev era and all its achievements. "How is it that we have let people come to power who do not love their country, who kowtow to foreign patrons and seek advice and blessing abroad?" the authors asked. It included an undisguised call for "all of us, young and old, [to] wake up, come to our senses, rise in defense of our country and say No to those who have invaded it and are destroying it." And it was signed by two members of the Soviet government, General Boris Gromov, Pugo's deputy in the Ministry of Interior, and General Valentin Varennikov, deputy minister of defense. Ten other signatories, including writers and political activists, added their names to the declaration.*

A day after the publication of that provocative statement—and the day before the Central Committee was to meet—Gorbachev announced that he and his nine interlocutors, the republican leaders, had agreed on a text of the new Union treaty. A few details were left to be worked out, he said, but a marathon session of negotiating had brought agreement on the main points. The timing of his announcement was widely interpreted as an effort to strengthen his hand before confronting the Party's conservatives, by reminding them that only he had found a way to keep the country—or most of it—together.

The plenum was bizarre. Gorbachev introduced the new Party program, which simply abandoned all traditional Communist positions. Its outlines had been leaked to the press in advance, and many commentators predicted that it would provoke, finally, a definitive split in the Party. The new program condemned "the crimes of Stalinism," arguing that Stalin had taken the Party and country off the correct Leninist path as soon as he took power in 1928. It endorsed private property, private farming, and retail trade. It called for political pluralism, tolerance of religion, and the rule of law. Yet the old guard did not fight this heresy. The new program was approved overwhelmingly after two days of debate. No strong voices were raised against it. This seemed strange at the time and was widely interpreted as a sign that the conservatives had simply given up and could no longer fight Gorbachev on any front. Subsequent events cast some doubt on that interpretation.

•   •   •

Despite Gorbachev's public assurance a few days earlier, he still did not have full agreement on the Union treaty, particularly from Yeltsin. Nazarbayev, the Kazakh leader, cast himself in the role of mediator. On the evening of the 29th of July, the three men met at Gorbachev's huge country house outside Moscow.

The problem was an old one. Despite all that had happened since the previous fall, Gorbachev was still surrounded by Party conservatives whom Yeltsin and his people considered enemies of reform.

---

* Two of the signatories turned up as members of the Committee on the State of Emergency that presided over the attempted coup in August: Vasili Starodubtsev, chairman of the Farmers' Union, and Alexander Tizyakov, president of the Association of State Enterprises.

The military-industrial complex still enjoyed its privileged status. How could Yeltsin go into this new arrangement with Gorbachev if Kryuchkov, Yazov, Pugo, and the others still held important positions? How could he trust Gorbachev's personal staff of old Party bureaucrats?

Thanks to the resourceful reporting of Norma Percy, Angus Macqueen, and Masha Slonim, who produced remarkable documentary films on these events for the BBC and the Discovery Channel in the United States, we have firsthand accounts from Gorbachev, Nazarbayev, and Yeltsin of what happened the night of July 29. "We spent several hours at it," Gorbachev recalled during a recorded interview three and a half months later. "First we worked at a table like this, then we had dinner, then we got to work again."

"I asked Yeltsin to speak first," Nazarbayev recalled. "He said Gorbachev's people were against the free market and against the Union treaty. I asked him which individuals were getting in the way. I said Lukyanov was against the treaty. Yeltsin named Kryuchkov and Yazov. I added Pavlov. It was obvious these people had to be dealt with."

"These people knew the treaty would be the death of them," Yeltsin recalled. "They would be made redundant."

Gorbachev remembered saying, "We would have to tackle these matters as soon as the treaty was signed."

Nazarbayev remembered that Gorbachev said, " 'Everything will have to be reorganized, including the army and the KGB. Then we can take action.' But he defended Lukyanov and Yanayev [and said] Kryuchkov wasn't as bad as we thought."

Evidently this was an unusually blunt conversation for these three men. Gorbachev recalled: "Yeltsin became concerned that no one should know about this. These were sensitive matters, matters best kept to ourselves."

Nazarbayev said, "Yeltsin got up and went out on the balcony." Gorbachev also remembered that "He went out. I was sitting facing the balcony."

Nazarbayev asked Yeltsin, " 'Why did you go out?' He said, 'To see if anyone is eavesdropping.' "

"Nazarbayev and I had a laugh," Gorbachev recalled. "But now, looking back, we see Yeltsin was right. Someone was very interested in what we were saying. It really happened."

Nazarbayev concurred. "I was amazed to hear later that the KGB had us recorded. They even bugged Gorbachev."

"The man who did it was Plekhanov, my chief of security," Gorbachev said. "I suspect his reports brought things to a head."

.   .   .

At that moment, by coincidence, I was in Moscow for my first visit in three years. I'd come on the occasion of President Bush's first official trip to the Soviet Union, and I spent a week talking to officials and old acquaintances about the state of their country. I had no idea at the time that things were coming to a head. Nor did any of the people I talked to.

But it was clear that I had walked into great turmoil and confusion —into a genuine revolution. I wrote an article for *The Washington Post* at the end of that week in Moscow which began with the observation that "in the midst of a true revolution, it isn't easy to describe the surroundings. Revolutions don't offer signposts or maps or timetables. The new Russian revolution is destroying the old Soviet Union, but revolutionary destruction is chaotic and confusing. It is easy to see what is happening but impossible to see what will happen next."

I asked everyone I met for their evaluations of the curious manifestations of opposition to Gorbachev, from Pavlov's power-grab and the alarmist speeches by Kryuchkov, Pugo, and Yazov, to the "Word to the People." The latter was dismissed as idle chatter by Alexander Gelman, a playwright who had become a political activist. "Better a letter than a coup," he said.

None of the officials I talked with expressed the slightest alarm. Three of Gorbachev's close associates, Andrei Grachev, Georgi Shakhnazarov, and Yevgeni Primakov, dismissed the opponents as talkers who would do nothing. The conservative critics "are part of the reality Gorbachev is working in," Grachev said. Shakhnazarov said that "of course there is some discontent in military circles, especially in higher echelons, but I'm sure that isn't a reason to be afraid of a coup d'état or something like that." Shakhnazarov said that "nobody dares challenge" the emerging new power structure being negotiated by the nine plus one.

Yeltsin's people were similarly sanguine about the conservatives. Economic problems were their great concern. Gennadi Burbulis, Yeltsin's principal aide, expressed satisfaction that the new Union treaty would give the republics the leverage they needed to choke off the military-industrial complex. They would do it through their new control over the national budget, Burbulis explained.

My old friends nearly all agreed that the danger of a right-wing coup—something they had all feared since the early days of Gorbachev—had passed.* The bad guys were too divided among themselves, said one, and they understood that they had no popular following. Everyone I saw feared the coming winter, food shortages, and economic catastrophe, but not a coup d'état.

In a notebook I wrote that the assurances from all corners that there was nothing to fear struck me as "part of the eerie sense that no one is coming to grips with anything here—not with the economic crisis, or with the Pavlov government, or the Union treaty, or anything else, especially real economic reform." That observation and the realization that this was a period of utterly unpredictable revolutionary change was as close as I came to a sense of what was about to happen.

On August 2, after President Bush had signed the Strategic Arms Reduction Treaty and left for home, Gorbachev went on television to announce that the Union treaty would be ready for signing on August 20. Russia, Kazakhstan, and Uzbekistan would sign it that day, he said, and he expressed confidence that the others would soon follow suit. Later he recalled the exhilaration which accompanied that announcement. "It was a great feeling. It was like conquering Everest. We'd done it." He then went on holiday to his luxurious villa at Cape Foros in the Crimea.

On August 15, with Gorbachev out of town, the Communist Party's Control Commission issued a public recommendation that Alexander Yakovlev be expelled from the Party. The commission had been "investigating" Yakovlev's role in the new Movement for Democratic Reforms which clearly angered Party elders. Before any action could be taken on the recommendation, Yakovlev announced on August 16 that he was quitting the Party. The architect of *glasnost* issued a bitter statement to the press: "The truth is that the Party leadership, contradicting its own declarations, is ridding itself of the democratic wing of the Party and is preparing for social revenge, and for a Party and state coup."

The coup began two days later. For months afterward I wondered just what Yakovlev had known when he issued that statement. Then in mid-November Yakovlev came to Washington, and we invited him

---

* One friend, V. V. Ivanov, director of the foreign language library in Moscow, was emphatically not part of this optimistic school of thought. He predicted in late July that some kind of coup backed by the military was still very likely—as he had thought it was for a long time.

to the *Post* for breakfast. What did he know when he predicted a coup?

"Actually, I knew nothing," he answered. "I just felt it in the air."

Yakovlev knew nothing of the plans for the coup, but he felt he knew the men who executed it exceedingly well. That, he explained, was the basis of his confident prediction. "I just knew everybody on that team. I worked closely with many of them in the Politburo and the Central Committee. I knew their moods very well, their positions. . . . There was nothing unexpected about that coup on the 19th of August except the date."

Yakovlev not only knew the coup plotters well, he had repeatedly warned Gorbachev not to trust them—one reason why Yakovlev lost influence with the president at the end of 1990. After the coup Yakovlev said he had repeatedly warned Gorbachev of the danger he faced from these men—after the killings in Vilnius, at the time of the March 28 demonstrations in Moscow, and in two letters written in the summer of 1991. Just before the coup, Yakovlev said, he had put it to Gorbachev bluntly: "The people you have around you are rotten. Please, finally, understand this."

Yakovlev favored making a break with the conservative Party barons and building stronger alliances with the emerging democratic forces. Gorbachev disagreed. "He always told me, 'Strategically you are right, but tactically you are mistaken,'" Yakovlev said.

Yakovlev's warnings were hardly the only ones Gorbachev heard. Shevardnadze had electrified the country with his prediction that dictatorship was about to return in his unexpected resignation speech in December 1990. Virtually all of the reformers considered Kryuchkov, Pugo, Pavlov, Yazov, and the others enemies—not just opponents, but old-line Party men determined to preserve Party power and the old system. Suspicions of their motives were openly discussed in political debate and in the press. Politicians and others complained that Gorbachev was surrounded by conservative Party men who distorted the information the president received to discredit the democrats. Especially after the crackdown in Lithuania in January, Kryuchkov and Pugo were widely described as architects of that clandestine attempt to reverse the course of democratization.

Even President Bush joined the chorus warning Gorbachev of danger. On June 20, 1991, he conveyed a detailed account of an impending coup to Gorbachev—a coup involving the same people who led the August putsch. (Moscow Mayor Gavril Popov had passed the information to the Americans.) Nazarbayev and Yeltsin spoke of the need to remove those men from office in their bugged conversation with Gorbachev on July 29, just three weeks before the coup. Even the form of the coup—declaring a state of emergency as a way of suspending democratic procedures and reestablishing traditional discipline— had been openly promoted by the Soyuz faction of Supreme Soviet deputies for many months.

An investigation conducted by the KGB after the putsch found that Kryuchkov began plotting a coup in November 1990. With the help of a few trusted aides, he compiled a careful plan of action that included names of people to be arrested and the phones to be tapped.

Yazov told the prosecutors investigating the putsch—according to an account of his interrogation leaked to *Der Spiegel,* the German newsmagazine—that he had been meeting for months with a group of senior officials later involved in the coup. They met to share their common dismay that Gorbachev was distancing himself from the Party while the country was falling apart. Often their discussions centered on Gorbachev's dealings with foreigners; Yazov and his comrades didn't like the way Gorbachev was making their country more dependent on the West, particularly the United States. They were especially unhappy with the president's hat-in-hand trip to the G-7 leaders in London in July. That group, Yazov said, included Kryuchkov; Valeri Boldin, Gorbachev's chief of staff; and Oleg Baklanov, who had been Central Committee secretary in charge of the military-industrial complex. All joined the conspiracy that led to the August coup; Kryuchkov and Baklanov were probably the putsch's principal architects. In their conversations, Yazov said, "gradually, the idea ripened that Gorbachev had exhausted himself as a statesman." (However, Yazov denied plotting the actual coup itself in advance; he said he learned about it just a day ahead of time.)

The coup was a fools' folly virtually from the moment it began. Its perpetrators were *apparatchiks,* not politicians, and they hadn't a clue how to take control of the country. They could only try to maneuver the Moscow-based institutions they knew well into position to support their putsch. Initially they succeeded in this, largely because the Russians who worked in those institutions—the army, the police, the KGB, the Party, and government—had long been psychologically prepared for a coup of some kind. They knew how to obey orders, including orders that contradicted previous orders.

We may never learn the whole story of the putsch. In fact there isn't a single story but a multitude of parallel stories. It may not be possible to sort them out retrospectively. Gorbachev's own part in the drama, especially its early stages, is one of these stories, and I'm afraid it may remain a mystery. A telephone log maintained by the KGB that kept track of Gorbachev's calls from Cape Foros showed that he and Kryuchkov exchanged four telephone calls on the morning of August 18, beginning at 7:00 A.M. That morning Gorbachev also spoke to Vice President Gennadi Yanayev, Premier Pavlov, and Politburo member Oleg Shenin—all participants in the coup plot.* Shenin was one of the conspirators who came to Cape Foros a few hours later to confront Gorbachev with their demands that he step aside in favor of a new State Committee on the State of Emergency.†

The only account we have of that confrontation is Gorbachev's own, which he gave to a press conference when he returned to Moscow on August 22. He described himself as firm and outspoken in rejecting the suggestion that he turn power over to Yanayev as vice president or simply resign. But he also acknowledged that he volunteered to call into session the Supreme Soviet or the Congress of People's Deputies. "If there are doubts among parts of the leadership, then let us gather, let us discuss it," Gorbachev quoted himself as saying. Was that an offer to cut a deal? I doubt it, but we can't be sure.

It was ironic that Gorbachev should meet his fate at Cape Foros. Khrushchev was vacationing not far from there in 1964 when his comrades decided to oust him—the event Gorbachev had cited anxiously to colleagues since 1985 when he worried about his own fate. One of his worries, of course, was that resentful Party hacks would eventually turn against him and his reforms to protect their power, privileges, and comfortable lives. Now these would-be coup makers—led by Boldin, who had been the president's principal assistant since 1985—confronted Gorbachev in the palatial villa in the Crimea that he had built for himself at enormous public expense. It was one of three such palaces he had built, according to Yeltsin—there was another in Moscow and a third just outside the capital. This one was an ugly modernistic structure of poured concrete, a hodgepodge of abrupt arches

---

* Stuart H. Loory of the Cable News Network acquired a copy of the KGB phone log and generously shared it with me. It is described in the book *Seven Days that Shook the World,* CNN's excellent account of the coup written by Loory and Ann Imse.

† Another member of the delegation—the rudest and most aggressive, by Gorbachev's account—was General Valentin Varennikov, the deputy minister of defense who had signed the "Word to the People" manifesto published in *Sovetskaya Rossiya* a month earlier.

under a steep yellow-tile roof. It must have suited the czarist streak in Gorbachev's personality.

By all indications Gorbachev conducted himself admirably once he realized that he was the victim of a putsch. On the first morning of his captivity he told Anatoli Chernayev, an aide who was with him in Cape Foros, about the way he had reacted to the delegation that confronted him the previous day. "You know, Anatoli, when I was talking to these people, my face did not give a single twitch. I was absolutely calm. I am still calm. I am convinced that I am right. I am also convinced that this is a roll of the dice. They will never achieve this! It's a criminal adventure!" (This is Chernayev's recollection, and it certainly sounds like Gorbachev's self-confidence.)

Later that day Gorbachev watched Yanayev's pitiable press conference, when the vice president—flanked by other members of the emergency committee—announced with trembling hands that although Gorbachev had to step aside because he was too ill to govern now, he hoped "my friend" would be able to return to the presidency. Gorbachev decided to demonstrate at least to the guards assigned to hold him under house arrest that this was a lie, and he took a vigorous walk on the beach. He decided that the household should only eat food that was already in the house before the putsch began. In the middle of the night after the first day of the putsch, Gorbachev recorded a strongly worded message to his countrymen and the world on his son-in-law's camcorder. "On the basis of a lie, an anticonstitutional coup has been carried out," he said. He and his entourage then tried unsuccessfully to find a way to smuggle the videotape out of the villa to the outside world. Gorbachev's staff did find a working shortwave radio which allowed him to follow events in Moscow through the BBC and Voice of America.

When Kryuchkov, Yazov, Baklanov, Lukyanov, and Vladimir Ivashko, the deputy general secretary of the Party, flew back to Gorbachev's villa when it was evident on Wednesday, August 21, that the coup was crumbling,* he refused even to see the first three ringleaders. He did meet briefly with Lukyanov, his old classmate and comrade. According to Chernayev, who witnessed the scene, Lukyanov tried to tell Gorbachev that he had worked against the putsch.

---

* There is no good explanation for why they flew to Cape Foros. For Yazov, at least, it was apparently a desire to seek forgiveness from Gorbachev. "I wanted to sink into the ground," he told investigators after his arrest. "I felt eternally guilty for what we had done to Gorbachev and Raisa."

"Listen," Gorbachev shot back, "we've known each other for forty years. Don't try to make a fool out of me! You should have thrown yourself in front of the guns! You delayed [calling a session of] the Supreme Soviet for six days, a week! What are you telling me, you did this, you did that! The very next day you should have summoned the Supreme Soviet if you're on the side of legality and the president."

But once he had refused to sanction the state of emergency, Gorbachev had no real part in the main drama of the putsch. That was played out in Moscow by other actors.

•   •   •

As it turned out, the coup was Gorbachev's undoing, but not at all in the way the plotters had hoped. It was his undoing because it became a demonstration of the way the country had been transformed by years of *glasnost* and *perestroika,* and because that transformation —once it was recognized by a large part of the population—left no real place for the sort of benign czar that Gorbachev wanted to be. The coup revealed a country—or more accurately, a collection of countries that were ready to fend for themselves without further guidance from the man who initiated the revolution that had set them free.

The plotters themselves were the first to demonstrate how the country had changed when they decided to stage a "legal" coup. Their first declaration said Vice President Yanayev had assumed the duties of president "in accordance with Article 127, clause 7, of the Soviet Constitution due to Mikhail Gorbachev's inability to perform his duties for health reasons." The constitutional provision they cited concerns the incapacitation of the president. The plotters wanted legal cover.

Equally revealing, the principal plotters had to lie to their comrades in order to win support for the coup. At a late-night meeting just hours before the state of emergency was declared, Kryuchkov and General Yuri S. Plekhanov, head of Kremlin security, told a group including Premier Pavlov, Yazov, Yanayev, and others that the KGB had information "that a military coup would be attempted in the next few hours, that gangs of thugs were already gathering around a whole series of buildings. They detailed the weapons they had, including mortars. They showed four lists of people who were to be liquidated immediately. So, they said, we've only got a few hours in which to act. If the news of Gorbachev's illness comes out, it will be impossible to keep the country under control." (This is the account of Vladimir

Shcherbakov, deputy premier to Pavlov, recalling what Pavlov told him about this meeting.)

Pavlov then repeated essentially the same story to the ministers of his government, who decided to support the putsch. Part of the story was that all ministers were on the lists of people these mythical rebels were planning to assassinate.

Evidently Kryuchkov had no confidence he could win over these men with truthful arguments about the need to stop Gorbachev from signing the Union treaty and undermining all of their power. Instead, apparently, he felt he had to scare them with threats to their own security. Shcherbakov said later he heard Pavlov "several times" during the short-lived putsch ask Kryuchkov personally "whether the militants had been seized . . . and whether their weapons had been confiscated."

In other words, even members of the Pavlov cabinet, mostly conservatives long associated with the military-industrial complex, could not be counted on as natural allies of a coup against Gorbachev. And when a coup was launched, not even Kryuchkov could organize the sort of violent action that would have been necessary to enforce the putsch's control. There was just no appetite for spilling blood.

Much more compelling evidence of how the society had changed was provided by the chain of events that unhinged the putsch. From Boris Yeltsin, to the commander of the air force, to the deputy director of Soviet television, to twenty-year-old soldiers driving armored personnel carriers through Moscow, to citizens who flooded the streets of many cities in protest, hundreds of thousands of individuals stood up against the coup. They demonstrated qualities of courage and independence that flew in the face of the traditional clichés portraying Russians as sheeplike followers.

Yeltsin can fairly be called the most heroic of these individuals because he so deliberately risked his own life for the cause. As the single most legitimate political leader in the country, he might have fled or hidden when the coup began. He might well have stayed in his bunker in the basement of the headquarters of the Russian government, the "White House" on the Moscow River, once he got there. But instead he marched out of the White House and stood atop a friendly tank to declare the coup illegal and urge all military personnel to disobey the orders of its organizers. This was an act of political genius as well as courage, for it created an indelible image of defiance that undermined the coup throughout the world.

Amazingly, that image was also seen inside the Soviet Union. This happened because a correspondent for Soviet television named Vladimir Medvedev included film of Yeltsin on the tank in a report he prepared for the main evening newscast that night; and because his boss, Valentin Lazutkin, the deputy director of Soviet television, had calculated that the coup would fail and decided to let Medvedev's report go on the air; and because a KGB colonel named Vladimir, who had been stationed at the television studio as a censor, also decided for his own unstated reasons to wink at what the other two were doing.*

At the Ministry of Defense the air force commander, General Yevgeni Shaposhnikov, decided he would have no part in the coup, despite the important role being played by his boss, Yazov. The commanders of Alpha Group, a highly trained team of KGB commandos, decided out of patriotism or fear or both to ignore orders to storm the White House. Thousands of ordinary citizens—at least 12,000 according to one participant—made their way to the White House to offer themselves up as human shields for Yeltsin and his colleagues. No doubt because of their presence many of the troops deployed in the area made personal decisions not to obey any orders that could result in civilian deaths—and they announced their decisions to inquiring citizens and reporters.

Although Yeltsin demanded from the outset that Gorbachev be set free and permitted to speak to the nation, the president's name was rarely invoked by those who resisted the putsch. The heroism on display during those three days of August was not inspired by love for Gorbachev, or a sense that heroism was needed to save him. No, the heroism was directed at saving what Gorbachev had made possible— the beginnings of a free, normal country.

Around the country the new elected bodies stood up for Yeltsin against the coup. In Leningrad Mayor Anatoli Sobchak led a demonstration of perhaps 200,000 people against the putsch. The Russian parliament rushed into session and became a continuing forum for the democrats. The new people and new institutions created by Gorbachev's reforms proved resilient and courageous.

The voice of the protesters who came into the streets sounded like that of Rima Tikhonovna, forty-six: "The coup has sounded an alarm.

---

* The story of what happened that Monday night at Soviet television is reported in *Seven Days that Shook the World.*

All of us had complaints about Mikhail Sergeyevich, but we can't let a bunch of hoods think they can take all power into their hands. We won't allow it." When the coup failed, many in the streets understood the event as evidence of the birth of a new Russia. "The people had been beaten down," said Vladimir Bayarkin, thirty-two, a computer programmer. "But now the people have awakened to democracy and showed their initiative." Some in the crowds were sharply critical of Gorbachev, blaming him for allowing the coup to happen by remaining loyal to the men who ran it. Others were more sympathetic. Olga Lenskaya, a thirty-year-old engineer, offered the thought that during the three days of the putsch the country had outgrown Gorbachev: "We suffered for three days without him, and because of his faults. Now we don't need him."

•   •   •

Gorbachev returned to Moscow in the early hours of Thursday, August 22. It might have been a dramatic political moment, particularly if he had driven directly to the White House to thank the crowds there for saving him, and to personally embrace Yeltsin as the hero of the resistance. He would also have benefited enormously from a speedy apology for his own errors in protecting and promoting the key plotters. But that chance was lost. Instead Gorbachev made a brief statement to television cameras at the airport which seemed to be devoted primarily to himself, not to the historic events the country had just survived. He did "congratulate our Soviet people for having a feeling of self-esteem" and expressed his "respect" for Yeltsin, but talked mostly about how he had been treated and what he had said to the plotters. "What did they do to the president and his family? What they attempted to do to the president and his family in these days, when for seventy-two hours they surrounded him with troops on sea and on land, [they] wanted to break his willpower. But they lost."

Then Gorbachev went home to bed. The next day he gave a press conference which he began with a detailed account of his experiences since the plotters' delegation first showed up at his villa on Sunday afternoon. Again he put much more emphasis on his personal experience than on the trauma the country had just been through. After a long account about himself, Gorbachev did acknowledge the contribution of Yeltsin and others to the resistance. He acknowledged the error of trusting the men who plotted the coup. But he also made a point of defending the Party, saying it could still be "a vital force for *perestroika."* He claimed that senior Party officials had eventually made "a correct decision" to oppose the putsch (two days later he had to admit this was not true). "I will fight to the end for the renewal of this Party," he declared. And he repeated his old mantra: "I am a convinced adherent of the socialist idea." It was a long-winded performance all too reminiscent of the old "Baltoon" who earned a reputation for talking too much.

On that first day back in Moscow Gorbachev made three quick appointments to replace the heads of the Ministry of Defense, Ministry of Interior, and the KGB. In all three cases he picked deputies to their discredited predecessors, all of whom turned out to have been involved in the coup too. They were all replaced within twenty-four hours. The spectacle of Gorbachev picking the wrong people once again was painful.

Thursday night, shortly after Gorbachev had spoken out in defense of the Party, crowds of Muscovites flooded into Dzerzhinsky Square in front of the Lubyanka, the headquarters of the KGB. The crowd wanted to tear down the statue of Felix Dzerzhinsky, the Polish Communist who was Lenin's first chief of secret police. Mayor Popov brought city workers in to do the job professionally, and this symbol of Communist oppression was suddenly gone from its place of honor.

The next day, Friday, Gorbachev had to confront his new place in Soviet society. He went to the Supreme Soviet of the Russian Republic for a joint appearance with Yeltsin and was greeted on his arrival by protesters shouting, "Resign! Resign!" Inside the hall members posed aggressive, even hostile questions. Gorbachev was pressed to ban the "criminal enterprise" known as the Communist Party. He was told in strong terms that henceforth the republics would be running the country. Yeltsin toyed with him. First he showed him the notes made by one of the lone members of the Soviet government who had refused to embrace the coup—notes of the meeting of Pavlov's Council of Ministers where nearly all of them backed the putsch. "I haven't read this yet," Gorbachev said, apparently trying to brush Yeltsin off.

"Go ahead," Yeltsin said sternly, waving a finger at Gorbachev, "read it now!"

Gorbachev did so. He had to read the names of minister after minister who had turned against him to support the putsch. "This whole government must resign," Gorbachev said finally. "I must say this has been a great drama for me, a severe trial."

At another point while they were both at the podium, Yeltsin suddenly interrupted Gorbachev and said, "Now for a bit of relaxation, let me sign a decree banning the activity of the Russian Communist Party."

Gorbachev stammered Yeltsin's name: "Boris Nikolayevich . . . Boris Nikolayevich . . . I think you'll be—I don't know what you're signing there." He said it would be undemocratic to ban the entire Party for the offenses of a few.

Yeltsin paid no heed and put his signature to the document. "There, it's been signed!" he said to cheers from the deputies. It was nearly four years since Gorbachev had subjected Yeltsin to brutal public denunciation before the old Moscow Party committee. How dramatically the wheel of history had turned!

Gorbachev spent hours the next morning debating with himself and colleagues whether or not to abandon the Party by resigning as general secretary. Yakovlev was with him. "I said, 'This is a meaningless conversation,' " Yakovlev recalled later. " 'We're discussing something that no longer exists. It's like trying to offer tea to a corpse and discussing how to do it.' " Angry crowds were gathering around the headquarters of the Central Committee on *Staraya Ploshchad,* or Old Square, threatening to ransack the building. In fact there was no way to avoid closing the Party down altogether.

"For me it is a personal tragedy," Gorbachev said later. "I put all my energy into reforming the Party. I wanted to make it truly democratic, a Party for the people and not the governing élite." Instead, late Saturday, he resigned as general secretary and ordered the state to seize all Party property.*

The great Communist experiment—begun by a tiny band of radicals in the early years of the century, empowered with unexpected victory in 1917, able to reshape the modern world before stumbling under the weight of its own failures—had come to an end.

.   .   .

Despite humiliation at the hands of Yeltsin and the collapse of the system over which he had presided, Gorbachev did not give up. Initially this suited Yeltsin and his people. They made clear their intention to renegotiate the Union treaty to give still more autonomy to

---

* The state acquired Party records showing that Gorbachev had personally authorized the transfer of millions of dollars to Western Communist Parties. Russian officials launched a criminal investigation into these transfers.

the republics, but they seemed to want to preserve a role for Gorbachev as a ceremonial figurehead who could preside over a common defense and perhaps several other governmental functions to be shared by the republics.

But there could be no restoration of his old status. In fact it had been permanently undermined by the election results in June, when Yeltsin had achieved a degree of legitimacy that had eluded Gorbachev. Now his relative weakness was aggravated by the widespread perception that the coup, staged by his people, was in large measure his fault—that Gorbachev's stubborn loyalty to thugs who didn't deserve it brought the country to the edge of an abyss from which it might never have returned.

"Who chose the officials [who staged the coup]? He did," Yeltsin said in a televised interview three days after the putsch failed. "Who confirmed them? He did. He was betrayed by his closest people. Almost all the cabinet members. They betrayed him. He chose them himself."

"Gorbachev trusted those people whom he should not have trusted, and he did not trust those who were ultimately prepared to fight for his freedom," said Nikolai Vorontsov, the environment minister and sole member of Pavlov's government to denounce the coup.

Shevardnadze said Gorbachev could have prevented the coup if he had respected the many warning signals that came from the conservatives in June and July and stayed put in Moscow. "He had no right in such a difficult situation to go on vacation and leave the capital."

Gorbachev struggled with these accusations, and over time developed a rationale for what had happened that seemed to give him comfort. His explanation was complex, and not entirely consistent from conversation to conversation.

First he embraced the argument that the coup failed primarily because the country had been transformed by his *glasnost* and *perestroika*. "Society was completely changed," he wrote in his brief and unrevealing book, *The August Coup*. "It had breathed the air of freedom and no one could take that away from it." Second he had built fundamentally new relationships with the West that resulted in the Western governments' open opposition to the coup—after "some hesitations . . . at the outset," Gorbachev acknowledged.* "The interac-

---

* President Bush and President François Mitterrand of France initially indicated willingness to work with the Committee on the State of Emergency, then changed their tune when they heard Yeltsin's defiant opposition to it.

tion of these two factors—the democratic achievements of *perestroika* and the new relationship with the world outside—predetermined the plotters' defeat," Gorbachev wrote.

Elaborating subsequently, Gorbachev argued that his six-and-a-half-year high-wire act was absolutely necessary to bring the country to the point where it could resist the August coup. Speaking of the old Party apparatus, he said in an interview in December 1991, "Had I left it, we would not have gotten this far." He meant that the Party conservatives would have squelched reform without Gorbachev standing in their way at the head of the Party. In another interview that month he added, "I tried to drag things out as long as I could, I delayed to the last so that no one could halt the country which had surged ahead."

In one interview Gorbachev argued that he knew all along what would someday happen. "Do you think I did not know that the Party's conservative circles, which had united with the military-industrial complex, would make a strike? I knew, and I kept them beside me. . . . But they procrastinated too, also afraid that the people would not follow them, and they waited for the people's discontent. . . . I will tell you: if they had acted twelve or eighteen months earlier the way they did in August, it would have come off. It is worth realizing this."

But a few weeks before he said that, he offered quite a different interpretation in an interview with Yuri Shchekochikhin of *Literaturnaya Gazeta*. The interviewer observed that "everyone had a feeling" there would be some kind of coup attempt.

Gorbachev replied, "But after all, we had all done our jobs. I believed I had fulfilled my mission; society had changed, so that any attempted coup was doomed. And therefore what I thought was this: If those who intend to perpetrate a coup have even a grain of common sense, even in the interests of saving their own skins, they would only have to calculate five or six moves ahead to realize that they would be disgraced and routed. . . . I certainly did not think they would go as far as a putsch."

The greatest difficulty for Gorbachev was trying to explain away the trust he had put in people who clearly didn't deserve it—people he'd been warned against repeatedly by his closest allies. He did acknowledge he had been mistaken in some of his personnel decisions, but his acknowledgments were curt. They lacked the quality of a genuine apology or confession. In fact he seemed genuinely puzzled by the fact that he was betrayed by people he really thought he could trust.

Kryuchkov was the most interesting example: "For me, to a significant extent, what mattered, apart from what I knew myself, was that Andropov had supported him," Gorbachev told Shchekochikhin.

"And Andropov's opinion was very important to you?" the interviewer asked.

"For all Andropov's shortcomings—and I don't want to idealize him, his ideological views and his involvement in combating dissidence, all this was clear to me—he was a man of great intellect and was resolutely determined against corruption. I was associated with him for a long time. I would not say we had a very close relationship, but I knew him well, and we used to meet regularly. And that is why I took on Kryuchkov, of whom Andropov had a good opinion."

This was the voice of a Party man, one who definitely was, as he himself said over and over again, a product of his times. Of course Kryuchkov was not his only embarrassment. Boldin, Gorbachev's principal aide since he became leader, his doorkeeper and right-hand man, was also a member of the plot. His oldest friend in the government, Lukyanov, was at least a collaborator, and in all likelihood an early and full participant too. These were also Party men, products like Gorbachev of life in the *apparat,* careful and deliberate men who knew how to hide their feelings and mislead their superiors. After the coup Gorbachev had to acknowledge that these people had systematically misled him, fed him disinformation while burying true facts they disapproved of. This was hardly news to people like Yakovlev and Shevardnadze, who had seen this happening for years, but it was a painful admission for Gorbachev, who always prided himself on his ability to make shrewd political calculations. How shrewd could he be if he was calculating on the basis of disinformation?

Gorbachev had countless opportunities to bring new people, and new kinds of people, into his inner circle, but he never did so. Just a year before the coup he seemed on the verge of joining what he himself called the "center-left," the real reformers. But then he backed away, rejected the 500-day plan, and fell into the embrace of Kryuchkov, Pugo, and Yazov. Those were calculated moves too. The calculations may have been reactions to crude threats from the military and its allies in industry, the police, and the Party, but they were rational calculations nevertheless. Gorbachev had a choice in the summer and fall of 1990, and he decided then to turn away from the reformers and toward the conservative power centers.

"At some point I misjudged the situation," he admitted in one of his farewell interviews. "For all the importance of strategy, it is important in politics to make the right decision at the right moment. It is like a battle in war. . . . I should have forged a strong common front with the democrats. . . . I should have realized that earlier, in August 1990. I should have looked for some form of cooperation then, held a round-table discussion or some other meeting. I missed that opportunity and paid dearly for it."

That was the second-guessing of a politician on his way out of power. Of course he might have saved himself in August 1990—or in 1989, if he had let the people elect him president, and thus won a popular mandate. But his alternative analysis might have been right too—if he had made an alliance with the democrats in 1990, a coup might have come much sooner and succeeded. We will never know. But the choice he did make cut him off from the democrats his reforms had spawned. As events would demonstrate, the break was irreparable.

•   •   •

The first week after the coup was a bad one for Gorbachev, but he quickly reestablished his political footing and reentered the fray. He refused to see the putsch and its aftermath as a signal that his own part was being written out of the drama. He intended to carry on.

For nearly four months Gorbachev resisted the tide that was running against him. At first he simply presumed the continued importance of his role, even as Yeltsin signed a steady stream of decrees transferring what used to be Soviet responsibilities to the Russian Republic. Gorbachev took control of what turned out to be the last meeting of the Congress of People's Deputies in early September, and pushed through changes in the constitution to create new governmental institutions for a looser Union. After that he missed no opportunity to speak out for the Union, to argue that its survival would serve the best interests of all.

He also adjusted his foreign policy to the new circumstances. He announced the withdrawal of nearly all Soviet troops from Cuba, then matched and exceeded a new offer from President Bush for unilateral reductions of nuclear weapons below levels previously agreed to. He established diplomatic relations with Israel, then traveled to Madrid at the end of October to participate in the opening of the Mideast peace talks. In November he even persuaded Eduard Shevardnadze to return to his old post as foreign minister of the Soviet Union.

But the Soviet Union was fading away. Right after the coup, the individual republics began to declare their total sovereignty and in-

dependence, one after another. Though initially there were indications that a loose new union might be achievable, a series of events in
the fall began to suggest otherwise. The Ukraine loomed as the biggest
obstacle to agreement. Nationalist sentiment seemed to strengthen
there every month. Cooperation with Gorbachev and the Union came
to be seen as a means of perpetuating the bad old arrangements that
had always allowed Russians to dominate Ukrainians. On December 1
more than 90 percent of all citizens of the Ukraine voted for complete
independence. Even ethnic Russians living in the republic voted overwhelmingly in favor of a sovereign Ukraine. Leonid Kravchuk was
elected president on the same day, and he concluded he had no choice
but to refuse to join a new Union. Even Yeltsin saw the inevitability
of Ukrainian independence; his Russian government formally recognized it on December 3.

A week after the Ukrainian vote, Yeltsin, Kravchuk, and Stansilav
Shushkevich, leader of the republic that had renamed itself Belarus,
met in a hunting lodge outside Minsk. There they agreed to dissolve
the Soviet Union and create a new Commonwealth of Independent
States. They envisioned a loose confederation that would coordinate
economic, foreign, energy, transportation, and military policies, but
with virtually no central bureaucracy, and no relinquishing of republican sovereignty. They invited all other members of the old Soviet
empire to join.

Gorbachev was pointedly excluded from the weekend meeting
where the Commonwealth was formed. He wasn't even told what had
happened until after Yeltsin had telephoned President Bush to explain the Commonwealth to him. Gorbachev's initial reaction was
anger, but in a matter of days he seemed to realize that the idea was
going to catch on. The leaders of the Central Asian republics quickly
decided that they would join, assuring that the new arrangement
would indeed come into being. On December 17 Yeltsin and Gorbachev met at the Kremlin and agreed to dissolve the U.S.S.R. by the
end of the year.

Ever the actor, Gorbachev struggled to end his presidency with
dignity. His farewell interviews were statesmanlike, and he showed no
outward sign of bitterness. But he was angry. "For me they have
poisoned the air," he confided to one reporter. "They have humiliated
me." It was, fittingly, an entirely unprecedented moment. Gorbachev
was not just a politician losing his job but a leader losing his country.
First he had presided over the demise of Soviet communism, which

went up in smoke in the aftermath of the August coup. Now he watched the nation itself disappear.

December 25 was his last day in office. There was little business to be done, but Gorbachev wanted to bid his countrymen a proper farewell. He did so with a remarkable speech to the nation that deserves to be quoted at some length:

> . . . Fate had it that when I found myself at the head of the state, it was already clear that all was not well in the land. We have plenty of everything: land, oil and gas, other natural riches, and God gave us lots of intelligence and talent. Yet we lived much worse than developed countries, and kept falling farther and farther behind them.
>
> The reason for this could already be seen. The society was suffocating in the vise of the bureaucratic-command system, doomed to serve ideology and bear the terrible burden of the arms race. It had reached the limit of its possibilities. All attempts at partial reform, and there had been many, had been defeated, one after another. The country was losing perspective. We could not go on living like that. Everything had to be changed radically.
>
> That is why not once—not once—have I regretted that I did not take advantage of the post of general secretary to rule like a czar for several years. I considered that idea irresponsible and immoral. I realized that to start reforms on a grand scale in a society like ours was a most difficult and even risky endeavor. But even today I am convinced of the historic correctness of the democratic reforms that were started in the spring of 1985.
>
> The process of renovating the country and of making radical changes in the world community turned out to be far more complicated than could have been anticipated. However, what has been done ought to be given its due. This society has acquired freedom, liberated itself politically and spiritually—and this is the foremost achievement, which we haven't fully understood yet because we have not yet learned how to use freedom.
>
> However, work of historic significance has been accomplished. The totalitarian system that long ago deprived the country of an opportunity to succeed and prosper has been eliminated. . . . Free elections, freedom of the press, religious freedoms, representative organs of power, a multiparty system have all become reality. Human rights are recognized as the supreme principle.
>
> Movement toward a mixed economy has begun, equality of all types of property is being established, people who work the land are coming to life again in the framework of land reform, farmers have appeared, millions of acres are being handed over to people who live in the

countryside and in towns. The economic freedom of the producer has been legalized, and entrepreneurship, shareholding, and privatization are all gaining momentum. . . .

We live in a new world. The cold war has ended; the arms race has stopped, as has the insane militarization that mutilated our economy, public psyche, and morals. The threat of a world war has been removed. . . .

We opened ourselves to the world, gave up interfering in other people's affairs, and ended the use of our troops beyond the borders of the country; trust, solidarity, and respect came in response. We have become one of the main foundations for the transformation of modern civilization onto peaceful, democratic grounds. . . .

I am leaving my post with apprehension, but also with hope, with faith in you, your wisdom and force of spirit. We are the heirs to a great civilization; and its rebirth into a new, modern, and dignified life now depends on one and all.

I wish to thank with all my heart all those who have stood together with me all these years in a fair and good cause. Some mistakes could surely have been avoided; many things could have been done better. But I am convinced that sooner or later our common efforts will bear fruit, our nations will live in a prosperous and democratic society.

I wish the best to all of you.

Gorbachev had initiated a new Russian revolution, but in the manner of all revolutions it had taken on a life of its own, and he had lost control. This was not surprising. Gorbachev himself understood the risks.

"Take any revolution in history," he told the conference of military deputies that gave him such a hard time in November 1990, "and you will find that they have all been very acute and painful."

CHAPTER TWELVE

TRIUMPH
AND FAILURE

How could so much happen in so short a time? The world that Gorbachev destroyed in less than seven years took decades to construct, and until he started to dismantle it, there was no obvious sign that it was as fragile as it proved to be. And yet it did crumble, as if shaken by a gigantic earthquake.

The amazing pace of change was an important clue. It was possible because energies had accumulated beneath the surface comparable to the natural forces that build up where two plates of the Earth's crust meet, finally erupting in a shattering earthquake. Once the first tremors were felt, the Soviet Union's stale and rigid economic and political structures began to shake. Eastern Europe's false front—a slapdash façade of Stalinism forcibly and unnaturally attached to ancient Central European cultures—crumbled under the temblor's strength.

Events could only move so fast because as long as he was dismantling the old system, Gorbachev was working with the forces of history, not against them. He understood this himself, more clearly as he went along. He knew from the outset that his country was in dire straits—this knowledge was the source of his urge to reform. The more he tried to put things right, the better he grasped how bad things were. We heard him say time and again that plans had to be changed—usually radicalized—after he and others understood the seriousness of the problems they faced. What they thought they knew repeatedly turned out to be less than the full truth. At the Central Committee plenum of April 1989 Gorbachev admitted: "None of us had a good knowledge of the country we live in." This observation was confirmed when the country they lived in fell apart after the attempted coup of August 1991.

The truth was that the Stalinist model had long outlived its utility and was ready to collapse after doing immeasurable damage to the country. The idea that a huge industrial economy could effectively be planned and controlled by relatively few officials in Moscow had proven false. The system this idea created was static, not dynamic, and was based on a simple-minded distinction between preindustrial and industrial life. The planned economy would take Russia from backwardness to modernity—that was its authors' vision. But their vision left no room for the actual dynamics of technological innovation, improvisation, market mechanisms, and so on. It was the vision of economic illiterates. It created a hapless economic monster that was backward, inefficient, and clumsy. Its managers did not know how to manage, its workers did not know how to work, its currency was worthless in any competitive marketplace. This was the Stalinist legacy.

Despite the inherent disadvantages of their system, Soviet leaders from Stalin to Chernenko had sought to compete for power and influence with the Americans and their allies, a formidable collection of free societies and strong economies. Operating from a position of profound weakness, they tried to establish the Soviet Union as a superpower equal to the United States. They could succeed only in the realm of military might, and only at immense cost. As Shevardnadze acknowledged in the summer of 1990, Soviet governments routinely spent a quarter of their resources on their military establishment—and more to sustain alliances with n'er-do-well third world allies. This squandering of the nation's wealth over more than forty years certainly hastened the collapse of the Stalinist system.

So did the worsening corruption of Soviet society. The corruption of a nation is a dynamic process; once begun, it tends to proceed apace. I saw this happen in the Soviet Union over the last twenty years, as bribe takers became ever bolder and everyday survival grew more and more dependent on corrupt relationships with various kinds of black marketeers. By the time Gorbachev came to power, it was common for a Soviet citizen to be asked for a bribe for the most basic services, even health care. The high-minded principles of the Bolshevik Revolution had lost all relevance; the society was rotting from within. This was obvious just from the statistics about life expectancy and consumption of alcohol, which showed a country that was killing itself.

The reasons for Gorbachev's revolution were similar to the causes of the first revolution of 1917: Stubborn retention of an outmoded social and economic structure—the monarchy then, the Stalinist system in the 1980s—and reckless commitments to ruinously expensive foreign ambitions had caused a crisis for the old order. By the time Gorbachev became general secretary, his country's economy could no longer grow and was falling farther and farther behind the rest of the world. Conditions of life were deteriorating ominously. The people were alienated and isolated from their so-called leaders. Either there would be change, or disaster.

The nature of the change that had to be made was widely understood—not as a blueprint for specific reforms but as a set of general principles. Sakharov laid many of them out in his 1968 essay. Some had been obvious as early as 1956. Gorbachev's generation included thousands of intelligent people who realized that the Soviet system had to loosen up, had to allow more freedom, and had to connect work to rewards and prices to values.

The modernization of the Soviet Union and the breakdown of its isolation actually began in the early 1970s, in the time of the Nixon-Brezhnev détente, when thousands of Soviet citizens first saw the West and realized how far their country lagged behind. Stalinism required isolation; only in ignorance would successive generations continue to accept the myths that propped it up. In the seventies Soviet young people discovered and joined the international youth culture; large numbers of Western tourists began to visit the U.S.S.R.; Soviet scientists caught on to the computer revolution and what it might mean, though because of the country's inability to produce the hardware they could not easily take part.

Gorbachev's arrival at the center of power was also a manifestation of the changes going on in his country. His promotion to general secretary was not a bolt from the blue. As Alexander Bovin said to me in the spring of 1990, "Understanding Gorbachev means understand-

ing the Soviet Union." I don't mean to denigrate Gorbachev's enormous personal contribution, but it is important to see him in the
context of Soviet history and society. "We are all children of our
times," as Gorbachev said often. His times did not begin in 1985. Nor
did the ideas for change that he embraced suddenly fall from the
heavens after he became general secretary.

Similarly, the troubles Gorbachev encountered beginning late in
1990, the tragic crackdown in Lithuania and Latvia in early 1991, then
six months of intrigue and the coup in August of that year can also be
understood only in the context of Soviet history. The changes instigated by Gorbachev crashed into the realities of the Stalinist inheritance: an unnatural multinational state, a pathetic economy, and the
enduring power of the core groups that had made the old system work,
however feebly. The army, the KGB, the police, the still hidden but
still powerful military-industrial complex, and the Party apparatus
could not be maneuvered out of the way, or tricked into standing
aside.

They had pushed Gorbachev toward a new, hard line that led directly to the clumsy showdown with the Baltic states and then to
tragedy in January 1991. Not that those conservative forces could be
blamed for what happened. It was Gorbachev's own fear and ambition
that made him susceptible to their pressure. The blood of the fifteen
Lithuanians killed when army troops stormed the television station in
Vilnius was blood on Gorbachev's hands. For nearly six years he had
avoided this; he had built a great international reputation and col-
lected the Nobel Prize as an implacable foe of violence. But when the
first great test of his moral position came at home, he failed it.

It is a tribute to his resilience that four months after the killings in
Vilnius and Riga Gorbachev was again looking for ways to renew his
license as a reformer. He seemed to recognize that he had committed
a terrible error in January and tried to rectify it. He made one last
stab at reconstructing his country on a new basis, in order to hold
most of its component parts in a new kind of Union. But by the spring
and summer of 1991, when he was finally willing to acknowledge that
some of the Soviet republics could leave the Union, events had moved
far beyond his control. What he offered was too little and it came too
late.

But what he offered was too much for the old Party barons in the
military, the KGB, the Party, and the police to endure, so they tried
to depose Gorbachev in their pathetic putsch. It failed, but in failing

it finally freed the country entirely from the Soviet harness. Soon Gorbachev's country and with it Gorbachev's role were gone.

Ultimately, Gorbachev failed because he was unable to go beyond the dismantling of Stalinism to the creation of something new and successful to replace it. Dismantling the old was an enormous accomplishment, and it created great new possibilities. But Gorbachev turned out to be unable to exploit them.

Gorbachev's historical role was that of a great *transitional* leader who led his people from one historical epoch into another. Moses was the archetypal transitional leader. Moses took the Jews out of slavery in Egypt and led them on a forty-year march to the Promised Land. He could not enter that Promised Land—he could only look into it across the Jordan River. We remember Moses not for what he built but for what he made possible. Joshua led the Jews into their homeland and began to build a new nation, but Moses is the giant in history, and justly so.

Gorbachev is no Moses, but he too will be a giant in history. Vast changes in world politics and a radical break in the history of his country will be associated with his name. How did this lad from Privolnoye end up in such a big role? This is surely one of the great stories of the twentieth century.

•   •   •

We don't know much about the formation of Gorbachev's character —that combination of genes and reflexes, taught or absorbed, that defines a human personality. I will resist the temptation to speculate on the effects of his grandfathers' arrests, his father's absence from home during the war, his close association with his mother's parents, his early exposure to Russian Orthodoxy, and other intriguing but inconclusive details from his early biography. Gorbachev's own description of his boyhood home as a "plague house" after Grandfather Gopkolo returned from fourteen months of imprisonment and interrogation—a house "where no one, not even relatives, dared to come" for fear of being associated with this "enemy of the people" who had been the first chairman of the collective farm—is haunting. Those few words (Gorbachev gave no further details) suggest the sort of searing childhood memory that can affect the course of a life.

It is clear from the evidence of his adolescence that Gorbachev emerged from childhood as a poised, confident, outgoing, and ambitious person. In adolescence he learned theatrical skills that make me wary of more elaborate psychological interpretation. He has been acting for more than forty years. His is a masked personality, and he is a lonely man who has apparently shared little that was truly personal with comrades and colleagues. He has the extra gene—a source of drive and ambition beyond normal human scale—that separates the most successful political leaders from their fellow mortals. That gene provides another mask.

But if the formation of character cannot be divined, the character itself isn't so mysterious. It is formidable, and made Gorbachev stronger than those around him in Soviet politics. He has intimidated and impressed everyone who has worked near him. Yeltsin admitted this in his autobiography:

> What he has achieved will, of course, go down in the history of mankind. I do not like high-sounding phrases, yet everything that Gorbachev has initiated deserves such praise. He could have gone on just as Brezhnev and Chernenko did before him. I estimate that the country's natural resources and the people's patience would have outlasted his lifetime, long enough for him to have lived the well-fed and happy life of the leader of a totalitarian state. He could have draped himself with orders and medals; the people would have hymned him in verse and song, which is always enjoyable. Yet Gorbachev chose to go another way. He started by climbing a mountain whose summit is not even visible. It is somewhere up in the clouds and no one knows how the ascent will end: Will we all be swept away by an avalanche or will this Everest be conquered?

Gorbachev was truly a child of his times; he saw firsthand many of the most important dramas of the Stalin years. They helped shape him. He grew up on an early collective farm, and surely came to understand how costly it had been to reorganize the countryside. He disclosed just before he left office that three aunts and uncles died of starvation in the famine of 1933, when he was just two. We know that he understood the difference between reality and the lyrical descriptions of collective farms in official propaganda. From the window of a train riding off to university in Moscow he saw some of the worst devastation of the war. At Moscow State University he was exposed to the first period of palpable intellectual ferment in Russia in a generation. He joined the crowds who mourned Stalin's death, and then joined the intense student conversations that his death made possible. As a Komsomol official he participated in the excitement initiated by

Khrushchev's secret speech to the 20th Party Congress, and was a delegate to the 22nd Congress where Khrushchev put his assessment of Stalin's crimes on the public record. Those were the years of the Thaw, when thoughtful people began to exchange candid thoughts about the plight of the country, and a new literature gave hope of a more honest and fruitful future. These were experiences Gorbachev shared with countless of his contemporaries—the so-called children of the 20th Congress.

He also had experiences shared by few others which must have been critical to the evolution of his independent outlook. An important one was his exposure at university to Zdenek Mlynar, the young Czech Communist, a sophisticated European who must have been an exotic figure to the bumpkin from Privolnoye. I am most intrigued by Gorbachev's long trips to France and Italy in the mid-1960s, when he was able to see how starkly the imperialist camp differed from the portrait of it drawn in Soviet propaganda.

Westerners cannot easily appreciate the way the Stalinist mythology overpowered Gorbachev's generation. It successfully defined reality for millions of Soviet citizens, including many who considered themselves free-thinking and cynical but who still could not escape the worldview inculcated by official propaganda from kindergarten onward. The myths became a kind of political and intellectual straitjacket, limiting the freedom of movement of several generations of Soviet leaders. Gorbachev broke out of the straitjacket; he was able to call things by their real names. The experiences of his life which taught him from an early age that the propaganda could be misleading also enabled him to make this critical break with the conventional thinking of his time and caste—the caste of Communist Party officials.

Gorbachev cannot be understood apart from his membership in that caste. He grew up in the Communist Party of the Soviet Union; it shaped him, taught him political analysis and political rhetoric, gave him a style and manner that he never abandoned. As I have written many times already, he was a Party man, instantly recognizable as such by other Party men.

The Russians use the word *partinost,* roughly translatable as "partyness," to signify qualities somehow related to the Party. Gorbachev has always had it. Just as Richard Nixon's conservative credentials enabled him to open relations with Mao Zedong's China, so Gorbachev's *partinost* allowed him to go so far toward destroying the Soviet

Communist Party. Other Party men saw him as "one of ours," and initially they accepted his prescriptions as necessary to preserve the Party's leading role. As time passed and his initial efforts to whip the country into shape failed, Gorbachev was pushed to redefine his own brand of communism. He became more radical and found the Party *apparat* increasingly hostile and recalcitrant.

He came to an important turn in the road in the preparations for the Central Committee plenum in January 1987, the one that was postponed several times before Gorbachev finally got a chance to introduce his ideas about new political reforms. But the decisions taken then and six months later, at the June 1987 plenum on economic reform, met further obstructionism from the Party *apparat*. So another important turn came during the preparations for the 19th Party Conference in June 1988; the theses for that meeting outlined a new kind of Soviet state in which the Communist Party clearly had a secondary role. Some of the Party elders became openly hostile, and there was no sign of greater cooperation from the *apparat*. Then the 28th Party Congress in July 1990 ratified the withdrawal of the Party from the running of the country—apparently a great victory for Gorbachev. But in fact the Party elders were angrier than ever; in 1991 their hatred for Gorbachev's reforms (displayed only behind closed doors at the Party Congress) burst into the open.

Through all of this, Gorbachev never even hinted at a loss of faith in communism. Only after the coup attempt in August 1991 (and not immediately afterward, either!) did he stop defending the Party and describing himself as a convinced Communist. And even then he kept insisting he was still a socialist.

He called himself a socialist even after he had embraced free-market economic reforms that looked more like capitalism than socialism. "Socialism . . . is entrenched among the people," he said at the end of November 1990, "and I don't think it is necessary to destroy it, as some are trying to do.

"Yes," he went on, "we have bid farewell to the past—an agonizing process." He acknowledged that young people without roots in the earlier phases of Soviet experience might not feel as he did. "But we are all from those times," he said, "and it is not so simple for us. Should we renounce things? What shall I do, renounce my grandfather, who was dedicated to everything right until the end and who, having returned [from prison, apparently], spent another seventeen years as chairman of the collective farm? . . . I cannot go against my grandfather. I cannot go against my father, who fought [the Germans] in the Kursk salient, who crossed the Dnepr, flowing with blood . . ." He was happy to reject "the barrackslike mentality of Stalinism," Gorbachev said, but he would not "renounce my grandfather and what he did. This would mean rejecting generations and what they did. Well then, did they live in vain?" He was certain they did not, and he would respect "the memory of those who gave their all, who believed that if it wasn't for themselves [that they sacrificed], then it was for the country, for the motherland."

In other words, if we had to admit that the whole Bolshevik experiment was a terrible mistake, we would have nothing to live for. That, I think, is what Gorbachev believed. Don't take away the very essence of our cause, lest we have nothing at all.

He perceived himself as part of a continuum that began with Lenin. He often compared himself to Lenin, publicly and privately. He believed that the Bolsheviks had produced something important, something worth salvaging.

Gorbachev's insistence on trying to preserve his communism ultimately undermined his position in the country, which by 1990 was in full flight away from the political doctrine that had done so much damage during the previous seventy-three years. Relatively few of his countrymen shared his concern with redeeming Lenin's revolution— they wanted something to eat, some sign of progress toward a normal society in which normal lives were possible.

But if Gorbachev held on to his Communist identity, he was never hidebound. Once he committed himself to "revolutionary change," he was willing to accept wholesale revision of Party tradition and to break nearly all the old rules that governed Soviet society. But there were always limits. He was never willing to go as far, or as fast, as the reformers he initially encouraged wanted to go. This tension between his willingness to break the china and his reluctance to break it all at once became a hallmark of his political personality. I think it also made him a more successful transitional leader.

For a long time Gorbachev saw himself overhauling Soviet communism to create a better Soviet Union, and better communism. But communism held little appeal for large numbers of people, and the Soviet Union had no appeal for many, probably most of the non-Russian citizens of the U.S.S.R. Ultimately Gorbachev fell out of step with the majority of his countrymen—they marched off in a new direction, leaving him behind.

Yet, as I hope I have made clear, there has been much more to Gorbachev's revolution than an effort to preserve communism and the Soviet Union. At certain moments there was nobility, even morality. I am convinced that Gorbachev is, in some way I cannot precisely define, a man of faith. Part of that faith was the secular, political belief in Lenin's revolution, but Gorbachev has hinted at religious faith too. He did so in his 1988 interview with *The Washington Post,* when he said he could not perform miracles like Christ's. After the failed coup he began comparing socialism and Christianity as two noble ideas for the betterment of mankind.

The idea that Gorbachev is a believer is certainly beguiling; I hasten to add that there is no concrete evidence to support it. One of my wisest friends in Moscow, a member of the Congress of People's Deputies who worked closely with Sakharov and who has gotten to know Gorbachev too, suggested the novel theory that a shared religiosity bound those two men together—not so much a conventional churchy religion, but a faith that "history and life have a purpose," as Sakharov put it. Sakharov's moral strength grew out of his conviction that men were obliged to treat each other humanely; one could argue that Gorbachev has been striving for a similar moral authority in his renunciation of the use of force and his more tolerant attitude toward virtually everyone.

In 1987 Gorbachev declared that democracy was as necessary to society as oxygen, but in July 1990, at the Party Congress, he reformulated that metaphor. "Spiritual rebirth is as essential to society as oxygen," he declared.

One of the least trumpeted consequences of Gorbachev's years in power was a religious resurgence in Russia. Many Russian Orthodox churches that had been abandoned or turned over to secular uses were reopened and reconstructed after 1985. At Easter in 1991 even St. Basil's Cathedral on Red Square was once again used for its original religious purpose. Official harassment of religion ended. In the fall of 1990 the Supreme Soviet adopted a new law legalizing religion and formally eliminating atheism as a state doctrine. Christmas and Easter services were broadcast on television. The long-suppressed Ukrainian Catholic Church was legally recognized; even the dwindling Jewish community staged a revival, exploiting new opportunities to practice Judaism appropriately.

None of this proves that Gorbachev was personally religious; nor does his admission that his grandmother baptized him. But I am convinced that he had serious moral concerns, that he was interested in spiritual values, and that he felt he was serving a larger purpose than most politicians. I don't think he could have taken on the challenges he did without some measure of faith.

.   .   .

It is a large jump from questions of belief to matters of tactics, but Gorbachev cannot be understood without an appreciation of his great gifts as a political tactician. His deftness at moments of crisis has sometimes been breathtaking—for example, when he used Mathias Rust's landing in Red Square to sweep away the upper echelon of his reactionary military establishment; or when he turned Chernobyl into a reason for more aggressive *glasnost;* or his sudden decision to accept a smaller Union and negotiate a new Union treaty with Yeltsin and other republican leaders as a last attempt to save his country.

Generations of future historians will argue over the degree to which Gorbachev was a modern Machiavelli who knew from the start what he hoped to achieve but never revealed a card in his hand until he absolutely had to. To my mind this is the wrong way to think of him. As he conducted his revolution, Gorbachev improvised, reacted. Yes, he did set off with a body of ideas in his head about what needed to change—the ideas of his December 1984 speech. But there was no blueprint, just guiding principles.

"In 1985 we came to the conclusion that one could not live that way," Gorbachev said in a reflective speech in November 1990. "We began looking for ways in which one might live. A concept came into being for the country. In one case, internally, we called this *perestroika,* and we put forward a simple formula: more democracy, more *glasnost,* more humanity. Everything must be developed so that the individual in this society feels like a human being. That is a simple formula. We used exactly the sort of language that people would understand."

"He didn't have a plan," Yevgeny Velikhov said when we discussed the mysteries of Gorbachev, "but he did have a direction. And he was willing to experiment." Sergei Stankevich put it like this: "Gorbachev is not a man who has one set of ideas, one vision. He carries lots of ideas in his head, and if conditions push him, he'll take up one of them."

Similarly, Gorbachev the revolutionary could take a break and pass the baton to Gorbachev the *apparatchik,* who would then behave like a reliable Party man in some situation or other, and pass the baton back to the revolutionary. He switched between the two roles as he saw fit—usually infuriating those who sympathized with whichever role he had just given up. His recurrent incarnations as a Party man led to hesitation and delay, often to the exasperation of reformers waiting for him to recommence his revolutionary crusade. But these interludes of retrenchment probably smoothed the way for further change. Gorbachev could not have bulled ahead stubbornly without any pause or hesitation; the system could not have tolerated the strain of such incessant movement. Again, his sense of timing, of when to push ahead and when to pull back, helped make him a successful transitional leader.

The ability to change his mind made Gorbachev a better tactician. Think how often he did it! In the case of Boris Yeltsin alone, Gorbachev changed his mind a dozen times. In early 1986 he could speak harshly of Andrei Sakharov as a criminal; at the end of the same year he could make the dramatic phone call that led to Sakharov's release and eventual transformation into Gorbachev's political ally. One month the idea of a multiparty political system was "rubbish"; the next month he was urging the repeal of Article 6 of the Constitution to open the way for a multiparty system. Desperately, he sanctioned violence in Lithuania and Latvia at the beginning of 1990; a few months later he was adamantly refusing demands that he impose sterner "discipline" against the democrats. Gorbachev proved the old saw about consistency being the hobgoblin of small minds.

At the heart of Gorbachev's tactics was the idea that he should always be somewhere in the middle. Yuri Afanasyev described him to me in May 1990 as "a vector politician" who constantly looked for the median position between left and right. For years Gorbachev cast himself as a wise and moderate leader who could thread a path between "conservatives" unprepared for change and "ultraleftists" who wanted to "skip stages" and jump ahead too quickly. Sometimes this effort to plant himself in the middle was transparently preposterous, but often it worked. He did maneuver the Party out of direct power. And he avoided a confrontation with the Party establishment that his policies were destroying for six years and five months.

Eventually the center he wanted to occupy all but disappeared. The new democratic forces drew many of those who long stood with Gorbachev in the center to the left; the deterioration of conditions in the country and the rise of nationalism drew others to the right. For five years after he came to power Gorbachev was, on balance, a man of the left, a liberal reformer; but in the sixth year he found himself on the right, a reactionary trying to stem the tides that his own reforms had created. When that ploy failed, he tried to move back toward what he called "the center left" again.

But by the spring of 1991, when he made that last feint to the left, the society had moved beyond the game he had been playing. This was ironic. For years Gorbachev had argued—and seemed to believe— that democratization was the key to success. When old comrades complained that democracy resulted in the wholesale defeat of traditional Communists at the polls, Gorbachev rebuked them. We wanted to give the people a voice, he said—this is why we began our reforms. But when the popular voice turned against him personally, and when democracy threatened the survival of the Union, Gorbachev didn't like it. At first he tried not to accept it. But in the end, to his credit, he yielded to a new group of legitimately elected political leaders who concluded that they didn't need him anymore.

●   ●   ●

From 1985 onward Gorbachev was hobbled by a number of personal shortcomings. One that I have mentioned repeatedly was his inability to choose the right aides and associates, a serious disability for a political revolutionary trying to push a giant nation in a new direction. Apart from Yakovlev and Shevardnadze, Gorbachev never found reliable, resourceful peers who could help him achieve his goals. He made many bad appointments, from Ligachev as his first number-two man, to Ryzhkov as his premier, to Murakhovsky, his first patron in Stavropol, as minister of the agricultural superministry created in 1986. His worst appointments, arguably, were of Kryuchkov, Yazov, Pugo, Boldin, Lukyanov, and the other supposed allies who led the coup against him.

Yeltsin, when he became president of Russia in 1990, quickly surrounded himself with bright young men in their thirties and forties, but Gorbachev never built a staff of younger associates. Nor did he establish close working relationships with the new political figures his reforms had thrown up, people like Stankevich and Popov in Moscow and Sobchak in Leningrad. He stuck to Party *apparatchiks* with a loyalty that exasperated his liberal intellectual supporters.

Was this tactics, or genuine preference? I suspect the latter. Gorbachev never seemed comfortable with unconventional people who might be in his intellectual class—he preferred good Party men. (Sakharov was one exception, though he too made Gorbachev uncomfortable in their public clashes.) But his preference suited his tactics: Party men would have been alarmed if Gorbachev had suddenly embraced a retinue of liberal intellectuals without Party backgrounds.

One reason why Gorbachev did not reach out for more talented associates may have been his excessive confidence in himself. At the outset Gorbachev seemed overconfident of his ability to carry the Party apparatus with him as he initiated reforms. His overconfident belief that he could deal with the Yeltsin affair in the fall of 1987 led to the horrendous display of Stalinist discipline at the Moscow Party plenum, an event that gravely undermined Gorbachev's efforts at the time. He overconfidently thought he could win a majority of the delegates to the 19th Party Conference of 1988 by instituting democratic selection procedures, which proved easy to manipulate. In 1989 and 1990 he seemed to think he could overcome Yeltsin's great popularity and head off his election first to the Congress, then to the Russian presidency. In both cases Gorbachev's intervention seems to have helped Yeltsin, not hurt him. And of course he was fatally overconfident in his ability to keep the hardliners around him in check.

He was also overconfident about what he could afford *not* to do. Perhaps the most egregious example of this was his failure to confront the need to create a new system to replace the one he was so successfully destroying. Gorbachev seemed to convince himself that he could postpone this task for three years, then four, then five. In the sixth year his procrastination caught up with him.

Vanity also tripped him up. He came to believe excessively in his own talents, and particularly to exaggerate his popularity. Gorbachev's first years were such a great triumph at home and abroad that when the country began to turn against him late in 1989 (pushed initially by disappearing food supplies and deteriorating economic conditions), he could not adjust. In 1990, when it became clear that the Soviet Union was in real danger of falling apart, Gorbachev allowed himself briefly to become one of the very people he spent his first five years struggling against—a stubborn officeholder determined above all to retain power. Perhaps his love of power shouldn't have been surprising. This was the man who invested twenty-three years in Stavropol to get his shot at power in Moscow. Power was important to him long before democratization was.

Vanity may also have fed Gorbachev's appetite for the privileges of office. His huge new dacha outside Moscow and his grand villa at

Cape Foros on the Black Sea betray a certain self-absorption and weakness for luxury.

"Gorbachev lived like a czar for so long that he got used to living like one and acting like one," said his longtime aide Sergei Grigoriev just after he left office. "He was so separated from what was going on, he relied on sycophants and gave more attention to bootlickers than the truth-tellers, because they said unpleasant things. . . . I was always amazed at how convinced he was that he had the right answers to all the questions. He would not tolerate it if someone tried to say, 'You know, Mikhail Sergeyevich, people are fed up with this socialism business. They despise it.' When he would say socialism is so deep-rooted in our people, they adore it, well, everyone would either say, 'Oh yes, absolutely,' or they'd keep silent. If they contradicted him, he'd go crazy."

His inclination to take offense was another weakness. It aggravated his relations with many who ought to have been close allies, helping to create a real schism among the liberal intellectuals. Gorbachev never seemed comfortable with the new people created by his own policies—the aggressive liberals who actually believed in democracy and acted accordingly. His intolerant attitude toward the Inter-Regional Group of Deputies, sharpened by the debate over his election to the presidency, worsened the situation. Many like Yuri Afanasyev, who quit the Party in 1990, became bitterly anti-Gorbachev, arguing that he could not keep up with the pace of change and had become an impediment. After the coup, many of the democrats decided there was no further need for Gorbachev's services.

Two of the chinks in Gorbachev's armor were substantive areas that he could never master: nationalities issues, as the Russians call them, and economics. They were two of the most important matters he faced, and he had a tin ear for both of them.

In his second speech to the 28th Party Congress he admitted his ignorance about the true state of relations among the many national groups of the Soviet Union and accused his comrades of sharing it. "All of us—go on, admit it—honestly believed that all of this [ethnic strife] had been happily resolved," Gorbachev said. "For the most part it was toasts to the friendship of peoples at the tables of meetings and at Party gatherings. That's what our work in the area of nationalities policy amounted to. And suddenly we saw it all revealed, and the problems that faced us. . . . Nor did we immediately reach a correct assessment and understanding . . ."

It is tempting to dismiss that confession as disingenuous; perhaps it was. Certainly it required a certain systematic obtuseness to miss the hostility that Lithuanians and Latvians felt toward Russians, for example, or to disregard the hatred dividing Azerbaijanis and Armenians. But it's possible that Gorbachev's idealism—or wishful thinking—had led him to overlook the evidence and believe the propaganda about a harmonious multinational Soviet state. This was one of the strongest myths that he had grown up with.

Whatever the explanation, the consequences of Gorbachev's obtuseness were obvious. Only after five years in power did he really begin to come to grips with the ethnic divisions that ultimately made it impossible to preserve the Soviet Union. Perhaps it was always doomed. Ironically, Gorbachev's reforms hastened its demise. Once Latvians, Ukrainians, Moldavians, Armenians, and all the others felt free to speak their minds, organize politically, and express their aspirations, the days of the old Union were clearly numbered. The logic of *glasnost* and democratization led inexorably to stronger nationalist sentiment, and from there to separation.

Gorbachev's incompetence as an economist was also serious. His only real accomplishment in the economic sphere was the launching of a private or cooperative sector of the economy, which began at once to fill in some of the many holes in the state-run system. In many other sectors the only progress was negative.

From his first months in office Gorbachev convinced the economists who advised him that he had no grasp of their subject, and no confident sense of where to try to take the country. Several of those economists confided to colleagues that in the early phases Gorbachev just could not grasp the seriousness of the economic situation, or come to terms with the pain that real reform might inflict. His early working groups produced no blueprint or consensus.

The general secretary's uncertainty was clearly reflected in the contradictory initiatives undertaken as *perestroika* unfolded—unraveled might be a better word. Gorbachev did seem to believe, as he told Zdenek Mlynar in 1967, that the system needed less central control and more autonomy for localities and enterprises. Ostensibly these were the objectives of his reforms. But the most important of them, designed to make every enterprise "self-financing," was hopelessly compromised by a system of fixed prices that hid real values, so "cost accounting"—the subject of many slogans—was meaningless. When the "self-financing" system introduced at the beginning of 1988 began to falter, Ryzhkov, with Gorbachev's support, issued numerous new decrees revoking key elements of the independence that had been promised. By the end of 1989 the economy had been effectively recentralized. No progress was made after that.

The dark realm of economics brought Gorbachev face-to-face with the true consequences of Stalinist rule. This is where much of the worst damage had been done. The Soviet economy had grown according to arbitrary planners' preferences, so it was hopelessly out of balance. The men and women who ran it had no experience with independent decision making or basic notions like profit maximization. In a system where prices did not reflect values, the whole idea of profit was confused. Left to its own devices, the economy would more likely collapse than thrive.

Unfortunately, this was the logical result of halfhearted reforms introduced over the opposition of those who had to implement them. Gorbachev ultimately had to confront the fact that the conventional tools he relied on for more than five years to improve economic performance were ineffectual. Managers who did not want to be responsible for the fate of their enterprises simply refused to take responsibility. Bureaucrats in Moscow who did not want to give up their power over individual enterprises found ways to hold on to it. Incentives could not be found to induce farms to grow more food or factories to produce more goods, largely because there were so many extra rubles in circulation already chasing too few consumer goods that higher wages provided no tangible benefits. The entire mechanism had devoured its lubricants and was locked, frozen.

The fact that Gorbachev was unable to brag of any positive economic results was disastrous for his standing in the country. This failure to produce goods that people wanted to eat and buy was also an incentive to the old-guard reactionaries who felt defeated by the first five years of Gorbachev's rule. They revived themselves in the sixth year when they realized that they could discredit all Gorbachev's liberalizing reforms by blaming them for food shortages and worsening economic conditions.

Ultimately the facts of Soviet life—objective reality, as a Marxist might put it—were Gorbachev's greatest enemy. He could open up the Soviet Union, restore its history, initiate debate on fundamental issues, even convert a nation of sheeplike followers into a vibrant new political organism, but he could not overcome the fundamental terms of existence in his country. So after nearly seven years he had succeeded brilliantly but also failed miserably. He had thrown off the yoke of Stalinism, an astounding accomplishment; but even without the yoke the country was crippled by the consequences of its past.

I don't think Gorbachev's failures are surprising. Consider what he proposed to do: Take a huge multinational empire that had been created by force and coercion; give it a large measure of democracy while loosening all the traditional bonds that held it together—thus encouraging the rebirth of long-suppressed local nationalisms; allow its citizens to travel quite freely around the world, but at home deprive them of attractive consumer goods, food, housing, and so on— deprive them *increasingly* while proclaiming the benefits of your reforms; do all this in a backward land whose citizens have little training and less experience useful for building a democratic society of self-reliant citizens, a country whose economic infrastructure was collapsing. This is obviously no formula for success. In fact it was a formula for disaster.

•   •   •

Mikhail Gorbachev was a Soviet Communist politician—in the end that was the critical fact. For the breed, he was enlightened, talented, even principled, but he was one of the breed.

When they launched their putsch, strangely, Kryuchkov and his comrades were throwing a last roll of the dice for the old Soviet political culture to which Gorbachev belonged. Of course they had a different sense of it than Gorbachev did. They wanted to change the balance of forces, to restore preeminence to the police, the military, and the Party *apparat*.

The available evidence suggests that when they hatched their plot the conspirators thought they had a chance of persuading Gorbachev to join them. They initially asked for his concurrence in their state of emergency. And of course they knew they had won him over before, the previous January, when he went along with the crackdown in the Baltics.

How could they have thought Gorbachev might join them? Because Gorbachev was duplicitous. He told different factions and different individuals different stories. He conducted an elaborate balancing act for more than six years. A prominent lawyer in Moscow, Alexander Yakovlev (no relation to the former Gorbachev associate of the same name), speculated after the coup that Gorbachev's duplicity had served the country well. "If he had shown his hand, the hardliners would have acted much more decisively" in the coup. But "they thought that they might be able to persuade him to come over to their side. His duplicity saved us from enormous bloodshed."

His duplicity, like all his skills as a "vector politician" weaving a tricky path between reformers and reactionaries, was enormously valuable as long as reformers and reactionaries were at each other's throats. But when the coup collapsed, so did the reactionaries—and so did the old political culture. For those of us who had spent long years engrossed in its intricacies, the spectacle of its sudden evaporation was astounding. In just three days the entire Communist apparatus crumbled. Statues of Lenin and other Communist icons tumbled from one end of the country to the other.

Gorbachev wasn't the least bit ready for this turn of events. He came back to Moscow after the coup failed still talking about making the Communist Party "a vital force for *perestroika*," suddenly a laughable proposition. In the new political culture—a democratic culture dominated by the democratically elected president of Russia—Gorbachev was a wasting asset. Events raced ahead of him; he never caught up.

It is important to remember that Gorbachev's inability to compete with Yeltsin in this new political culture was a consequence of the deliberate choices Gorbachev had made earlier. In the spring of 1989 he decided to take one of the seats reserved for Communist Party officials in the new Congress of People's Deputies instead of standing for election. (Yeltsin won the biggest victory of any candidate who ran for popular election to the Congress that March.) In the spring of 1990 Gorbachev decided to let the Congress elect him president of the U.S.S.R., when some of his aides favored going to the people for a mandate. Soon afterward he tried in every way he could to block Yeltsin's election as chairman of the new parliament of the Russian Republic. In the early summer of 1991 he and his comrades orchestrated a campaign to block Yeltsin's election as president of Russia. In other words, he chose *not* to establish his own position by popular vote, and he tried repeatedly to prevent Yeltsin from winning his own mandate.

Gorbachev made all of these choices (and many more in a similar vein) to pacify the conservative Party politicians whom he feared most. This was a pattern in his leadership—arguably a wise one. Gorbachev could be the transitional leader who destroyed the Stalinist system and guided his country to the brink of democracy precisely because he was so careful to make neutralizing the conservatives his first priority. Or so it seems to me.

This is the crucial fact about Gorbachev: Only a reliable Party man, one to whom his comrades would entrust the Party's leadership, could have been in a position to initiate a revolution. Gorbachev discussed this in one of his last interviews as president with Yuri Shchekochikhin of *Literaturnaya Gazeta,* in which he acknowledged that he knew things he would not disclose.

"I am not about to reveal everything," Gorbachev told Shchekochikhin.

"Yes," the interviewer replied, "you have repeated that enigmatic sentence several times."

And Gorbachev said, "And everyone thinks: So what is it that he knows?"

"Well, what is it?" Shchekochikhin asked.

"The system!" Gorbachev replied. "The system, which I studied from the inside." Only a man who knew the Communist system intimately could unravel it as effectively as Gorbachev did. "I had to outmaneuver them," he told Shchekochikhin.

It takes special talents, even a special genius, to perform the role of transitional leader. One of the most important of those talents was the ability to hide his true feelings, which Gorbachev has done masterfully for half a century. His wife, Raisa, confirmed this in the memoir she published in 1991, which included a letter Gorbachev wrote to her from Stavropol during his first year as a Komsomol *apparatchik,* when she was still a student in Moscow.

"I am so depressed by the situation here," he wrote. "How disgusting my surroundings are here. Especially the manner of life of the local bosses. The acceptance of convention, subordination, with everything predetermined, the open impudence of officials and the arrogance. When you look at one of the local bosses, you see nothing outstanding but his belly. But what aplomb, what self-assurance, and the condescending, patronizing tone!" And this was a description of the milieu in which he willingly spent the next twenty-three years! *

Since he was a young boy and first learned of the arrest of his paternal grandfather (arrested in 1933 for failing to meet the plan for

---

* This snippet suggested that Gorbachev's letters to Raisa were a treasure trove for future historians. But in the traumatic aftermath to the August coup, she decided to burn a lifetime of correspondence from Mikhail Sergeyevich.

spring sowing, and subjected to abusive interrogation), Gorbachev
had understood that something was terribly wrong with the Soviet
system. He began to admit this quite freely as his presidency drew to
a close. "All of that is inside me," he told Shchekochikhin, speaking
of the horrors of the 1930s. It helped lead him to "an inner conviction
that everything had to change," he said.

Many members of his generation developed a similar understanding, but most of them reacted by fighting against the system, or ignor-
ing it. Gorbachev's decision to join up was unusual. As his letter to
Raisa makes clear, he spent years of stupefying boredom and demean-
ing servility to numerous undeserving bosses in Stavropol to get a shot
at power in Moscow. He achieved power, then set about improving
what he thought was wrong. Before very long, the "improvements" he
initiated turned into revolutionary change.

For five years at least the old barons might have been able to stop
the Gorbachev revolution, even to reverse it, at least temporarily. But
when, after nearly six and a half years, they finally tried, it was too
late. The barons themselves were worn out, irrelevant figures who
could command no broad support in any important institution of the
society. And the country really had changed.

Gorbachev had fulfilled his role—he had led the country through
the most difficult stage of the transition away from Stalinism and
communism.

He will be remembered as the leader of the prologue to true *perestroika*—the real renewal of Russia. This is no small accomplishment.
On the contrary his is a heroic achievement, because Machiavelli was
right: Nothing is more difficult than taking the lead in the introduction of a new order of things. And because he was able to leave office
gracefully—the first Russian leader ever to do so in a thousand years
of history—Gorbachev even reserved the right to a second chance.
There are precedents. Charles DeGaulle ceased to be president of
France in 1946—but was again president of France in 1958. Winston
Churchill's political career appeared at an end when he resigned as
chancellor of the exchequer in 1929; eleven years later he was prime
minister. Gorbachev resigned as president of the defunct Soviet
Union two months before his sixty-first birthday.

His resignation did not diminish his appetite for politics in the
slightest. "I do not intend to leave the political stage, this is for sure,"
he said to a group of us from *The Washington Post* who interviewed
him in Moscow in March, 1992. Gorbachev said he would stay in

politics even if this "is inconvenient for some people," adding unnec-
essarily, "I do not have weak nerves." He was as alert, lively, and eager
to make his case three months after resigning the presidency of the
Soviet Union as he had been in our first interview nearly four years
earlier. I mentioned De Gaulle's biography to him and he laughed,
saying it was typical of journalists to try to make such parallels. But
when we asked him specifically if he could see himself leading the
country again someday, he answered with great care: "You know, now,
I don't have such plans, not yet . . ."

In the end Gorbachev did resemble the man he liked to compare
himself to. Like Lenin, Gorbachev was a missionary figure who led a
crusade to a new Russia. He had the personality of a missionary:
zealous, utterly self-confident, solemn to a fault. His determination
to turn away from the past and start afresh was his greatest strength.
In this he succeeded. But his zealotry and his self-confidence were
confining; he could begin the process of reinventing his country, but
at the critical moment he could not reinvent himself.

CHRONOLOGY

A GLOSSARY OF SOVIET TERMS

NOTES ON SOURCES

Chronology

1985

March 11: Mikhail Sergeyevich Gorbachev named general secretary of the Communist Party of the Soviet Union.

April 4: Politburo discusses antialcohol campaign.

April 8: In a speech to Communist Party officials Gorbachev backs Andropov's economic reforms and emphasizes giving enterprises more independence. He announces suspension of deployment of SS-20 missiles in Europe.

April 17: Gorbachev tours the Proletarsky region of Moscow and meets with workers at the ZIL auto factory, schoolchildren, and a young family, his first "walkabout" as leader.

April 23: The "April plenum" of the Central Committee endorses a vague reform program outlined by Gorbachev. Personnel changes also announced: Viktor Chebrikov, Nikolai Ryzhkov, and Yegor Ligachev named full members of the Politburo; Defense Minister Sergei Sokolov named a candidate member of the Politburo; Viktor Nikonov named a Central Committee secretary.

May 8: In a speech commemorating the fortieth anniversary of the Great Patriotic War, Gorbachev draws prolonged applause when he mentions Joseph Stalin.

May 15: Gorbachev visits Leningrad, the first visit by a Soviet leader to a city outside Moscow in two and a half years. He is greeted with much support for his policies, especially the antialcohol campaign, and delivers a strong speech, later shown on national television, that is much praised for its candor and directness.

May 16: Specific elements of the antialcohol campaign are announced, including a reduction in the annual production of strong alcoholic beverages, increased penalties for public drunkenness and drunken driving, the introduction of treatment programs for heavy drinkers, and raising the legal drinking age from eighteen to twenty-one. The government said "strict measures" would be applied to those brewing their own alcoholic beverages.

May 24: Increased pensions and family benefits announced.

June 11: Gorbachev delivers a major economic address to a Central Committee conference on Scientific and Technical Progress.

June 18–19: The U.S. and the Soviet Union hold talks on Afghanistan in Washington; the negotiations were the first between the two countries on the subject in three years, but were fruitless.

June 25: Gorbachev travels to Kiev, tours the city, and speaks with citizens. On June 26, his tour of the Ukraine continues to Dnepropetrovsk, where he addresses the workers of the city's largest steel mill.

July 1: Central Committee plenum makes personnel shifts: Georgi Romanov is removed from the Politburo; Eduard Shevardnadze is named a full member of the Politburo; Boris Yeltsin and Lev Zaikov are named Central Committee secretaries.

July 2: Supreme Soviet approves Gorbachev's nomination of Andrei Gromyko as chairman of the presidium. Shevardnadze becomes foreign minister.

July 2: U.S. officials announce that Gorbachev and Reagan will meet at a summit meeting in Geneva in November.

July 10: Gorbachev travels to Minsk to address military commanders. The next day he speaks to the Belorussian Central Committee.

August 3: Central Committee and Council of Ministers issue a decree calling for modest economic reforms.

August: Alexander Yakovlev is named head of the propaganda department of the Central Committee.

September 1: Time magazine publishes Gorbachev's first interview with an American publication.

September 4–7: Gorbachev visits Tyumen and Kazakhstan.

September 27: Nikolai Tikhonov resigns as chairman of the Council of Ministers and is replaced by Nikolai Ryzhkov.

September 30: At arms-control talks in Geneva the Soviet Union proposes sweeping cuts that would eliminate half of Soviet and U.S. offensive nuclear weapons.

October 1: Gorbachev is interviewed by French television and takes a tough stand on the question of dissidents.

October 2–6: Gorbachev visits France, his first official visit to the West as Soviet leader.

October 15: Plenary meeting of Central Committee discusses the draft of the new Party program. Gorbachev devotes his speech to the economy, emphasizing its potential for growth. Nikolai Talyzin is elected a candidate member of the Politburo.

November 18–21: Gorbachev travels to Geneva for a summit meeting with President Ronald Reagan. The two men seem to hit it off, and agree they can work together to reduce armaments. They tentatively schedule a series of additional summits.

November 18: A new superministry for agriculture is created; Gorbachev's old patron from Stavropol, Vsevolod Murakhovsky, is appointed its head.

December 24: Boris Yeltsin replaces Viktor Grishin as first secretary of the Moscow City Party Committee.

1986

February 8: In an interview with *L'Humanité,* the French Communist newspaper, Gorbachev dismisses Stalinism as "a concept made up by opponents of communism and used on a large scale to smear the Soviet Union and socialism as a whole." He says Andrei Sahkarov had committed "illegal acts," that he had been punished as provided by Soviet law, and that he could not be allowed to leave the Soviet Union because "he still has knowledge of secrets of particular importance to the state."

February 11: Anatoli Shcharansky, Jewish activist and dissident, is released and flown to the West as part of a spy swap. Shcharansky and his wife fly on to Israel, where he pledges to campaign for the right of Soviet Jews to emigrate. He is subsequently stripped of his Soviet citizenship.

February 18: Central Committee plenum discusses the upcoming Party Congress and the economic plan for 1990–2000. Viktor Grishin is removed from the Politburo; Boris Yeltsin is named a candidate member.

February 25: 27th Party Congress opens in Moscow. Gorbachev's speech lasts five hours. He calls for "radical reform" of the economic mechanism. The meetings last until March 6. On the last day of the Congress Lev Zaikov is named a full member of the Politburo, and Yuri Solovev and Nikolai Slyunkov are named candidate members. Vasily Kuznetsov and Boris Ponomarev retire. Yeltsin speaks to the Congress on the touchy issue of privileges.

April 7: Gorbachev tours Kuibyshev and conducts one of his walkabout tours. On April 8 he speaks in Togliatti.

April 24: Ogonyok publishes poems by Nikolai Gumilev, who was executed as a counterrevolutionary in 1921; some of his poems have appeared previously but there is no volume of his works available in the U.S.S.R. May 14, 1986: Writing in *Literaturnaya Gazeta* Yevgeny Yevtushenko gives details about Gumilev's death that were not printed in *Ogonyok,* disclosing that the poet was executed in 1921. In September *Novy Mir* publishes ten letters Gumilev wrote to his wife, Anna Akhmatova, and eighteen more of his poems.

April 26: An explosion occurs at the Chernobyl nuclear reactor. The first official Soviet statements are reassuring, announcing that two persons had died and that there was no additional danger of radiation.

April: A new edition of Boris Pasternak's works (poems, speeches, essays, etc.) is published and sold out as soon as it reaches bookstores.

May 14: Gorbachev addresses the nation on the Chernobyl accident. He gives few details and denounces Western reaction to the accident.

June: Melodiya Records releases a collection of Vladimir Vysotsky's songs, some of which appear for the first time. Vysotsky, a famous actor and author of a unique genre of protest folk songs, died in 1980, becoming a sort of folk hero in death. His songs were never officially recognized or published while he was alive.

June 8: Gorbachev flies to Hungary for bilateral and Warsaw Pact meetings.

June 16: Central Committee holds a one-day plenum in Moscow devoted principally to economic issues.

June 18: At a session of the Supreme Soviet, Premier Ryzhkov presents the proposal for the twelfth five-year plan.

June 30: Gorbachev arrives in Poland for the Party Congress there.

June: Vitali Korotich, a little-known Ukrainian writer, is appointed chief editor of *Ogonyok.*

July 28: Gorbachev arrives in Vladivostok for a tour of the Soviet Far East. In a speech there he says six Soviet regiments—about six thousand men—will be withdrawn from Afghanistan, and that discussions have begun with Mongolia about withdrawals of Soviet forces from that country. On August 1 Gorbachev speaks to the Party *aktif* in Khabarovsk on the need for more extensive *perestroika.*

August: Yegor Yakovlev is appointed chief editor of *Moscow News.* Yuri Afanasyev is appointed director of the Moscow State Institute of Historian-Archivists.

August 11: Sergei Zalygin, a writer who is not a member of the Communist Party, is named editor of *Novy Mir.*

August: A small chess magazine is the first Soviet journal to publish Vladimir Nabokov, the first step in his literary rehabilitation.

August 23: Gennadi Zakharov, a low-ranking Soviet official at the United Nations, is arrested in the U.S. on espionage charges.

August 30: Nicholas Daniloff, Moscow correspondent of *U.S. News & World Report* magazine, is detained by the KGB. He is subsequently charged with espionage and held in Moscow's Lefortovo prison.

September 17: Gorbachev visits Krasnodar *krai,* where he discusses domestic problems with citizens. He continues on to his native Stavropol *krai.*

September 26: U.S. expels twenty-five Soviet officials working at the United Nations.

September 29: Zakharov and Daniloff are both allowed to return home after a negotiated resolution to the crisis provoked by their arrests. Yuri Orlov, a prominent Soviet dissident then in Siberian exile, is also allowed to emigrate to the United States. On the same day, plans are announced for a Reagan-Gorbachev summit to be held in Iceland.

September 30: A Central Committee resolution complains of the slow progress of *perestroika,* specifically criticizing several ministries. This is the first such resolution.

October 10: Gorbachev arrives in Reykjavík for a two-day summit with Reagan. After tantalizing discussions about deep cuts in offensive arms and even the elimination of nuclear weapons, the meeting breaks up without reaching any agreements.

October: The first showings of the film *Repentance* to select audiences in Moscow.

November 6: The Ministry of Defense says the withdrawal of six regiments from Afghanistan is complete and that the troops will not be replaced. Western officials say that the number of troops had been raised before the announcement, and thus the withdrawal is not significant.

November 15: Gorbachev speaks to a Central Committee plenum on economic issues, describing new state quality-control bodies independent of enterprises that will be empowered to reject low-quality products.

December 16: Dinmukhamed Kunaev is replaced as first secretary of the Communist Party in Kazakhstan by Gennadi Kolbin. The change prompts street demonstrations and riots in the streets of Alma Ata.

December 16: Gorbachev places a telephone call to Sakharov in Gorki, inviting the physicist and his wife, Elena Bonner, to return to Moscow after six years of involuntary exile.

1987

January 6: The writers' union announces that a commission has been formed under the leadership of Andrei Voznesensky to examine Pasternak's works; the commission will oversee the publication of *Doctor Zhivago,* long suppressed in the Soviet Union. Soviet news media report for the first time that Pasternak had won the Nobel Prize for literature.

January 26: A plenum of the Central Committee convenes after several postponements. Gorbachev introduces his ideas for political reforms, including the introduction of multicandidate elections conducted by secret ballot and the promotion of non-Party members to senior government posts. He proposes that workers participate in the election of the directors of their enterprises, and recommends that cooperative ownership be expanded. Kunaev is retired from the Politburo; Alexander Yakovlev is named a candidate member. Nikolai Slyunkov and Anatoli Lukyanov are appointed secretaries of the Central Committee.

January: At the end of the month the anti-Stalin film *Repentance* is released for public showing around the country.

January: Jamming of Russian-language broadcasts of the BBC stops.

February 3: Yuri Churbanov, Brezhnev's son-in-law, is arrested on charges of corruption.

February 13: Gorbachev, addressing representatives of the mass media, pledges that *glasnost* will continue, but seeks to assure conservatives that this will not be at their expense.

February 17–22: Gorbachev visits Latvia and Estonia.

February 24: Gorbachev addresses the Trade Union Congress in Moscow, calling on workers to support the Party against bureaucrats who are resisting reform. He reportedly discloses that January's Central Committee plenum was postponed several times because of disagreements within the leadership over the extent of reforms.

February 28: Gorbachev proposes breaking the logjam in arms-control negotiations by separating discussions on medium-range missiles from the talks on strategic missiles and space weapons.

March 6: On a visit to Saratov, Yegor Ligachev says that not every aspect of Soviet history should be criticized since there were accomplishments even during the era of stagnation—the Brezhnev period.

March 21: The journal *Oktyabr* publishes Anna Akhmatova's famous, long-suppressed, anti-Stalinist poem "Requiem."

March 31: Alexander Yakovlev tells officials of the mass media to be more open and critical.

April: The journal *Druzhba Narodov* (Friendship of the Peoples) begins publishing Rybakov's anti-Stalinist novel *Children of the Arbat.*

April 10: Visiting Prague, Gorbachev makes new arms-control proposals to limit tactical nuclear weapons and improve verification of future treaties, and he calls for a meeting of the foreign ministers of thirty nations to accelerate reductions in conventional troops and weapons in Europe. Gorbachev says the U.S.S.R. no longer manufactures chemical weapons, and pledges to destroy all stockpiles.

May 6: About six hundred members of Pamyat, a new Russian nationalist organization, stage a demonstration in Moscow; afterward they are received by Boris Yeltsin, first secretary of the Moscow Party organization.

May 20: In an interview with the Italian Communist newspaper *L'Unità*, Gorbachev discusses his personal interests and the internal affairs of the U.S.S.R. He says that privileges for the élite will be necessary for some time to come, and asserts that there is resistance to reform.

May 28: Mathias Rust, a West German teenager, lands a single-engine airplane on Red Square, near Lenin's mausoleum.

May 30: Sweeping changes announced in the senior military command as a result of Rust's successful penetration of Soviet airspace. Dmitri Yazov replaces Sergei Sokolov as minister of defense.

May: Jamming of the Voice of America's Russian-language program stops.

June: The journal *Znamya* publishes Mikhail Bulgakov's *Heart of a Dog.*

June 11: The Politburo announces that all state enterprises are to become self-financing by the end of the decade.

June 25: A Central Committee plenum opens in Moscow. Gorbachev outlines new economic reforms, and announces that a special Party Conference will be held a year later. He criticizes the head of the state planning commission, Nikolai Talyzin, and the head of the state committee for material and technical supply, Lev Voronin, for economic shortcomings. Viktor Nikonov, Nikolai Slyunkov, and Alexander Yakovlev are promoted to full membership in the Politburo; Dmitri Yazov is named a candidate member.

June 28–30: The Supreme Soviet meets to consider the economic reforms approved by the Central Committee. Ryzhkov criticizes central management of Soviet industrial enterprises, which he calls "obsolete," and calls for radical changes. A new law on enterprises, intended to increase their independence, is adopted; it will go into effect at the beginning of 1988.

July 22: Gorbachev says the U.S.S.R. is ready to accept "the global elimination of all intermediate-range nuclear missiles." The next day the idea is formally presented in Geneva.

September 2: Mathias Rust put on trial in Moscow. Two days later he is sentenced to four years in a labor camp.

September 24: The Politburo decrees that individuals and cooperatives can run small shops and kiosks, a new departure.

September 29: Gorbachev returns to the public eye after a seven-week absence, which has provoked many rumors about his fate. He was writing his book, *Perestroika,* at his dacha in the Crimea. In his first appearance he meets a visiting French delegation in the Kremlin; he appears to be in fine form.

September 30: Gorbachev travels to Murmansk, warns the local citizenry that perestroika has entered a decisive stage. He tells city officials that price increases are under discussion.

October 12: Gorbachev visits Leningrad, beginning ceremonies to honor the seventieth anniversary of the October Revolution. Meeting with citizens, he campaigns for *glasnost* and cautions that if Party leaders do not support reform, the Party could lose its leading role.

October 18: About one thousand people demonstrate in Yerevan against continued Azerbaijani control of the predominantly Armenian area of Nagorno-Karabakh, apparently the first demonstrations on this issue.

October 21: At a Central Committee plenum, Boris Yeltsin defies Communist Party tradition by criticizing both Gorbachev and Ligachev; he is quickly denounced by other members, though a few come to his defense. Yeltsin asks to be relieved of his duties as a candidate member of the Politburo and first secretary of the Moscow Party organization. Geidar Aliyev is removed from the Politburo.

November 1: Gorbachev's book *Perestroika* is published in Moscow.

November 2: In a long-awaited speech on the occasion of the seventieth anniversary of the Revolution, Gorbachev disappoints liberal intellectuals with a tepid critique of Stalin's rule, but he invites further investigation into the dark periods of Soviet history. He defends Stalin's pact with Adolf Hitler as necessary to give the Soviet Union time to prepare for war.

November 11: Boris Yeltsin is publicly denounced by Gorbachev and many Moscow Party officials at an extraordinary meeting of the Moscow Party Committee. He is replaced as first secretary of the Moscow City Party Committee by Lev Zaikov. On November 18 Yeltsin is appointed first deputy chairman of the State Committee on Construction.

November 24: In Geneva, Secretary of State George P. Shultz and Shevardnadze agree to ban all medium-range missiles.

November 30: Gorbachev is interviewed by Tom Brokaw of NBC; the interview is subsequently broadcast on Soviet TV with one excision—Gorbachev's remark that he discusses all political issues with his wife.

November 30: Yegor Ligachev leaves for Paris. In an interview with *Le Monde* he says that he has been asked by the Politburo to chair meetings of the Central Committee, raising questions about Gorbachev's authority.

December: *Novy Mir* publishes poems by the émigré poet and Nobel laureate Joseph Brodsky, whose work has never before appeared in the Soviet Union.

December 6: *Moscow News* publishes an interview with the widow of Nikolai Bukharin, an early Bolshevik leader. The newspaper describes Bukharin's arrest, trial, and execution, and prints his "last testament," a bitter denunciation of Stalin.

December: Gorbachev travels to London and Washington for meetings with Margaret Thatcher and Ronald Reagan. In Washington he signs the new treaty banning medium-range nuclear missiles. His first visit to the United States is a personal triumph.

December 10: In an interview in honor of international Human Rights Day, Andrei Sakharov says that two hundred political prisoners have been released during 1987, but that many are still incarcerated.

1988

January 1: New law on state enterprises goes into effect. Enterprises accounting for 60 percent of Soviet industrial output will switch to a system of "self-accounting" and "self-financing." All enterprises are supposed to adopt the new system by 1991.

January 8: Gorbachev addresses representatives of media organizations, emphasizing the need for more openness and democracy.

January 9: First official announcements that the antidrinking campaign is being relaxed. Two hundred new liquor stores will open in Moscow.

January 12: Novy Mir begins publication of Boris Pasternak's *Doctor Zhivago*.

February 3: The Council of Ministers orders a 40 percent reduction in the number of cars used by government organizations.

February 5: Nikolai Bukharin and Alexei Rykov are rehabilitated by the Supreme Court of the Soviet Union.

February 8: Gorbachev proposes to withdraw all Soviet troops from Afghanistan over a ten-month period beginning May 15.

February 12: Soviet and U.S. warships bump as two Soviet vessels attempt to deter the American ships from entering the Black Sea; the Soviets charge that the American ships were violating Soviet territory.

February 20: New mass demonstrations in Armenia over Nagorno-Karabakh.

February 27–March 4: Ethnic violence and turmoil in Stepanakert, the capital of Nagorno-Karabakh, and Sumgait in Azerbaijan. On March 2 Politburo members Pyotr Demichev and Georgi Razumovski tour Azerbaijan and meet with citizens there; on March 4 Tass reports that thirty-one people had been killed in Sumgait.

March: Announcement of the creation of a new public-opinion institute, to be headed by Tatyana Zaslavskaya.

March 13: Sovetskaya Rossiya publishes Nina Andreyeva's letter attacking liberal reformers and criticizing those who have raised new questions about Stalin.

March 14: Gorbachev begins a five-day visit to Yugoslavia.

March: The Latvian journal *Rodnik* begins publication of George Orwell's *Animal Farm* in Russian.

March-April: Strikes and disorder in Armenia and Nagorno-Karabakh over the issue of unification of the enclave with the Armenian republic. On March 23 the U.S.S.R. Supreme Soviet issues a decree apparently precluding the transfer of any territory from Azerbaijan to Armenia. A general strike virtually shuts down Stepanakert from March 25 to April 7.

April 5: Pravda prints a strongly worded reply to Nina Andreyeva's letter, reestablishing the reformist line and rebuking conservatives who want to return to old ways.

April 6: Gorbachev travels to Tashkent to meet Najibullah, the Afghan leader. He makes the final decision to begin withdrawal of Soviet troops. On April 8 the Geneva accords on Afghanistan are announced.

April 10: Easter services broadcast on Soviet television for the first time.

April 14: Accords on settlement of the Afghan war are signed: Afghanistan and Pakistan must respect each other's sovereignty and nonalignment; the United States and the Soviet Union will guarantee the accords and pledge not to interfere in the internal affairs of Afghanistan or Pakistan.

May 11: Literaturnaya Gazeta publishes excerpts from Orwell's *1984,* which has been banned in the Soviet Union for thirty years.

May–June: Selection of delegates to the 19th Party Conference. Conservatives largely succeed in electing their candidates through manipulation of the election process. Many demonstrations throughout the country protest unfair elections and promote liberal candidates.

May 15: Soviet troops begin to leave Afghanistan.

May 18: Gorbachev interviewed by *The Washington Post* and *Newsweek.*

May 21: Leaders of the Communist Party organizations of Armenia and Azerbaijan are replaced.

May 23: Central Committee plenum approves the theses for the 19th Party Conference on the further development of economic and political reforms. They include recommendations that would radically weaken the Party's administrative powers, stimulate new, democratically elected councils, and promote new legal institutions and protections for citizens' rights.

May 25: For the first time, a Soviet general provides casualty statistics from the Afghan war: 13,310 dead, 35,478 wounded, and 311 still missing.

May 29–June 2: President Reagan visits Moscow for his fourth summit with Gorbachev.

May 30: Yeltsin is interviewed by the BBC and CBS and calls for Ligachev's ouster.

June 5: Celebrations begin of the millennium of Christianity in Russia, including the first church service celebrated inside the Kremlin in modern times. On June 10, Raisa Gorbacheva and top Soviet officials attend a special ceremony to mark the millennium in the Bolshoi Theater.

June 10: History exams canceled in secondary schools pending rewriting of history textbooks.

June 13: Supreme Court annuls the sentences of thirty-three officials purged under Stalin, including Grigori Zinoviev and Lev Kamenev.

June–July: Increased tensions in Armenia and Azerbaijan. The Armenian Supreme Soviet votes June 15 to annex Nagorno-Karabakh, a move rejected by Azerbaijan's Supreme Soviet two days later. Demonstrations and violence are common in both republics through the summer. On July 20 the U.S.S.R. Supreme Soviet declares that Armenian annexation of Nagorno-Karabakh is "unacceptable."

June 28: 19th Party Conference opens in Moscow. Gorbachev proposes a presidential system for the Soviet Union, an increase in the power of the local soviets, and a new parliament, to be called the Congress of People's Deputies.

July 2: Soviet inspectors arrive in California for the first inspections under the terms of the INF treaty signed in December, 1987. American teams begin to take up their positions around Soviet installations during the month.

July 11: Gorbachev goes to Poland for a six-day visit.

July 29: At a Central Committee plenum, Gorbachev calls for determined implementation of reform measures. He announces that elections to the new Congress of People's Deputies will be held in March; the Congress's first session will take place in April 1989, when it will elect a president. He also proposes granting fifty-year leases of land to farmers.

August 3: Mathias Rust is released after serving one year of his four-year sentence.

August: The journal *Yunost* publishes the memoirs of Nadezhda Mandelshtam, widow of the poet Osip Mandelshtam, who was killed by Stalin.

August 15: An Estonian newspaper publishes the secret protocols of the Molotov-Ribbentrop pact, the first time they have been published in the U.S.S.R.

September 5: The corruption trial of Yuri Churbanov, Brezhnev's son-in-law, opens in Moscow.

September 19: Pravda reports that restrictions on the sale of beer, wine, champagne, and cognac are to be lifted.

September 30: Major personnel changes are made at a Central Committee plenum. Gromyko and Solomentsev are retired from the Politburo, and Ligachev is transferred to new and obviously less significant responsibilities as chairman of a new Central Committee commission on agriculture.

October 1: Gorbachev elected chairman of the presidium—in effect, president of the Soviet Union—at a special session of the Supreme Soviet.

October 6: First report of a Soviet death due to AIDS.

October 21: Andrei Sakharov is elected a member of the governing presidium of the Academy of Sciences.

October 23: First mass in almost fifty years is celebrated in the cathedral in Vilnius, capital of Lithuania.

October 25: Four top political leaders of Uzbekistan, including former Party chief Inamzhon Usmankhodzhaev, are arrested for corruption.

October 26: After a visit to Moscow West German chancellor Helmut Kohl says that the Soviet Union will release all remaining political prisoners.

October 27: Minister of Finance Boris Gostev tells the Supreme Soviet that the Soviet Union will have a budget deficit in 1989 of 36 billion rubles, or 7.3 percent of the total budget.

November: Little Vera, the first Soviet movie that includes nudity and explicit sexual allusions, becomes a nationwide hit. The film depicts a society despoiled by decades of Party rule.

November 16: Estonia declares its sovereignty; the Estonian Supreme Soviet claims the right to veto Soviet laws.

December 1–3: Supreme Soviet session approves political changes, including new laws to govern the election of a Congress of People's Deputies.

December 7: Addressing the United Nations in New York, Gorbachev announces that the U.S.S.R. will reduce its military by 500,000 men within two years without asking for reciprocal concessions from the United States or its allies; six tank divisions will be withdrawn from Czechoslovakia, Hungary, and East Germany by 1991 and disbanded. He calls for a new world order built on the United Nations, and renounces the use of force.

December 7: Marshal Sergei Akhromeev resigns as deputy minister of defense and chief of staff of the U.S.S.R. armed forces.

December 7: A massive earthquake strikes Armenia. Prime Minister Ryzhkov immediately flies to the scene to organize rescue efforts; initial reports indicate 50,000 to 70,000 dead. Gorbachev abandons plans to visit Cuba and Britain after the UN so he too can fly to Armenia to inspect the damage.

December 29: A government decree strips Brezhnev and Chernenko of all posthumous honors and removes their names from Soviet towns and institutions.

December 30: Yuri Churbanov, Brezhnev's son-in-law, is sentenced to twelve years in prison for corruption.

1989

January 10: Central Committee plenum nominates the Party's candidates for membership in the Congress of People's Deputies; one hundred candidates are nominated to fill one hundred vacancies. Later it is revealed that in the voting twelve members of the Central Committee had voted against Gorbachev. Seventy-eight had voted against Ligachev.

January 18: Estonia approves a new language law that would force minorities in the republic to learn Estonian within four years. On January 26, Lithuania adopts a similar measure, and on May 4 so does Latvia. Later in the year other republics adopted similar acts: Tadzhikistan on July 22; Kirghizia on August 24; Moldavia on August 28; Uzbekistan on October 21; and the Ukraine on October 28.

January 18: Sakharov is rejected by the Academy of Sciences as a candidate for the Congress of People's Deputies. After much maneuvering, he is chosen one of the Academy's candidates in April.

February 3: Czechoslovakia announces that Soviet troops will begin a withdrawal from that country.

February 6: Round-table discussions begin between the government of Poland and the Solidarity trade union.

February 15: The last Soviet troops leave Afghanistan.

March 6: Speaking on Hungarian television, Foreign Ministry spokesman Gennadi Gerasimov says every East European country's future "is in its own hands," renouncing the Brezhnev doctrine.

March 15: At a Central Committee plenum on agricultural reforms, Gorbachev describes agriculture as the country's main problem and says a "green revolution" is necessary. He calls for cuts in the agricultural bureaucracy, more land leasing and family farming, and greater reliance on market mechanisms.

March 15: Approximately 75,000 Hungarians demonstrate in Budapest on the anniversary of the 1848 revolt against Austrian rule. Police do not disrupt the demonstration.

March 26: Nationwide elections are held for the Congress of People's Deputies. Party officials in Moscow, Leningrad, Kiev, Minsk, and Kishinev are defeated; Sajudis, the pro-independence popular front, wins 31 of Lithuania's 42 seats; the Popular Front of Latvia wins 25 of the republic's 29 seats; and Estonia's Popular Front takes 15 of that republic's 21 seats. Perhaps the biggest winner of the day is Boris Yeltsin, who receives 90 percent of the vote in Moscow.

March 29: Gorbachev tells media officials that the defeat of Party candidates is a natural part of democracy. He says the elections show that the Soviet Union does not need a multiparty system.

March 30: The Ministry of Defense announces that university students will no longer be drafted.

April 3: Gorbachev travels to Cuba on the trip he had postponed because of the earthquake in Armenia. On April 5 he goes on to Britain.

April 6: The Kremlin rescinds the antireligion edicts of the 1960s.

April 7: The government of Poland and Solidarity sign an agreement legalizing the trade union and calling for elections in which the opposition can contest 35 percent of the seats in the lower house and all one hundred seats in a new senate.

April 9: Nineteen people are killed in Tbilisi when police and soldiers attack a crowd of peaceful demonstrators with poison gas, shovels, and clubs.

April 25: A Central Committee plenum accepts the resignations of 110 elderly members of the Central Committee and the Central Auditing Commission. Conservatives voice their misgivings about the recent election results and other developments. Gorbachev hails the election results, and announces that for the first time since the 1920s a transcript of the plenum proceedings will be published in the press.

May 2: The Hungarian government begins to remove the barbed-wire fence along its border with Austria, making Hungary the first East European country to have an open border with Western Europe.

May 14: Gorbachev travels to China. His visit sparks demonstrations and appears to inspire the democracy movement.

May 18: Lithuania and Estonia adopt legislation declaring their sovereignty. On July 29 Latvia does the same.

May 25: The first session of the Congress of People's Deputies opens in Moscow. The meetings, televised in full, will be watched by millions. Gorbachev is quickly elected president, and on May 26 the members of the permanent standing legislature, the Supreme Soviet, are elected.

June 3: The Supreme Soviet opens its first session.

June 4: Clashes are reported between Uzbeks and Meskhetian Turks in the Fergana Oblast of Uzbekistan. Dozens are killed. Thousands of troops from the Ministry of Internal Affairs are dispatched to the scene.

June 4: The Polish Communists are defeated in national elections; Solidarity candidates win all 161 of the lower house seats that they were allowed to contest, and 99 of 100 seats in the Senate.

June 12: Gorbachev travels to West Germany. At a press conference on June 15 he says of the Berlin Wall that "nothing is eternal in this world."

June–July: The Supreme Soviet rejects a number of nominees for ministerial posts in the new government. One of them is Gorbachev's handpicked candidate for deputy premier, Vladimir Kalashnikov. Defense Minister Dmitri Yazov was confirmed only after Gorbachev pleaded for his approval.

June 26: Live coverage of the Supreme Soviet proceedings is halted on the grounds that there has been a 20 percent drop in industrial output since televised sessions began. Henceforth, the proceedings will be rebroadcast in the evening.

July 4: Gorbachev travels to France.

July 7: Addressing a Warsaw Pact summit in Bucharest, Gorbachev declares that the member nations are free to choose their own road to socialism.

July: Coal miners strike in Siberia, then walkouts spread to the Kuzbass and Donbass mining regions in Russia and the Ukraine.

July 18: Speaking at a Central Committee meeting, Gorbachev proposes advancing the next Party Congress from 1991 to the fall of 1990.

July 23: Alexander Yakovlev, head of the Congress of People's Deputies commission evaluating the 1940 Molotov-Ribbentrop Pact, officially acknowledges for the first time that the pact included secret protocols that divided Poland between the Soviet Union and Germany and ceded the Baltic states to the Soviet Union.

July 23: In a televised interview, Gorbachev supports the striking coal miners.

July 29: The Inter-Regional Group is formed in the Congress of People's Deputies to promote liberal reforms. The 250 deputies who join the group choose Gavril Popov, Yuri Afanasyev, Boris Yeltsin, Viktor Palm, and Andrei Sakharov as their leaders.

August 22: Gorbachev telephones Mieczyslaw Rakowski, the leader of Poland's Communist party, and urges the Polish Communists to join a Solidarity-led coalition government in Warsaw.

August 23: The fiftieth anniversary of the Molotov-Ribbentrop Pact is met with mass protests in the Baltic republics.

August 24: Tadeusz Mazowiecki is elected prime minister of Poland; this is the first time in the history of the Soviet empire that a Communist party is voted from power.

September 10: Hungary opens its border with Austria, allowing thousands of East German refugees to travel west.

September 19: At a Central Committee plenum on nationalities' issues, Nikonov, Chebrikov, Shcherbitsky, Solovev, and Talyzin are all retired from the Politburo; Kryuchkov and Maslyukov are named full members, and Primakov and Pugo are named candidate members.

September 25: The Supreme Soviet begins its second session.

September: More than 17,000 East Germans emigrate to West Germany by traveling through Czechoslovakia and Poland.

October 7: Gorbachev travels to East Germany for talks with Honecker and to attend celebrations marking the fortieth anniversary of the East German state. "Life itself punishes those who delay," Gorbachev told Honecker, widely interpreted as a signal that he should begin reforms in East Germany.

October 7: The Hungarian Communist party abandons Leninist ideology and renames itself the Hungarian Socialist Party.

October 9: Seventy thousand people march in Leipzig for democracy.

October 13: In a meeting with media officials, an angry Gorbachev criticizes outspoken periodicals such as *Ogonyok* and *Argumenti i Fakti* and some members of parliament for "irresponsible" and "inflammatory" statements. He suggests that the editor of *Argumenti i Fakti* should resign.

October 18: Honecker is removed as the head of the East German Communist party and replaced by Egon Krenz.

October 27: After a meeting in Warsaw, Warsaw Pact nations issue a statement endorsing the right of each to choose its own political course, while ruling out any intervention by one member nation in the affairs of another.

November 9: The Berlin Wall is opened.

November 13: A motion in the Supreme Soviet to debate eliminating the Party's leading role fails by only three votes.

November 15: Gorbachev tells a students' forum that every article of the constitution could be amended, including Article 6, which provides for the Party's leading role.

November 19: At a rally in Prague attended by ten thousand people the Civic Forum reform group is founded.

November 24: Czechoslovak Communist party general secretary and other leaders resign, and Alexander Dubček addresses a crowd of 250,000 in Prague.

November 27: Supreme Soviet adopts a draft law on the press that bans censorship of the media and allows individuals to put out their own publications. Another new law gives limited economic autonomy to the Baltic republics.

November 28: Czechoslovakia formally abandons the leading role of the Communist party.

November 29: Gorbachev travels to Rome; on December 1 he meets with the Pope.

December 2–4: Gorbachev and Bush meet at the Malta summit. The two discuss recent developments in Eastern Europe, arms control, Nicaragua, and other topics. Bush offers economic assistance to the Soviet Union.

December 3: Egon Krenz, the ruling Politburo, and the Central Committee all resign in East Germany.

December 4: The Warsaw Pact officially denounces the invasion of Czechoslovakia in 1968.

December 7: Sovetsky Pisatel (Soviet Writer) publishing house begins the distribution of the complete text of Solzhenitsyn's *Gulag Archipelago.*

December 9: Central Committee holds a plenum on the economy and other issues that will be discussed at the next session of the Congress of People's Deputies.

December 10: A new, non-Communist-majority government is installed in Prague; President Gustav Husak resigns.

December 12: The second session of the Congress of People's Deputies opens.

December 14: Andrei Sakharov dies; Gorbachev takes part in ceremonies honoring him on December 16.

December 15–17: Thousands riot in the Romanian town of Timosoara, beginning the Romanian revolution.

December 16: Ryzhkov's economic plan is approved by the Congress of People's Deputies after much debate. The Congress also abolishes automatic allotments of seats to "social organizations," including the Communist Party, in future Congresses.

December 20: Lithuanian Communist Party declares its independence from the national Party organization in Moscow.

December 25: Nicolae Ceauşescu and his wife are tried by a military tribunal, found guilty, and executed by firing squad.

December 29: Václav Havel becomes the first non-Communist president of Czechoslovakia in more than forty years.

1990

January 2: Thousands of Azerbaijanis riot near the Soviet border with Iran. On January 3 Soviet troops are sent to quell the fighting.

January 4: After a meeting between Gorbachev and Lithuanian Communists, Communist Party authorities decide to accept the republic Party's break with Moscow.

January 10: Gorbachev arrives in Lithuania for discussions with the breakaway republic's leaders. On January 11, 250,000 Lithuanians gather in Vilnius to show their support for an independent Lithuania. His visit lasts until the 13th. On that day he says, "I don't see a tragedy in a multiparty system if it serves the people."

January 11: Armenia declares that it has the right to veto Soviet laws, following the first step taken by the Baltic republics on their path to independence.

January 14: Armenia and Azerbaijan both mobilize troops as the conflict between the two republics escalates. The number of victims after two days of rioting in Azerbaijan has already reached thirty and troops are sent to the area on January 15; within a few days the number of deaths has doubled. On January 19–20 Soviet military forces occupy Baku in an operation that takes more than sixty lives.

January 15: Crowds in Moldavia call for reunification with Romania.

February 4: A mass rally for democracy in Moscow on the eve of a Central Committee plenum. Crowds of 100,000 to 300,000 people take part.

February 5: In his speech to a Central Committee plenum, Gorbachev proposes that the Party give up its "leading role," embrace a multiparty system, and adopt as its new goal "humane, democratic socialism." After a bitter debate, his proposals are adopted on February 7.

February 12: The presidium of the Supreme Soviet calls for a special session of the Congress of People's Deputies to enhance the powers of the president.

February 13: Anti-Armenian rioting in Dushanbe, the capital of Tadzhikistan, leaves thirty-seven dead.

February 13: Mstislav Rostropovich returns to Moscow for the first time since being stripped of his Soviet citizenship, and gives several concerts.

February 25: Demonstrations across the Soviet Union in support of democracy; 50,000–100,000 gather in Moscow. Army and KGB troops are also reported to have surrounded Moscow; an armed KGB detachment is seen around Gorbachev's dacha outside the capital.

February–March: Elections to local soviets, or councils, are held throughout the country, and opposition candidates register many victories. In Lithuania, candidates backed by the national front, Sajudis, win overwhelmingly; Party *apparatchiks* suffer humiliating defeats in all three Slavic republics; in Moscow and Leningrad, voters reject the Party apparatus in electing new city councils.

February 27: The Supreme Soviet passes a draft law greatly expanding presidential powers. The Congress of People's Deputies approves the measure on March 13. On the same day the Congress formally nullifies Article 6 of the constitution, which formalized the leading role of the Communist Party.

March 11: Lithuania declares itself independent and elects Vytautas Landsbergis the first non-Communist president of a Soviet republic. There follows a period of intense political maneuvering and threats by the central government. Armored personnel carriers roll through Vilnius, central authorities seize factories and Party buildings, military deserters are seized in hospitals, and the chief public prosecutor is replaced. After two months of tense confrontation, Gorbachev meets with the Lithuanian premier, Kazimiere Prunskiene, on May 17 after she says that Lithuania will postpone enactment of new independence legislation.

March 15: Gorbachev is reelected president by the Congress of People's Deputies. The next presidential election—in 1995—will be by popular vote.

March 24–26: Gorbachev chooses a fifteen-member Presidential Council, or cabinet, which includes representatives from left and right.

April 9: Gorbachev declares that he will use his new presidential powers to institute sweeping economic reforms.

April 13: For the first time the Soviet government admits that the NKVD, the precursor to the KGB, and not Nazi troops, massacred Polish officers at Katyn.

April 17: Moscow announces cuts in oil and natural-gas deliveries to Lithuania.

April 19: Yuri Afanasyev resigns from the Communist Party.

April 24: Gorbachev shelves a reform package that would have begun shifting the Soviet economy toward a market system. He cites fears of social disorder.

May 1: Gorbachev and other Kremlin leaders standing atop Lenin's mausoleum are jeered by protesters who have joined the May Day parade.

May 12: A draft law is published that would allow a punishment of up to six years for insulting the Soviet president.

May 15: Gorbachev is elected a delegate to the 28th Party Congress, but he wins just 61 percent of the votes cast by members of the Party committee in Moscow's Frunzenskaya district.

May 23: The Ryzhkov government outlines its program for economic reform; it calls for higher prices, including tripling the heavily subsidized price of bread. The government proposes a national referendum to gauge support; the program envisions a gradual transition to a market economy.

Late May: Goods of all kinds disappear from shops in Moscow and around the country in a spree of panic buying—the public response to the government's proposals for price increases.

May 28: Twenty-two Armenians are killed in Yerevan in clashes with police.

May 29: Boris Yeltsin is elected chairman of the ruling presidium of the Supreme Soviet of the Russian Republic—in effect, president of Russia.

May 30: Gorbachev arrives in Washington for his second summit with Bush. The visit ends with a trip to Minneapolis and San Francisco. Gorbachev departs for home on June 4.

June 6: Troops are sent to Kirghizia after three days of riots, principally in the holy city of Osh; forty people were killed. Communist Party leaders are stoned in Frunze. By June 10 the death toll had reached 115.

June 8: The parliament of the Russian Republic declares the primacy of its laws over Soviet law.

June 19: Russian Communist Party Congress opens in Moscow.

June 22: Ivan Polozkov, a conservative opponent of free-market economics, is elected leader of the Russian Communist Party.

June 29: The Lithuanian parliament votes to suspend the republic's declaration of independence for at least one hundred days. On June 30 the oil and gas embargo against Lithuania is lifted.

July 2: The 28th Communist Party Congress opens in Moscow. Initially delegates are openly hostile to Gorbachev and his allies. Yeltsin warns the delegates that they and other Party officials may someday be put on trial for the damage they have done to the country. On July 10 the Congress votes to expand the Politburo to include representatives of all fifteen republics, a change that will dilute its power. Gorbachev is reelected as head of the Party. On July 11 Vladimir Ivashko, Gorbachev's choice, defeats Ligachev for the post of deputy Party chief. Ligachev announces he will retire and write his memoirs. On July 12 Yeltsin and Vyacheslav Shostokovsky, director of the Higher Party School, resign from the Communist Party. A new Politburo and a new Central Committee are elected that are both dominated by Gorbachev loyalists. The new Politburo will have no role in governing the country.

July 15: Gorbachev issues a decree ending Party control of the media and broadcasting.

July 16: The Ukraine declares its sovereignty.

July 20: The Russian Republic's "500 Days" plan—a program to lead the country to a free market system in seventeen months—is unveiled.

August 1: Gorbachev and Yeltsin agree to pursue a common approach to economic reform.

August 13: Gorbachev issues a decree rehabilitating all victims of Stalinism.

August 15: Gorbachev issues a decree that restores Soviet citizenship to Alexander Solzhenitsyn and twenty-two others, mostly dissident intellectuals who had been forced to emigrate during the 1970s and '80s.

August 20–25: Riots provoked by a shortage of cigarettes reported in Chelyabinsk, Leningrad, Gorki, and Moscow.

August 23: Armenia declares its independence.

August 23: Turkmenistan declares its sovereignty.

August 24: Tadzhikistan declares its sovereignty.

Early September: Bread briefly disappears from stores in Moscow.

September 5: Details of the Gorbachev-Yeltsin economic plan are published. It closely parallels the five-hundred-day plan drawn up by economists led by Stanislav Shatalin.

September 9: Gorbachev and President Bush meet for a one-day summit in Helsinki to discuss the crisis in Kuwait. Both agree to cooperate to convince Iraqi president Saddam Hussein to withdraw his invading forces.

September 11: After weeks of temporizing, Gorbachev announces that he supports a radical economic reform plan drawn up by a committee under one of his advisers, Stanislav Shatalin, in preference to a more cautious plan proposed by Prime Minister Ryzhkov.

September 12: A new four-power treaty signed in Moscow effectively allows for the reunification of Germany.

September 13: The Soviet Union and West Germany sign a twenty-year treaty of friendship.

Mid-September: Unusual military maneuvers around Moscow give rise to rumors of a possible coup, which are discussed in the press and by Yeltsin in an address to the Russian parliament. On September 26 Defense Minister Dmitri Yazov denies that the military has any designs on gaining power, and describes the exercises in question as routine. Some troops were helping bring in the potato harvest, Yazov says.

September 17: The USSR and Saudi Arabia reestablish diplomatic relations after a break of fifty-two years—a result of the two countries' cooperation in the international coalition against Iraq's invasion of Kuwait.

September 18: Alexander Solzhenitsyn's article "How to Revitalize Russia" is printed in *Komsomolskaya Pravda.*

September 24: The Supreme Soviet grants Gorbachev new powers to rule by decree during the transition period to a market economy. But the Supreme Soviet could not agree on a new program for economic reform and delayed a decision until at least mid-October.

September 26: The Supreme Soviet adopts a new law that ends state control of religion and atheist education in the schools and permits organized religious instruction.

September 27: Gorbachev utilizes his new powers to issue his first emergency economic decree ordering state-run enterprises to fulfill their contracts for providing raw materials to the state.

September 27: General Mikhail Moiseyev, chief of staff of the Soviet military, says that armed forces have moved nuclear weapons from trouble spots around the country to secure locations.

September 30: The Soviet Union establishes diplomatic relations with South Korea and agrees to exchange consulates with Israel in Moscow and Tel Aviv.

October 1: Mass protests are held across the Ukraine to protest against Communist Party control. On October 17 Ukrainian Prime Minister Vitaly Masol offers his resignation in response to the demonstrations.

October 3: East and West Germany are reunited.

October 3: James A. Baker III and Eduard Shevardnadze announce completion of a treaty on conventional forces in Europe that will sharply reduce arsenals on both sides.

October 9: The Russian parliament votes to implement the Shatalin five-hundred-day plan whether or not the central government follows suit.

October 9: The U.S.S.R. Supreme Soviet adopts legislation providing that all political parties have equal status with the Communist Party and ending the legal status of Communist Party cell organizations in the workplace.

October 15: Gorbachev is awarded the 1990 Nobel Peace Prize.

October 16: Gorbachev presents his own economic reform program, combining elements from the Shatalin and Ryzhkov plans. Reformers express great disappointment. On October 19, the Supreme Soviet adopts the plan.

October 24: The Supreme Soviet declares invalid the assertions of individual republics that their laws take precedence over the Union's; the Russian and Ukrainian legislatures vote the primacy of their republics' law over all-Union laws immediately after the central government's declaration is announced.

October 26: Gorbachev issues two economic decrees authorizing the foreign ownership of Soviet enterprises and sharply devaluing the ruble.

October 29: The Georgian Round Table, a nationalist group, defeats the republic Communist Party in legislative elections by a margin of two to one.

November 2: Violence erupts in Dubossary, Moldavia, between Russians and Moldavians; six are killed.

November 7: Competing official and unofficial demonstrations mark the seventy-third anniversary of the October Revolution. One man in Red Square attempts to fire a shotgun in the direction of Gorbachev and other leaders standing atop Lenin's mausoleum, but he is quickly disarmed.

November 13: After hearing their angry complaints, Gorbachev pledges to military leaders that he will preserve the unity of the country and of the military, and warns of a "bloodbath" if the Soviet Union disintegrates.

November 17: Supreme Soviet approves Gorbachev's proposal to reorganize the government so that it includes the leaders of all fifteen republics in a presidential cabinet to be called the Federation Council.

November 23: The draft of a new Treaty of the Union is circulated: it changes the country's name to the Union of Sovereign Soviet Republics.

November 27: Gorbachev issues decrees barring republics from controlling nuclear weapons on their territory and authorizing Soviet soldiers to use force when attacked or harassed by citizens.

November 28: Gorbachev tells a meeting of intellectuals in the Kremlin that both of his grandfathers had been arrested and imprisoned during the Stalinist repressions of the 1930s.

November 29: A first shipment of food aid from Germany arrives in Moscow.

December 1: Leningrad institutes a policy of food rationing modeled on the system that was used during the Nazi siege of the city in 1941. Earlier, authorities in the Ukraine took comparable steps to ration food and consumer goods.

December 2: Vadim Bakatin is fired as minister of the interior and replaced by Boris Pugo, former Communist Party leader and KGB chief in Latvia. General Boris Gromov, the last commander of Soviet troops in Afghanistan, is appointed Pugo's chief deputy.

December 3: The Russian Republic's parliament legalizes private ownership of land.

December 4: The Supreme Soviet grants Gorbachev new executive powers to ease the transition to a market economy. (The Congress of People's Deputies affirms the decision later in the month.)

December 8: The Communist party of the republic of Georgia breaks with the national Communist party, pledging to work for the republic's independence.

December 9: Lech Walesa is elected president of Poland.

December 11: Vladimir Kryuchkov, head of the KGB, says on Soviet television that the organization will fight "with all the means at its disposal" the "anti-Communist forces" that are working against central power in the U.S.S.R.

December 12: The republic of Kirghizia declares its sovereignty, the fifteenth and final republic to do so.

December 14: President Gorbachev declares null and void all decisions by republic and local governments that have interrupted delivery of food and other necessary supplies.

December 17: Opening the fourth session of the Congress of People's Deputies, Gorbachev accepts responsibility for past mistakes but defends the accomplishments of his years in power. He warns of the "dark forces" of nationalism, and says the country needs twelve to eighteen months of firm executive rule to prevent it from falling apart.

December 20: Foreign Minister Eduard Shevardnadze resigns unexpectedly after warning the Congress that "a dictatorship is approaching."

December 23: In a speech to the Congress, Vladimir Kryuchkov, head of the KGB, implies that bloodshed may be necessary to restore order in the country. He accuses the CIA and other Western intelligence agencies of fomenting dissent in the U.S.S.R.

December 24: Gorbachev uses his new executive powers to try to quell dissident nationalists for the first time, ordering Moldavia to rescind recent laws that limit the power of the central government and favor the local language, Romanian, over Russian.

December 25: The Congress of People's Deputies orders nationwide referenda on the new Union treaty and on private ownership of land.

December 25: The Congress approves new executive powers for Gorbachev, and a reorganized executive branch that includes a new vice president and cabinet reporting directly to the president.

December 25: Premier Nikolai Ryzhkov suffers a heart attack.

December 26: Gorbachev names Gennadi Yanayev, fifty-three, a Communist Party official, the new vice president of the Soviet Union. He is confirmed a day later by the Congress, but only on a second ballot demanded by Gorbachev after Yanayev fails to get the necessary majority on the first vote.

December 27: The Russian Republic's parliament makes the Russian Orthodox Christmas, January 7, an official holiday.

December 30: The legislature in Moldavia, responding to Gorbachev's decree of December 24, agrees to reconsider nearly all the points raised by the president, apparently heading off a direct confrontation.

December 31: In a New Year's address to his countrymen, Gorbachev describes 1990 as "one of the most difficult years in our history." He declares, "There is no more sacred cause than the preservation and renewal of the Union."

1991

January 2: Soviet "black beret" security troops seize the main newspaper publishing plant in Riga, Latvia.

January 7: The Ministry of Defense announces that it is sending paratroop units to seven republics to enforce the military draft and help find deserters. The seven are Estonia, Latvia, Lithuania, Georgia, Armenia, Moldavia, and the Western Ukraine.

January 8: Lithuanian prime minister Kazimiera Prunskiene meets with Gorbachev in Moscow. Gorbachev instructs her to "go back home and restore order" or he will do the job himself. She asks if she can assure Lithuanians that the central government will not use force against them. "You cannot give them any assurances that I have not given you," Gorbachev replies. The same day Prunskiene announces her resignation after the Lithuanian parliament defeated her proposed program of price increases.

January 9: Soviet troops surround the television tower in Vilnius, Lithuania, while pro-Russian demonstrators stage protests outside the parliament building. The troops leave the television tower after several hours without explanation.

January 10: In a message to the Lithuanian government, Gorbachev accuses it of "implementing a policy aimed at restoring a bourgeois system," and demands "the restoration of constitutional order, reliable guarantees of security, and normal living conditions." He indicates he is considering imposing presidential rule.

January 11: Soviet paratroopers firing live ammunition and accompanied by tanks seize the main printing plant in Vilnius, where the principal Lithuanian newspapers are published. The airport and railroad station are closed. Local Communists loyal to Moscow announce creation of a "national committee of salvation."

January 11: The State Committee on Radio and Television tries to close the independent Interfax news agency by impounding most of its equipment. (Interfax had used offices on the committee's premises.) However, the agency was able to quickly resume operations after being given new offices and equipment by the Moscow city and Russian republican governments.

January 13: Shortly before 2:00 A.M., Soviet Army troops attack and seize the Lithuanian television station. Using their rifles as clubs, the paratroopers beat and fire on the crowds that have gathered around the station. Another group of paratroopers assaults the television transmission tower. Thirteen people are killed that night (another will die later). At least one victim is crushed by a tank. During the paratroopers' attacks, loudspeakers play a prerecorded message that declares again and again that power has passed to the national salvation committee.

January 13: About eighteen hours after the assaults in Vilnius, Boris Pugo, the minister of the interior, says on the main evening news program on television that the violence was caused by the Lithuanians.

January 14: Gorbachev says he knew nothing of the decision to use force in Vilnius until after the fact, "when they woke me up." He expresses no regret about what has happened, and says the army acted at the request of the national salvation committee, which he implicitly recognizes as a legitimate body.

January 14: Finance Minister Valentin Pavlov, a staunch opponent of radical economic reform, is named premier in Gorbachev's new presidential government.

January 15: Alexander Bessmertnykh is appointed foreign minister, succeeding Eduard Shevardnadze.

January 16: Gorbachev, reacting angrily to newspaper articles on the violence in Lithuania, proposes that the law guaranteeing freedom of the press be suspended, and that the Supreme Soviet take responsibility for supervising the news media. After angry protests from members, he withdraws this proposal.

January 19: A national salvation committee in Latvia—its members anonymous, like those of the similarly named committee in Lithuania—claims to have taken power.

January 19: Nikolai Petrakov, an economic adviser to Gorbachev, resigns his post, saying there is no hope of instituting reform under the present circumstances.

January 20: Soviet troops attack the Interior Ministry of Latvia, killing four.

January 22: Gorbachev appears before reporters at the Foreign Ministry press center and reads a statement pledging that he will stick to reform policies at home and abroad. He expresses condolences to the families of victims of the violence in Lithuania and Latvia, but says the "root cause" of the killings was the "unlawful acts" of the parliaments in both republics.

January 22: A presidential decree orders the confiscation of all fifty- and hundred-ruble notes, a move described by government officials as a blow at black marketeers and speculators, but attacked by reform economists as an attempt to undermine entrepreneurs and discourage the free market.

January 22: The European Parliament votes to detain $1 billion worth of food aid for the Soviet Union to protest the violent crackdown in the Baltics.

January 25: The Moscow city council announces it will begin rationing meat, grain, and vodka on March 1.

January 25: The Ministries of Defense and the Interior announce plans for joint patrols of policemen and soldiers in Soviet cities, described as an attempt to maintain public order.

January 26: In a presidential decree Gorbachev gives the police and the KGB unlimited powers to search business offices and accounting ledgers to combat economic crimes. The order applies to foreign businesses and joint ventures.

January 30: In an interview published in Moscow, Boris Pugo says nearly all the extra troops sent into the Baltics since early January are being withdrawn. Lithuanian officials confirm that many troops seem to be leaving Vilnius, though some remain.

February 1: Joint patrols of policemen and soldiers begin in Moscow.

February 5: In a decree Gorbachev denounces the forthcoming independence referendum in Lithuania as "without legal foundation" and says the vote will be invalid.

February 6: In a televised speech Gorbachev urges voters to support a vaguely worded March 17 ballot initiative backing the maintenance of a federation of republics that preserves the freedoms of all nationalities.

February 7: The parliament of the Russian Republic decides to add a question to the March 17 referendum to propose the direct election of a new president of Russia.

February 9: Lithuanians vote overwhelmingly for independence.

February 18: Premier Pavlov announces plans for price increases, but also indicates continued opposition to the creation of a real free market.

February 19: Speaking on national television, Yeltsin calls on Gorbachev to resign. The next day, the U.S.S.R. Supreme Soviet denounces Yeltsin, while the city soviet of Leningrad endorses his statements. On February 24 tens of thousands of Muscovites gather in Manezh Square to support Yeltsin.

February 26: Speaking in Minsk, Gorbachev accuses Yeltsin, Popov, and other democrats of trying to break up the Union, describing them as "anti-Communists" hungry for power.

March 1: A new round of coal miners' strikes begins. They will continue for March and most of April, eventually involving hundreds of thousands of miners all over the country.

March 2: Mikhail Gorbachev's sixtieth birthday.

March 3: Voters in Estonia and Latvia vote overwhelmingly for independence in referendums in both republics.

March 7: Gorbachev creates a new U.S.S.R. Security Council. The Supreme Soviet confirms as members Yanayev, Pavlov, Bessmertnykh, Pugo, Kryuchkov, Yazov, and Bakatin. Primakov and Valery Boldin, Gorbachev's longtime chief of staff, are rejected. Primakov wins approval in a second round of voting and Gorbachev gives Boldin an administrative position on the council that did not require confirmation.

March 9: In a speech criticizing Gorbachev, Yeltsin proposes that the country "declare war on the leadership" in the Kremlin and expresses disapproval of Gorbachev's proposals for preserving the Union.

March 10: Hundreds of thousands turn out for a rally in Moscow organized by Democratic Russia to show support for Yeltsin.

March 17: Nearly three-fourths of those voting in a national referendum support Gorbachev's vaguely worded proposal for preserving a Union of republics. In the Russian Republic 70 percent of the voters back a proposal, offered by Yeltsin supporters, for the direct election of a president of Russia.

March 25: The Council of Ministers bans all political rallies in Moscow for three weeks.

March 26: Gorbachev decrees that the Moscow police will report to the national Ministry of Internal Affairs rather than to city authorities.

March 28: In an extraordinary session, the Congress of People's Deputies of the Russian Republic rejects the ban on rallies in Moscow. The rally planned by Democratic Russia proceeds; more than 100,000 take part. The government deploys 50,000 soldiers and policemen to prevent the demonstrators from approaching the Kremlin. Violence is averted when the demonstrators decide not to challenge the armed guards but to meet instead at two squares each about half a mile from the Kremlin. Negotiations between Gorbachev and a Yeltsin aide appointed by the Russian Congress lead to the withdrawal of demonstrators and most troops on the 29th.

March 31: The Warsaw Pact is officially dissolved.

April 1: Georgia holds a referendum on independence. More than 99 percent of those voting (90 percent of the electorate) support an independent Georgian Republic.

April 2: Price increases go into effect, doubling and tripling the cost of many consumer goods.

April 5: After beating back attempts to force him from office, the Russian Congress of People's Deputies votes to give Yeltsin expanded executive powers. The Congress also approves a direct election of the Russian president, scheduled for June 12.

April 6–7: Russian Orthodox believers celebrate Easter; central television broadcasts special programs and services. Yeltsin and Pavlov both attend services. St. Basil's Cathedral on Red Square is used for religious services for the first time since 1917.

April 9: Georgia declares independence but says that it will not secede immediately.

April 9: Gorbachev outlines a new anticrisis plan that would ban strikes and partially reimpose central controls to guide transition to a market economy.

April 10: One hundred thousand people demonstrate in Minsk against the Soviet and Belorussian governments.

April 14: After amending the republic's constitution to create a new position of republic chief executive, the Georgian Supreme Soviet elects Zviad Gamsakhurdia president and gives him broad powers. Direct elections for the Georgian presidency are scheduled for May 26.

April 16–19: Gorbachev visits Japan but fails to satisfy Japan's desired for a more forthcoming policy on the Kurile islands, longtime sticking point in Soviet-Japanese relations. After leaving Japan he stops briefly in South Korea.

April 23: Gorbachev and the leaders of nine republics conduct secret and unexpected negotiations, then sign the "nine-plus-one" agreement calling for greater republican autonomy, a new union treaty and constitution, and new elections. Their announcement catches the country by surprise and indicates for the first time that Gorbachev will accept a new Soviet Union with a weaker center that could consist of fewer than the fifteen original republics.

April 24–25: At a Central Committee plenum, Party hardliners attack Gorbachev ferociously, but then back off after he announces his resignation, which he then withdraws. The plenum ends with an overwhelming vote of confidence in Gorbachev.

May 1: Yeltsin signs a decree transferring control of Russian coal mines to his republican government, hoping this will help him end miners' strikes that have continued for more than a month.

May 13: A new Russian TV service independent of the State Committee on Television and Radio begins broadcasting for six hours a day.

May 20: The U.S.S.R. Supreme Soviet approves a law liberalizing procedures for emigration, satisfying a longtime U.S. condition for the granting of Most Favored Nation trading status.

May 26: Zviad Gamsakhurdia is elected president of the Georgian Republic, winning 87 percent of the vote.

June 3: Gorbachev and the republic leaders of the nine-plus-one agreement decide to drop the word "Socialist" from the country's name and replace it with "Sovereign."

June 5: Gorbachev delivers his Nobel Prize lecture in Oslo. The lecture had originally been scheduled for December.

June 12: In Russia's elections, Boris Yeltsin is elected president with 57.4 percent of the vote. Former Premier Nikolai Ryzhkov, the candidate backed by the Communist Party establishment, wins 17.3 percent of the votes. In Leningrad voters choose the reformer Anatoli Sobchak to continue as their mayor and decide to restore the original name of their city, St. Petersburg. Reformer Gavril Popov is again elected mayor of Moscow.

June 17: Premier Valentin Pavlov unexpectedly asks the Supreme Soviet to give him vastly enhanced powers, effectively yielding him control over Soviet economic policies at Gorbachev's expense. Liberal critics accuse him of trying to stage a legislative coup d'état. On the second day of debate, conservative legislators ask for a closed session, where Yazov, Pugo, and Kryuchkov speak in alarmist terms about the fate of the country. Kryuchkov says the Soviet Union is on the edge of catastrophe and accuses the CIA of masterminding a plot that had brought the country to its knees. On June 21, after hearing Gorbachev defend himself and criticize the plan Pavlov had put forward, the Supreme Soviet votes 262–24 to reject Pavlov's proposals.

June 26: Reform economist Grigori Yavlinsky and Graham Allison of Harvard University give Gorbachev a new plan for sweeping economic reform, including significant Western aid, that has been drawn up by Soviet and American specialists.

June 26: Tass publishes a draft of a new Union treaty; it is ambiguous on the relationship between the republics and the center, and on the status of the republics that do not sign.

July 1: Prominent reformers, including Shevardnadze, Alexander Yakovlev, Stanislav Shatalin, Popov, and Sobchak, announce the formation of a new "Movement for Democratic Reforms" and call for a united front of democrats and reformers.

July 4: Shevardnadze quits the Communist Party.

July 17: Gorbachev meets with leaders of the G-7 industrial nations in London. All express support for his reforms and offer him technical assistance and a new associate membership in the International Monetary Fund, but they do not offer large-scale financial aid.

July 20: Yeltsin issues a "de-Partyization" decree banning Communist Party activities from workplaces in Russia, which would put an end to the Party's special status. The order is to take effect on August 4.

July 23: Deputy Interior Minister Gromov and Deputy Defense Minister Varennikov are among a dozen signatories of an outspoken "Word to the People" published in *Sovetskaya Rossiya*. The document denounces the Gorbachev era and all its works and appears to call for a popular uprising to oust the government.

July 25: A Central Committee plenum convenes to debate the draft of a new liberal Party program introduced by Gorbachev. The program denounces Stalin's crimes, endorses private farming and other private enterprise, embraces the idea of private property, and endorses political pluralism and the practice of religion. Despite its radical character, the draft provokes surprisingly mild debate and is approved overwhelmingly.

July 29: Yeltsin and Vytautas Landsbergis sign a treaty on Russian-Lithuanian relations, recognizing both countries as "sovereign states."

July 30–31: President Bush and Gorbachev hold a summit meeting in Moscow. They discuss economic matters and sign the Strategic Arms Reduction Treaty cutting by roughly 30 percent the arsenals of strategic long-range nuclear weapons held by both countries. Bush travels to Kiev on August 1, where he urges support for the nine-plus-one treaty. He also indicates opposition to the breakup of the Soviet Union into independent parts, a position that angers Ukrainian nationalists.

August 2: Gorbachev announces that Russia, Kazakhstan, and Uzbekistan will sign the Union treaty on August 20, with other republics signing later.

August 16: Alexander Yakovlev resigns from the Communist Party after the Party's central control commission recommends that he be expelled for his role in setting up the Movement for Democratic Reforms. Yakovlev warns that Party officials are preparing "a state and Party coup."

August 17: The Presidium of the Council of Ministers—the Pavlov government— criticizes the new Union treaty, saying it transfers too much authority from the center to the republics.

August 18: The coup begins. Gorbachev is placed under house arrest in the Crimea and held there incommunicado.

August 19: Muscovites awake to radio broadcasts announcing that because of Gorbachev's "ill health" his duties will be performed by Vice President Gennadi Yanayev. Yanayev and seven other senior officials will compose a "State Committee for the State of Emergency in the U.S.S.R." The other members include Oleg Baklanov, a former Central Committee secretary responsible for military industry: Kryuchkov of the KGB; Premier Pavlov; Pugo, the minister of the interior; Vasili Starodubtsev of the peasants' union; Alexander Tizyakov, president of an organization of military industries; and Yazov, the minister of defense. The committee issues numerous decrees throughout the day that are designed to brake Gorbachev's reforms. Anatoli Lukyanov, who is later identified as a participant in the coup, denounces the Union treaty as unconstitutional. The Council of Ministers announces its support for the coup. Tanks roll through the streets of Moscow; a defiant Yeltsin climbs atop a tank in front of his office, asks soldiers to disregard the orders of the coup organizers, and calls for a general strike. Yanayev, with shaking hands, holds a press conference this evening and says the country is collapsing; he states that he hopes Gorbachev will return to power when he becomes well.

August 20: Large crowds demonstrate against the coup in a number of cities, including more than 200,000 in St. Petersburg. Tens of thousands of people gather around the White House in Moscow to support Yeltsin. Yanayev promises Yeltsin that force will not be used against the Russian government, but rumors persist that military action is imminent. Andrei Kozyrev, foreign minister of the RSFSR, arrives in Paris, saying that he will set up a government-in-exile if necessary. Three are killed in fighting near the White House, the only deaths in coup-related struggles.

August 21: The coup crumbles. Key leaders fly to Gorbachev's villa in the Crimea, apparently hoping for forgiveness, but all are arrested. Pugo shoots himself to death. Gorbachev is reinstated as president and arrives back in Moscow in the early hours of the 22nd.

August 22: Gorbachev describes his captivity at a Moscow press conference. He defends the Communist Party and repeats that he is a socialist. Yeltsin bans Communist Party cells in the army. The statue of Felix Dzerzhinsky, founder of Lenin's political police, is removed from Dzerzhinsky square in front of KGB headquarters on the order of Mayor Popov as crowds in the square threaten to pull down the statue themselves.

August 23: During a joint appearance with Gorbachev before the Russian parliament, Yeltsin suspends the activities of the Communist Party inside the Russian Republic. Gorbachev is asked aggressive and sometimes hostile questions. Party offices in Moscow and St. Petersburg are sealed. Vadim Bakatin is named chairman of the KGB, General Evgeni Shaposhnikov is named defense minister, and Viktor Barannikov is chosen to head the Ministry of Internal Affairs. Foreign Minister Alexander Bessmertnyk is dismissed for failing to oppose the coup. Anatoli Lukyanov is dismissed from his chairmanship of the U.S.S.R. Supreme Soviet.

August 24: Gorbachev resigns as general secretary of the Party and orders the state to seize all Party property. The Russian Council of Ministers begins taking over all Union ministries. The archives of the Party and the KGB are sealed. Marshal Sergei Akhromeev, former chief of staff and a military adviser to Gorbachev, commits suicide. Ukraine declares independence and Leonid Kravchuk resigns from Party leadership positions. Russia recognizes independence of Estonia and Latvia.

August 25: Belarus declares independence.

August 26: Yeltsin spokesman Pavel Voshchanov sets off anger in other republics by declaring that the Russian Republic "reserves the right to raise the issue of revising borders" in future. Later Yeltsin repudiates his statement.

August 26: Uzbekistan declares independence.

August 27: Gorbachev urges the republics to sign the Union treaty and threatens to resign if they don't.

August 27: Moldavia declares independence.

August 28: The coup leaders are charged with high treason and murder. Kravchuk hints that Ukraine will not sign the Union treaty. Boris Pankin is appointed foreign minister.

August 29: Gorbachev's presidential powers are curtailed and a new Security Council is approved by the U.S.S.R. Supreme Soviet. It will consist of leaders of the republics that participated in the nine-plus-one talks, Bakatin, Primakov, Yakovlev, Popov, Sobchak, Yuri Ryzhov, and Grigori Revenko.

August 30: Azerbaijan declares independence.

August 31: Uzbekistan and Kirgizstan declare independence.

September 2: Opponents of Georgian President Gamsakhurdia begin demonstrations against him in Tbilisi. This begins months of turmoil in Georgia as the new president behaves in an increasingly authoritarian manner to try to hold on to power.

September 4: Gorbachev recognizes the independence of the Baltic states.

September 5: The Congress of People's Deputies, under pressure from Gorbachev, approves creation of a new bicameral Supreme Soviet and a new State Council that will consist of Gorbachev and the leaders of the republics. In its first official act, the State Council recognizes the independence of the Baltic states.

September 9: Tadzhikistan declares independence.

September 21: Armenians vote overwhelmingly for secession from the Union.

September 30: Evgeni Primakov named chief of a newly constituted foreign intelligence service, consisting of the former foreign intelligence branches of the KGB.

October 1: The twelve non-Baltic former Soviet republics agree to form an economic community.

October 5: Responding to President Bush's proposal to make additional cuts in nuclear arms, particularly short-range tactical weapons, Gorbachev announces unilateral reductions that go beyond those Bush had announced.

October 7: The Ukrainian government approves draft laws authorizing creation of a Ukrainian army and national guard.

October 12: Askar Akayev wins the first direct presidential election in Kirgizstan.

October 15: An aide to Yeltsin says the Russian president now doubts the need for a new Union treaty, since the republics plan to sign an agreement on economic cooperation.

October 16: Armenians elect Levon Ter-Petrosyan their president.

October 17: Ukraine refuses to sign the new interrepublican economic agreement. The next day eight other republics do sign.

October 21: The revamped Supreme Soviet opens in Moscow, but only seven republics send representatives.

October 28: Yeltsin announces steps to confront "a paralysis of power," including liberalization of prices and other economic reforms. He proposes that he become the premier of the Russian government to take full responsibility for implementing new policies. He announces that the Russian government will cease to finance some seventy ministries and institutions of the old Soviet regime as of November 1.

November 6: Ukraine and Moldavia sign the economic treaty that Gorbachev backs, leaving only Georgia, Azerbaijan, and the Baltic states as the former republics that have not signed. Ukraine also signs security and economic agreements with Russia.

November 14: Russia, Belarus, Kazakhstan, Azerbaijan, Kirgizstan, Tadjikhistan, and Turkmenistan "tentatively" agree to a revised Union treaty which provides for a confederative union to be known as the "Union of Sovereign States." Ukraine's refusal to join this group raises questions about the treaty's future.

November 15: Yeltsin suspends all export licenses for Soviet oil in order to protect winter supplies of this much-needed commodity.

November 19: Eduard Shevardnadze is appointed foreign minister of the U.S.S.R.; Boris Pankin is sent to Great Britain as ambassador.

November 21: Officials of the G-7 countries end four days of meetings with representatives of eight of the former Soviet republics by agreeing to a debt-relief package which includes a $1 billion loan and a deferral of $3.6 billion in foreign debt payments.

November 25: The seven republics that had earlier conditionally approved the new Union treaty decline to sign the document at the official ceremony, raising doubt that there will be a new federation.

November 28: The Russian cabinet approves measures to raise prices on all commodities, although the cost of many basic items will still be controlled by the government. Later it is announced that the law will go into effect on January 2, 1992.

November 30: Yeltsin announces that Russia will assume control of the Union budget for the rest of 1991.

December 1: In Ukrainian elections, more than 90 percent of the electorate vote for independence as Leonid Kravchuk is elected president of Ukraine with 60 percent of the vote. Countries around the world begin to recognize Ukraine as an independent country, including Russia on December 3.

December 5: Nursultan Nazarbayev is elected president of Kazakhstan.

December 8: After two days of meetings in a hunting lodge near Minsk, Yeltsin, Ukrainian President Kravchuk, and Belorussian Supreme Soviet Chairman Stanislav Shushkevich agree to the formation of a Commonwealth of Independent States. The republics will coordinate economic, foreign, transportation, communication, customs, defense, arms, and migration policies and leave the door open to other republics that may want to join later. The capital of the new Commonwealth will be Minsk. On December 9 Yeltsin meets with Gorbachev and Nazarbayev at the Kremlin to explain the terms of the new Commonwealth treaty. Gorbachev calls the treaty a positive development because Ukraine is participating, but says the three leaders did not have legal authority or a mandate from the people to negotiate the accord. On December 12, when it appears that Yeltsin is winning support for the Commonwealth from military leaders, Gorbachev says he will resign if the Union is destroyed.

December 13: After meeting in Ashkhabad, Central Asian leaders announce that they would like to join the Commonwealth.

December 16: Kazakhstan declares independence.

December 17: Yeltsin and Gorbachev agree that the Soviet Union will cease to exist on January 1. Yeltsin says he has asked Shevardnadze to resign and plans to merge the Soviet Ministry of External Relations and the Russian Foreign Ministry.

December 18: Yeltsin signs decrees enabling the Russian Republic to assume control of all Soviet ministries except those of defense and nuclear energy.

December 21: Eleven former republics, all except Georgia and the Baltic states, formally agree to the Commonwealth.

December 21: Fighting breaks out in Tbilisi that leaves seven dead and many injured. Violence between pro- and anti-Gamsakhurdia forces escalates over the next few days.

December 25: Gorbachev resigns as president of the U.S.S.R., which has effectively disappeared.

A Glossary of Soviet Terms

APPARATCHIK An official who works in the Communist Party bureaucracy, or *apparat*. By conservative estimate, there were several million of them when Gorbachev came to power—in addition to tens of millions of officials attached to government, as opposed to Party, organizations.

CADRE A more formal term for a paid official of the Party.

CENTRAL COMMITTEE Until 1990, the de facto governing body of the Soviet Union. It traditionally consisted of approximately three hundred members plus nonvoting alternate or candidate members, most of them senior Party officials. The Central Committee also included a number of symbolic worker and peasant members and key military officers. Its members were formally elected by the Party Congress, which traditionally met every five years. The Central Committee selected the membership of the Politburo, which was responsible for day-to-day management of the country until the system was changed in 1990. After those changes, the Central Committee and the Politburo gave up any direct role in managing the country, leaving that to the organs of state power, particularly the president, the council of ministers, the Congress of People's Deputies, and the Supreme Soviet.

CENTRAL COMMITTEE SECRETARIAT The permanent staff of the Central Committee. The country's leader, who has carried the title of general secretary, traditionally ran the secretariat with a small group of other secretaries. With day-to-day administrative authority over the entire Party bureaucracy, the secretariat under the old system was the locus of enormous power. After 1990 the secretariat lost its influence.

COMMUNIST PARTY OF THE SOVIET UNION (CPSU) The political organization established by Vladimir Lenin after the Bolshevik Revolution of 1917. It was not a party in the Western sense of the term, but more a political organization through which the Bolsheviks could dominate the country. By 1985 it had twenty million members, many of whom joined because they knew the most influential positions in society were generally reserved for Party members. Over time the Party became a mammoth bureaucratic organization with elaborate facilities for work and recreation. Until the Soviet constitution was changed in 1990 it had a formal monopoly on political power.

CONGRESS OF PEOPLE'S DEPUTIES The new representative body created in 1988, whose first members were chosen in 1989. Initially the Congress was to consist of both popularly elected deputies and others chosen by officially recognized "social organizations," including the Communist Party, the official trade unions, the Academy of Sciences, the unions of writers, cinematographers, composers and many more. In 1990 it was decided to eliminate the seats reserved for social organizations, so that in the future all deputies are to be popularly elected. The Congress is expected to meet for relatively brief sessions twice a year.

COUNCIL OF MINISTERS The government of the Soviet Union. Led by a premier, its members, the many ministers of the Soviet government, managed the entire economy and society through a bureaucracy that often paralleled the Party's. From top to bottom it was traditionally subservient to Party organs. Each of the fifteen Soviet republics has its own council of ministers and government bureaucracy, each of them under the control of the government in Moscow. At the end of 1990 Gorbachev announced plans to abolish this structure.

FIRST SECRETARY From town committees to republic Party organizations, every Communist Party organization is run by a first secretary. The term "Party leader" could be used as a substitute in all cases. Traditionally these officials were appointed by the next-higher Party authority. First secretaries in important geographical areas like Stavropol *krai* were chosen by the Central Committee secretariat in Moscow.

GENERAL SECRETARY The title used in recent times by the national leader of the Communist Party.

KGB The initials of the Committee for State Security *(Komitet Gosudarstvennoi Bezopastnosti)*, a vast security force responsible for gathering foreign intelligence, guarding the borders of the Soviet Union, and preserving political order and orthodoxy inside the country.

KOLKHOZ A collective farm, whose members theoretically share ownership of the land and equipment used to farm it. In fact, collectives have always been controlled by Party and state authorities. A *sovkhoz* is a state farm owned by the government.

KOMSOMOL The Young Communist League *(Kommunisticheskii Soyuz Molodezhi)*, a mass Party organization which, before Gorbachev's reforms, most young people joined. Komsomol membership was a necessary prerequisite to Party membership.

The organization itself was designed to propagandize the young and exhort them to work hard for Party and country.

KRAI The Russian word for "region." The term is used to describe territories that are autonomous administrative units.

KULAK A derisive term for a successful and relatively well-off farmer, popularized by Stalin during the campaign to collectivize agriculture, in which millions of alleged kulaks were killed or forcibly removed from their land.

NOMENKLATURA A list of important posts in the Party and government *apparats,* which had to be filled by Party organizations. The Party retained tight control over the entire society through the *nomenklatura* system until 1990.

OBLAST The Russian word for "province."

PLENUM A meeting of one of the Party committees. The regular plenums of the Central Committee were traditionally important gatherings called to debate and ratify Party policies.

POLITBURO In effect, the board of directors of the Central Committee. Until 1990 the Politburo ran the country, making all key decisions about policy and most important personnel decisions as well.

PRESIDENT Under the laws approved in 1989 and 1990 by the Congress of People's Deputies, the Soviet president is a powerful chief executive, able to rule unilaterally by decree in many circumstances. The Congress of People's Deputies elected Gorbachev to a five-year term in 1990; in 1995 the president is to be chosen by direct popular vote.

PRESIDENTIAL COUNCIL A kind of presidential cabinet or committee of advisers, created by the 1990 law on the presidency. Its members, all selected by the president, can help him exercise presidential power, but have no direct administrative responsibilities comparable to those of cabinet members in Western European nations and the United States. In November 1990, Gorbachev announced he would disband the council.

SOVIET The Russian word for "council." Lenin coined the slogan "All Power to the Soviets," then named the country the Union of Soviet Socialist Republics, to convey the idea that the power of the councils—Soviet power—ran the country.

SUPREME SOVIET The highest council. There are supreme soviets in each republic, and a national one in Moscow as well. Until 1990 the national Supreme Soviet was a compliant appendage of Party power, whose members were "elected" in ritualized elections that invariably featured one candidate for each seat. Under the new system, the membership of the national Supreme Soviet is chosen by the Congress of People's Deputies from within its own ranks. It is now considered the permanent legislative body, but the Congress has the final word on major issues.

Notes on Sources

The sources of most of the quotations in this book are self-evident, either because I explain them in the text or because I identify the occasion on which someone spoke or wrote a quoted comment. I have used the dispatches of *Washington Post* correspondents for accounts of day-to-day events in Moscow. I have kept precise citations for all quotations; if any scholar has trouble finding one, I will reply to all queries. Here I will try to provide a general guide to sources that may not be obvious or that are not mentioned in the text.

Chapter One: An Independent Man

I have drawn on several Gorbachev biographies for details of his early life, especially Zhores Medvedev's *Gorbachev* (New York, 1986) and *Mikhail S. Gorbachev, An Intimate Biography,* by the editors of *Time* magazine (New York, paperback, 1988). Hedrick Smith's *The New Russians* (New York, 1990) also provides interesting recollections of Gorbachev from people who knew him as a young man. The important *Washington Post* article on Gorbachev's youth by David Remnick appeared on December 1, 1989. Zdenek Mlynar's recollections appeared in *L'Unità* April 9, 1985; they were translated into English by the Foreign Broadcast Information Service (FBIS) and published on June 4, 1985. Gorbachev revealed the arrests of his grandfathers in a speech on November 28, 1990; it was broadcast the next day and published in the FBIS bulletin on November 30, 1990. Gorbachev recalled his memories of the war damage he saw from the train to Moscow. The description of how he was transferred to Komsomol work soon after his return to Stavropol comes from a speech he gave on April 27, 1990, in Nizhny Tagil. Gorbachev spoke about his trip to Italy in an interview with *L'Unità* published May 20, 1987. Michel Tatu of *Le Monde* had an opportunity to confirm with Gorbachev directly the story of his trip around France, which is recorded in Tatu's biography of Gorbachev, which will soon be published in English.

Chapter Two: Moscow, at Last

Zhores Medvedev's *Andropov* (New York, 1983) and Dusko Doder's *Shadows and Whispers* (New York, 1986) are helpful on Andropov and his time. Evgeny Velikhov's description of Gorbachev as a boss is from *Voices of Glasnost,* a collection of interviews conducted by Stephen F. Cohen and Katrina vanden Heuvel (New York, 1989).

Chapter Three: Struggle for Power

Zhores Medvedev's *Gorbachev* is useful on his accession to power. So is Mark Frankland's *The Sixth Continent* (New York, 1987). Yeltsin's intriguing memoir is *Against the Grain* (New York, 1990). Yakovlev's observation that the ideas of *perestroika* had been nourished for years is from his interview with Cohen and vanden Heuvel.

Chapter Four: Slow Beginnings

Gorbachev's dramatic first visit to Leningrad was recorded both by the CIA's Foreign Broadcast Information Service and by the British Broadcasting Corporation's short-wave broadcast monitoring service. Both publications are invaluable tools for students. Yakovlev's vivid memories of childhood and the war appeared in an interview published by *Komsomolskaya Pravda* on June 5, 1990. His account of his visit to Iowa is from *Voices of Glasnost.* Bill Keller's profile of Yakovlev in *The New York Times Magazine* of February 19, 1989, was very helpful. My account of the 27th Party Congress is drawn from the stenographic record of the meeting published in *Izvestia.* Zhores Medvedev's *The Legacy of Chernobyl* (New York, 1990) is helpful for detail on that accident. Sakharov published the transcript of his conversation with Gorbachev in his *Memoirs* (New York, 1990). Here and elsewhere I made use of excerpts from the official press in the invaluable *Current Digest of the Soviet Press,* published weekly at Ohio State University and available in most large libraries.

Chapter Five: Real Politics, and Real Change

Time of Change by Roy Medvedev and Giulietto Chiesa (New York, 1990) is a useful volume, which I have drawn on here. Chiesa reports on events in Moscow from 1986 through 1988, while Medvedev provides recollections, analysis, and gossip in conversations that intersperse Chiesa's reportage. Shmelyov's *Novy Mir* article is published in English in *Gorbachev & Glasnost,* Isaac J. Tarasulo, ed. (Wilmington, 1989). Some of the interesting events of 1987 were explored by Steven Wheatcroft in the first issue of the journal *Australian Slavonic and East European Studies,* in 1987, in an article called "Unleashing the Energy of History." Most of the quotations from outspoken new publications were taken from the originals. The fullest account of Gorbachev's meeting with editors in February 1987 can be found in the BBC's short-wave radio summary of February 16, 1987. A transcript of the November 1987 Central Committee plenum, where Yeltsin first voiced his criticisms of Gorbachev and Ligachev, was published in 1989 in the new publication *News of the Central Committee of the CPSU (Izvestia Ts.K. K.P.S.S.,* No. 2, 1989). Gorbachev's historical speech of November 2, 1987, was printed in *Pravda* and *Izvestia* the next day. I have used the translation of the *Current Digest of the Soviet Press* (Vol. XXXIX, No. 44). On November 13, 1987, *Moskovskaya Pravda* published the transcript of the Moscow Party committee meeting where Yeltsin was publicly denounced. Seweryn Bialer's article "The Yeltsin Affair" is an insightful account. It appears in *Inside Gorbachev's Russia,* edited by Bialer (Boulder, 1989). Here as elsewhere I use *Washington Post* accounts of events in Moscow.

Chapter Six: Breaking with the Past

My account of the publication of Bukharin's testament is based on interviews with knowledgeable editors. Journalists and officials in Moscow helped me compile the story of the Andreyeva letter. *Izvestia* published a stenographic report of the 19th Party Conference, which I used as the basis of my account. I also used the *Current Digest's* excerpts.

Chapter Seven: The Birth of a New Russia

The letter to *Izvestia* from N. Belous was published on January 10, 1989. Yeltsin's account of his election campaign is from *Against the Grain.* Viktor Pasternak's interview with *Izvestia* was published on April 6. *Pravda* published the proceedings of the Central Committee when elderly members retired on April 27. My account of the first session of the Congress of People's Deputies is drawn from the transcript published by *Izvestia,* supplemented by dispatches from *The Washington Post.* Yeltsin's commentary on the Congress is also from his book.

Chapter Eight: The Magician Runs Out of Tricks

Timothy Garton Ash's *The Magic Lantern* is helpful on events in Eastern Europe in 1989. Daniel Granin's important article on the December 1989 Central Committee plenum appeared in issue No. 51 of *Moscow News* for 1989. Soviet and American press accounts provided many of the details of the events described.

Chapter Nine: The End of the Party

Gorbachev's dramatic visit to Lithuania in January 1990, can be followed in detail in the accounts of the FBIS and BBC's short-wave broadcast report. Quotations from the participants in the February Central Committee plenum are from *Izvestia* and *Pravda* (February 6–8). *Izvestia* on anarchy appeared February 22; its sheepish report on demonstrations was published on the 26th. *Nedelya*'s report on informal political groups appeared in its issue No. 7 for 1990. Georgi Khastsenkov's commentary on the open letter "For Consolidation on a Principled Foundation" appeared in *Moscow News* No. 17, 1990. Yakovlev's candid remarks about the conservatives to Moscow University students were reported in *The Washington Post* on June 22. Quotations from speakers at the 28th Party Congress are taken from the special FBIS issues devoted to it, dated July 2–16, 1990. Anatoli Yurkov's account of the bitter meeting between Gorbachev and the Party secretaries from city and regional committees appeared in *Rabochaya Tribuna* of July 7. Pavel Gutionov's political diary was published in *Izvestia* on July 8. Yeltsin's comment on his collaboration with Gorbachev is from Giulietto Chiesa's helpful account of the Congress in *Problems of Communism*, July–August 1990.

Chapter Ten: A Time of Troubles

Alexander Bozhko's glum account of his attempt to become an entrepreneurial farmer is recounted in a dispatch by Michael Dobbs in *The Washington Post* on July 8, 1990. David Remnick reported Anatoli Strelyani's account of the meeting with Gorbachev in which he spoke of the importance of the center-left coalition and also Shatalin's recollections of his conversation with Gorbachev in *The Washington Post* on September 13, 1990. Nikolai Petrakov's observation on the desirability of getting rid of Stalinist socialism was quoted in *The Washington Post* on September 14, 1990. Petrakov's description of "blackmail" by conservatives and Grigory Yavlinsky's comment that the system could not approve a plan that would kill it were quoted in *The Wall Street Journal* on January 28, 1991. Gorbachev's comment that overhauling the entire system would be "a gift to all manner of claimants of public office" is quoted in a helpful analysis by Seweryn Bialer that appeared in *U.S. News & World Report*, October 8, 1990. Quotations from Gorbachev's meeting with military deputies of November 13 appeared in the army newspaper *Krasnaya Zvezda* (Red Star) on November 16, 1990. Stanislav Govorukhin's article appeared in *Sovetskaya Kultura* on November 24, 1990. Gorbachev's November 28 speech was circulated by Tass; I saw a copy distributed by the Soviet embassy in Washington.

Alexander Yakovlev's comments on the "vengeful and merciless" resurgent conservatives were quoted by Peter Reddaway in *The New York Review of Books*, January 31, 1991. Tatyana Zaslavskaya's explanation of the new power struggles in Soviet society appeared in *Izvestia* on December 18, 1990. Comments by Vladimir Chernyak and Nikolai Fyodorov on Shevardnadze's resignation were quoted in *The New York Times* on December 22, 1990. My account of events in Vilnius leading up to and including the violence of January 13, 1991, is taken from reconstructions of those events by Michael Dobbs in *The Washington Post* on January 14, 1991, and Bill Keller in *The New York Times* on January 16, 1991. The denunciation of violence in Lithuania on the front page of *Moscow News* appeared in issue no. 3 of 1991. Stanislav Shatalin's open letter to Gorbachev was published in *Komsomolskaya Pravda,* January 22, 1991. Gorbachev's remarks to the meeting of military deputies were quoted in a Tass dispatch of November 13, 1990, by Vladimir Isachenkov.

Chapter Eleven: The Final Act

Gorbachev's comments on the need to keep maneuvering are from his book *The August Coup* and from a fascinating interview with Yuri Shchekochikhin that appeared in *Literaturnaya Gazeta* on December 4, 1991. Alexander Yakovlev's comments in this chapter come from an interview at *The Washington Post* on November 14, 1991, and from episode seven of "The Second Russian Revolution," a marvelous series of documentary films produced by Norma Percy for the BBC and the Discovery Channel. This series of eight one-hour documentaries is a unique source of firsthand descriptions of key events in the Gorbachev years. Transcripts of the programs and of the interviews on which they are based have been placed in the library of the London School of Economics and Political Science. I have also used these films for Gorbachev's admission that he erred on March 28; Georgi Shakhnazarov's description of Gorbachev's view that democracy required a new relationship between the republics and the center; for Gorbachev's remark about "an open attack on me"; and for quotations from the interrogations of participants in the coup.

The helpful *Seven Days that Shook the World* by Stuart Loory and Ann Imse provides more detail from the interrogation reports that were leaked to *Der Spiegel.* Anatoli Chernayev's recollections of the coup are taken from an article he wrote for *Time* magazine (October 7, 1991), and from his interviews with the authors of *Seven Days.* It was Chernayev who recounted Gorbachev's tongue lashing of Lukyanov after the coup.

Deputy Premier Shcherbakov recounted his recollection of the way coup organizers lied to government ministers in an August 25 interview on Mayak radio, which I found in the Foreign Broadcast Information Service. Gorbachev's farewell interviews appeared in *Literaturnaya Gazeta* (cited above), *Nezavisamaya Gazeta* of December 14, 1991, and *Komsomolskaya Pravda* of December 24, 1991. My running account of events comes from the Soviet press and accounts published in *The Washington Post.*

Chapter Twelve: Triumph and Failure

Sergei Grigoriev made his comments on Gorbachev living like a czar to Remnick; they appeared in the *Post* on December 26, 1991. The comments on Gorbachev's duplicity by the lawyer Alexander Yakovlev were printed in *The Washington Post* of December 15, 1991.

Acknowledgments

A book is a great collaboration; some of the collaborators don't even know that they helped. I want to thank some of my collaborators formally here.

But first a note about some that I will not name. Russian friends, many of them friends for twenty years, are my most important sources. Russians are great talkers, and great speculators. I owe my sense of their country to the willingness of countless Russians to devote long hours to my education. When I first lived in Moscow in the early 1970s, identifying a Soviet source was a cardinal sin—lives could be destroyed by such an indiscretion. When I wrote the hardback version of this book in 1990 the future of the Soviet Union still seemed so uncertain that I decided to play by traditional Moscow rules and avoid naming my personal sources. By 1992 those rules had changed, but it was impractical to try to recontact all of my informants to ask their permission to put their names in this edition.

The Washington Post has been an exemplary employer for more than a quarter century. The paper sent me to school to learn Russian, sent me to Russia, sent me back for visits after my tour of duty was over, and supported this project in many different ways. Katharine Graham, our proprietor, took me with her to interview Gorbachev in May 1988, one of the great thrills of my years as a reporter. Don Graham, Ben Bradlee, and Len Downie, who ran the paper, indulged my need for time off to write, for which I am most grateful. The *Post*'s research staff under Jennifer Belton and Kathy Foley were enormously helpful. So was my secretary, Carol Van Horn. And the computer wizards at the newspaper, especially David Hoffman and Chris White, gave me a wonderful education in IBM and Xywrite, which made my tasks much easier. Some of the material in this book is based on articles I wrote for the *Post.*

Jennifer Long, my research assistant, made it possible for me to write the book on a very tight schedule. She assembled the chronology of Gorbachev's six years that appears in the back of the book, provided many helpful translations, and located critical documents with remarkable speed. Her greatest triumph was finding the full text of Gorbachev's December 1984 speech in the bowels of the Library of Congress after the ordinary search process had ended in failure.

I would also like to thank Greg Guroff, Steve Luxenberg, Thomas Powers and David Remnick, each of whom read the manuscript with care and made extremely useful suggestions. Others who helped were Murray Feshbach, Loren Graham, Brian Reed, and Jane Lester of Radio Free Europe–Radio Liberty, Don Graves of the Department of State, Gertrude Schroeder, Dimitri Simes, and George Soros.

My understanding of the Gorbachev era has been enriched by a talented group of American journalists in Moscow. There has never been a better group of Moscow correspondents. I would like to mention a few whose dispatches have been most helpful to me: Michael Dobbs, Gary Lee, and David Remnick of *The Washington Post;* Bill Keller and Serge Schmemann of *The New York Times;* Peter Gumbel of *The Wall Street Journal;* and Scott Shane of the *Baltimore Sun.*

Alice Mayhew of Simon and Schuster has been my friend and supporter for more than twenty years, but this is our first project together. I began with a half-baked idea for a Gorbachev book, which she poked and prodded into a more ambitious and vastly more rewarding endeavor. Her help in conceptualizing the project was invaluable; so were her suggestions for improving it once I thought I was finished writing. John Hawkins is that rare literary agent who actually likes to participate in the creation of books; his critical readings of my initial proposals and then of the manuscript were a great help.

My best critic is Hannah Jopling Kaiser, to whom my debts are legion and unrepayable. She was first to see a critical flaw in my initial approach to this book, and saved me from it. Charlotte and Emily Kaiser put up with a single-minded father who denied them a family vacation in the summer of 1990 so he could selfishly write a book. My special thanks to them.

Index

rehabilitation of, attempts at, 65
ritualized patterns of, 151
socialism of, 363
terror of, 22, 106–7, 235
totalitarianism of, 316
and Ukrainian Catholic Church, 307
victims of, 284
Stalinism, 26, 174, 180n, 229, 236, 237,
    245, 262, 456
  active, 157
  and *apparatchiks,* 87–88
  authoritarianism of, 342
  "barracks-like mentality" of, 447
  of Ceauşescu, 313
  central control of, 153
  collapse of, 20, 439, 440, 443, 457
  consequences of, 455
  damage of, 228
  destructiveness of, 123
  discipline of, 452
  fundamentals of, 135
  inheritance of, 442
  as model of socialism, 341, 440
  mythology of, 445
  orthodoxy of, 153
  privations of, 37
  roots of, 92
  stench of, 145
  and Supreme Soviet, 281
  true, 29
"Stalin's Eagles," 216–17
Stalin's Successors (Bialer), 86
Stankevich, Sergei, 295, 323, 326, 330,
    395, 398, 449, 451
Starkov, Vladislav, 303–4, 305, 306
Starodubtsev, Vasili, 418n
Steibliene, Dalia, 394
Stern (German magazine), 62, 378
Stolypin, Pyotr, 69
Strategic Arms Reduction Treaty, 421
Strategic Defense Initiative (Star Wars),
    65, 116, 120n, 139
Strelyani, Anatoli, 359
Sukhov, L. I., 278
Sumtsova, Yulia, 24
Supreme Soviet, 80, 168, 172, 244, 246,
    248, 278, 286, 289, 298, 301, 323,
    336, 364, 365, 367, 371–72, 373,
    388, 395, 396, 399, 426
  and Article 6, 310
  and budget deficit, 378
  and Central Committee, 169

and coal strikes, 294
committee on "Questions of Defense
    and State Security," 291
and Congress of People's Deputies,
    245
discipline of, 324
and freedom of conscience, 307
new power of, 226
oversight committee of, 284
and Pavlov's transfer-of-power
    proposal, 414, 415, 416
and Politburo, 43, 63n
and presidency, 326, 332
presidium of, 273, 317
radicalizing, 295
and religion, 448
shake-up at, 243
and Shatalin plan, 361, 363
Soyuz faction of, 407, 414–15, 423
and Stalinism, 281
Supreme State Inspectorate, 390
Suslov, Mikhail, 39, 40, 42, 44, 49
  death of, 52
Suvadevidze, V. G., 369

Tadzhikistan, 232, 360
Talmud, 131
Tass (state news agency), 80, 208, 264,
    272, 394
Tchaikovsky, Pyotr Ilich, 13
Thatcher, Margaret, 75
"The Thaw," 15–16, 32–33, 35, 70, 87–
    88, 445
Third Party Program, 114
Tiananmen Square massacre (China),
    277, 298, 299
Tikhomirov, V. P., 262, 263, 264
Tikhonov, Nikolai, 49–50, 58, 63, 80,
    81n, 105
Tikhonov, Vladimir, 320
Tikhonovna, Rima, 428–29
Time of Change (Chiesa/Medvedev),
    174n
Time magazine, 29, 30, 42, 116, 117
  biography of, 41–42
Tito, Josip Broz, 237
Titorenko, Raisa Maximovna. *See*
    Gorbacheva, Raisa Maximovna
Tiulkin, Viktor, 338
Tizyakov, Alexander, 418n
Togliatti, Palmiro, 201
Tolpezhnikov, V. F., 278

Robert G. Kaiser, author of *Russia: The People and the Power,* has worked at *The Washington Post* since 1963, where he is now Managing Editor. He has served as a foreign correspondent in London, Saigon, and from 1971 to 1974, Moscow. Kaiser's dispatches from Moscow won the Overseas Press Club's prize for the best foreign correspondence of the year. He lives in Washington, D.C., with his wife and two daughters.